In the Kitchen

more than 1000 recipes for every day

In the Kitchen

more than 1000 recipes for every day

Allan Campion and
Michele Curtis

Hardie Grant Books
MELBOURNE · LONDON

CONTENTS

intro
preface ix
everyday ingredients x

brunch
breakfast + lunch; ease into it 3

starters
appetisers, nibbles + entrees 39

soups
stocks, broths, hearty soups + bread 113

pasta + polenta
quick + easy 157

rice + noodles
risotto, pilafs + stir-fries 195

everyday dinners
family-friendly meals 245

barbies
outdoor food from the grill 289

roasts
classic + contemporary 337

slow cooking
braises + casseroles 381

curries + tagines
a bit of spice 423

vegies
seasonal side dishes 467

salads + dressings
fresh flavours 501

sauces + preserves
salsa, relish + jams 547

pastry
sweet + savoury; roll your dough 587

desserts + puddings
sweet treats 641

cakes
stickybuns, cheesecakes + muffins 699

biscuits + slices
bite-sized delights 763

lunchbox ideas
healthy + quick 801

notes
glossary 808
references + inspirations 811
acknowledgements 812
index 814

INTRO
preface + everyday ingredients

Good food is all about sharing. Whether it's sharing pancakes with the kids for breakfast, swapping recipes with your mates or cooking your grandmother's favourite cake, good food enriches our lives. Barbecues with your friends, long winter nights with a decent curry and a bottle of red, picnics on the beach in summer – many of life's memorable moments revolve around food.

Welcome to *In the Kitchen*, a book that has been many years in the making. We've gathered the recipes we loved the most over years of writing and cooking – our absolute favourites from *Fresh, Sizzle, Chilli Jam, Tucker for Tots, Food with Friends, Every Day Cooking*, the many editions of *The Foodies' Diary*, and, of course, the original *Campion and Curtis in the Kitchen* from 2002.

Never in our wildest dreams did we imagine this book would end up quite so large, but with more than 1000 recipes, plus lots of good kitchen advice, the personal stories behind the recipes and terrific food photography, that's what happened. The recipes we selected are those we feel represent modern Australian home cooking. Simplicity, seasonality and freshness are the key to each and every one of them.

We've also listened to our readers in the selection process. Dishes such as Spaghetti with Breadcrumbs, Tuna, Parsley and Lemon caused a wave of emails from adoring fans; likewise, muffins that taste like doughnuts have an enthusiastic fan club.

For us, food is usually about getting something quick and tasty on the table with minimal fuss, although some of these recipes reflect our passion for food. When a craving for The Pork Dish or Slow-Cooked Leg of Lamb grabs us, we will happily spend hours in the kitchen.

Part of the enjoyment of food comes from sharing it with family and friends. Over the years we would have fed hundreds of hungry mouths, many willing participants in our own style of recipe development. No test kitchen here, just real people with great appetites. Our children, Mia and Luke, are still a delight to feed. They are always ready for French Toast Sandwiches Filled with Chocolate or Spaghetti with Braised Chicken Meatballs in Tomato Sugo. What's changed is that as they are now teenagers, they too are starting to cook. We couldn't ask for more.

We are both excited about *In the Kitchen* and how it reflects our approach to good food and good cooking. More importantly, we are glad to finally have all our favourite recipes in one place, so we can find them easily! We hope you enjoy cooking from this book for family and friends for many years to come.

Allan Campion and Michele Curtis

everyday ingredients

It's often the basic ingredients that raise the most queries in a recipe. Chefs and food writers take huge leaps of faith, assuming that everybody else knows as much about the ingredients as they do. In order to prevent any confusion, here's our take on the basic stuff to get you started.

black pepper	All pepper used in these recipes is freshly ground black pepper, unless otherwise stated. It brings freshness and spice to any dish. As these properties will dissipate with cooking, add a little more before you serve a dish.
chicken	We use only free-range chickens. Given the amount of chicken we eat, this is our compromise on flavour and cost, though we do upgrade to corn-fed or organic poultry for special occasions. It's worth it for the flavour.
egg wash	Egg wash is lightly beaten egg yolk with a little milk, usually brushed onto raw pastry to add a shiny finish when cooked.
eggs	We use free-range eggs, medium sized and 59 g each.
herbs	All herbs used in these recipes are fresh unless otherwise stated.
oil for cooking	We tend to use only extra-virgin olive oil for cooking, except in a few cases where peanut or sesame oil is called for to give a different flavour. Depending on your budget and tastes, you may prefer to use virgin olive oil or just plain vegetable oil.
olive oil	Extra-virgin olive oil has the best flavour, as well as healthy qualities, so use one that suits your taste buds and budget. Prices can vary from $10 to $40 a bottle. We tend to buy Australian oil as it is cheaper and obviously hasn't travelled too far. We also try to buy recently pressed oil. Consider buying a large tin, then decant the oil into a clean, dry wine bottle and seal it with an olive-oil pourer. This is more economical if you use a lot of oil.

parmigiano reggiano	Be sure to buy parmigiano (or grana padano) rather than imitation parmesan, as true parmigiano comes only from Italy. To ensure freshness, it's best to buy a block and grate it as you need it.
pulses and beans	We have become healthier as we have grown older, and we now eat pulses, chickpeas and beans much more often. So often, in fact, that due to time constraints we often use canned beans. We recommend you soak them in lots of cold water for 15 minutes to get rid of the metallic taste. Some recipes, however, require long, slow cooking, for which only dried pulses will do. If using dried beans they are best soaked overnight in plenty of cold water, then cooked in boiling water until tender.
red chilli	Unless otherwise stated, small red chillies (not bird's eye) are used. Take care when removing the seeds and membrane as these contain the capsaicin (the source of the heat).
salt	We prefer to use sea salt, as it has a finer mineral flavour than common table salt. Murray River pink salt flakes are our favourite for cooking with, though we also use Sicilian Iblea fine crystals as they dissolve easily in dressings and are ideal for last-minute seasoning.
seasonal produce	We are big fans of seasonal produce – mostly because it tastes the best and requires little work to enhance its flavour, but also because quality and price are at their best when produce is in season.
stock	Stocks provide the essential base for all good sauces, casseroles and stews. The variety and quality of ready-made stocks are now better than ever, but it is very easy to make your own. Put 2 kg chicken bones in a large saucepan and cover with water. Add chopped onion, carrot, leek and celery, along with a few peppercorns, a bay leaf, thyme and a parsley stalk. Bring to the boil, reduce to a simmer and cook for 30 minutes to 2 hours, removing scum as necessary from the surface. Strain and use.
tomato sugo	Tomato sugo is simply a ready-to-use tomato sauce. The best sugos come from Italy and are an essential pantry item for pasta sauces and casseroles. We have stopped using canned tomatoes in some dishes as we prefer the smoothness of this sauce.
vanilla extract	As the name suggests, this is a pure extract from crushed vanilla pods, producing a thick, aromatic liquid. Use it wherever vanilla is called for. Vanilla essence is a poor substitute.

BRUNCH
breakfast + lunch
ease into it

Far from being a chore, the first meal of the day should be something to savour and enjoy. Breakfast is fast disappearing as a meal to be enjoyed at home, so if you are one of those people who eat in the car or on the way to work, try getting up a few minutes earlier. It doesn't take long to pour some muesli into a bowl or make a few slices of toast, and it will give you enough energy to at least get through to elevenses.

In this chapter we've included the basics: how to poach an egg, make an omelette, prepare a pot of porridge and put together a simple bowl of muesli. We've also given you plenty of creative ideas for weekends, when breakfast can easily be turned into brunch with friends by preparing a selection of dishes and adding coffee and perhaps a glass of sparkling wine. Don't forget that muffins and savoury tarts are also a great addition to brunch, and see the Sauces and Preserves chapter for ideas on making your own jams and marmalades.

brunch recipes

Apricot and almond muesli	6
Bircher muesli	6
Porridge with stewed apple, raisins and honey	7
Moroccan spiced breakfast couscous	7
Grilled peaches with goat's curd and honey	8
Fruit compote	8
Winter fruit compote	9
Ricotta hotcakes with poached raspberries	10
Blueberry pikelets	12
French toast sandwiches filled with chocolate	13
Gingerbread wafflecakes with honeycomb butter and banana	14
Croque monsieur	16
Grilled tomatoes with basil butter and bacon	16
Mushrooms on toast	17
Poached eggs	18
Eggs Benedict	19
Scrambled eggs	19
Bacon and eggs	20
The big brekkie	20
Hangover breakfast	21
Omelettes	22
Omelette wraps filled with smoked salmon, spinach and soft cheese	23
Cherry tomato and parmigiano frittata	24
Potato tortilla	26
Baked eggs with spinach and cheddar	26
Deep-fried eggs with sweet chilli, coriander and lime sauce	27
Basil frittata with smoked salmon, rocket and horseradish cream	29
Egyptian spiced eggs	30
Sweetcorn and ricotta hotcakes with smoked salmon	31
Mediterranean eggs with tomato and chorizo	32
Corn fritters with crisp bacon and spiced tomatoes	34
Zucchini and feta fritters	35
Haloumi and potato cakes with smoked salmon	35
Baked beans with smoky ham hock	36
Smoked salmon and prawn kedgeree	37

Things you need to know about brunch

1 Whether you choose to eat breakfast at 6 a.m. or midday, this first meal of the day is essential to jump-start your metabolism.

2 You will need a large heavy-based pan for frying eggs and bacon, making scrambled eggs, hotcakes, fritters and French toast.

3 A Sunday breakfast can be as simple as warmed croissants with jam and a cup of properly brewed coffee.

4 Try making your own freshly squeezed juices every now and then.

5 Eggs have to be free-range, and organic free-range eggs are even better. You don't need to buy barn-laid or omega 3 enhanced eggs.

6 Eggs usually benefit from a little salt, so buy some top-quality sea salt flakes from a specialist food store – it'll be well worth the extra expense.

7 Breakfast doesn't have to mean a fry-up, but that style of food is okay every now and then. It's been proven that a big fry-up is the most effective way of sorting out a hangover – what more excuse do you need?

8 Liven up toast for breakfast by making your own jams and marmalades (pages 581–584).

Apricot and almond muesli

Makes just over 1½ kg

Easy to make and much more delicious than bought pre-mixes. We vary the flavours every time we make it, often adding additional ingredients such as desiccated coconut, wheat germ and sunflower seeds. Make a huge batch, divide into smaller bags and give these to your friends as Christmas presents.

1 kg (10 cups) rolled oats
125 g (¾ cup) dried apricots, chopped
90 g (⅔ cup) toasted almonds, chopped
150 g (1½ cups) bran
200 g (1¼ cups) sultanas

Combine all ingredients. Divide into plastic containers with tight-fitting lids and store in a cool dark place. Will keep for 2–3 months.

Apple and hazelnut muesli
Substitute hazelnuts for almonds and dried apple rings for apricots.

Date and walnut muesli
Substitute walnuts (or pecans) for almonds and dried dates for apricots.

Bircher muesli

Serves 6–8

We've played around with the traditional bircher muesli recipes and discovered that you don't need to add cream to make a good bircher. That's great news for our waistlines! Bircher muesli is lovely served with poached fruit such as plums, quinces or rhubarb.

150 g (1½ cups) rolled oats
55 g (⅓ cup) sultanas
30 g (⅓ cup) flaked almonds
250 ml (1 cup) milk
250 g (1 cup) natural yoghurt
1 apple, grated
150 g (1 cup) berries
1 banana, sliced
honey (optional)

Mix oats with sultanas, almonds, milk and yoghurt. Refrigerate overnight.

In the morning add apple, berries and banana.

Add honey to taste, and more milk or yoghurt if needed to adjust the consistency; it should be moist, but not runny.

Quick bircher muesli
Soak 1 cup of muesli with 1 cup of milk and 1 cup of yoghurt overnight. Serve with fresh fruit in the morning.

Porridge with stewed apple, raisins and honey

Serves 4

Porridge is perfect for cold winter mornings when you need a warming start to the day. Here, the simple combination of stewed apple and raisins on top adds a real flavour boost.

2 apples, peeled, cored and thinly sliced
85 g (½ cup) raisins
60 ml (¼ cup) water
2 tbsp caster sugar
pinch of cinnamon

150 g (1½ cups) rolled oats
500 ml (2 cups) water, additional
375 ml (1½ cups) milk
pinch of salt (optional)
milk and honey to serve

Place the apple slices in a small saucepan with the raisins, 60 ml water, caster sugar and cinnamon. Cover and cook over a medium heat for 10–12 minutes, stirring often, until the apples are tender but not cooked to a puree.

Place the oats, 500 ml water and milk in a heavy-based saucepan. Add salt, if using. Bring to the boil, and then reduce to a gentle simmer. Cook for 10–15 minutes, stirring occasionally. Serve immediately with a dollop of stewed apple and raisins on top. Add milk and a drizzle of honey if desired.

Moroccan spiced breakfast couscous

Serves 4–6

A very sophisticated and exotic way to start the day. It is also delicious served with poached or stewed fruit (see pages 644–645) on top.

250 ml (1 cup) orange juice
½ tsp ground cinnamon
¼ tsp ground nutmeg
2 tsp caster sugar

250 g (1 cup) instant couscous
100 g (⅓ cup) natural yoghurt
2 tbsp honey
60 g (⅔ cup) flaked almonds

Place orange juice, cinnamon, nutmeg and sugar in a small saucepan. Heat to almost boiling. Remove from the heat, stir in the couscous, cover and allow to rest for 2 minutes. Place saucepan over a low heat and stir with a fork to break up the grains.

Mix yoghurt and honey together and refrigerate until required.

To serve, heap couscous into bowls, spoon sweet yoghurt on top and scatter with almonds.

Grilled peaches with goat's curd and honey

Serves 4

A rather decadent breakfast – and it makes a great dessert too.

4 peaches, cut in half and stone removed
100 g (½ cup) fresh goat's curd or ricotta
90 ml (⅓ cup) full-flavoured honey

Place peach halves skin side down on a grill tray. Cook under a hot grill until golden and slightly softened. Place peaches onto plates; divide goat's curd between halves and drizzle with honey.

Fruit compote

Serves 4–6

Make this with the season's best available ingredients: nectarines, apricots and berries in summer; plums and quinces in autumn; rhubarb and apples in winter; cherries in spring. This compote is great with muesli or porridge, or simply with a dollop of yoghurt.

3 nectarines, cut into thick wedges
6 plums, quartered
6 apricots, quartered
pulp from 4 passionfruit
pinch of saffron threads
80 ml (⅓ cup) water
55 g (¼ cup) caster sugar

Place the prepared fruit, saffron, water and caster sugar in a heavy-based saucepan and cook over a medium heat until the liquid comes to the boil. Reduce heat and simmer for 20 minutes, stirring occasionally. Allow to cool slightly before serving.

Winter fruit compote

Serves 6–8

Winter is a great time to prepare dried fruits as a delicious compote to serve with breakfast. The choice of fruits that can be used is quite extensive – anything from prunes, apricots and raisins to figs, dates and peaches. Simply choose the combination that appeals to you. You can also substitute orange juice for the sugar and water if you prefer.

220 g (1 cup) caster sugar
500 ml (2 cups) water
1 vanilla pod
4 cardamom pods (split open)
2 cinnamon sticks
1 kg dried fruit of your choosing, as mentioned above
natural yoghurt to serve

Place sugar and water in a large heavy-based saucepan over medium heat. Dissolve sugar in water. Once dissolved add vanilla, cardamom and cinnamon sticks and bring to a gentle boil. Allow to simmer for 5 minutes.

Prepare dried fruits by removing stones from the prunes, if using. Then place all the fruits into the simmering syrup. Cook gently for 20 minutes, then allow fruit and syrup to cool.

Remove cardamom pods and cinnamon stick if preferred. Serve compote with a dollop of natural yoghurt on top and a drizzle of the poaching liquid.

Seasonal winter fruit compote
The compote recipe can use in-season winter fruits instead of dried; try a similar quantity of apple and pear wedges, quince slices and chopped rhubarb instead. Cook as directed.

Ricotta hotcakes with poached raspberries

Serves 4–6

These ricotta hotcakes make a perfect brunch dish. They can be served with a range of different fruit, from banana and maple syrup to oven-roasted apricots or poached berries.

165 g (¾ cup) caster sugar
180 ml (¾ cup) water
300 g (2⅓ cups) raspberries
2 eggs
250 g (1 cup) ricotta
60 ml (¼ cup) milk
125 g (½ cup) natural yoghurt
2 tbsp caster sugar, additional
150 g (1 cup) self-raising flour
½ tsp baking powder
½ tsp salt
oil

Preheat oven to 180°C.

Place the caster sugar and water in a medium-sized saucepan over a low heat to allow the sugar to dissolve. Raise heat and bring to the boil. Place the berries in the hot syrup and heat through. Strain the berries immediately, reserving the cooking liquid. Return the cooking liquid to the saucepan and boil to reduce by half. Allow syrup to cool a little, and then add the berries.

Beat the eggs and ricotta together. Add milk, yoghurt and additional 2 tbsp caster sugar, and beat until smooth. Sift the flour with baking powder and salt, and add to the ricotta base. Stir until combined. It should be quite thick.

Heat a heavy-based pan over a medium–low heat. Add a splash of oil, then add ladlefuls of ricotta mix to form pikelet-sized hotcakes. Cook until the bases are golden brown. Turn the hotcakes over and cook for a further 2–3 minutes. Repeat until the mixture is used up, adding more oil as needed and keeping the cooked hotcakes warm in the oven. This mixture makes at least 12 hotcakes.

Serve hotcakes with poached raspberries on top.

Ricotta hotcakes with banana and maple syrup
Once the hotcakes are cooked, turn the heat up slightly and add a splash more oil. Add 2 sliced bananas and cook for 1–2 minutes on each side. Serve hotcakes with bananas on top and drizzle with maple syrup.

Blueberry pikelets

Makes 12–15 pikelets

Pikelets are one of our son Luke's favourite brekkie foods. We vary the fruit according to the season. In winter we cook the pikelets with no fruit and serve them with poached quinces or rhubarb and with yoghurt on top.

250 ml (1 cup) milk
1 medium egg
150 g (1 cup) self-raising flour
oil
150 g (1 cup) blueberries
maple syrup and natural yoghurt to serve

Beat milk, egg and flour together until smooth. Heat a heavy-based pan over medium–low heat. Add a splash of oil and wipe it with kitchen paper so it is a thin coating. Add 3–4 spoonfuls of batter to the hot pan. Add 4 or 5 blueberries to each pikelet and cook until bubbles start to form on the surface. Turn pikelets over and continue to cook for 2–3 minutes.

Repeat with remaining batter. Serve with maple syrup and natural yoghurt.

Banana pikelets
Replace blueberries with banana slices.

Summer berry pikelets
Omit blueberries from the mix, instead serve pikelets with 150 g (1 cup) mixed berries and a generous spoonful of mascarpone.

French toast sandwiches filled with chocolate

Serves 4

Just when you thought French toast couldn't get any better, along come these little beauties. Try serving them with a tart cherry jam or a drizzle of maple syrup.

3 eggs
60 ml (¼ cup) milk
salt and freshly ground black pepper
8 pieces of brioche or day-old bread
chocolate and hazelnut spread (Nutella)
oil
raspberries to serve (optional)

Whisk the eggs, milk, salt and pepper together until combined. Spread Nutella on 4 slices of brioche or bread. Top with remaining slices.

Take each sandwich and soak one side and then the other in the egg mixture until well coated on both sides. Heat a large heavy-based frypan over a medium–high heat. Add a generous splash of oil and the bread (you may need to cook in 2 batches, depending on the size of the bread). Cook for 3–4 minutes on each side until well browned.

Cut in half diagonally and serve immediately, with raspberries if desired.

Gingerbread waffle cakes with honeycomb butter and banana

Serves 6

We love waffles, so when we came across this recipe on an American website we were instantly smitten. If, like us, you don't have a waffle machine, just cook small circles of the batter in a warm frypan. I have dreams about these waffle cakes, and on waking I proceed to the kitchen instantly to make a batch. MC

125 g soft butter
60 g honeycomb, crushed
200 g (1⅓ cups) self-raising flour
1 tsp ground cinnamon
1 tsp ground ginger
¼ tsp ground cloves

4 eggs, separated
250 ml (1 cup) milk
50 g (¼ cup) brown sugar
60 ml (¼ cup) golden syrup
oil
4 bananas

Preheat oven to 180°C.

Mash butter with a fork and fold in honeycomb. Place butter on a piece of greaseproof paper. Roll up tightly to form a large sausage. Chill until required.

Sift together the flour, cinnamon, ginger and cloves. Beat the egg whites until stiff peaks form. Beat together the egg yolks, milk, brown sugar and golden syrup until thoroughly blended.

Add the egg yolk mixture to the sifted ingredients and stir until combined. Fold through egg whites.

Place a large frypan over a medium heat and add a splash of oil. Make sure the frypan isn't too hot or the waffle cakes will burn. Spoon in waffle mix to form 6 cm circles. Cook until bubbles form on top and the bases are golden brown. Turn the waffle cakes over and cook for a further 2–3 minutes. Repeat until the mixture is used up, adding more oil as needed and keeping the cooked waffle cakes warm in the oven.

Slice bananas and honeycomb butter. Top waffle cakes with slices of both.

Croque monsieur

Serves 4

Croque monsieur is an up-market toasted sandwich dish with a rich filling of cheese, mustard and smoked ham. It'll help bring a taste of Paris to your breakfast table.

90 g (1 cup) mix of grated cheese, such as gruyere, cheddar and parmigiano
2 tbsp sour cream
freshly ground black pepper
pinch of grated nutmeg
1 tsp Worcestershire sauce (optional)
½ tsp Dijon mustard
4 slices smoked ham
8 slices white bread
soft butter

Mix cheese with sour cream, pepper, nutmeg, Worcestershire sauce and mustard to form a smooth paste.

Spread the cheese mixture on four slices of bread, top each with a ham slice and another slice of bread to form sandwiches. Butter the outside of both slices of bread.

Heat a heavy-based pan over a medium–high heat. Add sandwiches and cook for 3–4 minutes on each side until golden brown and crisp.

Grilled tomatoes with basil butter and bacon

Serves 4

Most people love the flavours of tomatoes, bacon and basil together. In summer we cook the tomatoes and bacon on the barbecue and enjoy breakfast outside. It's called driving the neighbours wild.

60 g soft butter
2 tbsp chopped basil leaves
freshly ground black pepper
2–4 ripe tomatoes, stalks removed, and cut in half
8 thin slices bacon
oil
4 slices sourdough bread

Mix butter, basil and a little pepper until well combined. Turn basil butter onto a square of greaseproof paper and roll paper around butter to form a sausage shape. Refrigerate until firm.

Place tomatoes and bacon on grill tray and drizzle tomatoes with olive oil. Place under a medium-heat grill and cook for 6–7 minutes, or until tomatoes soften and bacon is crisp. Turn regularly to ensure even cooking.

Toast sourdough until golden. Serve toast topped with grilled bacon and tomatoes and sliced rounds of basil butter.

Mushrooms on toast

Serves 4

Mushrooms are one of the simplest things to pan-fry. In autumn wild mushrooms such as pines and slippery jacks are excellent. Try mixing wild mushrooms with button mushrooms, or use your favourite mix of exotics such as oyster or shiitake.

500 g mushrooms of your choice
2 tbsp olive oil
salt and freshly ground black pepper
fresh chopped herbs
toast for serving

Cut mushrooms to a similar size if necessary, to allow even cooking. Heat a heavy-based frying pan over medium–high heat, then add oil. Add mushrooms and toss to coat. Continue cooking, moving mushrooms so that they cook evenly, until they start to soften. Add salt, pepper and fresh chopped herbs to taste. Serve straight away on toast.

Poached eggs

Serves 2 eggs per person

Cooking poached eggs is like riding a bike. Learning is often painful and messy, but once mastered it's a skill to relish for life. You will need a deep-sided frypan and a slotted spoon. An egg poacher will make things much easier, but patience and the freshest eggs are the real essentials. Some people say that adding a teaspoon of acid, such as vinegar or lemon juice, will help keep the eggs in shape. To my way of thinking, this just adds an unnecessary sour flavour. MC

eggs, 2 per person toast to serve
salt and freshly ground black pepper

Fill your deep-sided frypan with 2–3 cm of water. Place over a medium heat and bring to a slow simmer, with bubbles gently popping on the surface. Some people like to swirl the water as they add the eggs to get the whites to stay together. This works for the first egg but is very tricky for the second. (If you are using fresh eggs you won't have this problem anyway; and if a bit of white floats away it's hardly the end of the world, is it?)

Crack eggs gently into simmering water. Add as many eggs as you are comfortable dealing with (4 is good and we eat in groups as the eggs are ready). Leave them to cook for 3 minutes, making sure the water doesn't boil. Gently spoon the cooking water over the top of the eggs, as this helps them to cook.

Okay, nearly there. Have a gentle poke at the eggs; the whites should be firm, but the yolks still soft. Have a paper towel nearby. Lift out the eggs, one by one, using the slotted spoon. Rest the spoon briefly on the paper towel to absorb water, then carefully slide each egg onto a slice of hot buttered toast and serve. Bear in mind that the yolk is about to be broken in 5 seconds, so if you do it at this stage, just think of it as an extra service to your breakfast companions. Serve with salt and pepper.

Eggs Benedict

Serves 4

Now that we are poached eggs experts, let's make Eggs Benedict. If you are still struggling with poached eggs, treat yourself to a morning off and go out for breakfast. Then try them again next weekend.

16 slices bacon
4 English muffins, each split in two
8 medium eggs
chives to garnish
Hollandaise Sauce (page 555)

Place pan on as directed for poaching eggs. Start cooking the bacon by pan-frying until brown and crispy. Place in oven to keep warm as it becomes ready. Toast muffins and also keep warm. Then, last but not least, begin poaching eggs.

When eggs are ready place 2 toasted muffin halves on each plate. Add a piece of cooked bacon to each muffin. Place eggs on top of bacon, then add a spoonful of Hollandaise Sauce (page 555). Garnish with chives.

Eggs Florentine
Omit bacon and spoon hot blanched spinach onto the toasted muffins just before eggs. Then top with a spoonful of hollandaise sauce and garnish with chives.

Scrambled eggs

Serves 2

The trick with scrambled eggs is to take the mixture from the heat when just under-cooked, as it will continue to cook a while longer. When just done, serve immediately. If you overcook your eggs, simply add another raw egg to the pan and stir gently. It will bring them back to moist, fluffy gorgeousness.

2 tbsp clarified butter
6 eggs
60 ml (¼ cup) cream
salt and freshly ground black pepper
chopped chives
toast to serve

Heat a heavy-based saucepan or frypan over a medium heat. Add butter, then beat together the eggs, cream, salt and pepper and pour into the pan. Cook for 3–4 minutes, stirring frequently. Serve with chopped chives and slices of hot buttered toast.

Herbed scrambled eggs
In place of chives add 2 tbsp chopped fresh herbs of your choice to cooked eggs. Basil and flat-leaf parsley are particularly good.

Saffron scrambled eggs
Cook 10 saffron threads in the butter for 2–3 minutes, or until fragrant, before adding the egg mix.

Bacon and eggs

A classic in its own right.

oil
2 or 3 slices bacon per person
1 or 2 medium eggs per person
salt and freshly ground black pepper
toast and tea to serve

Heat a large heavy-based frying pan over a medium–high heat. Add a splash of oil and cook bacon until crispy on each side. (If you are cooking for a few, place bacon in warm oven to keep hot while you cook the eggs.) Everyone has their own view on how much oil to use when frying eggs: some say lots, others keep it to a minimum. Practice and experience will teach you how much oil to add, but start with enough to coat the base of the pan.

Crack eggs into pan and cook for 2–3 minutes. If eggs are spluttering a lot, turn heat down. Serve them sunny side up or turn eggs over and allow to cook for 1–2 minutes on the other side.

Serve on hot buttered toast with a big pot (or two) of Irish breakfast tea.

The big brekkie

Serves 4

A big brekkie doesn't always have to include meat, as you'll see here. Instead, it focuses on fried eggs, grilled tomatoes and mushrooms, all served on sourdough toast. Rather than using a selection of pans, you may find it easier to use a flat-plate barbecue. This big brekkie is also great with Corn Fritters (page 34) or Zucchini and Feta Fritters (page 35).

oil
4 large ripe tomatoes, halved
8 medium mushrooms
salt and freshly ground black pepper
2 tbsp butter
4 eggs
8 slices sourdough bread
pesto

Heat an oiled barbecue plate to medium. Place the tomatoes and mushrooms on the grill and season with salt and pepper. Dot the butter over the mushrooms. Allow the tomatoes and mushrooms to cook for 3–4 minutes, then turn them over.

Crack the eggs onto the hotplate and cook for 2–3 minutes. If the eggs are spluttering a lot, turn the heat down. Serve the eggs sunny side up or turn them over and allow to cook for 1–2 minutes on the other side.

Toast the sourdough bread and spread lightly with pesto. Divide the tomato, mushrooms and eggs between the slices of toast and serve immediately, with more pesto on the side.

Hangover breakfast

Serves 4

It has been proven that fried food is the best cure for a hangover. It's true, we saw it on television! Not only that, we have first-hand experience. MC

oil
8–12 slices bacon
150 g mushrooms
2 tomatoes, halved
salt and freshly ground black pepper
4 eggs
toast to serve

Preheat oven to 150°C.

Heat a large heavy-based frypan over a medium–high heat. Add oil and bacon and cook for 2–3 minutes, until brown and crispy. Remember that the bacon is going to sit in the oven for at least 5 minutes, so don't overcook it or it will be too crispy. Place in oven to keep warm.

If necessary, add a splash of oil to the pan. Add mushrooms and tomatoes, cut side down. Season with salt and pepper. Cook for 3–4 minutes, tossing the mushrooms occasionally. Turn the tomatoes and cook for a further 2–3 minutes. Transfer to oven.

Again, if necessary, add a splash of oil to the pan. Add eggs and cook for 3–4 minutes, or until the whites are firm but the yolks are still runny. If you don't like your eggs sunny side up, flip them over and cook for 1–2 minutes.

Serve eggs on toast with bacon, mushrooms and tomatoes alongside, with plenty of strong coffee. We promise you'll be feeling better in no time at all. If all else fails, try a glass of Coke and a nanna nap.

Omelettes

Makes 1 omelette

Knowing how to make a great omelette is an essential life skill. It's also a handy little thing to have up your sleeve for those times when there's nothing in the refrigerator except, hopefully, a couple of eggs. Finishing the omelette under a grill or in the oven helps to puff it up, so it's worth doing.

3 eggs
salt and freshly ground black pepper
1 tbsp clarified butter
handful of grated parmigiano or your favourite cheese
chopped fresh herbs

Whisk the eggs together with a pinch of salt and freshly ground black pepper. Heat a heavy-based frypan over a medium heat. Give the pan plenty of time to heat properly.

Add butter and allow it to melt. Pour the egg mix into the pan, spread evenly and cook for 1–2 minutes, or until the base has set. Place cheese and fresh herbs on half of the omelette and fold the remaining half over. Finish under a grill or in a hot oven and serve straight away.

Ham and tomato omelette
Add a handful of sliced ham and 2–3 tomato slices along with the cheese.

Mushroom omelette
Allow 2 button mushrooms per person. Cook sliced mushrooms in a little butter with fresh herbs and salt and pepper until soft. Add to omelette with cheese and herbs.

Spinach and feta omelette
Substitute feta for parmigiano and add a handful of chopped blanched spinach.

Omelette wraps filled with smoked salmon, spinach and soft cheese

Serves 6

These omelettes can be made in advance and cut when you're ready to serve them. You can also slice them into thin 5 mm strips and serve them as a pre-dinner nibble or with cocktails. The wraps are spread with soft curd cheese but you could try them with labne, a yoghurt cheese from the Middle East.

6 eggs
60 ml (¼ cup) milk
salt and freshly ground black pepper
oil
100 g (½ cup) soft curd cheese or yoghurt cheese (labne)
6 slices smoked salmon
100 g baby spinach leaves or rocket

Whisk the eggs together with milk, a pinch of salt and freshly ground black pepper. Heat a heavy-based frypan over a medium heat. Give the frypan plenty of time to heat properly.

Add a splash of oil, then add enough egg to thinly coat the base of the frypan. Cook briefly until the egg sets. Place the omelette onto a plate and allow to cool. Repeat with the remaining egg mix until you have 6 thin omelettes.

Spread cheese over half of each omelette, top with a slice of salmon and divide spinach leaves between the 6 omelettes. Roll up the omelettes, encasing all the ingredients. If needed, refrigerate until ready to serve.

Cut each omelette in half on the diagonal. Arrange on plates and serve.

Cherry tomato and parmigiano frittata

Serves 4–6

This is a really light frittata packed with sweet cherry tomatoes and full-flavoured parmigiano cheese.

olive oil
2 onions, finely diced
½ red capsicum, diced
100 g cherry tomatoes, cut into halves
6 medium eggs
100 g (¾ cup) parmigiano, grated
¼ cup chopped fresh herbs such as parsley, thyme and chives

Preheat oven to 190°C.

Heat a small frying pan over a medium heat. Add two tablespoons of olive oil and cook onion and capsicum until slightly softened. Add tomato halves and cook together for 5 minutes. Beat together eggs, cheese and herbs in a large bowl. Pour onto cooking tomatoes. Cook for 4–5 minutes on stovetop until egg forms a cooked base. Place pan in preheated oven to finish cooking, about 10–15 minutes. Serve warm.

Broccoli frittata
Use the onion as a base, add blanched broccoli florets, parmigiano and cook in the same way.

Roast vegetable frittata
Add a selection of roasted vegetables, such as zucchini, eggplant or capsicum, parmigiano and cook in the same way.

Roasted pumpkin and feta frittata
Beat eggs together with salt and pepper. When pumpkin is cooked remove pan from oven and return to a medium heat on the stovetop. Pour eggs on top of pumpkin and arrange feta and thyme leaves in egg mix. Cook for 4-5 minutes on stovetop until egg forms a cooked base. Return pan to oven to finish cooking, approximately 10-15 minutes. Serve warm.

Prosciutto and olive frittata
Cook 3 or 4 slices of prosciutto with onions. Add egg mix, parmigiano, 90 g (½ cup) pitted kalamata olives and cook in the same way.

Potato tortilla

Serves 6

This classic Spanish dish is very similar to a frittata, combining a simple trio of eggs and vegetables. The secret is in the free-range eggs, the slow-cooked onions and the addition of flavour-filled potatoes such as nicolas, desiree or kipfler.

6 potatoes (800 g), peeled
80 ml (⅓ cup) olive oil
4 onions, sliced
2–3 sprigs of thyme (optional)
salt and freshly ground black pepper
6 eggs

Place the peeled potatoes in a saucepan and cover with water. Cook until just tender. Drain and set aside.

Heat a large heavy-based frypan over a medium–low heat. Add oil, onions and thyme (if using), and season with salt and pepper. Cook for 15–20 minutes, stirring often, until the onions soften and caramelise, turning golden brown.

Beat the eggs together with salt and pepper. Cut potatoes into 1 cm slices and add to the caramelised onions, tossing gently to combine and taking care not to break up the potatoes. Pour the egg mix over the onions and potatoes; it should just cover the potatoes.

Cook for 8–10 minutes over a low heat until well set. Slide the tortilla onto a plate and turn it over gently, then slide it back into the frypan. Cook for a further 5–6 minutes on a low heat, or until the egg is set and cooked. If you prefer, you can finish cooking the tortilla in a preheated 180°C oven.

Baked eggs with spinach and cheddar

Serves 6

Take fresh eggs, add the best farmhouse cheddar you can find and you'll soon have a delicious egg dish for breakfast, without the need to boil, poach or scramble anything.

1 bunch spinach leaves, thoroughly washed
12 medium eggs
200 g (2 cups) grated cheddar

Preheat oven to 180°C.

Blanch spinach leaves in boiling water, squeeze out excess water and chop roughly. Divide this between 6 buttered ramekin dishes. Break 2 eggs into each dish, add a handful of grated cheddar and bake in preheated oven for 15 minutes, or until cheese is golden and eggs are puffy.

Deep-fried eggs with sweet chilli, coriander and lime sauce

Serves 6

A very decadent dish guaranteed to get rid of all hangovers, or at least make you forget about them for a short time. Serve with fresh crusty bread.

220 g (1 cup) caster sugar
250 ml (1 cup) water
⅔ cup coriander roots and stems, finely chopped
1 small red chilli, cut in half
2 cm ginger, thinly sliced
80 ml (⅓ cup) lime juice
finely chopped zest of 2 limes
1 tbsp fish sauce
12 eggs
100 g bean shoots
¼ cup coriander leaves, sliced
½ red capsicum, thinly sliced
500 ml (2 cups) olive oil

Put the sugar and water in a small saucepan and cook over a medium heat until the sugar has dissolved. Continue cooking until the liquid has reduced by half, approximately 5 minutes. Add chopped coriander, chilli and ginger and simmer for 5 minutes more. Remove from heat, add lime juice, zest and fish sauce and allow to cool. Strain the sauce into a small saucepan.

Fill a frypan with 2–3 cm of water. Place over a medium heat and bring to a gentle simmer, with bubbles gently popping on the surface (you don't want large bubbles to break the surface). If necessary turn the heat down a little. Crack eggs 2 or 3 at a time into simmering water, and cook for 1 ½ minutes, or until the whites are just set and the yolks still runny. Spoon eggs gently onto a tray lined with paper towel, pat dry and allow to cool. Continue until all eggs are poached.

Mix together bean shoots, sliced coriander leaves and capsicum strips. Toss with ⅓ cup of the sweet chilli, coriander and lime sauce you made earlier.

Pour olive oil into a wok or a deep saucepan to a depth of 4 cm and heat.

If the oil begins to smoke it is too hot. Re-heat the remaining lime sauce, season to taste and keep warm. Deep-fry the eggs 3 at a time until golden. Keep the fried eggs warm until all are cooked.

To serve, place 2 deep-fried eggs on the centre of each plate and a mound of dressed salad on top. Drizzle lime sauce over to finish.

Basil frittata with smoked salmon, rocket and horseradish cream

Serves 4

This frittata makes a simple but sophisticated brunch. You can serve it cold or warm, depending on your personal preference.

1–2 tsp horseradish cream
250 ml (1 cup) sour cream
6 eggs
80 ml (⅓ cup) cream
⅓ cup shredded basil
40 g (½ cup) grated parmigiano
salt and freshly ground black pepper
oil
16 slices smoked salmon
100 g rocket

Mix horseradish and sour cream together. Add more horseradish if you like the kick. Set aside.

Lightly beat the eggs, then add the cream, basil, parmigiano, salt and pepper. Heat a medium-sized heavy-based frypan over a medium–high heat. Add a splash of oil and pour in the egg mix. Lower heat and cook for 4–5 minutes, or until the frittata is mostly set. Finish under a grill or in a hot oven. Allow to cool.

Slide the frittata out of the pan while still warm. You may need to run a palette knife under the frittata to ease it out. Cut into 8 wedges.

Arrange 1 wedge on each plate and top with 1 slice of smoked salmon. Top with another piece of frittata, some rocket and 1 more slice of smoked salmon. Finish with a dollop of the horseradish cream.

Egyptian spiced eggs

Serves 6

A twist on fried eggs. Sprinkle as much spice as you like on the eggs as they are cooking and serve the remainder alongside the cooked eggs, allowing guests to add more to suit their taste. Serve the eggs on toasted pide bread with Spiced Tomatoes (page 34) and crispy bacon.

1 tsp ground coriander
1 tsp ground cumin
1 tsp sweet paprika
½ tsp salt
freshly ground black pepper
oil
12 medium free-range eggs
toasted pide bread

Mix spices, salt and pepper together.

Heat a large heavy-based frypan over a medium–high heat. Add a splash of oil. (Everyone has their own view on how much oil to use when frying eggs: some say lots, others keep it to a minimum. Experience will teach you how much oil to add, but start with enough to coat the base of the frypan.) Crack 2 or 3 eggs into the frypan and cook for 2–3 minutes. If the eggs are spluttering a lot, turn heat down. Sprinkle with a little of the spice mixture. Turn the eggs over and cook for 1 minute more. Repeat with remaining eggs.

To serve, pile eggs onto toasted pide bread and add an extra sprinkle of the spice mix if desired.

Sweetcorn and ricotta hotcakes with smoked salmon

Serves 6

These hotcakes work well as breakfast, a light lunch or an entree. Make smaller versions and you have a pre-dinner nibble.

- 2 eggs
- 250 g (1 cup) ricotta
- 60 ml (¼ cup) milk
- 125 g (½ cup) natural yoghurt
- 150 g (1 cup) self-raising flour
- ½ tsp baking powder
- ½ tsp salt
- 2 corn cobs, kernels removed with a sharp knife
- 2 tbsp chopped parsley
- oil
- rocket to serve
- 12 slices smoked salmon

Preheat oven to 180°C.

Beat the eggs and ricotta together. Add milk and yoghurt, and beat until smooth. Sift the flour with baking powder and salt, and add to the ricotta base. Stir until combined. Stir the corn kernels and parsley through the pancake mixture.

Heat a heavy-based pan over a medium heat. Add a splash of oil, then add ladlefuls of ricotta mix to form pikelet-sized hotcakes. Cook until bubbles form on top and the bases are golden brown. Turn the hotcakes over and cook for a further 2–3 minutes. Repeat until the mixture is used up, adding more oil as needed and keeping the cooked hotcakes warm in the oven. You will need at least 12 hotcakes.

Place 1 hotcake on each plate. Top each one with a handful of rocket leaves, followed by another hot cake. Add more rocket leaves and arrange 2 slices of smoked salmon on top. Serve immediately.

Mediterranean eggs with tomato and chorizo

Serves 4

This tomato, onion and chorizo sauce is cooked in a large pan with eggs, and served on toasted sourdough bread. It makes a full-flavoured brunch dish to share.

1 red capsicum
oil
salt and freshly ground black pepper
1 onion, diced
1 hot chorizo, cut into ½ cm slices
1 garlic clove, crushed
1 tsp harissa
4 tomatoes, diced
125 ml (½ cup) water
1 tbsp chopped basil or parsley
4 eggs

Preheat oven to 180°C.

Rub capsicum with oil, salt and pepper. Place in a baking tray and roast for 20 minutes, or until the skin blisters. Set aside to cool. Peel skin, remove seeds and slice the capsicum flesh into 1 cm slices.

Heat a large frypan over medium–high heat. Add a generous splash of oil and the onion and chorizo. Cook for 7–8 minutes, until the onion is softened and golden brown. Add garlic and harissa and cook for 1–2 minutes, until fragrant. Add tomatoes, water, herbs and capsicum, season with salt and pepper, and simmer for 10–15 minutes, until the tomatoes are cooked to a rich sauce. Check seasoning. Crack the eggs on top of the sauce and cook until the whites are cooked but the yolks are still runny. Don't stir the sauce after adding the eggs.

Divide the eggs, tomato and chorizo mix between slices of toasted sourdough.

Corn fritters with crisp bacon and spiced tomatoes

Serves 4–6

We've made these corn fritters as an alfresco breakfast wherever we've happened to find ourselves, whether it be the lighthouse at Wilsons Prom or Pambula beach.

1 tsp ground cumin
1 tsp ground coriander
¼ tsp smoky paprika
salt and freshly ground black pepper
2 tbsp oil
500 g cherry tomatoes
75 g (½ cup) self-raising flour
180 g (1 cup) polenta
½ tsp salt
1 tsp baking powder
1 egg
250 ml (1 cup) milk
2 corn cobs, kernels removed with a sharp knife
oil
8–12 slices bacon

Preheat oven to 180°C.

Mix the cumin, coriander, paprika, salt, pepper and oil together. Brush the tomatoes with the mix and place on a baking tray. Roast in the preheated oven for 20 minutes or until softened. Keep warm until needed.

Combine the flour, polenta, salt and baking powder. Add egg and milk, and mix until the batter is smooth. If the batter is too thick, add a little more milk. Add the corn kernels to the mixture.

Heat a heavy-based frypan over a medium heat. Add 1–2 tbsp oil and spoonfuls of batter. Cook on one side until golden brown, with bubbles forming on top. Turn the fritters over and cook until golden brown on the other side. Repeat until the mixture is used up, adding more oil as needed and keeping the cooked fritters warm in the oven.

Using the same frypan, cook bacon until crisp. To serve, place crisp bacon on top of corn fritters with tomatoes on the side.

Zucchini and feta fritters

Makes 20–24

These zucchini fritters make a great brunch dish and are terrific served alongside bacon and tomatoes. If you've ever wondered what to do with zucchinis, wonder no more!

2 zucchinis, coarsely grated
2 eggs, separated
125 ml (½ cup) milk
125 g (½ cup) natural yoghurt
100 g soft feta, chopped
½ cup chopped basil leaves

150 g (1 cup) self-raising flour
½ tsp baking powder
¼ tsp salt
freshly ground black pepper
oil

Put the grated zucchinis in a clean tea towel. Tightly squeeze the tea towel to force out as much liquid as you can.

Mix the egg yolks, milk, yoghurt, feta and basil leaves together. Sift the flour with baking powder and salt, and add to wet mix. Stir until combined. Stir in the grated zucchini and plenty of freshly ground black pepper. Whisk the egg whites until thick, then fold gently into the fritter mix. It should be a nice dropping consistency.

Heat a heavy-based pan over a medium–high heat. Add a ½ cm layer of oil. Deep-fry spoonfuls of the fritter mix until golden brown on both sides and allow to drain on kitchen paper.

Haloumi and potato cakes with smoked salmon

Serves 6

Use waxy potatoes such as bintje, desiree or spunta for this recipe.

4 potatoes, peeled
125 g haloumi
chopped fresh herbs
salt and freshly ground black pepper

oil
100 g rocket
12 slices smoked salmon
sour cream

Preheat oven to 180°C.

Coarsely grate the potatoes and squeeze away excess starch. Grate the haloumi and place in a bowl along with the potato, chopped herbs, salt and pepper. Mix well.

Heat a heavy-based pan over a medium–high heat. Add a generous amount of oil. Spoon in the potato mix, aiming for rough circles 6 cm wide. Allow to cook for a couple of minutes, without stirring. The mixture will begin to brown and hold itself together. Using a palette knife, loosen the base of each potato cake. Turn them over and cook for a further 5 minutes. Remove from the pan, place on a baking tray and cook in the preheated oven for 10–12 minutes.

To serve, top each cake with a handful of rocket, 2 slices of smoked salmon and a spoonful of sour cream.

Baked beans with smoky ham hock

Serves 6

Give Heinz the flick and make your own baked beans. It takes a little effort to prepare the beans and the ham hock but the end result is well worth it. If your tastebuds prefer a hit of spice, add 1–2 chopped chillies.

- 1 ham hock
- 250 g (1⅓ cups) white beans, soaked in cold water
- oil
- 2 onions, diced
- 2 cloves garlic, crushed
- 250 ml (1 cup) tomato sugo
- salt and freshly ground black pepper
- 2 tbsp chopped parsley
- fresh crusty bread

Place ham hock in a large saucepan. Cover with water and bring to the boil. Reduce to a simmer and cook for 1 hour, or until the meat is cooked and beginning to fall off the bone. Remove any scum that comes to the surface during cooking. Set the meat aside to cool in the cooking liquid.

Place the beans in a saucepan, cover with plenty of water and bring to the boil. Reduce heat and cook for 30–40 minutes, until the beans are tender. Remove any scum that comes to the surface during cooking.

Remove the ham hock from the cooking liquid. Remove skin, bone and tendons, and discard. Chop ham meat into chunks. Strain the cooking liquid and set aside.

Preheat oven to 180°C.

Heat a large heavy-based saucepan over a medium–high heat. Add a splash of oil and the onions. Cook for 3–4 minutes, until the onions have softened. Add garlic and cook for 1–2 minutes, until fragrant. Add 1 cup of the reserved ham cooking liquid and the tomato sugo. Bring to the boil and add the cooked beans and chopped ham. Cover and cook in the preheated oven for 15–20 minutes, stirring occasionally. Add more cooking liquid if needed.

Check seasoning, add parsley and serve with crusty toast.

Smoked salmon and prawn kedgeree

Serves 4

Traditionally a kedgeree is made with smoked haddock, but this can be hard to find, so we tend to make it with salmon and prawns. It's a great rice dish that's good for brunch or even supper.

1 tbsp olive oil
2 onions, diced
2 tsp mild curry paste
400 g (2 cups) long grain rice
750 ml (3 cups) water
200 g green (raw) prawns, shells removed
2 medium eggs, hard boiled, peeled and cut into wedges
60 g butter, diced
150 g smoked salmon, cut into wide strips
2 tbsp chopped parsley

Preheat oven to 180°C.

Heat a medium-sized saucepan over a medium–high heat. Add oil and onion and cook until tender. Add curry paste and stir together for 1 minute. Add rice and water and bring to the boil. Reduce heat to low, cover and cook until all water is absorbed. Place rice in a buttered casserole dish and add the prawns and egg wedges on top. Dot rice with butter and cover casserole with foil. Place in the preheated oven and cook for 15 minutes. Remove foil and gently stir in the smoked salmon. Scatter parsley on top.

STARTERS

appetisers, nibbles + entrees

Dim sum, tapas, mezze, dips ... Australians just love to graze. Tasty little morsels appeal to our more casual style of eating, whether it's nibbles and drinks with a few friends or as a meal in itself.

Dates filled with blue cheese, felafel, Peking duck rice-paper rolls, crispy fritters, delicate pastries and blinis can all be served as appetisers or entrees, and are excellent with a glass of sparkling wine, a dry aromatic white or a good sherry.

Along with the recipes in this chapter, there are many other dishes you can try. The Moroccan Chicken Rolls (page 608) and Spiced Eggplant Parcels (page 612) from the Pastry chapter make great finger food. For more formal entrees see the following entree section and don't forget soups and light pasta dishes.

starter recipes

appetisers

Platters	42
Quick dip ideas	42
Pita crisps	43
Baba ghanoush	43
Hummus	44
Beetroot dip	44
Guacamole	45
White bean dip	45
Blinis	46
Crostini	46
Bruschetta	47
Spiced nuts	48
Dukkah	48
Warm garlic and fennel olives	49
Roasted chestnuts with jamon	49
Cherry tomato and buffalo mozzarella sticks	50
Grissini with prosciutto and truffle oil	50
Artichoke, prosciutto and buffalo mozzarella parcels	51
Grilled haloumi in vine leaves	51
Eggplant and feta rolls	52
Dates with blue cheese	54
Sushi rice	55
California rolls	55
Chicken liver pâté	56
Smoked trout pâté	57
Baccala	57
Country pork, veal and pistachio terrine	58
Pissaladière	59
Crispy stuffed mushrooms	59
Cauliflower polpetti	60
Spinach and haloumi fritters	61
Thai corn fritters	62
Zucchini-flower fritters with feta and basil	64
Lentil balls with chilli and sweet paprika	65
Dolmades	66
Cheese and zaatar kataifi parcels	67
Boreks	68
Onion bahjis	68
Chilli prawn balls	69
Chermoula prawns with tzatziki	70
Malaysian curry prawns	70
Pan-fried calamari	71
Deep-fried Thai calamari	71
Burghul-coated calamari	72
Oyster shooters	72
Oysters with jamon and harissa	73
Oysters with Vietnamese flavours	73
Steamed oysters with Asian flavours	74
Paper-wrapped chicken	74
Pandan chicken parcels	75
Pork gyoza	75
Wontons with Thai curry sauce	76
Spring rolls	78
Roast duck, chilli and coriander rolls	79
Peking duck and hoisin rice-paper rolls	80
Egg nets with noodle and herb salad	91
Sichuan chicken and fungi salad	92
Moorish prawn and mint salad	93
Tunisian prawns with fattouche	94
Moroccan mussel and fennel salad	95
Steamed mussels with garlic	96
Mussels with Thai chilli broth	97
Green chilli and coriander steamed mussels	98
Mussels with chorizo, tomato and couscous	101
Spiced pipis with risoni	102
Crab cakes with Thai cucumber salad	103
Stir-fried crabs with black beans and ginger	104
Seared calamari with chilli and balsamic dressing	105
Smoked trout and avocado toasts	106
Smoked salmon rillettes	107
Coriander-cured salmon	108
Hot and sour crispy salmon salad with lime dressing	110
Crispy-skin quail with Sichuan pepper and salt	111

entrees

Summer vegetable terrine	85
Goat's cheese souffle	86
Prawn cocktail	86
Twice-cooked goat's cheese souffles	87
Baked mushrooms with beetroot salad	88

Things you need to know about appetisers and nibbles

1 If you plan to serve cocktail food, make sure it can be eaten with one hand.

2 Remember to offer serviettes.

3 Serve 2-3 pieces per person before dinner or 8-10 pieces per person to substitute for a meal.

4 For a full-on cocktail party experience, allow at least 7 items per person for the first hour and add 2 more for each hour after that.

5 If you expect your guests to be drinking a lot of alcohol, increase the amount of food you'll be serving to help soak up the liquor.

6 Keep the dishes small – they're supposed to be a beginning to your meal rather than filling.

7 Another idea is to buy antipasto ingredients from your favourite deli, then serve up a platter.

8 Antipasto can range from marinated artichokes, olives and sun-dried tomatoes to baby bocconcini, thinly sliced prosciutto or salami and strips of roasted red capsicum.

9 Antipasto can also be supplemented with crispy grissini breadsticks or sliced ciabatta bread, plus a few fresh ingredients such as sliced capsicum, baby tomatoes, asparagus, green beans and radishes.

platters

A mixed platter is an excellent way to provide tasty nibbles before a meal and can be made up well in advance so that you can enjoy the party too. Remember to arrange the components so that foods with different colours and flavours are alongside each other to help make the platter more attractive to the eye.

ANTIPASTO PLATTER

The following can be considered for an antipasto platter: frittata wedges, black or green olives, bocconcini, sun-dried tomatoes, marinated artichoke hearts, diced feta cheese, strips of roasted red capsicum plus thinly sliced prosciutto, ham and salami. A bowl of tapenade is also good here. Serve with plenty of sliced focaccia bread or grissini sticks.

MIDDLE EASTERN PLATTER

A Middle Eastern platter might include small dolmades, felafel balls, black or green olives, marinated artichoke hearts and wedges of cucumber, capsicum and tomato. Thinly sliced bastourma (a spice-coated air-dried beef) and thinly sliced salami are also good, along with hummus, baba ghanoush and tzatziki. A bowl of Dukkah (page 47) and olive oil is also an excellent match with these foods. Serve with toasted crisp breads or pita bread.

VEGETABLE CRUDITÉ PLATTER

A typical crudité platter might include carrots, red capsicum, fennel and stalks of celery, all cut into long sticks; mushrooms, washed and quartered; cucumber cut into thin circles; tomatoes cut into wedges; and cherry tomatoes. Provide a few dips such as guacamole, beetroot dip or hummus. Serve with grissini sticks, corn chips and crisp breads.

Quick dip ideas

Here are some quick dip ideas for when unexpected guests arrive and you need to whip up a last-minute dip or dress up a store-bought one.

HUMMUS

Drizzle with olive oil and a sprinkling of smoky paprika, or top with a sprinkle of dukkah or zaatar.

JULIA'S HUMMUS

Whether you are making your own hummus or dressing up a bought one, for an extra zesty touch add chopped preserved lemon as our friend Julia Kelly does.

YOGHURT

Mix natural yoghurt with tahini, lemon juice, black pepper and garlic, or try it with grated cucumber, garlic and fresh herbs.

CANNED BEANS

Puree cannellini beans with garlic, olive oil, salt and freshly ground black pepper to make white bean dip. Take chickpeas and whiz with tahini, lemon juice, garlic and olive oil for hummus.

CREAM CHEESE

Make a creamy dip by pureeing cream cheese with garlic, fresh herbs, salt, freshly ground black pepper and lemon juice.

Pita crisps

Makes 80

Using pita bread to make your own crispbreads may sound like a lot of work, but they are so good it's well worth the effort.

1 × 450 g packet pita bread
olive oil as required
salt flakes
poppy seeds or toasted cumin seeds

Preheat oven to 180°C.

Using scissors, cut around the pita bread to produce 2 large circles. Brush the brown side of each pita bread circle with oil, then sprinkle on salt and poppy seeds. Lay the circles on top of each other.

Cut into crisps by cutting each circle in half, then quarters, then into 3 triangles. Lay them flat on baking trays and cook in the preheated oven for 5–10 minutes or until crisp.

Lemon and pepper pita crisps
The lemon and pepper mix you can buy from the supermarket is perfect on pita crisps.

Cheese and sesame seed pita crisps
Brush pita bread with oil, then sprinkle on grated parmigiano and sesame seeds. Cut and cook.

Baba ghanoush

Serves 6–8

Baba ghanoush is a classic Middle Eastern dip made with eggplants that have been cooked over a flame – best done over a gas stove or on a barbecue. It's this cooking that gives the dip its distinctive smoky flavour and aroma.

2 medium eggplants
½ tsp crushed garlic
1–2 tbsp lemon juice
3 tbsp tahini
80 g (⅓ cup) natural yoghurt
pinch of ground allspice
white pepper and salt

Cook each eggplant over a gas flame until the skin is charred and the flesh is completely softened inside. If eggplants are not completely softened they can be finished in a 180°C preheated oven. Allow to cool completely.

Peel away charred skin carefully and spoon flesh into a bowl. Mash with a fork until smooth. Stir in garlic, lemon juice, tahini and yoghurt along with allspice, white pepper and salt. Mix well and season to taste.

Serve with slices of Turkish pide bread or as part of a Middle Eastern antipasto platter.

Hummus

Serves 8–10

Hummus is probably the most famous of all the Middle Eastern dips. It's easy to make and the chickpeas give it a delicious nutty taste.

150 g (1 cup) chickpeas, soaked overnight
2 cloves garlic, chopped
90 ml (⅓ cup) tahini
2 tsp ground cumin
2 tsp ground coriander
2 tbsp lemon juice
60 ml (¼ cup) olive oil
salt and freshly ground black pepper
sweet paprika

Drain chickpeas and place in a saucepan, cover with plenty of water and bring to the boil, reduce heat and cook for 30–40 minutes, or until chickpeas are soft. Drain and retain cooking liquid.

Place cooked chickpeas in a food processor and pulse until they are smooth. Add garlic, tahini, spices, lemon juice, oil, salt and pepper.

Blend until all ingredients are smooth and well combined. If it's still thick add some of the cooking liquid. Adjust the seasoning by adding extra spices, lemon juice or salt and pepper.

Place the dip into a serving bowl. Drizzle a little olive oil on top, and sprinkle with sweet paprika. Serve with Lebanese bread.

Beetroot dip

Serves 6–8

We were first introduced to beetroot dip many years ago in Turkey, where it is often called beetroot salad. Basically we love it, and we think you will too.

3 medium beetroots
1–2 tbsp red wine vinegar
60 ml (¼ cup) olive oil
2 cloves garlic, crushed
1–2 tsp horseradish cream
salt and freshly ground black pepper

Place beetroots in a saucepan, cover with plenty of water and bring to the boil over a medium heat. Once boiling, reduce heat, cover and cook for 30–40 minutes, until beetroots are tender.

Allow beetroots to cool, remove skins and chop flesh roughly. Place beetroot in food processor; add vinegar and oil and process until smooth. Add garlic, horseradish, and salt and pepper to taste.

Serve with pita crisps or slices of baguette.

Creamy beetroot dip
For a milder, creamier dip, add 125 g (½ cup) sour cream or natural yoghurt with garlic and horseradish.

Guacamole

Serves 6–8

This dip is famous all over the world, and when you taste a good'un, you realise why. It's tasty, fresh and completely more-ish. Here is our favourite variation, just one of many hundreds in the world.

2–3 ripe avocados
1 tbsp lemon or lime juice
1–2 green chillies, de-seeded and diced
2 tbsp chopped coriander
1 spring onion, sliced
1 tomato, finely diced
salt and freshly ground black pepper
Tabasco, optional

Peel avocados and place flesh in a bowl. Mash to a coarse consistency with a fork. Add lemon juice, chilli, coriander, spring onion and tomato. Season with salt and pepper, adding a few drops of Tabasco if desired. Stir gently and taste, adding more citrus juice or chilli to suit.

Serve with toasted pita triangles or warmed corn chips.

White bean dip

Serves 6–8

This light and tasty dip is made from haricot beans and flavoured with lashings of garlic, fresh herbs and freshly ground black pepper. Serve with a drizzle of your best olive oil on top.

200 g (1 cup) haricot beans, soaked overnight
2–3 cloves garlic, crushed
2 tbsp lemon juice
salt and freshly ground black pepper
60 ml (¼ cup) chopped flat-leaf parsley
olive oil

Drain beans and place in a saucepan. Cover with plenty of water and bring to the boil, reduce heat and cook for 20–30 minutes, or until beans are soft. Drain well.

Place beans in food processor and puree until smooth. Add garlic and lemon juice, then season to taste with salt and pepper.

Place in a bowl and stir in chopped parsley. Drizzle olive oil on top before serving.

Blinis

Serves 20–25

Blinis are small buckwheat pancakes from Russia that were traditionally served with caviar. Even if you're not serving caviar, they make a great base for many other toppings.

1 sachet (7 g) dried yeast
2 tbsp warm milk
200 ml (¾ cup) milk
125 g (¾ cup) buckwheat flour
2 eggs, separated
pinch of salt
2 tbsp melted butter

Whisk yeast and warm milk together in a large bowl. Leave in a warm place until bubbles form on the surface. Whisk in 200 ml milk, flour, egg yolks and salt. Cover and leave until bubbles again form on the surface.

Beat egg whites until stiff. Fold whites into the blini mixture.

Heat a heavy-based pan over a medium heat. Brush melted butter into the pan, then spoon in level tablespoons of the blini mix. Allow to cook until bubbles appear on the surface, then turn them over and cook on the other side for 1–2 minutes, until just golden brown.

Place cooked blinis on a flat tray to cool. Continue cooking until all the mixture is used. When all the blinis are cooked, cover them with cling film until you are ready to add the toppings.

Crostini

Serves 20–30

Crostini are slices of French breadstick that have been baked until they are crisp. They can be topped with an endless array of ingredients or served with dips.

1 French breadstick
olive oil as required

Preheat oven to 160°C.

Slice bread into 1 cm slices. Brush each slice with oil. Place on flat baking trays and cook in the preheated oven for 10–15 minutes, or until crisp on top. Turn crostini slices over and continue cooking for a further 10 minutes, or until golden.

Crispbreads
Thinly slice focaccia bread and brush with olive oil as directed above.

TOPPINGS FOR BLINIS AND CROSTINI

Goat's cheese and tapenade
Goat's cheese and pesto
Pesto with roasted capsicum and a dollop of ricotta
Sun-dried tomato with salami, feta and basil
Marinated artichoke with roasted capsicum
Rocket leaves with pesto and goat's cheese
Thinly sliced ham with Dijon mustard
Salami with tapenade
Smoked salmon, sour cream, freshly ground black pepper and dill
Smoked salmon with sour cream and horseradish
Salmon caviar, crème fraîche and chives
Green Olive Salsa (page 564)

Bruschetta

Makes 6

You can go all out with this recipe and use slices of sourdough bread and add chopped coriander to the tomato mix, or even diced fresh chilli.

4 ripe tomatoes
6 basil leaves, thinly sliced
¼ cup roughly chopped parsley
½ small red onion, finely diced
salt and freshly ground black pepper
6 slices day-old bread
olive oil
1–2 cloves garlic, peeled (optional)

Dice tomatoes finely. Mix the tomato, basil, parsley and onion together and season to taste with salt and pepper.

Heat a char-grill pan, or a good heavy-based frypan, over a medium heat. Brush the bread with oil and cook until quite toasty. Remove from the pan and rub with peeled garlic (if using). While the bread is still warm, top with the tomato mix and serve straight away.

Bruschetta with goat's cheese
Spread toasted bread with soft goat's cheese, then top with tomatoes.

Bruschetta with tapenade
Spread toasted bread with tapenade, then top with tomatoes.

Spiced nuts

Makes 7 cups

Great as a nibble any time, these nuts will keep in an air-tight container for up to 1 month. You can use any combination of nuts you like in this recipe as long as they total 7 cups. The larger the nut (macadamia and pecans, for example), the better.

- 150 g (1 cup) macadamias, halved
- 160 g (1 cup) pecans
- 160 g (1 cup) almonds
- 150 g (1 cup) cashews
- 150 g (1 cup) peanuts
- 150 g (1 cup) pistachios
- 100 g (1 cup) walnuts
- 1 tbsp ground coriander
- 1 tbsp ground cumin
- 1 tbsp salt
- 2 tsp chilli powder
- freshly ground black pepper
- 1 tbsp chopped rosemary
- 2 egg whites
- 110 g (½ cup) caster sugar

Preheat oven to 180°C.

Line 2 deep baking trays with baking paper.

Place the nuts in a large bowl. Sift spices together and stir through rosemary. Beat the egg whites until stiff peaks form. Add sugar and beat until dissolved. Sift spices and rosemary into egg whites and fold nuts through. Spread the nuts in a single layer in the prepared baking trays.

Bake for 10–15 minutes. Stir well to ensure the nuts separate and cook evenly. Return to the oven for a further 10–15 minutes, or until the nuts are golden brown and crisp.

Dukkah

Serves 10–12

Dukkah is an Egyptian spice blend that can be used in myriad ways. The simplest is to offer it with a bowl of olive oil and fresh bread. Dunk the bread into the oil, then into the dukkah. Delicious!

- 75 g (½ cup) sesame seeds
- 30 g (⅓ cup) coriander seeds
- 30 g (⅓ cup) cumin seeds
- 50 g (⅓ cup) hazelnuts
- 55 g (⅓ cup) almonds
- salt flakes to taste

Toast all the seeds and nuts separately until fragrant, either in a dry frypan or on a baking tray in a preheated 180°C oven.

Allow to cool, then crush roughly in a mortar and pestle or pulse in a food processor. They should not be too finely ground. Add salt to taste.

Warm garlic and fennel olives

Serves 10–12

Warm olives in this aromatic spice and garlic mix for a treat to remember.

oil
1 tbsp fennel seeds
2 cloves garlic, crushed
500 g (3 cups) kalamata olives

Heat a large heavy-based frypan over medium heat. Add a splash of oil and fennel seeds and cook for 1–2 minutes until fennel seeds are fragrant. Add garlic and cook for a further 1–2 minutes, making sure neither fennel nor garlic burns. Add olives and cook for a further 3–4 minutes, stirring occasionally to warm olives through. Serve immediately.

Roasted chestnuts with jamon

Serves 6

When chestnuts are in season we make the most of them by wrapping the roasted nuts in a thin slice of jamon or prosciutto. The combination of the salty, raw ham and tender chestnut is a sensational start to a good meal.

1 kg chestnuts
20 thin slices jamon or prosciutto

Preheat oven to 180°C.

Using a small knife, cut a large cross into the skin of each chestnut. Line a baking dish with newspaper, place the chestnuts inside it and fold the paper over to form a parcel.

Bake for 20 minutes, or until tender, and remove the chestnuts from the oven. Keep them wrapped up until ready to serve as this helps to soften the skins, making them easier to peel.

Peel the chestnuts then wrap each one in a slice of jamon or prosciutto and serve with a glass of dry sherry.

Cherry tomato and buffalo mozzarella sticks

Makes 20

The combination of fresh creamy mozzarella and sweet tart cherry tomatoes is always a hit with a glass of bubbles.

2 buffalo mozzarella
3–4 basil leaves, torn
extra virgin olive oil
salt and freshly ground black pepper
1 punnet cherry tomatoes
toothpicks

Dice mozzarella into 1 cm chunks. Place in a bowl and add basil, olive oil, salt and pepper. Allow to marinate for 20 minutes. Take toothpicks, thread one cherry tomato onto each and top with a piece of mozzarella.

Cherry tomato and bocconcini sticks
Substitute bocconcini for mozzarella.

Grissini with prosciutto and truffle oil

Makes 24–36

A very simple nibble requiring just three ingredients.

12–18 slices prosciutto
grissini breadsticks
truffle oil

Cut each slice of prosciutto in half. Wrap around the end of each grissini stick. Arrange on a platter, and drizzle over truffle oil just before serving.

Artichoke, prosciutto and buffalo mozzarella parcels

Makes 12

These parcels are an excellent pre-dinner snack with drinks. If you can't get buffalo mozzarella use regular cow's milk mozzarella.

12 slices prosciutto, not too thin
3 buffalo mozzarella, each cut into 3 slices
12 basil leaves
6 baby artichoke hearts, cut in half
toothpicks

Lay prosciutto slices out flat. Lay a slice of mozzarella on top, followed by a basil leaf and an artichoke half. Roll up to encase the fillings and secure with a toothpick.

Cook each parcel for 6–8 minutes on a barbecue plate, in a pan or in a 180°C preheated oven.

Grilled haloumi in vine leaves

Makes 12

This is a simple dish, but to make it even simpler, you can just grill the haloumi cheese and squeeze some lemon juice over to serve it.

200 g haloumi
12 vine leaves, soaked in cold water for 30 minutes
oil

Cut haloumi into 12 equal pieces. Dry vine leaves and lay out flat. Place a piece of haloumi in the centre of each leaf. Roll leaf up to cover haloumi.

Brush with oil. Barbecue or grill until golden brown on each side and serve immediately.

Eggplant and feta rolls

Makes 12

A simple, yet stylish nibble. If you don't want to cook the eggplant slices you could buy grilled eggplant from the deli, or substitute grilled capsicum if you wish.

2 eggplants
salt
oil
shredded basil leaves
100 g feta, crumbled

Cut eggplants lengthways into thin slices and sprinkle with salt. Allow to drain in a colander for 30 minutes.

Rinse the eggplant slices and dry them well. Pan-fry in oil until golden brown on both sides. Drain and allow to cool.

Top the eggplant slices with chopped basil and crumbled feta, and roll up. Place the rolls on a platter and serve immediately.

Dates with blue cheese

Makes 20

The contrast of the sweet dates and savoury blue cheese is a flavour-packed sensation.

20 large dates   200 g blue cheese

Split each date lengthways and remove the pip. Cut cheese into 1 cm cubes and insert a cube into each date.

Dates with blue cheese and truffle honey
Drizzle the dates with truffle honey as you are about to serve them.

Sushi rice

Makes 6 cups

This is the rice that is used to make the ever-popular California rolls and sushi.

400 g (2 cups) medium-grain (sushi) rice
625 ml (2½ cups) water
60 ml (¼ cup) rice wine vinegar
1 tsp sugar
1 tsp salt

Place rice and water into a saucepan. Cover with a lid, bring to the boil, then reduce to a low simmer. It is important to keep covered with a lid, so as not to allow the steam to escape. This helps the rice to cook correctly.

It will take about 8–10 minutes for all the water to be absorbed. Allow the covered rice to stand covered for 5 minutes before using.

Warm rice wine vinegar in a small saucepan, add sugar and salt, stir until dissolved. Stir this into the rice while still hot. Allow rice to cool slightly before using to make sushi or California rolls.

California rolls

Makes 4–5 rolls (40–48 pieces)

California rolls make perfect party food. However, they take a bit of practice to get just right. You'll need a bamboo mat to make the rolling easier, plus a few other Japanese ingredients, including wasabi and pickled ginger.

1 quantity Sushi Rice
1 packet nori sheets
wasabi
1 cucumber, cut into a thin julienne
1 carrot, cut into a thin julienne
1 avocado, peeled and thinly sliced
pickled ginger, as required
seafood such as smoked salmon, cooked peeled prawns or crab meat (optional)

Prepare Sushi Rice as directed. Lay out one nori sheet on your bamboo mat. Cover most of the nori with cooked rice, leaving the top 1 cm free of rice.

Near the bottom spread a small layer of wasabi across the rice. Add a row of cucumber, carrot, avocado and pickled ginger. Add a layer of seafood if desired. Wet the top 1 cm of nori with a little pickled ginger juice. Roll nori around fillings, compressing tightly with the bamboo mat. Continue rolling until all rice and nori is used.

Chill rolls for 20 minutes before slicing each one into 10 pieces.

Serve with pickled ginger, wasabi and soy sauce.

Chicken liver pâté

Serves 8–10

This pâté recipe is from our good friend Ruth Wirtz and is one of the smoothest, most delicious pâtés we've ever tasted. It is cooked at a fairly low temperature to retain its smooth texture and has a great flavour combination of bacon, onion, garlic and chicken livers. Make it just once and you too will be hooked.

250 g butter
2 onions, diced
2 garlic cloves, crushed
salt and freshly ground black pepper
4 bacon slices, diced
500 g chicken livers, trimmed of any white sinew
1 tbsp brandy (optional)

Preheat oven to 160°C.

Heat a heavy-based pan over a medium heat. Melt 2 tbsp butter, add onion and garlic. Cook gently until onion begins to soften, about 6–7 minutes. Season well with salt and pepper. Add the bacon and livers to the pan and continue to cook over a low heat for 5–6 minutes. Transfer ingredients to an ovenproof dish, cover and cook in the preheated oven for 20 minutes. Melt remaining butter.

Allow livers to cool for 5 minutes, then place in a food processor. Puree until smooth, then add melted butter. Puree again until very smooth. Add brandy if using, then season to taste as required. Pour the mixture into a sieve and strain any remaining lumps. Spoon the pâté into a terrine dish or a few small bowls. Cover with cling film and chill overnight.

Serve with hot toast triangles or crackers.

Duck liver pâté
For a richer pâté replace chicken livers with duck livers, or any combination of pheasant, duck or even goose livers.

Other pâté flavours
This pâté can easily be varied by the addition of green peppercorns, port, Madeira, orange zest or cooked mushrooms.

Smoked trout pâté

Serves 8–10

We often use this recipe for smoked fish other than trout. Smoked mackerel is also excellent. However, it will need a little more lemon juice to cope with the oiliness of the fish.

200 g smoked trout
100 g cream cheese
2 tsp horseradish cream
2–3 tbsp lemon juice
salt and freshly ground black pepper

Remove the skin and all of the bones from the smoked trout. Flake the fish pieces and place in a food processor. Add the cream cheese and process until smooth. Add horseradish and enough lemon juice to get a good consistency, then season with salt and pepper.

Smoked mackerel pâté
Substitute mackerel for trout.

Baccala

Serves 8–10

Baccala is a puree made with salted cod, which is often available at good delis. It works well served as a pre-dinner dip with lavash, warm crostini or toasted focaccia.

300–500 g salted cod fillet
250–500 ml (1–2 cups) milk
4 peppercorns
1 bay leaf
1 medium potato, peeled, diced and boiled
125–150 ml (½–⅔ cup) olive oil
2–3 tbsp lemon juice
freshly ground black pepper

Soak cod in cold water for 48 hours, changing the water often.

Place cod in a saucepan and add enough milk to cover, along with the peppercorns and bay leaf. Gently bring to the boil, then simmer for 3–4 minutes. Remove from heat and allow to cool for 5–10 minutes.

Remove the fish from the milk and, while still warm, remove any bones and skin. Place in a food processor and pulse briefly to break the fish down. Add the cooked potato and, with the processor running, start to add the oil in a drizzle, as if making mayonnaise. Continue adding the oil until a soft mixture is achieved.

Add lemon juice and black pepper to taste. Serve as a dip or on top of grilled polenta.

Salt cod fritters
Add 100 g (1 cup) dry breadcrumbs and mix well. Deep or shallow fry tablespoon amounts of the batter in olive oil. Drain well, sprinkle with salt and serve.

Country pork, veal and pistachio terrine

Serves 8

You'll need thin rashers of bacon for this terrine. Avoid 'Australian' bacon, with its thick slices and large eye piece, and go for thin, fatty rashers from a European butcher instead. Make the terrine the day before you want to serve it, to allow the flavours to develop overnight. This also firms up the terrine, making it easier to slice.

oil	1 tbsp thyme leaves
1 onion, finely diced	pinch of ground nutmeg
16–20 thin slices bacon	1 tsp salt
2 cloves garlic, crushed	freshly ground black pepper
3–4 juniper berries	2 tbsp brandy
300 g pork mince	1 egg
300 g veal mince	1 bay leaf
50 g (⅓ cup) pistachios	cornichons to serve
50 g (1 cup) fresh breadcrumbs	

Heat a small frypan over a medium heat. Add a splash of oil and cook the onion for 3–4 minutes, until soft but not coloured. Dice 4 slices of bacon and add to onion, along with the garlic. Cook for 2–3 minutes, until fragrant. Place ingredients in a large bowl and allow to cool.

Crush juniper berries lightly using either a mortar and pestle or knife handle. Add to onion and bacon, along with both minces, pistachios, breadcrumbs, thyme leaves, nutmeg, salt, a decent grind of black pepper and brandy. Add egg to mix and combine.

Line a medium terrine dish (21 cm × 9 cm × 6 cm) with the remaining bacon slices, allowing the slices to hang over the sides of the dish. You want to be able to encase the mix with the bacon. Place the terrine mix in the dish, pushing it down into the corners. Place the bay leaf on top and fold the bacon slices over the terrine. Cover with foil or a lid.

Preheat oven to 180°C.

Half-fill a deep baking tray with boiling water to make a water bath. Place the terrine in the water and cover the tray with foil. Cook in the preheated oven for 1–1 ½ hours, or until firm to the touch. Remove from the water bath and allow to cool at room temperature. Refrigerate overnight.

Slice the terrine into 1 cm slices. Arrange on plates with 5–6 cornichons and slices of hot toast or crusty baguette.

Pissaladière

Makes 1 pizza

Pissaladière is a pizza topped with caramelised onions, anchovies and olives. As you can imagine, it is for those, like us, who enjoy robust, concentrated flavours on their pizza. Cut into fingers and serve as a nibble.

80 ml (⅓ cup) olive oil
4 onions, sliced
2 cloves garlic, peeled
1 small red chilli, halved
2 sprigs fresh thyme
salt and freshly ground black pepper
½ quantity Pizza Dough (page 248)
anchovies as required, halved lengthways
pitted kalamata olives as required

Heat oil in saucepan, then add onions, garlic, chilli and thyme. Add salt and freshly ground black pepper. Cook for 20–30 minutes on medium–low heat, stirring often until onions soften.

Roll dough to a rough rectangle shape of around 30 × 15 cm. Spread onions on top. Arrange anchovy halves in a diamond lattice formation and stud each diamond centre with an olive.

Preheat oven to 190°C.

Set aside to prove in a warm place for 15 minutes. Bake in preheated oven for 15–20 minutes, or until risen and golden brown.

Crispy stuffed mushrooms

Serves 4 as an entree or makes 24

Whoever said life's too short to stuff a mushroom hasn't tasted these!

150 g (⅔ cup) goat's cheese or ricotta
2 cloves garlic, crushed
2 tbsp chopped fresh herbs (basil, parsley, thyme and oregano)
freshly ground black pepper
1 tbsp thickened cream
350 g medium button mushrooms (6 per person)
1 egg
125 ml (½ cup) milk
flour for coating
50–100 g (½–1 cup) dry breadcrumbs
oil for deep-frying
500 g salad leaves
Lemon Dressing (page 504)

Mix the goat's cheese, garlic, herbs, pepper and cream. Remove stems from the mushrooms. Use a teaspoon to fill the mushroom cavities with the cheese mixture, rounding the tops to form 'balls'.

Lightly beat the egg with milk. Fill a bowl with flour and another with breadcrumbs. Coat the mushrooms with flour, egg, then breadcrumbs, one at a time. Repeat this coating to prevent the mushrooms from leaking during cooking.

Heat oil to 180°C and deep-fry 6–8 mushrooms at a time until golden brown. Drain on absorbent paper.

Dress salad leaves and pile onto 4 plates. Arrange 6 mushrooms around each salad and serve.

Cauliflower polpetti

Makes 20–25

Our friend Rosa Mitchell showed us the knack of making polpetti (Italian fritters) when we helped out at a big Slow Food dinner in Mildura. As with all batters, you need to adjust the amount of milk you add to get the right consistency. If you prefer, you can use zucchini instead of cauliflower in this recipe.

½ cauliflower
75 g (½ cup) self-raising flour
2 eggs
20 g (¼ cup) grated parmigiano
2 tbsp chopped parsley
2–3 tbsp milk
salt and freshly ground black pepper
oil

Cut the thick stalk out of the cauliflower and discard. Cut the remainder into small florets. Bring a large saucepan of water to the boil. Add a sprinkle of salt and cook the florets for 3–4 minutes. Drain cauliflower and set aside to cool.

In a large bowl mix the flour with the eggs, parmigiano and parsley until smooth. Add cauliflower and mix until combined. Add 2–3 tbsp milk, as needed, and season well with salt and pepper.

Heat a large heavy-based frypan over a medium heat. Add a generous splash of oil. Drop large spoonfuls of polpetti mix into the pan: you want them around 8 cm wide and 1 cm thick. Pan-fry until golden brown on each side. Serve immediately.

Zucchini polpetti
Substitute 4 grated zucchini for the caulifower, and add ½ tbsp chopped mint if desired.

Spinach and haloumi fritters

Makes 20

I love haloumi and I love fritters. You can serve them as finger food or dress them up with a Beetroot, Rocket and Yoghurt Salad (page 515) as an entree.

100 g baby spinach leaves
60 ml (¼ cup) water
60 ml (¼ cup) milk
pinch of salt
50 g butter
75 g (½ cup) plain flour

2–3 eggs
125 g haloumi, grated
1–2 tbsp grated parmigiano
salt and freshly ground black pepper
olive oil
Yoghurt and Tahini Sauce (page 564) to serve

Preheat oven to 180°C.

Blanch spinach leaves in boiling water for 30 seconds to soften. Refresh spinach under cold water, drain well and then chop roughly.

Place water, milk, salt and butter in a saucepan and bring to the boil. Tip in flour, stir and return to a low heat. Cook for 2–3 minutes, stirring constantly, until the mixture begins to come away from the sides of the saucepan.

Tip contents into a food processor. Start the processor and beat for 1–2 minutes to allow the mixture to cool slightly. Beat the eggs lightly, then slowly add to the pastry mixture in the food processor, ensuring that the eggs are well incorporated each time before adding more. Continue adding the eggs until the pastry is of a dropping consistency – not too runny. Add the cooked spinach, haloumi, parmigiano, salt and pepper, and process until combined.

Heat a heavy-based frypan over a medium heat. Add 1–2 tbsp oil and spoonfuls of batter. Cook on one side until golden brown, with bubbles forming on top. Turn fritters over and cook until golden brown on the other side. Repeat until the mixture is used up, keeping the cooked fritters warm in the oven.

Serve with Yoghurt and Tahini Sauce.

Thai corn fritters

Makes 30

This is a variation of our favourite corn fritters that we often top with smoked salmon or serve with grilled bacon. Light and easy to eat, they can be enjoyed on their own or dressed up with rocket, smoked salmon and cucumber.

75 g (½ cup) self-raising flour
180 g (1 cup) polenta
½ tsp salt
½ tsp baking powder
1 egg
250 ml (1 cup) milk

2 corn cobs, kernels removed with sharp knife
½ cup chopped coriander leaves
4 spring onions, thinly sliced
1 small red chilli, de-seeded and diced
oil
sweet chilli sauce to serve

Preheat oven to 180°C.

Combine flour, polenta, salt and baking powder. Add egg and milk, and mix until batter is smooth. Add the corn kernels to the mixture, along with the coriander leaves, spring onions and chilli. If the mixture seems too thin, add 1–2 tbsp more flour; if it's too thick, add 1–2 tbsp more milk.

Heat a heavy-based frypan over a medium heat. Add 1–2 tbsp oil and spoonfuls of batter. Cook on one side until golden brown, with bubbles forming on top. Turn fritters over and cook until golden brown on the other side.

Repeat until the mixture is used up, keeping the cooked fritters warm in the oven. Serve with sweet chilli dipping sauce.

Zucchini-flower fritters with feta and basil

Serves 4

These zucchini-flower fritters are filled with a creamy combination of feta and fresh basil, then fried until crisp. If you have a wok burner on the side of your barbecue, use it to cook the fritters and keep all the cooking aromas outside. Serve the flowers in a paper napkin with a sprinkle of salt.

150 g (1 cup) plain flour
½ tsp salt
250 ml (1 cup) water
1 tsp olive oil
1 egg, separated
16 zucchini flowers
150 g soft feta (or Persian feta)
10 basil leaves
freshly ground black pepper
oil for deep-frying
salt

Sift flour and salt together in a bowl. Whisk water, olive oil and egg yolk together, then whisk into the flour until combined. Allow to rest for 30 minutes. Beat egg white until soft peaks form, then fold through the batter just prior to using.

Gently open each zucchini flower and remove the stamens. Wash gently if needed and dry well.

Mash feta slightly with a fork. Chop basil leaves and add to the feta, seasoning with pepper. Place a heaped teaspoonful of the filling into each flower and press the petals back around it firmly.

Pour a 4–5 cm layer of oil in a large saucepan or wok and heat over a medium–high heat.

Dip the zucchini flowers, one at a time, into the batter. Fry in the hot oil until golden. Drain on kitchen paper, season with salt and serve immediately.

Lentil balls with chilli and sweet paprika

Makes 16

You can serve these lentil balls with a spoonful of cooling tzatziki as a pre-dinner treat.

2 tbsp olive oil
1 onion, diced
1 carrot, diced
1–2 green chillies, de-seeded and flesh chopped
½ tsp sweet paprika
180 g (1 cup) red lentils, washed
500 ml (2 cups) vegetable stock
½ cup roughly chopped coriander leaves
1 egg
100 g (1 cup) dry breadcrumbs
salt and freshly ground black pepper
oil

Heat a medium-sized saucepan over a medium heat. Add the 2 tbsp oil, onion and carrot, and cook for 3–4 minutes, or until soft. Add chillies and sweet paprika and cook for 30 seconds. Add the lentils and stir well, then pour in enough stock to cover. Bring to the boil, then reduce the heat.

Cook for 15 minutes, adding more stock as necessary. Cook until the lentils are tender and all the liquid is absorbed. Place the cooked lentils in a bowl and allow to cool slightly.

Add coriander, egg and enough breadcrumbs to make a mix that's not too dry. Season to taste. Divide into 16 portions and roll into small balls. Flatten slightly to ensure even cooking.

Heat a heavy-based frypan over a medium–high heat, add a splash of oil and cook for 5–6 minutes on each side, until golden brown.

Dolmades

Makes 25–30

These vine-leaf parcels are becoming increasingly popular as interest in Middle Eastern cooking grows. There's no doubt that the very best dolmades are those made at home. Commercially produced dolmades are typically laden with oil and lack texture and flavour.

25–30 preserved vine leaves
2 tbsp olive oil
1 onion, finely diced
2 cloves garlic, crushed
100 g (½ cup) long-grain rice
50 g (⅓ cup) toasted pine nuts
50 g (⅓ cup) currants
1 tbsp chopped mint
1 tbsp chopped parsley
pinch each of allspice and cinnamon
salt and freshly ground black pepper
375 ml (1½ cups) water or chicken stock
1 tbsp lemon juice
olive oil

Carefully unfold the vine leaves and discard any brine. Separate the leaves and place them in a large bowl. Pour boiling water over to completely cover them and leave to soak for 20 minutes. Drain well, then cover with cold water and leave to soak for another 20 minutes. Finally, drain the leaves well and pat them dry with kitchen towel. They are now ready to use.

Heat a small frypan over a medium–high heat. Add 2 tbsp oil and the onion and cook for 4–5 minutes, until soft. Add garlic and rice and cook for 1–2 minutes, until fragrant. Remove from heat and transfer to a bowl.

To the onion mix, add pine nuts, currants, herbs, spices, salt and pepper. Mix well. Spread out the leaves, shiny side down, and place 1 heaped tbsp of the filling at one end of each leaf. Fold over the 2 sides and roll it up. Continue with the remaining leaves until all the filling is used.

Line a pan that's big enough to hold all the dolmades snugly in one layer, with 3–4 parcels in each row. Pack the vine leaves as close together as possible. Cover with water or chicken stock, lemon juice and a drizzle of olive oil. Put a plate on top to stop the parcels moving around. Place over a medium–high heat and bring to the boil. Reduce heat and simmer for 40–45 minutes, or until the dolmades are soft and shiny. You may like to remove one of the dolmades to check that the rice is completely cooked. If necessary, add some more water or stock and cook for a further 5 minutes. Allow to cool in the saucepan. Serve warm or at room temperature.

Chicken and pistachio dolmades
Add 500 g minced chicken to the onion while cooking. Substitute chopped pistachios for the pine nuts. Makes an extra 12–15 dolmades.

Lamb and mint dolmades
Add 500 g minced lamb to the onion while cooking. Add an additional 1 tbsp chopped mint. Makes an extra 12–15 dolmades.

Cheese and zaatar kataifi parcels

Makes 20

These great little parcels look and taste fantastic, but beware when eating them as the pastry tends to fall everywhere. Serve with napkins! You can buy zaatar from Middle Eastern food shops and good delis.

100 g (1 cup) haloumi, grated
100 g feta, crumbled
80 g (½ cup) toasted pine nuts
1 tbsp chopped parsley
180 g kataifi pastry
125 g (½ cup) melted butter
zaatar as required

Preheat oven to 180°C.

Line a baking tray with baking paper.

Mix cheeses, pine nuts and parsley together. Form into 20 small 2 cm balls.

Separate pastry into strands of 10–12 lengths. Place one ball of cheese on each pastry section and roll up, enclosing the filling entirely. Place on the prepared baking tray. Brush pastries with melted butter and bake for 10–12 minutes, or until crisp.

Pile kataifi parcels on a platter, sprinkle with zaatar and serve.

Boreks

Makes 20–30

Boreks are a cheese pastry we learned to make in Turkey. In a way they are not unlike a spring roll, except the filling is cheese with a hint of garlic and mint.

250 g (2½ cups) haloumi cheese, grated
125 g feta, chopped
1 clove garlic, crushed
12 mint leaves, chopped
12 flat-leaf parsley leaves, chopped
freshly ground black pepper
1 egg
250 g Turkish pastry (which can be hard to find), filo pastry or spring roll wrappers
vegetable oil

Mix cheeses, garlic, mint and parsley with plenty of freshly ground black pepper. Taste the mix to ensure it has a good flavour. Stir egg into the mixture.

Cut pastry into 8 cm squares. Lay out pastry squares and brush edges with cold water. Place a spoonful of the mixture onto the centre of each pastry (or spring roll wrapper).

Place a teaspoon of mixture near the bottom of the pastry; fold the bottom corner up over the filling, then fold the sides in. Roll up to the top and ensure wrapper seals well.

Pour vegetable oil into a wok or a deep saucepan to a depth of 4 cm and heat. Deep-fry boreks 4 at a time until golden brown, then allow to drain on kitchen paper.

Onion bahjis

Makes 20–24

Onion bahjis are deep-fried fritters of crisp onions and spices, but to many English people onion bahjis also mean a late-night Indian snack on the way home from the pub.

3 onions
150 g (1 cup) chickpea flour
150 g (1 cup) plain flour
2 tsp baking powder
1 egg
1 tsp salt
3 tsp ground cumin
3 tsp ground coriander
oil

Finely dice onions and blanch in a pot of boiling water. Drain onion well and reserve 250 ml (1 cup) of cooking liquid for batter mixture. Combine chickpea flour, plain flour, baking powder, egg, salt, ground cumin, ground coriander and reserved cooking liquid. Whisk until smooth. Add onion and mix well.

Pour vegetable oil into a wok or a deep saucepan to a depth of 4 cm and heat. Deep-fry spoonfuls of the onion bahji mix until golden brown and allow to drain on a wok rack or kitchen paper.

Chilli prawn balls

Makes 20–25

These make a fantastic nibble, although the deep-frying is a bit of a drama. We fry ours outside on the wok burner attached to our barbecue. You can cook the balls in advance and reheat in a hot oven if you prefer.

500 g minced prawns
2 spring onions, finely sliced
2 tbsp chopped coriander leaves
1 tbsp sweet chilli sauce
1 tsp chilli paste
salt

75–100 g (¾–1 cup) dried breadcrumbs
seasoned flour
1 egg beaten with 2 tbsp milk
100 g (1 cup) dried breadcrumbs, additional
vegetable oil
sweet chilli sauce to serve

Mix prawns, spring onions, coriander, sweet chilli sauce, chilli paste, salt and enough dried breadcrumbs to bring mix together. Shape into balls about 2 cm in diameter. Roll each ball in flour, then egg mix and finally additional breadcrumbs. Refrigerate.

Pour vegetable oil into a wok or a deep saucepan to a depth of 4 cm and heat. Deep-fry prawn balls until golden brown, 6–8 at a time, and allow to drain on a wok rack or kitchen paper. Serve with a dipping bowl of sweet chilli sauce.

Chilli fish balls
Swap half the prawn mince for white fish or salmon mince, for a difference.

Chermoula prawns with tzatziki

Makes 30 skewers

One of Michele's favourite nibbles. You can also serve these as an entree with a simple rocket salad. Make them with chicken or beef instead of the prawns if you fancy.

2 tsp sweet paprika
1 tsp ground ginger
1 tsp chilli powder
1 tsp ground cumin
1 tsp ground coriander
1 tsp ground white pepper
½ tsp ground cardamom
½ tsp ground cinnamon
½ tsp allspice
1 tsp salt
2 tbsp lemon juice
60 ml (¼ cup) olive oil
1 kg green (raw) prawns
30 wooded skewers, soaked in cold water
Tzatziki (page 563)

Mix spices and salt with lemon juice and olive oil to form a smooth paste. Shell and de-vein prawns. Coat prawns with chermoula paste and marinate for 30 minutes. Thread one prawn onto each skewer, through the centre lengthways.

Grill on an oiled barbecue plate for 2 minutes on each side, or bake in an oven preheated to 180°C for 5–6 minutes.

Serve with Tzatziki.

Malaysian curry prawns

Makes 30

Cooking curry paste and coconut milk to a thick sauce is a grand way of adding good flavours to barbecued food. Any type of curry paste can be used in this way; you can try a Thai or Indian paste for something different next time.

2 tbsp Malaysian curry paste
200 ml (¾ cup) coconut cream
1 kg green (raw) prawns
salt
30 skewers

Place curry paste and coconut cream in a small saucepan. Bring to the boil. Simmer for 2–3 minutes and add salt to taste.

Shell and de-vein prawns. Thread one prawn onto each skewer, through the centre lengthways.

Brush with coconut curry sauce.

Place prawns on the oiled barbecue plate. Cook for 2 minutes, basting often. Turn over and cook for a further 2 minutes, continuing to baste.

Pan-fried calamari

Serves 4 as an entree

'Roundy things' (calamari rings) according to our son Luke, are meant to be eaten at least once a week. This is how we do it at home.

500 g calamari rings (can be cut from tubes 1 cm wide)
seasoned flour
oil
lemon wedges

Toss calamari with flour to coat, then shake well; a sieve does a good job of removing the excess flour.

Fill a shallow frying pan with 1 cm oil and place over a medium–high heat. Add calamari rings one by one, cooking as many as will fit into the pan without overlapping. Cook for 30 seconds, turn over and cook until golden brown. Drain on absorbent paper and serve with lemon wedges.

Deep-fried Thai calamari

Serves 4 as an entree

We're usually so greedy that we eat these spicy calamari rings as they are already, but they would probably be good with a salad too.

500 g calamari rings
1 tbsp Thai red curry paste
2 tbsp potato starch (or cornflour)
peanut oil
handful Thai basil leaves
lime wedges to serve

Mix calamari with Thai paste and set aside to marinate for 30 minutes. When ready to cook, stir through potato starch to coat.

Heat peanut oil in a wok and deep-fry calamari rings, adding one by one to stop them sticking together and frying no more than 5–6 at a time. Cook for 30 seconds, turn over and cook until golden brown. Continue cooking until all calamari are ready, serve on a platter with basil leaves and lime wedges to garnish.

Burghul-coated calamari

Serves 6–8

The burghul used in this recipe gives the calamari an extra crunch and helps prevent it from becoming overcooked and chewy. Serve the calamari rings as a nibble or bump it up to an entree with the addition of dressed salad greens.

3 medium-sized calamari tubes (750 g)
75 g (½ cup) seasoned flour
2 eggs
65 g (⅓ cup) burghul
1 tsp salt
75 g (¾ cup) dry breadcrumbs
oil for deep-frying
salt
150 g wild rocket, washed
1 lemon, cut into wedges
Almond Skordalia (page 550) to serve

Remove any loose bits of skin from the calamari tubes. Cut tubes into ½ cm rings.

Place flour in a bowl. Beat the eggs together in another bowl and place the burghul, tsp salt and breadcrumbs in a third bowl. Take each calamari ring and dip first in flour, shaking off excess, then in egg and finally in the burghul mix. Refrigerate until needed.

Heat a 4 cm layer of oil in a deep frypan. Cook the calamari rings in batches until golden brown. Drain on absorbent paper. Season with salt.

Divide rocket between plates, arrange calamari on top, add a lemon wedge to each plate and serve with a dollop of Almond Skordalia.

Oyster shooters

Makes 24

These oysters look fantastic served in shot glasses, but if you don't have any to hand simply spoon the oysters back into their shells. Liven them up by adding a splash of vodka, if you like.

250 ml (1 cup) tomato juice
1 Lebanese cucumber, finely diced
1 tomato, finely diced
½ red onion, finely diced
2–3 tbsp lemon juice
salt and freshly ground black pepper
Tabasco to taste
2 dozen oysters, freshly opened and with juices intact, if possible

Mix the tomato juice, cucumber, tomato and onion together. Season to taste with lemon juice, salt, pepper and Tabasco. Tip the oysters into the tomato mixture, along with any juices. Allow the oysters to absorb the flavours for at least 10 minutes, but no longer than 30 minutes.

Either spoon the oysters back into their shells, adding some of the liquid, or into shot glasses, covering with liquid. Serve immediately.

Oysters with jamon and harissa

Makes 24

Here's a twist on the dreaded Oysters Kilpatrick – and it's much more grown-up. If you can't find jamon use prosciutto or pancetta. For a sophisticated entree you could serve 6 oysters nestled around a mound of bitter lettuce leaves such as frisee, radicchio, rocket or mizuna, with a light dressing.

6–8 slices jamon
1 tsp harissa
½ cup good-quality mayonnaise
2 dozen oysters, freshly opened

Preheat oven to 180°C.

Place jamon slices on a baking tray and cook for 4–5 minutes, until crispy. You can also pan-fry them if you prefer.

Mix the harissa with the mayonnaise. Arrange the oysters on a platter and top each one with ½ tsp harissa mayonnaise. Break the jamon into small pieces and place 1 segment on top of the mayonnaise. Serve immediately.

Oysters with Vietnamese flavours

Makes 24

You should be able to make an Asian-inspired dressing with the ingredients you have to hand in the cupboard. We love the zingy combination of Vietnamese mint with fish sauce and chilli – perfect on a hot night with a glass of riesling.

2 tsp grated palm sugar
2 tsp fish sauce
2 tsp lime juice
freshly ground black pepper
1 spring onion, shredded
¼ cup coriander leaves
¼ cup Vietnamese mint leaves
1 green chilli, de-seeded and sliced
2 dozen oysters, freshly opened and with juices intact, if possible

Place palm sugar in a small bowl. Add the fish sauce, lime juice and black pepper. Stir until the sugar dissolves. Add spring onion, coriander, mint and chilli. Toss to combine.

Tip the oysters into the Vietnamese mixture, along with any juices. Allow the oysters to absorb the flavours for at least 10 minutes, but no longer than 30 minutes.

Spoon the oysters back into their shells, adding some of the liquid. Serve immediately.

Steamed oysters with Asian flavours

Serves 4 as an entree

Lightly steaming oysters is a really great way of serving them if you're not too keen on them raw. It's also a good way of adding in new flavours such as the Asian marinade here. If you prefer your oysters raw, this same marinade is ideal as an accompaniment. Simply spoon it over freshly opened oysters and enjoy.

2 tbsp mirin
1½ tbsp lime juice
1 tbsp sweet chilli sauce
2 spring onions, thinly sliced
2 tsp light soy sauce
6 Vietnamese mint leaves, thinly sliced
½ tsp fish sauce
2 dozen oysters, freshly opened

Mix all of the marinade ingredients together in a bowl. Add the oysters, with their juices, to the bowl. Allow to marinate for 10 minutes.

Pour 10 cm of water into a wok and bring to a gentle boil. Place the empty oyster shells into a bamboo steamer (you may need two decks to cook two dozen at the same time). Spoon an oyster into each shell with plenty of the marinade. Place over the steaming water and cover. Cook for 1½ minutes.

Gently place the bamboo steamer onto a large platter, taking care not to spill the delicious juices. Place on the dining table and allow your guests to pick the oysters out, one by one.

Paper-wrapped chicken

Makes 20

These can be made in advance and popped in the oven to cook just before your guests arrive.

1 tsp chilli paste
2 tbsp kecap manis
2 tbsp hoisin sauce
4 skinless chicken thigh fillets, cut into 3 cm chunks
20 small rice paper wrappers
4 spring onions, thinly sliced
3 Chinese sausages, sliced thinly on the angle
vegetable oil

Mix together chilli paste, kecap manis and hoisin sauce. Add chicken pieces. Stir to coat chicken and leave to marinate for 30 minutes. Drain well.

Fill a bowl with hot tap water. Dunk 2–3 rice paper wrappers into water to soften. Drain on a tea towel. Take a rice paper wrapper; place a piece of chicken towards the bottom of it. Top with a slice of sausage and a piece of spring onion. Roll towards the top, folding in the sides of the wrapper as you go. Continue soaking and wrapping rice paper parcels until all ingredients are used. Refrigerate until needed.

Preheat oven to 180°C. Line baking trays with baking paper. Arrange chicken parcels on baking trays and cook in preheated oven for 30 minutes until crisp, turning over halfway through cooking. Serve immediately.

Pandan chicken parcels

Makes 20

Pandan chicken parcels are pieces of black bean–marinated chicken wrapped in an aromatic pandan leaf. They are easily cooked in the oven.

1 tbsp black beans, soaked and drained
1 tsp chilli paste
1 tbsp kecap manis
1 kg skinless chicken thigh fillets
20 pandan leaves
toothpicks

Finely chop black beans, then mix with chilli paste and kecap manis. Cut each thigh fillet into 4 evenly sized pieces. Marinate chicken in black bean mixture for 1 hour.

Preheat oven to 180°C.

Place one piece of chicken at one end of each pandanus leaf, then roll the pandanus leaf around the chicken. Secure the pandanus leaf by putting a toothpick through it and the chicken.

Place parcels onto a baking tray and cook in preheated oven for 10–15 minutes, turning once. Serve them and advise guests to remove toothpick and pandan leaf before eating.

Pork gyoza

Makes 20–25

Gyoza dumplings make an excellent start to a Japanese meal and are really very easy to prepare. Chilli jam and round dumpling wrappers for making gyoza can be easily sourced at Asian food stores.

500 g minced pork
2 spring onions, sliced
1 tbsp grated ginger
2 tbsp chilli jam
gyoza wrappers
1 tbsp caster sugar
125 ml (½ cup) red wine vinegar
1 tbsp lime juice
2 tbsp water
60 ml (¼ cup) soy sauce

Combine pork with spring onions, ginger and chilli jam. Place a teaspoon of the mixture in the centre of a gyoza wrapper. Brush the edges of the gyoza wrapper with water, then pull them together so that they meet. Crimp to seal. Keep making gyoza until all of the filling is used. For the sauce, combine sugar, vinegar, lime juice, water and soy sauce, stirring to dissolve the sugar. Poach the dumplings in simmering water for 5–6 minutes. Toss the cooked gyoza with the sauce and serve immediately.

Wontons with Thai curry sauce

Makes 40

I made hundreds of these wontons for Allan's fortieth birthday party and served them on white Asian soup spoons. Very spectacular, but simple. MC

250 g pork or chicken mince
2 spring onions, sliced
2 tsp grated ginger
1 tbsp soy sauce
1 tbsp chopped coriander
180 g packet wonton wrappers

250 ml (1 cup) coconut cream
1 tbsp red Thai curry paste
fish sauce
lime juice (optional)
crispy fried shallots to serve

Mix together the mince, spring onions, ginger, soy sauce and chopped coriander. Arrange 4–5 wonton wrappers and place 1 tsp of mince in the centre of each one. Brush the edges with water and fold over diagonally to form a small triangular parcel. Press the edges together and hold firmly to seal. Repeat until all the mince mixture is used.

Place the coconut cream and Thai paste in a small saucepan and bring to the boil. Stir and allow to simmer for 5 minutes. Season to taste with fish sauce and, if desired, add a squeeze of lime juice. Keep the sauce warm until required.

Bring a large saucepan of water to the boil. Cook in batches of 8–10 wontons for 5 minutes. Remove and drain well. Place a wonton on each spoon, drizzle with hot sauce and garnish with crispy fried shallots.

Spring rolls

Makes 36

We like to make tiny finger-sized spring rolls to serve before a meal, particularly if it's to be one with Asian flavours.

50 g vermicelli noodles
250 g pork mince
1 clove garlic, crushed
1 tsp grated ginger
½ red capsicum, finely diced
4 spring onions, green tops only, thinly sliced
1 tbsp kecap manis
1 tbsp sweet chilli sauce
½ tbsp fish sauce
200 g packet small spring roll wrappers
1 egg, lightly beaten
vegetable oil
80 ml (⅓ cup) soy sauce
2 small red chillies, chopped

Place noodles in a large bowl and cover completely with boiling water. Stand for 5 minutes to soften, then drain well.

Place noodles, pork mince, garlic, ginger, capsicum, spring onions, kecap manis, sweet chilli sauce and fish sauce together in a large bowl and mix well.

Peel a spring roll pastry wrapper off the stack and place in front of you with one corner facing downwards (like a diamond). Brush liberally with beaten egg. Place a teaspoon of the mixture near the bottom of the pastry; fold the bottom corner up over the filling, then fold the sides in. Roll up to the top and ensure wrapper seals well. Repeat with remaining ingredients.

Pour vegetable oil into a wok or a deep saucepan to a depth of 4 cm and heat. Deep-fry spring rolls 4 at a time until golden brown and allow to drain on a wok rack or kitchen paper.

Mix the soy and chilli together in a small bowl and serve as a dipping sauce with the spring rolls.

Roast duck, chilli and coriander rolls

Serves 8–10

Roast duck from an Asian roast house is one of our all-time favourite takeaway foods. It's crispy, it's full flavoured and it's ready to eat. Here it's rolled up in roti bread with sweet chilli, coriander leaves and fresh salad ingredients to create a real taste sensation. We love this for its simplicity.

1 roast duck
½ iceberg lettuce
2 Lebanese cucumbers
3 tomatoes
4 pieces roti bread or pita bread
60–80 ml (¼–⅓ cup) sweet chilli sauce
1 cup coriander leaves

Preheat oven to 180°C.

Remove meat from roast duck, discarding any visible fat as you go. Cut the meat and crispy skin into thin shreds. Thinly slice the lettuce, cucumbers and tomatoes.

Heat bread in preheated oven for 3–4 minutes and remove. While still warm spread each with sweet chilli sauce, then scatter lettuce, cucumber, tomato and a few coriander leaves over the bread. Add a few strips of duck meat and roll the bread up, enclosing all ingredients. Cut into four equal-sized pieces and serve while still warm.

Peking duck and hoisin rice-paper rolls

Makes 12

Rice-paper rolls are perfect for a light pre-dinner nibble, particularly in warmer weather. You can add any filling you like, from roast chicken through to prawns or vegetables – or even crayfish if you're feeling flash.

50 g cellophane noodles
½ roast duck, flesh removed and thinly sliced
75 g (½ cup) chopped roasted peanuts
2 tbsp chopped coriander
1 small carrot, finely grated
1 tbsp hoisin sauce
12 Vietnamese mint leaves, shredded
12 large rice-paper wrappers
Vietnamese Dipping Sauce (page 564)

Place noodles in a large bowl and cover completely with boiling water. Stand for 5 minutes to soften, and then drain well.

Place noodles, duck meat, peanuts, coriander, carrot, hoisin sauce and Vietnamese mint in a large bowl and mix well. Season to taste.

Fill a large bowl with hot tap water, then soak the rice-paper wrappers one at a time until softened. Remove carefully and drain on absorbent paper or a tea towel. Lay the wrappers out flat, then place the filling on the bottom centre of each softened wrapper. Roll end up over filling, fold in the sides and continue rolling up to the top.

Serve with Vietnamese Dipping Sauce.

Vegetable and egg rice-paper rolls
Beat 2 eggs lightly. Heat a small frypan or wok, add a splash of oil, then enough beaten egg to form a thin layer, as you would with an omelette. Cook briefly on both sides, then remove from heat and allow to cool. Slice thinly and toss with noodles, as described in the rice-paper rolls recipe, but add more vegetables such as bean sprouts, shredded cucumber and capsicum.

Prawn rice-paper rolls
Instead of duck, use 6 cooked prawns cut in half. Swap hoisin sauce for sweet chilli sauce.

entrees

At a typical dinner party we would serve 2–3 nibbles followed by a more formal entree that we would sit at the table to enjoy. Most of our entrees tend to be vegetarian or seafood-based, mostly because we are saving the meat for the main course, but there are many options. Light salads, steamed mussels, smoked salmon and cheese-based dishes largely make up our repertoire, though pasta sneaks in from time to time, and soups, of course.

Balance the first course with what you will be serving next. Consider the style of food; keep to one type of cuisine to avoid confusing the palate, for instance, serve Asian-style entrees before an Asian-style main course.

If serving shellfish, check with your guests that no one has an allergy; there's nothing worse than everyone tucking into a delicious crab salad while one guest nibbles miserably on a piece of bread.

Things you should know about entrees

1 Keep it simple and seasonal: light dishes for spring and summer and hearty dishes for winter.

2 Don't drink too much, too early.

3 Never attempt something outside your capabilities.

4 Don't serve the same food group for entree and main.

5 Allow 250 g shellfish (mussels or prawns), 75 g fish, 75–100 g raw meat or 250 ml (1 cup) soup per person.

6 Keep the dishes small – they're supposed to be a beginning to your meal.

7 If you're game enough to serve souffles, make sure all guests are sitting down before you bring them to the table – there's nothing quite like the 'wow' reaction.

Summer vegetable terrine

Serves 6–8

Layers of our favourite summer vegetables sandwiched together with basil and goat's cheese equals totally yum. Although it takes a little bit of time to put together, come dinnertime it's just a matter of slicing and serving.

2 eggplants
salt
3 small zucchinis
olive oil
2 red capsicums
3 Roma tomatoes
150 g firm goat's cheese
100 g rocket, washed and dried
⅓ cup basil leaves

red wine vinegar
freshly ground black pepper and salt
1 × log baking tin, 23.5 × 13.5 × 7 cm

RED WINE DRESSING
2 tbsp red wine vinegar
salt and freshly ground black pepper
125 ml (½ cup) extra virgin olive oil

Preheat oven to 200°C.

Slice eggplants lengthways into ½ cm slices and sprinkle with salt; allow to drain in a colander for 30 minutes. Rinse under cold running water, then dry well. Slice the zucchini lengthways into ½ cm slices.

Heat a heavy-based pan over a medium–high heat. Add a splash of olive oil and cook eggplant, then zucchini slices, until tender and golden brown, then set aside.

Rub red capsicums over with olive oil and roast for 20–25 minutes until skins blister. Place capsicums in a plastic bag and seal to allow steam to lift skins. When cool, remove and discard the skins and seeds. Cut capsicums into thick strips. Slice the tomatoes and goat's cheese.

Line the baking tin with cling film lengthways and across, leaving plenty of overhang. Begin layering vegetables starting with one third of eggplant slices across the bottom. Sprinkle with a few drops of vinegar, olive oil, salt and pepper. Continue to sprinkle with vinegar, oil, salt and pepper between each layer.

Add a layer of zucchini slices, then half of the rocket, half of the capsicum, all the basil, tomato and goat's cheese, then another third of eggplant slices. Add remaining rocket, capsicums and finish with eggplant slices. Push down firmly when adding the rocket leaves.

Fold the overhanging cling film over the vegetables. Place filled baking tin on a baking tray to catch any overflowing juices. Cut a piece of thick cardboard to fit snugly in the top of the terrine. Weigh down with a heavy weight such as 2 × 2 litre juice or milk cartons (around 4 kg in total is required to compress the ingredients together). Refrigerate overnight with the weights on top of the terrine.

To serve, remove weights and cardboard from terrine. Peel back the top layer of cling film and place a chopping board on top. Turn board and the tin over carefully. Remove tin and cling film from the pressed terrine. Wipe away any excess juices.

Make dressing by stirring together red wine vinegar with salt and pepper, then lightly whisk in oil. Evenly slice the terrine and carefully place onto serving plates, add a splash of the dressing and serve.

Goat's cheese souffle

Serves 6

Souffles are rumoured to be tricky to make, but they are, in fact, quite easy. A fan-forced oven will help them to rise and it is important not to open the oven door during cooking, as a cold draught may make them collapse. It's a good idea to make sure everyone is seated in time to have the souffles served straight from the oven.

350 ml (1⅓ cups) milk
40 g (2 tbsp) butter
40 g (¼ cup) plain flour
300 g goat's cheese, mashed
3 eggs, separated
salt and freshly ground black pepper
6 × 175 ml ramekins/souffle dishes, buttered

Preheat oven to 180°C.

Place milk in a small saucepan and bring to the boil. Melt butter in another pan over a low heat. Add flour to melted butter and cook for 2 minutes, stirring occasionally. Increase heat and add the hot milk, whisking well to avoid lumps. Cook for 2–3 minutes over low heat, stirring the thick sauce occasionally. Remove from the heat.

Add goat's cheese and stir until melted. Stir egg yolks through and check seasoning.

Whisk egg whites until stiff and fold into warm cheese sauce. Divide mixture between buttered souffle dishes and place immediately into preheated oven. Bake for 20–25 minutes, or until well risen and golden brown.

Serve immediately.

Prawn cocktail

Serves 6

For those of you who couldn't care less about food fashion, here is our take on this great dish: pan-fried juicy prawns tossed with fresh salad ingredients and topped with a lime and chilli mayonnaise.

1 iceberg lettuce
150 g rocket leaves
1 avocado
2 Lebanese cucumbers
1 punnet cherry tomatoes
olive oil
1 kg green (raw) prawns, peeled and de-veined
Lime and Chilli Mayonnaise (page 554)

Carefully remove 6 large outside leaves from lettuce to use as cups to hold salad. Break remaining lettuce into bite-sized pieces. Wash iceberg and rocket leaves, then dry using a salad spinner.

Cut avocado in half, remove stone, peel and cut into thin slices. Slice cucumbers thinly. Cut tomatoes in half. Toss lettuce, avocado, cucumber and tomatoes together. Arrange salad in iceberg cups.

Heat a large frying pan over a medium heat, add 1–2 tbsp oil and cook prawns for 1–2 minutes on each side. Arrange prawns on top of each salad cup. Top with a generous spoonful of Lime and Chilli Mayonnaise.

Twice-cooked goat's cheese souffles

Serves 6

Don't be put off by the 'scary souffle' tag, as they're not as tricky to make as most people think. It's just a basic cheese sauce, with whipped egg whites folded through. This one is particularly easy as you do the majority of the cooking well beforehand, then reheat them before you serve. This avoids those anxious moments of whether the souffles will rise or not. Go get 'em.

1 tbsp butter
40 g (2 tbsp) butter, additional
40 g (2 tbsp) plain flour
350 ml (1⅓ cups) milk, warmed
150 g fresh goat's cheese
1 tbsp grated parmigiano reggiano
3 eggs, separated
salt and freshly ground black pepper
500 ml (2 cups) cream
6 × 150 ml ramekins

Preheat oven to 180°C. Melt 1 tbsp butter and grease ramekins. Line a deep baking dish with a tea towel and place buttered ramekins in the dish.

Melt additional butter in a small saucepan over a low heat. Add flour and stir together. Cook for 2 minutes, stirring occasionally. Gradually add milk, stirring well with each addition to ensure it makes a smooth sauce. Allow sauce to come to the boil, then reduce heat and simmer for 2 minutes.

Remove from heat, crumble in goat's cheese and parmigiano reggiano. Allow to cool for a few minutes, and then add egg yolks and seasoning (if you add the egg yolks while the sauce is really hot you run the risk of curdling the egg yolks).

Whip egg whites until stiff. Stir a spoonful of the beaten egg whites through the sauce first – this helps the remaining whites to fold through easily. Add remaining egg whites and fold through carefully using a flat spoon or spatula. Divide mixture between buttered ramekins. Pour enough boiling water into the baking dish to come two-thirds up the side of the ramekins. Place in preheated oven and bake for 20 minutes, until well risen and firm to touch.

Set aside for 5 minutes, allowing the souffles to deflate. Ease them out of their ramekins and place them in a greased ovenproof dish. Cover with cling film and refrigerate for several hours now if desired.

When you are ready to serve, preheat oven to 180°C. Pour cream over the top of the souffles. Bake in oven for 15 minutes. Place each souffle on individual plates, spoon cooking cream around souffles and serve.

Baked mushrooms with beetroot salad

Serves 6

We've yet to find anyone who doesn't like this entree. You could also serve a larger version of this for lunch – perfect if you have vegetarians on the guest list.

18 large mushrooms
oil
salt and freshly ground black pepper
12–18 baby beetroots
2 tbsp oil
1 tbsp balsamic vinegar
200 g goat's cheese
2 tbsp chopped parsley
2 cloves garlic, crushed
1 tbsp cream
100 g wild rocket

Preheat oven to 180°C.

Brush mushrooms with oil. Place skin side down in a baking tray and season with salt and pepper. Bake for 20–30 minutes or until the mushrooms are tender.

Trim stalks off the beetroots and discard. Toss the beetroots with oil and vinegar, and season with salt and pepper. Place in a roasting dish, cover with foil and cook for 40 minutes, or until tender. Set aside to cool.

Mix the goat's cheese, parsley, garlic and cream together to form a smooth paste. Add more cream if needed. Remove stalks from the mushrooms and place 1 tsp goat's cheese mix in the centre of each mushroom. Place on a baking tray and set aside until ready to serve. Peel beetroots and cut into halves.

Cook the mushrooms in hot oven or under a grill until the cheese is golden brown and the mushrooms are hot. Divide salad leaves between plates. Place 3 mushrooms on each plate, scatter beetroot halves over and serve.

Egg nets with noodle and herb salad

Serves 6

This recipe first appeared in *Food with Friends*, with full credit to Martin Boetz at Longrain restaurant for his egg nets, an effective web for holding this salad together. You could make 1 large net and ask your guests to cut themselves a piece, or do as we do and make cocktail-sized nets and serve them as a pre-dinner nibble.

4 eggs	75 g (½ cup) roasted peanuts
oil	100 g bean sprouts
100 g cellophane noodles	4 spring onions, thinly sliced
100 g snow peas	1 cup coriander leaves
½ red capsicum, finely diced	¼ cup Vietnamese mint leaves (optional)
1 carrot, shredded	2 tbsp grated palm sugar
1 Lebanese cucumber, thinly sliced	2 tbsp fish sauce
4 red shallots, thinly sliced	2 tbsp lime juice

Beat eggs together, strain and set aside for 1–2 hours to allow the protein in the eggs to break down.

To make the egg nets successfully you need to drizzle thin strands of the egg mix into a frypan (or a wok), criss-crossing them to form a net that will hold the ingredients together. We use a plastic squeezy bottle, as that way we can control the amount of egg coming out. You can use your fingers or even a spoon to drizzle the egg across the frypan, but be warned it can end up very messy. You may like to protect your stove with foil before starting.

Heat a medium-sized frypan over a medium heat. Add a splash of oil, swirl it around the frypan and then tip the excess away. Return the frypan to the heat and drizzle the egg across to form a net. Once set, remove the egg net carefully and transfer it to a plate. The mixture should make 6 nets. Cover them with foil to prevent them drying out and refrigerate until needed.

Cook noodles in plenty of boiling water for 3–4 minutes. Refresh under cold running water. Cook snow peas in boiling water for 2 minutes. Refresh under cold running water and slice thinly.

Toss noodles, snow peas, capsicum, carrot, cucumber, shallots, peanuts, bean sprouts, spring onions and herbs together. Dissolve palm sugar in fish sauce and add lime juice.

Toss the dressing through the salad. Place an egg net on each serving plate, divide the noodle salad between the egg nets, fold the net over to encase the filling and serve.

Egg nets with prawn noodle and herb salad
Add 500 g peeled cooked prawns to the salad mix.

Egg nets with crab noodle and herb salad
Add 300 g freshly cooked crab meat to the salad mix.

Sichuan chicken and fungi salad

Serves 6

This is a great salad if you really love the slippery textures of mushrooms. If you have some of the Salt and Pepper Spice (page 295), it will be good sprinkled over the top too.

500 ml (2 cups) water
125 ml (½ cup) Chinese rice wine
125 ml (½ cup) soy sauce
4 spring onions, chopped
5–6 ginger slices
2 chicken breast fillets, on the bone if possible
1 cucumber, peeled
½ cup coriander leaves

100 g oyster mushrooms or black ear fungus
100 g bean shoots
4 shallots, thinly sliced
1 small red chilli, de-seeded and diced
1 tbsp light soy sauce
1 tsp sesame oil
freshly ground black pepper

Put water, wine, soy sauce, spring onions and ginger in a medium saucepan and bring to the boil. Put the chicken in the saucepan, making sure the liquid covers the chicken. Reduce heat, cover with a lid and cook for 15 minutes (if chicken isn't on the bone, cook for 10 minutes). Remove from heat and set aside until the chicken cools.

Once cool remove the chicken from the stock. Remove flesh from the bones, discarding the skin, and pull the chicken meat apart. Put in a bowl.

Use a vegetable peeler to cut long strips from the cucumber. Discard seeds and squeeze excess moisture out of the cucumber strips. Add to the chicken along with the coriander. Thinly slice the mushrooms or fungus, and add to the chicken along with bean shoots, shallots and chilli. Toss to combine. Refrigerate until needed.

To serve, ensure the chicken is at room temperature. Add soy sauce, sesame oil and pepper. Toss to combine and divide between 6 bowls. Sprinkle with Salt and Pepper Spice if using.

Moorish prawn and mint salad

Serves 4–6

This combination of spicy prawns, creamy feta and bitter salad leaves is sensational. Lately, I've been having a bit of a love affair with lemon-infused olive oil, used to dress the salad – it adds a lovely richness to just about any dish, but particularly those featuring seafood. MC

- 500 g green (raw) prawns, shelled
- 80 ml (⅓ cup) extra-virgin olive oil
- grated zest of 1 lemon
- 1 tsp smoky paprika
- 1 tsp harissa
- 1 tsp sumac
- pinch of allspice
- salt and freshly ground black pepper
- 1 baby fennel bulb
- 4 red onions, cut into wedges
- 2 tbsp olive oil
- 2 tbsp sherry vinegar, plus extra for dressing
- 2 witlof
- 1 radicchio
- 1 cup flat-leaf parsley leaves
- 6–8 mint leaves, shredded
- 100 g (⅔ cup) Ligurian black olives
- oil for frying
- lemon-infused olive oil or extra-virgin olive oil
- 100 g feta

Place the prawns in a bowl. Add the olive oil, lemon zest, paprika, harissa, sumac, allspice, salt and pepper and mix together well. Refrigerate until needed.

Preheat oven to 180°C.

Remove stalk from the fennel and discard. Cut the bulb in half, remove the core and slice thinly. Place in a deep baking tray with the onion and toss with the olive oil, sherry vinegar, salt and pepper. Roast in the oven for 20–25 minutes, until golden brown. Set aside to cool.

Wash the witlof and radicchio leaves; break into bite-size pieces if necessary. Mix together with the parsley, mint and olives. Place in a large serving bowl with roasted fennel and onion.

To cook the prawns, heat a heavy-based frypan over medium heat. Add a splash of oil and the prawns and cook for 1–2 minutes on each side, or until they change colour. Depending on the size of your pan, you may need to cook the prawns in 2 batches.

Dress the salad with lemon-infused or extra-virgin olive oil and extra sherry vinegar. Arrange the prawns on top and crumble on the feta. Serve immediately.

Tunisian prawns with fattouche

Serves 6

We love fattouche as it's a clean crisp salad, perfect for warmer weather. Serving Tunisian spiced prawns on top makes it even better.

1 red onion, sliced
1 tsp sumac
125 g pide bread or focaccia
extra virgin olive oil
1 baby cos lettuce, washed
1 Lebanese cucumber, halved and sliced
generous handful of flat-leaf parsley leaves
2 tbsp lemon juice
salt and freshly ground black pepper
60 ml (¼ cup) extra virgin olive oil
2 tsp ras el hanout
½ tsp salt
2 tbsp olive oil, additional
36 green prawns, approximately 1 kg, peeled and de-veined
12 wooden skewers, soaked in cold water

Pour hot tap water onto the onion and allow to stand for 2 minutes before draining. When cool toss onion slices with sumac.

Dice the pide bread into 1 cm chunks. Heat a heavy-based frypan over medium heat, and then add a generous splash of olive oil and the bread chunks. Stir until the bread becomes quite toasty, about 3–4 minutes.

Mix onion, bread chunks, lettuce leaves, cucumber and parsley. Whisk lemon juice, salt and pepper together, then whisk in oil.

Mix ras el hanout, salt and additional oil together. Coat the prawns with this mix and marinate for up to 2 hours. Thread 3 prawns onto each skewer.

Barbecue the prawns on the grill or pan-fry for 2–3 minutes on each side. Toss the dressing through the salad. Divide the salad between 6 plates and top with 2 skewers each.

Moroccan mussel and fennel salad

Serves 6

This is perfect entree food. Light but full of interesting textures and flavours.

1 kg mussels, shells scrubbed and beards removed
1 red onion, sliced
1 tsp sumac
½ tsp allspice
1 fennel bulb
2 tbsp lemon juice
1 clove garlic, crushed
generous handful of flat-leaf parsley leaves
salt and freshly ground black pepper
60 ml (¼ cup) extra virgin olive oil
100 g rocket

Heat wok over high heat, add about 2 cm water and bring to the boil. Toss in mussels. Cover with a lid and leave to steam for 3–4 minutes. Remove lid, shake pan well and remove cooked mussels as they open. Discard any that do not open. Remove cooked mussels from shells and place in a small bowl.

Pour hot tap water onto onion and allow to stand for 2 minutes. Drain, then toss onion slices with sumac and allspice. Remove tough outer layer from fennel bulbs. Cut in half, remove core and slice fennel thinly (a mandolin is perfect for this if you have one).

Whisk lemon juice, garlic, chopped parsley, salt and pepper together, then whisk in oil.

Combine onion, fennel, rocket and parsley leaves and toss with salad dressing. Divide salad between six plates, or one large platter. Surround salad with mussels and serve.

Steamed mussels with garlic

Serves 4

A bowl of garlicky mussels makes a great start to any meal; it's also a dish that takes only a few minutes to prepare. Remember to purchase mussels with their shells closed and discard any that fail to open during cooking. You can serve the mussels in individual portions, but it's more fun to throw them into a big bowl and invite everyone to dive in and share.

2 tbsp olive oil
4 cloves garlic, crushed
125 ml (½ cup) dry white wine
pinch of saffron threads
1 kg mussels, shells scrubbed and beards removed
chopped parsley
knob of butter
salt and freshly ground black pepper

Heat a wok or large frypan over high heat. Add a swirl of oil, then the garlic. Stir for 1 minute, or until fragrant. Add white wine and saffron. Allow the liquid to come to the boil, then toss in the mussels. Cover with a lid and leave to steam for 3–4 minutes.

Have 4 bowls to hand. Remove the lid, shake the pan well and remove the cooked mussels as they open, placing them directly in the bowls.

Remove the pan from the heat and discard any mussels that didn't open during cooking. Add chopped parsley and butter to the cooking liquid and whisk through. Check seasoning and add salt and pepper if needed.

Pour the cooking juices over the mussels and serve immediately.

HOW TO CLEAN MUSSELS

Rinse under cold running water and pull sharply at beards to remove, discarding any open shells. Scrub shells if necessary. Place clean mussels under a damp cloth in the refrigerator until needed.

Mussels with Thai chilli broth

Serves 6 as an entree or 4 as a main course

This dish is great for lunch, or as a smart entree for a dinner party. You have to believe us when we say mussels are easy to cook; they just sound, and look, terrifying.

3 tomatoes, quartered
2 small red chillies, halved
3 cloves garlic, bruised
1 × 5 cm piece fresh ginger, sliced
2 sticks lemongrass, sliced
400 ml can coconut cream
2 tbsp fish sauce
250 ml (1 cup) fish or chicken stock
1 bunch coriander
6 red shallots, sliced
½ red capsicum, sliced
250 g chow mein noodles
2 kg fresh mussels, cleaned

Place tomatoes, chillies, garlic, ginger and lemongrass in a heavy-based saucepan. Add coconut cream, fish sauce and stock.

Wash coriander well, roughly chop roots and stems, reserving leaves for later, and place in the saucepan. Bring to a gentle boil and allow to simmer for 20 minutes.

Remove from the heat and strain infused coconut milk into a clean saucepan. With a ladle force any remaining liquid through the sieve and set aside until ready to serve.

Bring infused coconut milk to the boil. Add shallots and capsicum, and allow to simmer until needed.

Put a kettle of water on to boil. Pour boiling water over noodles and set aside. Heat wok, add 2 cm of boiling water and toss mussels in. Cover with a lid; allow to steam for 2 minutes. Remove mussels as they open and keep warm until remainder are opened. Drain noodles.

To serve, divide noodles into bowls, add 8 mussels per person for an entree or 12 for a main course, discarding any that are not open. Add a handful of coriander leaves to infused coconut milk, pour over the noodles and serve.

Green chilli and coriander steamed mussels

Serves 4

Mussels are a foolproof but impressive standby when we have friends over for dinner. For extra flavour you can use chicken, fish or vegetable stock in this recipe.

- 2 tbsp grated ginger
- 4 cloves garlic, crushed
- 1 tsp turmeric
- 2 tsp ground coriander
- ½ tsp salt
- oil
- 1 onion, thinly sliced
- 2–3 large green chillies, thinly sliced
- 125 ml (½ cup) stock or water
- 1 kg mussels, shells scrubbed and beards removed
- large handful of coriander leaves

Make a spice paste by blending the ginger, garlic, turmeric, coriander and salt together. Add 2–3 tbsp oil to form a paste.

Heat a large wok over a high heat. Add a generous splash of oil to coat the base. Add the onion and chillies and cook for 3–4 minutes, stirring often, until they start to soften. Add the spice paste and cook for a further 3–4 minutes, until fragrant, taking care that it doesn't burn. Add the stock (or water) and allow it to come to the boil.

Add mussels to the wok, cover and cook for 4–5 minutes. Remove the lid and place any opened mussels in a serving bowl. Continue cooking, stirring often and removing the mussels as they open. Discard any mussels which fail to open during cooking.

Pour cooking liquid over the top of the cooked mussels, sprinkle over coriander leaves and serve immediately.

Mussels with chorizo, tomato and couscous

Serves 6 as an entree, 4 for lunch

This dish was inspired by one we saw demonstrated by chef Karen Martini. We've simplified it somewhat, creating a dish with an amazing taste that needs only crusty bread for an entree, or a salad to make lunch for four.

- 1 dry chorizo sausage, approximately 250 g
- olive oil
- 1 onion, finely diced
- 2 cloves garlic, crushed
- pinch of saffron threads
- 1 tsp smoky sweet paprika
- 2 bay leaves
- 150 ml (⅔ cup) white wine
- 250 ml (1 cup) tomato sugo
- 250 ml (1 cup) chicken stock
- 100 g (⅔ cup) medium-sized couscous
- 1½ kg mussels
- ¼ cup chopped flat-leaf parsley

Cut the chorizo in half lengthwise and slice thinly. Heat a saucepan over a medium heat, add chorizo and dry fry, rendering out some of the fat. Tip excess fat away and remove the chorizo. Add a splash of olive oil along with the onion and cook for 4–5 minutes until the onion softens but doesn't brown. Add garlic and saffron and cook for 2–3 minutes until fragrant. Add paprika, bay leaves and white wine. Bring to the boil, and then add tomato sugo, chorizo and stock. Bring to the boil, add couscous and cook for 5 minutes. Remove from the heat and set aside.

Rinse the mussels well, pulling at the beards to remove them. Line a large bowl with a wet towel, place the mussels in the bowl, cover and refrigerate until needed.

Reheat sauce over a low heat, check seasoning and add more stock if necessary to adjust consistency. Heat a wok over a high heat, add ½ cup of water, cover with a lid and bring to the boil. Add mussels, cover and cook for 4–5 minutes. Remove lid and any opened mussels. Place cooked mussels in a serving bowl. Continue cooking, stirring often and removing mussels as they open. This will take 4–5 minutes. Discard any that do not open after 10 minutes of cooking.

To serve, pour the hot sauce over the mussels and sprinkle with parsley.

Spiced pipis with risoni

Serves 4

Risoni is pasta shaped like a grain of rice and pipis are small, silvery coloured shellfish. Together they make a delicious combination. If one were having a candle-lit supper this would be just the dish to prepare.

500 g pipis
2 tbsp olive oil
1 onion, finely diced
1 carrot, finely diced
1 leek, thinly sliced
1 clove garlic, crushed
2 small red chillies, de-seeded and finely diced
1 tbsp tomato paste
1 litre (4 cups) chicken stock
220 g (1 cup) risoni
1 tbsp chopped parsley
salt and freshly ground pepper

Rinse the pipis under cold water and discard any opened shells. Keep refrigerated until needed.

Heat a large saucepan over a medium heat. Add oil and onion, carrot and leek. Cook for 5 minutes, stirring often. Add garlic, chillies and tomato paste, cook for a further 2 minutes. Add stock and bring to the boil. Once boiling add a pinch of salt and risoni. Return to the boil, then lower the heat, cover with a lid and cook for 6 minutes.

Check risoni is al dente, add the pipis, cover again and cook for 2 minutes. Uncover and watch for pipis beginning to open. Remove pipis as they open and place in a warm bowl. Continue cooking until most of the pipis have opened, discard any which won't open. Add parsley to the risoni and check the seasoning.

Divide pipis and risoni evenly between 4 warmed soup bowls. Serve with crusty bread.

Crab cakes with Thai cucumber salad

Serves 4

These crab cakes were on the menu when we welcomed in the year 2000 with friends at home. It was a great start to a memorable meal. One large crab weighing about 1.5 kg will be perfect for this recipe, otherwise smaller crabs to the weight. Or even easier buy fresh crab meat from your local fishmonger. This recipe is just as delicious with lobster or crayfish meat.

200 g fresh crab meat
1 egg
2 tbsp chopped coriander
1 tbsp lime juice
200 g (4 cups) fresh breadcrumbs
4 spring onions, very finely chopped
salt
Tabasco sauce
2 cucumbers
½ cup coriander leaves
6 shallots, thinly sliced
1 small red chilli, de-seeded and finely diced
½ tbsp palm sugar
1 tbsp lime juice
1 tbsp fish sauce
freshly ground black pepper
2 tsp rice vinegar
2 tbsp peanut oil
ghee or olive oil for cooking
2 limes, cut into wedges

Place crabmeat, egg, coriander, lime juice, breadcrumbs and spring onions in a bowl and mix lightly. Add a pinch of salt and a few drops of Tabasco to season and combine. Divide mixture into 8 and pat into burger shapes. Refrigerate until needed.

Peel cucumbers, then, using the vegetable peeler, slice strips of cucumber from one end to the other, discarding centre seeds. Place cucumber strips in a colander and leave to drain for 30 minutes. Toss cucumber with coriander leaves, shallots and chilli and set aside until ready to serve.

Prepare dressing by dissolving palm sugar in lime juice and fish sauce. Add freshly ground black pepper to season and whisk in vinegar. Finally add the oil. Toss dressing with cucumber strips just before serving.

To serve, heat a heavy-based frypan over medium heat. Add 1–2 tbsp ghee (or olive oil), add crab cakes and cook for 5–8 minutes on each side until golden brown on the outside and hot in the middle. It is essential to cook crab cakes slowly over a medium heat to ensure they cook right through to the centre, without browning too much. You can pan-fry them until crispy on the outside and put them in a 180°C preheated oven for 10 minutes if you prefer.

Meanwhile toss cucumber with dressing and divide between 4 plates. Place 2 crab cakes on each plate and serve with lime wedges.

Stir-fried crabs with black beans and ginger

Serves 4 as an entree

A classic Chinese dish that is easy to prepare and a stunner to serve.

- 4 blue swimmer crabs, about 200–300 g each, preferably live
- 1 tbsp black beans, soaked in cold water
- 2 tsp grated ginger
- 2 cloves garlic, peeled and crushed
- 2 small red chillies, de-seeded and finely diced
- 1 tbsp peanut oil
- 150 ml (⅔ cup) water
- coriander leaves to garnish
- steamed rice to serve

If using live crabs, freeze for 30 minutes to put them to sleep. Cut each crab into quarters, leaving claws attached. Rinse each piece under cold running water to remove innards. Drain well and refrigerate until needed.

Rinse black beans well and chop finely. Place in a small bowl with ginger, garlic and chillies. Mix well.

Place wok over high heat for 5 minutes without oil. The wok has to be really hot to cook the crabs quickly. Prepare yourself and get the range hood or extractor going full blast. Add the peanut oil, swirl to coat surface and add black bean mixture. Stir for 20 seconds, allowing the kitchen to fill with the fragrant aromas. Add crab pieces, and cook and stir for 2–3 minutes. Add the water. Cover with a lid and cook for 5 minutes, stirring occasionally.

Place crabs, liquid and all, on a hot platter and top with coriander leaves. Serve with steamed rice. Napkins and finger bowls of water are probably a good idea too.

Spicy pipis with black bean and ginger
Replace crab with 1 kg pipis (or mussels). Get the spice mix cooked and just throw the pipis in along with the water and cook until shells open.

Seared calamari with chilli and balsamic dressing

Serves 4

This is the type of recipe where you need to get everything ready before you start cooking, as the actual cooking part takes only about 5 minutes.

4 calamari tubes, about 125 g each
oil
2 small red chillies, de-seeded and finely diced
2 tsp grated ginger
1 tbsp balsamic vinegar
salt and freshly ground black pepper
2 tbsp lemon or lime juice
2 tbsp chopped parsley
2–3 tbsp olive oil
250 g salad leaves

Slit the calamari along one side. Remove any loose skin. Using a sharp knife, score the inside skin on an angle to create a crosshatch pattern. Refrigerate until needed.

Place a large heavy-based frypan, or preferably two, over high heat. Add a splash of oil to the pan and cook chilli and ginger briefly. Add calamari, cut side down. Cook for 2–3 minutes until calamari starts to turn opaque. Turn over and continue cooking for a further 2–3 minutes. Add 1–2 tbsp water and continue cooking until calamari forms a roll. Remove from the heat.

Add vinegar, salt, pepper, juice, parsley and oil to the pan. Divide salad leaves between plates. Add one piece of calamari to each plate and drizzle sauce over the top. Serve immediately.

Smoked trout and avocado toasts

Serves 6

This dish is really a combination of a delicious salad on toasted Italian bread. We love it – firstly because the ingredients are readily available at delicatessens and supermarkets, and secondly because it's quick and easy to make.

1 whole smoked trout
500 g asparagus, ends trimmed off
200 g watercress sprigs, tips picked (or rocket)
18 basil leaves, torn roughly
100 ml (⅓ cup) Lemon Mayonnaise (page 554)
a little lemon juice
1 tsp Dijon mustard
6 thick slices crusty casalinga bread
1 ripe avocado, diced
150 g cherry tomatoes, halved
2 tbsp chives, finely chopped

Gently peel skin from fish. Remove flesh from the bones and flake into large pieces.

Cook asparagus in boiling water for 2 minutes, then refresh immediately under cold running water. Place asparagus in a bowl with watercress sprigs (or rocket) and basil leaves.

Mix mayonnaise with lemon juice and mustard to taste. It should be fairly runny so add a little boiling water if needed.

Lightly toast the sourdough and spread each with the mayonnaise. Place each slice of toast on a serving plate and top with asparagus and greens. Then divide the avocado, cherry tomatoes and smoked trout between each plate. Spoon more mayonnaise over the top and scatter with chopped chives.

Smoked salmon rillettes

Serves 6

It's more formal to serve everyone their own ramekin of rillettes, but you can just as easily produce one large dish with toast and pickles so that people can help themselves as they are having a drink.

300 g salmon fillet, skin and bones removed
100 g melted butter
100 ml (⅓ cup) cream
80 ml (⅓ cup) lemon juice
salt and freshly ground black pepper
200 g smoked salmon, cut into ½ cm dice
French toast, lavoche or crackers to serve
pickles to serve
6 × 150 ml ramekins

Fill a deep frypan with water, place over a medium heat and bring water to the boil. Add salmon, ensure that the water covers the fish, and simmer for 5–6 minutes, turning the fish over once, to cook the salmon to medium-rare. Remove from the liquid and set aside to cool.

When the salmon is cool put it into a food processor and blend until almost smooth. Add butter in a constant stream. Add cream to bring to a stiff paste consistency, then add lemon juice and check seasoning. Fold diced smoked salmon through. Spoon into 6 small ramekins, or in one large dish, and refrigerate for at least 6 hours or overnight.

To serve, place the ramekins of rillettes on plates. Serve with warm toast, lavoche or crackers and a small pile of pickled cornichons, olives or gherkins on each plate.

Coriander-cured salmon

Serves 8–10

This recipe takes the theory behind gravlax salmon and cures it in a similar manner using coriander in place of dill, making it more Middle Eastern than Scandinavian. Add a splash of soy sauce to make it more Asian.

1 Atlantic salmon fillet, approximately 1 kg
2 tbsp coriander seeds
1 tbsp juniper berries
200 g (¾ cup) sea salt
150 g (⅔ cup) caster sugar
zest of 1 lemon

1 bunch coriander with roots
2 cloves garlic, crushed
1½–2½ tbsp lemon juice
80–125 ml (⅓–½ cup) olive oil
salt and freshly ground black pepper
wild rocket leaves to serve

Ask your fishmonger to remove the fine bones that run down the centre of the salmon – you can do it yourself if you have tweezers. Place the salmon skin side down in a deep baking dish. Crush coriander seeds and juniper berries coarsely in a mortar and pestle. Mix with salt, sugar and lemon zest. Chop the roots of the coriander and mix through salt mix. Pack the salt–sugar mix down on the salmon flesh, cover with cling film and weigh it down with something heavy such as a bag of rice. Refrigerate for 12 hours. Turn salmon over and refrigerate for a further 6 hours.

Remove the cling film and salt mixture. Rinse the salmon under cold water and pat dry. Take a sharp knife and, starting at the tail, on an angle (as you would smoked salmon) slice paper-thin slices. Don't worry if the first few are a bit uneven, you'll get better. You can slice the salmon whenever you are ready; place it on a tray or large platter and put cling film between layers. Refrigerate until needed.

Make dressing by placing the coriander leaves and stems in a food processor along with the garlic. Process until chopped. Add 2 tbsp lemon juice, blend, then start to drizzle in oil to form a smooth sauce. Check seasoning, adding salt and pepper as needed. Add more lemon juice if needed and refrigerate.

Toss the rocket leaves with 1–2 tbsp of dressing. Arrange 4–5 slices of salmon in the centre of each plate. Arrange a handful of dressed rocket leaves in the centre and drizzle a spoon of dressing on the salmon. Grind a little black pepper over the top if desired.

Hot and sour crispy salmon salad with lime dressing

Serves 4–6

This salad is just the thing to liven up your tastebuds in the depths of winter. The tangy dressing is the perfect complement to the rich fish.

- 2 tbsp fish sauce
- 2 tbsp grated palm sugar
- 4 small red chillies, finely chopped
- 2 × 200 g salmon fillets
- peanut oil
- 2 tbsp lime juice
- 1 Lebanese cucumber
- 3 spring onions, finely sliced
- 10 mint leaves, shredded
- 1 cup coriander sprigs
- 100 g (⅔ cup) peanuts, roasted
- freshly ground black pepper

Combine half of each of the fish sauce, palm sugar and chilli. Place the salmon in a shallow dish and coat it in the mixture. Set aside to marinate for at least 40 minutes, but no longer than 4 hours, then drain the fish.

Heat a small frypan or grill pan over medium–high heat. Add a splash of oil and cook the fish for 4 minutes on each side, or until medium–rare. Set aside to cool.

Prepare the dressing by dissolving the remaining palm sugar in the lime juice. Add the remaining fish sauce and chilli.

Peel the cucumber, then use the peeler to cut the cucumber into long thin strips. Discard the inner seeds. Place the strips in a colander and leave to drain for 10 minutes.

Place the spring onion, mint, coriander and peanuts in a large bowl.

Remove the skin and any bones from the salmon. Flake the flesh into pieces and add to the bowl along with the cucumber. Pour on the dressing, season with black pepper and toss to combine.

Divide between plates or arrange on a large platter and serve.

Crispy-skin quail with Sichuan pepper and salt

Serves 6

This dish can easily be served as a main course by adding an extra half quail per person. If you have a wok burner on your barbecue we suggest you cook the birds outside. To spatchcock the quails, insert a sharp knife into the cavity and out through the neck. Hold the point of the knife and cut through beside the backbone, pressing down firmly. Trim backbone away and remove any excess skin. Press bird flat. Trim rib bones, if desired, and you're ready to go.

2 tbsp Sichuan pepper
3 tbsp salt
Master Stock (page 118)
6 quails, spatchcocked
oil
lime wedges and additional Sichuan pepper and salt mix to serve

To make the Sichuan pepper and salt mix, place Sichuan pepper and salt in a dry frypan and cook over a medium heat. Stir for 3 minutes, or until the salt turns golden. Crush in a mortar and pestle until very fine, and store in an airtight jar.

Bring the Master Stock to a gentle boil in a medium-sized saucepan. Add the quails and cook for 10 minutes, making sure the liquid doesn't boil, just trembles. Remove the quails and allow them to cool. Once cool, lay them skin side down on paper towel and refrigerate.

When you're ready to fry the quails, make sure that their skin is completely dry. Heat 4 cm oil, or enough oil to deep-fry the birds 2–3 at a time. Cook the quails until crispy. Drain on absorbent paper.

Arrange quail pieces on a platter and sprinkle with Sichuan pepper and salt mix. Serve with lime wedges and an additional bowl of the Sichuan mix.

SOUPS

stocks, broths
hearty soups + bread

As a general rule of cooking, the higher the quality of the raw ingredients, the better the dish will be. This is definitely the case with soup. It's well worth the effort to ensure you have good stock, fresh vegetables, quality meats and noodles.

We're big soup fans, especially for lunch in cooler weather and to provide an energy boost to keep us going. Everyone should learn how to make a few soups – they're very easy to prepare and it only takes 10 minutes or so to get a pot of soup onto the stove. Then it simmers away gently and virtually cooks itself.

Good stock is essential for most soups. The best stock is homemade, but of course we don't all have the time to make our own stock and there are plenty of good alternatives available: quality food stores sell homemade stock; there are cartons of stock at the supermarket; and if you're really stuck, a stock cube can do the job. We have to confess that we are big users of packaged liquid stock, mostly the low-salt ones.

soup recipes

stock

Beef stock	116
Chicken stock	117
Master stock	118
Vegetable stock	118
Fish stock	119

soup

Potato and leek soup	119
Vegetable soup	120
Roast tomato soup	121
Classic tomato soup	122
Roast capsicum soup	122
Asian-inspired pumpkin soup	123
Sweet potato and ginger soup	124
Cauliflower, chilli and coconut soup	124
Carrot and coriander soup	125
Spring pea soup	126
Broad bean and crispy prosciutto soup	128
Creamy corn soup	128
Beetroot soup	129
Curried parsnip soup	129
Roast pumpkin and Moroccan lentil soup	130
Chicken noodle soup	132
Minestrone	133
Duck and pine mushroom bread soup	133
French onion soup	134
Italian spring vegetable and pasta broth	135
Pasta e fagioli	136
Lentil and ham hock soup	137
Lamb shank, vegetable and barley broth	138
Oxtail soup	139
Roasted vegetable gazpacho	140
Sweetcorn chowder	141
Fish and fennel chowder	141
Tom yum	142
Laksa	143
Prawn and coconut tom yum	144
Miso soup	146
Duck and macadamia wonton soup	147
Beijing dumpling soup	147

bread

Soup accompaniments	148
Soda bread	150
Bread rolls	151
A great crusty loaf	152
Polenta bread	153
Focaccia	154
Naan bread	155

Things you need to know about soups and stocks

1 If you make a large saucepan of stock you can reduce it until the flavour is very concentrated. Freeze this in small quantities, even in ice-cube trays, and reconstitute it later in water.

2 Virtually all soups freeze well, so you can usually make enough for more than one meal.

3 Stock and soup will keep well for 2–3 days in the refrigerator and up to 3 months in the freezer.

4 We prefer to thicken our soups with potato where possible, rather than using flour and butter in a roux. Simply add a peeled and diced potato to soup that will be pureed to ensure a good consistency, or add a grated potato to broth soups that are to be served as they are.

5 Take care when pureeing soups: hot soup will cause nasty burns if it splashes onto your skin.

6 Deep bowls are perfect for serving soup, keeping the liquid hot to the very last spoonful.

7 Don't forget to try barley, rice, pasta, noodles, lentils, borlotti beans, split peas, chickpeas and haricot beans in your soup.

8 We cook dried beans in a separate saucepan until they are tender, and then add them to the soup in the later stages. This ensures that they are completely tender and it stops the soup going cloudy.

9 Bay leaves add an essential background herb flavour to all stocks. They are best fresh and are easy to grow if you have a sunny spot in the garden. Bay trees provide way more leaves than you could ever use and they look beautiful, too.

10 It's best to add cream to soup after it has been taken from the heat. Boiling liquid can curdle the cream.

11 Stock and soup recipes sometimes call for a bouquet garni. This is a bundle of fresh herbs that includes bay leaves, thyme, parsley and celery leaves, tied with string or wrapped in muslin. You add it while the stock is simmering and remove it during straining. We always have the basics of a bouquet garni growing in the backyard with a plot of thyme and parsley plus bay leaves.

12 Use chicken or vegetable stock at your discretion in vegetable soups. We prefer chicken for its fuller flavour, but vegetable stock is just as good.

Beef stock

Makes 2–3 litres

Beef stock can be made with a mix of beef and veal bones. The beef lends a hearty flavour, while the veal will bring a hint of richness and a slight stickiness to the stock.

500 g veal bones, such as shanks
500 g beef bones, such as shins
1 onion, roughly chopped
1 leek, roughly chopped
2 carrots, roughly chopped
2 celery stalks, roughly chopped
a few whole black peppercorns
2 bay leaves
parsley stalks
2–3 litres water

Preheat oven to 180°C.

Arrange bones in a baking tray and roast in preheated oven for 30–40 minutes, draining excess oil off occasionally and turning once or twice until golden brown.

Place bones in a large saucepan. Add vegetables, peppercorns, herbs and water, and bring to the boil. Remove any scum from the surface, reduce to a simmer and cook for 2–3 hours. Strain and press down hard on the ingredients to extract all the flavour. Set aside. When the stock has cooled slightly, refrigerate to allow fat to set on the surface. Skim fat off the surface and the stock is ready to use.

Veal stock
Use only veal bones in the beef stock recipe in order to make a stock that can be reduced to an almost sticky consistency for sauces and gravy.

Game stock
Prepare a mix of veal bones with bones from duck, venison or quail and prepare as directed, to produce a more full-flavoured stock. This, too, can be reduced to an almost sticky consistency for sauces and gravy.

Chicken stock

Makes 2–3 litres

Keep chicken stock on hand for many uses besides soup – risotto, gravy, casseroles and curries also benefit from the addition of good-quality stock.

1 kg chicken bones
1 onion, roughly chopped
1 leek, roughly chopped
2 carrots, roughly chopped
2 celery stalks, roughly chopped
a few whole black peppercorns
2 bay leaves
parsley stalks
2–3 litres water

Place chicken bones in a large saucepan. Add vegetables, peppercorns, herbs and water, and bring to the boil. Remove any scum from the surface, reduce to a simmer and cook for 2–3 hours. Strain and press down hard on the ingredients to extract all the flavour. When the stock has cooled slightly, refrigerate to allow fat to set on the surface. Skim fat off the surface and the stock is ready to use.

Asian chicken stock
Add a 3 cm piece of ginger, sliced, 2 tbsp soy sauce, 1 sliced lemongrass stem and, optionally, a sliced chilli or two.

Rich chicken stock
Place the bones in a baking tray and roast in a preheated 180°C oven for 30-40 minutes until golden brown, turning once or twice and draining excess oil off occasionally. The bones can then be added to the vegetables and herbs and cooked in the usual way.

Duck stock
Use the same quantities of duck bones as directed in the chicken stock recipe, and roast them as described for Chicken Stock. This stock can also be reduced to 250 ml (1 cup) for an amazingly rich, sticky duck sauce.

Turkey stock
Use the same quantities of turkey bones as for chicken stock, and roast them as directed for Chicken Stock. This stock can also be reduced to 250 ml (1 cup) for a rich turkey sauce.

Master stock

Makes 1¾ litres

Master stock can be used as a base for Asian soups, but more commonly it is used for the Chinese practice of cooking poultry and pork in stock to keep moisture and add flavour. The stock can be reused for poaching time and time again, becoming more flavourful each time it is used. We use this recipe for twice-cooked pork ribs, crispy duck, and Sichuan pepper and salt quail.

- 1½ litre (6 cups) water
- 250 ml (1 cup) soy sauce
- 125 ml (½ cup) Chinese rice wine
- 3–4 slices ginger
- 1 lemongrass stem, sliced
- 2–3 pieces tangerine peel (optional)
- 2 star anise
- 75 g (⅓ cup) caster sugar

Place all ingredients in a large saucepan and bring to the boil. Reduce to a simmer then use to poach the meat as directed in your recipe. When finished, the stock can be refrigerated and used many times.

Vegetable stock

Makes 2–3 litres

Vegetable stock is perfect when you want a lightly flavoured base for your finished dish or are cooking a strictly vegetarian meal. It's quick to prepare and is easily made as required.

- 2 tbsp oil
- 3 onions, roughly chopped
- 2 leeks, roughly chopped
- 3 carrots, roughly chopped
- 2 celery stalks, roughly chopped
- 2 tomatoes, chopped
- a few whole black peppercorns
- 2 bay leaves
- parsley stalks
- 2–3 litres water

Heat oil in a stockpot, add the vegetables and stir for a few minutes. Add pepper, herbs and water, and bring to the boil. Remove any scum from the surface, reduce to a simmer and cook for 20 minutes. Strain and press down hard on the vegetables to extract all the flavour. Set aside.

Roasted vegetable stock
Place the vegetables in a baking tray and drizzle with a little olive oil. Roast in a preheated 180°C oven for 20–30 minutes, stirring once or twice until golden brown. The vegetables can then be added to the stockpot and cooked as described. This stock is great in full-flavoured dishes.

Fish stock

Makes 1–2 litres

Fish bones need only 20 minutes of cooking to produce a well-flavoured stock – any longer and the stock may turn bitter. It's best to use bones from white fish rather than oily varieties. We also recommend ladling the fish stock into a sieve before using it.

1 kg fish bones
250 ml (1 cup) white wine
1 onion, roughly chopped
1 leek, roughly chopped
2 carrots, roughly chopped
2 celery stalks, roughly chopped
top of 1 fennel bulb, if available
a few whole black peppercorns
2 bay leaves
parsley stalks
2–3 litres water

Heat a stockpot over a medium heat. Add the bones and white wine, and then cook for 2–3 minutes. Add the vegetables, peppercorns, herbs and water, and heat until almost boiling. Remove any scum from the surface, reduce to a simmer and cook for 20 minutes. Strain by ladling into a sieve and set aside. When the stock has cooled slightly, refrigerate it.

Potato and leek soup

Serves 4

Potato and leek soup is nutritious, tasty and easy to make. Everyone should learn how to make this soup before leaving home.

olive oil
1 onion, diced
2 celery stalks, diced
2 leeks, sliced
4 potatoes, peeled and diced
1 clove garlic, crushed
1 litre (4 cups) chicken or vegetable stock
salt and freshly ground black pepper
cream and fresh herbs to taste

Heat a heavy-based saucepan over a medium–high heat. Add a generous splash of oil, onion, celery and leek. Cook for 5–6 minutes, stirring often. Add potatoes and garlic and cook for a further 3–4 minutes. Add enough stock to just cover and a little salt and pepper, and bring to the boil. Reduce heat and simmer for 15 minutes, or until potatoes are tender.

Remove from heat, puree soup using a food processor and pass through a strainer back into a clean saucepan. To serve, bring soup back to the boil, check seasoning, and add cream if desired and chopped herbs to garnish.

Potato and watercress soup
Use only 1 leek and cook as described. Adding a few handfuls of freshly picked watercress to the soup as it is about to be pureed will give it a fresh green colour and a gutsy watercress flavour.

Vegetable soup

Serves 4

This is your basic everyday vegetable soup. You can make it from a mix of vegetables or use just 1 or 2 varieties, such as mushrooms, tomato or potato and leek. Choose your vegetables, scrub or peel them as needed, cut them into similar-sized pieces so they will all cook at the same time, and have fun playing around with different combinations to come up with your favourite soup.

oil
1 onion, diced
2 celery stalks, diced
1 leek, sliced
1 potato, peeled and diced
300 g mixed vegetables (for example, carrot, pumpkin and tomato)
1 clove garlic, crushed
1 litre (4 cups) vegetable or chicken stock
salt and freshly ground black pepper
cream and fresh herbs to taste

Heat a heavy-based saucepan over a medium–high heat. Add a generous splash of oil and the onion, celery and leek. Cook for 5–6 minutes, stirring often. Add the potato, mixed vegetables and garlic, and cook for a further 3–4 minutes. Add a little salt and pepper and enough stock to just cover the vegetables, and bring to the boil. Reduce heat and simmer for 15 minutes, or until the potato is tender.

Remove from heat. Puree the soup using a food processor, then pass through a strainer back into a clean saucepan.

To serve, bring the soup back to the boil, check seasoning, and add cream if desired and chopped herbs to garnish.

Mushroom soup
Omit mixed vegetables. Add 300 g mushrooms along with the potato and garlic.

Asparagus soup
Make as vegetable soup, but omit mixed vegetables and add 300 g asparagus tips to the soup just before pureeing.

Tomato and fennel soup
Omit mixed vegetables. Add 300 g diced tomatoes and 1 chopped fennel bulb along with the potato and garlic.

Roast tomato soup

Serves 4

Roasting tomatoes brings an extra intensity to this soup. Adding a dollop of pesto as you serve it takes it one step further.

1 red capsicum
500 g Roma tomatoes
olive oil
freshly ground black pepper
1 onion, diced
1 clove garlic, crushed

1 small red chilli, halved
2 small celery sticks, chopped
1 carrot, sliced
2 potatoes, peeled and diced
1 litre (4 cups) vegetable stock
pesto to serve (optional)

Preheat oven to 200°C.

Cut the capsicum in half and remove seeds. Cut the tomatoes in half and place on a baking tray along with the capsicum halves. Lightly drizzle with oil, sprinkle with ground pepper and cook in the preheated oven for 30 minutes, or until the tomatoes are soft and browned. Place capsicums in a plastic bag and seal to allow steam to lift skins. When the tomatoes and capsicums have cooled, peel and discard skins.

Heat a large saucepan over a medium heat. Add a splash of oil, onion, garlic, chilli, celery and carrot. Cook for 5 minutes, stirring occasionally, until softened. Add potatoes, cook gently for another 5 minutes, and then add peeled tomatoes and capsicum. Add vegetable stock and bring to the boil. Simmer gently for 20 minutes or until the potatoes are soft. Puree and pass through a strainer into a clean saucepan.

Return soup to the boil, check seasoning and adjust consistency.

Add a dollop of pesto to each bowl of soup if desired.

Roast tomato and coriander pesto soup
Serve with a spoonful of Coriander Pesto (page 551) and coriander leaves to garnish.

Classic tomato soup

Serves 4

You can't go too far wrong with this old favourite. A good tip is to add a pinch of sugar after pureeing the tomatoes, as it increases the soup's sweetness.

oil
1 onion, peeled and quartered
2 cloves garlic, peeled
8 ripe tomatoes, chopped
250–500 ml (1–2 cups) vegetable or chicken stock
salt and freshly ground black pepper
125 ml (½ cup) cream
½ cup chopped basil leaves

Heat a large heavy-based saucepan over a medium heat. Add oil and the onion and cook for 5–6 minutes, stirring well. Add the garlic and tomatoes, then reduce heat to low and cook for 10 minutes, stirring often.

Add enough stock to cover the tomatoes. Raise the heat and bring to the boil. Reduce to a simmer, cover the saucepan and cook for 20 minutes, or until the tomatoes are tender. Puree the soup and strain into a clean saucepan.

Return the soup to the boil and add more stock if it is too thick. Remove from heat, whisk in the cream and season to taste with salt and pepper. Stir in chopped basil and serve immediately.

Roast capsicum soup

Serves 4–6

Despite the roasting and pureeing involved, this soup is very quick to make. The flavour is so good it can also be served chilled on a hot summer night.

4 red capsicums
oil
6 tomatoes, halved
1 onion, peeled and quartered
2 cloves garlic, peeled
1 red chilli
salt and freshly ground black pepper
250–500 ml (1–2 cups) vegetable or chicken stock

Preheat oven to 180°C.

Rub the capsicums with oil. Place them in a baking tray and roast them for 30 minutes, or until their skins blister. Put the tomatoes, onion, garlic and chilli in another baking tray, toss with oil, salt and pepper and roast at the same temperature for 30 minutes, or until soft.

Remove and discard the seeds and skins from the tomatoes and capsicums. Puree the tomato, capsicum, onion, garlic and chilli with the cooking juices. Pass through a sieve.

Place the puree in a saucepan and add enough stock to bring the soup to a good consistency. Bring to the boil. Check seasoning and serve.

Asian-inspired pumpkin soup

Serves 6–8

This soup came about when we got totally fed up with regular pumpkin soup. All we've done is add some Thai paste for flavour and coconut milk for creaminess, and now it's anything but boring. We were delighted when this recipe was included in Stephanie Alexander's updated version of *The Cook's Companion*.

- 2 tbsp vegetable oil
- 2 tbsp red Thai curry paste
- 1 onion, diced
- 1 celery stalk, diced
- 1 tomato, chopped
- 1 kg pumpkin, peeled and diced
- salt and freshly ground black pepper
- 1 litre (4 cups) vegetable or chicken stock
- 1 × 400 ml can coconut milk
- coriander leaves to serve

Heat a large heavy-based saucepan over a medium heat. Add oil and Thai curry paste and cook for 5 minutes, stirring often, until fragrant. Add the onion, celery, tomato and pumpkin, and season with salt and pepper. Reduce heat and cook for 15 minutes, stirring often.

Add stock to the saucepan, raise the heat and bring to the boil. Reduce to a simmer, cover the saucepan and cook for 20 minutes, or until the pumpkin is tender. Puree soup and strain into a clean saucepan.

Return the soup to the boil, whisk in the coconut milk and adjust seasoning. Serve with coriander leaves as a garnish.

Sweet potato and ginger soup

Serves 4

Sweet potato is very similar to pumpkin in that it produces a soup with an excellent texture. The ginger gives it a lift too.

olive oil
1 onion, diced
2 celery stalks, diced
1 leek, sliced
2 sweet potatoes, peeled and diced
3 cm ginger, peeled and sliced
1 clove garlic, crushed
1 litre (4 cups) chicken or vegetable stock
salt and freshly ground black pepper
cream and fresh herbs to taste

Heat a heavy-based saucepan over a medium–high heat. Add a generous splash of oil, onion, celery and leek. Cook for 5–6 minutes, stirring often. Add sweet potato, ginger and garlic and cook for a further 3–4 minutes. Add enough stock to just cover, and salt and pepper, and bring to the boil. Reduce heat and simmer for 15 minutes, or until sweet potato is tender.

Remove from heat, puree soup using food processor and pass through a strainer back into a clean saucepan. To serve, bring soup back to the boil, check seasoning, and add cream if desired and chopped herbs to garnish.

Cauliflower, chilli and coconut soup

Serves 6

I am always amazed at how good this soup is. Cauliflower isn't one of the great soup vegetables in my mind, but the addition of chilli and coconut makes this a great lunch dish. Serve in small bowls to stimulate the appetite as an amuse-bouche on a cold winter's night. MC

oil
1 celery stalk, diced
1 leek, diced
2 small red chillies, de-seeded and diced
2 potatoes, peeled and diced
½ cauliflower, roughly chopped
1 litre (4 cups) vegetable or chicken stock
300 ml (1¼ cups) coconut milk
salt and freshly ground black pepper
coriander leaves to serve

Heat a large heavy-based saucepan over a medium heat. Add a splash of oil, the celery and leek. Cook for 5 minutes, stirring often. Add chillies, potato and cauliflower and cook for a further 2–3 minutes.

Add the stock and coconut milk. Season with salt and pepper, raise the heat and bring to the boil.

Reduce to a simmer, cover the saucepan and cook for 20 minutes, or until the cauliflower is tender. Puree the soup and strain into a clean saucepan.

Return the soup to the boil and adjust seasoning. Sprinkle coriander leaves as a garnish.

Carrot and coriander soup

Serves 4

Fresh carrots are wonderfully highlighted by the aromatic spice of ground coriander, while the fresh coriander adds a lovely zing.

oil
1 onion, diced
2 celery stalks, diced
1 leek, sliced
4 carrots, peeled and diced
1 clove garlic, crushed
½ bunch coriander
60 ml (¼ cup) orange juice
1 litre (4 cups) chicken or vegetable stock
salt and freshly ground black pepper
cream to taste

Heat a heavy-based saucepan over a medium–high heat. Add a generous splash of oil, then add the onion, celery and leek. Cook for 5–6 minutes, stirring often. Add carrots and garlic and cook for a further 3–4 minutes. Wash coriander well and chop the roots and stems, reserving the leaves for a garnish. Add chopped coriander to saucepan and cook for 2–3 minutes. Add orange juice, enough stock to just cover the vegetables, and salt and pepper and bring to the boil. Reduce heat and simmer for 15 minutes, or until carrots are tender.

Remove from heat. Puree the soup using a food processor, then pass through a strainer back into a clean saucepan.

To serve, bring the soup back to the boil, check seasoning, and add cream if desired and coriander leaves to garnish.

Spring pea soup

Serves 6

Soup made with fresh green peas is a real taste sensation; it's also very easy to make. Here the peas are lightly cooked, then added to a simple potato base and pureed until smooth. A few fresh herbs, a splash of cream and it's ready.

60 g (3 tbsp) butter
1 onion, diced
1 stick celery, sliced
1 leek, white only, washed and sliced
2 cloves garlic, crushed
3 medium potatoes, peeled and diced
salt and freshly ground black pepper
500 ml (2 cups) light chicken stock
1 kg peas in the pod (450–500 g podded peas)
12 basil leaves, sliced
12 mint leaves, sliced
80 ml (⅓ cup) cream

Melt butter in a heavy saucepan over medium heat. Add onion, celery and leek; cook for 5 minutes, stirring often. Add garlic, potato, salt and pepper, and cook for a further 3 minutes. Pour in stock. Bring to the boil; reduce heat and simmer until all ingredients are tender, about 10–15 minutes.

Bring a pot of water to the boil. Add a pinch of salt, then the podded peas and cook until vibrant green and tender, about 5 minutes. Pour into a colander; refresh by running under cold water. It is essential to cook the peas separately to avoid overcooking them and turning the soup grey-green.

Puree peas and stock together and pass through a fine sieve. Return to a clean saucepan. To serve, bring the soup to a gentle boil. Remove from the heat and add the chopped herbs and cream. Adjust the consistency with more stock if required, season to taste and serve.

Broad bean and crispy prosciutto soup

Serves 4

Broad beans can be a delicious ingredient, especially when they are small and sweet. Avoid large beans – these are likely to be woody and bitter. It's best to pod them and also to remove the thin inner layer that encases each bean before use.

olive oil
1 onion, diced
1 clove garlic, crushed
1 potato, diced
1 litre (4 cups) chicken or vegetable stock
sprig of sage
salt and freshly ground black pepper
1 kg broad beans, podded
80 ml (⅓ cup) cream
8 slices prosciutto

Heat a large heavy-based saucepan over medium heat, add oil and onion. Cook for 5 minutes, stirring often until soft but not coloured. Add garlic and potato and cook for a further 2–3 minutes. Add stock, sage and a pinch of salt and bring to the boil. Cook for 15–20 minutes, or until potato is cooked. Add broad beans and cook for a further 5 minutes.

Remove soup from the heat, puree in a food processor and strain into a clean saucepan. Return to the boil, remove from the heat, whisk in the cream and adjust seasoning. Heat a small pan over medium heat, add a splash of oil and cook prosciutto slices until crisp. Remove and place on paper towel to drain excess oil. Chop roughly and sprinkle on top of each bowl of soup.

Creamy corn soup

Serves 4–6

This thick and creamy corn soup would be equally at home as part of a summery lunch or served in tiny cups as a mini starter for a smart dinner party.

oil
1 onion, chopped
1 celery stalk, chopped
1 carrot, chopped
2 medium potatoes, peeled and diced
2 cloves garlic, crushed
4 corn cobs, kernels removed with a sharp knife
1 litre (4 cups) vegetable or chicken stock
125 ml (½ cup) cream
2–3 tbsp chopped parsley

Heat a heavy-based saucepan over a medium–high heat. Add a splash of oil and the onion, celery, carrot and potatoes. Cook for 5–6 minutes, stirring often. Add garlic and cook for 1–2 minutes, until fragrant. Add corn kernels and stock, raise the heat and bring to the boil. Reduce to a simmer and cook for 10–15 minutes, or until potatoes are cooked. Puree the soup and strain into a clean saucepan.

Return the soup to the boil. Remove from heat, whisk in the cream and season to taste with salt and pepper. Stir in chopped parsley and serve immediately.

Beetroot soup

Serves 4

This soup is rich, warming and restorative. It's also easy to prepare as it's a simple matter of cooking diced beetroot in an aromatic broth until tender. It's also a great use of beetroot, a vegetable that we happen to adore.

2 tbsp olive oil
1 onion, diced
1 stalk celery, diced
1 clove garlic, crushed
3 large beetroots, peeled and diced 1 cm
80 ml (⅓ cup) orange juice
750 ml (3 cups) chicken or beef stock
1 tbsp balsamic vinegar
salt and freshly ground black pepper
natural yoghurt or sour cream to serve

Heat a heavy-based saucepan over a medium heat. Add oil, onion and celery and cook for 4–5 minutes, stirring often. Add garlic and diced beetroot and cook for a further 5 minutes, stirring often. Add orange juice, stock and vinegar and bring to the boil. Lower heat and cook for 15–20 minutes, or until beetroot is tender.

Add lots of pepper, check seasoning and serve each bowl with a spoonful of yoghurt or sour cream.

Curried parsnip soup

Serves 4

Just the thing for lunch on a cold winter's day, don't forget loads of crusty bread and butter.

2 tbsp olive oil
1 onion, diced
1 leek, sliced
1 clove garlic, crushed
1 celery stalk, chopped
1 carrot, diced
2 tbsp curry paste
4 parsnips, chopped
salt
500–750 ml (2–3 cups) vegetable or chicken stock
2 tbsp coconut cream
chopped parsley to garnish

Heat a heavy-based saucepan over medium heat. Add oil, onion, leek, garlic, celery and carrot. Cook for 5–7 minutes, stirring often, or until softened. Add curry paste and cook for 2–3 minutes until fragrant. Add parsnips, cook for a further 5 minutes. Add salt and enough stock to cover. Bring to the boil, reduce heat and simmer for 15–20 minutes or until all vegetables are cooked.

Puree soup and strain into a clean saucepan. Return soup to the boil, and then remove from the heat. Add coconut cream and adjust the seasoning. Sprinkle chopped parsley on top to serve.

Parsnip, lemon and ginger soup
Omit curry paste and substitute cream for coconut cream. Add a 5 cm peeled and chopped piece of ginger along with the onion. Add ½ lemon when adding the stock. Allow the lemon to cook, but remove it before pureeing.

Roast pumpkin and Moroccan lentil soup

Serves 6

This is a great winter warmer that makes the most of pumpkin – one of our favourite soup vegetables – and the Moroccan flavours add a touch of spice. This soup is perfect for a Sunday lunch or a casual meal with friends – just serve with crusty bread and a good cheese.

500 g pumpkin, peeled, de-seeded and chopped into 3 cm chunks
oil
salt and freshly ground black pepper
1 onion, finely diced
1 leek, thinly sliced
2 celery stalks, finely diced
2 carrots, finely diced
2 cloves garlic, crushed
20 saffron threads
2 tsp harissa
1–1½ litres (4–6 cups) vegetable stock
150 g (¾ cup) red lentils
2 tbsp chopped parsley
2 tbsp chopped coriander

Preheat oven to 180°C.

Place the pumpkin in a baking dish, toss with oil and season with salt and pepper. Roast in the preheated oven for 20–30 minutes, until the pumpkin is tender. Set aside.

Heat a medium-sized saucepan over a medium heat and add a splash of oil. Add the onion, leek, celery and carrots. Cook for 5 minutes, stirring often, until the vegetables begin to soften. Add garlic, saffron and harissa and cook for 2–3 minutes, until fragrant. Add enough stock to cover the vegetables and bring to the boil.

Rinse the lentils under cold running water, then add to the soup. Reduce heat and simmer for 15–20 minutes, or until the lentils are completely tender.

Take half the soup, add the roast pumpkin and puree. Mix both soups together and bring back to the boil, adding more stock if necessary. Check seasoning, add chopped herbs and serve.

Chicken noodle soup

Serves 6

Here is the ultimate chicken noodle soup, the dish that's said to be able to cure anything.

- 1 whole chicken
- 2–3 litres water
- a few whole black peppercorns
- 2 bay leaves
- 2 onions
- 2 carrots
- 1 leek
- 2 celery stalks
- olive oil
- 100 g thin spaghetti, broken into 5 cm pieces, or egg noodles
- 2 tbsp chopped parsley to serve
- salt and freshly ground black pepper

Place the chicken in a large saucepan and cover with water. Add peppercorns and bay leaves. Roughly chop 1 onion and 1 carrot, add to the pot along with the tops of the leek and celery, and bring to the boil. Remove any scum from the surface, reduce to a simmer and cook for 1–2 hours. Remove the chicken and set aside to cool.

Strain the liquid and press down hard on the ingredients to extract all the flavour. When the cooking liquid has cooled slightly, refrigerate to allow fat to set on the surface. Skim fat off the surface and the stock is ready to use.

Remove skin and bone from the chicken and thinly slice the chicken meat. Finely dice the remaining vegetables.

In a clean saucepan, add oil and cook the finely diced vegetables gently without colour for 4–5 minutes, stirring often. Add stock and bring to the boil. Add spaghetti or noodles and simmer for 10 minutes, until the pasta is cooked. Add the chicken, return to the boil, check seasoning and add parsley to serve.

Chinese chicken noodle soup
Instead of spaghetti use thin Chinese noodles, either fresh or dried, and season with soy sauce. Serve with sliced spring onions instead of parsley.

Vietnamese noodle soup
Flavour broth with grated ginger, sliced chilli, thinly sliced lemongrass and a few drops of fish sauce. Replace spaghetti with rice noodles and serve topped with coriander leaves, a handful of bean sprouts and some crispy fried shallots.

Chicken and corn soup
Add kernels from 2 cobs of corn (or a small can of kernels) to the broth after cooking the chicken. Instead of spaghetti use thin Chinese noodles, either fresh or dried, and season with a little soy sauce. Just before serving, lightly whisk 1 egg and stir into the soup. Serve with sliced spring onions instead of parsley.

Minestrone

Serves 4

The ingredients list might look somewhat daunting, but don't be alarmed. You can use any or all of what we suggest, or even more, depending on what you have available. Sweetcorn, peas, green beans, spinach leaves, chopped cabbage and cooked chickpeas are some of our other favourite ingredients to add. Be warned: minestrone seems to grow and grow.

oil
1 onion, diced
1 celery stalk, diced
1 leek, thinly sliced
1 carrot, diced
½ red capsicum, diced
1 potato, diced
2 cloves garlic, crushed
250 ml (1 cup) tomato puree
750 ml (3 cups) chicken or vegetable stock
salt and freshly ground black pepper
75 g (⅓ cup) risoni
⅓ cup chopped parsley and basil or a dollop of pesto

Heat a large heavy-based saucepan over a medium–high heat. Add a generous splash of oil and add onion, celery, leek, carrot, capsicum and potato. Cook for 8–10 minutes, stirring often. Add garlic and cook for 1–2 minutes more. Add tomato puree, stock, salt and pepper and bring to the boil. Add risoni and reduce heat to a simmer. Cook for 10 minutes, check seasoning and add herbs to taste.

Duck and pine mushroom bread soup

Serves 4

This is a more complex version of bread and cheese soup. It's wonderful in early autumn, when pine mushrooms start to appear on market stalls, though any full-flavoured mushroom may be used.

1 litre (4 cups) duck stock
olive oil
2 duck breasts
1 clove garlic, crushed
200 g pine mushrooms, thinly sliced
250 ml (1 cup) light red wine
4 slices day-old sourdough bread
½ cup chopped flat-leaf parsley

Preheat oven to 180°C.

Place duck stock in a medium-sized saucepan and bring to the boil. Reduce to a gentle simmer. Heat a heavy-based frying pan over a medium–hot heat, add a splash of oil and cook duck breasts for 2–3 minutes on each side. Place in the preheated oven for 10 minutes, or until cooked to medium–rare. Remove and allow to rest for 10 minutes.

Drain excess fat from the pan, leaving just enough to cook the mushrooms. Add garlic and mushrooms to the hot pan and cook for 3–4 minutes until soft and fragrant. Add wine, stir well, then add this mixture to the simmering stock.

Cut duck breast into thin slices. Arrange a piece of bread in each bowl, top with parsley and duck slices. Divide hot broth and mushrooms over bread and duck.

French onion soup

Serves 4–6

Serve huge bowls of this intensely flavoured soup with a loaf of good bread, a wedge of full-flavoured cheese (such as English farmhouse cheddar) and a green salad. It will prove once and for all our theory of how satisfying the holy trinity of soup, bread and cheese can be.

- 2 tbsp butter
- 1 tbsp olive oil
- 6 onions, diced
- 2 cloves garlic, crushed
- salt and freshly ground black pepper
- 2 tbsp flour
- 1½ litres (6 cups) beef stock
- 12–18 slices French bread
- grated cheese

Heat a heavy-based saucepan over a medium heat. Add butter and oil, allow to melt then add the onions and garlic. Cook and stir occasionally for 30 minutes, by which time the onions should develop a pale golden colour. Sprinkle in the flour and cook for 3–4 minutes, stirring often.

Add stock and bring to the boil, whisking occasionally to ensure that the flour is incorporated. Reduce to a simmer, cover the pot and cook for 45 minutes. By this stage it should have achieved a good gutsy flavour. Season to taste.

Top bread slices with grated cheese and cook under a hot grill until cheese melts. Pour soup into bowls and place cheese croutons on top.

Creamy onion soup
Add one diced potato to cooked onions, use chicken instead of beef stock and puree soup when cooked. Stir in a few tablespoons of cream just before serving. Sprinkle with chopped parsley and freshly grated black pepper.

Italian spring vegetable and pasta broth

Serves 6–8

A sophisticated version of chicken broth, this soup makes the most of spring vegetables such as asparagus, broad beans and peas. For the best results, use home-made stock rather than a packaged one.

200 g broad beans (optional)
oil
1 onion, diced
1 celery stalk, diced
1 leek, thinly sliced
2 potatoes, peeled and diced into 1 cm chunks
2 carrots, diced into 1 cm chunks
1½ litres (6 cups) chicken stock
salt
100 g (½ cup) pasta (risoni or a very small macaroni)
1 corn cob, kernels removed with a sharp knife
100 g (⅔ cup) fresh or frozen peas
100 g asparagus
freshly ground black pepper
2 tbsp chopped parsley

Remove broad beans from their large pods (if using). Bring a large saucepan of water to the boil. Add the broad beans and cook for 1 minute. Drain and refresh under cold running water. Remove the pale green skins from the beans. This is easily done by inserting a small knife or your thumbnail into the skin to create a slit, then pushing the vivid green bean halves from their skins. Set the beans aside and discard the skins.

Heat a large saucepan over a medium–high heat. Add a generous splash of oil, the onion, celery and leek. Cook for 5–6 minutes, stirring occasionally. Add the potatoes and carrots and cook for a further 2–3 minutes. Add the stock, season with salt and bring to the boil. Add the pasta, reduce to a simmer and cook for 8–10 minutes. Add the corn kernels and peas and cook for 2–3 minutes. Cut the asparagus into 2 cm pieces and add to the soup, along with the broad beans (if using). Check seasoning, adding loads of black pepper, and add parsley. Serve with crusty bread.

Pasta e fagioli

Serves half the neighbourhood, and then some

This classic Italian dish is part soup, part stew. Some people reckon it's a hangover cure, and without a doubt it's a lifesaver that cures most ailments – hunger being the main one.

- 500 g (2½ cups) borlotti beans, soaked in cold water
- 6 potatoes, peeled and diced
- 2 carrots, chopped
- 2 onions, diced
- 2 celery stalks, diced
- 2 cloves garlic, crushed
- 1 small red chilli, de-seeded and diced
- 2 tbsp tomato paste
- 1 tsp salt
- 2–3 litres water
- 200 g pasta (such as spaghetti or fettuccine)
- parmigiano to serve
- extra-virgin olive oil
- chopped parsley

Place the drained borlotti beans, potatoes, carrots, onions, celery, garlic, chilli, tomato paste and salt in a large saucepan. Add enough cold water to cover everything completely. Bring to the boil, reduce heat and simmer gently for 1–2 hours. Take care to stir often and well to prevent the beans and vegetables sticking to the bottom of the saucepan. Cook until the vegetables and beans are well cooked.

Cool slightly, then puree half of the soup. Return the pureed soup to the saucepan. Bring back to the boil, adding more water if necessary. Add the pasta and cook for 10 minutes. Check seasoning.

To serve, ladle soup into bowls, add a generous sprinkle of parmigiano, a swirl of extra-virgin olive oil and some chopped parsley.

Lentil and ham hock soup

Serves 4–6

A personal favourite – there's often a tub of this soup in the fridge or freezer on stand-by for a winter's lunch. MC

1 ham hock
oil
2 onions, diced
2 carrots, diced
1 leek, sliced
2 celery stalks, diced
2 cloves garlic, crushed
1 small red chilli, de-seeded and diced (optional)
200 g (1 cup) green lentils
salt and freshly ground black pepper
chopped parsley to serve

Place the ham hock in a large saucepan. Cover with at least 1 litre of water, and bring to the boil. Reduce heat and cook for 1 hour, or until the ham is cooked and beginning to fall off the bone. I often do this the day before, allowing the stock to be refrigerated and the fat to set overnight. Set ham hock aside to cool and keep the strained cooking stock.

Heat a large saucepan over a medium heat. Add a splash of oil and the onions, carrots, leek and celery. Cook for 5–6 minutes, stirring often, until the vegetables soften. Add the garlic and chilli (if using) and cook for a further 1–2 minutes. Pour in the strained cooking stock and bring to the boil. Add lentils and cook for 30–45 minutes, or until the lentils are tender.

Remove the skin from the ham hock and dice the meat, discarding any sinew and gristle. Add the ham meat to the soup. Check seasoning – you may not need to add salt as ham hocks are sometimes very salty. Serve with a good pinch of chopped parsley.

Lamb shank, vegetable and barley broth

Serves 6

A great Aussie classic that's so substantial it can easily be served as dinner on a chilly winter's night.

2 lamb shanks
200 g (1 cup) pearl barley
2 onions, diced
1 leek, thinly sliced
2 celery stalks, diced
2 carrots, diced into 1 cm chunks
1 swede, diced into 1 cm chunks
2 small turnips, diced into 1 cm chunks
¼ green or savoy cabbage, sliced
salt and freshly ground black pepper
chopped parsley to serve

Place the lamb shanks in a large saucepan. Cover with 2–3 litres water and bring to the boil. Remove any scum that comes to the surface and discard. Reduce heat and simmer for 1 hour, or until lamb is tender. Remove shanks and strain the broth. If you refrigerate the broth when it has cooled, the fat will rise to the top and set, allowing it to be easily removed.

Place the barley in a small saucepan. Cover with water and bring to the boil. Reduce to a simmer and cook for 20–30 minutes, or until the barley is tender. Drain and set aside.

Pour the broth into a clean saucepan and bring to the boil. Add the onions, leek, celery, carrots, swede and turnips, and cook over a low heat for 30 minutes, or until the vegetables are tender. Add cabbage, check seasoning and cook for a further 10 minutes.

Cut the meat off the lamb shank bones, discarding any skin, sinew and the bones. Add to the broth along with the pearl barley. Cook for a further 10 minutes, check seasoning again and serve with a generous handful of chopped parsley.

Oxtail soup

Serves 6

Oxtail soup is delicious and rich – perfect for a warming meal. It's a soup that requires a hefty 3–4 hours of simmering in order to draw out the best flavours. Oxtail soup was a constant in my winter diet as a child growing up in Ireland, so perhaps I still make it for nostalgic reasons. AC

- 1 kg oxtails, cut into 3–4 cm pieces
- seasoned flour
- olive oil
- 2 onions, diced
- 2 carrots, diced
- 3 stalks celery, diced
- 2 leeks, sliced
- ¼ cup tomato paste
- 750 ml (3 cups) red wine
- 1½ litres (6 cups) beef stock
- 2–3 bay leaves
- 2–3 sprigs thyme
- salt and freshly ground black pepper
- chopped parsley

Coat each piece of oxtail with seasoned flour, shaking well to remove any excess.

Heat a large saucepan over a medium heat and add a generous splash of oil. Add onion, carrot, celery and leek, and cook for 5–10 minutes, stirring regularly. Remove vegetables from pan and set aside. Return pan to a medium–high heat, add more oil if needed and cook each piece of oxtail until brown.

Add tomato paste and cook briefly for 1–2 minutes, stirring occasionally. Return vegetables to pan and add red wine, stock, herbs and a pinch of salt, and bring to the boil. Remove any scum as it rises to the surface and reduce heat to low. Allow soup to simmer for 3–4 hours.

Remove oxtail and set aside to cool. Puree soup and strain liquid into a clean saucepan. When oxtail is cool enough to handle, remove all meat from the bones and dice finely. When ready to serve bring soup to the boil; add oxtail meat, return to the boil and check seasoning. Add chopped parsley.

Roasted vegetable gazpacho

Serves 6

This soup takes the classic gazpacho idea and combines it with roasted vegetables, which we find adds a terrific depth of flavour and richness. It's a soup that takes a little time to prepare and requires top-quality ingredients – the sort of thing we make on a lazy Sunday afternoon in summer.

THE ROASTED VEGETABLE PUREE
3 red capsicums
olive oil
6 tomatoes
1 onion, peeled and quartered
1 small red chilli, halved
3 cloves garlic, peeled
salt and freshly ground black pepper

Preheat oven to 200°C.

Rub capsicums with oil and place in a baking tray. Put tomatoes, onion, chilli and garlic in another baking tray and toss with oil, salt and pepper. Roast until capsicum skins blister and tomatoes become soft, about 30 minutes. Place capsicums in a plastic bag and seal to allow steam to lift skins.

Allow tomatoes and capsicums to cool, then set aside 2 capsicums for later use. Remove and discard seeds and skins from tomatoes and capsicum. Puree the tomato, capsicum, onion, garlic and chilli with cooking juices. Pass through a sieve and refrigerate.

THE DICED VEGETABLES
1 Lebanese cucumber
3 tomatoes, blanched and skins removed
½ green capsicum
salt and freshly ground black pepper
125 ml (½ cup) olive oil
¼ cup chopped parsley
½ cup shredded basil
500 ml (2 cups) vegetable or chicken stock
shredded basil to garnish

Remove the skin and seeds from the cucumber, dice finely and place in a colander with salt and set aside to drain.

Quarter tomatoes, remove seeds and dice remaining flesh finely. Dice green capsicum the same size. Take the reserved roasted capsicums, remove skins and seeds, and dice the flesh the same size as the tomato. Rinse cucumber and pat dry.

COMBINING In a large bowl mix the pureed roasted vegetables, the diced vegetables, the oil and herbs. Add enough stock to adjust the consistency, keeping in mind the soup will thicken as it chills. Check seasoning.

Place the soup and serving bowls in the refrigerator for 1 hour before serving.

Give chilled soup a final taste test, and then pour into bowls and garnish with the shredded basil.

Sweetcorn chowder

Serves 4

We have been making and enjoying this creamy, chunky sweetcorn soup forever. Make it once and it's sure to become a favourite of yours too. Remember to keep all the vegetables finely diced, as this soup is not pureed.

2–3 tbsp olive oil
1 onion, finely diced
2 cloves garlic, crushed
1 leek, chopped finely
2 sticks celery, chopped finely
1 zucchini, chopped finely
2 carrots, chopped finely
2 tbsp plain flour
1 litre (4 cups) vegetable or chicken stock
2 corn cobs, kernels removed with a sharp knife
250 g (1 cup) creamed cottage cheese
2 tbsp sour cream
1 tbsp chopped parsley
1 tbsp chopped basil

Heat a heavy-based saucepan over medium heat. Add oil, onion, garlic, leek, celery, zucchini and carrot. Cook for 7–8 minutes, stirring often. Stir in the flour. Lower the heat to allow the flour to cook completely. Pour in stock and return to the boil, whisking occasionally.

When boiling, add corn kernels, then simmer for 10 minutes. Remove from the heat, whisk in cheese and sour cream. Add the chopped parsley and basil then check seasoning.

Fish and fennel chowder

Serves 4

Chowder with seafood is yet another great favourite of ours. The flavour of the fish, the sweetness of sweetcorn and a tiny hint of chilli is a combination we really enjoy. Take care to choose a variety of fish that will keep its shape during cooking. Ask your fishmonger if you're not sure.

olive oil
1 onion, finely diced
2 cloves garlic, crushed
2 small red chillies, de-seeded and diced
1 fennel bulb, diced 1½ cm
1 red capsicum, diced 1½ cm
2 potatoes, diced 1½ cm
2 tbsp plain flour
2 corn cobs, kernels removed with a sharp knife
1 litre (4 cups) fish stock
500 g trevally fillets, skin removed and diced 2 cm
125 g (½ cup) crème fraîche
¼ cup torn basil leaves

Heat a large heavy-based saucepan over medium heat. Add oil, onion, garlic, chillies and fennel, stir and cook for 4–6 minutes until soft. Add capsicum and potato, and cook for a further 5 minutes. Reduce heat, add the flour, stir and cook for 2 minutes.

Add corn kernels and enough fish stock to just cover. Bring to the boil, stirring. Reduce to a simmer and cook for 5 minutes, ensuring potato is soft. Add fish and cook briefly. Remove from the heat, add crème fraîche and herbs, check the seasoning and adjust the consistency as required with remaining fish stock.

Tom yum

Serves 4

The ingredients and food of Thailand really opened up our palates to the possibilities of other Asian countries. For that we'll be forever thankful. This is a simple broth that uses many of the aromatic Thai ingredients we have come to know and love.

1 skinless chicken breast fillet, thinly sliced
2 tbsp tom yum paste
500 ml (2 cups) chicken stock
500 ml (2 cups) water
2 kaffir lime leaves, shredded
3 spring onions, chopped
1 lemongrass stem, thinly sliced
4 shallots, sliced
4 coriander stems and roots, chopped
1 tbsp shaved palm sugar
2 tbsp fish sauce
2 tbsp lime juice
coriander leaves to garnish
sliced red chillies (optional)

Marinate chicken in tom yum paste for 30 minutes.

Place stock and water in a large saucepan. Add lime leaves, spring onions, lemongrass, shallots, coriander, palm sugar and fish sauce. Bring to the boil over a medium heat. Reduce to a simmer and cook for 20 minutes. Strain into a clean saucepan. Add chicken and lime juice, and simmer for 5 minutes. Check seasoning, adding more fish sauce if necessary. Serve with coriander leaves and chillies if desired.

Laksa

Serves 4

We were tossing up as to which chapter this dish should be in – is it a noodle dish, a curry or a soup? As you can see, the soup chapter won. But boy, oh boy, what a soup!

200 g dried vermicelli noodles
2 tbsp vegetable oil
2 tbsp laksa paste
500 ml (2 cups) chicken stock
250 ml (1 cup) water
400 ml can coconut milk
2 tbsp fish sauce
2 tomatoes, diced (optional)
½ red capsicum
12 green (raw) prawns, heads and shells removed
handful of bean sprouts
100 g deep fried bean curd, sliced
1 cup of mixed herbs, to include Vietnamese mint, coriander, Thai basil
2 limes, cut into wedges
crispy shallots to serve

Place the vermicelli noodles in a large bowl and cover with boiling water. Soak for 8–10 minutes, or until the noodles soften. Drain and set aside.

Heat a large saucepan or wok over a medium heat and add the vegetable oil. Add the paste and stir for 2–3 minutes, or until aromatic. Add chicken stock, water and coconut milk, and bring to the boil. Add fish sauce, tomato, capsicum and prawns. Simmer until prawns are cooked, about 3–4 minutes.

To serve, divide noodles between four bowls. Add bean sprouts and slices of bean curd. Ladle broth into bowls and top with a large handful of fresh herbs and shallots. Serve with lime wedges.

Chicken laksa
Substitute 1 sliced chicken fillet for prawns.

Prawn and coconut tom yum

Serves 4

Tom yum is a classic Asian soup and one of the most popular dishes on Thai menus. For many people it is their first introduction to ingredients such as kaffir lime leaves, lemongrass, coriander, chillies, palm sugar and fish sauce. Here, prawns and coconut milk are added to the base ingredients to make a creamy version of this soup.

500 g green (raw) peeled prawns
2 tbsp tom yum paste
750 ml (3 cups) chicken stock
750 ml (3 cups) water
2 kaffir lime leaves, shredded
3 spring onions, chopped
1 lemongrass stem, thinly sliced
4 shallots, sliced

½ bunch coriander stems and roots, chopped
1 tbsp grated palm sugar
2 tbsp fish sauce
2 tbsp lime juice
125 ml (½ cup) coconut milk
coriander leaves to serve
sliced red chillies (optional)

Brush the prawns with tom yum paste and marinate for 30 minutes.

Place stock and water in a large saucepan. Add the lime leaves, spring onions, lemongrass, shallots, coriander, palm sugar and fish sauce. Bring to the boil, then reduce to a simmer and cook for 20 minutes.

Strain into a clean saucepan. Add the prawns, lime juice and coconut milk, and simmer for 5–6 minutes. Check seasoning, adding more fish sauce if necessary. Serve with coriander leaves and chillies, if desired.

Miso soup

Serves 4

Miso is our son Luke's favourite soup, whether as an after-school snack or late-night treat. Not only is it quick to make, requiring just 3 ingredients, but the addition of udon noodles means Luke may even be weaned off 2-minute noodles.

1 litre (4 cups) vegetable or chicken stock
80 ml (⅓ cup) tamari
60 ml (¼ cup) miso paste

Bring chicken stock to the boil. Mix miso paste and tamari together, and add to the boiling stock. Allow to cook for 3–4 minutes.

Miso soup with tofu
Dice 300 g soft tofu and add it to the broth just before serving.

Chicken, bok choy and udon miso
Cut 1 skinless chicken breast fillet thinly and add to simmering miso. Cook for 5 minutes. Add the washed leaves of 1 bunch of baby bok choy and 250 g udon noodles, and cook for 1–2 minutes. To finish, add ½ cup of coriander leaves.

Udon soup with shiitake mushrooms and roast duck
To boiling miso add 250 g udon noodles, 150 g sliced shiitake mushrooms and 1 cup sliced broccoli. Cook for 2 minutes. Add ½ roast duck (flesh removed from bone and sliced) and 2 thinly sliced spring onions. Return to the boil then remove from heat. Add coriander leaves and check seasoning.

Duck and macadamia wonton soup

Serves 4

Roast duck is widely available from all Asian roast-house restaurants. They will often supply a little tub of cooking juices if requested. If they do, this makes a great addition to the cooking stock.

¼ roast duck
750 ml (3 cups) water
60 ml (¼ cup) light soy sauce
5 cm piece ginger, sliced
1 small red chilli, split
6 shallots, sliced
2 tbsp chopped coriander
60 g (⅓ cup) macadamia nuts, chopped
1 packet wonton wrappers
4 spring onions, chopped

Remove meat from duck. Thinly slice meat and set aside. Place duck bones, cooking juices (if available), water, soy sauce, ginger and chilli in a saucepan and bring to the boil. Reduce to a simmer and cook for 25 minutes, removing scum as it comes to the surface. Strain into a clean saucepan. You should have 1 litre. Add water if necessary.

Combine duck meat with shallots, coriander and macadamia nuts. Season to taste.

Lay 6–8 wonton wrappers out flat in front of you. Brush two edges of each wonton with water. Place one teaspoon of duck mixture in the centre of each wrapper. Fold each wonton in half, press edges together and hold firmly to seal. Repeat until all mixture is used.

To serve, bring stock to the boil. Add wontons and poach for 3–4 minutes. Divide wontons between bowls, ladle broth over and garnish with spring onions.

Beijing dumpling soup

Serves 6

We love this style of soup, where the simplicity of the broth is combined with the silky softness of delicate wontons.

250 g pork or chicken mince
4 spring onions, sliced
3 tsp grated ginger
2 tbsp soy sauce
2 tbsp chopped coriander leaves
1 packet wonton wrappers
1¼ litres (5 cups) chicken stock
soy sauce as required
2 spring onions, sliced
coriander leaves to garnish

Mix together mince, spring onion, ginger, soy sauce and chopped coriander. Take wonton wrappers, lay 4–5 out at a time. Place a teaspoon of prepared mix in the centre of each. Brush edges with water. Fold over diagonally to form a small triangular parcel. Press edges together and hold firmly to seal. Repeat until all mince mixture is used.

Bring chicken stock to the boil, and then reduce to a simmer. Carefully add the wontons to the simmering stock and cook for 3–4 minutes. Season to taste with soy sauce.

To serve, spoon 4–5 wontons into each bowl, ladle hot broth over and garnish with sliced spring onions and coriander leaves.

bread

The world of bread offers a range of wonderful things to eat. It's also an area of cooking that's quick and easy to learn if you consider the following two points:
1. The base of virtually every recipe uses the same ingredients: flour, salt, water and yeast.
2. Once you've mastered making the simplest bread dough, you're set: with all other breads the method changes only slightly. Most of the recipes here are for fairly rustic breads – the type that we make at home – and are easy to execute.

Bread makers are a recent introduction to the kitchen and many swear by them. However, we're not convinced that they are that easy to use, or that the bread is all that good. Many of them seem to require special ingredients and the ones we've tried all produce a square loaf with a hole in one end where it was cooked. If we could teach everyone how easy to it is to make a simple loaf of bread they would soon find their bread machine unnecessary. However, if you love your bread maker and it stops you buying fluffy white loaves from the supermarket, don't let us stop you. Either way, bread is an essential accompaniment to soups. Once you have mastered dough, you may want to consider making your own Pizza Dough (page 248); it's well worth the effort.

Soup accompaniments

CROUTONS

Take day-old bread; sourdough is particularly good as it has an excellent flavour. Cut into 2 cm cubes and pan-fry in oil until golden all over. Drain on kitchen towel to remove any excess oil. Sprinkle on bowls of soup to add crunch and texture.

CHEESY CROUTONS

Cut thin slices from a French breadstick and top with a mix of grated parmigiano and gruyere cheese. Place slices on a baking tray and cook under a hot grill until cheese melts. Place 1 or 2 cheesy croutons in a bowl of soup just before serving.

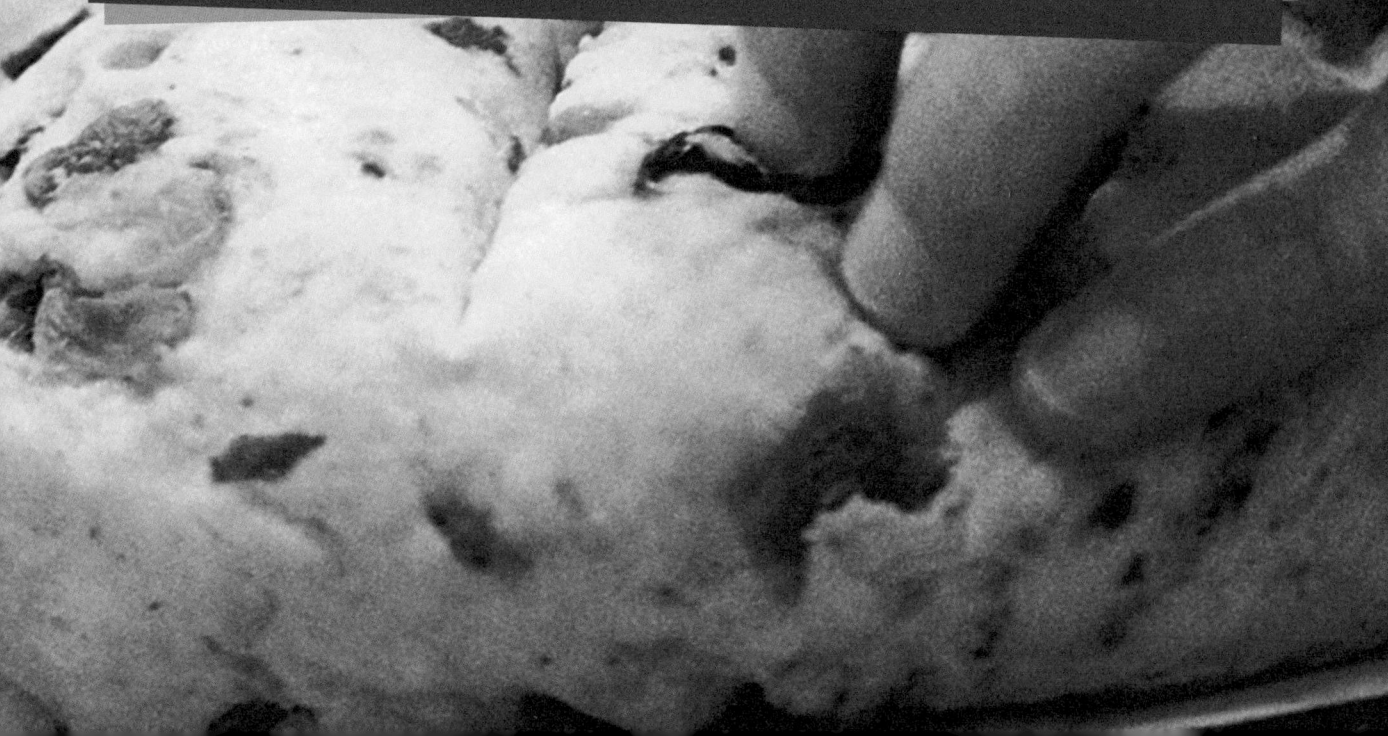

Things you need to know about bread and doughs

1 Yeast is available in two main forms: fresh and dried. Fresh is good if you bake on a daily basis; sachets of dried yeast are better if you use it no more than once a week, as these will keep for many months in the pantry.

2 Yeast is often mixed with a little warm water and a pinch of sugar in order to bring it to life.

3 One sachet contains 7 g of dried yeast.

4 Use plain unbleached flour, unless otherwise stated. If you have a supply of baker's or strong flour, use that instead.

5 Kneading the dough is an essential part of making any yeast product. To knead, sprinkle a little plain flour onto a smooth surface. Place the dough in front of you and bring the far edge of the dough towards the centre with your fingers. Press it down with the heel of your hand. Repeat this until the dough takes on a smooth, almost silky feel. This can be anywhere from 5 to 10 minutes. This is wonderful, physical work. It's also much better for everyone in the house if you take any frustrations out on the dough rather than on them.

6 Kneading can be done in a large mixer using a dough hook attachment, if you have one, running on the lowest speed.

7 All doughs need a warm place to prove – this is sometimes not easy on a cool day. Here are a few things to try:

Place the covered bowl of dough on top of a warm heater.

Float the covered dough in a sink of warm water.

Keep the covered dough on top of the stove with the oven on a low temperature below.

Warm the oven for 5 minutes then turn it off and use this as a warm place for your dough to rise.

8 On hot days you can pop your dough in a sunny spot in the garden to prove.

9 Flat baking trays are best for baking bread and pizza. If you're really keen you can also buy ceramic or terracotta trays. These hold the heat well and will give nice crusty bottoms to your baked goods.

10 A light brushing of butter or olive oil is enough to stop bread and pizza sticking to trays. We often add a light sprinkle of fine polenta or semolina, a little of which sticks to the finished bread, adding a nice texture and crunch. Baking paper can also be used if you don't want to deal with greasing trays, and this will also leave your baking tray much cleaner.

Soda bread

Makes 1 loaf

Soda bread is perfect for those who want a quick and easy loaf. This old-fashioned Irish recipe uses bicarbonate of soda and baking powder for rising and the dough is simply stirred together, shaped and baked until golden.
I have been eating this bread all my life, as it's what my mother whips up at the drop of a hat. It's excellent served warm with butter and jam. AC

- 375 g (2½ cups) wholemeal self-raising flour
- 375 g (2½ cups) self-raising flour
- 2 tsp baking powder
- 1 tsp bicarbonate of soda
- 1 tsp salt
- 500 ml (2 cups) buttermilk, or milk soured with lemon juice
- additional buttermilk for brushing

Preheat oven to 210°C.

Sift together the flours, baking powder, bicarb soda and salt. Stir in buttermilk and mix until combined to a firm dough. Shape the dough into a round about 4 cm high on a lined baking tray. Slash a deep cross into the top of the bread, then brush it with additional buttermilk.

Bake in preheated oven for 20 minutes. Remove from oven and brush with additional buttermilk. Reduce oven to 180°C and cook bread for a further 40 minutes. A perfectly cooked loaf will sound hollow when tapped on the bottom. Wrap in a dry tea towel as it cools; this will help keep moisture in.

Fruity soda bread

Add 250 g (1½ cups) of dried fruit to the dough; try a mix of raisins, apricots, currants and sultanas. Adding ½ tsp of cinnamon, mixed spice or nutmeg goes well with the fruit.

Bread rolls

Makes 12 rolls

This bread roll recipe is so easy that absolutely everybody should try it.

1 sachet (7g) dried yeast
1 tsp sugar
100 ml (⅓ cup) warm water
450 g (3 cups) unbleached plain flour

60 g soft butter
1 tsp salt
175 ml (¾ cup) water, additional
egg wash

Mix dried yeast with sugar and warm water. Leave in a warm place until mixture bubbles. In a large bowl rub the butter into the flour and salt. Add yeast and additional water. Mix together well, then place onto a floured surface.

Knead until smooth and no longer sticky, around 6–8 minutes. Place dough in a large bowl and cover with cling film. Prove in a warm place until dough doubles in size, 1–2 hours.

Preheat oven to 200°C.

Take proven dough and knead for 1–2 minutes. Divide dough into 12 evenly sized pieces. Shape into balls and place on greased baking tray. Cover with a cloth and leave to prove in a warm place for 20 minutes.

Brush rolls with egg wash and bake in preheated oven for 10–12 minutes, or until golden brown.

Sesame seed rolls
When rolls are proven, brush with egg wash and sprinkle with sesame seeds, then bake as described.

Poppyseed rolls
When rolls are proven, brush with egg wash and sprinkle with poppyseeds, then bake as described.

Square white loaf
Turn this recipe into a simple white loaf by placing the risen dough into a tin lined with baking paper. Allow to prove for 30 minutes in a warm place, then bake for 30 minutes. A perfectly cooked loaf will sound hollow when tapped on the bottom.

Knot rolls
Take divided dough and roll each piece into a long snake-like shape about 15 cm in length. Tie each piece into a knot, then prove and bake as directed.

A great crusty loaf

Makes 1 loaf

We find that this loaf is best on the day it is made, after which we usually slice it and use it for toast.

500 g (3⅓ cups) unbleached flour
2 tsp salt
60 g (⅓ cup) soft butter
1 sachet (7 g) dried yeast
250–300 ml (1–1¼ cups) warm water
egg wash

Sift flour and salt into a large bowl. Rub in butter. Add yeast and mix briefly. Add water – 250 ml should do it, but you may need more. Mix with a wooden spoon until mixture comes together. Tip onto a floured surface.

Knead until smooth and no longer sticky, around 6–8 minutes. Place dough in a large bowl and cover with cling film. Prove in a warm place until dough doubles in size, 1–2 hours.

Preheat oven to 200°C.

Take proven dough and knead for 1–2 minutes. Make into a loaf shape and either place on a greased and lined baking tray, or into a greased and lined loaf tin 23½ × 13½ × 7 cm . Cover loosely with a tea towel and set aside to prove in a warm place for 30 minutes. Brush top with egg wash and slash the top 3–4 times with a small knife.

Bake in preheated oven for 25–30 minutes, or until well risen and golden brown and base sounds hollow when tapped.

Polenta bread

Makes 2 loaves

Adding polenta to bread dough introduces a delightful yellow colour, and robust flavour and texture, to the finished loaf. It is good for making sandwiches with fillings of roasted vegetables, goat's cheese and pesto.

2 sachets (14 g) dried yeast
1 tsp caster sugar
275 ml (1 cup) warm water
500 g (3 ⅓ cups) unbleached plain flour
250 g (1½ cups) polenta
1 tsp salt
2 eggs, lightly beaten
egg wash

Mix yeast with sugar and warm water. Leave in a warm place until mixture bubbles. In a large bowl sift together flour, polenta and salt. Add yeast and eggs. Mix together well, then place onto a floured surface.

Knead until smooth and no longer sticky, around 6–8 minutes. Place dough in a large bowl and cover with cling film. Prove in a warm place until dough doubles in size, 1–2 hours.

Preheat oven to 200°C.

Take proven dough and knead for 1–2 minutes. Divide dough into 2 equal-sized pieces. Shape into loaves and place on greased baking tray. Cover with a cloth and leave to prove in a warm place for 20 minutes.

Brush with egg wash and bake in preheated oven for 15–20 minutes, or until golden brown and bottom sounds hollow when tapped.

Rosemary polenta bread
Add 1 tsp chopped fresh rosemary to the polenta.

Focaccia

Makes 2 focaccias

Focaccia is one of the easiest styles of bread to make. It's just the usual blend of yeast, water, salt and flour with a little olive oil added. It's also easy to work with and can be made into virtually any shape you prefer: a huge oval loaf, a couple of thin round ones or even small individual ones.

1 sachet (7g) dried yeast
pinch of sugar
80 ml (⅓ cup) tepid water
1 tsp salt
250 ml (1 cup) tepid water, additional
60 ml (¼ cup) olive oil
500 g (3⅓ cups) unbleached plain flour
additional olive oil
salt flakes

Mix dried yeast with sugar and tepid water. Leave in a warm place until mixture bubbles. Stir in salt, additional water and oil. Stir in flour until combined. Place on a lightly floured surface. Knead until smooth and no longer sticky, around 6–8 minutes. Place dough in a large bowl and cover with cling film. Prove in a warm place until dough doubles in size, 1–2 hours.

Preheat oven to 200°C.

Take proved dough and knead for 1–2 minutes. Shape into 2 × 25 cm rounds about 2 cm thick, or another size if you prefer. Place on greased baking trays and allow to prove for 15 minutes. Brush bread with olive oil and sprinkle with salt flakes.

Bake in preheated oven for 10–12 minutes, or until golden brown.

Olive focaccia
Press 125 g (¾ cup) pitted kalamata olives into proved loaves, then brush with oil and sprinkle salt over.

Rosemary focaccia
Roughly chop a few rosemary leaves and spread them onto the dough after the olive oil and salt.

Garlic focaccia
Slice 4 or 5 large peeled garlic cloves and press them into the dough after the olive oil and salt.

Naan bread

Makes 16 naan

Naan bread is loved by one and all at our place, so we were determined to master it ourselves. This recipe follows a similar principle to other doughs, with the addition of a few other simple ingredients. When it's ready it can be cooked in a hot pan or, even better, outside on the barbecue hot plate.

2 sachets (14 g) dried yeast
1 tsp caster sugar
50 ml (¼ cup) warm water
3 tsp caster sugar, additional
1 egg
1 tsp salt
125 ml (½ cup) natural yoghurt
125 ml (½ cup) milk
125 ml (½ cup) water
50 g melted butter
700 g (4⅔ cups) unbleached plain flour
olive oil

Mix yeast with sugar and water. Leave in a warm place until mixture bubbles. Stir in additional sugar, egg, salt, yoghurt, milk, water and melted butter. Add flour, mix briefly, and then tip dough onto a lightly floured surface. Knead until smooth and no longer sticky, around 6–8 minutes. Place dough in a large bowl and cover with cling film. Allow to prove in a warm place until dough doubles in size, 1–2 hours.

Take proved dough and knead for 1–2 minutes. Divide into 16 × 80 g portions, and roll into balls.

Using a rolling pin or your fingers, make each bread 20 cm across. Place a tight layer of cling film on a dinner plate and lay bread on it. Cover with more plastic and repeat until all portions are flattened.

Heat a flat barbecue plate or a heavy-based pan over a medium–high heat. Brush with a thin layer of olive oil, then cook naan until golden, about 2 minutes each side.

Garlic naan
Brush both sides of each naan with melted garlic butter as it finishes cooking.

Spice naan
Add 3 tsp of spice, such as ground cardamom, cumin and coriander, to the dough.

PASTA
+ polenta
quick + easy

We can remember a time when a bowl of spaghetti bolognaise was considered exotic. Today, pasta is served at least once or twice a week in many homes. And we've moved on from bolognaise to meatballs in tomato sauce.

The recipes in this chapter cover the basics through to more glamorous dishes. We think veal ragu is the ultimate pasta accompaniment, but tuna with rocket and lemon comes a very close second. While writing this chapter we came across an idea for a cheesy pasta bake. Luke calls it lasagne, but call it what you like, it's a great meal and now a regular addition to our repertoire.

The cooking time for pasta we've given in these recipes is for dried pasta, simply because that is what we tend to cook most often. If you're cooking fresh pasta, reduce the cooking time from 8 minutes to 3–4 minutes, depending on the type you're using.

pasta + polenta recipes

pasta

Quick-and-easy bolognaise	160
Spaghettini carbonara	160
Veal ragu	161
Tomato sauce #1	162
Tomato sauce #2	163
Tomato, olive and anchovy pasta sauce	164
Eggplant, tomato and basil sauce	164
Rich duck sauce	165
Penne with Italian sausage, tomato and red wine sauce	166
Penne with prosciutto, peas and mint	167
Spaghetti with smoked chicken and asparagus	168
Chicken, mushroom and olive sauce	169
Orecchietti with rich mushroom sauce	170
Penne tossed with caramelised onion, rocket and olive	170
Linguini with chilli, anchovies, breadcrumbs and basil	172
Spaghetti with silverbeet, raisins and pine nuts	173
Linguini with roasted pumpkin, spinach and goat's cheese	175
Troffiette with chestnuts and smoked ham hock	176
Spaghetti with tuna, rocket and lemon	177
Pasta with tuna and artichokes	177
Spaghetti with breadcrumbs, tuna, parsley and lemon	179
Spaghetti with blue-swimmer crab, fennel and tomato	180
Macaroni cheese	181
Spaghetti with braised chicken meatballs in tomato sugo	182
Cheesy bean and tomato pasta bake	184
Roast vegetable and goat's cheese lasagne	186
Potato gnocchi	187
Goat's cheese gnocchi	187
Semolina gnocchi	188
Gnocchi with blue cheese sauce	189
Roast tomato, pancetta and sweet onions with gnocchi	189

polenta

The best soft polenta	192
Polenta wedgies	193

pasta essentials

FRESH OR DRIED?

Fresh pasta produces a soft eating experience and is perfect for filled pastas such as ravioli, lasagne and cannelloni.

Dried pasta, which is an essential modern pantry item, is firmer to bite into than fresh pasta. Choose one that suits your taste and budget.

WHAT SHAPE?

It all comes down to personal taste. We always cook spaghetti for pasta bolognaise; it just doesn't seem right with anything else. Likewise, it has to be macaroni in macaroni cheese, though at a pinch penne will do. However, if you want farfalle with bolognaise sauce, be our guest. Younger members of the family love the different shapes of pasta, so it's well worth experimenting.

PARMIGIANO REGGIANO

Parmigiano reggiano (often labelled as parmesan) is the classic Italian pasta cheese. It's quite expensive, but the flavour is so good that only a little is needed. For the best flavour buy it in large chunks rather than pre-grated, and grate it as required. Serve a bowl of grated or shaved parmigiano with most pasta dishes, although seafood and cream sauces rarely need cheese.

A BIG PASTA POT

We're talking a 10-litre pot here, one that's especially made for cooking pasta. Inside each pasta pot is a large colander so you lift your cooked pasta from the boiling water, rather than pouring the boiling water over the cooked pasta. The drained pot is then perfect for tossing the pasta with its sauce.

TOMATO SUGO

Simply heat this ready-to-use Italian tomato sauce while your pasta is cooking – you can add chilli and olives, a few chunks of tuna, a spoonful of pesto, or nothing at all!

Depending on the acidity of the tomatoes, you may need to add a pinch of sugar to tomato-based recipes.

OLIVE OIL

Good olive oil is an essential ingredient when cooking pasta. You'll need it for making pasta sauces; to toss with pasta so that that the strands don't stick to each other; and for pan-cooking or oven-roasting vegetables to go with your dish. The better the quality, the deeper the flavour that olive oil will bring to your pasta dishes.

Things you need to know about pasta

1 Unless you are making a slow-cooked dish like ragu, remember to put a saucepan of water on to boil for the pasta before starting to prepare your sauce.
2 Allow 100 g dried pasta per person.
3 Allow 150 g fresh pasta per person.
4 Cook pasta in plenty of gently boiling salted water.
5 Always drain your pasta well.
6 Toss pasta with the sauce before serving.
7 Always serve pasta piping hot.
8 Never overcook your pasta.

Quick-and-easy bolognaise

Serves 4–6

This is a strictly no-fuss and no-frills recipe. The sauce can also be used in cottage pie, tacos or lasagne, so why not double the quantities and stash some away in the freezer for those days when cooking is just too hard?

- 1 kg lean beef mince
- 2 onions, diced
- 2 cloves garlic, crushed
- 1 small red chilli, de-seeded and diced (optional)
- 250 ml (1 cup) tomato puree
- 375 ml (1½ cups) beef stock
- 150 g (½ cup) tomato paste
- 2 tbsp chopped fresh herbs (basil, thyme, parsley)
- salt and freshly ground black pepper

Place all the ingredients in a large saucepan. Cook over a high heat until the mixture starts to bubble. Stir well to incorporate all the ingredients and break up the mince. Once boiling, reduce heat to a simmer and cook for 1 hour, stirring often. Check seasoning and consistency.

Spicy bolognaise
Add 2 finely diced and de-seeded chillies along with the onions.

Beef and mushroom bolognaise
Add 150 g sliced mushrooms.

Spaghettini carbonara

Serves 4

Spaghettini is a thin spaghetti, and it's perfect for a creamy sauce such as this.

- 400 g dried spaghettini
- olive oil
- 125 g bacon, thinly sliced
- 4 egg yolks
- 2 tbsp cream
- 2 tbsp grated parmigiano
- salt and lots of freshly ground black pepper
- 2 tbsp chopped parsley

Bring a large saucepan of water to a boil over a high heat. Add a good pinch of salt. Add the pasta and stir until the water has returned to the boil. Reduce heat, cover and cook the pasta at a fast simmer for 8 minutes.

Heat a frypan over a medium heat. Add oil and cook the bacon until crispy. Chop into small pieces. Beat egg yolks, cream, cheese, salt and pepper together. The pepper needs to be plentiful, so it dominates in the finished dish.

Drain pasta and toss with the egg mix, bacon and parsley, and serve.

Veal ragu

Serves 4–6

This is it: the king of pasta sauces – rich, decadent and well worth the effort involved. Make this sauce, transform it into lasagne and you have perfect 'going-away-for-the-weekend' food.

olive oil
1 onion, diced
2 celery stalks, diced
1 carrot, diced
1 clove garlic, crushed
125 g pancetta, diced
1 kg coarse ground veal (silverside is excellent)
2 tbsp tomato paste
125 ml (½ cup) white wine
375 ml (1½ cups) beef stock
250 ml (1 cup) tomato puree
sprig of rosemary
2–3 sprigs of thyme
salt and freshly ground black pepper
2 tbsp chopped parsley

Heat a heavy-based saucepan over a medium heat. Add a splash of oil and the onion, celery and carrot. Cook for 5–6 minutes, stirring often. Add garlic and cook for a further 1–2 minutes, or until the garlic is fragrant. Add the pancetta and veal and cook until well browned, stirring well. Add the tomato paste, then lower the heat and cook for 2–3 minutes. Raise heat, then add wine, stock, tomato puree, rosemary and thyme. Bring to the boil, then reduce heat and simmer for 1 hour, stirring often.

Check seasoning, add parsley and serve.

Traditional lasagne
Make a large batch of Cheese Sauce (page 557). Put half amount of ragu in a lasagne dish. Top with lasagne sheets, then a layer of cheese sauce, another layer of lasagne sheets, the remainder of the ragu, more lasagne sheets and a final layer of cheese sauce. Sprinkle with grated cheese and bake in a preheated 180°C oven for 30–40 minutes.

Beef lasagne
A simpler dish made with Quick-and-easy Bolognaise (page 160).

Tomato sauce #1

Serves 6–8

This recipe is your classic tomato sauce for pasta of all types. Sergio de Pieri, musician brother of cook Stefano de Pieri, revealed the secret of this sauce to us a few years back. We were amazed at the depth of flavour that comes from the simple method of cooking the garlic in a decent amount of olive oil before adding any tomatoes. Sergio is also a keen exponent of the need for a 'big' pasta pot.

80 ml (⅓ cup) olive oil
2–3 cloves garlic, coarsely crushed
2 × 400 g cans chopped peeled tomatoes or 800 g chopped tomatoes
salt and freshly ground black pepper
pasta of your choice, 100 g dried per person
2 tbsp chopped parsley

Bring a large saucepan of water to a boil over a high heat. Add a good pinch of salt.

Heat a medium-sized saucepan over a low heat. Add oil and heat for 3–4 minutes. Add garlic and cook for 1–2 minutes, until light brown. Add chopped tomatoes, salt and pepper. Simmer sauce for 10 minutes.

Add the pasta to the boiling water and stir until the water has returned to the boil. Reduce heat, cover and cook the pasta at a fast simmer for 8 minutes.

Check that the pasta is cooked, drain and toss with the sauce and chopped parsley.

Tomato sauce with basil
Add chopped basil to the sauce for a fresh taste.

Tomato sauce with roasted eggplant
Add diced roasted eggplant with the tomatoes.

Tomato sauce with roasted capsicum
Add 1 diced roasted red capsicum with the tomatoes.

Tomato sauce with olives
Add 80 g (½ cup) pitted olives to the sauce.

Tomato sauce with tuna
Add 300 g canned tuna chunks to the sauce.

Tomato sauce #2

Serves 4

This sauce is simpler in flavour than Tomato Sauce #1. We would serve it with a filled tortellini or ravioli, or over penne for an uncomplicated meal.

olive oil
1 onion, diced
1 clove garlic, crushed
1 tbsp tomato paste
6 tomatoes, diced, or 1 × 400 g can chopped tomatoes
salt and freshly ground black pepper
chopped fresh herbs (basil and flat-leaf parsley are both good)
pasta of your choice, 100 g dried per person

Bring a large saucepan of water to a boil over a high heat. Add a good pinch of salt.

Heat a medium-sized saucepan over a medium heat. Add oil and the onion and cook for 3–4 minutes, stirring often, until the onion softens slightly. Add garlic and cook for a further 1–2 minutes, or until garlic is fragrant. Add tomato paste and cook briefly before adding the tomatoes. Bring to the boil, reduce heat and cook for 5–8 minutes, stirring often. When the sauce has thickened to the desired consistency, check seasoning and add fresh herbs to taste.

Add the pasta to the boiling water and stir until the water has returned to the boil. Reduce heat, cover and cook the pasta at a fast simmer for 8 minutes.

Check that the pasta is cooked, drain and toss with the sauce.

Tomato sauce with pesto
Finish sauce with a spoonful of pesto per person.

Tomato sauce with mushrooms
Add 100 g sliced mushrooms after cooking the onion for 3-4 minutes.

Tomato sauce with spinach
Add 100 g washed spinach leaves for the last 3-4 minutes of cooking.

Tomato sauce with bacon
Add 150 g diced bacon (or pancetta) after cooking the onion for 3-4 minutes and continue cooking for another 4-5 minutes. You could also use salami.

Tomato sauce with chilli
Add 2 de-seeded and finely diced red chillies with cooking onions.

Tomato, olive and anchovy pasta sauce

Serves 4

Try this tomato-based pasta sauce, which has a few other goodies thrown in for good measure.

2 tbsp olive oil
1 onion, finely diced
1 clove garlic, crushed
500 g fresh tomatoes, chopped
2–3 anchovies, chopped
2 tbsp tiny salted capers, rinsed
100 g (⅔ cup) pitted kalamata olives
fresh herbs (basil and parsley are excellent)
salt and freshly ground black pepper
pasta of your choice, 100 g dried per person

Heat a medium-sized saucepan over a medium heat. Add oil and onion and cook for 3–4 minutes, stirring often, until onion softens slightly. Add garlic and cook for a further 1–2 minutes or until garlic is fragrant. Add the tomatoes and allow to come to the boil. Reduce heat; add anchovies, capers and olives. Cook for 5–8 minutes until sauce reduces. Add fresh herbs and check seasoning.

Bring a large pot of water to a boil over a high heat. Add a good pinch of salt. Add the pasta to the boiling water and stir until the water has returned to the boil. Reduce heat, cover and cook the pasta at a fast simmer for 8 minutes.

Check that the pasta is cooked, drain and toss with the sauce.

Eggplant, tomato and basil sauce

Serves 4

This combination is a bit of a *menage à trois*, as eggplant, tomato and basil have a natural affinity. Add parmigiano and you have a party.

olive oil
2 anchovies, diced
1 onion, finely diced
1 red capsicum, diced
1 eggplant, diced
2 cloves garlic, crushed
5 Roma tomatoes, quartered lengthways
125 ml (½ cup) white wine
pasta of your choice, 100 g dried or 150 g fresh pasta per person
¼ cup chopped basil
handful of pitted black olives
salt and freshly ground black pepper

Heat a large frypan over a medium–high heat and add a splash of oil. Cook the anchovies, onion, capsicum, eggplant and garlic for 5–10 minutes, stirring often, until soft and fragrant. Add more oil if needed. Add tomatoes to the pan, along with the white wine. Cover and cook over a medium–low heat for 20–30 minutes, stirring occasionally.

Bring a large saucepan of water to a boil over a high heat. Add a good pinch of salt. Add the pasta and stir until the water has returned to the boil. Reduce heat, cover and cook the pasta at a fast simmer for 8 minutes.

Remove the sauce from the heat. Stir in the basil and olives and check the seasoning. Drain the pasta and toss together with the sauce.

Rich duck sauce

Serves 4

This opulent sauce is probably a bit too rich to enjoy in warmer weather. In autumn and winter, however, it is just perfect – especially with a glass of pinot noir to help it along.

olive oil	250 ml (1 cup) red wine
50 g pancetta, diced	250 ml (1 cup) tomato puree
1 onion, finely diced	375 ml (1½ cups) beef or chicken stock
1 carrot, finely diced	pasta of your choice, 100 g dried or 150 g fresh pasta per person
2 duck legs	
1 clove garlic, crushed	grated parmigiano
sprig of thyme	2 tbsp chopped parsley

Heat a heavy-based saucepan over a medium–high heat. Add 1 tbsp oil, pancetta, onion and carrot. Cook for 6–8 minutes, stirring often.

Meanwhile, remove duck meat from bones and cut into rough dice. Add to the pan, along with the garlic and thyme. Cook until the meat is lightly browned. Add the wine, tomato puree and stock, and bring to the boil. Cover and simmer for 1 ½–2 hours, stirring occasionally.

Bring a large saucepan of water to a boil over a high heat. Add a good pinch of salt. Add the pasta and stir until the water has returned to the boil. Reduce heat, cover and cook the pasta at a fast simmer for 8 minutes.

Drain the pasta, toss with the duck ragu and serve topped with parmigiano and parsley.

Penne with Italian sausage, tomato and red wine sauce

Serves 4

This pasta sauce can be made with either a dried or fresh Italian sausage. Our ideal preference would be to use a fresh pork and fennel sausage, or perhaps pork and chilli for an extra flavour boost.

olive oil
200 g Italian sausage, cut into chunks
1 onion, diced
1 clove garlic, crushed
1 tbsp tomato paste
6 tomatoes, diced, or 400 g can chopped tomatoes
125 ml (½ cup) red wine
salt and freshly ground black pepper
400 g dried penne

Heat a large heavy-based frypan over a medium–high heat. Add a generous splash of oil and the sausage. Cook for 4–5 minutes, until golden brown. Remove from the pan and set aside.

Return the pan to the heat and add more oil if necessary. Add the onion and cook for 2–3 minutes, stirring often. Add garlic and cook for 1–2 minutes, until fragrant. Add tomato paste and tomatoes and cook for 3–4 minutes, then add red wine and cooked sausage to the pan. Season with salt and pepper and cook for 6–8 minutes, until the wine reduces and the tomatoes are cooked.

Bring a large saucepan of water to a boil over a high heat. Add a good pinch of salt. Add the pasta to the boiling water and stir until the water has returned to the boil. Reduce heat, cover and cook the pasta at a fast simmer for 8 minutes.

Check that the pasta is cooked, drain and toss with the sauce.

Penne with prosciutto, peas and mint

Serves 4

With this type of dish it's easy to serve the sauce on the side for fussy eaters, then toss the rest of the sauce together for those with grown-up tastes.

400 g dried penne
60 ml (¼ cup) olive oil
1 onion, chopped
1 clove garlic, crushed
90 g prosciutto, about 8 thin slices, chopped
250 ml (1 cup) chicken stock
250 g (2 cups) peas
2 tbsp butter
salt and freshly ground black pepper
1 tbsp chopped fresh mint

Bring a large pot of water to a boil over a high heat. Add a good pinch of salt. Add the pasta to the boiling water and stir until the water has returned to the boil. Reduce heat, cover and cook the pasta at a fast simmer for 8 minutes.

Heat a large shallow pan over a medium heat. Add oil and onion and cook for 3–4 minutes, stirring often, until onion softens slightly. Add garlic and cook for a further 1–2 minutes or until fragrant, then add prosciutto. Cook until prosciutto begins to crisp, stirring often.

Add stock, bring to the boil, and then reduce heat. Simmer for 5 minutes, allowing stock to reduce slightly. Add peas; cook for 3–4 minutes, turning heat up if necessary. Remove from heat; add butter, salt and loads of pepper. Whisk to incorporate butter, salt and pepper, and add mint.

Drain pasta, toss with sauce and serve.

Broad bean and bacon pasta sauce
Substitute bacon for prosciutto, double-podded broad beans for peas and basil for mint.

Spaghetti with smoked chicken and asparagus

Serves 4

Smoked chicken and asparagus is a gorgeous combination, especially in spring when the new season's asparagus arrives.

400 g dried spaghetti
60 ml (¼ cup) olive oil
1 onion, chopped
1 clove garlic, crushed
2 smoked chicken breast fillets, sliced
250 ml (1 cup) chicken stock
1 bunch asparagus, cut into 2 cm lengths
2 tbsp butter
salt and freshly ground black pepper
2 tbsp chopped parsley

Bring a large saucepan of water to a boil over a high heat. Add a good pinch of salt. Add the pasta to the boiling water and stir until the water has returned to the boil. Reduce heat, cover and cook the pasta at a fast simmer for 8 minutes.

Heat a frypan over a medium–high heat. Add the oil and onion and cook for 3–4 minutes, stirring often, until the onion softens slightly. Add garlic and cook for a further 1–2 minutes, or until the garlic is fragrant. Add smoked chicken and stock and bring to the boil. Add asparagus and cook for 2–3 minutes.

Remove the pan from the heat and add butter, salt and loads of pepper. Whisk to incorporate the butter and add parsley.

Drain the pasta, toss with the sauce and serve.

Smoked trout and asparagus cream sauce
Swap the smoked chicken for smoked trout, being sure to remove all bones.

Chicken, mushroom and olive sauce

Serves 4

Serve this sauce with penne or spaghetti, or toss it through potato gnocchi.

olive oil
1 onion, diced
125 g mushrooms, sliced
2 chicken thigh fillets, diced
1 clove garlic, crushed
125 ml (½ cup) chicken stock
125 ml (½ cup) tomato sugo
pasta of your choice, 100 g dried or 150 g fresh pasta per person
100 g (¾ cup) pitted black olives
salt and freshly ground black pepper
2 tbsp chopped parsley

Heat a medium-sized saucepan over a medium–high heat. Add a generous splash of oil and the onion, and cook for 3–4 minutes. Add the mushrooms and cook for 2–3 minutes, stirring often. Add the chicken and garlic and cook for 3–4 minutes, or until the chicken is beginning to brown. Add the stock and tomato sugo, and bring to the boil. Reduce to a simmer and cook for 10–15 minutes.

Bring a large saucepan of water to a boil over a high heat. Add a good pinch of salt. Add the pasta and stir until the water has returned to the boil. Reduce heat, cover and cook the pasta at a fast simmer for 8 minutes.

Add the olives to the sauce and check the seasoning. Drain the pasta and toss with the sauce. Add parsley to serve.

Chicken, mushroom and spinach sauce
Substitute 100 g spinach leaves for the olives and cook for 1–2 minutes in the sauce before tossing with the pasta.

Orecchietti with rich mushroom sauce

Serves 4

If wild mushrooms such as pine mushrooms or slippery jacks are in season they will add extra oomph to this sauce. If not, a combination of readily available Swiss browns, field and shiitake is good.

olive oil
1 onion, diced
500 g mushrooms, sliced
2 cloves garlic, crushed
125 ml (½ cup) white wine
125 ml (½ cup) chicken stock
125 ml (½ cup) tomato sugo
400 g dried orecchietti
salt and freshly ground black pepper
2 tbsp chopped parsley or basil

Heat a medium-sized saucepan over a medium–high heat. Add a generous splash of oil and the onion and cook for 3–4 minutes. Add mushrooms and cook for 4–5 minutes, stirring often. Add garlic and cook for 1–2 minutes, until fragrant. Pour in the wine and cook until reduced by half. Add stock and tomato sugo, and bring to the boil. Reduce to a simmer and cook for 10–15 minutes.

Bring a large saucepan of water to a boil over a high heat. Add a good pinch of salt. Add the orecchietti and stir until the water has returned to the boil. Reduce heat, cover and cook the pasta at a fast simmer for 8 minutes.

Check seasoning. Drain the pasta and toss with the sauce and herbs to serve.

Penne tossed with caramelised onion, rocket and olive

Serves 4

A favourite combination of ours: caramelised onions, salty olives and peppery rocket leaves.

80 ml (⅓ cup) olive oil
4 onions, sliced
2 cloves garlic, peeled
1 small red chilli, halved (optional)
2 sprigs of thyme
salt and freshly ground black pepper
400 g dried penne
100 g (¾ cup) pitted black olives, halved
125 g rocket, washed and chopped

Heat the oil in a saucepan. Add the onions, garlic, chilli (if using) and thyme. Season well. Cook for 20–30 minutes on a low heat, stirring often, until the onions soften and turn a golden caramel colour.

Bring a large saucepan of water to a boil over a high heat. Add a good pinch of salt. Add the pasta to the boiling water and stir until the water has returned to the boil. Reduce heat, cover and cook the pasta at a fast simmer for 8 minutes.

Drain excess oil away from the onions. Toss with the olives, rocket and cooked, drained pasta. Serve immediately.

Linguini with chilli, anchovies, breadcrumbs and basil

Serves 4

The lightly toasted sourdough breadcrumbs in this recipe add flavour and texture to create a memorable dish.

- 400 g dried linguini
- olive oil
- 175 g sourdough bread, chopped into coarse breadcrumbs
- 4 anchovies, diced
- 2 small red chillies, de-seeded and diced
- 2 cloves garlic, crushed
- 2 tbsp chopped parsley
- handful of torn basil leaves
- 80 g (1 cup) grated parmigiano
- salt and freshly ground black pepper

Bring a large saucepan of water to a boil over a high heat. Add a good pinch of salt. Add the pasta and stir until the water has returned to the boil. Reduce heat, cover and cook the pasta at a fast simmer for 8 minutes.

Heat a large heavy-based frypan over a medium–high heat. Add a very generous splash of oil and the breadcrumbs and cook for 4–5 minutes, stirring often, until the breadcrumbs are golden and crunchy. Remove from heat and set aside.

Return the pan to the heat and add a splash of oil, the anchovies, chillies and garlic. Cook for 30 seconds, stirring often, until fragrant. Add to breadcrumbs. Drain the pasta and toss with the anchovy and breadcrumb mix, parsley, basil and parmigiano. Season to taste and serve immediately.

Spaghetti with silverbeet, raisins and pine nuts

Serves 4

Good friend Daniele blew me away with this simple pasta recipe. We agreed we just had to share it with you. MC

85 g (½ cup) raisins
60 ml (¼ cup) brandy
400 g dried spaghetti
3–4 silverbeet stems
olive oil
1 onion, diced
50 g (⅓ cup) pine nuts
1 clove garlic, crushed
1 small red chilli, de-seeded and diced
zest of 1 orange, diced
125 ml (½ cup) chicken stock
salt and freshly ground black pepper

Soak the raisins in brandy.

Bring a large saucepan of water to a boil over a high heat. Add a good pinch of salt. Add the pasta and stir until the water has returned to the boil. Reduce heat, cover and cook the pasta at a fast simmer for 8 minutes.

Wash silverbeet well. Discard stalks and roughly chop leaves.

Heat a frypan over a medium–high heat and add a splash of oil, the onion and pine nuts. Cook for 4–5 minutes, stirring often, until the pine nuts turn golden brown. Add the garlic, chilli, orange zest and silverbeet, and cook for 2–3 minutes. Add the stock, cover with a lid and cook for 1–2 minutes, until the silverbeet collapses. Check seasoning.

Add the brandy-soaked raisins and toss everything together well. Drain the pasta and toss with the sauce.

Linguini with roasted pumpkin, spinach and goat's cheese

Serves 4

This is a simple combination of sweet roasted pumpkin chunks freshened up with spinach and goat's cheese. It's a style of pasta we regularly enjoy as you don't have to create a sauce.

- 200 g pumpkin, peeled, de-seeded and diced 2 cm
- olive oil
- salt and freshly ground black pepper
- 400 g dried linguini
- 1 onion, diced
- 1 clove garlic, crushed
- 1 small red chilli, de-seeded and diced
- 125 ml (½ cup) chicken stock
- 75 g spinach leaves, washed
- 100 g goat's cheese, crumbled

Preheat oven to 180°C.

Toss the pumpkin with oil, salt and pepper, and roast in the preheated oven for 30 minutes, or until soft and golden brown.

Bring a large saucepan of water to a boil over a high heat. Add a good pinch of salt. Add the pasta and stir until the water has returned to the boil. Reduce heat, cover and cook the pasta at a fast simmer for 8 minutes.

Heat a small frypan over a medium heat. Add a splash of oil and the onion and cook for 5–6 minutes, stirring often. Add garlic and chilli and cook for 1–2 minutes, until fragrant but not coloured. Add stock and bring to the boil, then reduce by half.

Just before you drain the pasta, add the spinach leaves to the onion and allow them to cook briefly until they wilt. Add the roasted pumpkin and season with salt and pepper. Drain the pasta and toss with the pumpkin and goat's cheese until combined.

Pasta with roasted pumpkin, spinach and blue cheese
Substitute blue cheese for goat's cheese.

Troffiette with chestnuts and smoked ham hock

Serves 4–6

We're big fans of this corkscrew-shaped pasta, which is a speciality of Liguria in northern Italy. It keeps its shape when cooked, picks up other flavours beautifully and retains its texture. This dish is perfect in autumn and early winter when fresh chestnuts are available.

- 1 × 500 g ham hock
- 12 large chestnuts (375 g)
- 400 g dried troffiette
- 2 tbsp olive oil
- 1 tbsp butter
- 1 onion, finely diced
- 2 cloves garlic, sliced
- 1 small red chilli, de-seeded and diced
- 125 ml (½ cup) white wine
- 125 ml (½ cup) chicken stock
- salt and freshly ground black pepper
- 200 g baby spinach leaves
- grated parmigiano

Place the ham hock in a saucepan of cold water and bring to the boil. Reduce to a simmer, cover and cook for 1 hour, or until tender.

Remove ham hock from water and allow to cool. Peel and discard the skin, then remove the ham from the bone and chop into 1 cm dice. Refrigerate until needed.

Bring a saucepan of water to the boil. Meanwhile, cut a slit in the bottom of each chestnut. Add the chestnuts to the boiling water, cover and reduce to a simmer. Cook for 15–20 minutes, or until tender. Remove from heat and, while still warm (it's easier), peel the hard shell and the inner skin from each chestnut. Roughly chop the cooked chestnuts.

Bring a large saucepan of water to a boil over a high heat. Add a good pinch of salt. Add the pasta and stir until the water has returned to the boil. Reduce heat, cover and cook the pasta at a fast simmer for 8 minutes.

Heat a frypan over a medium heat and add the oil, butter and onion. Cook for 3–4 minutes, until the onion softens. Add the garlic and chilli and cook for 1–2 minutes, until fragrant. Pour in the wine and cook until reduced by half. Add ham, chestnuts and stock and simmer for 6–8 minutes. Check seasoning. Add the spinach leaves and cook for 1–2 minutes, until they wilt.

Drain the pasta and toss with the ham sauce. Serve with grated parmigiano.

Spaghetti with tuna, rocket and lemon

Serves 4

This dish is super-easy to make and it tastes terrific, too. What more could you possibly want from a pasta recipe?

400 g dried spaghetti
olive oil
2 cloves garlic, crushed
350 g canned tuna, drained

75 g rocket leaves, roughly chopped
chopped zest and juice of 1 lemon
salt and freshly ground black pepper

Bring a large saucepan of water to a boil over a high heat. Add a good pinch of salt. Add the pasta and stir until the water has returned to the boil. Reduce heat, cover and cook the pasta at a fast simmer for 8 minutes.

Heat a large heavy-based frypan over a medium–high heat. Add a very generous splash of oil, along with the garlic. Cook for 1–2 minutes. Add the tuna, rocket, lemon zest and juice, salt and pepper. Cook briefly.

Drain the pasta and toss to coat well with rocket and tuna mix.

Pasta with tuna and artichokes

Serves 4

Nothing tricky here – simply a pan of ingredients like onion, artichokes, tuna, lemon and parsley being cooked together. Then you add the cooked pasta, do the hokey-pokey and shake it all about.

olive oil
1 onion, diced
1 clove garlic, crushed
200 g marinated artichoke hearts, quartered
300 g canned tuna, drained

2 tbsp chopped parsley
squeeze of lemon juice
salt and freshly ground black pepper
400 g dried orecchietti

Bring a large pot of water to a boil over a high heat. Add a good pinch of salt. Add the pasta and stir until the water has returned to the boil. Reduce heat, cover and cook the pasta at a fast simmer for 8 minutes.

Heat a heavy-based pan over a medium–high heat. Add a splash of oil and onion and cook for 4–5 minutes, stirring often until the onion begins to soften. Add garlic and artichokes, cook, stirring often for 2–3 minutes. Add tuna, parsley, a squeeze of lemon juice, and salt and pepper to taste. Toss well to combine all ingredients.

Add drained, cooked pasta to the pan, toss to combine ingredients well, then serve straight away.

Spaghetti with breadcrumbs, tuna, parsley and lemon

Serves 4

This is one of those recipes that we have had lots of feedback on – how much people enjoy it and what a perfect, easy dinner it makes. We just had to include it. A good sourdough bread is best as it has a strong, gutsy flavour.

- 400 g dried spaghetti
- olive oil
- 175 g sourdough bread, chopped into coarse breadcrumbs
- 2 cloves garlic, crushed
- ⅔ cup chopped parsley
- chopped zest and juice of 1 lemon
- 350 g canned tuna, drained
- salt and freshly ground black pepper
- 125 g (1⅓ cups) parmigiano, grated

Bring a large pot of water to a boil over a high heat. Add a good pinch of salt. Add pasta and stir until water has returned to the boil. Reduce heat, cover and cook pasta at a fast simmer for 8 minutes.

Heat a large heavy-based frypan over a medium–high heat. Add a very generous splash of oil and breadcrumbs and cook for 4–5 minutes, stirring often until breadcrumbs are golden and crunchy. Add garlic, parsley, lemon zest, juice, tuna, salt and pepper. Cook briefly.

Drain pasta and toss to coat well with tuna mixture and parmigiano and serve.

Spaghetti with blue-swimmer crab, fennel and tomato

Serves 6

This dish celebrates the end of autumn by using the last of the season's basil and tomato in a luxurious combination of spaghetti, fennel and crab meat. Fresh blue-swimmer crabs are readily available and are only $10 to $15 per kilo. You will save yourself some effort if you can source fresh crab meat from a reputable fishmonger, although we enjoy spending the time picking out the crab meat.

- 2 kg blue-swimmer crabs or 600 g crab meat
- salt
- 6 tomatoes
- ½ cup basil leaves
- ½ cup flat-leaf parsley leaves
- 2 tbsp capers, soaked in cold water
- 2 small red chillies, de-seeded and sliced
- 2 fennel bulbs, thinly sliced
- 400 g dried spaghetti
- 80 ml (⅓ cup) extra-virgin olive oil
- 2 tbsp lemon juice
- salt and freshly ground black pepper

If the crabs are still alive, put them to sleep by placing them in the freezer for 30 minutes before cooking. Bring a large saucepan of water to the boil. Add a generous handful of salt. Add the crabs and cook them for 15 minutes. Remove from heat and allow to cool.

When the crabs are cool, crack their shells open and remove the flesh, taking care that no stray pieces of shell make their way into the meat. Refrigerate until needed.

Mark a cross on the base of each tomato with a sharp knife. Blanch the tomatoes in boiling water for 10–20 seconds, refreshing immediately in cold water. Peel off the skins, cut into quarters and remove the seeds. Dice the tomato flesh into 1 cm squares. Mix with basil, parsley, capers, chillies and fennel.

Bring a large saucepan of water to a boil over a high heat. Add a good pinch of salt. Add the pasta and stir until the water has returned to the boil. Reduce heat, cover and cook the pasta at a fast simmer for 8 minutes. Drain the pasta and return it to the saucepan. Add the crab meat and tomato and fennel mix, along with the extra-virgin olive oil and lemon juice.

Add salt and pepper to taste and serve immediately.

Macaroni cheese

Serves 4

This is a classic you just can't pass up. Littlies love it, especially when it's all crispy on top. Be sure to remove the white sauce from the heat before adding the cheese, as otherwise the sauce may curdle.

400 g dried macaroni
2 tbsp butter
2 tbsp flour
750 ml (3 cups) hot milk
1 tsp Dijon mustard
200 g (2¼ cups) grated cheese (mix of parmigiano and cheddar)
salt and freshly ground black pepper

Bring a large saucepan of water to a boil over a high heat. Add a good pinch of salt. Add the pasta and stir until the water has returned to the boil. Reduce heat, cover and cook the pasta at a fast simmer for 8 minutes.

Place a medium saucepan over a medium heat and melt the butter, without browning. Add the flour and stir well to incorporate and form a roux. Reduce heat and 'cook' the flour for 2–3 minutes, stirring often.

Raise the heat under the roux and add 1 ladleful of hot milk. Whisk in well, then continue to add milk, 1 ladleful at a time, until it's all incorporated. Add mustard, reduce heat and cook for 3–4 minutes, stirring often. Remove from heat, add ¾ of the grated cheese and stir well until melted. Season well with salt and pepper.

Drain the pasta and stir through the cheese sauce. Pour into an ovenproof dish. Sprinkle the remaining cheese on top and place under a hot grill until golden brown.

Michele's macaroni cheese
Sounds weird, tastes fantastic. Cook 1 diced onion in olive oil with a diced fresh chilli. Add 2 good-quality sliced frankfurters and cook for a further 3–4 minutes. Add a drained can of sweetcorn, then incorporate everything into the sauce, along with the cheese. Don't waste time browning the top, just get stuck in. MC

Macaroni cheese with ham
Dice 2 x 1 cm thick slices of leg ham and add it to the sauce with the cheese.

Macaroni cheese with corn
Add 200 g sweetcorn to the sauce with the cheese.

Spaghetti with braised chicken meatballs in tomato sugo

Serves 6

We've fallen in love with the simplicity of this dish. It can easily be made in advance and be cooking away in the oven when your guests arrive.

1 kg chicken mince
2 tbsp chopped parsley
1 tbsp chopped basil
salt and freshly ground black pepper
1 egg
50 g (½ cup) dry breadcrumbs
olive oil
2 onions, diced
2 small red chillies, de-seeded and diced
2 cloves garlic, crushed
125 ml (½ cup) dry white wine
500 ml (2 cups) chicken stock
250 ml (1 cup) tomato sugo
600 g dried spaghetti
2 tbsp chopped parsley to serve

Preheat oven to 180°C.

Mix the chicken mince, chopped parsley, basil, salt, pepper, egg and breadcrumbs together. Roll into 3 cm balls.

Heat a heavy-based frypan over a medium–high heat. Add a generous splash of oil and cook the meatballs until golden brown. Transfer to an ovenproof casserole dish.

Heat a large saucepan over a medium heat. Add 80 ml (⅓ cup) oil and the onions. Cook for 5–6 minutes, stirring often and ensuring that the onions don't colour. Add the chillies and garlic and cook for a further 1–2 minutes, until fragrant. Pour in the white wine, bring to the boil and cook until reduced by half (around 10–15 minutes). Add the stock and tomato sugo and bring to the boil. Season with salt and pepper.

Pour the hot sauce over the meatballs. Cover the dish with foil and bake in the preheated oven for 1 hour.

After 1 hour, bring a large saucepan of water to a boil over a high heat. Add a good pinch of salt. Add the spaghetti and stir until the water comes back to the boil. Cook the pasta at a fast simmer for 8 minutes.

Drain the pasta and serve with the meatballs and sauce, sprinkled with chopped parsley.

Cheesy bean and tomato pasta bake

Serves 4

This reliable option for a mid-week family-friendly dinner includes carbs and protein as an added bonus.

250 g dried penne
olive oil
2 onions, diced
1 clove garlic, crushed
1 small red chilli, de-seeded and diced
375 ml (1 ½ cups) tomato sugo
375 ml (1½ cups) chicken or vegetable stock
400 g can cooked cannellini beans
125 g (1 cup) grated cheddar
100 g (1 cup) grated mozzarella
salt and freshly ground black pepper

Preheat oven to 180°C.

Bring a large saucepan of water to a boil over a high heat. Add a good pinch of salt. Add the pasta to the boiling water and stir until the water has returned to the boil. Reduce heat, cover and cook the pasta at a fast simmer for 8 minutes. If making in advance, drain and refresh the pasta under cold running water. Toss the cold pasta with 1 tbsp oil to prevent it sticking together and set aside until needed. If baking straight away, add the hot pasta to the finished sauce.

Heat a large frypan over a medium–high heat. Add oil and the onions and cook for 3–4 minutes, stirring often, until the onions soften slightly. Add the garlic and chilli and cook for a further 1–2 minutes, or until the garlic is fragrant. Add the tomato sugo and stock and bring to the boil. Add the beans, then reduce to a simmer and cook for 8–10 minutes, stirring often.

Mix the cheddar and mozzarella together. Add the pasta to the sauce along with half the cheese and stir well to combine. Check seasoning. Pour the pasta mix into a 3-litre ovenproof dish. Scatter remaining cheese over pasta and bake in the preheated oven for 30–40 minutes, or until the cheese is golden brown and pasta is heated through.

Bolognaise pasta bake
Omit bean and vegetable sauce. Add Quick-and-easy Bolognaise (page 160) to the cooked pasta along with cheese. Scatter the remaining cheese over the top as above and brown.

Roast vegetable and goat's cheese lasagne

Serves 4–6

This dish takes a bit of preparing as the eggplant, zucchini, capsicum and mushrooms need to be roasted before you start. But it's well worth every extra minute spent.

olive oil
1 red capsicum
1 eggplant
salt and freshly ground black pepper
2 zucchini
175 g mushrooms, quartered
6–8 instant lasagne sheets
1 batch of Tomato Sauce with Basil (page 162)
150 g goat's cheese
parmigiano shavings

Preheat oven to 200°C.

Rub capsicum all over with oil and roast until blistered, around 30 minutes. Place in a plastic bag until cool, then skin, de-seed and slice.

Slice eggplant, sprinkle with salt and set side until juices bead, about 20 minutes. Rinse, pat dry and lay in baking tray. Brush with oil, season and cook in preheated oven until brown and cooked, about 20 minutes.

Slice zucchinis lengthways into 4 slices. Place on baking tray, drizzle with oil, season and roast until just soft, 15–20 minutes.

Quarter mushrooms, place in a tray, drizzle with oil, season and roast for 10–15 minutes, until just cooked.

To assemble take a lasagne dish and arrange half of the vegetables in the base, starting with the eggplant and finishing with the capsicum and mushrooms. Cover with a lasagne sheet. Spoon tomato sauce over pasta and crumble half of the goat's cheese on top. Repeat with another layer of everything.

Scatter parmigiano shavings over the top. Wrap dish with foil and cook in preheated oven for 40 minutes. Remove foil and cook for a further 10 minutes, until cheese browns slightly.

Potato gnocchi

Serves 4

Toolangi delight or bintje potatoes are the best for making gnocchi. A pasta pot with a large colander will enable you to lift your cooked gnocchi from the boiling water, rather than pouring the boiling water over it (cooked gnocchi is quite fragile).

- 1 kg potatoes, peeled
- 75 g butter
- 3 eggs
- 3 egg yolks
- pinch of nutmeg
- 300 g (2 cups) plain flour
- salt and freshly ground black pepper
- plain flour for dusting

Boil or steam the potatoes until tender. Drain well. Mash the potatoes while they're still hot, then add the butter, eggs, egg yolks, nutmeg, flour, salt and pepper. Stir until incorporated.

Divide the potato mixture into 4 portions on a floured bench top. Roll each portion into 2 cm thick sausages. Cut into 2 cm lengths.

Plunge the gnocchi into boiling salted water. Allow the gnocchi to rise to the surface then cook for a further 2 minutes. Remove, and serve straight away with a piping-hot sauce.

If desired, gnocchi can be pre-cooked, set aside to cool and tossed gently with olive oil. Reheat by placing the gnocchi gently back into boiling water for 1 minute, or by reheating in a microwave.

Goat's cheese gnocchi

Serves 4

Depending on the potatoes, you may not need all the flour. Add most of it, check the texture and add more if necessary.

- 1 kg peeled potatoes
- 75 g diced butter
- 1 egg
- 2 egg yolks
- 100 g crumbled goat's cheese
- 300 g (2 cups) self-raising flour
- pinch of nutmeg
- salt and freshly ground black pepper

Boil or steam the potatoes until tender. Drain well. Mash the potatoes while they're still hot, then add butter, egg, egg yolks, goat's cheese, flour, nutmeg, salt and pepper. Stir until incorporated.

Divide the mixture into 4 portions on a floured bench top. Roll each portion into a sausage 2 cm thick. Cut into 2 cm lengths.

Plunge the gnocchi into boiling salted water. Allow the gnocchi to rise to the surface then cook for a further 2 minutes. Remove, and serve straight away with a piping-hot sauce.

If convenient, gnocchi can be cooked in advance, set aside to cool and gently tossed with a little olive oil. Reheat the gnocchi in boiling water for 1 minute or in a microwave.

Semolina gnocchi

Serves 4

Semolina makes soft and tender gnocchi. It's perfect for these gnocchi discs, which are grilled then served with a simple tomato salsa.

1¼ litres (5 cups) milk
1 bay leaf
pinch of grated nutmeg
6 black peppercorns
1 onion, peeled and roughly chopped
pinch of salt

160 g (1 cup) semolina
150 g (2 cups) parmigiano, finely grated
150 g gruyere, finely grated
3 egg yolks
50 g soft butter

Place milk in a heavy-based pan with the bay leaf, nutmeg, peppercorns, onion and salt. Bring to a gentle boil, reduce heat and allow flavours to infuse for 5 minutes.

Strain the milk into a clean heavy-based pan and return to the boil. Sprinkle in semolina and stir constantly as the mixture thickens and starts to bubble. Reduce heat and cook gently for 5–10 minutes until very thick, stirring all the time.

Combine the two cheeses. Remove the semolina from the heat, and stir in the egg yolks, butter and half of the cheese. Check seasoning, adding salt and pepper to taste. Pour into a greased deep dish (such as a large baking tray) and smooth down the top; it should be around 1 cm thick. Sprinkle the remaining cheese on top. Allow to cool in the refrigerator until set firm.

When cool, cut the gnocchi into 4 cm circles. Arrange the circles in small buttered gratin dishes, 3 circles per person, or place them on one large tray.

To serve, place the gnocchi under hot grill and cook until cheese melts and turns golden brown. If grilling on one large tray, divide the gnocchi between warmed plates. Serve topped with a simple Tomato and Basil Salsa (page 565).

Gnocchi with blue cheese sauce

Serves 4

This is a rich dining experience that demands the very best blue cheese to be enjoyed at its smooth-textured best.

125 ml (½ cup) cream
150 g blue cheese, such as gorgonzola
100 g (1¼ cups) grated parmigiano
freshly ground black pepper
800 g Potato Gnocchi (page 187) or packet gnocchi
60 g (½ cup) chopped walnuts (optional)

Place cream and cheeses in a saucepan and bring to the boil. Reduce heat and allow to simmer for 3–4 minutes. Season with black pepper.

Bring a large saucepan of water to a boil over a high heat. Add a good pinch of salt. Add the gnocchi and stir until the water has returned to the boil. Reduce heat, cover and cook the gnocchi at a fast simmer for 3–4 minutes, until the gnocchi is cooked through.

Drain the pasta and toss gently with the blue cheese sauce. Serve with chopped walnuts sprinkled over the top if you like.

Roast tomato, pancetta and sweet onions with gnocchi

Serves 2

You don't have to serve this chunky, rich sauce with gnocchi – but take it from us: it's a magic combination. This is usually a dinner for two of us.

4 tomatoes
olive oil
salt and freshly ground black pepper
pinch of caster sugar
60 ml (¼ cup) olive oil
2 onions, diced
2–3 sprigs thyme
150 g pancetta, diced
2 tbsp chopped parsley
2–3 tbsp shaved parmigiano
300 g gnocchi

Preheat oven to 180°C.

Cut tomatoes into quarters, lay on a baking tray, skin side down, drizzle with olive oil and season with salt, pepper and sugar. Roast in preheated oven for 30 minutes.

Heat 60 ml (¼ cup) of oil in a heavy-based frying pan. Add onions, thyme, salt and pepper. Cook over a low heat for 20–30 minutes or until onions are soft and slightly coloured. Turn heat up, add pancetta. Cook for 3–4 minutes until pancetta is crispy. Add roasted tomatoes, parsley and parmigiano. Check seasoning.

Bring a large pot of water to a boil over a high heat. Add a good pinch of salt.

Plunge the gnocchi into boiling salted water, allow them to rise to the surface and cook for a further 2–3 minutes. Toss sauce with cooked gnocchi and serve.

Roast pumpkin, pancetta and sweet onions with gnocchi
Substitute 200 g diced pumpkin for tomatoes.

polenta

Some people may be a little fed up with polenta, mostly due to a period of over-exposure in the food media. We, however, are not; we love it passionately. We like soft polenta served straight from the saucepan with a cheesy flavour and porridge-like consistency. And we love it set into a firm block, sliced and cooked on a barbecue plate or in an oven until it's crisp on the outside.

If you need something other than pasta, rice or potatoes to serve with dinner, polenta is your man. And what we are most thankful for is the fact that the children love it too. Halleluiah. There's not too much to the cooking process: as long as you get the proportion of polenta to liquid right, and you remember to stir it occasionally, you're set.

Things you need to know about polenta

1 Polenta is the grainy flour milled from maize.

2 Polenta is a seductive accompaniment to all dishes. Because of its subtle flavour, it's a perfect way to balance robust meat dishes or to soak up juices.

3 To cook it, bring the liquid to the boil and sprinkle in polenta gradually to prevent lumps forming. A whisk is excellent for this. Bring back to the boil, then reduce to the lowest possible heat. Stir the polenta with a wooden spoon as it cooks.

4 A saucepan of polenta retains a lot of heat inside the mixture, and because it's thick it will 'plop' (like porridge) while cooking. Watch out for the 'plops' because if they catch you on the hand, they will burn.

5 Polenta takes only 20 minutes or so to cook.

The best soft polenta

Serves 4

Using half water and half stock adds richness to the finished polenta. If you don't have stock available it's fine to just use water.

500 ml (2 cups) water
500 ml (2 cups) chicken or vegetable stock
180 g (1 cup) polenta
60 g (¾ cup) grated parmigiano
salt to taste

Bring water and stock to the boil in a heavy-based saucepan. Sprinkle in polenta, whisking well to prevent any lumps forming. Reduce to a low simmer and cook for 20–30 minutes, stirring often, until the mixture thickens. Take care, as the polenta can splutter and burn; a long-handled spoon is ideal.

Remove from heat and stir in cheese. Season to taste, then serve straight away.

Herb polenta
Add 1–2 tbsp chopped herbs (parsley, thyme, basil or rosemary) along with the cheese.

Goat's cheese polenta
Add 100 g fresh goat's cheese to polenta just before serving.

Truffle polenta
Add 1 tsp truffle oil to polenta just before serving. You may also like to add 250 g pan-fried mushrooms.

Polenta wedgies

Serves 6

These amazing wedgies are perfect with just about everything. We like to serve up smaller versions as a pre-dinner nibble, sometimes with a spicy tomato salsa.

500 ml (2 cups) water
500 ml (2 cups) chicken or vegetable stock
180 g (1 cup) polenta
60 g (¾ cup) grated parmigiano
salt to taste

Bring water and stock to the boil in a heavy-based saucepan. Sprinkle in polenta, whisking well to prevent lumps forming. Reduce to a low simmer and cook for 20–30 minutes, stirring often, until the mixture thickens. Take care, as the polenta can splutter and burn; a long-handled spoon is ideal. Add more stock or water if it becomes too thick to stir.

Remove from heat and stir in cheese. Season to taste, then pour cooked polenta into a deep baking dish and allow to set for at least 4 hours. Cut into wedges or triangles.

Preheat oven to 180°C.

Arrange wedges on an oiled baking tray and bake for 20 minutes, until crispy and golden. Alternatively, cook the wedges on a hot barbecue plate.

Cheesy wedgies

Omit parmigiano from recipe. Place wedgies on a baking tray and top with slices of fresh or aged mozzarella or gruyere cheese. Bake in a preheated oven for 20 minutes, until golden brown. You can also add olive paste, tomato slices, barbecued eggplant, artichokes, sun-dried tomatoes or whatever takes your fancy.

RICE
+ noodles
risotto, pilafs + stir-fries

It's said that more people throughout the world sit down to a meal that uses rice than to any other food. Not really surprising when you consider the fact that virtually every country has its favourite rice dishes. What would Italian food be without risotto, Japanese cuisine without sushi, North African food without pilaf or Spanish cooking without paella?

Both of our childhood experiences of rice were pretty basic in comparison. If we ate rice, it was likely to be part of a Chinese takeaway, as a rice pudding or as basic boiled rice (swamped in lots of water). Luckily, we have come a long way since then and extended our food horizons to see what the rest of the world does with this nutritious, versatile and delicious grain.

Rice is now essential to so many of the dishes we love to eat, and it seems the variety of different meals that can be prepared from rice is never-ending. We always have at least three types on hand in the cupboard: arborio rice for making risotto, fragrant jasmine rice to serve with curries and long-grain rice for pilaf.

rice + noodle recipes

rice

Steamed rice	198
Preserved lemon, almond and parsley pilaf	199
Pine nut, sultana and onion pilaf	200
Chicken pilaf	201
Persian rice	202
Pumpkin, chickpea and saffron pilaf	204
Chicken and asparagus risotto	205
Risotto of chicken, mushroom and taleggio cheese	206
Sweet potato, pancetta and pea risotto	207
Risotto of prawns with peas and radicchio	208
Asparagus and prawn risotto	209
Risotto with rocket and gorgonzola	210
Tuscan bean risotto	211
Spring risotto	212
Mushroom risotto with truffle oil	213
Roast pumpkin, feta and pine nut risotto	215
Wild mushroom risotto	216
Mushroom risotto cakes	217
Vegetable risotto cakes	218
Paella	219
Spring Spanish rice with chicken, peas and lemon	220
Nasi goreng (stir-fried rice)	221

noodles

Chicken, ginger and noodle stir-fry	225
Teriyaki chicken udon stir-fry for Mia	226
Beef, black bean and cashew nut stir-fry	227
Chilli beef stir-fry	228
Sour beef with lemongrass	230
Barbecue pork and bok choy stir-fry	230
Barbecue pork and noodle stir-fry	231
Honey roast pork with stir-fried noodles	233
Pad Thai (Thai rice noodles)	234
Chow mein	235
Singapore noodles	236
Spicy Sichuan noodles	237
Chilli prawns with asparagus, shiitake mushrooms and cellophane noodles	237
Stir-fried rice noodles with prawns and snow peas	238
Calamari with soy and chilli glaze	238
Chinese stir-fried vegetables with noodles	239
Vegetable stir-fry with Hokkien noodles and chilli jam	240
Fried tofu with cellophane noodles, shiitake mushrooms and cashews	241
Tofu and ginger stir-fry	242

types of rice

SUSHI RICE

Rice for sushi is usually labelled as sushi rice, which is a short-grain rice.

CALROSE RICE

Calrose rice is a medium-grain rice, which means the grains are shorter and plumper than long-grain. It's the ideal accompaniment to Chinese dishes. It releases starch during cooking and the grains stick together slightly, making it easy to eat with chopsticks. Calrose rice is best cooked by the absorption method; it can also be boiled in plenty of water, if necessary, but it should be washed first. This rice is commonplace at supermarkets, but you can purchase large bags at Asian grocery stores very cheaply.

ARBORIO RICE

Most rice for making risotto is labelled as arborio or risotto rice. This is a medium-grain rice which releases starch during cooking to bind the mixture lightly and add a distinctive creaminess to the finished dish. It also absorbs liquid and the flavours that have been added to the risotto. Vialone nano and carnaroli are other rice varieties grown in Italy especially for making risotto. Both are quite expensive here due to a limited supply. Look for them in specialist food stores.

LONG-GRAIN RICE

The most famous of the many varieties of long-grain rice are without doubt basmati and jasmine rice. Both are subtly perfumed grains which match well with hundreds of different dishes. This type of rice contains less starch than other varieties and the grains remain separate during cooking. It is best cooked by the absorption method. Long-grain rice can be flavoured with saffron threads, nuts and spices or cooked with stock to produce a more full-flavoured dish.

GLUTINOUS RICE

Glutinous rice is available in both black and white varieties and is so called not because of any gluten, but because of its stickiness when cooked. It needs to be soaked for at least 6 hours and thoroughly rinsed before being cooked, usually steamed. It can then be rolled into balls and served with coconut milk and fresh fruit or wrapped in banana leaves with sweet and savoury fillings and eaten as a snack. Black glutinous rice turns a lovely purple colour when cooked, particularly when coconut milk is added.

Things you need to know about rice

1 The best way to cook rice is by the absorption (steamed) method.

2 Even better is a rice cooker that does all the work for you.

3 Don't stir rice during cooking as this allows steam and heat to escape.

4 Generally speaking, rice doesn't have to be washed before cooking. You only need to wash rice if you want to get rid of the starch, but this isn't necessary if you use the absorption method.

5 1 cup of raw rice equals 3 cups of cooked rice.

6 The addition of salt is a personal taste.

7 Different rices have different flavours and uses, such as arborio for risotto and long-grain for pilaf.

8 Pilaf can be cooked on the stovetop or left to finish in a preheated oven.

9 Pilaf often needs a little more water or stock than steamed rice as the extra ingredients also soak up liquid.

10 Risotto is one of the quickest one-pot meals we know – it's a staple in our house.

Steamed rice

Serves 4–6

A rice cooker should take away the fear of cooking rice, but if that doesn't work for you, practise this absorption method until you have it down pat. It's one of the best things you can learn. Once cooked, rice will keep warm for up to 20 minutes. Salt is optional; we rarely add it to steamed rice.

400 g (2 cups) rice
625 ml (2½ cups) water
salt (optional)

Place rice, water and salt (if using) in a saucepan. Cover with a lid, bring to the boil and then reduce to a low simmer. It is important to keep the saucepan covered, so as not to allow the steam to escape. It will take 15–20 minutes for all the water to be absorbed. It is also beneficial to allow the rice to stand for 5–10 minutes, covered, at room temperature before using.

Coconut rice
Substitute half of the water with coconut milk.

Saffron rice
Add a large pinch of saffron threads to the cooking water.

Spiced nut rice
Cook 30 g each of almonds, pine nuts and pistachios in 1 tbsp oil until golden brown. Add a pinch each of ground turmeric, cinnamon and chilli. Then add uncooked rice and cook briefly together. Add water and continue as described.

Preserved lemon, almond and parsley pilaf

Serves 4–6

This Middle Eastern–flavoured pilaf is easy to prepare and goes well with dishes like the Chermoula Chicken (page 344) and Braised Lamb Shanks with Mint and Harissa (page 406). Stick to vegetable stock if you want a vegetarian dish or use chicken stock for a more full-flavoured result.

½ preserved lemon
2 tbsp oil
1 onion, diced
1 clove garlic, crushed
pinch of saffron threads
50 g (⅓ cup) blanched almonds
400 g (2 cups) long-grain rice
750 ml (3 cups) chicken or vegetable stock
salt and freshly ground black pepper
½ cup chopped parsley

Preheat oven to 180°C.

Soak the preserved lemon in cold water for 30 minutes. Drain the lemon, discard the pulpy centre and dice the rind.

Heat a large heavy-based ovenproof saucepan over a medium–high heat. Add the oil, onion, garlic and saffron and cook for 4–5 minutes, until fragrant and soft. Add almonds and cook until golden brown. Add rice and stir for 1–2 minutes. Add stock and preserved lemon rind and bring to the boil, stirring often.

Reduce heat, cover and cook in the preheated oven for 30 minutes, or until the rice is tender and the stock has been absorbed. Allow to stand for 5 minutes before serving.

Check seasoning, add parsley and serve.

Pine nut, sultana and onion pilaf

Serves 4–6

Pilafs are a touch more sophisticated than plain steamed rice and are perfect with spiced food, particularly Indian and Middle Eastern dishes. The addition of onion, garlic and saffron, and stock instead of water, gives pilaf its characteristic richness.

- oil
- 2 onions, diced
- 1 clove garlic, crushed
- pinch of saffron threads
- 50 g (⅓ cup) pine nuts
- 400 g (2 cups) long-grain rice
- 750 ml (3 cups) vegetable or chicken stock
- 110 g (⅔ cup) sultanas
- salt and freshly ground black pepper
- 2 tbsp chopped parsley

Preheat oven to 180°C.

Heat a large heavy-based ovenproof saucepan over a medium heat. Add the oil, onions, garlic and saffron and cook for 4–5 minutes, until fragrant and soft. Add pine nuts and cook until golden brown. Add the rice and stir for 1–2 minutes. Add stock and sultanas and bring to the boil, stirring often.

Reduce heat, cover and cook in the preheated oven for 30 minutes, or until the rice is tender and the stock has been absorbed. Allow to stand for 5 minutes before serving.

Check seasoning, add parsley and serve.

Chicken pilaf

Serves 4–6

Making a chicken pilaf is an easy introduction to this Middle Eastern style of cooking. Once mastered, you can move on to more complex versions by adding vermicelli noodles, nuts, pumpkin or chickpeas. Pilaf can easily be cooked over a low heat on the stovetop or in your oven, as in this recipe.

2 tbsp oil
2 onions, diced
1 clove garlic, crushed
pinch of saffron threads
500 g diced chicken
400 g (2 cups) long-grain rice
750 ml (3 cups) chicken stock
salt and freshly ground black pepper
2 tbsp chopped parsley

Preheat oven to 180°C.

Heat a large heavy-based ovenproof saucepan over a medium heat. Add the oil, onions, garlic and saffron and cook for 4–5 minutes, until fragrant and soft. Add the chicken and cook until it starts to colour. Add the rice and cook for 2–3 minutes, stirring often, then add stock.

Bring to the boil, stirring often. Reduce heat, cover and cook in the preheated oven for 30 minutes, or until the rice is tender and the stock has been absorbed. Allow to stand for 5 minutes before serving.

Check seasoning, then add parsley and serve.

Chicken, almond and harissa pilaf
Add 80 g (½ cup) blanched almonds and 1 tsp harissa to the pilaf along with the onions.

Persian rice

Serves 4–6

With its flecks of ruby red, green and brown, you could call this dish jewelled rice it's so pretty. Don't worry if you need to omit the pomegranate because it isn't in season.

2 tbsp oil
1 onion, diced
80 g (½ cup) blanched almonds
100 g (⅔ cup) pistachios or pine nuts
pinch of saffron threads
3 cardamom pods
400 g (2 cups) basmati rice
750 ml (3 cups) vegetable or chicken stock
110 g (⅔ cup) sultanas
salt
1 pomegranate, skin and pith discarded
1 cup coriander leaves

Heat a heavy-based saucepan over a medium heat. Add the oil, onion, almonds, pistachios, saffron and cardamom pods. Cook for 7–8 minutes, stirring often, until the nuts turn golden and the saffron and onion are fragrant. Add rice and cook for 2 minutes, stirring to coat with oil. Add the stock, sultanas and a pinch of salt. Cover with a lid and bring to the boil.

Reduce heat and cook for 15–20 minutes, until the stock is absorbed and the rice is tender; add a splash more water if necessary. Allow to stand for 5 minutes before serving.

Stir through pomegranate seeds and coriander leaves. Spoon rice onto a large platter.

Pumpkin, chickpea and saffron pilaf

Serves 4–6

A variation of pilaf, this makes a substantial dish, certainly good enough for dinner.

2 tbsp olive oil
2 onions, diced
1 clove garlic, crushed
pinch of saffron threads
70 g vermicelli noodles, roughly broken
750 g pumpkin, diced into 2 cm chunks
400 g (2 cups) long grain rice
750 ml (3 cups) chicken stock
70 g (½ cup) currants
100 g (½ cup) chickpeas, soaked and cooked until tender
2 tbsp chopped parsley
½ cup coriander leaves

Preheat oven to 180°C.

Heat a large heavy-based saucepan over medium heat. Add oil, onions, garlic and saffron and cook for 4–5 minutes until fragrant and soft. Add noodles and cook until they just start to colour. Add rice and pumpkin, cook for 2–3 minutes, add stock, currants and cooked chickpeas. Bring to the boil, stirring often. Reduce heat, cover and cook in the preheated oven for 30 minutes, or until the rice is tender and the stock has been absorbed.

Allow to stand for 5 minutes before serving. Check seasoning, then add parsley and coriander and serve.

Lamb, chickpea and saffron pilaf
Omit pumpkin. Brown 500 g lean diced lamb in oil, remove and set aside. Cook onions, etc; return lamb to the pot with stock.

Chicken, sultana and sweet spice pilaf
Omit pumpkin; add 500g diced chicken to cooking onions and seal. Add 1 tsp each of cinnamon, allspice and cardamom. Cook until fragrant. Continue as directed by recipe, swapping currants for sultanas and chickpeas for a handful of toasted flaked almonds.

Chicken and asparagus risotto

Serves 4–6

This is arguably the most popular risotto of all. It's also one of the most adaptable, as you can add myriad other ingredients such as spinach, peas, sweet potato or pumpkin.

300 g asparagus
2 tbsp olive oil
1 onion, diced
1 clove garlic, crushed
1 leek, thinly sliced (optional)
1 carrot, finely diced (optional)
2 skinless chicken thigh fillets, diced
500 g (2½ cups) arborio rice
250 ml (1 cup) white wine
1–1¼ litres (4–5 cups) hot vegetable or chicken stock
80 g (1 cup) grated parmigiano
90 g butter, diced
2 tbsp chopped parsley
salt and freshly ground black pepper

Prepare asparagus by snapping off the woody ends and cutting the spears into 3 cm pieces. Blanch in boiling water for 2–3 minutes, then refresh under cold running water.

Heat a large heavy-based saucepan over a medium heat. Add the oil, onion, garlic, leek and carrot (if using) and cook for 3–4 minutes, until fragrant and soft. Add chicken and cook for 3–4 minutes, or until beginning to brown. Add rice and stir to coat with oil, and then cook briefly. Add wine and stir until it is absorbed.

Begin adding the hot stock – just enough to cover the rice at first, then a ladleful at a time as the stock is absorbed. Stir well with each addition of stock. Continue cooking for 15–20 minutes, until the rice is just done but each grain is still slightly firm in the centre. Add the prepared asparagus for the last 2–3 minutes of cooking.

Remove from heat. Add parmigiano, butter and parsley and stir until the risotto is creamy and the cheese has melted. Check seasoning and serve.

Chicken and pea risotto
Omit asparagus. Add 125 g (1 cup) cooked fresh (or frozen) peas for the last 2-3 minutes of cooking.

Chicken and mushroom risotto
Omit asparagus. Add 150 g sliced mushrooms with the chicken.

Risotto of chicken, mushroom and taleggio cheese

Serves 4–6

A good risotto is always a great stand-by for a successful dinner. If we have friends over mid-week or have last-minute dinner guests this is what we cook. To make it extra special, top each bowl of risotto with a slice of taleggio cheese.

2 tbsp olive oil
1 onion, diced
1 leek, thinly sliced (optional)
1 carrot, finely diced (optional)
125 g mushrooms, sliced
2 skinless chicken thigh fillets, diced
1 clove garlic, crushed
500 g (2½ cups) arborio rice

250 ml (1 cup) white wine
1¼–1½ litres (5–6 cups) hot chicken stock
90 g taleggio cheese, rind removed and diced
60 g (¾ cup) parmigiano, grated
60 g butter, diced
2 tbsp chopped parsley
salt and freshly ground black pepper

Heat a large heavy-based saucepan over a medium heat. Add oil, onion, leek and carrot (if using) and cook for 3–4 minutes until fragrant and soft. Add the mushrooms and chicken and cook for 3–4 minutes, or until beginning to brown. Add garlic and cook briefly. Add rice and stir to coat with oil, and then cook briefly. Add wine and stir until it is absorbed.

Begin adding hot stock – at first just enough to cover the rice, then a ladleful at a time as the stock is absorbed. Stir well with each addition. Continue cooking until rice is just done but each grain is still slightly firm in the centre, about 15–20 minutes.

Remove from the heat. Add the diced taleggio, parmigiano, butter and parsley and stir until the risotto is creamy and the cheese has melted. Check seasoning and serve.

Sweet potato, pancetta and pea risotto

Serves 4–6

Sweet vegetables and salty pancetta is another of our favourite flavour combinations. Ask your local deli to cut you a thick slice of pancetta, or substitute bacon or prosciutto.

1 large sweet potato, peeled, halved and cut into ½ cm slices
olive oil
salt and freshly ground black pepper
100 g pancetta, diced
1 onion, diced
1 clove garlic, crushed
1 leek, thinly sliced (optional)
1 carrot, finely diced (optional)

500 g (2 ½ cups) arborio rice
250 ml (1 cup) white wine
1–1¼ litres (4–5 cups) hot vegetable or chicken stock
100 g podded peas
80 g (1 cup) grated parmigiano
90 g butter, diced
2 tbsp chopped parsley

Preheat oven to 180°C.

Toss the sweet potato with oil, salt and pepper. Roast in the preheated oven for 15–20 minutes, or until the sweet potato is tender and golden. Set aside.

Heat a large heavy-based saucepan over a medium heat. Add oil and pancetta and cook for 5–6 minutes, until crispy. Remove pancetta from heat and set aside.

Wipe pan clean of any fat and return to the heat. Add 2 tbsp oil, the onion, garlic, leek and carrot (if using) and cook for 3–4 minutes, until fragrant and soft. Add rice and stir to coat with oil, and then cook briefly. Add wine and stir until it is absorbed.

Begin adding the hot stock – just enough to cover the rice at first, then a ladleful at a time as the stock is absorbed. Stir well with each addition of stock. Continue cooking for 15–20 minutes, until the rice is just done but each grain is still slightly firm in the centre. Add pancetta, sweet potato and peas for the last 5 minutes of cooking.

Remove from heat. Add the parmigiano, butter and parsley and stir until the risotto is creamy and the cheese has melted. Check seasoning and serve.

Risotto of prawns with peas and radicchio

Serves 4–6

Risotto with seafood gets even better when the seafood is prawns. Here it is balanced with peas and radicchio to create a classic summer meal. If you have the time, a seafood stock made with the prawn shells is best.

2 tbsp olive oil	200 g (2 cups) podded peas
1 onion, diced	500 g green (raw) prawns, peeled and de-veined
1 clove garlic, crushed	1 small radicchio, thickly sliced
1 leek, thinly sliced	80 g (1 cup) grated parmigiano
1 carrot, finely diced	90 g butter, diced
500 g (2½ cups) arborio rice	2 tbsp chopped parsley
250 ml (1 cup) white wine	salt and freshly ground black pepper
1–1¼ litres (4–5 cups) hot seafood, vegetable or chicken stock	

Heat a large heavy-based saucepan over a medium heat. Add the oil, onion, garlic, leek and carrot and cook for 3–4 minutes, until fragrant and soft. Add rice and stir to coat with oil, and then cook briefly. Add wine and stir until it is absorbed.

Begin adding the hot stock – just enough to cover the rice at first, then a ladleful at a time as the stock is absorbed. Stir well with each addition of stock. Continue cooking for 15–20 minutes, until the rice is just done but each grain is still slightly firm in the centre. Add peas for the last 5 minutes of cooking. When nearly ready, add the prawns and cook for 2 minutes. Add sliced radicchio and cook for a further 2 minutes.

Remove from heat. Add the parmigiano, butter and parsley and stir until the risotto is creamy and the cheese has melted. Check seasoning and serve.

Asparagus and prawn risotto

Serves 4–6

This dish is a must when spring arrives and asparagus comes into its own. If you have the time, a stock made with the prawn shells is best; otherwise use chicken or vegetable stock.

- 500 g asparagus spears
- 2 tbsp olive oil
- 1 onion, diced
- 1 leek, thinly sliced
- 1 carrot, finely diced
- 1 garlic clove, crushed
- 500 g (2½ cups) arborio rice
- 250 ml (1 cup) white wine
- 1½ litres (6 cups) hot seafood, chicken or vegetable stock
- 500 g green (raw) prawns, peeled and de-veined
- 80 g (1 cup) grated parmigiano
- 90 g butter, diced
- 2 tbsp chopped parsley
- salt and freshly ground black pepper

Prepare asparagus by snapping the woody ends off and cut tips into 3 cm pieces on the angle. Blanch in boiling water for 1–2 minutes, then refresh under cold running water. Set aside.

Heat a large heavy-based saucepan over a medium heat. Add oil, onion, leek, carrot and garlic and cook for 3–4 minutes until fragrant and soft. Add rice and stir to coat with oil, and then cook briefly. Add wine and stir until it is absorbed. Begin adding hot stock – at first just enough to cover the rice, then a ladleful at a time as the stock is absorbed. Stir well with each addition. Continue cooking until rice is just done but each grain is still slightly firm in the centre, about 15–20 minutes. Add prawns and cook for 2 minutes. Add asparagus and cook for a further 2 minutes. Remove from the heat.

Add parmigiano, butter and parsley and stir until risotto is creamy and cheese has melted. Check seasoning and serve.

Risotto with rocket and gorgonzola

Serves 4–6

This dish packs a punch with peppery rocket and salty gorgonzola. It makes a perfect entree, particularly for vegetarians.

- 2 tbsp olive oil
- 1 onion, diced
- 1 clove garlic, crushed
- 1 leek, thinly sliced (optional)
- 1 carrot, finely diced (optional)
- 500 g (2½ cups) arborio rice
- 250 ml (1 cup) white wine
- 1–1¼ litres (4–5 cups) hot vegetable or chicken stock
- 100 g wild rocket
- 60 g (¾ cup) grated parmigiano
- 120 g crumbled gorgonzola
- 90 g butter, diced
- 2 tbsp chopped parsley
- salt and freshly ground black pepper

Heat a large heavy-based saucepan over a medium heat. Add the oil, onion, garlic, leek and carrot (if using) and cook for 3–4 minutes, until fragrant and soft. Add rice and stir to coat with oil, and then cook briefly. Add wine and stir until it is absorbed.

Begin adding the hot stock – just enough to cover the rice at first, then a ladleful at a time as the stock is absorbed. Stir well with each addition of stock. Continue cooking for 15–20 minutes, until the rice is just done but each grain is still slightly firm in the centre.

Remove from heat. Add the rocket, parmigiano, gorgonzola, butter and parsley, and stir until the risotto is creamy and the cheese has melted. Check seasoning and serve.

Tuscan bean risotto

Serves 4–6

It's ideal if you had Tuscan Bean Stew (page 421) for dinner the previous night and have leftovers, as you can use them in this recipe. What usually happens, though, is that you start to crave this risotto and have to make the bean stew especially for this dish.

2 tbsp olive oil
1 onion, diced
1 clove garlic, crushed
1 leek, thinly sliced (optional)
1 carrot, finely diced (optional)
500 g (2½ cups) arborio rice
250 ml (1 cup) white wine
1–1¼ litres (4–5 cups) hot vegetable or chicken stock
½ quantity Tuscan Bean Stew (page 421)
80 g (1 cup) grated parmigiano
90 g butter, diced
2 tbsp chopped parsley
salt and freshly ground black pepper

Heat a large heavy-based saucepan over a medium heat. Add the oil, onion, garlic, leek and carrot (if using) and cook for 3–4 minutes, until fragrant and soft. Add rice and stir to coat with oil, and then cook briefly. Add wine and stir until it is absorbed.

Begin adding the hot stock – just enough to cover the rice at first, then a ladleful at a time as the stock is absorbed. Stir well with each addition of stock. Continue cooking for 15–20 minutes, until the rice is just done but each grain is still slightly firm in the centre. Add Tuscan Bean Stew for the last 5 minutes of cooking.

Remove from heat. Add the parmigiano, butter and parsley and stir until the risotto is creamy and the cheese has melted. Check seasoning and serve.

Spezzatino risotto
Any classic casserole can be added to the risotto for the last 5 minutes of cooking. Spezzatino (page 398) is another good example.

Spring risotto

Serves 4–6

We like to make this vegetable risotto with chicken stock because it creates a richer dish, but you can use vegetable stock if you prefer.

1 kg broad beans
500 g asparagus spears
2 tbsp olive oil
1 onion, finely diced
1 leek, thinly sliced
1 clove garlic, crushed
500 g (2½ cups) arborio rice
250 ml (1 cup) white wine
1–1¼ litres (4–5 cups) hot vegetable stock
80 g (1 cup) grated parmigiano
90 g butter, diced
2 tbsp chopped parsley
salt and freshly ground black pepper

Bring a large pot of water to the boil. Pod broad beans and blanch for 2–3 minutes, then remove and refresh under cold running water. Remove and discard pale green skins from broad beans. Prepare asparagus by snapping the woody ends off and cut spears into 3 cm pieces. Blanch in boiling water for 2–3 minutes, then refresh under cold running water.

Heat a large heavy-based pan over medium heat. Add oil and onion, leek and garlic and cook for 3–4 minutes until fragrant and soft. Add rice and stir to coat with oil. Pour in white wine and stir until it is absorbed. Begin adding the hot stock – at first just enough to cover the rice, then a ladleful at a time as the stock is absorbed. Stir well with each addition.

Continue cooking until the rice is done but each grain is still slightly firm in the centre, about 15–20 minutes. Add asparagus spears and broad beans and remove from the heat. Add cheese, butter and parsley and stir until risotto is creamy and cheese has melted. Check seasoning and serve.

Mushroom risotto with truffle oil

Serves 4–6

Being fairly rich, this risotto lends itself to small portions. We typically have it alongside things like roast chicken, pot-roasted veal or pan-fried steaks.

- 2 tbsp olive oil
- 1 onion, diced
- 1 clove garlic, crushed
- 1 leek, thinly sliced (optional)
- 1 carrot, finely diced (optional)
- 250 g Swiss brown mushrooms, sliced
- 500 g (2½ cups) arborio rice
- 250 ml (1 cup) white wine
- 1–1¼ litres (4–5 cups) hot vegetable stock
- 80 g (1 cup) grated parmigiano
- 90 g butter, diced
- 2 tbsp chopped parsley
- 2–3 tsp truffle oil
- salt and freshly ground black pepper

Heat a large heavy-based saucepan over a medium heat. Add oil, onion, garlic, leek and carrot (if using) and cook for 3–4 minutes until fragrant and soft. Add mushrooms and cook for 3–4 minutes, or until soft. Add rice and stir to coat with oil, and then cook briefly. Add wine and stir until it is absorbed.

Begin adding hot stock – at first just enough to cover the rice, then a ladleful at a time as the stock is absorbed. Stir well with each addition. Continue cooking until the rice is just done, about 15–20 minutes. Remove from the heat. Add parmigiano, butter, parsley and truffle oil and stir until risotto is creamy and cheese has melted. Check seasoning and serve.

Porcini and truffle oil risotto
Use only half of the mushrooms. Soak 10 g dried porcini mushrooms in 90 ml (⅓ cup) of boiling water. Add this soaking liquid to the risotto, reducing the stock by the same amount, and combine porcini mushrooms with the other mushrooms.

Roast pumpkin, feta and pine nut risotto

Serves 4–6

The feta in this risotto adds a lovely salty hit to the rice, while the toasted pine nuts bring a nutty crunch.

200 g pumpkin, diced 2 cm
2 tbsp olive oil
salt and freshly ground black pepper
2 tbsp olive oil, additional
1 onion, diced
1 clove garlic, crushed
1 leek, thinly sliced (optional)
1 carrot, finely diced (optional)

500 g (2½ cups) arborio rice
250 ml (1 cup) white wine
1–1¼ litres (4–5 cups) hot vegetable stock
60 g (¾ cup) pine nuts, toasted
30 g (⅓ cup) parmigiano, grated
60 g feta, crumbled
90 g butter, diced
2 tbsp chopped parsley

Preheat oven to 180°C.

Toss pumpkin with oil, salt and pepper. Roast in the preheated oven for 15–20 minutes, or until pumpkin is tender and golden. Set aside.

Heat a large heavy-based saucepan over a medium heat. Add oil, onion, garlic, leek and carrot (if using) and cook for 3–4 minutes until fragrant and soft. Add rice and stir to coat with oil, and then cook briefly. Add wine and stir until it is absorbed.

Begin adding hot stock – at first just enough to cover the rice, then a ladleful at a time as the stock is absorbed. Stir well with each addition. Continue cooking until rice is just done, about 15–20 minutes. Add pumpkin and pine nuts and stir through, then cook for 1–2 minutes. Remove from the heat. Add cheeses, butter and parsley and stir until risotto is creamy and cheese has melted. Check seasoning and serve.

Wild mushroom risotto

Serves 4–6

Although a complete dish in its own right, this risotto makes a great side dish for meals such as roast meats or Spezzatino (page 398).

- 50 g dried porcini mushrooms
- 250 ml (1 cup) boiling water
- 2 tbsp olive oil
- 1 onion, diced
- 1 clove garlic, crushed
- 1 leek, thinly sliced (optional)
- 1 carrot, finely diced (optional)
- 500 g (2½ cups) arborio rice
- 250 ml (1 cup) white wine
- 1–1¼ litres (4–5 cups) hot vegetable or chicken stock
- 80 g (1 cup) grated parmigiano
- 90 g butter, diced
- 2 tbsp chopped parsley
- salt and freshly ground black pepper

Pour boiling water over the porcini mushrooms and allow to stand for 20 minutes.

Heat a large heavy-based saucepan over a medium heat. Add the oil, onion, garlic, leek and carrot (if using) and cook for 3–4 minutes, until fragrant and soft. Add rice and stir to coat with oil, and then cook briefly. Add wine and stir until it is absorbed.

Drain the mushrooms, reserving the soaking water. Add the mushrooms to the pan, cook briefly, then add the reserved soaking water.

Begin adding the hot stock – just enough to cover the rice at first, then a ladleful at a time as the stock is absorbed. Stir well with each addition of stock. Continue cooking for 15–20 minutes, until the rice is just done but each grain is still slightly firm in the centre.

Remove from heat. Add the parmigiano, butter and parsley and stir until the risotto is creamy and the cheese has melted. Check seasoning and serve.

Mushroom risotto cakes

Makes 12

Risotto cakes are an easy way of enjoying the flavours of risotto in a patty that can be cooked on the barbecue or in a pan. We've yet to come across someone who doesn't like them. Try them with your favourite salad.

2 tbsp olive oil
1 onion, finely diced
½ small carrot, finely diced
1 clove garlic, crushed
90 g Swiss brown mushrooms, thinly sliced
200 g (1 cup) arborio rice
750 ml (3 cups) hot vegetable or chicken stock

60 g (¾ cup) parmigiano, grated
15 basil leaves, thinly sliced
1 egg
25 g (¼ cup) dry breadcrumbs
salt and freshly ground black pepper
additional dry breadcrumbs
olive oil

Heat a large saucepan over a medium heat. Add oil, onion, carrot and garlic and cook for 2 minutes, stirring regularly. Add mushrooms and cook for 3–4 minutes. Add rice and cook for 1 minute, stirring well. Add stock to saucepan and simmer until liquid is absorbed, about 12 minutes. Allow to cool slightly, and then stir in parmigiano, basil, egg and breadcrumbs. Season to taste.

Divide into 12 and pat into round cakes. Sprinkle each cake with additional breadcrumbs. Heat a heavy-based frying pan over a medium–high heat. Add a splash of oil and risotto cakes. Cook for 3–4 minutes on each side until golden brown.

Roasted eggplant risotto cakes
Dice, salt, rinse and roast 1 eggplant until soft. Omit mushrooms and add cooked eggplant to the rice for the last 2 minutes of cooking. Try this with any other vegetables, such as asparagus or pumpkin.

Arancini
Roll mushroom risotto mix into small balls. Coat with breadcrumbs and deep-fry until golden brown. Serve with Quince Aioli (page 550).

Vegetable risotto cakes

Makes 12

You can make these risotto cakes from scratch or use leftover risotto to create a similar result.

2 tbsp olive oil
1 onion, finely diced
1 clove garlic, crushed
½ small carrot, finely diced
1 small zucchini, finely diced
1 small eggplant, finely diced
50 g pumpkin, finely diced
200 g (1 cup) arborio rice
750 ml (3 cups) hot vegetable or chicken stock
60 g (¾ cup) grated parmigiano
15 basil leaves, thinly sliced
1 egg
35 g (⅓ cup) dry breadcrumbs
salt and freshly ground black pepper
dry breadcrumbs, additional
oil

Heat a large saucepan over a medium heat. Add the oil, onion, garlic and carrot and cook for 2 minutes, stirring regularly. Add the zucchini, eggplant and pumpkin and cook for 5–6 minutes. Add rice and cook for 1 minute, stirring well. Pour in the stock and simmer for 12 minutes, until the liquid is absorbed. Allow to cool slightly, and then stir in the parmigiano, basil, egg and breadcrumbs. Season to taste.

Divide into 12 portions and pat into round cakes. Sprinkle each cake with additional breadcrumbs. Heat a heavy-based frypan over a medium–high heat. Add a splash of oil and the risotto cakes and cook for 3–4 minutes on each side, until golden brown.

Paella

Serves 4

Paella is made with short-grain rice, or you can purchase special paella rice at most top quality food stores. A paella pan makes light work of keeping all the ingredients together.

2 tbsp olive oil
2 onions, diced
6–8 small cloves garlic
pinch of saffron threads
1 tsp smoked paprika
400 g (2 cups) paella rice
1 litre (4 cups) chicken stock
90 g (½ cup) pitted olives
500 g chicken drumettes, roasted until golden
1 red capsicum, roasted, peeled and de-seeded and cut into long strips
500 g green (raw) prawns, peeled and de-veined
500 g mussels, de-bearded
2 tbsp chopped parsley

Place a large heavy-based frypan over a medium heat. Heat oil, add onions, garlic and saffron and cook for 4–5 minutes, stirring often. Add paprika, cook for 1–2 minutes, then add rice and cook briefly for 2–3 minutes, stirring often. Add most of the stock and allow to come to the boil, stirring often.

Add olives, roasted chicken and capsicum. Reduce heat and allow to cook for 15 minutes, stirring often. You may need to add more stock. Check that the rice is nearly cooked, add prawns and mussels and cook until mussels open (discard any that do not) and prawns turn pink.

Serve immediately with chopped parsley.

Spring Spanish rice with chicken, peas and lemon

Serves 4–6

This dish is inspired by the wonderful tapas restaurant MoVida in Melbourne. It is basically a paella using chicken, and is livened up with fiery harissa, the crunch of new-season peas and the zest of lemons. A one-pot meal, all it needs is a green salad.

2 red capsicums
olive oil
600 g skinless chicken thighs, diced 2 cm
2 cloves garlic, chopped
grated zest of 1 lemon
2 tsp harissa
2 tsp smoky paprika
salt and freshly ground black pepper

2 red onions, chopped
pinch of saffron threads
500 g (2½ cups) paella rice
125 ml (½ cup) white wine
750 ml (3 cups) chicken stock
250 g (2 cups) podded peas
¼ cup chopped flat-leaf parsley
2 tbsp lemon-infused olive oil

Preheat oven to 180°C.

Rub the capsicums with oil. Place them on a baking tray and roast for 30 minutes, or until their skins blister. Allow to cool, and then remove the skin and seeds. Cut the flesh into 1 cm strips.

Meanwhile, place the chicken in a bowl with the garlic, lemon zest, harissa, smoky paprika and 60 ml (¼ cup) olive oil. Season with salt and pepper. Marinate for at least 20 minutes.

Heat a large paella pan or frypan over medium heat. Add the chicken and fry for 6–8 minutes, stirring often, until golden brown. Remove from the pan and set aside.

Return the pan to the heat, add a splash more oil if needed and fry the onions for 4–5 minutes. Add the saffron and cook for 1–2 minutes until fragrant. Add the rice and cook for 2–3 minutes, stirring often, until lightly toasted. Add the wine, stirring well, and cook until it has reduced slightly, then add the stock. Bring to the boil, return the chicken to the pan, reduce the heat to a simmer and cook for 15–20 minutes, stirring often, until almost all the stock has been absorbed by the rice. Add the peas and capsicums and cook for another 3–4 minutes. Stir well for the last 2–3 minutes, ensuring the peas cook through and the remaining stock is absorbed. Add more stock or water if necessary. Taste for seasoning and add the parsley and lemon-infused olive oil. Stir through and serve.

Nasi goreng (stir-fried rice)

Serves 2

For those times when you have leftover rice, here's the perfect thing to do with it. You can add anything to this, any cooked meat or fish that is on hand.

2 eggs
peanut oil
4 red or golden shallots, diced
1 small red chilli, de-seeded and finely diced
1 carrot, finely diced
½ chicken breast, finely diced
60 g bean sprouts
1 bunch bok choy, thinly sliced
2 tbsp soy sauce
3 cups cold cooked rice
fried onions (optional)
coriander leaves to garnish

Beat eggs together lightly. Heat wok over a high heat, add a splash of oil, add eggs and swirl well to coat the sides of the wok with egg mix. Cook briefly, then lift one edge away from wok and roll omelette up. Tip onto a chopping board, allow to cool.

Return wok to the heat, add another splash of oil, and then add shallots, chilli and carrot. Cook for 2–3 minutes, stirring often. Add chicken, bean sprouts and bok choy and cook for a further 2–3 minutes, stirring. Add soy sauce, then add rice, breaking up if needed. Continue cooking and stirring constantly until rice is coloured by the sauce and heated through.

Slice omelette thinly, add to the wok with fried onions if using and toss to combine. Serve immediately, topped with coriander.

noodles

Noodles are a great resource to have on hand in the kitchen cupboard. We typically have dried vermicelli, udon and buckwheat noodles, and purchase fresh Hokkien and chow mein noodles to refrigerate or freeze for longer storage. We also source fresh rice noodles from Asian grocers as the need arises.

Things you need to know about noodles

1 When preparing fresh noodles we usually pour boiling water over them and set them aside.

2 Hokkien and flat egg noodles are our fresh noodles of choice. They need to be set aside in boiling water for 4-5 minutes to heat through.

3 You can also add fresh noodles to a pot of boiling water, allow the water to return to the boil and then drain the noodles before using.

4 When preparing dried noodles we add them to a saucepan of boiling water.

5 Vermicelli and rice noodles are our dried noodles of choice. They need to be boiled for a few minutes to become tender.

6 Dried noodles can be added to soups and broths straight from the packet.

7 Dried soba noodles and udon noodles are also great to have on hand for use in Japanese salads and soups. They need to be cooked in boiling water for 6-8 minutes, until tender.

types of noodles

CELLOPHANE NOODLES

Cellophane noodles are made with mung beans and are often labelled as mung bean vermicelli. They are usually sold in clear plastic packets with the noodles tied up with distinctive striped strands of string. Cellophane noodles need to be cooked in boiling water to soften them before they are used. Once softened in this manner they will keep for many hours before using, and will not stick together.

CHOW MEIN EGG NOODLES

Chow mein egg noodles are used extensively in Chinese cooking for wok stir-fried dishes; the name chow mein literally means fried noodles. As there is such a wide choice of top-quality fresh chow mein noodles, we rarely bother with the dried variety. The noodles come in a variety of widths – thin, round or flat ribbons. Fresh noodles will keep refrigerated for 3–4 days, and they freeze well. They can be used in the last moments of stir-frying and tossed to combine with the other ingredients. The thin round noodles can also be served cold in salads.

HOKKIEN NOODLES

Fat, round and fabulous, Hokkien noodles are made in much the same way as chow mein noodles, but they are softer and thicker. You will find them in white and yellow varieties, and they are generally fresh rather than dried. The noodles take 3–4 minutes to cook in boiling water and they have a satisfying gluey texture. You can never get them crispy-fried like chow mein noodles, but you can stir-fry them quite satisfactorily. They are often called Shanghai noodles.

RICE RIBBON NOODLES

Rice ribbon noodles can be purchased either dried or fresh; fresh noodles are superior in texture and they're easier to handle. You will find fresh pre-packed rice ribbon noodles or rice noodle sheets in Asian grocers. There are also loose rice noodles available in plastic trays or waxed boxes. Pre-packed rice noodles or rice noodle sheets need to sit at room temperature for 30 minutes before using to allow them to soften. Unfold the sheets carefully and cut them into desired thickness. Rice ribbon noodles are most frequently used in broth, such as the traditional Vietnamese pho. Add rice ribbon noodles only at the last moment of cooking and take care not to boil the broth, or the noodles will disintegrate.

RICE VERMICELLI NOODLES

Rice vermicelli noodles are made from ground rice and water. Look for packets marked with the word rice so as not to confuse them with the similar-looking mung bean vermicelli variety. They are also sometimes labelled rice stick noodles. Rice vermicelli noodles are difficult to separate without breaking, so buy a quantity to suit your purpose. The noodles need to be cooked in boiling water to soften. Don't prepare them too far in advance as they stick together. Once drained, rice vermicelli noodles can be eaten cold as a salad base for grilled meats, or hot in curry laksa, stir-fried Singapore noodles and spring rolls.

SOBA AND UDON NOODLES

Japanese soba noodles get their distinctive colour from a combination of wheat and buckwheat flours. Typically bought dried (like pasta), these noodles can occasionally be found fresh at good Japanese stores or health-food shops. Udon noodles are a white Japanese variety made from wheat, and they're used in similar ways to soba noodles. Soba and udon noodles are cooked in the same way as pasta – plunged into boiling salted water straight from the packet and cooked until tender. Drain the noodles in a colander, and refresh them under cold running water if serving them cold. Soba and udon noodles can be used in stir-fries and soups, but traditionally they are served cold as an appetiser with a mirin dipping sauce.

Chicken, ginger and noodle stir-fry

Serves 3–4

This stock-standard stir-fry has a gutsy flavour base of garlic and chilli, with plenty of ginger to spice things up.

375 g fresh chow mein noodles
2 tbsp peanut oil
1 clove garlic, crushed
1 small red chilli, de-seeded and finely diced
2–3 tsp grated ginger
4 spring onions, sliced
2 skinless chicken breast fillets, sliced
chicken stock or water
soy sauce

Put the kettle on to boil, then pour boiling water over the noodles and set them aside.

Place a wok over a high heat. Add oil, then garlic, chilli, ginger and spring onions. Cook for 1–2 minutes, stirring often to avoid burning, until fragrant. Add sliced chicken and cook for a further 2–3 minutes, until browned.

Add a splash of stock or water, cover with a lid and cook for 3–4 minutes. Add more stock if necessary.

Drain the noodles and add them to the wok with soy sauce to taste. Serve immediately.

Chicken, cashew and noodle stir-fry
Add 100 g (⅔ cup) roasted cashews with the noodles.

Chicken, black bean and noodle stir-fry
Add 2 tbsp soaked and chopped black beans with the chicken.

Chicken, oyster sauce and noodle stir-fry
Add 1 tbsp oyster sauce with noodles, omitting soy sauce.

Chicken, broccoli and noodle stir-fry
Add 100 g broccolini or broccoli florets when about to cover.

Teriyaki chicken udon stir-fry for Mia

Serves 3–4

This dish appeals to all ages, and our daughter Mia just loves it. This one's for you, baby.

- 2 skinless chicken breast fillets, sliced into strips
- 80 ml (⅓ cup) soy sauce
- 2 tbsp mirin
- 2 tsp grated ginger
- 1 tsp sesame oil
- 1 tsp caster sugar
- 1 clove garlic, crushed
- 375 g udon noodles
- oil
- 1 onion, sliced
- 1 carrot, sliced
- 1 small bunch baby bok choy, washed
- 2 spring onions, green tops only, thinly sliced

Place the chicken in a bowl then add the soy sauce, mirin, ginger, sesame oil, caster sugar and garlic. Leave to marinate in the refrigerator for 1 hour. Drain the chicken well and retain the marinade.

Put a saucepan of water on to boil for the noodles.

Place a wok over a high heat. Add a splash of oil and onion, cook for 1–2 minutes until soft. Add carrot and the drained chicken and cook for 2–3 minutes, stirring often. Add the marinade and bok choy, cover the wok. Allow to simmer for 5 minutes.

Cook the udon noodles in boiling water for 2–3 minutes, until tender. Drain well, and then add them to the wok, tossing them briefly with the chicken.

Scatter with spring onions and serve immediately.

Teriyaki beef
Substitute 500 g beef fillet for the chicken fillet.

Beef, black bean and cashew nut stir-fry

Serves 4

This is our spin on the beef and black bean flavour combination we're all very familiar with. Using steak, as we do here, guarantees the finished dish will be tender and delicious.

2 × 200 g porterhouse steaks
2 tbsp black beans, soaked and chopped
2 tsp chilli paste
2 tbsp peanut oil
375 g Hokkien noodles
1–2 tbsp peanut oil
½ red capsicum, sliced
4 spring onions, sliced
2–3 bok choy
90 g (⅔ cup) roasted cashew nuts
soy sauce to taste

Coat steaks with black beans and chilli paste and marinate for at least 30 minutes.

Preheat oven to 180°C.

Heat a heavy-based frying pan over a medium heat, add oil and brown steak well, then transfer to baking dish and cook in preheated oven for 10 minutes until medium–rare. Allow steaks to rest, and then slice.

Put the kettle on to boil, then pour boiling water over noodles and set aside.

Place wok over high heat; add peanut oil, then capsicum, spring onions and bok choy. Cook briefly until vegetables soften. Add hot noodles, cashew nuts, soy sauce to taste and sliced beef. Cook briefly, stirring occasionally to combine. Serve immediately.

Chilli beef stir-fry

Serves 4

This is one of the quickest stir-fries around, and one of the tastiest. I like it because it's quick, spicy and great for an iron hit, not to mention the decadence of using eye fillet. All you'll need is a bowl of steamed rice or some noodles to serve with it. MC

400 g eye fillet
1 tbsp peanut oil
1 bunch baby bok choy, leaves separated and washed
80 ml (⅓ cup) sweet chilli sauce
80 ml (⅓ cup) soy sauce
3 spring onions, thinly chopped
100 g (⅔ cup) roasted peanuts (optional)
Steamed Rice (page 198) or hot noodles to serve

Cut eye fillet into 1 cm slices, and then cut each slice into 1 cm strips.

Heat a wok over a high heat, add oil, swirl around wok and add beef. Toss and cook for 2–3 minutes, or until beef is well browned. Add bok choy, stir well, and then add chilli sauce, soy sauce, spring onions and peanuts (if using). Allow to heat through and serve immediately with Steamed Rice or hot noodles.

Chilli kangaroo stir-fry
Substitute sliced kangaroo sirloin for beef fillet.

Chilli beef and mushroom stir-fry
Add 125 g quartered mushrooms at the same time as the beef.

Sour beef with lemongrass

Serves 4

As the name suggests, sour beef with lemongrass is a full-flavoured dish with the gutsy taste of tamarind, blended with the fresher fragrance of lemongrass and lime juice.

1 lemongrass stem, sliced thinly
2 green chillies, de-seeded and finely diced
1 onion, peeled and chopped
1–2 tbsp peanut oil
60 g tamarind
125 ml (½ cup) boiling water
oil
400 g scotch fillet
1 bunch snake beans, cut into 3 cm lengths (optional)
1 tbsp shaved palm sugar
1 tbsp fish sauce
juice of 1 lime
Steamed Rice (page 198) or noodles to serve

Place the lemongrass, chillies, onion and oil in food processor. Process until the paste is smooth. Soak the tamarind in boiling water for 15–20 minutes. Use your fingers to work the pulp free from the tamarind seeds, strain and reserve liquid. Cut steak into 1 cm slices, and then cut each slice into 1 cm strips.

Place wok over a high heat, add oil, swirl around wok and add paste. Cook for 2–3 minutes, or until distinctly fragrant. Add beef. Toss and cook for 2–3 minutes, or until the beef is well browned. Add beans if using, then pour tamarind liquid in. Add palm sugar and fish sauce. Toss, still cooking, for 2–3 minutes, until well combined. Season with lime juice to taste. Serve immediately with Steamed Rice (page 198) or noodles.

Barbecue pork and bok choy stir-fry

Serves 3–4

Barbecue pork, or char siew or as it is sometimes called, can be bought at any Asian roast house.

200 g cellophane noodles
1 tbsp peanut oil
4 spring onions, thinly sliced
½ red capsicum, thinly sliced
250 g barbecue pork, thinly sliced
2 bunches bok choy, washed and sliced
chicken stock or water
90 g bean sprouts
2 tbsp soy sauce
crispy fried shallots to garnish

Put the kettle on to boil, then pour boiling water over noodles and set aside.

Place wok over a high heat; add peanut oil, then spring onions and capsicum. Cook for 1–2 minutes, stirring often. Add the barbecue pork, bok choy and a splash of stock. Cover with lid and cook for 3–4 minutes.

Drain the noodles and add to the wok with bean sprouts and soy sauce. Stir until hot, top with crispy fried shallots and serve.

Barbecue pork and noodle stir-fry

Serves 3–4

This is a really flavoursome mix of barbecue pork with noodles and greens. It can be easily whipped up for a quick dinner.

375 g Hokkien noodles
1 bunch Chinese broccoli
2 tbsp peanut oil
1 clove garlic, crushed
1 small red chilli, de-seeded and finely diced
2–3 tsp grated ginger
4 spring onions, sliced
200 g barbecue pork, thinly sliced
chicken stock or water
soy sauce to taste

Put the kettle on to boil. Pour boiling water over noodles and set aside.

Wash Chinese broccoli well, remove tough outer leaves and slice stems and leaves on the angle into 2 cm slices.

Place wok over high heat; add peanut oil, then garlic, chilli, ginger and spring onions. Cook for 1–2 minutes, stirring often to avoid burning, until fragrant. Add pork and Chinese broccoli, cook briefly, then add a splash of stock or water, cover with lid and cook for 2 minutes.

Drain noodles. Add hot noodles to wok and more stock if necessary. Toss, still cooking, for 2–3 minutes, until well combined. Season with soy sauce to taste. Serve immediately.

Barbecue pork and sweet chilli noodles
Use just 1 tsp ginger and add 1–2 tbsp sweet chilli sauce (depending on your tastes) with noodles.

Barbecue duck and Hokkien noodles
Substitute half a roast duck for pork. Remove flesh from bones, discarding excess fat; slice into 1 cm pieces.

Honey roast pork with stir-fried noodles

Serves 3–4

Whether it's served at a dinner-party or as an everyday meal, this pork dish is an absolute winner.

2 tbsp soy sauce	1 clove garlic, crushed
2 tbsp honey	1 small red chilli, de-seeded and diced
½ tsp sesame oil	2–3 tsp grated ginger
500 g pork fillet	4 spring onions, sliced
375 g dried rice noodles	100 g (¾ cup) roasted cashews
1 bunch Chinese broccoli	chicken stock or water
2 tbsp peanut oil	soy sauce

Preheat oven to 180°C.

Place the 2 tbsp soy sauce, honey and sesame oil in a small saucepan. Cook over a medium heat until reduced to a thick syrup.

Place the pork in a baking dish. Brush honey mixture over and cook in the preheated oven for 15–20 minutes, by which stage it should be cooked to medium.

Put the kettle on to boil. Pour boiling water over the noodles and set them aside.

Wash the broccoli well. Remove the tough outer leaves and slice the stems and leaves on an angle into 2 cm slices.

Place a wok over a high heat. Add peanut oil, then the garlic, chilli, ginger and spring onions. Cook for 1–2 minutes, stirring often to avoid burning, until fragrant. Add the sliced Chinese broccoli and cashews. Cook briefly, and then add a splash of stock or water. Cover with a lid and cook for 2 minutes.

Drain the noodles and add them to the wok, along with more stock or water if the stir-fry is looking a little dry. Toss while cooking for 2–3 minutes, until well combined. Season with soy sauce to taste.

Slice the roast pork. Place the stir-fried noodles on a serving platter and arrange the pork over the top. Serve immediately.

Pad Thai (Thai rice noodles)

Serves 2–3

What we really like about this dish is that we generally have most of these ingredients on hand, so it's become a cupboard-dinner stand-by.

100 g thin rice stick noodles
oil
3 spring onions, thinly sliced
1 clove garlic, crushed
2 small red chilli, de-seeded and finely diced, or 2 tsp chilli sauce
2 eggs, lightly beaten
2 tbsp fish sauce
1 tbsp shaved palm sugar
120 g bean sprouts
60 g (⅓ cup) roasted peanuts
fresh coriander leaves
lime wedges to serve

Put the kettle on to boil. Pour boiling water over noodles and set aside.

Place wok over high heat; add oil, then spring onions, garlic and chilli. Cook for 1–2 minutes, stirring often to avoid burning, until fragrant. Push to one side, add eggs, allow them to just set lightly, and then scramble them by stirring well. Drain noodles and add to wok with fish sauce, palm sugar, bean sprouts and peanuts. Stir constantly until heated through, 3–4 minutes.

Serve immediately with coriander leaves and lime wedges.

Chow mein

Serves 3–4

For many people, chow mein brings back memories of very ordinary Chinese take-away dinners. In fact, it is a classic Chinese dish and when made correctly it's excellent.

375 g fresh chow mein noodles
peanut oil
4 mushrooms, thinly sliced
1 clove garlic, crushed
3 spring onions, sliced
¼ Chinese cabbage, chopped
50 g bamboo shoots, sliced (optional)
500 g pork fillet, cut into thin strips
2 tbsp soy sauce
1 tsp sugar
2 tbsp Chinese cooking wine
salt and freshly ground black pepper

Put the kettle on to boil, then pour boiling water over the noodles and set them aside.

Place a wok over a high heat. Add 1–2 tbsp oil, then the mushrooms, garlic, spring onions, cabbage and bamboo shoots (if using). Stir-fry for 2 minutes, stirring well, then set aside in a separate dish.

Reheat the wok with 1–2 tbsp oil. Add the pork and cook for 2–3 minutes, stirring well. Add the soy sauce, sugar and wine. Stir well, and then set aside with the other cooked ingredients.

Drain the noodles well, and then reheat the wok over a high heat. Add 1–2 tbsp oil, then the drained noodles. Stir-fry well to ensure the noodles get a little colour into them. Add the pre-cooked vegetables and pork, cover with a lid and cook for 2 minutes.

Stir well, season to taste and serve immediately.

Chicken chow mein
Substitute 500 g chicken for the pork fillet.

Beef chow mein
Substitute 500 g beef for the pork fillet.

Vegetable chow mein
Substitute 500 g sliced capsicum, carrot and bok choy for the pork fillet.

Singapore noodles

Serves 3–4

Singapore noodles are great to make if you have left-over cooked chicken or pork, as either can easily be used in place of the chicken breast in the recipe. Likewise, any cooked vegetable you have can easily be incorporated.

- 375 g Hokkien noodles
- oil
- 2 eggs, whisked lightly
- 2 cloves garlic, crushed
- 1 tsp grated ginger
- 1 small red chilli, de-seeded and finely diced
- 1 skinless chicken breast fillet, thinly sliced
- ½ capsicum, finely diced
- 4 broccoli florets, chopped
- 1 carrot, peeled and thinly sliced
- 90 g sugar snap peas
- ¼ Chinese cabbage, thinly sliced
- 150 g cooked shrimp
- chicken stock or water
- 4 spring onions, thinly sliced
- 2–3 tbsp soy sauce
- fresh coriander leaves to garnish

Put the kettle on to boil. Pour boiling water over noodles and set aside.

Beat eggs together lightly. Heat wok over a high heat, add a splash of oil, add eggs and swirl well to coat the sides of the wok with egg mix. Cook briefly, then lift one edge away from wok and roll omelette up. Tip onto a chopping board and allow to cool.

Return wok to the heat. Add another splash of oil, then garlic, ginger and chilli, and cook briefly, stirring frequently, until fragrant. Add chicken and cook until browned, stirring often. Add capsicum, broccoli, carrot and sugar snap peas, cook briefly, tossing occasionally. Add wonga bok, shrimp (and cooked meat if using), stir briefly, and then add stock (or water).

Cover wok with lid and cook for 2–3 minutes, stirring once or twice. Add more stock if necessary to prevent vegetables from catching. Drain noodles and add to wok with the spring onions and soy sauce. Cook briefly, and then serve immediately with coriander leaves scattered on top.

Spicy Sichuan noodles

Serves 3–4

This is a traditional Asian dish which is often called Chinese spaghetti bolognaise. It does in fact look like bolognaise and it is served on noodles, but it cooks in a fraction of the time and has flavours of ginger, chilli and soy sauce.

375 g Hokkien noodles
1–2 tbsp peanut oil
2 cloves garlic, crushed
2 tsp grated ginger
2 small red chillies, de-seeded and finely diced
4 red or golden shallots, peeled and diced
500 g pork mince
2 tbsp Chinese rice wine
2 tbsp soy sauce
125 ml (½ cup) chicken stock
1 tsp Sichuan peppercorns, roasted and ground

Put the kettle on to boil. Pour boiling water over noodles and set aside.

Heat wok until hot. Add a splash of oil, garlic, ginger, chillies and shallots, then cook until fragrant. Add pork mince and cook, stirring often, until colour changes. Add Chinese rice wine, soy sauce and enough chicken stock to just cover. Stir until well combined, and then simmer for 5–6 minutes, lowering heat if necessary.

Check the seasoning of the pork. Drain noodles and serve immediately with sauce on top. Sprinkle with Sichuan pepper.

Chilli prawns with asparagus, shiitake mushrooms and cellophane noodles

Serves 2–3

This recipe has been specially created for those who love their seafood and noodles with plenty of chilli kick.

100 g cellophane noodles
2–3 tbsp peanut oil
1 clove garlic, crushed
2 tsp grated ginger
4 small red chillies, finely diced
250 g peeled green (raw) prawns
100 g shiitake mushrooms, sliced
100 g asparagus, cut into 3 cm pieces
2 tbsp soy sauce
¼ cup crispy fried shallots

Put the kettle on to boil. Pour boiling water over the noodles and set them aside.

Place a wok over a high heat. Add the oil, garlic, ginger and chillies. Cook for 1 minute, stirring often to avoid burning. Add the prawns and cook for 1 minute, then add the shiitake mushrooms and asparagus plus a small ladleful of water.

Cover and cook for 2 minutes.

Drain the noodles and add them to the wok, along with the soy sauce. Stir for 3–4 minutes, until heated through.

Serve immediately with crispy fried shallots on top.

Stir-fried rice noodles with prawns and snow peas

Serves 2–3

In this recipe, a classic combination of rice noodles, garlic, ginger and chilli is tossed with fresh prawns and tender snow peas to make a special meal.

100 g dried rice stick noodles
2–3 tbsp peanut oil
3 spring onions, sliced
1 clove garlic, crushed
2 tsp grated ginger
2 small red chillies, de-seeded and diced

250 g peeled green (raw) prawns
100 g snow peas, strings removed
1 tbsp fish sauce
2 tbsp soy sauce
500 g bean sprouts
1 lime, cut into wedges

Put the kettle on to boil. Pour boiling water over the noodles and set them aside.

Place a wok over a high heat. Add the oil, spring onions, garlic, ginger and chillies. Cook for 1 minute, stirring often to avoid burning. Add the prawns and cook for 1 minute, then add the snow peas plus a small ladleful of water. Cover and cook for 2 minutes.

Drain the noodles and add them to the wok with the fish sauce and soy sauce. Stir for 3–4 minutes, until heated through. Add bean sprouts and serve immediately with lime wedges.

Calamari with soy and chilli glaze

Serves 4

Calamari seems luxurious, but it's actually a very reasonably priced ingredient. This soy and chilli glaze is as good with calamari as it is with prawns or crabs. I'd like to say that we keep some calamari frozen for emergency dinners, but I can't claim any such forward planning. Any calamari that is brought into the house gets cooked and eaten straight away.

60 ml (¼ cup) soy sauce, light soy for preference
1 tsp grated ginger
2 small red chillies, de-seeded and finely diced
1 tbsp sweet chilli sauce
90 ml (⅓ cup) mirin

1 tbsp peanut oil
500 g calamari rings
1 cup Thai basil or coriander leaves
Steamed Rice (page 198) or noodles to serve

Mix together soy sauce, ginger, chilli, sweet chilli sauce and mirin.

Place wok over a high heat; add oil and calamari rings and cook, stirring with a chopstick for 2–3 minutes to ensure even cooking. When the calamari changes from translucent to white, pour in soy–chilli glaze and add basil leaves. Allow to bubble, then remove from the heat and serve immediately with Steamed Rice or noodles.

Chinese stir-fried vegetables with noodles

Serves 3–4

There are times when it's vegetables and noodles that you crave, and meat or seafood doesn't enter into the picture. This is just the thing to satisfy that need.

375 g Hokkien noodles
oil
1 clove garlic, crushed
1 tsp grated ginger
1 small red chilli, de-seeded and finely diced
4 spring onions, thinly sliced
½ capsicum, finely diced
1 carrot, peeled and thinly sliced
4 broccoli florets, chopped
90 g sugar snap peas
1 bunch Chinese broccoli, cut into 5 cm chunks
stock or water
2–3 tbsp soy sauce
fresh coriander leaves to garnish

Put the kettle on to boil. Pour boiling water over the noodles and set aside.

Place wok over a high heat, add a splash of oil and garlic, ginger, chilli and spring onions, cook briefly, stirring frequently, until fragrant. Add capsicum, carrot, broccoli and sugar snap peas, add stock (or water). Cover wok with a lid and cook for 2–3 minutes, stirring once or twice. Add Chinese broccoli and more stock if necessary, cover and cook for 1–2 minutes.

Remove the lid, stir, add soy sauce to taste and serve immediately with coriander leaves scattered on top.

Stir-fried vegetables and egg with noodles
Make an omelette using 2 eggs as in Singapore Noodles (page 236). Add with Chinese broccoli.

Stir-fried vegetables with tofu and noodles
Add 300 g firm, diced tofu with the Chinese broccoli.

Chilli stir-fried vegetables with noodles
Add another chilli and a dash of sweet chilli sauce to taste.

Vegetable stir-fry with Hokkien noodles and chilli jam

Serves 3–4

This stir-fry is for those times when you want a great vegetable dish which is easy to prepare and packed with great flavours and textures. It's also perfect if you're serving a range of meat-based Asian dishes and are looking for a way to incorporate more vegetables.

- 375 g Hokkien noodles
- peanut oil
- 2 cloves garlic, crushed
- 1 tsp grated ginger
- 1 small red chilli, de-seeded and diced
- 4 spring onions, thinly sliced
- ½ red capsicum, thinly sliced
- 1 carrot, peeled and thinly sliced
- 90 g snow peas, strings removed
- 90 g sugar snap peas, strings removed
- ¼ Chinese cabbage, thinly sliced
- 2 tbsp soy sauce
- 2 tbsp Chilli Jam (page 578)
- 2 tbsp sweet chilli sauce
- salt and freshly ground black pepper

Put the kettle on to boil. Pour boiling water over the noodles and set them aside.

Place a wok over a high heat. Add 1–2 tbsp oil, then the garlic, ginger, chilli and spring onions. Cook for 1–2 minutes, stirring well. Add capsicum, carrot, snow peas, sugar snap peas and Chinese cabbage. Stir well together for
1 minute. Add ½ cup water to the wok and cover with a lid. Leave to steam for 2–3 minutes.

Drain the noodles and add them to the wok with the soy sauce, chilli jam and sweet chilli sauce. Stir well and check seasoning. Serve immediately.

Fried tofu with cellophane noodles, shiitake mushrooms and cashews

Serves 4

This recipe includes the deep-fried golden squares of tofu which are readily available nowadays. If you find the custard-like texture of fresh tofu off-putting, then these crisp puffs are for you.

100 g cellophane noodles
2 tbsp peanut oil
100 g shiitake mushrooms, sliced
3 spring onions, green tops only, thinly sliced
160 g packet tofu puffs, cut in half if large

100 g (⅔ cup) roasted cashews
chicken stock or water
1 tbsp oyster sauce
1 tbsp light soy sauce

Put the kettle on to boil. Pour boiling water over the noodles and set them aside.

Heat a wok over a high heat. Add the oil, shiitake mushrooms and spring onions and cook for 1–2 minutes, stirring well. Add the tofu puffs and cashews, and then add a splash of stock or water. Cover with lid and steam for 2–3 minutes.

Drain the noodles and add them to the wok, along with the oyster sauce and soy sauce. Toss to combine ingredients and serve immediately.

Tofu and ginger stir-fry

Serves 2

Cleansing and refreshing, this dish always makes us feel better, especially if we've been over-indulging. Must be something to do with that ginger, so add as much as you like or need.

oil
3 spring onions, sliced
1 small red chilli, de-seeded and finely diced
2–3 tsp grated ginger
1 bunch Chinese broccoli, chopped
100 g snow peas
stock or water
300 g tofu, cut into 1 cm cubes
60 g bean sprouts
soy sauce to season
Steamed Rice (page 198) or noodles to serve

Heat wok over high heat. Add a splash of oil and spring onions, chilli and ginger and cook for 1–2 minutes, stirring, until fragrant. Add broccoli, cook and stir briefly, and then add a splash of water or stock. Cover with a lid and steam for 2–3 minutes.

Remove the lid, add snow peas, plus more liquid if required, cover and steam for 1 minute. Add tofu and bean sprouts, cover and steam for a further 2 minutes. Toss to combine ingredients, but do so carefully so as not to break up the tofu.

Serve immediately with Steamed Rice or noodles.

EVERYDAY
dinners
family-friendly meals

Whether cooking for one or for 10, the hardest question you face every day is: what's for dinner? What's ideal is something that's quick and easy, can be made from ingredients to hand and which everybody is going to enjoy. Not to mention something that results in minimal washing up.

Some families follow a strict order of meals for dinner each week. Monday is tuna mornay, Tuesday spaghetti bolognaise, and so on. We find this hard to imagine as we generally decide what we are going to eat for dinner based on the contents of the fridge at 5.30 p.m. each day. But if you can get organised, preparing a menu at the beginning of each week is a lifesaver come 5.30 p.m. when the cry goes up.

Hopefully this chapter will give you some new ideas. Most recipes can be prepared in under 30 minutes and the dishes are fairly straightforward, though we have included a bit of variety for the more adventurous palate. Stir-fries, pasta and barbecues are all ideal quick dinners, too, so don't forget to look at those chapters when dinnertime comes around.

everyday dinner recipes

Pizza	248
Roasted vegetable calzone	249
Pan-fried herb chicken fillets	250
Pan-fried chicken with mushroom sauce	250
Chicken saltimbocca	251
Chicken schnitzel	252
Luke's favourite chicken dinner	253
Chicken fajitas	254
Southern fried chicken	255
Chicken drumsticks with Italian flavours	255
Chicken fillets poached in soy and star anise	256
Spiced coriander and yoghurt chicken	256
Steamed ginger chicken	258
Chicken and veal polpettini	259
Danish beef burgers	259
Thai chicken balls	260
Lemon chicken polpettini	260
Steak with oven chips	262
Corned beef (silverside)	263
Pan-fried steak with mushroom sauce	263
Beef stroganoff	264
Birgit's frikadella	265
Savoury mince	265
Swedish meatballs	266
Lamb cutlets with red wine onions	267
Spiced lamb steaks	267
Tikka-yoghurt lamb chops	268
Lamb kofta skewers	268
Moussaka	269
Olive and thyme crumbed pork schnitzels	270
Barbecued pork sausage with spiced lentils	271
Moorish lamb with quince glaze	272
San choy bau	274
Chinese twice-cooked pork spare ribs	274
Lion's head meatballs	275
Plum and soy pork steaks	275
Katsudon (Japanese crumbed pork)	276
Veal, sage and onion meatloaf	277
Parmigiano crumbed veal cutlets	277
Salmon and potato cakes	278
Pan-fried fish fillets	279
Fish fingers	279
Seven-spice fish fillets	280
Pan-fried fish with coconut curry sauce	280
Crispy skin fish with spring onions	281
Deep-fried fish fillets in beer batter	281
Pan-fried fish with yellow miso dressing	282
Pan-fried swordfish with olive ratatouille	283
Pan-fried salmon with chilli coriander udon broth	284
Steamed Thai fish	286
Soy ginger salmon	286
Baked fish parcels with coconut milk and kaffir lime	287
Sweet chilli and mirin steamed tofu	287

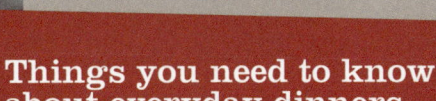

Things you need to know about everyday dinners

1 You need a large heavy-based frypan such as a Le Creuset – this is what we use all the time. We also have a smaller pan which is great for 2 chicken breasts or 2 steaks.

2 A grill pan is also fantastic for cooking meats as the flesh cooks on the hot metal ridges while most of the oil drains away.

3 Just how much oil you fry with depends largely on what you are cooking. Crumbed food will soak up a lot of oil, as does some meat, though generally 1–2 tbsp will do it.

4 When we are feeling indulgent, we cook with a splash of oil and a knob of butter. This adds the richness of butter to the high cooking temperature of oil. Butter also turns food a lovely golden brown.

5 Forty minutes is the ideal amount of time for marinating meat, but less is acceptable when you need to get dinner on the table.

6 Try to serve a bowl of salad with every evening meal. Not only is this a good standard to set for the younger generation, but it's also a fantastic way to cleanse your palate after dinner. It also makes you less likely to stray towards the treat box later on.

7 It's a great idea to get your children used to sitting at a dinner table with adults from the earliest age possible. This means no television, good table manners and joining in conversations. It's the perfect way to find out exactly what your children have been up to. Encourage your children's friends to join you for dinner, too.

8 Rather than serving up food on individual plates for everyone, place it on platters and ask them to help themselves. There's less waste and it encourages children to come back for seconds or, heaven forbid, thirds.

Deglazing and reducing

Deglazing and reducing are the two basic principles for making a sauce. Deglazing is the process of adding liquid (usually alcohol such as wine, but when we're cooking for the family we simply use stock) to a hot pan after meat has been browned and transferred to the oven to finish cooking. Tip any oil from the pan away and return to the heat. Always take care when adding alcohol as it may ignite; this is fine – good, actually – but you don't want to have your hand in the way. Let the alcohol evaporate, but make sure some liquid stays in the base of the pan.

Reducing is adding stock to the remaining juices in the pan and boiling rapidly in order to evaporate the liquid. Usually the liquid is reduced by half; any more, and the flavour can become too concentrated. Once the stock is reduced, any finishing ingredients such as herbs or cream are added. Don't add the cream any earlier as it will curdle, but you want it to reduce a little to thicken the sauce. A knob of butter whisked in at the end will also thicken slightly, as well as adding sheen and richness.

Pizza

Makes 2 pizzas

Pizza, it seems, is loved by one and all. No matter what your favourite topping might be, your enjoyment of pizza can only be improved by making your own base. This recipe makes a thick and chewy pizza base and is the sort of thing we prepare on weekends so the children can get involved in the mixing and kneading.

1 sachet (7 g) dried yeast
pinch of caster sugar
80 ml (⅓ cup) tepid water
80 ml (⅓ cup) olive oil
250 ml (1 cup) tepid water, additional
500 g (3⅓ cups) unbleached plain flour
1 tsp salt

Mix the dried yeast with caster sugar and tepid water. Leave in a warm place until the mixture bubbles. Stir in the oil and additional 250 ml water. Add the flour and salt and mix briefly, and then tip the dough onto a lightly floured surface. Knead for 6–8 minutes, until smooth and no longer sticky. Place the dough in a large bowl and cover with cling film. Allow to prove in a warm place until dough doubles in size (1–2 hours).

Preheat oven to 190°C.

Take the proven dough and knead for 1–2 minutes. Divide into 2 equal pieces and roll each into a ball. Place on oiled baking trays and use your fingers to press the dough out until 20 cm across and 2 cm thick. Cover and prove for 20 minutes.

Add toppings of your choice and bake in the preheated oven for 10–15 minutes, or until the pizza base is dry and golden underneath.

Pizza toppings

While we usually make our own pizza bases, we consider good-quality pre-bought bases to be a must in the freezer as an after school-snack or for those times when unexpected guests drop in for dinner.

The only rule for pizza is to limit yourself to 2–3 toppings on each one so you can enjoy the flavours.

Given that most pizzas have a tomato base and include mozzarella, here are some topping suggestions:

- ham, olives and sun-dried tomatoes
- ham, tomato and grilled eggplant
- salami, tomato and olives
- salami, artichokes and goat's cheese
- roasted capsicum, basil and goat's cheese
- artichokes, eggplant and bocconcini
- tapenade, tomato and goat's cheese
- chicken, mascarpone and mushroom
- caramelised onion and anchovies

Pizzas are also often topped with tomato, baked and then finished with raw ingredients such as:

- smoked salmon and horseradish cream
- prosciutto, mozzarella and figs
- prosciutto, blue cheese and rocket

Pizza bianco, white pizza, has no tomato base and is usually brushed with olive oil and topped with ingredients such as the following:

- potato, rosemary and onion
- roast pumpkin, pine nuts, spinach and goat's cheese
- three cheeses: mozzarella, blue cheese and parmigiano

Roasted vegetable calzone

Makes 6 calzone

Calzone is basically an enclosed pizza parcel, so anything you can put on pizza you can put into a calzone. Calzone can be cooked with a sweet filling as well.

1 eggplant, diced 1 cm chunks, salted and rinsed
1 zucchini, halved and cut 1 cm slices
1 onion, diced
¼ pumpkin, peeled and diced
1 red capsicum, diced
olive oil
salt and freshly ground black pepper
3–4 oregano sprigs
1 quantity Pizza Dough (page 248)
125 ml (½ cup) tomato puree
125 g (½ cup) mozzarella
egg wash

Preheat oven to 200°C.

Toss together eggplant, zucchini, onion, pumpkin, capsicum, oil, salt, pepper and oregano. Place in a deep baking tray and cook in a preheated oven for 40 minutes, until soft and cooked. Set aside to cool.

Divide dough into 6 × 150 g pieces. Roll each piece of dough into an oval 20 cm long. Toss roasted vegetables with tomato puree and cheese. Divide vegetables between each dough oval, placing on lower half. Brush around vegetables with egg wash. Fold dough over and press edges together firmly. Transfer to greased baking dishes sprinkled with polenta. Brush the top of each calzone with egg wash. Set aside to prove in a warm place for 15 minutes.

Bake in a preheated oven for 20 minutes, or until golden brown.

Pan-fried herb chicken fillets

Serves 4

A chicken fillet coated lightly with fresh herbs is a great-tasting mix. If anyone partaking of this meal has a problem with herbs, leave a fillet or two plain. This dish is good with soft polenta or mashed potato.

handful of chopped herbs: parsley, thyme, rosemary, oregano
salt and freshly ground black pepper
2 tbsp olive oil
4 small chicken breast fillets

Mix herbs, salt, pepper and oil together. Rub over chicken fillets and set to marinate, at least 10 minutes or up to 3 hours if time permits.

Preheat oven to 180°C.

Heat a heavy-based frying pan over a medium–high heat; add oil and chicken fillets and cook for 2–3 minutes on each side until well browned. Place in preheated oven and continue to cook for 10 minutes. Remove and rest, covered, in a warm place for 5 minutes before serving.

Pan-fried chicken with mushroom sauce

Serves 4

This dish is the equivalent to the pan-fried steak with mushroom sauce. It too is excellent served with baked potatoes.

olive oil
4 skinless chicken breast fillets
1 onion, diced
150 g mushrooms, sliced
250 ml (1 cup) chicken stock
90 ml (⅓ cup) cream
salt and freshly ground black pepper
2 tbsp chopped parsley

Preheat oven to 180°C.

Heat a heavy-based frying pan over a medium–high heat, add oil and chicken fillets and cook for 2–3 minutes on each side until well browned. Place chicken fillets in preheated oven and continue to cook for 10 minutes.

Return pan to the heat and add more oil if needed. Add onion and mushrooms and cook for 5–6 minutes, stirring often, until softened. Add stock, bring to the boil and reduce by half. Add cream and allow to simmer for 1–2 minutes. Check seasoning, add parsley and serve sauce over chicken.

Chicken saltimbocca

Serves 4

This is a chicken version of veal saltimbocca. What you end up with is thin slices of chicken with prosciutto wrapped around each one and sage leaves in the centre. They are beautiful with a simple mushroom risotto.

4 skinless chicken breast fillets
sage leaves
8 slices prosciutto
salt and freshly ground black pepper
olive oil
250 ml (1 cup) white wine
250 ml (1 cup) chicken stock
90 g butter
2 tbsp chopped parsley

Cut chicken fillets in half. Take each piece of chicken and use a meat hammer to pat gently 2–3 times on each side until they are flat and have an even thickness. (Lay a large square of cling film on a chopping board, put 1–2 pieces of chicken inside, fold half of cling film over the top and then pat gently; the cling film prevents the meat sticking to the hammer.)

Lay 3–4 sage leaves on each piece of chicken. Season lightly with salt and pepper and wrap 1 piece of prosciutto around each piece of chicken. Pat with meat hammer to bond prosciutto to the chicken.

Heat a heavy-based frypan over a medium–high heat. Add a splash of oil and brown chicken pieces, in batches if necessary, until golden brown on each side. Place cooked chicken in a warm oven while you prepare the sauce.

Tip any oil from pan and return to high heat. Add wine and reduce by half. Add stock and again reduce by half. Remove from heat and whisk in butter in small amounts. Check seasoning and add parsley.

Serve 2 chicken pieces per person, drizzle with sauce and serve with mushroom risotto or polenta.

Chicken schnitzel

Serves 4–6

Schnitzel is an ever-popular dish, as the variations are endless – you can change not only the meat but also the breadcrumbs. Serve schnitzel with lemon wedges, mashed potatoes and peas.

- 2–3 skinless chicken breast fillets
- seasoned flour
- 1 egg
- 125 ml (½ cup) milk
- 100 g (1 cup) dry breadcrumbs
- oil
- lemon wedges to serve

Remove the small fillet from underneath each larger fillet, and then cut the remaining piece into 3 or 4 pieces lengthways, depending on the original size.

Using a meat hammer, pat each piece of chicken gently 2–3 times on each side until flat and of an even thickness. The easiest way to do this is to lay a large square of cling film on a chopping board, put 1 or 2 pieces of chicken on it, fold half the cling film over the top and then pat gently; the cling film stops the chicken sticking to the hammer (as it does with all meats).

Put the flour in a shallow bowl. Beat the egg and milk together in another bowl, then put the breadcrumbs in a third bowl. Dip the chicken pieces into the flour, shaking off excess, and then dip into the egg and finally into the breadcrumbs, making sure each piece of chicken is well coated at each stage. If desired, the chicken can now be placed in the refrigerator until you are ready to cook it.

Preheat oven to 160°C.

Heat a large heavy-based frypan over a medium–high heat. Add a generous splash of oil and chicken pieces to the pan. Make sure that the chicken doesn't overlap or it won't cook properly. Cook for 2–3 minutes, until golden brown on one side. If the pan becomes dry, add more oil as needed. Turn each piece of chicken over and cook for 2 minutes on the other side, or until golden brown. Remove and place on a tray in the warm oven. It's a good idea to line the tray with clean brown paper or kitchen paper to absorb excess oil and keep the food crisp.

Repeat this process until all the chicken is cooked.

Chicken parmigiano
While the schnitzels are hot, place them on a tray, spread them with Tomato Sauce (pages 162-163) and then sprinkle with grated mozzarella cheese. Grill until golden brown, or bake in the oven until the cheese melts.

Lemon and herb schnitzel
Add the grated zest of 1 lemon and 1 tbsp chopped parsley to the breadcrumbs.

Cheesy schnitzel
Substitute 30 g (⅓ cup) grated parmigiano for 30 g (⅓ cup) breadcrumbs.

Veal schnitzel
Use thin veal fillets instead of chicken.

Sesame schnitzel
Add 1-2 tbsp sesame seeds to the breadcrumbs.

Indian spiced schnitzel
Add 2 tbsp curry powder to the breadcrumbs.

Chicken nuggets
Chop chicken into 3 x 3 cm chunks, then crumb as directed.

Crumbed lamb chops
Use trim lamb chops (allow 3 per person) and crumb as directed. Serve with Caponata (page 482).

Luke's favourite chicken dinner

Serves 4

For our son Luke, eating gets in the way of watching television, messing up the house, harassing the dog and generally having a good time. If there's one meal that's guaranteed to keep him at the table it's make-your-own-wraps. Some of the things that go into Luke's wraps may not be to everyone's taste, but on the whole they're a great way to get fussy kids to eat. Sometimes we just pan-fry the chicken fillets and slice them thinly. Adding a bit of spice expands kids' tastebuds without them even noticing.

2 skinless chicken fillets
1 tbsp olive oil
1 tsp ground coriander
1 tsp ground cumin
salt and freshly ground black pepper
8 wraps (roti or pita bread)

hummus and/or tzatziki
grated carrot
cucumber slices
grated cheddar
lettuce leaves

Dice chicken into 2 cm chunks and mix with oil, coriander, cumin, salt and pepper. Thread onto 8 skewers. Pan-fry or grill for 8–10 minutes, until golden brown and cooked through.

Place the remaining ingredients on a platter. You can add whatever you like: boiled egg, radishes, beetroot slices, pesto, Tomato and Basil Salsa (page 565) or Chilli Salsa (page 565).

Warm the wraps in a hot pan. Allow everyone to help themselves to a wrap, add a chicken skewer, then their own personal combo of salad ingredients. The wraps can also be served with steamed rice.

From here, it's only a small step up to Chicken Fajitas (page 254) and Spiced Coriander and Yoghurt Chicken (page 256). You can also use lamb or beef in these wraps instead of chicken.

Chicken fajitas

Serves 4

Fajitas are a great family-friendly dinner. Just roll up the spiced chicken in a tortilla and add your choice of fillings.

500 g skinless chicken breast fillets	2 tomatoes, diced
1 tbsp oil	400 g can cooked cannellini beans
1 tbsp sherry vinegar	2 tbsp lemon juice
½ tsp ground allspice	2 tbsp chopped parsley
1 tsp dried oregano	1 small red chilli, de-seeded and diced
2 tbsp onion flakes	salt and freshly ground black pepper
1 tsp salt	8 wheat-flour tortillas
¼ tsp chilli powder	2 cups shredded lettuce (iceberg or cos)
½ red capsicum, diced	125 ml (½ cup) sour cream

Preheat oven to 180°C.

Cut chicken fillets into 1 cm wide strips and place in a bowl. Combine the oil, sherry vinegar, allspice, oregano, onion flakes, salt and chilli powder. Pour the marinade over the chicken, stirring to coat pieces thoroughly. Allow to marinate for 20 minutes.

Place the diced capsicum and tomatoes in a bowl with the drained and rinsed cannellini beans. Add the lemon juice, parsley and chilli, and season to taste. Set aside at room temperature until ready to serve.

Heat a heavy-based frypan over a medium–high heat. Add the chicken strips; you won't need to add any oil to the pan as there should be enough in the marinade. Cook the chicken by tossing and lifting the pieces, allowing them to brown.

Warm the tortillas in the preheated oven. Serve them with lettuce, chicken, bean salsa and sour cream, allowing everyone to assemble their own fajitas.

Southern fried chicken

Serves 4

You can use whichever cut of chicken you like for this recipe, though the cooking time will vary slightly. We prefer to use drumsticks as our children love eating with their fingers and this gives them the perfect opportunity. We can all forget about table manners now and again.

100 g (⅔ cup) cornflour
2 tsp sweet paprika
1 tsp ground coriander
1 tsp salt
½ tsp cayenne
1 tsp ground oregano
1 tsp ground cumin
½ tsp ground cardamom
1 egg
125 ml (½ cup) milk
8 chicken drumsticks, skin removed
oil
lemon wedges to serve

Preheat oven to 180°C.

Mix the spices with the cornflour in one bowl, and whisk the egg and milk together in another bowl. Dip the chicken pieces into the flour mixture, then into the egg mix, and then back into the flour again.

Heat a heavy-based frypan over a medium–high heat. Add a ¼ cm layer of oil. Shallow-fry the chicken until each piece is golden brown. Place the chicken pieces on a baking tray and cook in the preheated oven for 20 minutes.

Serve with lemon wedges and Baked Potatoes (page 490).

Chicken drumsticks with Italian flavours

Serves 4

We've become big fans of this method of preparing drumsticks – it requires almost no effort on the cook's part once it goes into the oven, other than to stir occasionally.

8 chicken drumsticks, skin removed
4 potatoes, diced
1 red onion, sliced
2–3 cloves garlic, peeled
80 g (½ cup) pitted olives
2 tbsp capers, soaked
2 tbsp balsamic vinegar
1 tbsp chopped rosemary and thyme
60 ml (¼ cup) olive oil
salt and freshly ground black pepper
250–500 ml (1–2 cups) chicken stock

Preheat oven to 180°C.

Place all ingredients except stock in a deep baking dish and toss well to combine. Pour over enough chicken stock to just cover and roast in the preheated oven for 45 minutes–1 hour. Stir occasionally.

The stock is absorbed as this dish cooks, resulting in a great one-pot dinner that needs only a green salad to complete.

Chicken fillets poached in soy and star anise

Serves 4–6

Transform simple chicken fillets into an Asian-inspired dish by poaching them in a broth of soy sauce and Chinese cooking wine.

60 ml (¼ cup) soy sauce
125 ml (½ cup) Chinese cooking wine
250 ml (1 cup) chicken stock
2 star anise

1 small red chilli, sliced (optional)
4 skinless chicken breast fillets
Steamed Rice (page 198) to serve

Place soy sauce, cooking wine, stock, star anise and chilli (if using) in a large heavy-based frypan. Bring to the boil over a medium–high heat. Add the chicken fillets, reduce liquid to a simmer and cook for 8–10 minutes, turning the chicken over halfway.

Remove the chicken from the pan and set aside in a warm place to rest. Raise the heat under the frypan and reduce the poaching liquid by half.

Slice the chicken, serve on Steamed Rice and pour the sauce over the meat. Perfect with Chinese Broccoli and Garlic Stir-Fry (page 480).

Spiced coriander and yoghurt chicken

Serves 4

This dish is for those times when it's chicken for dinner, but instead of the usual pan-fried fillets we've spiced it up just a little. Serve with a salad.

125 g (½ cup) natural yoghurt
3 tsp ground cumin
2 tbsp ground coriander
2 tsp chilli powder
1 tsp turmeric

salt and freshly ground black pepper
2 tbsp lemon juice
4 skinless chicken breast fillets
oil
Spiced Couscous (page 453) to serve

Preheat oven to 180°C.

Combine yoghurt, spices, seasoning and lemon juice. Lightly coat the chicken fillets with the spice mixture.

Heat a heavy-based frypan. Add oil and the chicken fillets and cook for 2–3 minutes on each side, until well browned.

Place the chicken fillets in the preheated oven and continue to cook for 5–6 minutes. Remove the chicken from the oven and rest, covered, in a warm place for 5 minutes.

Slice the fillets into 3–4 pieces and serve on top of Spiced Couscous.

Steamed ginger chicken

Serves 4

Steaming may not be the first thing that springs to mind when deciding how to cook chicken, but this is a dish that should be tried by everyone. The result is an incredibly tender and amazing-flavoured meal. Go on, try it.

- 4 chicken breast fillets on the bone, or off the bone if it's easier for you
- 125 ml (½ cup) light soy sauce
- 2 cloves garlic, peeled and sliced
- 2 small red chillies, sliced
- 1 tbsp fish sauce
- 80 ml (⅓ cup) water
- 60 ml (¼ cup) rice wine vinegar
- 2 tsp sesame oil
- 4 cm ginger, peeled and shredded
- Steamed Rice (page 198) to serve

Place chicken in a deep bowl. Mix together soy sauce, garlic, chilli, fish sauce, water, rice wine vinegar and sesame oil. Pour over chicken and leave to marinate in refrigerator for 4 hours, turning chicken once.

Place wok over a high heat, add 6 cm of water and bring to the boil. Rest a plate in the bottom of a bamboo steamer and place into the wok. Arrange chicken fillets on the plate and pour the marinade over. Spread ginger over the chicken, cover and steam for 20 minutes, or until chicken is just cooked. Remove and allow to rest for 5 minutes in a warm place.

Cut each piece of chicken into 4 and serve immediately with cooking juices and Steamed Rice.

Chicken and veal polpettini

Serves 4–6

These are a fairly adult type of meatball, which is not to say that children don't eat them like they're going out of fashion.

100 g day-old bread
250 ml (1 cup) milk
300 g veal mince
300 g chicken mince
salt and freshly ground black pepper
¼ cup chopped parsley
2 cloves garlic, crushed
zest of 1 lemon
60 g (¾ cup) parmigiano, grated
flour for dusting
olive oil
2 lemons, cut into wedges

Tear bread into small pieces. Soak in milk for 10–15 minutes. Squeeze well to remove excess liquid. Place bread in a bowl, add mince, salt, pepper, parsley, garlic, lemon and parmigiano. Mix well.

Roll mixture into small balls, about 3 cm in diameter. Roll each ball lightly in flour. When ready heat a heavy-based pan over a medium–high heat. Add a splash of oil. Add polpettini in batches and cook for 5–6 minutes, shaking often until polpettini are golden brown all over. Remove and keep warm in a 160°C preheated oven until all are cooked. Serve with lemon wedges.

Danish beef burgers

Serves 4

My mum, Birgit, who is Danish, is famed for her burgers. Although her Frikadella (page 265) are also good, these beef burgers have a special place in our memories as we ate them with my Morfar (grandfather) at his 89th birthday in Denmark. MC

1 kg beef mince
salt and freshly ground black pepper
oil
2 onions, sliced
250 ml (1 cup) red wine
250 ml (1 cup) beef stock

Preheat oven to 180°C.

Mix the beef mince with salt and pepper and form into 8 burger shapes.

Heat a heavy-based frypan over a medium–high heat. Add a splash of oil and cook the burgers for 3–4 minutes on each side until brown. Remove from the pan to a baking tray and place in the preheated oven to continue cooking.

Return pan to heat. Add the onions and cook for 4–5 minutes, stirring often, until soft. Add red wine and bring to the boil. Allow to reduce by half, then add the stock. Lower the heat and allow to simmer for 3–4 minutes.

Serve the burgers with the red wine and onion sauce and Mashed Potatoes (page 489).

Thai chicken balls

Serves 4

The old trick of hiding vegetables in minced meat always works. Sometimes we add even more, or sometimes none at all to suit our tastes. These chicken balls are also good as nibbles with a bowl of sweet chilli sauce.

500 g chicken mince
½ red capsicum, diced
3 spring onions, finely diced
1 carrot, grated
1 egg
1 tbsp soy sauce
1 tbsp sweet chilli sauce
2 tbsp chopped coriander
100 g (1 cup) dry breadcrumbs
olive oil
Steamed Rice (page 198) to serve

Mix chicken with all ingredients, adding enough breadcrumbs to bring mixture together. Roll into small balls. Heat a heavy-based frypan over a medium–high heat, add a splash of oil and cook chicken until golden brown all over.

Serve with rice and extra sweet chilli sauce.

Lemon chicken polpettini

Serves 4–6

These meatballs are one of our son Luke's favourite meals – alongside chicken wraps, that is. We often double this recipe, in the hope that there'll be leftovers for lunch boxes the next day. The polpettini also make a great pre-dinner nibble with Almond Skordalia (page 550) or Green Olive Salsa (page 564).

100 g day-old bread
250 ml (1 cup) milk
500 g chicken mince
salt and freshly ground black pepper
¼ cup chopped parsley
2 cloves garlic, crushed
zest of 1 lemon
60 g (¾ cup) grated parmigiano
plain flour for dusting
oil
2 lemons, cut into wedges, to serve

Tear bread into small pieces and soak in milk for 10–15 minutes.

Squeeze the bread well to remove excess liquid and place in a bowl with the mince, salt, pepper, parsley, garlic, lemon and parmigiano. Mix well.

Roll the mixture into small 3 cm balls. Roll each ball lightly in flour.

Preheat oven to 160°C.

Heat a heavy-based pan over a medium–high heat. Add a splash of oil, and cook the polpettini in batches for 5–6 minutes, shaking often, until the meatballs are golden brown. Remove from pan and keep warm in the preheated oven until all the polpettini are cooked.

Serve with lemon wedges and Polenta Wedgies (page 193).

Steak with oven chips

Serves 4

The oven chips included here are wicked. Seeing that they are so easy to make we can't understand why anyone buys those frozen ones. It's these or nothing as far as we are concerned.

½ kg desiree potatoes
olive oil
2 tbsp rosemary leaves
1 tbsp chopped parsley
salt and freshly ground black pepper
4 × 200 g fillet or porterhouse steaks

Preheat oven to 200°C.

Cut potatoes into thick wedges. Place oil, herbs, salt and pepper in a large bowl. Add potato wedges and toss well. Place wedges onto a large baking tray, skin side down, and cook in preheated oven for 45–55 minutes, turning tray occasionally. Potatoes will be golden brown when ready.

Heat a heavy-based frypan over a medium–high heat and add a splash of oil. Add steaks and cook for 4–5 minutes on both sides. Rest briefly in a warm place, then serve with lots of potato wedges and perhaps a green salad and fried mushrooms.

Corned beef (silverside)

Serves 4–6

Corned beef is regarded as an old-fashioned type of dish, but that doesn't mean we should underestimate it as a meal. Silverside should be soaked in cold water overnight to remove excess salt before cooking. Adding oranges, lemons, peppercorns and chopped vegetables to the poaching water dramatically boosts the final flavour.

- 1⅓ kg silverside
- 1 bouquet garni
- 1 lemon, sliced
- 1 orange, sliced
- 10 peppercorns
- 2 onions, sliced
- 2 carrots, peeled and chopped

Place silverside in a large pot or saucepan, add cold water to cover. Bring to the boil, discard water. Again add enough cold water to cover, add remaining ingredients and bring to the boil. Reduce to a simmer, skimming the surface if required. Cover with a lid and cook for 1 hour.

Remove pot from heat and allow to stand for 10–15 minutes. Remove silverside and slice. Serve with boiled potatoes and Parsley Sauce (page 556).

Pan-fried steak with mushroom sauce

Serves 4

A simple but stylish steak dish with a tasty sauce. It is excellent served with baked potatoes.

- 4 × 250 g porterhouse steaks
- olive oil
- 1 onion, finely diced
- 250 g Swiss brown mushrooms, cut into wedges
- 250 ml (1 cup) beef stock
- 90 ml (⅓ cup) cream
- salt and freshly ground black pepper

Preheat oven to 180°C.

Heat a heavy-based pan over a medium–high heat. Brush steaks with oil and cook for 3 minutes on each side, until well browned. Place steaks on a tray and cook in preheated oven for 5 minutes (medium–rare).

Return pan to the heat, add more oil if required, onion and mushrooms. Cook for 5–6 minutes, until onion and mushrooms are well softened. Stir occasionally. Add the stock, bring to the boil and reduce by half. Add cream to the sauce and simmer for a further 2–3 minutes. Season well, adding lots of pepper. Serve steaks with sauce on top.

Beef stroganoff

Serves 4

Avoid buying 'beef stroganoff cuts' from your butcher, as the mish-mash of odd pieces of beef will all have different cooking times and your dish will end up with some tough bits. It's better to purchase a cut such as scotch fillet and slice it yourself, then you know exactly what you are dealing with.

- 500 g scotch fillet, cut into strips
- oil
- 1 onion, thinly sliced
- 250 g button mushrooms, sliced
- 1 clove garlic, crushed
- 1–2 tbsp sweet paprika
- 250 ml (1 cup) beef stock
- 1 tbsp Worcestershire sauce
- 1 tbsp tomato paste
- 80 ml (⅓ cup) sour cream
- 2 tbsp chopped parsley
- Steamed Rice (page 198) to serve

Heat a large non-stick frypan over a medium–high heat. Add oil and half the beef and cook for 3 minutes, stirring, until brown. Transfer to a heatproof bowl. Repeat with the remaining beef.

Return the pan to the heat and add more oil, if required. Add the onion and mushrooms and cook for 5–6 minutes, stirring often, until softened. Add garlic and paprika and cook for 1 minute, until fragrant.

Return the beef to the pan, along with the stock, Worcestershire sauce and tomato paste. Bring to the boil. Reduce heat to low and simmer, covered, for 20 minutes, or until the beef is tender.

Check seasoning, add sour cream and parsley and stir to combine. Serve with Steamed Rice.

Birgit's frikadella

Serves 4

Frikadella are probably the simplest burgers you'll ever come across. The mix is easy to make and you just plonk the burgers into the pan as they come without forming them into patties. This is a standard family meal in Denmark where my mum, Birgit, comes from. I'm still trying to get the rest of my family to love it as much as I do, but I guess you just had to be there. MC

60 g (⅔ cup) rolled oats
500 g veal or pork mince (or a mix of the two if available)
salt and freshly ground black pepper
milk, as needed
olive oil
pickles to serve

Place rolled oats in a food processor and whiz until they are very fine. Add the mince, plus salt and pepper, and whiz until smooth and combined. Add a splash of milk if the mix is very thick.

Heat a heavy-based frypan over a medium–high heat and add a generous amount of oil.

Drop spoonfuls of the mix into the oil and cook for 10 minutes, turning occasionally. Each frikadella should be golden brown all over.

Serve with pickles.

Savoury mince

Serves 4–6

Savoury mince doesn't sound very exciting but we cook this from time to time and transform it into something else. For instance, it's good in baked potatoes, made into cottage pie, spiced up as chilli con carne or spooned into taco shells.

oil
2 onions, diced
1 kg lean beef mince
2 cloves garlic, crushed
150 g (½ cup) tomato paste
250 ml (1 cup) tomato puree
500 ml (2 cups) beef stock
salt and freshly ground black pepper
2 tbsp chopped parsley

Heat a large heavy-based saucepan over a medium–high heat. Add a splash of oil and the onions and cook for 5–6 minutes, stirring often, until soft. Add the beef and garlic and cook until the beef has changed colour. Add tomato paste, stir well and cook for 1–2 minutes. Add the tomato puree, stock, salt and pepper and bring to the boil. Reduce heat and cook at a simmer for 25–30 minutes, or until the stock has reduced.

Check seasoning and add parsley.

Swedish meatballs

Serves 4

These make a great change from our more usual Italian- or Australian-style meatballs. They are light, with a hint of nutmeg, and are great served with hot buttered noodles.

oil
1 onion, diced
100 g (2 cups) fresh breadcrumbs
165 ml (⅔ cup) milk
500 g beef mince
1 egg
salt and freshly ground black pepper
¼ tsp nutmeg
2 tsp sweet paprika
plain flour for dusting
Allan's Gravy (page 559)
80 ml (⅓ cup) sour cream

Preheat oven to 180°C.

Heat a small pan over a medium heat. Add a splash of oil and cook the diced onion for 4–5 minutes, until soft.

Mix the breadcrumbs and milk together in a bowl and allow to soak for a couple of minutes. Add the cooked onion, beef mince, egg, salt, pepper, nutmeg and paprika. Mix thoroughly until well blended. Shape the mixture into 20 small balls; dust your hands with flour frequently while shaping the balls. Add a handful of extra breadcrumbs if the mix seems too wet.

Heat a large heavy-based frypan over a medium–high heat. Add a generous splash of oil and cook the meatballs until golden brown all over. You may need to do this in 2 batches. As the meatballs are ready, place them in an ovenproof serving dish and keep them warm in the preheated oven.

Prepare a batch of Allan's Gravy (page 559). When ready to serve, remove the gravy from heat and stir in sour cream, a little at a time. Check seasoning then pour over the meatballs and serve.

Lamb cutlets with red wine onions

Serves 4

Just looking at all these recipes in this chapter has made us realise how much we eat pan-fried meat with some sort of sauce. Yikes.

2 tbsp olive oil
3 onions, sliced
1 tbsp chopped thyme leaves
1 tbsp Dijon mustard
½ tsp caster sugar
375 ml (1½ cups) pinot noir, or other light red wine
1 kg (about 16) small, trimmed lamb cutlets
1 tbsp olive oil
salt and freshly ground black pepper

Preheat oven to 180°C.

Heat a heavy-based saucepan over a medium–high heat. Add oil, onions and thyme. Cook for 8–10 minutes, stirring often until onions are soft. Add mustard, sugar and wine, bring to the boil, then reduce heat. Simmer until wine has evaporated and onions are a pale pink colour, about 15 minutes. Season to taste and keep warm until lamb is cooked.

Heat a large heavy-based frypan over a high heat. Add a splash of oil and cook lamb cutlets for 2 minutes on each side, a few at a time. Place on a baking tray as they are ready and cook remaining cutlets. When all cutlets are done, place in the preheated oven and cook for 5 minutes. Serve a spoonful of the red wine onions with lamb cutlets on top.

Spiced lamb steaks

Serves 4

You can use any manner of spices or herbs to jazz up these lamb steaks for dinner. They're even better when served with Quince Aioli (page 550) or a bowl of full-flavoured Romesco Sauce (page 552).

2 tbsp olive oil
1 tbsp ground coriander
1 tbsp ground cumin
½ tsp ground cinnamon
½ tsp ground allspice
½ tsp ground white pepper
2 tsp harissa or chilli paste
1 tsp salt
8 lamb steaks

Mix oil, spices, harissa and salt in a large bowl. Add the lamb steaks and toss to combine. Marinate for up to 2 hours.

Heat grill pan or barbecue and cook lamb for 4 minutes on one side. Turn over and cook for a further 2–3 minutes. Allow to rest for a few minutes before serving.

Tikka-yoghurt lamb chops

Serves 4

Tikka paste usually packs a bit more punch than tandoori and, naturally enough, matches lamb well. Serve with a pilaf and a green salad.

3 tbsp tikka curry paste
1 tsp ground coriander
1 tsp ground cumin
½ tsp ground cardamom
2 tbsp lemon juice
80 g (⅓ cup) natural yoghurt
8 lamb loin chops
oil
Pilaf to serve (pages 199–204)

Mix the tikka paste, spices, lemon juice and yoghurt together. Brush over the lamb and marinate for up to 30 minutes, if time permits.

Heat a heavy-based frypan over a medium–high heat. Add a splash of oil. Shake excess marinade from the lamb and cook the chops for 4–5 minutes on each side. If you prefer, you can grill or barbecue them.

Lamb kofta skewers

Makes 12

Minced lamb is becoming more widely available nowadays so making these kofta skewers is easy. They are also very good barbecued.

1 kg finely minced lamb
1 onion, finely minced
3 tsp ground coriander
4 tsp ground cumin
½ tsp ground cinnamon
½ tsp ground allspice
½ tsp ground white pepper
2 tsp oregano leaves, chopped
2 tsp harissa paste
1 tsp salt
90 g (½ cup) burghul
12 skewers
olive oil

Place lamb, onion, ground spices, oregano, harissa and salt in a large bowl. Knead well by hand for five minutes. Refrigerate for 1 hour so flavours can develop.

Soak burghul in plenty of cold water for 20 minutes. Drain well.

Divide kofta mixture into 12 equal pieces and shape into thick fingers. Scatter burghul onto a plate and roll lamb until coated. Thread skewers through the centre of each kofta.

Heat a heavy-based frypan over a high heat, add a splash of oil and cook lamb for 12–15 minutes, turning frequently. Serve with Tzatziki (page 563), Green Salad (page 506) and Turkish pide bread.

Moussaka

Serves 4–6

Our family remains divided on who likes this dish and who doesn't, but it's such a classic we just had to include it. Make sure your lamb mince is lean or there'll be oil everywhere. Here speaks the voice of experience.

2 tbsp olive oil
1 onion, diced
1 clove garlic, crushed
750 g lean lamb mince
500 ml (2 cups) tomato puree
2 tbsp tomato paste
½ tsp ground cinnamon
salt and freshly ground black pepper
2 eggplants
olive oil for cooking
6 potatoes, boiled and sliced
1 quantity Cheese Sauce (page 557)

Heat a heavy-based pan over a medium–high heat. Add oil and onion and cook for 4–5 minutes, until soft, stirring often. Add garlic and lamb and cook, stirring often, until lamb changes colour. Add tomato puree, tomato paste, cinnamon, salt and pepper. Bring to the boil, reduce heat and simmer for 45 minutes. Check seasoning.

Slice eggplants, sprinkle with salt and set aside until juices bead. Rinse and pat dry. Place on a flat tray, drizzle with oil and grill until tender.

Preheat oven to 180°C. Lay potatoes in the base of a deep baking dish, such as a lasagne dish. Spoon lamb mince on top. Lay eggplant slices on top and cover with Cheese Sauce. Bake in preheated oven for 40 minutes, until golden brown and heated through. Serve with Green Salad (page 506) or Greek Salad (page 506).

Olive and thyme crumbed pork schnitzels

Serves 4

Schnitzels are a popular choice at our place. This version is more suited to adult tastes, however, as a layer of olive paste is spread onto each schnitzel just before crumbing. It adds a salty burst of flavour to the finished dish.

4 large pork schnitzels
2 tbsp black olive paste
1 egg
1 tbsp milk
75 g (¾ cup) dry breadcrumbs
leaves from 2–3 sprigs of thyme
salt and freshly ground black pepper
50 g (⅓ cup) plain flour
oil
lemon wedges to serve

Lay pork schnitzels out flat and spread ½ tbsp olive paste evenly onto one side of each schnitzel.

Combine the egg and milk in a flat container and lightly beat. Mix the breadcrumbs, thyme leaves, salt and pepper in another flat container. Place flour in a third flat container.

Coat the schnitzels lightly with flour, shaking gently to remove excess, then dip them into the beaten egg. Allow excess to drain before coating each schnitzel in the breadcrumbs.

Preheat oven to 160°C.

Heat a large heavy-based frypan over a medium–high heat. Add a generous splash of oil and 1–2 pork schnitzels, making sure they don't overlap or they won't cook properly. Cook for 2–3 minutes, until golden brown on one side. If the pan becomes dry, add more oil as required. When brown on one side, turn the schnitzels over and cook them for 2 minutes on the other side, or until golden brown.

Remove and place on a baking tray in the preheated oven. It's a good idea to line the tray with kitchen paper to absorb excess oil and keep the food crisp. Repeat the process until all the pork is cooked.

Serve with lemon wedges and Potato Wedges (page 490).

Barbecued pork sausage with spiced lentils

Serves 4–6

If it's raining and we can't get to the barbecue, we cook the sausage slices for this dish in a pan before serving them on top of the spiced lentils. This means we can eat the dish all year round.

- 200 g (1 cup) green lentils
- 1 tbsp olive oil
- 1 onion, diced
- 1 clove garlic, crushed
- 2 carrots, peeled and finely diced
- 1 celery stick, finely diced
- 2 tbsp curry paste
- 500 ml (2 cups) vegetable or chicken stock
- salt and freshly ground black pepper
- chopped parsley
- 500 g Polish pork sausage
- olive oil

Sort through lentils, discarding any brown ones and pieces of grit, then rinse well.

Heat a heavy-based pan over a medium–high heat. Add oil, onion, garlic, carrots and celery and cook for 5–6 minutes until soft. Add curry paste and cook until fragrant. Add lentils and cook briefly for a few moments. Add enough stock to just cover and bring to the boil. Lower heat, season with salt and cook for 30–40 minutes, or until lentils are soft. Add more stock as necessary and stir frequently. Stir through parsley and check seasoning.

Slice pork sausage into ½ cm slices. Brush with olive oil and barbecue or grill for 3–4 minutes on each side, or until brown and crispy.

Spoon lentils into a bowl, arrange slices of grilled sausage on top and serve.

Moorish lamb with quince glaze

Serves 4

Quince, smoky paprika, garlic and fresh thyme combine to flavour the lamb and create a great tasting sauce to serve over it. This sauce would be equally good with chicken fillets.

2 cloves garlic, crushed
1 tsp smoky paprika
1 tbsp vinegar or lemon juice
1 tbsp thyme leaves
1 tbsp olive oil
salt and freshly ground black pepper
4 lamb back straps or steaks
oil
2 tbsp quince paste
125 ml (½ cup) white wine

Mix the garlic, paprika, vinegar, thyme leaves, oil, salt and pepper together. Brush over lamb and marinate for up to 1 hour.

Heat a heavy-based frypan over a medium–high heat. Add a splash of oil and cook the lamb for 3–4 minutes on each side until golden brown. Remove the lamb from the pan and set aside in a warm place to rest.

Tip away excess oil from the pan. Add the quince paste and white wine and bring to the boil. Whisk well and cook until the sauce reduces to a syrupy consistency. Check seasoning.

To serve, slice the lamb thickly and pour the quince glaze over. Goes well with Polenta Wedgies (page 193) and Rocket, Parmigiano and Pomegranate Salad (page 506).

San choy bau

Serves 4

San choy bau is a classic Asian dish, often made with minced quail though minced pork is easier to come by. You can add mushrooms, water chestnuts, bean sprouts, bamboo shoots or anything else that takes your fancy.

1 iceberg lettuce
1–2 tbsp peanut oil
2 cloves garlic, crushed
2 tsp grated ginger
2 small red chillies, de-seeded and finely diced
750 g pork mince
2 tbsp Chinese rice wine
soy sauce to taste
4 spring onions, chopped
fresh coriander leaves
chilli sauce

Peel whole leaves away from lettuce, wash well and chill until needed.

Heat wok until hot; add peanut oil, garlic, ginger and chillies, then cook until fragrant. Add pork mince and cook, stirring often, until meat changes colour. Add Chinese rice wine and soy sauce to taste, along with spring onions and coriander leaves. Toss until combined.

Spoon pork mince into lettuce cups, add coriander and chilli sauce to taste, roll up and away you go.

Chinese twice-cooked pork spare ribs

Serves 4

Pork ribs can be cooked and enjoyed in so many different ways. This is one of our favourites: the ribs are cooked in a master stock to make them tender, then grilled to crispy perfection.

Master Stock (page 118)
8 pork ribs
1 tbsp sweet chilli sauce
1 tsp Chinese five-spice powder
1 tbsp soy sauce
1 tbsp Asian plum sauce
oil
Steamed Rice (page 198) to serve

Bring the Master Stock to the boil. Add the pork ribs and cook at a gentle simmer for 5–7 minutes. Remove the ribs and set them aside to drain. Allow to cool.

Heat a grill or grill pan. Mix the sweet chilli sauce, five-spice powder, soy sauce and plum sauce together. Brush the sauce onto the pork and cook for 4–5 minutes on each side, until crispy and golden brown. If you have a grill in the top of your oven, place the pork ribs on a baking rack over a baking dish filled with water. This will catch any cooking drips and also allow the fat to drain away from the meat.

Serve with Steamed Rice and Chinese Broccoli and Garlic Stir-Fry (page 480).

Lion's head meatballs

Serves 4

Lion's head meatballs are an easy peasant dish, but they taste as if you've gone to a lot of trouble. Serve them with Wok-Fried Asian Greens (page 499).

500 g pork mince
6 shiitake mushrooms, finely chopped
90 g water chestnuts, finely chopped
1 egg white
4 spring onions, thinly sliced
2 tsp grated ginger
3 tsp cornflour
1½ tbsp Chinese rice wine
½ tsp salt
100 g vermicelli noodles
½ Chinese cabbage
extra cornflour
olive oil
500 ml (2 cups) chicken stock
60 ml (¼ cup) soy sauce
2 tbsp Chinese rice wine

Mix together pork, mushrooms, chestnuts, egg white, spring onions, ginger, cornflour, Chinese rice wine and salt until well combined. Divide mixture into 16 portions and roll into balls with extra cornflour if too wet.

Preheat oven to 180°C. Pour boiling water over noodles and set aside to soften, then drain. Chop cabbage into 3 cm chunks. Lay cabbage, then noodles, into the bottom of a deep baking tray.

Coat meatballs with extra cornflour. Heat a large heavy-based frypan over a medium–high heat. Add a splash of oil and cook meatballs for 3–4 minutes, or until brown all over. Place meatballs on top of noodles. Mix together stock, soy sauce and Chinese rice wine and pour over meatballs and other ingredients. Cover tray with foil and cook in preheated oven for 45 minutes. Serve with Steamed Rice (page 198).

Plum and soy pork steaks

Serves 4

Pork is a very adaptable meat that works with a range of marinades. Here, it's brushed with a simple mix of plum sauce, soy sauce and five-spice powder, which is bursting with flavour.

60 ml (¼ cup) Asian plum sauce
60 ml (¼ cup) soy sauce
1 tsp Chinese five-spice powder
4 pork butterfly steaks
oil
Steamed Rice (page 198) to serve

Mix the plum sauce, soy sauce and five-spice powder together. Brush over the pork steaks and marinate for up to 10 minutes.

Heat a heavy-based frypan or grill pan. Add a splash of oil and cook the pork steaks for 3–4 minutes on each side, or until golden brown and cooked through.

Serve with Steamed Rice and Choy Sum with Ginger (page 480).

Katsudon (Japanese crumbed pork)

Serves 4

This is a dish we've only recently begun cooking at home, although we've been eating it in Japanese restaurants for quite a while. It's essentially crumbed pork slices cooked in a pan with beaten egg and served on rice with dashi broth poured over it.

1 pork fillet, about 500 g
seasoned flour
1 egg
125 ml (½ cup) milk
100 g (1 cup) Japanese breadcrumbs
1 onion, sliced
250 ml (1 cup) dashi
60 ml (¼ cup) soy sauce
90 ml (⅓ cup) mirin
olive oil
3 eggs, additional
Steamed Rice (page 198) to serve

Cut pork into slices. Using a meat hammer, pat each piece of pork gently 2–3 times on each side until flat and of an even thickness (cover pork with cling film to prevent pork from sticking to hammer). Put flour in a shallow bowl. Beat egg and milk together in another bowl and put breadcrumbs in a third bowl. Coat pork in flour and shake off excess. Then coat with egg and finally breadcrumbs, making sure each piece of pork is well coated at each stage. If you want, you can now place pork in refrigerator until you are ready to cook it.

Make your broth by combining onion, dashi, soy and mirin in a small saucepan. Bring to the boil over a medium heat, reduce to a simmer and cook for 10 minutes.

Heat a large heavy-based frypan over a medium–high heat. Add a generous splash of oil and enough pork pieces to fit into the pan, making sure pork doesn't overlap or else it will not cook properly. Cook for 2–3 minutes until golden brown on one side. If pan becomes dry add more oil as needed. When brown on one side, turn over and cook for 2 minutes on the other side, or until golden brown.

Beat additional eggs together and pour into pan around pork pieces. (If cooking in batches, pour half the egg in and keep the remaining beaten eggs for the second batch.) Cook for 1–2 minutes until the egg sets. Serve pork over rice with a spoonful of the hot broth.

Veal, sage and onion meatloaf

Serves 4–6

Meatloaves are out of fashion. Sad, but true. But half of my wardrobe is out of fashion, too, and that doesn't stop me wearing it. In fact, it'll probably all be back in again next year, just like meatloaf. MC

olive oil
2 onions, diced
4 slices bacon, chopped
1 clove garlic, crushed
1 kg veal mince
2 tbsp chopped sage leaves
100 g (1 cup) dry breadcrumbs
1 egg

Heat a frypan over a medium–high heat. Add a splash of oil and cook onions for 3–4 minutes, stirring often. Add bacon and cook for a further 3–4 minutes until cooked. Add garlic and cook for 1–2 minutes. Remove from heat and allow to cool.

Preheat oven to 180°C.

In a large bowl mix veal, the onion and bacon mix, sage, breadcrumbs and egg together. Place into a greased loaf pan and bake for 40 minutes.

To test whether the meatloaf is cooked insert a small knife into it. If juices run clear the meatloaf is ready.

Allow to cool in the tin before slicing.

Parmigiano crumbed veal cutlets

Serves 6

This is a very refined way of serving veal cutlets. They are coated with parmigiano-flavoured breadcrumbs and then served with a sweet–sour caponata sauce, which contrasts beautifully with the richness of the meat.

seasoned flour
1 egg
125 ml (½ cup) milk
100 g (2 cups) fresh breadcrumbs
60 g (¾ cup) parmigiano, grated
1 tbsp finely chopped parsley
6 veal cutlets (one per person, or two if small)
olive oil

Preheat oven to 180°C. Place flour in one bowl, beat egg and milk together in a second bowl and mix breadcrumbs, cheese and parsley in a third bowl. Take veal cutlets one by one and coat first in flour, then egg mix, then breadcrumbs.

Place a heavy-based frypan over high heat, add a generous splash of olive oil and cook veal cutlets for 3–4 minutes on each side until golden brown. Remove veal to a baking tray and cook in oven for a further 5–10 minutes (depending on size), or until just cooked. Remove from oven, cover, and allow to rest in a warm place for 5–10 minutes.

Serve with Caponata (page 482).

Salmon and potato cakes

Serves 12

You can use any fish for this recipe, but the rich taste of Atlantic salmon works best for us every time. It's amazing how far 400 g of salmon can go and how good it can be. Just don't forget the Lemon Butter Sauce (page 555).

750 g potatoes
knob of butter
salt and freshly ground black pepper
1–2 tbsp olive oil
2 × 200 g pieces Atlantic salmon
1 tbsp chopped fresh dill (optional)

seasoned flour
1 egg
125 ml (½ cup) milk
100 g (1 cup) dry breadcrumbs
olive oil

Peel, boil and mash potatoes. Add butter, salt and pepper to taste. Heat a heavy-based frypan over medium heat, add olive oil and cook salmon for 2 minutes on each side. Allow fish to cool slightly, then flake the flesh discarding skin and bones (if any). Add fish to mashed potato along with dill, if using.

Divide mixture into 12 equal-sized pieces and pat into burger shapes. Put flour in a shallow bowl. Beat egg and milk together in another bowl and put breadcrumbs in a third bowl. Coat each fish cake in flour and shake excess off. Then coat with egg and finally breadcrumbs, making sure each cake is well coated at each stage. Fish cakes can be refrigerated until needed.

Preheat oven to 180°C. Place a heavy-based frypan over high heat, add a generous splash of olive oil and cook fish cakes for 3–4 minutes on each side until golden brown. You may have to do this in batches.

Place fish cakes on a baking tray and cook in preheated oven for a further 10 minutes. Serve with Lemon Butter Sauce (page 555) or a squeeze of lemon juice.

Pan-fried fish fillets

Serves 4

Once a week we will have this for dinner and the children eat just as much of it as we do, sometimes more. Usually we choose flathead or rockling for flavour and firmness. We eat fish with everything: rice; boiled, baked, mashed or fried potatoes; and sometimes noodles.

500 g firm white fish fillets
seasoned flour
oil and butter for cooking
lemon wedges to serve

Cut fish onto 10 cm pieces. Coat with flour, shaking excess away. Heat a heavy-based frypan over a medium–high heat. Add a splash of oil and a knob of butter (for flavour and browning). Cook fish for 3–4 minutes, or until golden brown. Turn over, add more oil and butter if needed and continue cooking for a further 2–3 minutes.

Remove and serve straight away with lemon wedges. We usually have to cook ours in two batches to fit in the pan, which means the children get a head start on dinner.

Fish fingers

Serves 4

Flathead is ideal for this recipe, but salmon adds an extra dimension altogether. Be sure to serve salmon fish fingers with boiled potatoes tossed with butter and fresh herbs.

500 g fish fillets, skin removed
1 egg
125 ml (½ cup) milk
75 g (½ cup) seasoned flour
75 g (¾ cup) dry breadcrumbs
oil

Cut the fish fillets on the angle into thick fingers. Beat the egg with milk and set aside in a shallow dish. Place the flour in a flat dish and the breadcrumbs in another flat dish. Coat the fish with flour, then dip into the egg mix and finally coat well with breadcrumbs.

Heat a large heavy-based frypan over a medium–high heat. Pour in a generous splash of oil and add the fish fingers to the pan. Make sure they don't overlap or they won't cook properly. Cook for 2–3 minutes on one side, until golden brown. If the pan becomes dry, add more oil as required. Turn fingers over and cook them for 2 minutes on the other side, or until golden brown. Continue cooking for 1–2 minutes, until all sides are golden brown.

Serve with Tartare Sauce (page 554) and Pear, Walnut and Rocket Salad (page 507).

Seven-spice fish fillets

Serves 4

Here fish fillets are dusted with a flavoursome spice mixture and flour with great results. Who said cooking was difficult?

60 g (⅓ cup) plain flour
1 tsp sweet paprika
½ tsp ground ginger
½ tsp chilli powder
½ tsp ground coriander
¼ tsp ground cinnamon
¼ tsp ground cardamom
¼ tsp allspice
1 tsp salt
500 g firm white fish fillets
oil
lemon wedges to serve

Mix flour, spices and salt together. Cut fish onto 10 cm pieces. Coat fish with spice mix, shaking excess away. Heat a heavy-based frypan over a medium–high heat. Add a splash of oil. Add fish (you may need to cook in two batches). Cook fish for 3–4 minutes, or until golden brown. Turn over, add more oil if needed and continue cooking for a further 2–3 minutes. Serve with lemon wedges and Couscous (page 453).

Creole fish fillets
Substitute Creole Spice Blend (page 295) for spice mix.

Pan-fried fish with coconut curry sauce

Serves 4

Every now and again the curry craving takes over and we jazz our fish up like this.

500 g firm white fish fillets
seasoned flour
oil and butter for cooking
300 ml (1¼ cups) coconut milk
2 tbsp Thai curry paste

Cut fish into 10 cm pieces. Coat with flour, shaking excess away. Heat a heavy-based frypan over a medium–high heat. Add a splash of oil and a knob of butter (for flavour and browning). Cook fish for 3–4 minutes, or until golden brown. Turn over, add more oil and butter if needed and continue cooking for a further 2–3 minutes. Remove fish; keep warm in a preheated oven.

Tip excess oil away and return pan to the heat. Add coconut milk and Thai paste and bring to the boil, stirring occasionally. Once boiling, reduce heat and cook for 2–3 minutes. Serve the sauce on top of the fish. This fish and sauce combination is great over a bowl of noodles.

Crispy skin fish with spring onions

Serves 4

Choose either 1 large fish, such as snapper or perch, or 4 small individual fish such as barramundi or red snapper.

- 8 spring onions, thinly sliced
- 2 cloves garlic, crushed
- 2 tsp grated ginger
- 1 tbsp light soy sauce
- 1 large fish (1 kg) or 4 (250 g each) small ones, gutted
- peanut oil
- 4 spring onions, sliced, green tops only for garnish
- soy sauce to serve

Preheat oven to 180°C.

Mix spring onions with garlic, ginger and soy sauce and stuff into the cavity of the fish. With a sharp knife, make 3 slashes on each side of the fish through to the bone. Heat a heavy-based frypan, add enough peanut oil to cover the base of the pan and cook fish until golden brown on each side.

Place on a baking tray and bake in preheated oven (20 minutes for large fish, 10 minutes for small fish). Heat 100 ml peanut oil over a high heat while fish is cooking (the oil must be very hot to get the fish skin to crackle). When the fish is removed from the oven, pour a small ladleful of the hot oil right over the entire fish. The skin will crackle instantly.

Garnish with green tops of spring onions and drizzle each fish with light soy sauce to serve.

Deep-fried fish fillets in beer batter

Serves 4

This batter is guaranteed to be light and fluffy because of the yeast in the beer. Small fish fillets like flathead and strips of rockling are perfect to use.

- 250 ml (1 cup) beer
- 2 tbsp olive oil
- 1 egg
- 170 g (1 cup plus 1 tbsp) plain flour
- pinch of salt
- 500 g firm white fish fillets
- seasoned flour
- oil for deep-frying

Whisk together beer, oil and egg. Sift flour and salt and add to beer, whisk until smooth. Set aside for 30 minutes. Coat fish in seasoned flour, then batter, allowing excess to drip off.

Ease fish gently into hot oil and cook until golden, turning fish over once. Drain on absorbent paper, sprinkle with salt and serve with lemon wedges, Lemon Mayonnaise (page 554) and salad.

Pan-fried fish with yellow miso dressing

Serves 4

What better way to serve fresh seafood than topped with this Asian-inspired warm salad of coriander leaves and red onion?

- 1 tbsp yellow miso
- 2 tbsp lemon juice
- 125 ml (½ cup) water
- 2 tbsp mirin
- 1 tbsp rice vinegar
- 2 tsp soy sauce
- 1 tsp grated ginger
- 1 clove garlic, crushed
- 2 tsp sesame seeds
- 500 g firm white fish fillets
- seasoned flour
- oil
- handful of coriander leaves
- ½ red onion, thinly sliced
- lime wedges to serve
- Steamed Rice (page 198) to serve

Combine the miso, lemon juice, water, mirin, rice vinegar, soy sauce, ginger, garlic and sesame seeds.

Dust the fish fillets with seasoned flour, shaking off excess. Heat a heavy-based frypan over a high heat, add a generous splash of oil and cook the fish for 3–4 minutes on each side, until golden brown and cooked through.

While the fish is cooking, toss the coriander leaves and red onion together.

Place the fish fillets on plates, add the coriander salad and pour 1–2 tbsp of the yellow miso dressing over the fish. Serve immediately with lime wedges and Steamed Rice.

Steamed fish with yellow miso dressing

Place a wok over a high heat. Add 6 cm of water and bring to the boil. Rest a plate in the bottom of a bamboo steamer and place in the wok. Arrange the fish fillets on the plate. Pour the dressing over the fish and steam for 5–6 minutes, or until the fish is cooked through. The timing will depend on the thickness of the fish fillets. Top with salad and serve with cooking juices and Steamed Rice.

Pan-fried swordfish with olive ratatouille

Serves 4

You can substitute the swordfish with any oily fish such as salmon, tuna or even marlin. Either way the olive ratatouille is a great match.

olive oil
1 onion, finely diced
1 long thin eggplant, finely diced
1 small zucchini, finely diced
freshly ground black pepper
2 cloves garlic, crushed
3 Roma tomatoes, finely diced
90 g (½ cup) kalamata olives, pitted and roughly chopped
1 tbsp tomato paste
2 tbsp chopped basil leaves
4 × 200 g swordfish steaks

Heat 3 tbsp oil in a small saucepan over a medium–high heat. Add onion, eggplant, zucchini and pepper. Stir and cook for 5 minutes or until soft. Add garlic, stir well, and then add tomatoes, olives, and tomato paste. Bring to the boil, reduce to a simmer, then cover and cook for 20 minutes, stirring occasionally.

Heat a heavy-based frypan over a medium heat. Brush swordfish with olive oil and grind a little black pepper over each steak. Cook fish for 2–3 minutes on each side for medium–rare, or 4–5 minutes for medium.

Serve fish fillets on top of ratatouille.

Pan-fried salmon with chilli coriander udon broth

Serves 4

Simple yet impressive enough for any occasion, this dish is an absolute beauty. The salmon fillets are served on udon noodles, surrounded by an aromatic broth.

- 750 ml (3 cups) chicken or vegetable stock
- 2 kaffir lime leaves (optional)
- 1 lemongrass stem, chopped
- 4 small red chillies
- ½ bunch coriander roots, chopped
- 3 cm piece of ginger, sliced
- oil
- 4 salmon steaks
- 200 g udon noodles
- 2–3 tbsp fish sauce
- 4 shallots, peeled and sliced
- 1½–2 tbsp lime juice
- salt and freshly ground black pepper
- 1 cup coriander leaves
- 2 small red chillies, sliced, for garnish

Place a medium-sized saucepan over a medium heat. Add stock and bring to the boil. Add lime leaves (if using), lemongrass, chillies, coriander roots and ginger. Reduce heat and simmer for 20–30 minutes to allow the flavours to infuse. Strain into a clean saucepan.

Heat a heavy-based frypan over a medium–high heat. Add a generous splash of oil and place the salmon flesh side down in the frypan. Cook for 4–5 minutes, then turn over and cook for a further 4 minutes.

Place the udon noodles in a heatproof bowl and pour boiling water over them.

Bring the infused stock back to the boil, then add the fish sauce, shallots and lime juice. Check seasoning, adding pepper and more fish sauce if necessary. Reduce to a simmer.

When salmon is cooked to medium, remove from heat. Drain the noodles and divide them between bowls. Top with 1 piece of salmon. Pour stock over the fish and garnish each bowl with coriander leaves and additional sliced red chillies.

Steamed Thai fish

Serves 4

Steaming is a simple way to cook delicate food such as fish, yet it's a method that's rarely used by most home cooks. Well, this could just be the recipe to inspire you to give it a try.

½ bunch coriander
½ tsp salt
2 cloves garlic, crushed
2 fresh green chillies, finely diced
60 ml (¼ cup) lime juice
2–3 tsp caster sugar
2 tbsp fish sauce
1 tsp sesame oil
4 fish fillets or 1 whole fish
2 tbsp julienne ginger
2 spring onions, thinly sliced
Steamed Rice (page 198) to serve

Trim roots from coriander and chop finely. Mix the coriander roots, salt, garlic, chillies, lime juice, caster sugar, fish sauce and sesame oil together. Pound briefly with a mortar and pestle or whiz briefly in a food processor. Pick the coriander leaves from the stems and set aside for garnish.

Place a wok over a high heat. Add 6 cm of water and bring to the boil. Rest a plate in the bottom of a bamboo steamer and place in the wok. Arrange fish fillets or the whole fish on the plate and pour the marinade over. Top with the julienne ginger. Cover and steam for 6–8 minutes, depending on the thickness of the fish. A whole fish may take up to 12–15 minutes.

Serve the fish with the cooking juices, spring onions and coriander leaves, along with Steamed Rice.

Soy ginger salmon

Serves 4

Soy and ginger are classic partners for fresh salmon. This dish can be served on top of stir-fried greens or with Ramen Noodle and Sesame Salad (page 528).

2 tsp grated ginger
1 small red chilli, de-seeded and diced
60 ml (¼ cup) soy sauce
1 tsp Salt and Pepper Spice (page 295) (optional)
4 × 200 g salmon fillets
oil

Combine the ginger, chilli, soy sauce and pepper mix (if using). Brush over the salmon fillets and marinate for up to 30 minutes, if time permits.

Heat a heavy-based frypan over a high heat. Add a generous splash of oil and cook the salmon fillets for 3–4 minutes on each side, until golden brown and medium–rare. Cook for 1–2 minutes longer if you prefer your fish cooked to medium.

Baked fish parcels with coconut milk and kaffir lime

Serves 4 as a side dish

We can't express how simple fish parcels are to make and how dramatic they look as you serve them.

1 carrot
8 choy sum stems
4 greaseproof paper squares
4 kaffir lime leaves
2 spring onions, sliced
1 lemongrass stalk, sliced
2 tbsp fish sauce
4 firm white fish fillets
60 ml (¼ cup) coconut milk
coriander sprigs

Preheat oven to 180°C.

Peel the carrot, then cut long strips from the carrot using the peeler. Cut choy sum into 6 cm lengths. Lay 4 greaseproof paper squares out flat. Divide carrot and choy sum between paper squares and lay one kaffir lime leaf on top of each pile. Divide spring onions and lemongrass between piles. Sprinkle with fish sauce.

Place fish on top and pour coconut milk over. Fold paper ends in and pull remaining two edges up together. Roll over tightly to finish on top of the fish. Cook fish in preheated oven for 15 minutes.

Serve with jasmine rice.

Sweet chilli and mirin steamed tofu

Serves 4 as a side dish

This is another steamed dish, this time using tofu flavoured with ginger, mirin, spring onion and sweet chilli sauce.

750 g soft tofu
2 tsp grated ginger
60 ml (¼ cup) mirin
6 spring onions, thinly sliced
2 tbsp sweet chilli sauce

Cut tofu into 1 cm chunks. Place on a plate. Mix remaining ingredients together. Pour over tofu. Place plate in bamboo steamer. Place steamer over wok filled with boiling water and cook for 5–6 minutes. Remove plate and serve immediately.

BARBIES

outdoor food from the grill

Australians have a patriotic duty to throw a snag or shrimp on the barbie, or so it seems. Whether it's in the backyard, at a local park or a large social gathering, barbecues are part of our culture. Thankfully we've moved on from fatty lamb chops and tough steaks to more sophisticated salmon steaks, chicken fillets, kebabs, quality steaks and even vegetables.

Barbecuing isn't just popular in Australia. You'll find barbecues in market places throughout Spain, Turkey and Greece, from the tropics of Thailand to Moroccan street vendors, Japan's hibachis and Caribbean beachside grills. We've included some of the very best recipes from these barbecue-loving nations so that you can re-create them in your backyard.

Barbecuing isn't just for summer either. Many of us use our barbecues all year round, braving the milder winter nights to fire up the beast. Alternatively, if you prefer, any of these recipes can be cooked on a grill or in a grill pan or frypan. But why not get out into the backyard, tongs in hand, and get sizzling!

barbie recipes

marinades

Ultimate barbecue marinade	292
Barbecue baste	292
Wine marinade	292
Asian marinade	292
Indian spice mix	293
Chilli and garlic marinade	293
Spicy Mexican marinade	293
Soy and garlic marinade	293
Caribbean fish marinade	294
Simple Moroccan blend	294
Creole spice blend	295
Sweet sticky marinade	295
Salt and pepper spice	295

barbies

Lemon spice chicken	296
Lemony chicken and veal burgers	297
Moorish chicken skewers	298
Spicy lip-smacking drumsticks	298
Barbecued lime and chilli chicken wings	299
Chicken saltimbocca skewers	299
Chicken satay kebabs	300
Chicken tandoori in naan bread	300
Whole barbecued chicken with lemon and herbs	301
Piri-piri chicken	301
The perfect porterhouse	302
Chilli rump steak	302
Classic beef and mushroom kebabs	303
Pinchito beef kebabs	303
Oriental beef	304
Spiced beef balls in basil leaves	304
Chimichuri barbecued beef	305
Rosemary lamb kebabs	305
Moroccan lamb cutlets	306
Asian lamb steaks	306
Lebanese lamb kebabs	307
Lamb souvlaki	307
North African lamb	308
Lime coriander lamb cutlets	308
Greek leg of lamb	309
Satay pork sugar-cane sticks	309
Harissa pork	310
Pork shish kebabs	310
Asian chilli pork steaks	311
American pork ribs	311
Sichuan pepper and honey pork fillet	312
Indonesian marinated baby chickens	312
Japanese glazed duck	313
Pomegranate and sumac glazed duck	313
Shiraz-glazed quails	314
Spanish barbecued quails	316
Cevapcici	317
Simple barbecued fish	317
Thai fish cakes	318
Barbecued whole snapper in banana leaves	319
Swordfish kebabs	319
Sizzlin' garlic prawns	320
Barbecued chermoula prawns	320
Thai barbecued prawns	321
Crayfish with roasted red capsicum butter	321
Coconut spiced prawn kebabs	322
Chilli crabs	324
Ginger mirin salmon	324
Soy and ginger salmon kebabs	325
Spice-coated tuna	325
Tuna teriyaki skewers	326
Yakitori chicken kebabs	326
Barbecued whole fish	328
Spice and salt sardines	328
Whole smoky salmon	329
Barbecued oysters	329
Moroccan eggplant and capsicum kebabs	330
Spiced green lentil burgers	330
Haloumi and couscous burgers	331
Mexican bean cakes with chilli salsa	332
Caramelised onion and chickpea burgers	333
Lentil and ricotta burgers	334
Grilled polenta with garlic vegetables	335

Things you need to know about barbecues

1 Get to know your barbecue's hot and cold spots, and then you can move food around accordingly.

2 Food will take longer to cook on a windy day as the wind will disturb the heat.

3 Never barbecue in bare feet, as you could be injured by falling embers.

4 Always bring food out from the kitchen just before cooking it.

5 Don't use the flip-flop approach to barbecuing meat. Instead, place the meat on the barbecue, cook it as recommended, then rotate it 180 degrees. Turn it over and rotate it once more. (Turn it only once.)

6 Never cut into the meat to see if it is cooked, as the juices will escape.

7 Allow large cuts of meat to rest for 5 minutes before serving them.

8 Freshness and quality are paramount to getting the best from seafood. Fresh-produce markets are great places to buy fish, as are local fishmongers. Always ask what's best on the day.

9 Snapper, Atlantic salmon and barramundi are great choices if you want to cook a whole fish. Check whole fish for signs of freshness such as clear eyes, no unpleasant smells and bright scales.

10 If you're cooking food with bones, such as a whole fish, you can shorten the cooking time by covering it with a lid. A wok lid makes a great cover, but if you don't have one try a deep baking tray or a few layers of foil. Either will work okay.

11 One of the great things about cooking seafood on the barbecue is that all the fishy cooking smells are left outside.

12 Try simple flavours such as fresh herbs, garlic and lemon when cooking everyday fish fillets.

13 Cook a few salmon steaks, then crumble them over a huge salad for one-platter dining.

14 Oily fish such as ocean trout, salmon, sardines, tuna and swordfish are all ideal for the barbecue, as the natural oils help keep the fish moist during cooking. Oily fish also copes better with strong flavours and spice such as ginger, fish sauce, lemongrass and chillies.

15 Cleaning up is a breeze, as the grill simply needs to be scrubbed with a wire brush and wiped over with newspaper or kitchen towel.

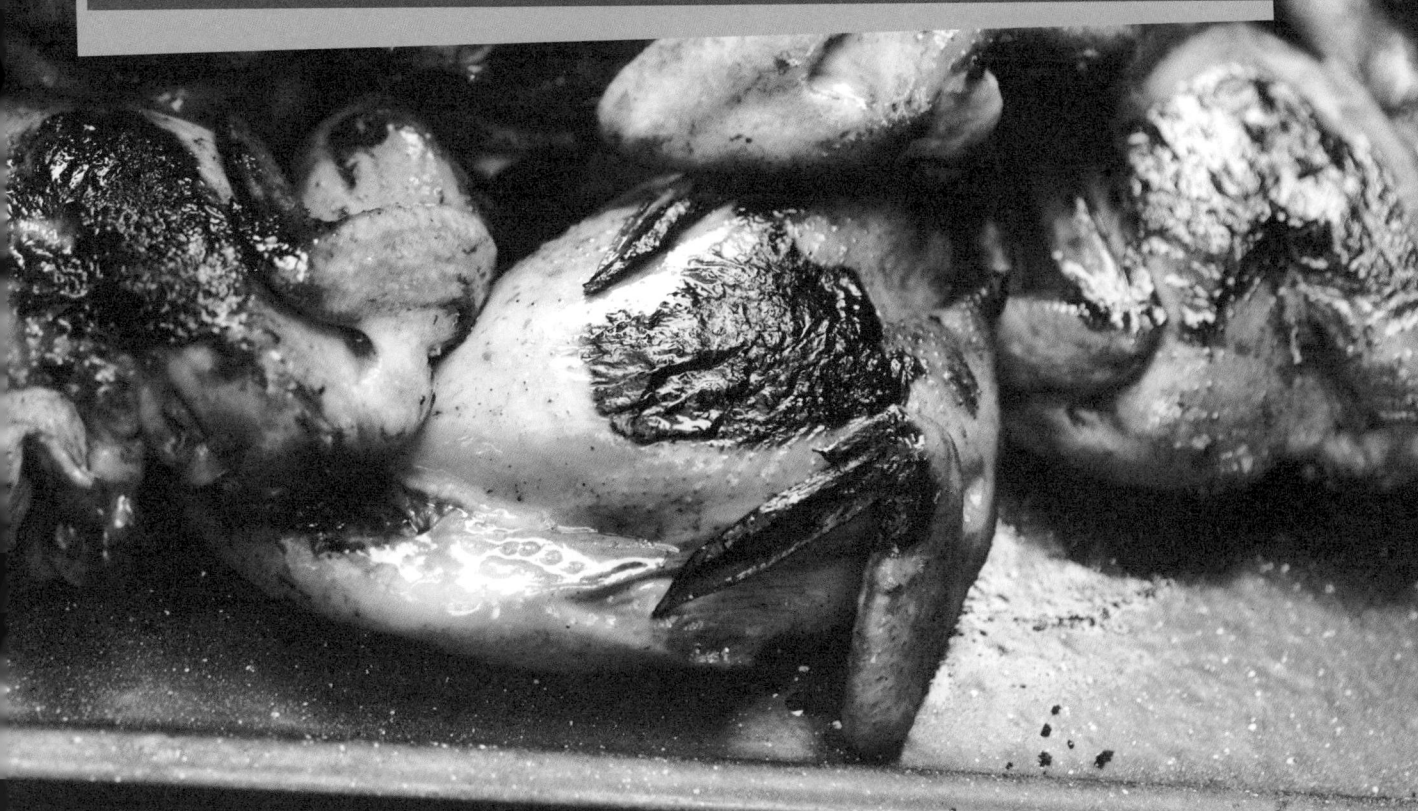

Ultimate barbecue marinade

This ultimate barbecue marinade is perfect for pork, beef or chicken.

60 ml (¼ cup) tomato ketchup
1 tbsp Worcestershire sauce
1 tbsp white vinegar
1 tbsp brown sugar
2 tsp Dijon mustard
1 tsp chilli powder
dash of Tabasco

Whisk all the ingredients together and brush onto the meat as it is barbecuing.

Barbecue baste

This baste packs a punch. My favourite way of using it is on chicken wings, chicken drumsticks and beef ribs. AC

1 onion, diced
125 ml (½ cup) tomato sugo
2 tbsp Worcestershire sauce
2 tbsp red wine vinegar
100 g (½ cup) brown sugar
1 tbsp smooth mustard
1 clove garlic, crushed
1 tsp sweet paprika
1 tsp ground coriander
1 tsp ground cumin
1 tsp freshly ground black pepper
½ tsp salt
250 ml (1 cup) water

Place all the ingredients in a saucepan and bring to the boil. Reduce to a simmer and cook for 30 minutes.

Place baste in a food processor and puree until smooth. Adjust seasoning and allow to cool. Brush onto meat as it is barbecuing.

Wine marinade

Use white wine if you are going to use this marinade on white meats, and red wine for red meats.

80 ml (⅓ cup) olive oil
80 ml (⅓ cup) wine of your choice
2 shallots, finely diced
2 cloves garlic, crushed
3 tsp chopped fresh herbs
salt and freshly ground black pepper

Mix all the ingredients together and brush onto the meat as it is barbecuing.

Asian marinade

This marinade is particularly good on chicken and pork.

1 tbsp black beans, soaked and drained
80 ml (⅓ cup) soy sauce
2 tbsp fish sauce
2 tsp chilli paste
1 tsp sesame oil
2 tsp grated ginger

Mash the black beans with a fork, then add the remaining ingredients. Brush the mix onto the meat as it is barbecuing.

Indian spice mix
A classic blend from the subcontinent.

2 tsp ground coriander
1 tsp turmeric
1 tsp ground cinnamon
1 tsp ground cumin
¼ tsp ground ginger
¼ tsp chilli

Mix the spices together well and coat chicken, lamb or beef just before barbecuing.

Chilli and garlic marinade
The perfect marinade for beef or lamb.

2 small red chillies, de-seeded and diced
2 cloves garlic, crushed
salt and freshly ground black pepper
80 ml (⅓ cup) olive oil

Mix all the ingredients together. Pour over the meat and allow to marinate for at least 30 minutes, or up to 4 hours, before barbecuing.

Spicy Mexican marinade
This one really packs a punch. It is great on chicken wings, drumettes and beef ribs.

1 clove garlic, crushed
½ tsp salt
½ tsp chilli powder
1 tsp sweet paprika
½ tsp ground coriander
½ tsp ground cumin
1 tsp mustard seeds, crushed
½ tsp freshly ground black pepper
2 tbsp olive oil

Mix all the ingredients together and brush onto the meat as it is barbecuing.

Soy and garlic marinade
This is a simple marinade that works wonders with chicken, fish and pork.

1½ tbsp rice vinegar
2 tbsp soy sauce
1 clove garlic, crushed
pinch of five-spice powder
1 tsp caster sugar
a few drops of Tabasco

Mix all the ingredients together and brush onto the meat as it is barbecuing.

Caribbean fish marinade

This is really good with fish, particularly oily fish like garfish, sardines and salmon.

60 ml (¼ cup) lime juice
1 tsp allspice
3 spring onions, thinly sliced
1 small red chilli, de-seeded and finely diced
½ tsp salt
2 tbsp olive oil

Mix all ingredients together and brush onto fish just before barbecuing.

Simple Moroccan blend

This blend can be added to just about any meat successfully, particularly lamb and quail.

1 tsp ground coriander
1 tsp ground cumin
1 tsp sweet paprika
½ tsp salt
1½ tbsp lemon juice
2 tbsp olive oil

Mix the ingredients together to form a smooth paste. Brush it onto lamb just before barbecuing.

Creole spice blend

This blend is an oldie but a goodie. We like it best on chicken and fish.

4½ tsp sweet paprika
3 tsp onion powder
3 tsp garlic powder
1½ tsp thyme leaves
1½ tsp ground oregano
1 tsp cayenne pepper
1 tsp white pepper
1 tsp freshly ground black pepper

Mix the spices together well and coat chicken or fish just before barbecuing.

Salt and pepper spice

A classic spice mix that's good with oily fish, quail, chicken and prawns.

3 tsp Sichuan pepper
½ tsp salt
½ tsp five-spice powder

Place the pepper and salt in a dry pan and cook over a medium heat. Stir until the salt turns golden, about 3 minutes. Crush until very fine in a mortar and pestle. Sieve to remove husks and stir five-spice powder through.

Sprinkle the mixture onto meat or seafood just before barbecuing.

Sweet sticky marinade

This marinade goes particularly well with pork neck, which can be bought from any butcher's shop in an Asian shopping area.

250 ml (1 cup) dark soy sauce
125 ml (½ cup) rice vinegar
2 tbsp honey
1 tsp sesame oil
2 cloves garlic, crushed
2 tsp grated ginger
2 tbsp hot bean paste
½ tsp five-spice powder

Mix all ingredients together. Marinate meat for 1–2 hours and drain excess marinade before cooking. Serve with Asian Noodle Salad (page 528).

Lemon spice chicken

Serves 4

This marinade is incredibly easy to make and tastes as if you've gone to lots of trouble. Sounds like just the thing for dinner tonight!

4 chicken breast fillets
80 ml (⅓ cup) olive oil
2 tbsp lemon juice
1 tbsp sweet paprika
¾ tsp salt
1 tsp ground cumin
¼ tsp ground cayenne pepper
2 tbsp chopped flat-leaf parsley leaves
1 lemon, cut into wedges, to serve

Place the chicken in a flat dish. Combine the oil, lemon juice, paprika, salt, cumin, cayenne and parsley. Brush the marinade onto the chicken and leave to marinate for at least 2 hours.

Place the chicken on a medium–hot barbecue grill and cook for 6–7 minutes, rotating once. Turn over and cook for a further 4–6 minutes, rotating once.

Serve with lemon wedges.

Lemony chicken and veal burgers

Serves 10

This recipe produces an Italian-inspired burger flavoured with garlic, lemon, chopped fresh herbs and parmigiano.

100 g day-old bread
250 ml (1 cup) milk
500 g veal mince
500 g chicken mince
salt and freshly ground black pepper
¼ cup chopped parsley
2 cloves garlic, crushed
zest of 1 lemon, chopped
60 g (¾ cup) grated parmigiano
plain flour for dusting
2 lemons, cut into wedges, to serve

Tear the bread into small pieces and soak in milk for 10–15 minutes.

Squeeze the bread well to remove excess liquid, then place in a bowl with the minces, salt and pepper, parsley, garlic, lemon zest and parmigiano and mix well. Divide into 10 and form into burger shapes. Roll each burger lightly in flour.

Place the burgers on a hot barbecue and cook for 6–7 minutes, rotating once. Turn over and cook for a further 5–6 minutes, rotating once.

Serve with lemon wedges.

Moorish chicken skewers

Serves 20

These are great if you are planning to have your meal outdoors, as you can easily cook them on the barbecue as you chat to the guests.

500 g skinless chicken thigh fillets
1 tsp ground coriander
1 tsp ground cumin
1 tsp ground fennel (optional)
1 tsp smoky sweet paprika
1 tbsp chopped oregano
2 tsp red wine vinegar
1 tbsp olive oil
salt and freshly ground black pepper
20 wooden skewers, soaked in cold water

Dice chicken into 2 cm chunks. Mix remaining ingredients together. Stir into chicken and marinate for at least 30 minutes, but no longer than 4 hours. Thread 3–4 pieces of chicken on to each skewer.

Place on a hot barbecue grill for 6–7 minutes, turning once or twice.

Pile on a platter and serve with a bowl of Quince Aioli (page 550).

Spicy lip-smacking drumsticks

Serves 4

The flavours in this garlic and spice mix are perfect on chicken drumsticks. Cooking the meat on the bone leaves the chicken beautifully moist.

1 clove garlic, crushed
1 tsp chilli powder
1 tsp sweet paprika
1 tsp mustard
½ tsp ground coriander
½ tsp ground cumin
½ tsp freshly ground black pepper
½ tsp salt
2 tbsp olive oil
1 kg chicken drumsticks

Mix the marinade ingredients together. Rub the mix over the chicken drumsticks and allow to marinate for at least 2 hours.

Place the drumsticks on a medium–hot barbecue plate and cook for 30 minutes, turning often.

Use any remaining marinade for basting during cooking.

Barbecued lime and chilli chicken wings

Serves 5–6

This one is finger lickin' good. Children wolf these wings down without even realising the chilli is in there.

125 ml (½ cup) lime juice
1 small red chilli, de-seeded and finely diced
½ tsp salt
1 tsp caster sugar
2 tbsp olive oil
1 kg chicken wings

Mix lime juice, chilli, salt, sugar and oil together. Marinate chicken wings for 1 hour. Drain off excess marinade and use for basting during cooking.

Place chicken on oiled barbecue grill. Cook for 20 minutes, turning often.

Lime and chilli lamb cutlets
Substitute 12 lamb cutlets for chicken wings and cook for 4–5 minutes on each side.

Chicken saltimbocca skewers

Makes 24

Anything on a skewer is a great hit at a barbecue. We sometimes make mini versions of these and serve them as a pre-dinner nibble.

2 tbsp olive oil
2 tbsp chopped fresh sage
salt and freshly ground black pepper
4 chicken breast fillets, skinless
12 thin slices prosciutto
24 skewers, soaked in cold water

Mix together oil, sage, salt and pepper. Cut each chicken fillet into 6 long strips. Mix sage oil and chicken together.

Cut prosciutto slices in half lengthways. Lay out one slice of prosciutto and place 1 strip of chicken on top. Thread prosciutto and chicken onto skewers.

Place skewers on oiled barbecue plate. Cook for 4 minutes on each side.

Chicken satay kebabs

Serves 10

These satay kebabs are ideal as a starter or as part of a larger spread of food.

500 g chicken breast fillets, skinless
1 small onion, diced
1 tbsp soy sauce
60 ml (¼ cup) peanut oil
2 tsp ground coriander
1 tsp ground cumin
1 tsp ground turmeric
¼ tsp ground cinnamon
1 tsp salt
1 tsp sugar
60 g (⅓ cup) roasted peanuts
20 skewers, soaked in cold water

Cut chicken into 3 cm chunks. Make satay by placing remaining ingredients in a food processor and blend until smooth. Marinate chicken in the satay for 1 hour. Thread 4–5 pieces of chicken onto each skewer.

Place chicken skewers on oiled barbecue grill. Cook for 10 minutes, turning 2–3 times.

Beef satay kebabs
Substitute beef fillet for chicken.

Chicken tandoori in naan bread

Serves 4

We eat this dish with alarming regularity. Sometimes we make our own Naan Bread (page 155), but usually we purchase it from the supermarket or Indian takeaway for convenience.

4 chicken thigh fillets, skinless
250 g (1 cup) natural yoghurt
2 tbsp tandoori paste
1 tbsp lemon juice
12 skewers
2 tomatoes, finely diced
1 Lebanese cucumber, finely diced
2 spring onions, thinly sliced
1 tbsp chopped mint
1 tbsp lemon juice, additional
2 tbsp olive oil
4 Naan (page 155)
natural yoghurt, additional

Dice chicken into 3 cm chunks. Mix together yoghurt, tandoori paste and lemon juice. Marinate chicken for 1 hour. Thread 4 or 5 pieces of chicken onto each skewer. Place chicken on an oiled barbecue plate. Cook for 12 minutes, turning 3 or 4 times.

Mix together tomato, cucumber, onion, mint, additional juice and oil. Place Naan Bread on an oiled barbecue grill for 1–2 minutes before serving. Serve skewers in hot bread with salad over the top. Add additional natural yoghurt.

Whole barbecued chicken with lemon and herbs

Serves 4

This marinade can also be used with chicken wings, chicken fillets or drumsticks.

1 size 16 chicken, spatchcocked
2 cloves garlic, crushed
½ cup chopped parsley, thyme, basil and oregano
1 tbsp lemon juice
salt and freshly ground black pepper
pinch of ground cumin
pinch of ground coriander
pinch of sweet paprika
60 ml (¼ cup) olive oil

Place the chicken in a flat dish. Mix the remaining ingredients together to create a marinade. Brush the marinade all over the chicken. Place the chicken on an oiled barbecue plate and cover it with a lid. Cook the chicken for 15 minutes, rotating 2–3 times. Turn the chicken over and cover again with the lid. Cook for a further 15 minutes, rotating the chicken 2–3 times. Remove the lid, baste well and continue cooking uncovered for a further 10 minutes.

Piri-piri chicken

Serves 4

Piri-piri is a fiery sauce that was created after the Portuguese were introduced to hot chillies in East Africa. It's now incredibly popular throughout much of the barbecue-loving world. In this version the chillies and garlic are lightly cooked then mixed with olive oil and vinegar. Brush with abandon onto virtually anything you're cooking on the barbecue.

1 size 16 chicken, spatchcocked
250 ml (1 cup) olive oil
8 hot chillies, chopped
4 cloves garlic, sliced
½ tsp salt
¼ tsp freshly ground black pepper
2 tbsp red wine vinegar

Place the chicken into a flat dish. Heat 2 tbsp olive oil in a saucepan and cook the chillies and garlic for 3–4 minutes. Add the remaining ingredients then remove the saucepan from the heat. Allow to cool then brush a little of the sauce over the chicken. Marinate for at least 2 hours.

Lay the chicken breast skin side down onto a medium–hot barbecue grill, baste, cover with a lid and cook for 15 minutes, rotating if needed.

Turn the chicken over, baste, cover and cook for a further 15 minutes, rotating if needed. Remove the lid, baste well and continue cooking uncovered for a further 10 minutes.

To serve, cut the chicken into portions and serve with a selection of cooling salads.

The perfect porterhouse

Serves 4

Porterhouse steak is one of the more tender cuts available. It offers a good balance between flavour and juiciness, with just a thin layer of fat across the top to keep it moist during cooking.

4 × 200g porterhouse steaks
salt and freshly ground black pepper
oil

Place porterhouse steaks on an oiled barbecue grill. Season and cook for 6 minutes, rotating once. Turn over and cook for a further 4–5 minutes, rotating once, for medium–rare steaks.

For medium, cook for an extra 2 minutes. Rest the steaks for 5 minutes before serving.

Chilli rump steak

Serves 4

Rump is a gutsy, full-flavoured meat that is perfectly suited to barbecuing. It also copes well with this searing chilli and garlic baste.

4 × 250 g rump steaks
1 tsp chilli paste
2 tbsp lime juice
2 tbsp olive oil
2 cloves garlic, crushed
½ tsp salt
½ tsp freshly ground black pepper

Place the steaks in a large dish. Combine the remaining ingredients and smear over the steaks. Set aside to marinate for at least 1 hour.

Place the steaks on a medium–hot barbecue grill and cook for 5–6 minutes, rotating as needed. Brush marinade onto them during cooking.

Turn the steaks over and cook for a further 4–5 minutes, rotating as needed. Continue to brush with the marinade.

Allow the steaks to rest on a cool part of the barbecue for 5 minutes before serving.

Chilli pork ribs
Double the chilli marinade recipe and use it on pork ribs. Pork and chilli is a magical combination, especially when cooked on the barbecue.

Classic beef and mushroom kebabs

Makes 14 kebabs

We call these our 'classic' kebabs because everyone loves them, children and grown-ups alike. I've been making them since I was 16, when I was training to be a chef. They are always a hit. MC

1 kg tender beef (fillet, porterhouse or rump)
2 tsp Dijon mustard
2 tsp chopped rosemary
2 tbsp olive oil
60 ml (¼ cup) red wine
salt and freshly ground black pepper
1 red capsicum
16 button mushrooms (200 g)
14 skewers
oil

Cut beef into 2 cm chunks. Mix the mustard, rosemary, oil, red wine, salt and pepper together. Pour over the beef and marinate for 1 hour.

Cut capsicum in half, remove the seeds and dice into 2 cm chunks. Wipe mushrooms clean and cut in half.

Drain excess marinade off the beef and set aside for basting during cooking. Thread ingredients onto 14 skewers. Heat a heavy-based frypan over a medium–high heat. Add a generous splash of oil and cook the kebabs for 8–10 minutes, turning often.

Pinchito beef kebabs

Makes 8 kebabs

Pinchito kebabs are a popular snack at travelling fairs in Spain. This version has fresh lemon and cumin flavours.

500 g rump steak
60 ml (¼ cup) lemon juice
2 tbsp ground cumin
60 ml (¼ cup) olive oil
2 cloves garlic, crushed
1 tsp smoky paprika
½ tsp salt
½ tsp freshly ground black pepper
8 skewers

Dice the meat into 2 cm chunks. Combine the remaining ingredients and marinate the beef for at least 2 hours.

Thread 8 skewers with 4–5 pieces of meat each.

Place the kebabs on a medium–hot barbecue grill and cook for 8 minutes, turning 3–4 times.

Oriental beef

Makes 8

Chinese flavours combine with beef for a real taste of the Orient.

500 g rump steak
2 tbsp soy sauce
1 tbsp brown sugar
1 tbsp Chinese cooking wine
1 tbsp olive oil
2 tbsp chopped coriander
2 cloves garlic, crushed
1 tbsp grated ginger
large pinch of Chinese five-spice powder
8 skewers

Cut the beef into 2 cm chunks. Combine the remaining ingredients and marinate the beef for at least 1 hour.

Drain any excess marinade from the beef. Thread 8 skewers with 5–6 pieces of beef each. Place the kebabs on a medium–hot barbecue grill and cook for 10 minutes, turning 3–4 times.

Spiced beef balls in basil leaves

Serves 4

This is an interesting way of spicing up some minced beef and then skewering it so it's easy to cook and eat. These balls are great with Watercress Tabouli (page 516) and a bowl of Tzatziki (page 563).

500 g minced beef
½ tsp ground nutmeg
½ tsp ground cinnamon
1 tsp ground coriander
1 tsp ground cumin
1 tbsp chopped mint leaves
1 tbsp chopped coriander leaves
¼ tsp salt
¼ tsp freshly ground black pepper
50 large basil leaves
10 skewers

Mix beef, spices and chopped mint and coriander together with salt and pepper. Divide mix into 10 × 50 g portions. Divide each portion evenly into 5 and roll into balls. Wrap each ball in a basil leaf.

Thread 5 basil-wrapped meatballs onto each skewer. Cook on grill for 9–10 minutes, turning once or twice.

Chimichuri barbecued beef

Serves 6–8

This method of marinating a large piece of beef in chimichuri and then cooking it over a slow and smoky fire will produce a meal that is a joy to behold.

1½–2 kg piece bolar blade
¼ cup finely chopped onion
1 clove garlic, crushed
2 tbsp thyme or oregano, finely chopped
2 tbsp white wine vinegar
½ tsp sweet paprika
¼ cup parsley, finely chopped
olive oil
salt and freshly ground black pepper
200 g mesquite wood chips, soaked

Place the beef in a dish. To make the chimichuri, mix together the onion, garlic, thyme or oregano, white wine vinegar, sweet paprika and parsley. Add enough oil to make the marinade moist and season well with salt and pepper. Rub the chimichuri over the beef and marinate overnight.

Prepare your kettle barbecue in the normal manner, and wait until the coals have reached the white ash stage. Place the damp smoking mesquite wood chips on the coals.

Place beef onto a tray and put onto the barbecue. Cover and cook for 2 ½ hours, brushing the beef with more chimichuri as it cooks.

To test whether the meat is cooked, insert a knife into the thickest part of the meat, then remove it. If the juices that come from the cut are a little pink, the meat is ready.

Remove beef from the barbecue when ready, cover with foil and rest for 10 minutes before carving.

Rosemary lamb kebabs

Makes 20 kebabs

This is a simple kebab recipe that makes the most of the classic combination of lamb and rosemary. Cook the lamb to medium only, to enjoy the kebabs at their juicy best.

8 lamb fillets
60 ml (¼ cup) olive oil
1 tbsp lemon juice
2 tbsp chopped fresh rosemary
salt and freshly ground black pepper
20 skewers, soaked in cold water

Dice lamb into 2 cm squares. Mix oil, lemon juice, rosemary, salt and pepper together. Pour over lamb and marinate for 2 hours.

Thread lamb onto skewers, about 6 pieces per skewer. Use remaining marinade for basting during cooking.

Place lamb on oiled barbecue plate. Cook for 8 minutes, turning 3–4 times.

Moroccan lamb cutlets

Serves 4

We just adore this blending of Moroccan spices on juicy lamb cutlets. Whenever we have them we feel compelled to eat some Moroccan Couscous Salad (page 525) and a bowl of Tzatziki (page 563).

1 tsp ground coriander
1 tsp ground cumin
1 tsp sweet paprika
½ tsp salt
1½ tbsp lemon juice
2 tbsp olive oil
16 trim lamb cutlets

Mix spices, salt, lemon juice and oil together to form a smooth paste. Brush onto lamb cutlets. Cook for 3–4 minutes on each side.

Asian lamb steaks

Serves 8

Asian sauces combine with ginger, chilli and garlic to create a great tasting marinade for lamb steaks.

1 tbsp soy sauce
1 tbsp sweet chilli sauce
1 tsp grated ginger
1 small red chilli, de-seeded and diced
1 clove garlic, crushed
8 lamb leg steaks

Combine the soy sauce, sweet chilli sauce, ginger, chilli and garlic. Brush over the lamb and marinate for at least 20 minutes, or up to 4 hours.

Place the lamb on an oiled barbecue grill. Cook for 6–8 minutes, turning 1–2 times.

Lebanese lamb kebabs

Makes 8

Serve these Lebanese-inspired kebabs with a sprinkle of onion and sumac.

½ tsp freshly ground black pepper
¼ tsp ground allspice
½ tsp salt
1 tbsp olive oil
1 tbsp chopped flat-leaf parsley leaves

8 skewers
500 g diced lamb
2 tsp sumac
¼ onion, thinly sliced

Mix the pepper, allspice, salt, oil and parsley together. Combine with the lamb and allow to marinate for at least 2 hours.

Thread 8 skewers with 5–6 pieces of lamb each. Place the kebabs on a medium–hot barbecue grill and cook for 10 minutes, turning 3–4 times.

Mix together the onion and sumac and sprinkle over the kebabs to serve.

Lamb souvlaki

Makes 12

Souvlaki is a classic of Greek cooking and the good news is it works well on the barbecue.

60 ml (¼ cup) lemon juice
2 tbsp olive oil
1 tbsp chopped oregano
2 cloves garlic, crushed
salt and freshly ground black pepper

500 g diced lamb
1 red capsicum, diced into 2 cm chunks
2 zucchini, sliced into 1 cm chunks
Tzatziki (page 563)

Mix the lemon juice, oil, oregano, garlic, salt and pepper. Pour over the lamb and marinate for at least 20 minutes, or up to 4 hours.

Thread the lamb, capsicum and zucchini onto 12 skewers, alternating the ingredients. Place the kebabs on a hot barbecue grill and cook for 8–10 minutes, turning 3–4 times.

Serve the kebabs with Tzatziki.

North African lamb

Serves 6

Here, lamb is cooked in a kettle barbecue, adding a roasted flavour to the finished dish. If you prefer, butterfly the leg of lamb and cook it on your barbecue plate.

1½ kg easy-carve leg of lamb
½ tsp salt
2 cloves garlic, crushed
2 tsp ground coriander
2 tsp ground cumin
1 tsp freshly ground black pepper
2 tsp sweet paprika
½ tsp cayenne pepper
60 ml (¼ cup) olive oil

Make small cuts all over the lamb to allow the flavour of the marinade to permeate the meat. Stir together the remaining ingredients and smear all over the lamb. Marinate overnight, if time permits.

Prepare your kettle barbecue in the normal manner and wait until the coals have reached the white ash stage. Place the lamb on a tray, put into the barbecue and cover with the lid.

Cook for 2–3 hours, rotating and turning the lamb over every 30 minutes or so. Brush with any remaining marinade from time to time.

After 2 hours, test the meat by inserting a knife into the thickest part of the leg, then remove it. If the juices that come from the cut are pink, the meat is ready. This means the lamb is still pink in the centre. If you prefer your lamb to be completely cooked through, keep cooking until the juices run clear.

Slice and serve with Spiced Couscous (page 453).

Lime coriander lamb cutlets

Makes 12

Lamb cutlets are one of our favourite barbecue meats. They are always succulent, plus they go down a treat with children.

2 tsp ground coriander
60 ml (¼ cup) lime juice
⅓ cup chopped coriander
60 ml (¼ cup) olive oil
salt and freshly ground black pepper
12 lamb cutlets

Mix the marinade ingredients together. Brush over the lamb and marinate for at least 20 minutes, or up to 4 hours.

Drain off excess marinade and place the lamb cutlets on an oiled barbecue grill. Cook for 4 minutes, rotating once. Turn over and cook for a further 3–4 minutes, rotating once.

Greek leg of lamb

Serves 6

A leg of lamb cooked on the grill with these flavours of lemon juice, garlic and fragrant herbs is a beautiful thing. Besides tasting great it's also a good way to feed a crowd. I think I've already mentioned how much I like lamb, garlic and herbs. No surprises, then, that this is one of my favourite barbecue recipes. MC

60 ml (¼ cup) olive oil
80 ml (⅓ cup) lemon juice
3 cloves garlic, crushed
½ cup chopped basil, oregano and parsley leaves
salt and freshly ground black pepper
1 leg of lamb, boned and pressed flat

2 cloves garlic, peeled
80 ml (⅓ cup) lemon juice
1 cup parsley leaves
½ cup basil leaves
250 ml (1 cup) olive oil

Prepare marinade by mixing together oil, lemon juice, garlic, herbs, salt and pepper. Place lamb in a deep baking tray. Rub marinade over and marinate for 1 hour.

Prepare dressing by putting garlic, lemon juice, parsley and basil in a food processor. Blend until smooth. Gradually add oil, then season to taste.

Place lamb on oiled barbecue plate. Cook for 10 minutes, rotating once. Reduce heat to low and turn lamb over. Cover and cook for 10 minutes. Remove cover, rotate and cook for a further 10 minutes. Rest the meat for 10 minutes.

Cut into thick slices. Pour dressing over lamb and serve with Greek Salad (page 506).

Satay pork sugar-cane sticks

Makes 10

These sticks look – and taste – impressive when served up at a barbecue. Canned sugar cane is available from Asian grocers.

500 g pork mince
60 g (¼ cup) crunchy peanut butter
3 tsp grated ginger

zest of 2 limes, finely diced
15 pieces peeled sugar cane (½ cm × 5 cm long)
Satay Sauce (page 563)

Mix the pork mince with the peanut butter, ginger and lime zest. Divide into 10 and shape into balls. Push 1 piece of sugar cane through each ball.

Place the pork on an oiled barbecue grill. Cook for 8 minutes, turning 3–4 times. Serve with hot Satay Sauce.

Harissa pork

Makes 12

Harissa is a smoky chilli paste which is used to great effect in this marinade, along with a small selection of other spices. It adds a great flavour boost to this pork.

1 kg pork fillets, cut into 2 cm cubes
1 tsp harissa
3 tsp ground cumin
3 tsp ground coriander
2 tsp caraway seeds
½ tsp chilli powder
1 clove garlic, crushed
1 tbsp chicken stock or water
12 skewers

Place the diced pork in a bowl. Combine the remaining ingredients in a small bowl. Rub the marinade over the pork to coat evenly. Refrigerate for 30 minutes to develop the flavours.

Thread 12 skewers with 5–6 pieces of pork each. Place the kebabs on a medium–hot barbecue grill and cook for 8–10 minutes, turning 3–4 times.

Pork shish kebabs

Serves 4–6

Marinated pork and capsicum are threaded onto skewers in this recipe, with great results.

2 bay leaves
2 tbsp olive oil
60 ml (¼ cup) lemon juice
2 cloves garlic, crushed
1 tsp chopped thyme
1 tsp chopped oregano
½ tsp paprika
500 g pork fillet, diced into 2 cm chunks
1 red capsicum, diced into 2 cm chunks
8 skewers

Chop the bay leaves into small pieces and mix with the oil, lemon juice, garlic, herbs and paprika. Add the diced pork and stir to coat. Marinate for up to 30 minutes, if time permits.

Thread the pork and capsicum onto 8 skewers, alternating the ingredients. Place the kebabs on a medium–hot barbecue grill and cook for 6–8 minutes, turning 3–4 times. Rest for 1–2 minutes before serving.

Serve with Catalan Potatoes (page 492) and Tomato, Bocconcini and Basil Salad (page 509).

Asian chilli pork steaks

Serves 4

Asian flavours sit well with pork. In this recipe, hoisin sauce combines with sweet chilli and ginger to produce a great result with pork steaks.

2 tbsp hoisin sauce
1 tbsp soy sauce
2 tbsp Chinese cooking wine
1 tbsp sweet chilli sauce
2 tsp grated ginger
1 clove garlic, crushed
4 pork steaks
Steamed Rice (page 198) to serve

Combine the hoisin sauce, soy sauce, Chinese cooking wine, sweet chilli sauce, ginger and garlic. Brush over the pork and allow to marinate for 30 minutes, if time permits.

Cook the pork steaks on a medium–hot barbecue grill for 3–4 minutes on each side, until golden brown and cooked through.

Serve with Steamed Rice and Choy Sum with Ginger (page 480).

American pork ribs

Serves 4–6

Large, flat pork ribs are rubbed with an aromatic dry spice mix, then cooked long and slow in a kettle barbecue. A barbecue sauce is brushed onto them for the last 30 minutes of cooking. The results have to be tasted to be believed.

2 × 1 kg pork rib racks, trimmed of excess fat
50 g (¼ cup) brown sugar
80 g (¼ cup) sweet paprika
3 tbsp freshly ground black pepper
3 tbsp salt
2 tsp garlic powder
2 tsp onion powder
2 tsp celery seeds
1 tsp cayenne pepper
1 batch Barbecue Baste (page 292)

Place the ribs in a flat dish. Mix the brown sugar and spices and rub well into the ribs. Leave to marinate for at least 4 hours.

Place the ribs in a baking dish, put in a hot kettle barbecue and cover with the lid. Cook for 1½–2 hours, rotating regularly. Brush the ribs with plenty of the Barbecue Baste during the last 30 minutes of cooking time.

Slice the ribs to serve.

Sichuan pepper and honey pork fillet

Serves 4

This recipe shows how good pork fillet can be when it's treated to a gutsy marinade. Just be sure to cook it for 15 minutes only, and rest the meat before slicing.

1 tsp Sichuan pepper
2 tsp sesame oil
1 tsp five-spice powder
½ tsp hot chilli sauce
2 tbsp honey
pinch of salt
750 g pork fillet

Toast Sichuan pepper in a small pan until fragrant. Crush with a mortar and pestle. Mix with oil, five-spice powder, chilli sauce, honey and salt. Brush over pork fillet and marinate for 1 hour.

Drain the pork and set aside remaining marinade for basting during cooking.

Place pork on a medium-heat oiled barbecue grill. Cook for 15 minutes, turning 2–3 times. Rest the meat for 5 minutes. Slice and serve.

Indonesian marinated baby chickens

Serves 4

This sensational recipe will wow your barbecue companions. Use the marinade on any poultry for amazing results.

4 × 250g baby chickens, spatchcocked
4 cloves garlic, crushed
4 green onions, thinly sliced
60 g (⅓ cup) brown sugar
50 ml (¼ cup) lemon juice
2 green chillies
60 ml (¼ cup) soy sauce
1 tsp ground turmeric
2 tsp ground coriander
2 tsp grated fresh ginger
100 g (⅔ cup) peanuts, ground
100 ml (⅓ cup) olive oil

Place baby chickens in a dish. Put the remaining ingredients in a food processor and process the marinade until smooth. Marinate baby chickens for 1 hour.

Place baby chickens on an oiled barbecue grill and cover with a lid. Cook for 15 minutes, rotating 2–3 times. Turn the baby chickens over and cover again with a lid. Cook for a further 15 minutes, rotating 2–3 times. Cut in half along the breastbone to serve.

Serve with Asian Coleslaw (page 517).

Japanese glazed duck

Serves 4

A simple way to enhance duck. The tamari nicely contrasts the richness of the duck flesh.

1 × 2 kg duck, spatchcocked
60 ml (¼ cup) tamari
1 tsp sesame oil
20 ml mirin
60 ml (¼ cup) orange juice

Trim excess fat and skin from the duck. Place the duck in a shallow dish.

Mix the remaining ingredients together to form a marinade. Pour marinade over the duck and leave to marinate for 2 hours.

Drain excess marinade, and reserve to use for basting during cooking.

Place duck on an oiled barbecue plate at medium heat. Cook for 10 minutes, rotating once. Cover and cook for a further 10 minutes. Turn duck over and cook uncovered for 10 minutes, rotating once. Cover and cook for a final 10 minutes. Rest for 5 minutes, then cut into 4 portions to serve.

Pomegranate and sumac glazed duck

Serves 4

Duck fillets are versatile and can be marinated in just about any type of flavour. This recipe is dedicated to our good friend Phillippa Grogan, who has a bottle of pomegranate syrup that is just waiting for a dish like this to come along. And you never know when a bottle of pinot may turn up too.

80 ml (⅓ cup) pomegranate syrup
2 tbsp olive oil
3 tsp sumac
salt and freshly ground black pepper
4 duck breast fillets

Combine syrup, oil, sumac, salt and pepper. Brush over duck fillets and marinate for 1 hour. Drain off excess marinade and set rest aside to use for basting during cooking.

Place duck fillets skin side down on an oiled barbecue grill. Cook for 9–10 minutes, rotating once or twice. Turn over and cook for a further 8–9 minutes, rotating once or twice. Rest for 5 minutes.

Slice thickly to serve.

Pomegranate and sumac glazed quail
Pour marinade over 4 spatchcocked quails and marinate for 30 minutes. Cook for 5 minutes on each side.

Shiraz-glazed quails

Serves 4 (2 per person)

Quail is one of the best meats you can barbecue. It has a slightly gamey flavour and copes well with the intense heat of the grill. This glaze is easy to make and tastes amazing.

8 quails
185 ml (¾ cup) shiraz
55 g (¼ cup) caster sugar
60 ml (¼ cup) sherry vinegar
pinch of salt
oil
salt and freshly ground black pepper

Spatchcock each quail by inserting a sharp knife into the cavity and out through the neck. Hold the point of the knife and cut through next to the backbone, pressing down firmly. Trim backbone away and remove any excess skin. Press the bird flat and trim rib bones, if desired.

Place the shiraz, caster sugar, vinegar and pinch of salt in a small saucepan. Bring to the boil, then allow to reduce for 4–5 minutes, until it reaches a syrup-like consistency. Remove from heat and allow to cool.

Brush the quails with oil and sprinkle with salt and pepper. Place the quails on the barbecue grill, skin side down, and cook for 5–6 minutes, rotating once. Brush liberally with the shiraz glaze while cooking.

Turn the quails over, brush with shiraz glaze and cook for 4–5 minutes, rotating once if needed. Remove from heat, cover and allow to rest in a warm place for 5 minutes.

Spanish barbecued quails

Serves 4 (2 per person)

These make a beautiful start to a barbecue and only take 10 minutes or so to cook. Refer to Shiraz-Glazed Quails (page 314) for instructions on how to spatchcock a quail or ask your butcher to do it for you. These are so delicious you'll want to allow at least two each.

8 quails, approximately 200 g each, spatchcocked
60 ml (¼ cup) olive oil
60 ml (¼ cup) lemon juice
2 cloves garlic, crushed
1 tbsp chopped basil
½ tsp smoky paprika
salt and freshly ground black pepper

Place the quails in a dish. Mix together the remaining ingredients and brush onto the quail. Marinate for at least 2 hours.

Place quails onto a hot barbecue. Cook for 5–6 minutes, rotating as required. Turn over, baste lightly and cook for a further 5 minutes, rotating as required.

Allow the quails to rest on a cool part of the barbecue for 2–3 minutes before cutting in half along the breastbone to serve.

Cevapcici

Makes 20

This cevapcici recipe is the base mix from which a multitude of different types of sausages can be made. You can swap the minced beef for lamb or veal, or vary the flavours to suit your tastes by adding more chilli, spices or fresh herbs.

500 g beef mince
500 g pork mince
1 tsp salt
¼ tsp ground white pepper
½ tsp freshly ground black pepper
1 clove garlic, crushed
large pinch of chilli powder

Mix all the ingredients together well, then divide the mix into 20 × 50 g portions. Pat them into thin sausage shapes, then flatten them slightly.

Cook the cevapcici on a medium–hot barbecue grill for 10 minutes, turning 3–4 times. Serve with rustic bread and Chilli Salsa (page 565).

Simple barbecued fish

Serves 4

As the name suggests, this is a simple way to cook fish. Use good-quality, firm fillets such as flathead or rockling.

50 g soft butter
2 tsp chopped fresh herbs
zest of 1 lemon, chopped
freshly ground black pepper
4 × 200g firm white fish fillets
oil

Combine the butter, herbs, lemon zest and pepper. Place butter mix in a heatproof bowl on the side on the barbecue. Place fish on the oiled barbecue plate. Cook for 2–3 minutes on each side while basting the fish regularly with the butter mix. Serve with Green Olive Salsa (page 564).

Thai fish cakes

Makes 20 small fish cakes

A classic in its own right and even better barbecued.

1 small red capsicum, diced
2 red chillies, finely diced
2 cloves garlic, peeled
1 lemongrass stalk, chopped
1 tbsp fish sauce
500 g white fish fillets, roughly diced
125 ml (½ cup) coconut milk
1 egg
oil

Place capsicum, chillies, garlic, lemongrass and fish sauce in a food processor and blend until smooth. Add fish and process until smooth. Add coconut milk and egg and mix until combined. Refrigerate for at least 1 hour, or up to 24 hours.

Form the fish mix into 20 burger shapes. Cook the fish cakes on an oiled barbecue plate for 4–5 minutes on each side. Serve with Coriander Pesto (page 551) or Sweet Chilli Sauce (page 578).

Barbecued whole snapper in banana leaves

Serves 4–6

A whole snapper is one of our absolute favourite fish to cook on a barbecue because of its ability to cope with the intense heat and long cooking times and still come out juicy and moist. Whole fish are best cooked in a kettle-style barbecue, but if you only have a trolley barbecue you can still do it by covering with a lid as directed here. If you can't find snapper, try small salmon, barramundi or perch – and if banana leaves are unavailable you can use aluminium foil.

1 × 1 kg whole snapper, cleaned
2 shallots, chopped
2 cloves garlic, crushed
2 tbsp grated ginger
2 tbsp kecap manis
125 ml (½ cup) coconut milk
zest and juice of 1 lime
2 small red chillies, de-seeded and diced
banana leaves

Slash the sides of the fish diagonally 3–4 times. Place the shallots, garlic, ginger, kecap manis, coconut milk, lime zest and juice, and chillies in a food processor and process until they form a smooth paste.

Place the fish in the centre of a banana leaf or piece of foil and rub the paste inside and all over the fish. Wrap the fish tightly in banana leaves or foil and tie the parcel tightly with string to hold it together.

Place the wrapped fish on a medium–hot barbecue, cover with a lid and cook for 20 minutes. Turn the fish over, replace the lid and cook for a further 15 minutes. Place the fish on a platter, then unwrap gently to serve.

Swordfish kebabs

Makes 8 kebabs

Swordfish is a real winner when it comes to barbecues. Its flesh is firm and won't fall apart during the cooking process, plus it's naturally oily and will keep moist when cooked. Other firm white fish or even tuna will work well, too.

500 g swordfish
2 tbsp olive oil
2 tbsp lemon juice
2 tbsp white wine
1 tbsp oregano leaves
large pinch of salt
large pinch of freshly ground black pepper
8 skewers

Cut the swordfish into 2 cm chunks. Mix the remaining ingredients together and marinate the swordfish for at least 1 hour.

Drain the fish well, then thread 8 skewers with 5–6 chunks of fish each.

Place the kebabs on a medium–hot barbecue plate and cook for 6–7 minutes, turning once only.

Sizzlin' garlic prawns

Serves 2 for lunch or 4 as an entree with salad and bread

The combination of prawns and garlic is a classic that goes back a long, long way. Now you can try it yourself at home to see how good it can be.

500 g green (raw) prawns
2 tbsp olive oil
4 cloves garlic, crushed
1 small red chilli, de-seeded and finely diced
pinch of saffron threads, soaked in 1 tbsp boiling water (optional)

Shell and de-vein prawns. Add oil, garlic and chilli to a medium–hot barbecue plate. Cook briefly for 1–2 minutes until fragrant. Add prawns and cook for 2 minutes, then turn over. Add saffron water, if using, and cook for a further 2 minutes.

Barbecued chermoula prawns

Makes 30 skewers

What's a barbie without a prawn on it? This chermoula paste is extremely versatile; as well as on prawns, we use it on roasted vegetables and to make tagines.

2 tsp sweet paprika
1 tsp ground ginger
1 tsp chilli powder
1 tsp ground cumin
1 tsp ground coriander
1 tsp ground white pepper
½ tsp ground cardamom
½ tsp ground cinnamon
½ tsp allspice
1 tsp salt
2 tbsp lemon juice
60 ml (¼ cup) olive oil
1 kg green (raw) prawns
30 skewers, soaked in cold water

Mix spices and salt with lemon juice and olive oil to form a smooth paste. Shell and de-vein prawns. Coat prawns with chermoula paste and marinate for 30 minutes. Thread one prawn onto each skewer, through the centre lengthways.

Cook on an oiled barbecue plate for 2 minutes on each side and serve with Tzatziki (page 563).

Thai barbecued prawns

Makes 30 kebabs

The potential fieriness of this magnificent marinade is tempered with coconut milk. Brush it onto skewered prawns for a real taste sensation.

250 ml (1 cup) coconut milk
2 tbsp lime juice
1 tbsp fish sauce
2 cloves garlic, crushed
1 tbsp grated ginger
½ tsp chilli paste
1 kg green (raw) prawns
5 limes, cut into 6 wedges
30 skewers, soaked in cold water

Place the coconut milk, lime juice, fish sauce, garlic, ginger and chilli in a saucepan. Bring to the boil, then simmer until reduced by half. Leave to cool.

Peel and de-vein the prawns, and remove the head. Thread 1 prawn onto each skewer, through the centre lengthways, followed by 1 lime wedge.

Brush the prawns with the coconut sauce, then place the kebabs on a medium–hot barbecue grill and cook for 3–4 minutes on each side.

The cooked lime wedge should be squeezed over the prawns as they are eaten.

Crayfish with roasted red capsicum butter

Serves 4

You can also try this recipe with smaller shellfish, such as scampi, langoustine, Moreton Bay bugs or another local shellfish.

1 red capsicum
2 tbsp olive oil
100 g soft butter
10 basil leaves, finely chopped
salt and freshly ground black pepper
2 × 250 g crayfish tails

Rub the capsicum with oil and barbecue or roast until the skin blisters. Allow it to cool and then remove the skin and seeds. Dice the flesh finely. Place the capsicum in a heatproof bowl with butter, basil, salt and pepper. Place bowl on the side of the barbecue. Cut the shellfish in half lengthways, and place it flesh side down on an oiled barbecue plate. Cook for 10–12 minutes, brushing with butter 2–3 times. Turn the shellfish over and cook for a further 10 minutes, brushing with butter 2–3 times.

Coconut spiced prawn kebabs

Makes 30 kebabs

These prawn kebabs have a touch of Indian spice, tempered with coconut milk once again.

1 dried red chilli
3 cardamom pods, lightly crushed
1 tsp coriander seeds
1 tsp fennel seeds
1 tsp black peppercorns
1 tsp salt
250 ml (1 cup) coconut milk
250 ml (1 cup) chicken stock
1 kg green (raw) prawns
5 limes, cut into 6 wedges
30 skewers, soaked in cold water

Heat a small frypan over a medium heat. Add the chilli, cardamom, coriander, fennel, pepper and salt. Stir well for 2–3 minutes, or until the spices are aromatic. Put in a mortar and pestle and crush lightly.

Place the crushed spices in a saucepan, along with the coconut milk and chicken stock. Bring to the boil, then simmer until reduced by half. Strain and allow the liquid to cool.

Peel and de-vein the prawns, and remove the head. Thread 1 prawn onto each skewer, through the centre lengthways, followed by 1 lime wedge.

Brush the prawns with the spiced coconut milk, then place on a medium–hot barbecue grill and cook for 3–4 minutes on each side.

Chilli crabs

Serves 4

There's something wicked about the combination of crab and chilli. Even better cooked outside to drive the neighbours wild.

4 blue-swimmer crabs, 200–300 g each
2 red chillies, finely diced
80 ml (⅓ cup) chilli jam or sweet chilli sauce
2 tbsp soy sauce
50 g (¼ cup) brown sugar

If using live crabs, freeze for 1 hour to put them to sleep. Cut the crabs into quarters and rinse to remove innards. Mix chillies, chilli jam, soy sauce and brown sugar together. Toss the crabs with the sauce. Place the crabs in a kettle barbecue, cover and cook for 15 minutes.

Ginger mirin salmon

Serves 4

This recipe shows how just a few ingredients can combine to create a terrific marinade and flavour base for barbecued salmon.

4 × 200 g salmon steaks
1 tbsp grated ginger
2 tbsp mirin
2 tbsp lime juice
2 tbsp peanut oil
pinch of sugar
salt and freshly ground black pepper

Put the salmon in a shallow dish. Place the remaining ingredients in a bowl and whisk well to combine. Brush the marinade over the salmon and leave to marinate for 20 minutes in the refrigerator.

Place the salmon steaks on a hot barbecue grill and cook for 4 minutes, rotating once. Turn them over and cook for a further 3 minutes, rotating once.

Soy and ginger salmon kebabs

Makes 10 kebabs

Cook these soy and ginger marinated salmon kebabs to medium–rare and you may never go back to lamb chops again.

- 750 g salmon fillet, skin removed
- 1 tsp grated ginger
- 1 small red chilli, de-seeded and finely diced
- 1 tbsp kecap manis
- 60 ml (¼ cup) soy sauce
- 60 ml (¼ cup) peanut oil
- 10 skewers, soaked in cold water

Dice salmon into 2 cm chunks. Mix remaining ingredients together. Pour over salmon chunks and marinate for 1 hour, turning once.

Drain salmon well and reserve remaining marinade for basting.

Thread salmon onto skewers. Place skewers on oiled barbecue plate. Cook for 3 minutes, basting as required.

Spice-coated tuna

Serves 4

A delicious combination of spice, just the thing to cut through the richness of the tuna.

- 3 tsp Sichuan pepper
- ½ tsp salt
- ½ tsp five-spice powder
- 4 × 200 g tuna fillet steaks
- olive oil

Place pepper and salt in a dry pan and cook over a medium heat. Stir until the salt turns golden, approximately 3 minutes. Crush pepper and salt mix until very fine in a mortar and pestle. Sieve mix to remove husks and stir five-spice powder through.

Brush tuna with oil and sprinkle on spice mix. Place tuna on an oiled barbecue plate. Cook for 4 minutes on each side, rotating once. Turn over and cook for 4 minutes more, rotating once. Serve with Fennel Relish (page 566).

Tuna teriyaki skewers

Makes 12 skewers

As with all oily fish, you should cook these tuna teriyaki skewers only to medium–rare to enjoy them at their best. Try them just once and they're sure to become a favourite, like they are for me. AC

750 g tuna
80 ml (⅓ cup) shoyu
2 tbsp mirin
2 tsp grated ginger
1 tsp sesame oil
1 tsp caster sugar
12 skewers
lime wedges to serve

Cut tuna into 2 cm chunks. Mix remaining ingredients together. Pour over tuna chunks and marinate for 30 minutes.

Thread 4 chunks onto each skewer. Set aside remaining marinade for basting during cooking.

Place tuna on an oiled barbecue plate and cook for 2 minutes. Turn over and cook for a further 2 minutes. Serve with lime wedges.

Yakitori chicken kebabs

Serves 8

Food cooked in this Japanese style has real subtlety, yet it never fails to produce terrific flavours, too.

500 g skinless chicken thigh fillets
80 ml (⅓ cup) soy sauce
1 tbsp caster sugar
2 tbsp mirin
1 clove garlic, crushed
salt and freshly ground black pepper
8 skewers

Cut the chicken into 2 cm chunks. Mix the soy sauce, caster sugar, mirin and garlic together. Season lightly. Brush the marinade onto the chicken and leave to marinate for at least 30 minutes or up to 4 hours.

Thread 8 skewers with 5–6 pieces of chicken each. Place the kebabs on a medium–hot barbecue grill and cook for 10 minutes, turning 3–4 times. Brush the kebabs with any remaining marinade as they cook.

Barbecued whole fish

Serves 4

Whole fish are best cooked in a kettle-style barbecue, but if you only have a trolley barbecue you can still do it by covering with a lid as directed. This is one of those dishes we can't believe people don't cook more often. It's extremely simple and fish tastes moist and magnificent when it has been cooked on the bone.

2 limes, sliced
10 cm ginger, peeled and sliced
4 × 400 g whole fish, cleaned
olive oil
2 tsp salt
freshly ground black pepper

Place lime and ginger slices inside the cavity of each fish. Slash sides of fish diagonally a couple of times. Brush fish with oil. Rub salt and pepper over skin and place fish on oiled barbecue grill.

Cover with lid and cook for 8 minutes, rotating once. Turn over, cover, and cook for 7 minutes, rotating once.

Spice and salt sardines

Makes 12

Try this wonderfully salty–spicy marinade with fresh seafood for a taste of Spain.

12 fresh sardines, cleaned and scaled
½ tsp salt
pinch of ground cinnamon
2 tsp ground cumin
pinch of nutmeg
1 tsp smoky paprika
1 tsp freshly ground black pepper
2 tbsp olive oil
coriander leaves to serve
lemon wedges to serve

Place the sardines in a dish. Mix the remaining ingredients except coriander and lemon together and brush all over the sardines, both inside and out. Leave to marinate for at least 1 hour.

Cook the sardines on a medium–hot barbecue plate for 3–4 minutes on each side. Sprinkle with fresh coriander and serve with lemon wedges.

Whole smoky salmon

Serves 10–12

Cooking a whole salmon in a kettle barbecue with smoking chips produces a moist, translucent fish with just a hint of smoky flavour. This could just be the perfect summer lunch dish.

200 g mesquite wood chips, soaked in water for 30 minutes

1 whole salmon or ocean trout, 2–3 kg, cleaned

piece of foil 60 cm × 30 cm

Prepare kettle barbecue in the normal manner. When coals have turned to white ash, it is ready to cook in.

Drain the smoking chips well, then place them on top of the hot coals.

Lay whole fish onto foil. Turn up the edges a little to form a small lip. Place salmon in barbecue.

Cover and cook for 1 hour or until the fish is just cooked through.

Excellent with lemon wedges, homemade Lemon Mayonnaise (page 554), good bread and a salad.

Barbecued oysters

Makes 2 dozen

The oysters don't need to be pre-opened for this recipe as the heat from the barbecue grill will open their shells. Spoon on your preferred sauce and enjoy. This sauce will make enough for at least 2 dozen oysters.

125 ml (½ cup) rice wine vinegar
2 tbsp caster sugar
60 ml (¼ cup) lime juice
2 tbsp fish sauce

1 small red chilli, de-seeded and finely diced
4 shallots, thinly sliced
2 dozen oysters, still closed in their shells

Place vinegar in a small saucepan and heat over a gently heat. Add sugar and stir until dissolved. When cool add lime juice, fish sauce, chilli and shallots. Place unopened oysters on a hot barbecue grill (they sit well on the bars). Cook for 3–4 minutes, or until the shells pop open. Using a small knife, pry shells off and place oysters on a platter. Spoon sauce into shells to serve.

Moroccan eggplant and capsicum kebabs

Makes 10 kebabs

Vegetable kebabs may seem an old-fashioned idea, but here they're combined with spices to make them more palatable for modern tastes.

2 cloves garlic, crushed
½ tsp ground turmeric
½ tsp ground cardamom
1 tsp ground coriander
1 tsp ground cumin
salt and freshly ground black pepper

60 ml (¼ cup) olive oil
1 eggplant, cut into 2 cm chunks
1 red capsicum, cut into 2 cm chunks
1 onion, cut into wedges
1 zucchini, cut into 2 cm chunks
10 skewers

Mix the garlic, spices, salt, pepper and oil. Toss with the vegetables until coated and marinate for 1 hour so all the flavours can infuse.

Thread the vegetables onto 10 skewers. Put the kebabs on a hot barbecue and cook for 10–15 minutes, turning 3–4 times.

Spiced green lentil burgers

Makes 10 burgers

The barbecue is often solely occupied by sausages, steak and burgers, but it is also excellent for cooking vegetarian food. Try these spiced lentil burgers and you'll see exactly what we mean. They're earthy and full-flavoured, and they pack a good amount of spice thanks to the Chermoula Paste, which we've taken from the Chermoula Chicken recipe in the Roasts chapter (page 344).

1 tbsp olive oil
1 onion, diced
1 clove garlic, crushed
1½ tbsp Chermoula Paste (page 344)
200 g (1 cup) green lentils, washed

500 ml (2 cups) vegetable stock or water
200 g (2 cups) dry breadcrumbs
1 egg
1 tbsp chopped mint leaves
salt and freshly ground black pepper

Heat a saucepan over a medium heat. Add the oil, onion and garlic and cook for 3–4 minutes, until the onion begins to soften. Add the chermoula paste and cook for a further 1–2 minutes, stirring often. Add the lentils and stock or water and stir well. Bring to the boil, then reduce heat, cover the saucepan and cook for 15–20 minutes, adding more stock if the mix looks dry. Continue cooking until the lentils are tender and all of the liquid is absorbed. Allow the lentils to cool.

Place the lentils in a bowl and add the breadcrumbs, egg and mint. Mix well to combine all the ingredients and season to taste. The mix should be just dry enough to hold together, but not wet. Add more breadcrumbs if needed.

Divide the mix into 12 equal portions and shape into burgers. Place the burgers on a hot barbecue plate and cook for 5–6 minutes, rotating as needed. Turn them over and cook for a further 5 minutes, again rotating as needed.

Haloumi and couscous burgers

Makes 10 burgers

Couscous makes an interesting base for a great vegetarian burger to cook on the barbecue.

- 250 ml (1 cup) water or vegetable stock
- 1 tbsp olive oil
- pinch of salt
- 250 g (1¼ cups) instant couscous
- small knob of butter
- 1 tbsp olive oil, additional
- 1 red capsicum, diced into 1 cm chunks
- 1 small eggplant, diced into 1 cm chunks
- 125 g haloumi, grated
- ½ cup chopped parsley
- 3 eggs
- salt and freshly ground black pepper
- 175 g (3½ cups) fresh breadcrumbs

Place the water or stock, 1 tbsp oil and pinch of salt in a saucepan and bring to the boil. Remove from heat, stir in the couscous, cover and allow to rest for 2 minutes. Add the butter to the soaked couscous and place over a low heat. Stir with a fork to break up the grains and mix the butter through. Place in a large bowl.

Heat a small frypan over a medium heat and add 1 tbsp oil, the capsicum and eggplant. Cook for 6–7 minutes, stirring often, until softened. Add the vegetables to the bowl with the couscous, along with the haloumi, parsley and eggs. Mix well and season with salt and pepper. Add enough breadcrumbs to make a mix which will hold its shape and combine well.

Divide the mix into 10 equal portions and shape into burgers. Place the burgers on a hot barbecue plate and cook for 5–6 minutes, rotating as needed. Turn them over and cook for a further 5 minutes, again rotating as needed.

Mexican bean cakes with chilli salsa

Makes 12

These bean cakes are well suited to both vegetarians and vegans. They can also be made smaller and served as an entree.

300 g (1½ cups) dried pinto beans, soaked in cold water	2 cloves garlic, crushed
oil	2–3 tbsp chopped coriander
1 onion, diced	1 tbsp ground cumin
1 red capsicum, diced	1 tbsp ground coriander
4 small red chillies, de-seeded and diced, or 1 tbsp chilli paste	salt and freshly ground black pepper
	90 g (½ cup) polenta
	Chilli Salsa to serve (page 565)

Place the soaked beans in a large saucepan, cover with cold water and bring to the boil. Cook for 30–40 minutes, until tender, topping up the water if needed. Drain and mash roughly.

Heat a small frypan over a medium heat. Add a splash of oil, the onion and capsicum and cook for 4–5 minutes, until soft. Add the chillies and garlic and cook for a further 1–2 minutes, until fragrant. Add to the mashed beans, along with the coriander and spices. Season with salt and pepper and shape into 12 cakes. Coat lightly with polenta.

Place the burgers on a hot barbecue plate and cook for 5–6 minutes, rotating as needed. Turn them over and cook for a further 5 minutes, again rotating as needed.

Serve with Chilli Salsa.

Caramelised onion and chickpea burgers

Makes 12

These burgers are a taste sensation. We love them cooked on the barbecue and served with a huge dollop of tomato relish on top. Even if you thought you didn't like chickpeas, you will after trying these.

250 g (1¼ cups) chickpeas, soaked overnight
80 ml (⅓ cup) olive oil
4 onions, sliced
2 tsp ground cumin
2 tsp ground coriander
1 tsp sweet paprika
½ tsp chilli powder
150 g spinach leaves, chopped
1 egg
100–150 g (2–3 cups) fresh breadcrumbs
½ cup coriander leaves
salt and freshly ground black pepper
oil

Cook chickpeas in boiling water until soft, about 30–40 minutes. Drain and mash roughly.

Heat oil in saucepan, add onion, cumin, coriander, paprika and chilli. Cook for 20 minutes on low heat, stirring often until onions soften. Add spinach and cook until soft. Mix onion and spinach with chickpeas. Add egg, breadcrumbs and coriander. Mix to combine and season to taste. Divide into 12 and form into burger shapes.

Add a splash of oil to a medium–hot barbecue plate and cook burgers for 5–6 minutes on each side, until golden brown.

Lentil and ricotta burgers

Makes 12

These burgers are devilishly more-ish. Again, we often cook them on the barbecue, or make small-sized ones and serve with relish as pre-dinner nibbles. We like to use red lentils for these burgers as they cook quickly.

1½ tbsp olive oil
1 onion, diced
1 tsp curry paste
200 g (1 cup) red lentils, washed
500 ml (2 cups) vegetable stock
2 tbsp chopped fresh herbs
125 g (½ cup) ricotta
100 g (1 cup) dry breadcrumbs
oil

Heat a medium-sized saucepan over a medium heat. Add oil and onion and cook for 3–4 minutes, until soft. Add curry paste and cook for 3–4 minutes, until aromatic. Add lentils, stir well, and add enough stock to cover. Bring to the boil, then reduce the heat. Cook for 15 minutes, adding more stock as necessary. Cook until lentils are tender and all liquid is absorbed.

Place cooked lentils in a bowl and add herbs, ricotta and breadcrumbs. Mix well, season to taste. Divide into 12 portions and form into burger shapes.

Add a splash of oil to a medium–hot barbecue plate and cook for 5–6 minutes on each side, until golden brown.

Grilled polenta with garlic vegetables

Serves 4

Polenta that is to be cooked on a barbecue plate or in a pan will need to be poured into a dish and left to set hard. It can then be cut into wedges or triangles and cooked to your liking.

1 quantity Best Soft Polenta (page 192), left to set in a dish
2–3 tbsp olive oil
3 cloves garlic, crushed
salt and freshly ground black pepper
2 zucchini, cut in half lengthways
1 small eggplant, cut into 8 wedges, salted and rinsed
8 mushrooms
2 tomatoes, cut in half
pesto (optional)

Cut polenta into 8 wedges. Mix oil, garlic, salt and pepper together in a bowl. Brush the vegetables with a little olive oil, then arrange them on a barbecue plate or in a hot pan, with polenta.

Cook for 10–15 minutes, turning as required. Baste the vegetables with garlic oil during cooking.

Serve the vegetables on top of the polenta wedges, then add a dollop of pesto.

ROASTS

classic + contemporary

A roast dinner is one of the most satisfying meals you can prepare. Anticipation builds from the moment the first aromas start to waft from the oven, culminating in the presentation of the cooked meat with all the trimmings. We grew up with the tradition of the weekly Sunday roast and, while we no longer regularly indulge, having a roast dinner on a Sunday is a treat we still savour.

Even our children get excited ...'There is going to be gravy, isn't there?' Whether you're a roast chook, lamb, pork or beef kind of person, a traditional roast deserves roast potatoes, a variety of seasonal vegetables and proper gravy. Try one of the time-honoured recipes, or go for something more modern and exotic.

roast recipes

stuffings

Sage and onion stuffing	341
Lemon, herb and almond stuffing	341
Saffron and almond couscous stuffing	342
Chestnut stuffing	342
Middle Eastern fruit and nut stuffing	343
Italian herb and salt rub	343

roasts

Roast chicken	344
Chermoula chicken	344
Oriental roast chicken	345
Hoisin chicken	346
Chinese crispy-skin chicken	347
Herby baby chickens with rocket and red onion salad	348
Pot-roasted chicken with red wine and mushrooms	350
Pot-roasted chicken with apples and cider	350
Stuffed turkey breast	351
Moroccan roast turkey	351
Pot-roasted chicken with 40 cloves of garlic	352
Christmas roast turkey with all the trimmings	354
Roast turkey breast with cranberry, walnut and orange stuffing	355
Roast beef with Yorkshire puddings	356
Roast rib of beef with potato gratin	357
Roast eye fillet with chilli and garlic marinade	358
Pomegranate-glazed beef	358
Roast sirloin with mustard and balsamic crust	359
Beef pot-roast	360
Garlic and rosemary roast lamb	361
Basil and pine nut stuffed lamb	362
Slow-roasted lamb shoulder	363
Lamb topsides with roasted ratatouille	364
Stuffed leg of lamb with zaatar, preserved lemon and herbs	365
French roast lamb with haricot beans and green olive salsa	366
Roast rack of pork	369
Prosciutto-wrapped pork fillet with roasted quinces	370
Sweet sticky pork	371
Slow-roasted pork belly with fennel and garlic	371
Roasted pork loin with porcini mushrooms and sherry	372
Roast duck	374
Roast duck with orange and cardamom caramel sauce	375
Crispy duck with spiced plum sauce	377
Duck confit	378
Duck confit with cherry and verjuice sauce	378
Nine-spiced roasted vegetables with chickpeas	379

Things you need to know about roasts

1 Good roasts mean top-quality meat.

2 A roast needs fat to keep it moist; no fat results in a dry, tasteless roast.

3 The oven must be preheated before the meat goes in.

4 Meat can be browned before roasting to create an outside crust. This can be done by placing the joint in a very hot 220°C oven for 10 minutes, then lowering the oven to 180°C and cooking as required. You can also brown the meat in a hot pan before placing the roast in the oven. The only exception to this rule is poultry, as the high temperatures can cause the flesh to dry out.

5 Poultry comes with its own rules. Stuff the bird, and it will repay you by taking up to an extra 30 minutes to cook. Start the bird off upside down, as this keeps the juices in the breast and prevents the flesh from drying out. Finish cooking by turning the bird the right way up for the last 30 minutes to crisp the skin.

6 A free-range chicken has loads more flavour than an ordinary chook.

7 If you want pork crackling, score the skin on your cut of pork with a sharp knife, then rub lots of salt into it.

8 Roast your vegies! They're delish cooked that way. Potatoes, obviously, but also carrots, parsnips – just about every root vegetable, in fact, as well as cauliflower and zucchini, but not green vegetables such as green beans and broccoli.

9 Good gravy can make or break a roast. For this reason alone we like to have an Allan in the kitchen. The second best option is to use Allan's Gravy Recipe (page 559).

10 Add trimmings such as mint sauce, bread sauce, mustards, horseradish, Yorkshire puddings and stuffing to suit your own tastes. These are all optional extras.

11 A good heavy-based roasting dish is a fantastic asset – one that doesn't wobble or warp during cooking, that's large enough to fit the meat and the potatoes together and that sits happily soaking in the sink while you enjoy the fruits of your labour.

12 Don't forget to rest your roast once it's cooked. Allow at least 10 minutes. Remove the meat from the baking dish, wrap it in foil, place it on a plate and cover with a dry tea towel. Add any juices to the gravy.

13 Always carve across the grain of the meat.

14 Meat cooked on the bone – such as racks, ribs, shoulders and leg – will have much more juice and meaty flavour than a boned roast.

roasting times

BEEF AND VEAL

NO BONE 15 minutes per 500 g plus 15 minutes (medium–rare)
Add 5 minutes per 500 g (medium)
Add another 5 minutes per 500 g (well done)
BONE IN 20 minutes per 500 g plus 15 minutes (medium–rare)
Add 5 minutes per 500 g (medium)
Add another 5 minutes per 500 g (well done)

PORK

NO BONE 25 minutes per 500 g plus 25 minutes – cooked through
BONE IN 30 minutes per 500 g plus 25 minutes – cooked through

LAMB

NO BONE 20 minutes per 500 g plus 15 minutes (medium–rare)
Add 5 minutes per 500 g (medium)
Add another 5 minutes per 500 g (well done)
BONE IN 25 minutes per 500 g plus 20 minutes (medium–rare)
Add 5 minutes per 500 g (medium)
Add another 5 minutes per 500 g (well done)

POULTRY

WHOLE CHICKEN 20 minutes per 500 g plus 20 minutes – cooked through
TURKEY 20 minutes per 500 g plus 20 minutes – cooked through
NOTE If roast is stuffed, allow at least an additional 20–30 minutes overall.

HOW TO TELL IF A ROAST IS COOKED

Insert a small knife into the meat as described below and leave it there for 5 seconds. Then test the temperature of the knife blade by placing it, cautiously, on the fleshy part of your thumb. (You may prefer to use a meat thermometer.)

The colour of the juices that come to the surface can also indicate how well the meat is cooked. It takes a bit of getting used to, as well as some trial and error, but it works.

POULTRY Insert the knife in between the leg and the body. If the juices that come to the surface are pink, return the roast to the oven for a further 5–10 minutes. If the juices run clear (no sign of blood), the poultry is ready and there's no need to test for temperature.

BEEF AND LAMB Insert a small kitchen knife into the centre of the roast. Count to five. If the knife feels warm (tepid), the meat is rare. If it feels bearably hot, the meat is medium – it will have some pink left but no rare bits. This is ideal.

PORK AND TURKEY Insert the knife into the thickest part of the joint. Unless the knife feels unbearably hot, indicating a high internal temperature, return the roast to the oven. These meats need to be thoroughly cooked through.

Sage and onion stuffing

Sage and onion are a classic combination for stuffing a chicken. This one uses sourdough bread, adding an extra gutsy flavour.

200 g day-old sourdough bread
2 tbsp butter
3 onions, sliced
2 tbsp chopped sage
1 tbsp chopped parsley
1 egg
salt and freshly ground black pepper

Tear bread into large chunks and soak in cold water. Squeeze the bread well to remove all liquid and place bread in a bowl.

Heat a small saucepan over a medium heat. Add butter and onions and cook for 7–8 minutes, stirring often, until the onions soften but don't burn. Add the cooked onion, sage, parsley, egg and lots of salt and pepper to the bread. Mix well to combine.

Spoon the stuffing into a bird and roast as directed. Alternatively, line a log tin with buttered aluminium foil and spoon the stuffing into it. Cook alongside the roast for 30 minutes, or until crunchy on top.

Makes enough for one chicken

Lemon, herb and almond stuffing

This is a fresh and zesty stuffing with fruit for sweetness, nuts for texture and herbs for a savoury flavour. We use a mix of whatever herbs are best at the time – perhaps thyme, rosemary, oregano, chives, parsley and a few mint leaves.

2 tbsp olive oil
knob of butter
1 onion, finely diced
2 cloves garlic, crushed
75 g (½ cup) dried dates, pitted and chopped
⅔ cup chopped fresh herbs
40 g (¼ cup) roasted blanched almonds
chopped zest and juice of 1 lemon
150 g (3 cups) fresh breadcrumbs
1 egg
salt and freshly ground black pepper

Heat a small saucepan over a medium heat. Add oil and butter. Allow butter to melt, then add the onion and garlic and cook for 7–8 minutes, until soft. Place in a large bowl and allow to cool. Add the dates, herbs, almonds, lemon zest and juice, breadcrumbs and egg. Season with salt and pepper and mix well.

Spoon the stuffing into a bird and roast as directed. Alternatively, line a log tin with buttered aluminium foil and spoon the stuffing into it. Cook alongside the roast for 30 minutes, or until crunchy on top.

Makes enough for two chickens

Saffron and almond couscous stuffing

This stuffing is excellent in a roast chicken. The couscous makes an interesting change from a bread-based stuffing, and the almonds, sultanas and saffron add great flavour and texture.

1 tbsp olive oil
1 small onion, finely diced
1 clove garlic, crushed
45 g (¼ cup) almonds
40 g (¼ cup) sultanas
pinch of saffron threads
100 ml (⅓ cup) water or stock
100 g (½ cup) instant couscous
small knob of butter
salt and freshly ground black pepper
1 egg

Heat a saucepan over a medium heat. Add oil, onion and garlic and cook for 4–5 minutes, until fragrant and soft. Add the almonds, sultanas and saffron and cook until the nuts begin to take on a little colour.

Add the water or stock and the couscous, then bring to the boil. Remove from heat, cover and allow to rest for 2 minutes. Add the butter to the couscous and place the saucepan over a low heat. Stir the couscous with a fork to break up the grains and to mix the butter through. Place couscous in a large bowl and allow to cool.

When cooled, season to taste with salt and pepper, then stir in the egg. Spoon the stuffing into a bird and roast as directed. Alternatively, line a log tin with buttered aluminium foil and spoon the stuffing into it. Cook alongside the roast for 30 minutes, or until crunchy on top.

Makes enough for one chicken

Chestnut stuffing

Chestnuts can be tiresome to prepare, but this recipe is your hard-earned reward. Good with chicken, pheasant or turkey (add 90 g (½ cup) raisins or cranberries at Christmas time).

250 g chestnuts
2 tbsp olive oil
1 onion, finely diced
2 cloves garlic, crushed
4 bacon rashers, chopped
2 tbsp chopped parsley
75 g (¾ cup) dry breadcrumbs
1 egg
salt and freshly ground black pepper

With a sharp knife make two slits in the chestnuts from top to bottom. Place in a saucepan, cover with water and bring to the boil. Reduce to a simmer and cook for 10 minutes. Allow to cool, then peel, removing both outside shell and inside skin. Chop roughly and place in a bowl.

Heat a small saucepan over medium heat; add olive oil, onion and garlic and cook until soft. Add bacon and cook lightly. Add this mixture to the chestnuts.

Add parsley, breadcrumbs, egg, salt, and pepper. Mix well.

Either stuff into bird and cook as directed or spoon into a small greased baking dish and cook alongside the roast for 30 minutes, or until crunchy on top. This recipe makes enough for two chickens, so we usually freeze half for another roast.

Makes enough for two chickens

Middle Eastern fruit and nut stuffing

This is an aromatic, sweet and nutty stuffing that is excellent in a big corn-fed chicken.

60 g butter
1 onion, diced
pinch of saffron threads
60 g (⅓ cup) almonds
60 g (⅓ cup) pine nuts
125 ml (½ cup) white wine
75 g (¾ cup) sultanas
75 g (¾ cup) dry breadcrumbs

Heat a heavy-based frypan over medium heat. Add butter and cook onion with saffron, almonds and pine nuts until onion is soft and nuts are brown. Add white wine and sultanas and cook until wine has evaporated.

Remove from heat. Stir onion mix into breadcrumbs. Spoon stuffing into chicken or other bird of your choice and cook as directed.

Makes enough for two chickens

Italian herb and salt rub

This is a great all-in-one seasoning to have on hand. Try rubbing a few tablespoons onto a leg of lamb or a chicken before roasting. It is also good with barbecued and grilled meats.

500 g (2 cups) salt flakes
1 tsp freshly ground black pepper
2 bay leaves
2 small sprigs of rosemary
6 sage leaves
2 sprigs of thyme
zest of 1 lemon, chopped
3 cloves garlic, crushed

Place the salt and pepper in a large bowl. Finely chop the bay leaves, rosemary, sage and thyme. Add the herbs to the salt, along with the lemon zest and garlic. The salt rub should be aromatic and full of herby, lemon and garlic flavour. The salt will dry out any liquid in the herbs, lemon zest and garlic over time.

Makes 500 g (2 cups)

Spanish herb and spice rub
Add 1 tsp Spanish smoky paprika and 2 chopped small red chillies to the mix.

Roast chicken

Serves 4

A proper roast chook is one of life's simple pleasures. Buy a free-range corn-fed bird if you can, and serve it with all the trimmings.

1 size 16 chicken
oil
salt and freshly ground black pepper

Preheat oven to 180°C.

Rub the chicken with oil and sprinkle salt and pepper all over, including in the cavity. Place the chicken upside down in a roasting tray, or better still use a baking rack in the roasting tray.

Cook in the preheated oven for 45 minutes, until the skin is crisp. Turn over and cook for a further 30 minutes, until the skin is golden brown and crisp. Check whether the chicken is cooked by inspecting the juices for any sign of blood (pinkness). Allow to rest for 10 minutes before carving.

Lemon roast chicken
Cut a lemon in half, rub all over the chicken and place lemon halves inside the cavity before cooking.

Honey roast chicken
Mix 2 tbsp oil and 2 tbsp warm honey together and brush all over the chicken.

Herb roast chicken
Roughly chop herbs such as thyme, rosemary or sage and mix with a little melted butter. Brush this all over the chicken and put some in the cavity.

Chermoula chicken

Serves 4

Chermoula is a beautiful North African spice mix which can be used to enhance the flavour of a simple roast chicken. If you have other favourite spice blends you can use them in a similar way.

2 tsp sweet paprika
1 tsp ground ginger
1 tsp chilli powder
1 tsp ground cumin
1 tsp ground coriander
1 tsp ground white pepper
½ tsp ground cardamom
½ tsp ground cinnamon
½ tsp allspice
1 tsp salt
2 tbsp lemon juice
60 ml (¼ cup) olive oil
1 size 16 chicken

Preheat oven to 180°C.

Mix spices and salt with lemon juice and oil to form a smooth paste. Rub the chicken with the chermoula paste. Place the chicken upside down in a roasting tray, or better still use a baking rack in the roasting tray.

Cook in the preheated oven for 45 minutes, until the skin is crisp. Turn over and cook for a further 30 minutes, until the skin is golden brown and crisp. Check whether the chicken is cooked by inspecting the juices for any sign of blood (pinkness). Allow to rest for 10 minutes before carving.

Oriental roast chicken

Serves 4

This chicken recipe is, in a word, delicious. It first appeared in a book of ours called *Tucker for Tots* in 1996, and we still make it today. You can forget the traditional roast trimmings and just serve it with rice and greens, or noodles. If you can marinate it for 3 hours it will have a more pronounced flavour; if not, no worries. Children love this and it's perfect for picnics too.

- 80 ml (⅓ cup) soy sauce
- ½ tbsp fish sauce
- 2 tsp chilli paste
- 1 tsp sesame oil
- 1 tbsp black beans, soaked and chopped, or 1 tbsp black bean sauce
- 2 tsp grated ginger
- 1 size 16 chicken

Mix soy sauce, fish sauce, chilli paste, sesame oil, black beans and ginger together. Rub all over chicken and, if time permits, marinate for 3 hours.

Preheat oven to 180°C.

Place chicken upside-down in roasting tray or, better still, on a baking rack across a baking tray, adding some water underneath to prevent burning. Place in the preheated oven and cook for 45 minutes until chicken bottom is crisp. Turn over and cook for a further 30 minutes, until skin is golden brown and crisp. Check that chicken is cooked by inspecting the juices for any sign of blood (pinkness). Allow to rest for 10 minutes before carving.

Serve with rice and steamed greens.

Hoisin chicken

Serves 4

We've long been fans of flavouring a chicken with Asian sauces and then roasting it to perfection. Not only does it add flavour to the skin, but it means it can be served with rice and Asian greens instead of the usual roast potato and vegetable accompaniments.

1 size 16 chicken
125 ml (½ cup) soy sauce
60 ml (¼ cup) hoisin sauce
60 ml (¼ cup) sweet chilli sauce
1 tbsp mirin
Steamed Rice (page 198) to serve

Preheat oven to 180°C.

Cut the chicken in half through the backbone and trim away rib bones. Cut off any excess fat and skin. You may prefer to ask your butcher to do it for you, but it's not difficult if you have a sharp knife and it's a great skill to learn.

Mix soy sauce, hoisin sauce, sweet chilli sauce and mirin together in a saucepan. Place over a medium heat and bring to the boil. Reduce to a simmer and cook until reduced by half. Allow the sauce to cool slightly then brush it all over the chicken. Leave to marinate for 20 minutes, if time permits.

Place chicken skin side down on a baking rack across a roasting tray. Place in the preheated oven and cook for 25 minutes. Turn over and cook for a further 20 minutes, until skin is golden brown and crisp. Check that the chicken is cooked by inspecting the juices for any sign of blood (pinkness). Allow to rest for 10 minutes before carving.

Serve with Steamed Rice and steamed greens.

Chinese crispy-skin chicken

Serves 4

Crispy-skin chicken is a bit of an addiction with us – we can't go to a Chinese restaurant without ordering it. To re-create it at home we rub the chicken with a Sichuan pepper and salt spice, fry it to give it a crispy skin, then roast it to finish cooking.

1 size 16 chicken
Salt and Pepper Spice (page 295)
4 cm piece of ginger, peeled and thoroughly crushed
1½ tbsp rice wine vinegar
1½ tbsp soy sauce
1½ tbsp Chinese cooking wine
vegetable oil
1 lemon, cut into wedges, to serve
Steamed Rice (page 198) to serve

Cut the chicken in half through the backbone and trim away rib bones. Cut off any excess fat and skin.

Place 1 tsp of the Salt and Pepper Spice in a deep bowl, along with the ginger, vinegar, soy sauce and sherry. Mix well, then add the chicken and rub the marinade all over it. Marinate the chicken skin side down for 1–2 hours, if time permits.

Preheat oven to 200°C.

Heat a wok over a high heat and add 3–4 cm vegetable oil. Remove the chicken from the marinade and pat dry on absorbent paper. Carefully place the chicken in the hot oil and cook skin side down for 3–4 minutes, until golden. Turn over and cook for a further 4–5 minutes. Place the chicken skin side up on a baking tray and cook in the preheated oven for 15 minutes.

To serve, chop the chicken into thick slices and sprinkle with extra Salt and Pepper Spice. Serve with Steamed Rice and lemon wedges.

Herby baby chickens with rocket and red onion salad

Serves 6

We usually serve 1 baby chicken per person. Quail would also work well with this recipe.

2 cloves garlic, crushed
½ cup chopped herbs (parsley, thyme and oregano)
2 small red chillies, de-seeded and diced
pinch of ground cumin
pinch of ground coriander
pinch of sweet paprika
salt and freshly ground black pepper

2 tbsp lemon juice
60 ml (¼ cup) olive oil
6 × 400 g baby chickens
½ preserved lemon, soaked in cold water
150 g rocket
1 red onion, thinly sliced

Mix the garlic, herbs, chilli, spices, salt, pepper, lemon juice and oil together. Place the baby chickens in a baking tray, spoon the marinade over them and massage well into the skin. Set aside to marinate for up to 4 hours in the refrigerator.

Discard the preserved lemon's pulpy centre. Thinly slice the rind and mix with the rocket and onion. Refrigerate until needed.

Preheat oven to 180°C.

Cook the baby chickens for 1 hour in the preheated oven, basting with marinade from the tray occasionally. Serve each chicken with a good handful of the rocket salad.

Herby baby squab
Substitute baby chickens with squab.

Pot-roasted chicken with red wine and mushrooms

Serves 4

This pot-roast produces something for everyone: you'll end up with crispy breast meat, tender drumsticks and thighs, plus amazingly flavoured juices. We often cook this dish for dinner on a Sunday night.

- 1 size 16 chicken
- 1 onion, diced
- 1 carrot, diced
- 4 mushrooms, sliced
- 125 ml (½ cup) red wine
- 250 ml (1 cup) chicken stock
- 250 ml (1 cup) tomato sugo
- salt and freshly ground black pepper
- oil

Preheat oven to 180°C.

Use a large ovenproof saucepan with a lid. Place the chicken upside down in the saucepan and add the remaining ingredients, seasoning with salt and pepper. Cover and cook in the preheated oven for 45 minutes.

Remove the saucepan from the oven and turn the chicken breast side up. Brush with oil and return the pan to the oven without the lid. Cook for a further 45 minutes.

Cut the chicken into portions and either return it to the sauce or arrange the meat on a plate and serve the sauce separately. Serve with a green salad and Mashed Potatoes (page 489).

Pot-roasted chicken with apples and cider

Serves 4

A good gutsy one-pot meal. Just the thing for a cold night – mashed potatoes compulsory.

- oil
- 1 onion, diced
- 4–6 rashers of bacon, diced
- 1 carrot, diced
- 1 tbsp chopped rosemary leaves
- 125 ml (½ cup) cider
- 250 ml (1 cup) chicken stock
- 1 size 16 chicken
- salt and freshly ground black pepper
- 2 apples, sliced

Preheat oven to 180°C.

Heat a large heatproof and ovenproof casserole dish (preferably one with a lid) over a medium heat. Add oil and onion, cook for 2–3 minutes. Add bacon and cook until golden brown. Add carrot, rosemary, cider and chicken stock. Place the chicken upside down in the dish and season with salt and pepper. Cover and cook in the preheated oven for 45 minutes. Remove from the oven and turn the chicken breast-side up. Brush with oil, add sliced apples and return the dish to the oven without the lid. Cook for a further 45 minutes. Cut the chicken into portions to serve.

Stuffed turkey breast

Serves 4–6

Ask your butcher to even out the thickness of the breast if necessary. Better still, if you ask nicely and bring your stuffing with you, your poultry person will stuff and roll the fillet for you. Just don't forget to say please.

1 kg turkey breast
stuffing of your choice (see pages 341–343)
olive oil
salt and freshly ground black pepper

Preheat oven to 180°C.

Lay turkey on chopping board skin side down. Push to one side the underfillet (small fillet under the main part of the breast), keeping it attached. Lay stuffing down the centre and wrap turkey around stuffing.

Roll fillet carefully so skin is uppermost. Take a piece of string, about 30 cm, and tie the thick part of the fillet tightly. Continue to wrap string around turkey 2 cm apart from first tie. Thread end of string under and pull tightly. Tie with a knot and repeat action until turkey is evenly rolled with string around.

Rub with oil; sprinkle with salt and pepper. Place in baking tray and cook in preheated oven for 1 hour and 20 minutes, or until turkey is cooked through. Remove from tray; wrap in foil and rest in a warm place for 10–15 minutes.

Carve and serve.

Moroccan roast turkey

Serves 10–12

A turkey buffe is a turkey with the legs removed. It takes a shorter time to cook than a whole turkey and has white meat only. We often prepare this dish for Christmas Day and cook it in our kettle barbecue. It comes out moist, tender and full of flavour. You can, of course, cook the turkey without the spice mix if you prefer.

1 turkey buffe, 3½–4 kg
4 tsp ground cumin
4 tsp ground coriander
2 tsp ground ginger
2 pinches saffron threads, about 20
½ tsp ground cinnamon
pinch of ground cloves
½ tsp salt
¼ tsp freshly ground black pepper
60 ml (¼ cup) olive oil

Preheat oven to 180°C.

Pat turkey dry. Mix spices, salt and pepper together with oil and brush over turkey skin. Place turkey in a large roasting tray, Roast in preheated oven for 1¼ hours. Turn over, baste well and cook for a further 45 minutes. Remove and rest for 20 minutes before carving. This is excellent with Moroccan Couscous Salad (page 525).

Pot-roasted chicken with 40 cloves of garlic

Serves 4

Don't worry too much if you don't like fresh garlic; it transforms completely during the cooking process and becomes sweet and nutty. There's no way anyone would ever guess that there are 40 garlic cloves in there, which means you don't really have to count them – just chuck in a generous amount. Even if you don't add the garlic cloves, you'll still have a delicious pot roast to enjoy. I adore this dish because it produces a roast chicken, yummy garlic cloves and a stunning sauce – all from the one pot. AC

1 lemon
1 size 16 chicken
2 tbsp olive oil
1 tsp thyme leaves
salt and freshly ground black pepper
40 cloves of garlic (no need to peel)
250 ml (1 cup) chicken stock
250 ml (1cup) white wine

Preheat oven to 180°C.

Cut lemon into quarters and stuff into the cavity of the chicken. Rub chicken with oil, thyme, salt and pepper. Place chicken, breast side up, in a heatproof casserole pot. Scatter garlic cloves around chicken. Pour the stock and wine around the chicken. Place the casserole over a medium heat and allow liquid to come to the boil. Place lid on the casserole and put into the preheated oven. Cook for 1 hour.

Remove lid and continue cooking chicken for a further 20–30 minutes or until chicken is golden brown. Remove chicken carefully to a serving platter and keep warm. Spoon the garlic cloves into a small serving dish. Strain the remaining liquid into a bowl. Spoon off the fat from the surface and pour liquid into a serving jug. Check the seasoning of the sauce then serve with the chicken.

At the table each person can squeeze the silky garlic puree from the cloves to eat with the chicken and the sauce.

Christmas roast turkey with all the trimmings

Serves 10–12

We're still traditionalists when it comes to the festive season. To us, it's just not Christmas without turkey, and as this is a special purchase we always take care to search out the very best organic, free-range bird we can find. The quality and flavour make the extra effort and expense well worthwhile.

1 × 3½–4 kg turkey
75 g butter
1 tbsp chopped parsley
2–3 sprigs of thyme, chopped
zest of 1 lemon, chopped
salt and freshly ground black pepper

10–12 slices streaky bacon
10–12 chipolata sausages
cranberry sauce to serve
Allan's Gravy (page 559) or Turkey Gravy (page 559) to serve

Preheat oven to 180°C.

Pat the turkey dry. Place the butter in a small saucepan and cook over a low heat until it just melts. Combine with the chopped herbs and lemon zest and brush the mix over the turkey skin. Season well with salt and pepper.

Place the turkey upside down in a large roasting tray and roast in the preheated oven for 1¼ hours. Remove the turkey from the oven and turn it over. Cook for a further 45 minutes.

Wrap 1 piece of bacon around each sausage. Add the bacon-wrapped sausages to the roasting dish with the turkey. Return to the oven and cook for a further 20–30 minutes. Check to see if the turkey is cooked by inspecting the juices for any sign of blood (pinkness). Remove the turkey from the oven and rest for 20 minutes before carving.

Serve with the bacon-wrapped chipolatas, cranberry sauce and gravy.

Roast turkey breast with cranberry, walnut and orange stuffing

Serves 4–6

A rolled fillet with a good stuffing in the centre is a great way to prepare turkey for Christmas. When purchasing the fillet, ask your butcher to even out the thickness of the breast, if necessary. Better still, if you ask nicely and bring your stuffing with you, your butcher may even stuff and roll the meat for you. However, it's fairly easy to do at home.

- 2 tbsp olive oil
- knob of butter
- 1 onion, finely diced
- 2 cloves garlic, crushed
- ¼ cup chopped parsley
- 40 g (⅓ cup) roasted walnuts, roughly chopped
- 70 g (½ cup) craisins (dried cranberries)
- chopped zest and juice of 1 orange
- 150 g (3 cups) fresh breadcrumbs
- 1 egg
- salt and freshly ground black pepper
- melted butter
- 1 kg whole turkey breast, skin on

Preheat oven to 180°C.

Heat a small saucepan over a medium heat. Add oil, butter, onion and garlic and cook for 7–8 minutes, until soft. Place in a large bowl and allow to cool. Add parsley, walnuts, cranberries, orange zest and juice, breadcrumbs and egg. Season with salt and pepper and mix well.

Spread out a large piece of aluminium foil and brush well with melted butter. Lay the turkey on the buttered foil, skin side down. Push the small fillet under the main part of the breast to one side, keeping it attached. You are aiming for fairly even thickness of turkey.

Spread the stuffing across the centre of the turkey and then wrap the turkey around it. Wrap the turkey gently in the buttered foil to create a sealed roll. Tie gently with string to keep it sealed.

Place in a baking tray and cook in the preheated oven for 1 hour. Test with a skewer: if the juices run clear, it's ready. If not, cook for 10 minutes more, then test again. When ready, remove the turkey from the oven and rest in a warm place for 10–15 minutes.

Unwrap and carve to serve.

Roast beef with Yorkshire puddings

Serves 6

We always had trouble finding a small cut of beef for roasting – until we tried scotch fillet. Scotch is usually considered to be a steak cut, rather than a roast, but it's actually very good for roasting, particularly with Yorkshire pudding. Just make sure any excess fat is trimmed from the top, leaving a nice thin layer to baste the meat while it's in the oven.

olive oil
salt and freshly ground black pepper
1½ kg scotch fillet, trimmed of excess fat
300 ml (1¼ cups) milk
150 g (1 cup) plain flour

2 tbsp olive oil
1 tsp salt
2 eggs
Allan's Gravy (page 559)

Preheat oven to 220°C.

Rub beef all over with oil, salt and pepper. Place beef on a baking rack over the baking tray and cook in preheated oven for 20 minutes. Lower temperature to 180°C and cook for a further 1 hour, for medium–rare. Remove beef; wrap in foil and rest in a warm place.

While beef is cooking, whisk milk, flour, oil, salt and eggs together until smooth. Allow to stand for 30 minutes. When beef is cooked and resting, raise oven temperature to 220°C. Brush muffin tins with oil and heat in oven for 5 minutes. Pour batter mix into hot tins and return to the oven for 15 to 20 minutes or until risen and golden brown.

Slice beef and serve with puddings and potatoes, and gravy in a warmed jug alongside.

Mustard roast beef
Rub beef with grain mustard.

Horseradish Yorkshire pudding
Add 2 tsp creamed horseradish to batter.

Roast rib of beef with potato gratin

Serves 4–6

Classic dinner-party stuff and minimal work once it's in the oven. You might like to serve it with some steamed vegetables or a simple green salad.

6–8 waxy potatoes, such as desiree or bintje
butter
185 ml (¾ cup) cream
185 ml (¾ cup) milk
2 cloves garlic, sliced
salt and freshly ground black pepper
nutmeg
oil
2 × 3 ribs of beef (1 rib per person)
250 ml (1 cup) red wine
250 ml (1 cup) beef stock

Peel potatoes and put in a large saucepan. Cover with water and bring to the boil. Cook for 5 minutes – you don't want them completely cooked. Drain. Butter an ovenproof dish, one that you can serve at the table. Slice potatoes into 5 mm thick slices and arrange in the dish. Mix cream and milk together and pour over potatoes. Scatter garlic slices over, season with salt and pepper and grate fresh nutmeg over the top. Cover with foil.

Heat a heavy-based frypan over medium heat. Add a splash of oil and brown ribs all over. Transfer to a baking tray. Return frypan to a high heat, add red wine and allow to reduce by half. Add stock and bring to the boil. Set aside.

Preheat oven to 180°C.

Place potatoes and beef in oven. Cook for 40 minutes then check beef, it should be medium-rare. Once cooked to your preference, remove from oven, cover with foil and rest for 10 minutes.

Remove foil from potatoes and return to the oven to cook until golden brown. Reheat red wine sauce.

To serve, slice beef, arranging a rib on each plate. Serve straight away with red wine sauce and potatoes.

Roast eye fillet with chilli and garlic marinade

Serves 6

Eye fillets generally take the same amount of time to cook, regardless of their length. We usually allow 200 g per person.

2–3 small red chillies, de-seeded and diced
4 cloves garlic, crushed
1 tsp freshly ground black pepper
1 tsp salt
oil
1½ kg eye fillet

Mix the chillies (use 3 if you like things extra spicy), garlic, pepper, salt and enough oil to combine into a smooth paste. Rub over the fillet and marinate for at least 20 minutes.

Preheat oven to 220°C.

Place the fillet in a baking dish and roast in the preheated oven for 30–40 minutes, or until cooked to your liking; medium–rare is ideal. To check if it is done, insert a small kitchen knife into the centre of the roast. Count to five. If the knife feels warm (tepid), the meat is rare. If it feels bearably hot, the meat is medium. Remove from the oven, wrap in foil and rest in a warm place for 10–15 minutes. Carve into 1 cm slices, allowing 2–3 slices per person.

Pomegranate-glazed beef

Serves 4

We just love the combination of the sweet-and-sour pomegranate and the meatiness of the roast beef. Serve with Walnut Tabouli Salad (page 517).

2 tbsp pomegranate syrup
60 ml (¼ cup) extra-virgin olive oil
2 tbsp lemon juice
2 tsp sumac
½ tsp ground coriander
½ tsp ground cumin
pinch of ground allspice
2 cloves garlic, crushed
salt and freshly ground black pepper
1 kg rolled beef porterhouse

Mix the pomegranate syrup, extra-virgin olive oil, lemon juice, spices, garlic, salt and pepper together. Rub over the beef and marinate in the refrigerator for 4 hours.

Preheat oven to 180°C.

Drain excess marinade from the beef and place the meat in a roasting tray. Roast for 1 hour, or until medium–rare. Set aside to rest for 20 minutes.

Carve into thick slices and serve.

Roast sirloin with mustard and balsamic crust

Serves 6

The crust on this roast beef adds extra texture and flavour. You may like to use grain mustard instead of Dijon, or different herbs to suit your tastes.

1½ kg beef sirloin
oil
2 tsp Dijon mustard
2 tsp balsamic vinegar
2 tsp olive oil
salt and freshly ground black pepper
2 tbsp chopped herbs (thyme, rosemary and parsley)
25 g (½ cup) fresh breadcrumbs

Heat a large frypan over a medium–high heat. Add a splash of oil and the beef and cook until golden brown on all surfaces. Remove from heat and allow to cool.

Mix the mustard, vinegar, 2 tsp oil, salt, pepper and herbs to form a smooth paste. Add enough breadcrumbs to hold the paste together. Spread the paste on top of the sirloin and press firmly to ensure that it sticks to the meat's surface.

Preheat oven to 180°C.

Place the beef in a roasting dish and cook in the preheated oven for 45 minutes. To check if it is done, insert a small kitchen knife into the centre of the roast. Count to five. If the knife feels warm (tepid), the meat is rare. If it feels bearably hot, the meat is medium. You're aiming for medium to medium–rare. If necessary, cook for a further 5 minutes and test again.

Remove the beef from the oven, wrap in foil and rest in a warm place for 10 minutes.

Carve into thin slices and serve immediately.

Beef pot-roast

Serves 4–6

This recipe is an absolute must for us to cook several times in the cooler months. The first sign of a cool night and we're into it. Simple method and ingredients combined with a long slow cooking time mean that you are still in good shape to enjoy it when it finally appears as a magnificent roast complete with its own gravy.

- 1½ kg beef, fresh silverside or bolar blade
- 2 tbsp olive oil
- 125 ml (½ cup) beef stock
- 125 ml (½ cup) red wine
- 2 tbsp tomato paste
- 1 onion, diced
- 2 carrots, diced
- 1 clove garlic, crushed
- 1 bay leaf
- 2–3 sprigs of thyme
- salt and freshly ground black pepper

Preheat oven to 180°C.

Heat a large heavy-based saucepan or roasting dish over a medium heat. Rub the beef with oil and add it to the saucepan. Cook the meat on all sides until well browned all over, about 10 minutes.

Add stock, wine and tomato paste. Scatter the vegetables around the meat. Add fresh herbs along with a sprinkle of salt and pepper. Cover with a tightly fitting lid or with foil and place in the preheated oven.

Cook for 2½ hours, then check the meat for tenderness and adjust the seasoning of the sauce if required.

Cut into thick slices and serve with vegetables and the sauce.

Garlic and rosemary roast lamb

Serves 4–6

Garlic and rosemary is the classic combination to enhance the flavour of roast lamb.

1 × 1½ kg easy-carve leg of lamb
10–12 cloves garlic, peeled
2–3 sprigs of rosemary
oil
salt and freshly ground black pepper

Preheat oven to 180°C.

Using a small knife make 10–12 cuts 2 cm deep evenly over the lamb. Push 1 garlic clove and a piece of rosemary into each cut. Rub lamb with oil and season well. Cook in the preheated oven for 1–1½ hours.

To check if the lamb is done, insert a small kitchen knife into the centre of the roast. Count to five. If the knife feels warm (tepid), the meat is rare. If it feels bearably hot, the meat is medium. You're aiming for medium to medium–rare. If necessary, cook for a further 5 minutes and test again.

Remove the lamb from the oven. Cover and rest for 10 minutes in a warm place before carving.

Pesto roast lamb
Smear 60 g (¼ cup) pesto all over the lamb and roast as described above.

Mustard roast lamb
Rub 2–3 tbsp grain mustard all over the lamb and roast as described above.

Basil and pine nut stuffed lamb

Serves 6

Easy-carve legs of lamb are a twenty-first century revolution, they're easy to deal with and they carve beautifully. We often cook a leg of lamb this way, which involves simply untying the lamb, filling it with pesto, then re-tying it. Basil and pine nut stuffed lamb has never been easier. I feel as Australian as Dame Edna Everage every time I have a mouthful of roast lamb. MC

90 g (⅔ cup) pine nuts
1 cup basil leaves
salt and freshly ground black pepper
50 g (⅔ cup) parmigiano, grated
1 x 1½ kg easy-carve leg of lamb
2 tbsp olive oil

Preheat oven to 180°C.

In the food processor, pulse pine nuts, basil, salt and pepper, leaving the mixture as chunky as possible. Add parmigiano and mix to incorporate. Untie the lamb, spread it with the pesto, and then re-tie it.

Cook in preheated oven for 1–1½ hours. Remove from the oven; rest for 20 minutes in a warm place before carving.

Slow-roasted lamb shoulder

Serves 6

Slow-roasted lamb is a sensation. The shoulder has more flavour, but a leg of lamb will work just as well. Keep the oven temperature low and roast for hours – the aromas will tantalise your tastebuds.

- 1 lamb shoulder (weighing approximately 2 kg)
- 60 ml (¼ cup) olive oil
- 2 tbsp lemon juice
- 2 cloves garlic, crushed
- 2–3 thyme sprigs
- salt and freshly ground black pepper
- 500 ml (2 cups) chicken stock
- 1 kg broad beans, podded

Preheat oven to 160°C.

Cut slashes all over the lamb going down to the bone. Combine the olive oil, lemon juice, garlic and thyme and season with salt and pepper. Rub the mixture all over the lamb, getting into the slashes. Place on a baking tray, cover with foil and roast for 5 hours, turning occasionally.

When the lamb has cooked for 5 hours, remove the foil and add the chicken stock to the tray. Return to the oven for a further hour, turning the lamb 2–3 times. Ensure the lamb is cooked until it is literally falling apart. Remove the lamb from the tray and keep warm. Place the tray over medium heat on your stove and bring the liquid almost to the boil. Use a wooden spoon to scrape the bottom of the tray, ensuring you get all the good flavours off. Add broad beans and check seasoning.

To serve, place the lamb on a serving platter. Use 2 forks to roughly pull the meat off the bone, breaking it into large chunks. Pour the hot stock over the top.

Lamb topsides with roasted ratatouille

Serves 4

Give ratatouille a modern day make-over with this delicious dish. Chop all the vegetables to a small dice, about 5 mm.

- 1 kg small potatoes, halved
- olive oil for cooking
- salt and freshly ground black pepper
- 1 small eggplant, chopped, salted and rinsed
- 1 onion, chopped
- 2 small zucchini, chopped
- 1 red capsicum, chopped
- 1 tomato, coarsely chopped
- 1 clove garlic, crushed
- 1 tbsp chopped flat-leaf parsley
- 1 tbsp chopped thyme
- 2 lamb topsides, about 400 g each

Preheat oven to 190°C.

Place potatoes in a roasting pan, drizzle with olive oil and season to taste. Combine chopped eggplant, onion, zucchini, capsicum and tomato in another roasting dish. Scatter with garlic, herbs, salt and pepper and drizzle with olive oil.

Place lamb topsides on a baking rack over the vegetables. Place both roasting dishes into the preheated oven and cook for 40 minutes, stirring ratatouille occasionally. Remove lamb from roasting pan, cover with foil and rest in a warm place for 10 minutes. Continue cooking potatoes and vegetables until potatoes are golden and vegetables are tender.

Slice lamb and serve with potatoes and roasted ratatouille.

Stuffed leg of lamb with zaatar, preserved lemon and herbs

Serves 4–6

With the ready availability of pre-boned and rolled easy-carve lamb, it's easy to make a stuffed and rolled roast leg of lamb.

1 preserved lemon
⅓ cup chopped flat-leaf parsley leaves
1 tbsp chopped basil
1–2 tbsp zaatar
1–1½ kg easy-carve leg of lamb
oil
salt and freshly ground black pepper

Preheat oven to 180°C.

Soak the preserved lemon in cold water for 10–15 minutes. Drain, discard the pulpy centre and dice the zest finely. Mix with the herbs and zaatar.

Remove the string from the leg of lamb and spread the meat out flat. Sprinkle the lemon and zaatar mix in the centre. Roll the lamb back up, enclosing the mixture. Tie with string to keep the lamb rolled in shape. Rub the lamb all over with oil, sprinkle with salt and freshly ground black pepper and place in a baking tray.

Cook the lamb in the preheated oven for 30 minutes. Turn the meat over and cook for another 30 minutes. Turn the meat over again and cook for a further 20–30 minutes, or until the lamb is medium. To check if it is done, insert a small kitchen knife into the centre of the roast. Count to five. If the knife feels warm (tepid), the meat is rare. If it feels bearably hot, the meat is medium. If necessary, cook for a further 5 minutes and test again.

When the meat is ready, remove it from the oven and allow it to rest, covered, in a warm place. Carve the lamb and serve it with Persian Rice (page 202).

French roast lamb with haricot beans and green olive salsa

Serves 6

This dish tastes delicious because the lamb is roasted over the beans and its juices drip down, adding great flavour to them. Always soak beans overnight so they don't take too much time to cook.

- 1 easy-carve leg of lamb, boned and rolled
- 8–10 cloves garlic, peeled
- 2–3 sprigs rosemary
- olive oil
- salt and freshly ground black pepper
- 200 g (1 cup) haricot beans, soaked overnight in cold water
- 1 onion, diced
- 1 carrot, finely diced
- 500–750 ml (2–3 cups) chicken stock
- 2 tbsp chopped parsley
- Green Olive Salsa (page 564)

Take lamb leg and using a small knife make deep cuts over it. Insert a garlic clove and 2–3 rosemary leaves into each cut. Rub the lamb with olive oil, season with salt and pepper and place on a roasting rack.

Preheat oven to 180°C.

Put soaked beans, onion, carrot and stock in a saucepan and bring to the boil. Transfer to a deep baking tray. Place lamb (on rack) over the top and cover baking tray with foil. Cook for 30 minutes, remove foil and cook for a further 30–45 minutes, until meat is medium-rare. Remove lamb, wrap in foil and rest for 15 minutes. Check beans are tender, if necessary add more stock or water and cook for a further 10 minutes. Check seasoning, add parsley. Carve lamb, adding any juices back to the beans.

To serve, spoon beans onto a large platter, arrange slices of lamb on top and serve with Green Olive Salsa.

Roast rack of pork

Serves 6

We often have a roast rack of pork for mid-year Christmas dinner. The tender slices of crackling-topped meat with creamy potatoes really hit the spot on a cold winter's night.

2 kg rack of pork, trimmed and scored
2 tbsp olive oil
2 tbsp salt
freshly ground black pepper
500 ml (2 cups) chicken stock
2 kg potatoes, peeled and sliced
2–3 tbsp butter

Preheat oven to 220°C.

Rub the pork with the oil, salt (yes, all of it) and pepper. Pour the stock into a deep roasting dish, place a baking rack across the dish and place the pork on top of it.

Cook the pork in the preheated oven for 20–30 minutes. The crackling should rise and become puffy; if it doesn't start to crackle at this stage, then it probably isn't going to. Lower the oven temperature to 180°C and cook for 40 minutes. Add the sliced potatoes to the stock in the roasting dish, top with dobs of butter and sprinkle with salt and pepper. Return the dish to the oven, with the pork still sitting on top of the baking rack. Cook for a further 1 hour.

Check that the pork is cooked by inserting a knife into the thickest part of the joint. Unless the knife is unbearably hot, indicating a high internal temperature, return the roast to the oven.

When the pork is ready, remove it from the oven, wrap it in foil and rest it in a warm place for 20 minutes. Return the potatoes to the oven and cook for a further 20 minutes, until tender and the stock is absorbed.

Carve the pork and serve with the potatoes.

Prosciutto-wrapped pork fillet with roasted quinces

Serves 4–6

Quinces impart a delicate flavour to this dish. Apples or pears could be used in their place, but they require less cooking time.

1½ litres (6 cups) water
220 g (1 cup) caster sugar
1 cinnamon stick
3 quinces, peeled, quartered and cored
1½ kg pork scotch fillet
oil
salt and freshly ground black pepper
1 tbsp finely chopped rosemary
8–10 slices prosciutto

Place the water, caster sugar and cinnamon in a large saucepan. Bring to the boil, stirring occasionally to dissolve the sugar. Add the quinces and cook in the simmering sugar stock for 20 minutes. Remove and drain well.

Preheat oven to 220°C.

Rub the pork scotch fillet with oil, salt, pepper and rosemary. Wrap the prosciutto slices around the pork, encasing it completely. Toss the quinces with oil, salt and pepper, and arrange in a deep baking tray. Place the pork in the centre of the tray and roast in the preheated oven for 20 minutes.

Reduce the oven temperature to 180°C and continue cooking the pork and quinces for a further 1 hour, turning the pork and quinces halfway through.

Check that the pork is cooked by inserting a knife into the thickest part of the joint. Unless the knife is unbearably hot, indicating a high internal temperature, return the roast to the oven. When cooked through, remove the pork from the oven, wrap in foil and rest in a warm place for 15 minutes.

Carve the pork and serve with roasted quinces alongside.

Sweet sticky pork

Serves 6

This incomparable roast has a flavoured crust from the marinade. It's incredibly moist and tender, and is also free of bones. You can buy pork neck from Asian butchers.

250 ml (1 cup) dark soy sauce
125 ml (½ cup) rice vinegar
2 tbsp honey
1 tsp sesame oil
2 cloves garlic, crushed
2 tsp grated ginger
2 tbsp hot bean paste
½ tsp Chinese five-spice powder
1–1½ kg pork neck or scotch fillet

Mix the soy sauce, rice vinegar, honey, sesame oil, garlic, ginger, hot bean paste and five-spice powder together. Rub onto the pork and set aside to marinate for 2 hours, turning occasionally.

Preheat oven to 190°C.

Drain excess marinade off the pork. Place the pork in a deep baking tray and cook in the preheated oven for 45–50 minutes, turning occasionally. Check that the pork is cooked by inserting a knife into the thickest part of the joint. Unless the knife is unbearably hot, indicating a high internal temperature, return the roast to the oven.

When ready, rest for 10 minutes before carving.

Slow-roasted pork belly with fennel and garlic

Serves 4–6

The longer you cook this fabulous pork roast, the more the fat will break down and the more the meat will melt in your mouth. For a twist on apple sauce, serve the pork with Quince Aioli (page 550), which will bring a beautiful sweetness to the meat.

4 cloves garlic, crushed
1 tbsp fennel seeds
1–2 tbsp salt
2 tbsp olive oil
1½ kg pork belly, skin scored
salt and freshly ground black pepper
Quince Aioli (page 550)

Preheat oven to 220°C.

Mix the garlic, fennel seeds, salt and oil together. Rub over the skin of the pork, massaging it well into the flesh. Set aside to allow the flavours to penetrate the pork.

Place the pork in a large baking tray, skin side up, and add enough water to half-cover the meat. Cook for 30 minutes, until the skin crackles. Lower the heat to 180°C and cook for a further 2–2½ hours. Check the water level during cooking and top up as necessary, as the liquid will evaporate.

Remove the pork from the oven. If the skin needs to be crisper, remove in 1 piece using a sharp knife, place on a cooking rack over a shallow baking tray and return to the oven or place under a hot grill to crisp up. Once crisp, chop into pieces

Cut pork into 2 cm thick slices and serve with crackling and Quince Aioli.

Roasted pork loin with porcini mushrooms and sherry

Serves 4–6

The combination of slow-cooked pork and porcini mushrooms in this dish is balanced by the sherry.

- oil
- 1½ kg pork loin, skin scored
- salt and freshly ground black pepper
- 500 ml (2 cups) boiling water
- 30 g dried porcini mushrooms
- 8 flat Swiss brown mushrooms, sliced
- sprig of rosemary
- 80 ml (⅓ cup) dry sherry
- 2 tbsp chopped parsley

Preheat oven to 220°C.

Rub oil into the scored pork skin. Sprinkle liberally with salt and season with pepper. Rub well to push the salt into the skin. Place the pork in a snug-fitting baking tray or dish. Cook in the preheated oven for 20 minutes.

Pour boiling water over the porcini mushrooms and allow to stand for 20 minutes.

Heat a large frypan over a medium–high heat. Add a generous splash of oil and cook the sliced Swiss brown mushrooms for 5–8 minutes, stirring often. Add the rosemary and sherry and remove from heat. Season with salt and pepper.

Reduce the oven temperature to 180°C, remove the dish from the oven and place the porcini mushrooms, their soaking liquid and the cooked Swiss brown mushrooms in the roasting dish around the pork. Return the dish to the oven and cook for a further 1½ hours.

Check that the pork is cooked by inserting a knife into the thickest part of the joint. Unless the knife is unbearably hot, indicating a high internal temperature, return the roast to the oven. When cooked through, remove the pork from the roasting dish and cut off the crackling; set it aside to serve. Wrap the pork loin in foil and rest in a warm place for 15–20 minutes. Check the sauce, and reduce if necessary. Check seasoning and add parsley.

Carve the pork into thin slices and chop up the crackling. Arrange on a platter and serve with the mushroom sauce.

Roast duck

Serves 6

Most people put roasting a duck into the too hard basket, but essentially it's no different to roasting a chicken. Quite a bit of fat will come from the duck as it cooks, but all you need to do is pour this away from time to time.

1 x 2–2½ kg duck
olive oil
salt and freshly ground black pepper
1 orange

Preheat oven to 200°C.

Remove any giblets, neck and loose fat from duck. Wipe inside and out to remove moisture. Rub duck all over with oil and season inside and out with salt and pepper. Cut orange into quarters and stuff into cavity. Place duck upside-down in roasting dish.

Roast for 20 minutes; remove and tip excess fat away. Return to oven for a further 20 minutes; remove. Again tip excess fat off and turn duck breast side up. Return to oven for a further 30 minutes, checking once to see if more fat needs to be drained away. Check to see if duck is cooked by inserting knife between thigh and body, looking for clear juices.

Rest duck in a warm place for 15 minutes before carving.

Chinese roast duck
Use Sweet Sticky Marinade (page 295) on duck. Roast as described.

Sumac and pomegranate roast duck
Mix 80 ml (⅓ cup) pomegranate syrup, 1½ tbsp olive oil and 3 tsp sumac. Rub over duck and marinate for 1 hour. Drain excess marinade away. Roast as described.

Roast duck with orange and cardamom caramel sauce

Serves 6

This is a jazzier version of the classic duck a l'orange. The cardamom adds a taste of the Middle East, so why not go all out and prepare Spiced Couscous (page 453) to accompany the dish?

1 × 2–2½ kg duck	2 oranges, additional
1 orange	110 g (½ cup) caster sugar
1–2 bay leaves	80 ml (⅓ cup) water
1–2 sprigs of thyme	250 ml (1 cup) orange juice
1 tsp ground Sichuan pepper	3–4 cardamom pods, smashed
1 tsp ground cardamom	250 ml (1 cup) chicken stock
salt and freshly ground black pepper	80–125 ml (⅓–½ cup) lemon juice

Preheat oven to 200°C.

Remove any giblets, neck and loose fat from the duck. Wipe inside and out to remove moisture. Make a few small cuts into the duck skin to allow some of the fat to come out during cooking. Cut the orange into 6 segments and stuff into the cavity with the bay leaves and thyme. Place the duck upside down in a roasting dish and sprinkle with half of the Sichuan pepper and cardamom, and season with salt and pepper.

Roast the duck for 30 minutes. Remove from the oven and tip excess fat away, if necessary. Turn the duck over and sprinkle with the remaining Sichuan pepper and cardamom, and season with salt and black pepper. Return the duck to the oven and continue cooking for a further 40 minutes.

Check to see if the duck is cooked by inserting a knife between the thigh and body; you are looking for clear juices to run out. Rest the duck in a warm place for 15 minutes before carving. Remove the zest from the 2 additional oranges and set aside. Using a small sharp knife, remove the orange segments from the pith and set aside. To make the sauce, place the caster sugar and water in a small saucepan. Cook over a low heat until the sugar dissolves. Raise the heat and bring to the boil, and continue boiling until the sugar turns to a dark caramel. Remove from heat and carefully add the orange juice; it will splutter as it hits the hot sugar. Bring back to the boil and add the orange zest, cardamom pods and stock. Continue to boil until reduced by half. Strain and return to a clean saucepan. Check seasoning. Add lemon juice to counteract the sweetness of the caramel sauce.

Just before serving, add the reserved orange segments to the sauce and allow to heat through. Serve the duck with the sauce.

Crispy duck with spiced plum sauce

Serves 4–6

Everyone seems to love the combination of crispy-skin duck with spiced plum sauce.

Master Stock (page 118)
4 duck breast fillets
110 g (½ cup) caster sugar
2 star anise
2–3 cinnamon sticks
4–6 plums, halved and stoned
oil
80 ml (⅓ cup) fish sauce
80–125 ml (⅓–½ cup) lime or lemon juice
Steamed Rice (page 198) to serve

Bring the Master Stock to the boil. Add the duck fillets, cover and cook for 10 minutes at a gentle simmer. Remove from heat and allow the duck to cool in the stock. Once cool, remove the duck from the stock and refrigerate.

Preheat oven to 180°C.

To make the sauce, place 2 cups of the Master Stock in a saucepan over a medium heat. Bring to the boil, add the caster sugar and stir to dissolve. Add the star anise and cinnamon and cook for 10 minutes to infuse the flavours. Add the plums and cook for 2–3 minutes. Remove the saucepan from the heat.

Heat a large frypan over a medium heat. Add a splash of oil and cook the duck fillets for 3–4 minutes on each side, until golden brown. Place on a tray and cook in the preheated oven for 10 minutes. Remove from the oven, cover and rest for 5 minutes.

Reheat the plum sauce, and add the fish sauce and lemon or lime juice to taste. The sauce should be tart, sweet and sour.

Carve each duck fillet into 6–7 slices. Arrange the duck pieces on a platter and pour on the hot sauce. Serve with Steamed Rice and Chinese Broccoli and Garlic Stir-Fry (page 480).

Duck confit

Serves 6

To make duck confit you are basically drawing out moisture with salt, then cooking the meat slowly in fat. Traditionally, this is done with duck fat or lard, but our mate Macka goes for the low-fat option (if you can call it that) with olive oil. The resulting meat can then be served in all manner of ways, from roasting or pan-frying, as a salad ingredient or to make the classic Duck Cassoulet (page 412).

100 g coarse salt
6 duck legs
1 kg duck fat or lard, or 1 litre olive oil

Rub the salt on the duck legs. Cover and refrigerate overnight.

Preheat oven to 180°C.

Rinse the duck legs well and dry the meat. Place a large ovenproof saucepan over a medium heat and melt the fat or lard. Submerge the duck legs in the fat, cover with a lid and cook in the preheated oven for 2–2½ hours, or until the duck meat is tender and the legs are almost falling apart. Allow to cool slightly before removing the legs and setting them aside to drain well.

Once the fat is tepid, strain it into a clean saucepan and bring to the boil, skimming if necessary. Strain once again and cool. Keep the fat for the next time you want to make confit.

Refrigerate the duck legs until needed.

Duck confit with cherry and verjuice sauce

Serves 6

Confit duck legs can be prepared at home or purchased at a specialist food store. Either way, once you have the confit duck, the rest of the recipe is easy to prepare.

6 confit duck legs
oil
1 onion, diced
1 carrot, finely diced
1 clove garlic, crushed
250 ml (1 cup) verjuice
2 bay leaves
250 ml (1 cup) beef stock
300 g cherries, halved and pitted
2 tbsp chopped parsley

Preheat oven to 180°C.

Place the confit duck legs in a roasting dish and roast in the preheated oven for 20–30 minutes.

To make the sauce, heat a medium-sized saucepan over a medium–high heat. Add a splash of oil and the onion and carrot. Cook for 4–5 minutes, stirring often. Add garlic and cook for 1 minute, until fragrant. Add the verjuice and bay leaves, and reduce by half. Add the stock and also reduce by half. Check seasoning.

Just before serving, add the cherries and parsley and serve the duck confit with the sauce.

Nine-spiced roasted vegetables with chickpeas

Serves 4

This is truly a memorable dish – lots of chunky vegetables covered in an aromatic spice paste and roasted to perfection. The long list of ingredients makes this recipe look much harder than it really is, so don't be put off by it.

- 150 g (¾ cup) chickpeas, soaked overnight
- 1 tsp sweet paprika
- ½ tsp ground ginger
- ½ tsp chilli powder
- ½ tsp ground coriander
- ½ tsp ground white pepper
- ¼ tsp ground cardamom
- ¼ tsp ground cinnamon
- ¼ tsp allspice
- 1 tsp salt
- juice of 1 lemon
- 2 tbsp olive oil
- 4 potatoes, peeled
- 1 eggplant
- 2 zucchini
- olive oil
- 2 large carrots
- 2 parsnips
- ½ pumpkin
- 375 ml (1½ cups) vegetable stock
- Couscous (page 453) and Tzatziki (page 563) to serve

Preheat oven to 180°C.

Place chickpeas in a medium-sized saucepan, cover with water and bring to the boil over a medium heat. Reduce heat and cook until soft, about 30–40 minutes. Drain and set aside.

Mix all of the spices together with the salt, lemon juice and oil to form a smooth paste. Cut potatoes and eggplants into thick wedges. Salt eggplant and stand for 30 minutes, until juices bead. Rinse well and dry. Cut zucchini in half lengthways, then halve again.

Heat a pan over a medium heat and cook eggplant and zucchini in a small amount of oil until golden brown. Peel carrots and parsnips. Cut as for zucchini. Cut pumpkin into thick fingers.

Rub the spice mix over all of the prepared vegetables.

Arrange potatoes, parsnips and carrots in a deep baking tray. Pour half of the stock over and bake in preheated oven for 30 minutes, turning occasionally.

Place eggplant, zucchini, pumpkin and chickpeas in another dish and pour remaining stock over. Cook for a further 20 minutes alongside potatoes.

Serve vegetables on top of Couscous accompanied by Tzatziki.

SLOW
cooking
braises + casseroles

Braises, casseroles, stews and pot-roasts – whatever you want to call them – are a convenience food. And we're not talking about the packets of powdered sauces on supermarket shelves. We're talking about the real thing here: fresh meat and vegetables combined with top-quality seasonings. Don't be put off by the long cooking time in these recipes.

You'll only spend 30 minutes or so dicing, chopping and frying before you put the whole thing in the oven and leave it alone for 1½–2 hours.

That will give you enough time to run down to footy practice, put the washing away, tidy up the bedroom or put your feet up and have a well-deserved drink before dinner. It's also very easy to transform a casserole into a pie. Simply cook as described until the meat is just tender. Transfer to a pie dish, cover with puff pastry, brush with egg wash and put it into a preheated oven for 30–40 minutes, or until the pastry is crisp and golden brown.

slow cooking recipes

Simple chicken casserole 384	Braised lamb shanks with mint and harissa 406
Mediterranean chicken casserole 385	Spanish lamb stew 407
French chicken casserole 386	Braised pork with star anise (The pork dish) 408
Catalan chicken 387	Rodriguez pork 409
Hungarian chicken casserole 389	Braised pork belly with chorizo sausage 410
Chicken and mushroom pie 390	Slow-cooked pork belly with Catalan potatoes and quince aioli 411
Moroccan chicken with tomatoes and olives 391	Duck cassoulet 412
Moroccan chicken pie 392	Osso buco 413
Soy-braised chicken 393	Pot-roasted veal shanks 414
Basic beef stew 394	Pot-roasted veal with pancetta and mustard 415
Dumplings 395	Rabbit casserole 416
Braised steak and onions 395	Braised rabbit with cider and rosemary 417
Beef and Guinness casserole with dumplings 396	Mediterranean fish stew 418
Spezzatino 398	Seafood casserole with saffron and cream 418
Beef goulash 399	Moroccan fish stew 420
Garlic confit with braised beef 400	Mediterranean bean stew with feta 420
Beef and Guinness pie 401	Chickpea and vegetable casserole 421
Slow-cooked leg of lamb with lemon and oregano 402	Tuscan bean stew 421
Braised lamb chops 402	
Braised lamb with cannellini beans 403	
Lamb hot pot 404	
Lamb navarin with root vegetables and rosemary 405	
Sicilian lamb stew with pecorino 406	

Things you need to know about slow cooking

1 The beauty of casseroles is that they only work if you use the cheaper cuts. You are never going to get a tender beef stew from topside or sirloin; chuck or blade steak will melt in the mouth though. Likewise, with lamb, go for diced leg; with chicken, choose thigh fillets ... You get the picture.

2 Casseroles only work with long, slow cooking – you can't cheat and turn the oven up and hope it does its thing in 45 minutes – but they are well worth the wait.

3 Flour is used to thicken most casseroles, to get that stick-to-your-ribs sensation that we love so much. You can either lightly cook the meat and then add 1–2 tbsp flour before adding any liquid, or you can toss the meat in the flour before cooking it.

4 To flour the meat, you can put it in a plastic bag with the flour and shake well to coat, or simply put the flour in a bowl, add the meat, then stir well. It's worth putting the flour-covered meat into a sieve and shaking well to ensure that any excess flour is removed; otherwise, you will end up with a thicker-than-normal stew. Try the different options, then decide which method suits you best. Always remember to add a little salt and pepper to the flour before use; this is what we call seasoned flour.

5 An important stage in most dishes of this type is cooking the meat until it is lightly browned. This provides depth of flavour as the dish cooks, as well as good colour. The vegetables are often lightly cooked, though there are some recipes that skip this step altogether. Be sure to deglaze the base of the pan with wine or stock to make sure all the flavour goes into the finished dish.

6 We use a variety of cookware for our casseroles. The one that we use most often is a large oval Le Creuset saucepan made from enamelled cast iron. The thick metal base is perfect for the initial cooking of the ingredients, and the casserole can then be covered and popped straight into the oven for 1–2 hours. We know these pots are expensive – that's why we only have one – but one is usually enough and they tend to last a lifetime.

7 Sometimes we cook the meat and vegetables in a frypan, then transfer them to a casserole dish as they are ready. We use Spanish terracotta pots for this purpose. Terracotta or earthenware dishes are perfect for casseroles, stews and braises, as they are excellent conductors of heat in the oven, while also presenting well at the table. They seem to be on sale everywhere these days and are much cheaper than other dishes. Terracotta dishes must be soaked in water for 24 hours, then dried in the oven, before their first use.

8 Try to purchase skinless chicken pieces. The fat in the skin breaks down during the cooking process and floats to the top of a casserole, producing a layer of chicken fat.

9 As well as the European-style dishes in this chapter we've included a range of Asian braises. These are cooked without the addition of flour and are served with a light broth rather than a thick sauce. They are incredibly easy to make and, again, terracotta pots are perfect for this style of cooking.

10 Casseroles can either be cooked over a low heat on the stovetop (a simmer pad makes sure the heat is spread over the base of the saucepan) or in the oven. It doesn't make any difference to the finished dish, though we fancy that cooking a casserole in the oven lessens the chances of the food catching or burning. If you have a crock pot lurking in the back of the cupboard, take advantage of it: these are ideal for cooking all casseroles, stews and braised dishes.

Simple chicken casserole

Serves 4

There are two main ways to make a chicken casserole: one with diced chicken, thigh fillets for preference, and the other with chicken on the bone. These cuts are often sold as casserole pieces. Again, leg portions are better, and you could make a casserole solely with chicken drumsticks or thigh pieces. Another option is to purchase a whole chicken and cut it into 8 or 10 pieces, or better still get your butcher to do this.

1 kg chicken casserole pieces
seasoned flour
olive oil
1 onion, diced
1 carrot, finely diced
1 clove garlic, crushed
1 tbsp tomato paste
750 ml (3 cups) chicken stock
chopped parsley to serve

Toss chicken pieces in flour and shake off excess. Heat a heavy-based saucepan over a medium heat, add a generous splash of olive oil and cook chicken pieces all over until golden brown. Remove chicken from the saucepan and set aside. Return saucepan to the heat and add more oil if necessary.

Cook onion, carrot and garlic until soft. Add tomato paste, cook briefly, then add stock and bring to the boil. Reduce heat to a simmer, return chicken to the saucepan, cover with a lid and cook for 1 hour, or until chicken is tender.

Check seasoning and when the casserole is ready to serve, sprinkle parsley on top. Serve with mashed potato.

Chicken casserole with wine
Substitute either white or red wine for half of the stock.

Chicken casserole with mushrooms
Add 100 g sliced mushrooms with onion and carrot.

Chicken casserole with red capsicum
Add 1 diced red capsicum with the onion and carrot. Try adding 1–2 tsp chilli powder to add a touch of warmth.

Mediterranean chicken casserole

Serves 4

This takes the simple chicken casserole recipe and introduces a few more ingredients, such as mushrooms and olives, to add more complexity and body to the dish.

1 kg skinless chicken casserole pieces
seasoned flour
olive oil
1 onion, diced
1 carrot, finely diced
1 clove garlic, crushed
100 g mushrooms, sliced
1 tbsp tomato paste
250 ml (1 cup) white wine
500 ml (2 cups) chicken stock
100 g (⅔ cup) pitted kalamata olives
chopped parsley to serve

Toss chicken pieces in flour and shake off excess. Heat a heavy-based saucepan over a medium heat, add a generous splash of olive oil and cook chicken pieces all over until golden brown. Remove pieces from the saucepan and set aside. Return saucepan to the heat and add more oil if necessary.

Cook onion, carrot and garlic until soft. Add mushrooms and cook for a further 3–4 minutes. Add tomato paste and cook briefly, then add wine and stock and bring to the boil. Reduce heat to a simmer, return the chicken to the saucepan, cover with a lid and cook for 1 hour, or until chicken is tender.

Add olives, check seasoning and, when ready to serve, sprinkle parsley on top. Serve with mashed potato.

French chicken casserole

Serves 4

This traditional French approach to making a chicken casserole uses shallots along with carrot and bacon to create the flavour base, while red wine produces a heartier result than many dishes cooked in this style. It's an absolute beauty of a meal to enjoy in cooler weather.

1 kg chicken casserole pieces	1 clove garlic, crushed
seasoned flour	1 tbsp tomato paste
oil	125 ml (½ cup) red wine
10–12 shallots, peeled	500 ml (2 cups) chicken stock
1 carrot, finely diced	salt and freshly ground black pepper
6 slices bacon, diced	chopped parsley to serve

Toss the chicken pieces in flour and shake off excess. Heat a heavy-based saucepan over a medium heat, add a generous splash of oil and cook the chicken pieces until golden brown all over. Remove the chicken from the saucepan and set aside.

Return the saucepan to the heat and add more oil, if necessary. Cook the shallots, carrot, bacon and garlic until soft. Add tomato paste and cook briefly, then add the wine and stock and bring to the boil. Reduce heat to a simmer, return the chicken to the saucepan, cover with a lid and cook for 1 hour, or until the chicken is tender.

Check seasoning, and sprinkle parsley on top. Serve with Mashed Potatoes (page 489) and Cauliflower Cheese (page 479).

Catalan chicken

Serves 4

This Spanish-flavoured dish is best served with creamy mashed potatoes or couscous and shared with a bottle of Spanish red and a couple of good friends.

170 g (1 cup) raisins
60 ml (¼ cup) dry sherry
1 kg chicken casserole pieces
seasoned flour
oil
1 onion, diced
½ red capsicum, cut into 2 cm chunks
2 cloves garlic, crushed
2 tsp harissa
250 ml (1 cup) tomato sugo
500 ml (2 cups) chicken stock
80 g (½ cup) toasted pine nuts
salt and freshly ground black pepper
chopped parsley to serve

Marinate the raisins in sherry for at least 30 minutes. Set aside until needed.

Toss the chicken pieces in flour and shake off excess. Heat a heavy-based saucepan over a medium heat, add a generous splash of oil and cook the chicken pieces until golden brown all over. Remove the chicken from the saucepan and set aside.

Return the saucepan to the heat and add more oil, if necessary. Cook the onion and capsicum until soft. Add the garlic and harissa and cook for 1–2 minutes, stirring often, until fragrant. Add the tomato sugo, stock, raisins and sherry and bring to the boil. Reduce heat to a simmer, return the chicken to the saucepan, cover with a lid and cook for 1 hour, or until the chicken is tender.

Add the pine nuts, check seasoning and sprinkle parsley on top. Serve with Spiced Couscous (page 453) or Catalan Potatoes (page 492).

Hungarian chicken casserole

Serves 4

Hungarian cooking is renowned for its use of aromatic paprika, which brings a deep, rich flavour to whatever it's used in. Use sweet paprika for a mild flavour or hot paprika if you like a bit of heat in this casserole.

1 tbsp butter
olive oil
1 kg skinless chicken thigh pieces
3 onions, thinly sliced
2 cloves garlic, chopped

2 tbsp sweet or hot paprika
2 tbsp flour
750 ml (3 cups) chicken stock
salt and freshly ground black pepper
sour cream (optional)

Preheat oven to 180°C.

Heat a heavy-based frypan over a medium heat. Add butter and a tablespoon of olive oil. Cook chicken pieces until golden all over. Set chicken pieces aside in an ovenproof casserole dish. Add additional oil to the pan, if needed, with the onions and garlic and cook until they begin to soften, about 5–6 minutes. Sprinkle the paprika and flour over the onions and stir well for 1–2 minutes. Add stock and stir until it comes to the boil. Season to taste with salt and pepper.

Pour onions and sauce over chicken, cover dish and place in the preheated oven. Cook for 1½ hours, by which stage chicken will be tender. Uncover the dish and cook for 30 minutes more to reduce the sauce and intensify the flavour.

Serve with noodles or mashed potatoes, and sour cream if using.

Chicken and mushroom pie

Serves 4

There's something special about serving a pie at the table. It always looks as if you've gone to a lot of trouble, whereas in fact it's just a casserole with pastry on the top – but don't tell anyone.

- 1 kg skinless chicken thigh fillets, diced
- seasoned flour
- olive oil
- 6 bacon slices, cut into strips
- 200 g mushrooms, sliced
- 125 ml (½ cup) white wine
- 125–250 ml (½–1 cup) chicken stock
- 1 tsp fresh thyme leaves
- 1 tbsp chopped parsley
- salt and freshly ground black pepper
- ½ quantity Puff Pastry (page 593) or 1 sheet frozen puff pastry
- egg wash

Toss chicken with flour and shake well to remove excess. Heat a heavy-based casserole pot or saucepan over a medium heat. Add oil and cook chicken in batches until golden brown. Set aside. Using the same pot, cook bacon and mushrooms until softened and beginning to colour. Add white wine and allow to come to the boil.

Return chicken to pot and add enough stock to just cover. Add herbs and season to taste, then reduce heat and allow to cook for 30–45 minutes.

Preheat oven to 180°C.

Spoon hot chicken mix into pie dish. Ensure pastry is rolled to a 3 mm thickness. Cover the chicken mix with puff pastry, trim edges and brush with egg wash. Place in preheated oven and bake for 20–30 minutes, or until pastry is cooked and golden brown. Remove and serve.

Moroccan chicken with tomatoes and olives

Serves 6

This shows how the simple casserole method can be adapted and transformed to include spices, preserved lemon and aromatic saffron. Serve it with pilaf or couscous.

1½ kg skinless chicken casserole pieces	pinch of saffron threads
seasoned flour	6 Roma tomatoes, diced or 1 × 300 g can tomatoes
olive oil	500 ml (2 cups) chicken stock
1 onion, sliced	½ preserved lemon, soaked for 30 minutes, pulp removed, then rind diced
2 tsp ground cumin	200 g (1¼ cup) green olives, pitted
2 tsp ground coriander	fresh parsley and coriander leaves
1 tsp sweet paprika	
½ tsp allspice	

Toss chicken pieces in seasoned flour and shake off excess using a sieve.

Heat a heavy-based casserole pot or saucepan over a medium heat, add a generous splash of olive oil and cook chicken pieces all over until golden brown. Remove chicken pieces from the pot and set aside. Return pot to the heat and add more oil if necessary.

Cook onion and spices until fragrant. Add tomatoes and stock and bring to the boil.

Return chicken to the pot, add preserved lemon, cover and cook over a low heat for 1 ½ hours. Add olives for the final 15 minutes of cooking. Check seasoning and add fresh herbs.

Moroccan chicken pie

Serves 4–6

This will produce a rich-tasting pie that needs only a green salad to go with it. If you want it a bit spicier add 1 tsp chilli powder and 1 extra tsp of both coriander and cumin.

- 1 kg skinless chicken thigh fillets, diced
- seasoned flour
- olive oil
- 1 onion, diced
- 2 tsp ground cumin
- 2 tsp ground coriander
- 1 tsp sweet paprika
- ½ tsp allspice
- ½ tsp ground ginger
- 500 ml (2 cups) chicken stock
- salt and freshly ground black pepper
- 1 tbsp pomegranate syrup (optional)
- handful of coriander leaves
- 3 small zucchini, halved and cut into 1 cm slices
- 6–8 sheets filo pastry
- melted butter
- sesame seeds

Toss chicken with flour and shake well to remove excess. Heat a heavy-based casserole pot over a medium heat. Add a generous splash of oil and cook chicken in batches until golden brown. Set aside.

Using the same pot, cook onion and spices until fragrant. Return chicken to the pot and add stock, salt and pepper. Bring to the boil; reduce heat and simmer, uncovered, until chicken is tender, about 45 minutes. Check seasoning, add coriander, zucchini, and pomegranate syrup (if using). Remove from heat.

Preheat oven to 180°C.

Grease a 20 cm springform cake tin. Brush butter on 6–8 sheets of filo and arrange them in cake tin, allowing excess to hang over the side. Spoon chicken filling into pastry and arrange excess pastry over the top, adding extra pastry if needed to enclose filling. Brush the top with butter and sprinkle with sesame seeds.

Bake in a preheated oven for 30 minutes, or until pastry is crisp and golden brown.

Soy-braised chicken

Serves 4–6

You're going to love this: only a handful of ingredients, no chopping – and it tastes fantastic. I feel like chicken tonight, at its best.

1 size 16 chicken
250 ml (1 cup) soy sauce
250 ml (1 cup) Chinese rice wine
250 ml (1 cup) chicken stock
250 ml (1 cup) water
3 whole star anise
220 g (1 cup) caster sugar
Steamed Rice (page 198) and Wok-Fried Asian Greens (page 499) to serve

Place chicken, breast side up, in a saucepan that will fit it snugly and that comes with a lid. Add all the other ingredients and place over a medium heat. Bring to the boil, then reduce heat, cover with a lid and cook for 30 minutes. Remove lid, turn chicken over, cover and cook for a further 15 minutes. Remove from heat and allow to stand, covered, for 15–20 minutes before serving.

Chop the chicken into 10–12 pieces and serve with Steamed Rice and Wok-Fried Asian Greens.

Basic beef stew

Serves 4

A traditional dish with classic flavours cooked on top of the stove, this will fill your home with hearty, appetite-inducing aromas. Master it, then adapt it with other flavours and ingredients that you love.

olive oil
6 slices bacon, cut into strips
16 shallots, peeled, or 2 onions, sliced
1 kg diced chuck or blade steak
seasoned flour
500 ml (2 cups) red wine
250 ml (1 cup) beef stock
bouquet garni
2 cloves garlic, crushed
salt and freshly ground black pepper

Preheat oven to 180°C.

Heat a large heavy-based casserole pot or saucepan over medium–high heat, add 1 tbsp oil. Add bacon and cook for 2–3 minutes, until it begins to brown. Remove with a slotted spoon and set aside. Add shallots, or onions, and more oil if needed, and cook until beginning to brown. Remove with slotted spoon and set aside with bacon.

Coat beef with seasoned flour and shake in a sieve to remove excess. Brown in batches, using more oil as needed. Tip off excess fat and return beef, bacon and shallots to pot with red wine and stock. Bring to the boil, stirring often, then reduce heat and add bouquet garni, garlic and a pinch of salt.

Cover with lid, and cook for 2 hours on minimum heat or in a 180°C preheated oven. Check to ensure beef is tender. If not, continue cooking for a further 15–20 minutes before checking again. When ready adjust seasoning if needed and serve with mashed potatoes and steamed vegetables.

Beef stew with dumplings
Add Dumplings (page 395) for the last 45 minutes to 1 hour of cooking.

Beef stew with mushrooms
Add 100 g sliced mushrooms with shallots/onions and cook for another 2–3 minutes.

Dumplings

Serves 4

Make these simple dumplings and add them with abandon to your favourite beef or chicken casserole for the last hour of cooking.

100 g (1 cup) dried breadcrumbs
150 g (1 cup) self-raising flour
75 g soft butter, diced
salt and freshly ground black pepper
1 tbsp chopped parsley
1 egg
50 ml (¼ cup) milk

Combine breadcrumbs and flour in a bowl. Rub butter through to form a sandy texture. Add salt, pepper and parsley and stir to combine. Add egg and enough milk to bring the mixture together.

Knead to form a smooth dough. Roll into 3 cm balls. Add to casseroles and stews during the last hour of cooking.

Horseradish dumplings
Add 50 g finely grated fresh horseradish (use 2 tsp creamed horseradish if you can't find fresh) with salt and pepper to add more flavour.

Braised steak and onions

Serves 4–6

Braised steak and onions is a dish that everyone should learn how to make. It's perfect during the cooler months, when you need some gutsy, rib-sticking food. Serve with mashed potatoes and lots of vegetables.

olive oil
4 onions, sliced
4 × 150 g pieces blade steak
250 ml (1 cup) red wine
250 ml (1 cup) beef stock
1–2 tbsp chopped fresh herbs
250 ml (1 cup) tomato puree
salt and freshly ground black pepper

Preheat oven to 180°C.

Heat a heavy-based saucepan over a medium heat. Add oil and onions and cook until soft. Add steak, red wine, stock, herbs, tomato puree and salt and pepper. Cover with a lid and cook in a preheated oven for 1½–2 hours, or until tender.

Beef and Guinness casserole with dumplings

Serves 4–6

The heart-warming power of this luscious casserole will be most appreciated on a cold winter's night. Dumplings may seem like a very old-fashioned thing to add, but these ones are beautifully light and really take the dish to a new level.

- 1½ kg diced skirt or blade steak
- seasoned flour
- oil
- 500 ml (2 cups) Guinness
- 500 ml (2 cups) beef stock
- 2 cloves garlic, crushed
- 250 g shallots, peeled and cut into quarters
- salt and freshly ground black pepper
- 100 g (1 cup) dry breadcrumbs
- 150 g (1 cup) self-raising flour
- 75 g soft butter, diced
- 1 tbsp chopped parsley
- 1 egg
- 50 ml (¼ cup) milk

Coat the beef with the seasoned flour and shake off excess flour, using a sieve. Heat a large heavy-based saucepan over a medium heat, add a splash of oil and cook the beef in small batches until golden brown, adding more oil if needed. Add the Guinness, stock, garlic and shallots and bring to the boil. Season lightly, cover and reduce heat to low. Skim the surface as needed. Cook for 1 hour.

While the beef is cooking, prepare the dumplings by combining the breadcrumbs and flour in a bowl. Rub the butter through to form a sandy texture. Add salt, pepper and parsley and stir to combine. Add the egg and enough milk to bring the mixture together. Knead to form a smooth dough and roll into 3 cm balls.

Add the dumplings to the casserole after the first hour of cooking and cook for an additional 1 hour.

After 2 hours of cooking, test if the beef is tender. If so, check seasoning and serve. If not, cook for a further 20–30 minutes.

Serve with Fresh Garden Peas (page 486).

Spezzatino

Serves 6

Only the Italians can make a humble beef stew sound so exotic. This version is inspired by the Australian godfather of Italian cooking, Stefano de Pieri.

oil
2 carrots, diced
2 onions, diced
2 celery stalks, diced
1 ½ kg diced blade steak
2 cloves garlic, peeled
250 ml (1 cup) red wine
4 potatoes, peeled and diced
400 g can chopped tomatoes
250 ml (1 cup) tomato sugo
1 bay leaf
salt and freshly ground black pepper
250–375 ml (1–1 ½ cups) beef stock

Heat a large heavy-based saucepan over a medium heat. Add a generous splash of oil and the diced carrots, onions and celery. Cook for 5–6 minutes, until soft but not coloured. Remove the vegetables from the pan and set aside.

Return the saucepan to the heat and add more oil, if needed. Cook the beef, in batches if necessary, until well sealed (browned). Return the vegetables to the saucepan, along with the garlic, red wine, potatoes, tomatoes, tomato sugo, bay leaf, salt and pepper.

Bring to a gentle simmer and add stock as needed to ensure that the meat is covered. Cook for 2 ½–3 hours over a low heat, partially covered, until the meat is tender. Check seasoning.

Spezzatino is great with Soft Polenta (page 192) and a Pear, Walnut and Rocket Salad (page 507).

Beef goulash

Serves 4

Beef goulash is the perfect meal for a wintery night. Add a glass or two of red wine and perhaps an open fire and you will be in seventh heaven.

oil
1½ kg diced blade steak
3 onions, thinly sliced
2 cloves garlic, chopped
2 tbsp sweet or hot paprika
2 tbsp flour
750 ml (3 cups) beef stock
salt and freshly ground black pepper
sour cream (optional)

Preheat oven to 180°C.

Heat a heavy-based frypan over a medium heat. Add a generous splash of oil and cook the beef until golden all over. Set the beef aside in an ovenproof casserole dish.

Add additional oil to the pan, if needed, along with the onions and garlic. Cook for 3–4 minutes, until the onions begin to soften. Sprinkle the paprika and flour over the onions and stir well for 1–2 minutes. Add stock and stir until the liquid comes to the boil. Season with salt and pepper.

Pour the onions and sauce over the beef. Cover the dish and place it in the preheated oven to cook for 1½–2 hours, or until the beef is tender. Uncover and cook for a further 30 minutes to reduce the sauce and intensify the flavour.

Serve with noodles or Mashed Potatoes (page 489), along with sour cream (if using).

Garlic confit with braised beef

Serves 4–6

In this unusual dish the garlic is cooked confit-style in olive oil, then served with braised beef steaks in a red wine sauce.

4–6 heads garlic	2 celery stalks, chopped
2–3 bay leaves	6 × 150 g pieces blade steak
2–3 sprigs of thyme	250 ml (1 cup) red wine
250–500 ml (1–2 cups) olive oil	250 ml (1 cup) beef stock
1 onion, sliced	1–2 tbsp chopped fresh herbs
2 carrots, sliced	salt and freshly ground black pepper

Preheat oven to 180°C.

Turn each head of garlic on its side and cut the top ½ cm away to expose the cloves inside. Place the garlic heads in a snug-fitting ovenproof dish. Add the bay leaves and thyme and pour over enough oil to cover. Cover the dish with a lid or foil and cook in the preheated oven for 1–1½ hours, or until the garlic is tender. You may like to do this in advance. The garlic-infused oil can be re-used for general cooking.

To prepare the braised beef, heat a heavy-based ovenproof saucepan over a medium heat. Add oil and the onion, carrots and celery, and cook for 3–4 minutes, until soft. Add the steak, red wine, stock, herbs, salt and pepper. Cover with a lid and cook in the preheated oven for 1½–2 hours, or until tender.

Serve each person 1 piece of beef steak, with a head of garlic on the side. Accompany with Mashed Potatoes (page 489).

Beef and Guinness pie

Serves 4–6

This is a luscious, rich pie whose heart-warming power will be most appreciated on a really cold night.

- 1½ kg diced skirt steak
- seasoned flour
- olive oil
- 500 ml (2 cups) Guinness
- 500 ml (2 cups) beef stock
- 2 cloves garlic, crushed
- 250 g shallots, peeled and cut into quarters
- 150 ml (½ cup) cold water
- 100 g butter
- 1 tsp salt
- 300 g (2 cups) self-raising flour
- egg wash

Coat beef with seasoned flour and shake excess off using a sieve. Heat a large heavy-based saucepan over medium heat, add a splash of olive oil and cook beef in small batches until golden brown, adding more oil if needed. Add Guinness, stock, garlic and shallots and bring to the boil. Season lightly, reduce heat to low, cover and cook for 1½–2 hours. Check seasoning. When beef is tender it's time to prepare the pastry.

Preheat oven to 180°C.

Combine water, butter and salt in a saucepan and place over medium heat until butter melts. Remove from heat, add flour and stir to combine quickly. Tip dough onto a floured board and knead quickly until smooth. Divide dough in two. Roll out a piece to fit into a 2 litre pie dish. Grease pie dish and line with pastry. Spoon hot pie filling into dish. Roll remaining pastry and cover the pie, trim edges and brush with egg wash. Bake in preheated oven until golden brown, about 15–20 minutes.

Slow-cooked leg of lamb with lemon and oregano

Serves 4–6

Cooking lamb with potatoes and garlic over a long period of time adds intensity to this dish. The potatoes will soak up all the fat from the lamb, making them irresistible.

oil
1 leg of lamb on the bone
80 ml (⅓ cup) lemon juice
1 tbsp chopped oregano
salt and freshly ground black pepper
250–375 ml (1–1½ cups) chicken stock
4–6 cloves garlic, peeled
6 large potatoes, diced

Preheat oven to 160°C.

Heat a heavy-based saucepan over a medium–high heat. Add a splash of oil and cook the lamb until brown all over.

Transfer the meat to an ovenproof dish. Rub lemon juice all over the lamb and season with oregano, salt and pepper. Pour stock around the meat and add the garlic and potatoes. Cover with foil.

Cook in the preheated oven for 3–4 hours. Check every 30 minutes or so, turning the lamb and potatoes to ensure they brown evenly. Add more stock or water, as needed, to keep the dish moist. Remove foil and cook for a further 30 minutes. The lamb should now be tender and falling to pieces.

To serve, simply break the meat into chunks and place on a large platter with the potatoes and cooking juices.

Braised lamb chops

Serves 4–6

This is a very basic dish, but with only 45 minutes' cooking time it's a very handy dinner suggestion.

12 lamb chops
1 onion, sliced
1 carrot, sliced
1 tbsp chopped rosemary
2–3 sprigs of thyme
2–3 cloves garlic, peeled
1–2 tbsp tomato paste
125 ml (½ cup) white wine (optional)
250–375 ml (1–1½ cups) chicken stock
salt and freshly ground black pepper

Preheat oven to 180°C.

Place the lamb chops in a single layer in a baking dish, then add the remaining ingredients. Cover with foil and cook for 45 minutes–1 hour, or until the lamb is tender.

Check seasoning and serve with Potato Gratin (page 492).

Braised lamb with cannellini beans

Serves 4–6

The beauty of cooking the lamb over the beans in this recipe is that all the cooking juices from the meat drip down and into the beans, adding an extra flavour boost.

1 leg of lamb
2–3 sprigs of rosemary
8–10 cloves garlic, peeled
oil
salt and freshly ground black pepper
200 g (1 cup) dried cannellini beans, soaked in cold water
1 onion, diced
1 carrot, finely diced
500–750 ml (2–3 cups) chicken stock
2 tbsp chopped parsley

Using a small knife, make deep cuts all over the lamb and insert a garlic clove and 2–3 rosemary leaves into each cut. Rub the lamb with oil, season with salt and pepper and place in a deep baking dish.

Preheat oven to 180°C.

Place the soaked beans, onion, carrot and stock in a saucepan and bring to the boil. Pour into the baking tray around the lamb and cover the dish with foil. Cook for 1 ½ hours, then remove the foil and cook for 30–45 minutes, until the lamb is golden brown.

Remove the lamb, wrap it in foil and rest for 15 minutes. Check that the beans are tender; if necessary, add more stock or water and cook for a further 10 minutes. Check seasoning and add parsley.

Carve the lamb, adding any juices back to the beans. Spoon the beans onto a large platter, arrange slices of lamb on top and serve with Romesco Sauce (page 552).

Lamb hot pot

Serves 4

A piping-hot lamb hot pot is the perfect meal on a cold winter's night. It's an all-in-one meal with a delicious mix of diced lamb and vegetables in a light sauce, all under a crust of golden potato slices. The traditional version uses lamb chops. If you prefer, use them in this recipe, but we choose to use diced lamb.

olive oil
1 kg diced lamb, shoulder for preference
1 onion, diced
1 clove garlic, crushed
1 carrot, diced
2 celery sticks, diced
1 tbsp flour

750 ml (3 cups) chicken or beef stock
400 g can chopped tomatoes
1 tbsp tomato paste
1 tbsp thyme leaves
salt and freshly ground black pepper
1 kg potatoes
2 tbsp melted butter

Preheat oven to 180°C.

Heat a large heavy-based frypan over medium–high heat, add a splash of olive oil and cook lamb in small batches until golden brown, adding more oil if needed. Set aside lamb in an ovenproof casserole dish.

Add extra oil to the pan if needed. Reduce heat, add onion, garlic, carrot and celery and cook for 5–6 minutes until vegetables soften, stirring often. Sprinkle flour over vegetables and stir in, then cook for 3–4 minutes. Add stock, tomatoes, tomato paste and thyme. Bring to the boil, reduce heat and simmer for 10 minutes. Season to taste. Pour sauce over lamb.

Peel potatoes and slice into rounds. Arrange the potatoes on top of the lamb. Melt the butter and brush over the layer of potato. Place the hot pot into the preheated oven, uncovered, and cook for 2 ½ hours. Brush the potato slices with some of the casserole juices every half hour.

Lamb navarin with root vegetables and rosemary

Serves 4–6

Another winter warmer, this recipe takes diced lamb and cooks it long and slow with root vegetables.

oil
1½ kg diced lamb
8 shallots, peeled
2 turnips, diced into 2 cm chunks
1 swede, diced into 2 cm chunks
2 carrots, sliced
2 cloves garlic, peeled
2 sprigs of rosemary
2 bay leaves
125 ml (½ cup) white wine
2 litres (8 cups) chicken stock
salt and freshly ground black pepper
75 g podded peas
2 tbsp chopped parsley

Heat a large heavy-based saucepan over a medium–high heat. Add a splash of oil and cook the lamb in batches until browned. Remove from heat and set aside.

Return the saucepan to the heat and add the shallots, turnips, swede and carrots. Cook for 3–4 minutes, stirring often. Add garlic, rosemary and bay leaves and cook for 1–2 minutes. Return the lamb to the saucepan, along with the white wine and enough stock to cover. Season with salt and pepper and bring to the boil.

Reduce heat, cover and cook for 1½ hours, or until the lamb is tender. Check seasoning, add peas and cook for 5 minutes.

Add parsley and serve with Potato Gratin (page 492).

Sicilian lamb stew with pecorino

Serves 4–6

The rustic flavours of this Italian-influenced slow-cooked stew include pancetta, garlic and red wine.

oil
2 onions, sliced
60 g pancetta, diced
1 kg diced lamb
2 cloves garlic, crushed
250 ml (1 cup) red wine
250 g small potatoes
250 ml (1 cup) chicken stock
125 ml (½ cup) tomato sugo
salt and freshly ground black pepper
100 g pecorino cheese, diced into 1 cm chunks
2 tbsp red wine vinegar
2 tbsp chopped parsley

Preheat oven to 180°C.

Heat a heavy-based ovenproof dish over a medium–high heat. Add a splash of oil and the onions and cook for 3–4 minutes, stirring often, until softened. Add the diced pancetta and cook for a further 3–4 minutes. Add diced lamb and cook for 3–4 minutes, until golden brown on all sides.

Add garlic and cook briefly, then add red wine. Allow to boil until reduced by half. Add the potatoes, stock and sugo and bring to the boil. Season with salt and pepper.

Reduce heat, cover with a lid and cook in preheated oven for 1–1½ hours or until the lamb is tender. Add the diced pecorino and red wine vinegar and return to the oven for 5 minutes. Check seasoning, add parsley and stir well to combine.

Serve with Soft Polenta (page 192).

Braised lamb shanks with mint and harissa

Serves 6

We love long slow-cooked lamb with a bit of spice; it helps to cut through the richness of the meat. If you like, you can add some vegetables to the lamb as it cooks. This is excellent with Spiced Couscous (page 453).

oil
6 lamb shanks
1½ tsp harissa
2 tsp ground cumin
1 tsp smoky sweet paprika
½ tsp allspice
⅓ bunch coriander with roots, chopped
2 sprigs mint, chopped
625 ml (2½ cups) chicken stock
375 ml (1½ cups) tomato sugo
salt and freshly ground black pepper

Preheat oven to 180°C.

Heat a large heavy-based saucepan over a medium heat. Add a splash of oil and shanks and cook until well browned on all sides. Add harissa, spices, herbs, stock and sugo and bring to the boil.

Transfer lamb and sauce to an ovenproof casserole dish, cover with lid or foil and cook for 2 hours, or until lamb is tender and almost falling off the bone. Season to taste.

Serve with Spiced Couscous (page 453), arrange shanks on top, pour sauce over and serve with a Green Salad (page 506).

Spanish lamb stew

Serves 6

We've cooked many variations of this dish over the years, the original hailing from our good friend Phillippa Grogan. We've added some almonds to increase the richness and we love including fresh broad beans if they are in season.

- 2 red capsicums
- olive oil
- 80 g (½ cup) blanched almonds
- 1 kg broad beans, podded (optional)
- 1½ kg diced lamb
- 2 onions, diced
- 2 cloves garlic, crushed
- 2 tsp smoky paprika
- pinch of saffron threads
- 2–3 bay leaves
- 160 ml (⅔ cup) white wine
- 500 ml (2 cups) chicken stock
- 375 ml (1½ cups) tomato sugo
- salt and freshly ground black pepper
- 2 tbsp chopped parsley

Preheat oven to 180°C.

Rub the capsicums with olive oil and roast in the oven until the skins blister, approximately 20–30 minutes. Put them in a plastic bag and seal to allow the steam to lift the skins. When cool enough to handle, peel, discard seeds and cut capsicum into 1 cm slices, then set aside.

Roast almonds in the oven until golden brown, allow to cool, and then grind in a food processor. Set aside for later use.

Bring a saucepan of water to the boil, blanch broad beans, and then refresh under cold water. Remove the outer pale green skins and set the beans aside.

Heat a large ovenproof casserole dish over a medium–high heat. Add a splash of olive oil and cook the lamb until brown all over, in batches if necessary. Remove lamb from the dish and return the dish to the heat. Add more oil if needed and cook the onions for 6–8 minutes until soft. Add garlic, paprika, saffron and bay leaves and cook for 1–2 minutes until fragrant, add wine, bring to the boil and allow to reduce by half. Add the stock and sugo and bring to boil. Reduce heat and simmer for 20–30 minutes. Return lamb to the dish and season with salt and pepper.

Cover the casserole and cook in the preheated oven for 1½–2 hours, or until lamb is tender. Add the cooked capsicum and enough roasted ground almonds to thicken the sauce. Add broad beans and parsley, and season to taste.

Braised pork with star anise (The pork dish)

Serves 4–6

Pork belly is braised with simple Asian ingredients to create a meal you will absolutely adore. All it needs is steamed rice and stir-fried greens to complete the experience.

1½ kg pork belly
3 spring onions, sliced
4 cm piece of ginger, sliced
2 tbsp soy sauce
2 tbsp Chinese cooking wine
2 tbsp fish sauce
2 star anise
1 tsp crushed Sichuan peppercorns
1 tsp crushed black peppercorns
2 small red chillies, halved
Steamed Rice (page 198) to serve

Preheat oven to 180°C.

Cut the pork into 1 cm thick slices. Place the meat in a heatproof casserole dish with a tight-fitting lid. Add the remaining ingredients and enough water to come halfway up the pork. Put the lid on and cook in the preheated oven for 3 hours.

Carefully lift the slices of pork onto a deep serving platter and spoon over the cooking liquid. Serve with Steamed Rice and Chinese Broccoli and Garlic Stir-Fry (page 480).

Rodriguez pork

Serves 6

Being movie fans, we were intrigued by the cooking lesson included by director Robert Rodriguez in the DVD of *Once Upon a Time in Mexico*. In the film, the character Sands, played by Johnny Depp, chows down in restaurants across Mexico in search of the best Puerco Pibil, a classic dish of slow-cooked pork, only to shoot the chef at the end because it was so good. Luckily, that hasn't happened to us yet.

⅓ cup annatto seeds
2 tbsp cumin seeds
1 tbsp black peppercorns
8 whole allspice
1 tsp whole cloves
125 ml (½ cup) orange juice
165 ml (⅔ cup) lemon juice
125 ml (½ cup) white wine vinegar
2 tbsp tequila
2 Habanero chillies, de-seeded and diced
8 cloves garlic, peeled
2 tbsp salt
2½ kg pork butt or leg
banana leaves (optional)
Steamed Rice (page 198) to serve

Grind the spices in a mortar and pestle until fine. Robert Rodriguez suggests that you use a coffee grinder, but not one you'd ever use for coffee.

Place the ground spices, orange juice, lemon juice, vinegar, tequila, chillies, garlic and salt in a blender and puree until smooth.

Dice the pork into 2 cm chunks. Pour the marinade over and refrigerate for at least 40 minutes or up to 4 hours.

Preheat oven to 180°C.

Line a baking dish with banana leaves (if using), add the pork and cover with more leaves. If not using banana leaves, place the pork in a baking dish and cover with foil.

Bake in the preheated oven for 3–4 hours. Test after 3 hours; the pork should have a fall-apart character. If you cook the meat for too long it will become dry and stringy.

Serve with Steamed Rice.

Braised pork belly with chorizo sausage

Serves 4–6

Pork belly is meltingly delicious when cooked long and slow. Here, it's combined with spicy chorizo sausage, smoky paprika and a haricot bean stew.

1 chorizo sausage (250 g), diced
oil
1 onion, diced
1 carrot, finely diced
2 celery stalks, chopped
2 cloves garlic, crushed
1½ tsp smoky paprika
1½ kg pork belly
150 g (¾ cup) haricot beans, soaked in cold water
125 ml (½ cup) tomato sugo
250–500 ml (1–2 cups) chicken stock
salt and freshly ground black pepper

Preheat oven to 180°C.

Heat a heavy-based ovenproof saucepan over a medium–high heat. Add the chorizo to the dry saucepan and cook for 4–5 minutes, stirring often, until golden brown and the fat breaks down. Remove from heat and set aside on absorbent paper.

Wipe the saucepan clean and return to the heat. Add a splash of oil and cook the onion, carrot and celery for 4–5 minutes, stirring often. Add the garlic and paprika and cook for 1–2 minutes, stirring well, until fragrant. Add the pork, beans and chorizo, along with the tomato sugo and enough stock to cover the beans and vegetables. Bring to the boil. Cover with a lid and cook in the preheated oven for 2–2 ½ hours.

Remove the pork from the pan. Check that the beans are cooked, and add more stock if necessary. Check seasoning.

Carve the pork into 1 cm thick slices. Serve the bean and chorizo braise in a large, flat bowl, topped with slices of the pork belly.

Slow-cooked pork belly with Catalan potatoes and quince aioli

Serves 6

This dish is basically a fabulous pork roast. The Quince Aioli adds a beautiful sweetness to the meat, not dissimilar to apple sauce. The longer you cook the pork the more the fat breaks down and the more it will melt in your mouth.

4 cloves garlic, crushed
1 tbsp fennel seeds
1–2 tbsp salt flakes
olive oil
2 kg pork belly, skin scored
1½–2 kg desiree potatoes
salt and freshly ground black pepper
1 tsp smoky paprika
500–750 ml (2–3 cups) chicken stock, as needed
black pepper
Quince Aioli (page 550)

Preheat oven to 220°C.

Mix garlic, fennel seeds and salt with 2 tbsp oil. Rub over the skin of the pork, massaging it well down into the flesh. Set aside to allow flavour to penetrate pork.

Place pork in a deep baking tray skin side up; add enough water to come halfway up the pork. Cook for 30 minutes until skin crackles.

Lower heat to 180°C and cook for a further 2–2 ½ hours. Water will evaporate during cooking.

Peel potatoes and cut in half lengthways. Put in a roasting tray, sprinkle with salt, pepper and paprika. Add a good splash of olive oil, and toss to coat potatoes with seasoning. Carefully pour stock around potatoes to come halfway up them. Cook for 1 ½ hours at 180°C, alongside pork, tossing them occasionally. Cook until golden brown and liquid has been absorbed.

Remove pork from oven. If skin needs to be crisper, remove using a sharp knife, place on a cooking rack over a shallow baking tray and return to oven or place under a hot grill to crisp up. Once crisp chop into pieces.

Remove pork from baking tray, cut into 2 cm thick slices. Arrange on a platter with potatoes and crackling. Serve with Quince Aioli and Green Salad (page 506).

Duck cassoulet

Serves 6

You'll be waiting for winter to kick in, just so you can enjoy this duck confit casserole. It's become a regular 'celebrate the start of winter' meal for our good friend Steve, who reckons he can't get through winter without this extra layer of fat.

6 duck confit legs (see page 378, or purchase in a specialist food store)
oil
300 g pork belly, skin removed and diced into 2 cm pieces
2 onions, diced
1 celery stalk, chopped
½ leek, chopped
2 carrots, diced
2 cloves garlic, crushed
125 ml (½ cup) white wine
250 g (1¼ cups) haricot beans, soaked in cold water
sprig of thyme
2 bay leaves
250 g saucisson lyonnaise or Polish sausage, sliced into 1 cm rounds
salt
250 ml (1 cup) tomato sugo
chicken stock as required
100 g (2 cups) fresh breadcrumbs
chopped parsley

Heat a large saucepan over a medium heat. Add a generous splash of oil and cook the pork belly for 15 minutes, until browned. Remove from the pan and set aside.

Return the saucepan to the heat and add more oil, if necessary. Cook the onions, celery, leek and carrot for 5–6 minutes, stirring often, until soft. Add garlic and cook for 1–2 minutes, until fragrant. Pour in the wine, and add the pork belly, beans, thyme and bay leaves. Cover with water, bring to the boil and simmer for 1 hour, until the beans are tender. Drain, reserving the stock, and set both aside.

Heat a large frypan over a medium heat. Add a splash of oil and lightly brown the sausage slices.

Place half the amount of cooked pork and beans in the bottom of a large ovenproof casserole dish. Arrange the duck legs on top and cover with the remaining pork and beans. Arrange the pork sausage on top of the beans, pushing the slices down into the bean mixture.

Bring the reserved stock to the boil, season with salt and add the tomato sugo. Pour the liquid over the beans, duck and sausage to almost cover. If you don't have enough liquid, top up with chicken stock. Sprinkle breadcrumbs over the top.

Cover the dish with foil and cook in the preheated oven for 40 minutes. Remove the foil and cook for a further 30–40 minutes, until golden brown.

Sprinkle with parsley and serve with a green salad.

Osso buco

Serves 4

A classic veal casserole that is delicious served with mounds of mashed potato or soft polenta to soak up all the lovely tasty juices.

1 kg veal osso buco	250 ml (1 cup) tomato puree
seasoned flour	250–500 ml (1–2 cups) chicken stock
olive oil	salt and freshly ground black pepper
1 onion, diced	1 clove garlic, crushed, additional
2 celery stalks, diced	zest of 1 lemon, chopped
2 carrots, finely diced	3 tbsp chopped parsley
2 cloves garlic, crushed	2 anchovy fillets, chopped
250 ml (1 cup) white wine	

Dust osso buco with flour, shaking well to remove excess. Place a large heavy-based casserole dish or saucepan over a medium heat. Add a splash of oil and brown osso buco well on both sides, in batches if necessary. Remove veal and set aside. Add more oil if required and cook onion, celery and carrots for 6–8 minutes, stirring often, until soft. Add garlic and cook for a further minute.

Return veal to pan, add white wine, bring to the boil and reduce by half. Add tomato puree and enough stock to cover veal. Season with salt and pepper. Bring to the boil, reduce to a simmer, cover with lid and cook for 1 hour. Check to see whether veal is tender. If not, cook for a further 10 minutes and try again.

Mix additional garlic, lemon zest, parsley and anchovy together. Sprinkle over veal to serve.

Pot-roasted veal shanks

Serves 4

As veal is not always available, some retailers sell beef labelled as veal. To make sure your shanks really are veal, buy them from a butcher who specialises in European cuts; and take the extra precaution of ordering a few days ahead to make sure you don't miss out.

olive oil
4 veal shanks
2 cloves garlic, crushed
1 onion, finely diced
1 carrot, finely diced
1 small turnip, finely diced
1 small swede, finely diced
1 celery stick, finely diced
2 tbsp plain flour
250 ml (1 cup) red wine
1 tbsp tomato paste
salt and freshly ground black pepper
1 bouquet garni of bay leaf, thyme and parsley
chopped parsley

Heat a heavy-based saucepan over a medium heat, add a dash of olive oil and brown the shanks all over. Remove shanks from the pan. Add the vegetables and cook until soft, stirring often, about 10 minutes. Sprinkle with flour, stir, lower heat and allow to cook for 2 minutes.

Increase heat; add wine and stir vigorously to remove any sediment from the base of the pan. Simmer for 3–4 minutes. Add tomato paste and a pinch of salt. Place the shanks back in the pan and add enough water to just cover. Add the bouquet garni and bring the liquid to the boil. Remove the scum as it rises to the surface. Lower heat; cover with a lid and cook for 1½ hours. Every 15 minutes, turn the shanks to allow even cooking. When tender, check seasoning and add chopped parsley.

Serve with Mashed Potatoes (page 489).

Pot-roasted veal with pancetta and mustard

Serves 4

Veal responds well to pot roasting, as the meat juices go directly into the sauce. This dish is great served with mashed potatoes, roast potatoes or polenta.

1 kg veal nut
oil
salt and freshly ground black pepper
2 tbsp chopped rosemary
150 g pancetta, diced into 1 cm pieces

2–3 cloves garlic, peeled
125 ml (½ cup) white wine
125 ml (½ cup) chicken stock
2 tsp wholegrain mustard
180 g button mushrooms, halved

Preheat oven to 180°C.

Heat a heatproof casserole dish over a medium heat. Add a splash of oil and brown the veal all over. Remove the dish from heat and season the veal with salt and pepper. Add the rosemary, pancetta, garlic, wine, stock and mustard. Cover the casserole and cook in the preheated oven for 1 hour.

Turn the veal over and add the mushrooms. Cover and continue cooking for 30 minutes. Cook the veal uncovered for 15 minutes to brown the outside and reduce the sauce a little. Remove the veal from the dish and allow it to rest for 5–10 minutes.

Carve the veal and check the seasoning of the cooking liquid. Serve the veal with the sauce.

Rabbit casserole

Serves 6

We always search out some top-quality farmed rabbits for this dish. It takes a bit of work to get it cooking. But, like all good casseroles, once it's in the oven your work is done.

- 125 g pancetta or streaky bacon
- 125 ml (½ cup) verjuice, or white wine
- 20 shallots or small pickling onions, peeled
- 2 cloves garlic, peeled
- 2 rabbits, skinned, cleaned and jointed
- seasoned flour
- olive oil
- 1 carrot, finely diced
- 2 leeks, thinly sliced
- 2 celery stalks, diced
- 1–2 bay leaves
- 2–3 thyme sprigs
- 250 ml (1 cup) white wine
- 500 ml (2 cups) chicken stock
- 20 button mushrooms
- 90 g (½ cup) sultanas
- salt and freshly ground black pepper
- 90 g (⅔ cup) pine nuts, toasted
- chopped parsley to serve

Preheat oven to 180°C.

Heat a large heavy-based casserole dish or saucepan over a medium–high heat. Cook pancetta in dry pan until golden. Add verjuice, shallots and garlic, cook until verjuice has evaporated and shallots begin to colour. Set aside.

Dust rabbit pieces with seasoned flour. Add a splash of oil to saucepan and cook rabbit pieces, in batches if necessary, until golden. Remove and set aside. Add more oil if required and cook carrot, leeks and celery until soft, about 6–8 minutes.

Return rear legs and saddle pieces to the pot along with herbs, wine and stock. Cover and cook in preheated oven for 40 minutes. Remove from the oven and add the pre-prepared verjuice, shallots and garlic mixture, along with the mushrooms, sultanas and remaining rabbit pieces. Season to taste, cover and return to the oven for a further 30 minutes.

Check to see whether rabbit is tender. If not, cook for a further 10 minutes and check again. Check seasoning, add pine nuts and parsley and serve.

Braised rabbit with cider and rosemary

Serves 6

We tend to cook rabbit only a couple of times each winter, so we like to ensure that the recipe we're using will produce a great result. This dish of braised rabbit flavoured with cider and rosemary is one which will do just that.

2 rabbits, skinned, cleaned and jointed
seasoned flour
oil
1 onion, sliced
1 leek, thinly sliced
2 cloves garlic, peeled
1–2 bay leaves
1–2 sprigs of rosemary
250 ml (1 cup) dry cider
250 ml (1 cup) chicken stock
250 ml (1 cup) thickened cream
2 tsp wholegrain mustard
salt and freshly ground black pepper
chopped parsley to serve

Preheat oven to 180°C.

Heat a large heavy-based heatproof casserole dish over a medium–high heat. Dust the rabbit pieces with seasoned flour. Add a splash of oil to the casserole dish and cook the rabbit pieces, in batches if necessary, until golden. Remove from the dish and set aside.

Add more oil, if required, and cook the onion and leek for 3–4 minutes, until soft. Add garlic and cook for a further 1–2 minutes. Add the bay leaves, rosemary, cider, stock, cream and mustard. Bring to the boil. Add the hind legs and saddle pieces of the rabbit to the casserole. Season with salt and pepper. Cover the dish and cook in the preheated oven for 40 minutes. Add the remaining pieces of rabbit and return to the oven for a further 40 minutes.

Check to see whether the rabbit is tender. If not, cook for a further 10 minutes and try again. Check seasoning.

Sprinkle with parsley and serve the dish at the table, allowing everyone to help themselves.

Mediterranean fish stew

Serves 4–6

Cooking fish with tomatoes, herbs and potatoes is one of the easiest ways to enjoy seafood for dinner. It's a true one-pot wonder.

- 4 potatoes, peeled and diced
- 1 onion, sliced
- 2–3 cloves garlic, peeled
- 4 tomatoes, diced
- a few sprigs of thyme
- 1 tbsp oregano leaves
- 1 kg firm white fish fillets
- olive oil
- juice of 1 lemon
- 375 ml (1½ cups) fish or chicken stock
- salt and freshly ground black pepper
- 2 tbsp chopped parsley

Preheat oven to 180°C.

Place the potato, onion, garlic, tomatoes and herbs in an ovenproof baking dish. Cut the fish into 3 cm chunks and place on top. Drizzle with a little olive oil and lemon juice.

Place the stock in a small saucepan and bring to the boil. Pour over the other ingredients. Season lightly and cover with foil.

Bake in the preheated oven for 45 minutes. Check to see if the potatoes are cooked; if not, cook for an additional 5 minutes. Check seasoning.

Scatter parsley over and serve with a loaf of crusty bread and good butter.

Seafood casserole with saffron and cream

Serves 4–6

This dish is just the thing to serve when you feel like going to a bit of extra effort to create a real seafood feast.

- 750 g firm white fish fillets
- 8 scallops
- 8–12 green (raw) prawns
- 250 ml (1 cup) fish stock
- 80 ml (⅓ cup) white wine
- 1 leek, sliced
- 2 bay leaves
- pinch of saffron threads
- salt and freshly ground black pepper
- 250 ml (1 cup) thickened cream
- 2 tbsp chopped parsley

Preheat oven to 180°C.

Cut the fish into 3 cm chunks. Place the fish, scallops and prawns in the base of a heavy-based ovenproof saucepan. Add the fish stock, wine, leek, bay leaves and saffron. Season with salt and pepper. Place the pan over a medium heat and bring to the boil. Reduce to a simmer, cover and cook in the preheated oven for 10 minutes. Carefully remove the fish and seafood from the pan and keep warm.

Place the saucepan over a medium–high heat and boil rapidly to reduce liquid by half. Add cream and bring back to the boil, then simmer for 2 minutes. Check seasoning.

Return the fish and seafood to the sauce, spoon into a large bowl and sprinkle parsley on top to serve.

Moroccan fish stew

Serves 4

Try this gutsy fish stew with couscous to soak up the spicy juices.

oil
1 onion, sliced
1 fennel bulb, sliced
1 small red chilli, de-seeded and diced
2 cloves garlic, crushed
½ tsp sweet paprika
pinch of saffron threads
4 tomatoes, diced
2 bay leaves
250 ml (1 cup) fish stock or water
300 g small potatoes
500 g mussels, cleaned
500 g firm white fish, diced into 2 cm chunks
salt and freshly ground black pepper
2 tbsp chopped coriander
Quick Couscous (page 453) to serve

Heat a large heavy-based saucepan over a medium–high heat. Add a splash of oil, the onion and fennel. Cook for 4–5 minutes, stirring often, until softened. Add the chilli, garlic, paprika and saffron, and cook for a further 1–2 minutes, stirring well. Add the tomatoes and cook briefly to soften, then add the bay leaves and stock and bring to the boil. Add potatoes, season with salt and cook for 10–15 minutes or until potatoes are cooked through.

Add the mussels and cook until they all open (discard any that remain closed). Add the fish pieces and allow to cook through.

Check seasoning and spoon into a large serving bowl. Top with coriander and serve with couscous.

Mediterranean bean stew with feta

Serves 4

There are times when all you crave is a great vegetarian bean stew. Well, here it is!

oil
1 onion, diced
2 cloves garlic, crushed
½ tsp paprika
250 ml (1 cup) vegetable or chicken stock
250 ml (1 cup) tomato sugo
200 g (1 cup) dried cannellini beans, soaked in cold water
2 bay leaves
salt and freshly ground black pepper
2 tbsp chopped parsley
100 g feta, chopped

Heat a heavy-based saucepan over a medium–high heat. Add splash of oil and the onion and cook for 3–4 minutes, stirring often. Add the garlic and paprika and cook for 1–2 minutes, until fragrant, then add the stock and tomato sugo. Bring to the boil. Add the cannellini beans and bay leaves and season. Cover saucepan, reduce to a simmer and cook for 1 hour, or until the beans are tender. Add more stock if it seems a little dry.

Check seasoning, add parsley and feta and serve with Spiced Couscous (page 453).

Chickpea and vegetable casserole

Serves 4

This simple but satisfying casserole is for lovers of chickpeas and vegetables.

- 100 g (½ cup) dried chickpeas, soaked in cold water
- 1 eggplant, diced
- oil
- 2 onions, diced
- 2 carrots, diced
- 1 red capsicum, diced
- 2 small red chillies, de-seeded and finely diced
- 2 cloves garlic, crushed
- 2 tsp ground turmeric
- 2 tsp sweet paprika
- 2 tbsp tomato paste
- 250 ml (1 cup) vegetable stock
- salt and freshly ground black pepper
- 1 tsp harissa (optional)
- Steamed Rice (page 198) to serve

Place the chickpeas in a medium-sized saucepan, cover with water and bring to the boil over a medium heat. Reduce heat to medium–low and cook for 30–40 minutes, until the chickpeas are soft. Drain and set aside.

Sprinkle the diced eggplant with salt and allow juices to bead. Rinse well and pat dry.

Heat a medium saucepan over a medium–high heat. Add a splash of oil and cook the onions, carrots, capsicum and eggplant for 6–8 minutes, or until softened. Add the chillies, garlic and spices and cook for a further 3–4 minutes, stirring occasionally, until aromatic. Add the tomato paste and cook for 1 minute. Add the chickpeas, stock, salt, pepper and harissa (if using), and bring to the boil. Reduce heat to a simmer and cook for w10–12 minutes, until the liquid thickens.

Check seasoning. Serve with Steamed Rice.

Tuscan bean stew

Serves 4

This simple bean stew can be added to Risotto (page 88) or eaten as is. You may like to up the chilli or throw in some spinach leaves.

- 200 g (1 cup) dried cannellini beans, soaked in cold water
- oil
- 1 onion, diced
- 1 carrot, diced
- 4 tomatoes, diced
- 1 small red chilli, de-seeded and diced (optional)
- 1 clove garlic, crushed
- 250 ml (1 cup) vegetable or chicken stock
- salt and freshly ground black pepper
- 2 zucchini, sliced

Place the beans in a medium-sized saucepan, cover with water and bring to the boil over a medium heat. Reduce heat to medium–low and cook for 30–40 minutes, until the beans are soft. Drain and set aside.

Heat a splash of oil in a medium-sized saucepan over a medium–high heat and cook the onion and carrot for 3–4 minutes, or until soft. Add the tomatoes, chilli (if using) and garlic and cook for 3–4 minutes, stirring often. Add the beans and stock, and season with salt and pepper. Allow to come to the boil, then reduce heat to a simmer, add zucchinis and cook for 10–12 minutes, until the liquid thickens.

CURRIES

+ tagines
a bit of spice

Curries have long been a part of everyday cooking in many parts of the world. Now, more than ever before, Australians are experimenting with spice combinations from Thailand, India, Malaysia and the Middle East, and curries are a regular feature on menus across the country.

Curry is a generic term applied to spicy food, usually from Asia, most commonly India. They are not called curries there, nor do traditional Indian chefs use pre-made curry pastes, sauces or spice mixes. Each dish is made up from selected spices, blended as they go into the saucepan. This is fine if you have plenty of time to spare, but most of us don't. Our curries are a mixture of simple spice combinations, our own curry pastes and (more often) quick curries using pre-bought curry pastes. We tend to eat one of these curries at least once a week.

curry + tagine recipes

pastes

Red Thai curry paste	426
Green Thai curry paste	426
Rendang curry paste	427

curries

Thai green chicken and cashew curry	428
Indian chicken curry	429
Coconut chilli chicken curry	430
Malaysian chicken curry	431
Thai red beef and bok choy curry	433
Bloody good beef curry	434
Sour and spicy beef braise	434
Beef rending	435
Hot and sour beef curry	436
Indian beef curry	437
Indian lamb, spinach and potato curry	438
Kashmiri lamb	440
Whole leg of lamb in spicy yoghurt sauce	441
Red curry of duck	442
Malaysian fish curry	443
Quick Thai fish curry	444
Fish curry	445
Thai prawn and asparagus curry	445
Thai red roasted pumpkin, spinach and chickpea curry	446
Potato, spinach and chickpea curry	447
Lentil dhal	448
Indian spiced beans	448
Kidney bean and vegetable chilli	449
Fragrant vegetable curry	450
Sweet potato and cashew nut curry	451

tagines

Quick couscous	453
Spiced couscous	453
Pine nut and coriander couscous	453
Chicken tagine with mushrooms, chorizo and sherry	454
Beef and prune tagine	455
Moroccan chicken with tomato saffron jam	456
Lamb and quince tagine	458
Lamb tagine	459
Tunisian lamb shanks	460
Aromatic vegetable tagine	461
Moroccan chickpea and pumpkin stew	462
Pan-fried blue eye with harissa lentils	462
Eggplant and root vegetable tagine	463
Tunisian vegetable and chickpea tagine	465

Things you need to know about curries

1 Curries don't require special cooking pots or equipment.

2 A heavy-based saucepan with a tight lid will handle just about every curry we know.

3 Curries make very inexpensive and flavoursome meals.

4 When making a traditional curry you must have fresh spices, or it's not even worth starting.

5 When pushed for time, we do use pre-bought curry pastes – they are convenient, easy and quick, and you can add more or less to suit your taste.

6 We often use two pastes, such as madras and hot, to get a more complex flavour.

7 Start with mildly spiced curries and build up to spicier blends over time.

8 Check the seasoning before serving, adding fish sauce for salt or freshly ground black pepper if needed, although the chillies should make the dish spicy enough.

9 You can choose to make quick curries using prime, tender cuts of meat, or there are slower curries using cheap meat which are cooked long and slow to impart wonderful flavours and aromas.

10 Virtually all recipes can have their meat component replaced with chunks of vegetables, although the cooking times will be shorter.

11 A big bowl of yoghurt or Tzatziki (page 563) is wonderful with curries, as well as plenty of fluffy Steamed Rice (page 198).

12 Many people find spice addictive. Expect to find yourself adding more chilli and other spices as your tastebuds are won over.

Red Thai curry paste

Before there was the plethora of good-quality curry pastes on the market that we currently enjoy, we had to make our own. We have included the recipes here for those curry purists who like to make everything from scratch, but we'll happily admit to using pre-bought curry pastes 90 per cent of the time.

4 long red chillies, de-seeded and roughly chopped
1 onion, diced
⅓ bunch coriander (roots, stems and leaves), roughly chopped
2 cm piece of galangal, thinly sliced and finely diced
1 lemongrass stem, thinly sliced and finely diced
2 cloves garlic, chopped
1 tbsp ground coriander
1 tbsp ground cumin
1 tsp ground turmeric
1 tsp paprika
2 tsp dried shrimp paste
1 tsp salt
2 tbsp peanut oil

Place the chillies and onion in a food processor and blend to a fine paste. It's best to blend the onion first as onions release their own liquid, making it easier to blend the other ingredients without the need to add water, which can dilute the overall flavour.

Add the coriander, galangal, lemongrass and garlic, and puree until smooth, stopping occasionally to push down ingredients with a spatula. Add the remaining spices, shrimp paste and salt, and blend until combined. Store in a clean, dry glass jar, and cover the surface with oil. This will keep in the refrigerator for up to 3–4 weeks or it can be frozen.

Makes 1 cup

Green Thai curry paste

This is the green version of the Red Thai Curry Paste. It packs quite a punch, so approach with caution.

4 large green chillies, de-seeded and roughly chopped
1 onion, diced
⅓ bunch coriander (roots, stems and leaves), roughly chopped
2 cm piece of galangal, thinly sliced and finely diced
2 cloves garlic, chopped
1 lemongrass stem, thinly sliced and finely diced
2 tsp ground coriander
1 tsp ground cumin
1 tsp ground turmeric
1 tsp dried shrimp paste
1 tsp salt
2 tbsp peanut oil

Place the chillies and onion in a food processor and blend to a fine paste. It's best to blend the onion first as onions release their own liquid, making it easier to blend the other ingredients without the need to add water, which can dilute the overall flavour.

Add the coriander, galangal, garlic and lemongrass, and puree until smooth, stopping occasionally to push down ingredients with a spatula. Add the remaining spices, shrimp paste and salt, and blend until combined. Store in a clean, dry glass jar and cover the surface with oil. This will keep in the refrigerator for up to 3–4 weeks or it can be frozen.

Makes 1 cup

Rendang curry paste

Rendang is a famous Malaysian curry paste that is slowly cooked to tender, aromatic perfection.

1 onion, diced
1 lemongrass stem, thinly sliced
2 cloves garlic, peeled
5 cm piece of ginger, peeled and chopped
1 tsp salt
2 tsp ground coriander
2 tsp ground cumin
2 dried red chillies, soaked in water
60 ml (¼ cup) water
35 g (½ cup) desiccated coconut

Place all the ingredients except coconut in a food processor and blend until smooth. Add more water if too thick. Transfer to a bowl and stir through coconut. Store in a clean, dry glass jar and cover the surface with oil. This will keep in the refrigerator for up to 3–4 weeks or it can be frozen.

Makes 1 cup

Thai green chicken and cashew curry

Serves 4

The basic method for all Thai curries is much the same. You heat coconut cream until the natural oils appear on the surface, then you add the curry paste and cook the spices in the coconut oil. It sounds unusual, but it produces a curry that's much more pungent and has fuller flavours than those produced in the conventional way of cooking the spices in oil, then adding the coconut milk and meat.

1 tbsp peanut oil
500 g skinless chicken thigh fillets, diced
1 × 150 ml can coconut cream
3 tsp Thai green curry paste
2 tbsp grated palm sugar
2 tbsp fish sauce
1 × 400 ml can coconut milk
400 g diced potato
100 g (¾ cup) toasted cashews
½ cup coriander leaves
Steamed Rice (page 198) to serve

Heat a large heavy-based saucepan over a medium heat. Add the oil and chicken and cook until browned. Remove the chicken from the saucepan and set aside. Spoon the coconut cream into the same saucepan and cook over a medium–high heat for 5 minutes, until it separates and the oil floats on the surface.

Add the curry paste and cook for 5 minutes, stirring constantly, until fragrant. Add the palm sugar and cook briefly before adding the fish sauce and coconut milk. Bring the liquid to the boil, then return the chicken to the saucepan, along with the diced potatoes. Reduce heat and simmer for 15–20 minutes, or until the potatoes are cooked.

Add cashews and coriander leaves to taste, check seasoning and serve with Steamed Rice.

Thai green chicken and spinach curry
In the last minutes of cooking, add 90 g washed spinach leaves – or other vegetables such as peas, green beans or capsicum.

Thai red chicken curry
Substitute red Thai paste for green.

Indian chicken curry

Serves 4

I've called this dish an 'Indian' chicken curry to differentiate it from the preceding curries. But to me it's just a basic curry that I cook all the time, varying the ingredients according to what I feel like – and whatever is in the fridge. I use a combination of both medium and hot curry pastes to alter the flavour; however, you can make your own, or of course make it hotter or milder to suit yourself. MC

oil
1 onion, diced
3 tbsp curry paste
500 g skinless chicken thigh fillets, diced
250 ml (1 cup) tomato puree
250 ml (1 cup) chicken stock
Steamed Rice (page 198) to serve

Heat a large heavy-based saucepan over a medium–high heat. Add oil and the onion and cook until the onion just begins to soften. Add the curry paste and cook for 5–10 minutes, until fragrant but not allowing the spices to burn. Add the chicken and cook briefly for 2–3 minutes, just browning the meat. Add the tomato puree and stock and bring to the boil. Reduce heat and simmer for 15–20 minutes, uncovered.

Indian chicken, potato and spinach curry
Add diced cooked potato and spinach leaves for the last 2–3 minutes of cooking.

Indian chickpea and spinach curry
Omit chicken and add cooked chickpeas. Add spinach and coriander leaves for the last 2–3 minutes of cooking.

Indian vegetable curry
Omit chicken and add a selection of vegetables such as sliced zucchini, capsicum, broccoli, green beans, peas, sliced red cabbage or bok choy to vary the textures.

Coconut chilli chicken curry

Serves 6

You can cook this curry in advance by following the recipe until you get to the 'bring to the boil' stage. Just remove it from the heat at this point, and set it aside until you are almost ready to serve. (Refrigerate the curry if this is longer than 15 minutes.) All you need to do is bring it back to the boil and let it simmer for 15–20 minutes.

oil	1 kg chicken thigh meat, diced
1 onion, sliced	2 tbsp grated palm sugar
1 red capsicum, sliced	2 tbsp fish sauce
5 cm piece of ginger, peeled and julienned	1 × 270 ml can coconut milk
2 coriander roots, cleaned and chopped	125 ml (½ cup) chicken stock
2 small red chillies, thinly sliced	1 cup Thai basil leaves
2 cloves garlic, sliced	Steamed Rice (page 198) to serve

Heat a heavy-based saucepan over a medium heat. Add a splash of oil, the onion, capsicum, ginger, coriander roots and chillies. Cook for 3–4 minutes, until the vegetables soften. Add garlic and cook for a further 1–2 minutes, taking care not to burn the garlic.

Remove the vegetables from the saucepan and return the pan to the heat, adding more oil if needed. Cook the chicken, in batches if necessary, until browned. Return the vegetables to the saucepan, along with the palm sugar, fish sauce and coconut milk. Bring to the boil and add chicken stock as needed to adjust the consistency. Cover and simmer for 20 minutes, or until the chicken is tender.

Check seasoning, adding more fish sauce if necessary, and add basil just before serving.

Malaysian chicken curry

Serves 4–6

Malaysian curries are great when you want a really flavoursome, satisfying meal. Serve this with lots of steamed rice, natural yoghurt and roti bread for a real feast.

6 shallots, peeled
2 cloves garlic, peeled
1 lemongrass stem, pale section only, chopped
3 small red chillies, chopped
3 cm piece of galangal, peeled and chopped
1–2 tbsp water
1 tbsp oil
1 tsp ground turmeric

oil
4 skinless chicken breast fillets
1 tbsp tomato paste
1 × 400 ml can coconut milk
2–3 kaffir lime leaves
200 g green beans
salt and freshly ground black pepper
Steamed Rice (page 198) to serve

Place the shallots, garlic, lemongrass, chillies, galangal, water, 1 tbsp oil and turmeric in a food processor and blend until smooth.

Heat a medium-sized saucepan over a medium–high heat. Add a splash of oil and cook the chicken fillets for 2–3 minutes on each side, until golden brown. Remove from heat and set aside.

Return saucepan to heat and add the blended curry paste, along with more oil if necessary, and cook for 3–4 minutes, until fragrant. Add the tomato paste, coconut milk and kaffir lime leaves. Return the chicken to the pan and bring to the boil. Reduce heat, cover and simmer for 6–8 minutes.

Trim the ends off the beans and cut them in half. Add them to the saucepan and cook for a further 1–2 minutes. Check seasoning and serve with Steamed Rice.

Thai red beef and bok choy curry

Serves 4

This is the same base recipe used in Thai Green Chicken and Cashew Curry, but it uses red curry paste instead of green. The beef is cooked separately to ensure it remains tender, and it's added to the sauce just before serving. We have made it this way hundreds of times and it's always been a success.

1 tbsp peanut oil
400 g scotch fillet
1 × 150 ml can coconut cream
3 tsp Thai red curry paste
2 tbsp grated palm sugar
2 tbsp fish sauce

1 × 400 ml can coconut milk
1 bunch baby bok choy, washed and sliced
½ red capsicum, thinly sliced
100 g (¾ cup) roasted cashews
½ cup coriander leaves
Steamed Rice (page 198) to serve

Preheat oven to 180°C.

Heat a heavy-based ovenproof frypan over a high heat. Add oil and cook the scotch fillet until browned all over. Place the beef in the preheated oven for 15–20 minutes, or until cooked to medium–rare. Allow to cool and reserve the pan juices. Slice the meat into thick strips, discarding fat and gristle.

Place the coconut cream in a heavy-based saucepan and cook over a medium–high heat for 5 minutes, until it separates and the oil floats on the surface.

Add the curry paste and cook for 5 minutes, stirring constantly, until fragrant. Add the palm sugar and cook briefly before adding the fish sauce and coconut milk. Bring the liquid to the boil, then reduce the heat and simmer for 8–10 minutes. Add the bok choy and capsicum, and cook until slightly softened. Add the beef and cashews and cook until heated through.

Add coriander leaves to taste, check seasoning and serve.

Thai red fish curry
Swap the beef for raw fish chunks and add them with the bok choy and capsicum. Vary the vegetables to suit your own tastes and finish with a squeeze of fresh lime juice to add zest.

Bloody good beef curry

Serves 6

It is indeed bloody good when you realise this dish needs few ingredients yet produces an aromatic curry that's perfect for Friday nights with a beer or two. Use any type of curry paste that takes your fancy. We like to use a mixture of two to add extra depth, usually half madras and half hot.

oil
2 onions, diced
2 tsp grated ginger
2 cloves garlic, crushed
4 tbsp curry paste
1½ kg blade steak, diced
2–3 cardamom pods
1 cinnamon stick
500 ml (2 cups) beef stock
250 ml (1 cup) tomato sugo
Steamed Rice (page 198) to serve

Heat a large heavy-based saucepan over a medium heat. Add oil, onions and ginger and cook until the onions just begin to soften. Add garlic and curry paste and cook for 5–10 minutes, until fragrant but not allowing the spices to burn.

Add the beef and cook briefly for 2–3 minutes, just browning the meat. Add the spices, stock and tomato sugo and bring to the boil. Reduce heat, cover and cook for 1½–2 hours, or until the beef is tender.

Sour and spicy beef braise

Serves 4

Anyone who tastes this dish would swear that whoever made it slaved over a hot stove for hours. Truth be known, it takes about 15–20 minutes – tops – to get it cooking.

100 g tamarind
250 ml (1 cup) boiling water
1 kg blade steak
4 small red chillies, split
8 red shallots, peeled and halved
2–3 kaffir lime leaves
3 cm ginger, sliced
2 lemongrass stems, sliced
250 ml (1 cup) beef stock
60 g (¼ cup) shaved palm sugar
60 ml (¼ cup) fish sauce
coriander leaves to serve

Soak tamarind in boiling water for 15–20 minutes. Use fingers to separate pulp from pips, then strain the liquid and discard the seeds.

Cut steak into about 6 cm pieces. Place beef, tamarind liquid, chillies, shallots, lime leaves, ginger, lemongrass, stock, sugar and fish sauce into a heavy-based saucepan.

Bring to the boil, reduce heat, cover with a lid and cook for 1½ hours.

Try beef to see if it's tender yet; it could require up to 2 hours' cooking. If not, return lid and continue cooking until meat is tender.

Sprinkle with coriander to serve.

Beef rendang

Serves 4

Rendang is perfect with the usual accompaniments of steamed rice and hot roti bread. Together with our friends Max and Sophie Allen, we've discovered that a magnum of Chimay stout with this dish will get us through a winter's night with considerable comfort. Allan and I disagree on how we prefer our rendang to be cooked. I like it dry and falling apart in the traditional way, while Allan prefers his moister. This doesn't stop us eating rendang with alarming frequency.

- 1 tbsp tamarind pulp
- 125 ml (½ cup) boiling water
- 1 tbsp peanut oil
- 200 g Rendang Paste (page 427)
- 1 kg blade steak, diced
- 250 ml (1 cup) coconut cream
- 1 star anise
- 1 cinnamon stick
- coriander leaves for garnish
- 2 tbsp toasted coconut (optional)
- Steamed Rice (page 198) to serve

Soak the tamarind in boiling water for 5–10 minutes. Use your fingers to work the pulp free from the tamarind seeds. Strain the tamarind, reserving the liquid.

Heat a heavy-based casserole dish over a medium–high heat. Add oil and the rendang paste and fry for 5–6 minutes, stirring often, until fragrant. Add beef and cook for 5–10 minutes, or until the beef starts to colour but before the spices begin to burn.

Add the tamarind liquid, coconut cream, star anise and cinnamon to the casserole dish. Allow to come to the boil, reduce to a simmer, cover with a lid and cook for 1 hour, stirring occasionally.

Remove the lid and continue cooking the rendang for a further 30–45 minutes, until the beef is tender and most of the liquid has evaporated. Stir often to prevent the sauce catching.

Sprinkle coriander leaves and coconut (if using) on top and serve with Steamed Rice and crisp roti bread.

Hot and sour beef curry

Serves 4–6

This is a very simple dish to make, yet it has a really interesting, complex flavour. It's packed with tender chunks of beef and potato in a sour tamarind and coconut sauce.

1 tbsp tamarind
125 ml (½ cup) boiling water
olive oil
2 tsp chilli powder
2 tsp ground coriander
¼ tsp ground cardamom
1 tsp turmeric

2 cloves garlic, crushed
2 tsp grated ginger
1 kg blade steak, diced
250 ml (1 cup) coconut cream
1 star anise
500 g potatoes, diced (optional)

Soak tamarind in boiling water for 5–10 minutes. Use your fingers to work pulp free from tamarind seeds, then strain liquid and reserve.

Heat a heavy-based casserole pot over a medium–high heat. Add oil and spices, garlic and ginger and fry for 5–6 minutes or until fragrant, stirring often. Add beef and cook for 5–10 minutes, or until beef starts to colour but before spices begin to burn.

Add tamarind liquid, coconut cream and star anise to the pot. Allow to come to the boil, reduce to a simmer, cover with a lid and cook for 1 hour, stirring occasionally.

Add potatoes and cook for a further 20–30 minutes or until beef and potatoes are tender. Check seasoning and serve.

Indian beef curry

Serves 4

This is based on a vindaloo recipe and it's quite fiery, so make sure there's plenty of thirst-quenching beer and a big bowl of natural yoghurt nearby.

2 tbsp vinegar
pinch of salt
3–4 curry leaves
1 tbsp ground coriander
1 tbsp ground cumin
1 tsp chilli powder
½ tsp turmeric
250 g (1 cup) natural yoghurt
1 kg blade steak, diced
2 tbsp oil
2 onions, diced
2 tsp grated ginger
2 cloves garlic, crushed
3 tomatoes, diced
1 tsp cumin seeds
2–3 cloves
2–3 cardamom pods
1 cinnamon stick
250 ml (1 cup) beef stock
coriander leaves to garnish
Steamed Rice (page 198) to serve

Mix vinegar, salt, curry leaves, coriander, cumin, chilli, turmeric and yoghurt together. Pour over beef and set aside to marinate for at least 2–3 hours, or ideally overnight. Stir once or twice if possible.

Heat a heavy-based saucepan over a medium heat. Add oil and onions, cook for 5–6 minutes or until onions are soft. Add ginger and garlic and cook for a further 1–2 minutes. Add marinated beef, tomatoes, cumin seeds, cloves, cardamom, cinnamon stick and stock and bring to the boil, stirring often. Cover with a lid, reduce heat and cook for 1–1 ½ hours. Check to see if beef is tender; if not, continue cooking. Serve curry with coriander leaves and Steamed Rice.

Indian lamb, spinach and potato curry

Serves 6

The long, slow cooking results in tender meat beautifully coated with a smooth rich curry sauce. Appealing, isn't it?

- 2 tsp ground coriander
- 2 tsp ground cumin
- 1 tsp ground turmeric
- 200 g (¾ cup) natural yoghurt
- 2 tbsp lemon juice
- 1 kg diced lamb, such as leg
- oil
- 2 onions, diced
- 1 clove garlic, crushed
- 1 kg potatoes, peeled and diced
- 1 × 400 g can crushed tomatoes
- 2 tbsp tomato paste
- salt and freshly ground black pepper
- 100 g spinach leaves, washed
- Steamed Rice (page 198) and Naan Bread (page 155) to serve

Combine spices, yoghurt and lemon juice in a large bowl. Add lamb, mix well and set aside to marinate for at least 2–3 hours, or better still overnight.

Place a large heavy-based saucepan over a medium–high heat. Add a splash of oil, the onions and garlic and cook for 5 minutes. Add lamb mixture, potatoes, tomatoes and tomato paste. Bring to the boil, season with salt and pepper, reduce heat and simmer uncovered for 1–1 ¼ hours or until lamb is tender. Check seasoning and add spinach. Cook for a further 2–3 minutes, or until spinach softens.

Serve with Steamed Rice and Naan Bread.

Indian beef, spinach and potato curry
Substitute diced blade steak for lamb.

Kashmiri lamb

Serves 6–8

Diced leg of lamb will work nicely with this recipe, which features dried apricots and sultanas. However, diced mutton, if you can find it, is even better. Because it's a tougher meat, it takes longer to cook, so the flavours of the dish have even longer to develop. Ask your local butcher if they can get some in for you; it will be well worth the effort.

- 2 tbsp garam masala
- 2 tbsp madras powder
- 1 tsp mixed spice
- 1 tbsp sweet paprika
- 1 tbsp ground ginger
- salt and freshly ground black pepper
- 125 g (½ cup) natural yoghurt
- 2 kg diced lamb or mutton
- 2 tbsp ghee
- 4 onions, diced
- 500–750 ml (2–3 cups) chicken stock
- 125 g (¾ cup) dried apricots, sliced
- 125 g (¾ cup) sultanas
- basmati rice to serve

Mix all the spices, salt and pepper and yoghurt together. Mix with lamb and marinate overnight or at least 2–3 hours.

Heat a large, heavy-based casserole dish over a medium–high heat. Add ghee and onions and cook until golden in colour, 5–6 minutes, stirring often. Add marinated lamb and enough chicken stock to just cover.

Simmer uncovered for 1–1 ½ hours, until almost tender. If using mutton this could easily take an extra hour. Add apricots and sultanas and cook for a further 30–45 minutes, or until meat is tender.

Serve with basmati rice.

Whole leg of lamb in spicy yoghurt sauce

Serves 6

This great curry does its magic all by itself. You can serve the sliced lamb with the sauce poured over the top or, if you prefer, serve the sauce in a jug to allow people to add their own.

- 55 g (⅓ cup) blanched almonds
- 2 onions, chopped
- 4 cloves garlic, peeled
- 4 cm piece of ginger, peeled and chopped
- 4 large green chillies
- 500 g (2 cups) natural yoghurt
- 2 tsp ground cumin
- 2 tsp ground coriander
- 1 tsp ground chilli
- 2 tsp salt
- 1 × 1½ kg easy-carve leg of lamb
- 2–3 cloves
- 6 cardamom pods, lightly crushed
- 2 cinnamon sticks
- coriander leaves for garnish
- Steamed Rice (page 198) to serve

Place the almonds, onions, garlic, ginger and chillies in a food processor (or mortar and pestle) and blend briefly. Add 3–4 spoonfuls of yoghurt and blend to form a smooth paste. Add the ground spices and salt and combine. Add the remaining yoghurt to the sauce.

Using a small knife, make deep slashes in the lamb. Place the meat in a deep baking dish and pour on the yoghurt sauce, working the sauce into the lamb. Cover and refrigerate to marinate for up to 24 hours or at least 4 hours.

Preheat oven to 180°C.

Remove the lamb from the fridge and allow it to come to room temperature. Add the cloves, cardamom and cinnamon to the marinade. Cover with foil and cook in the preheated oven for 1 hour. Remove the foil and turn the lamb over, then return the meat to the oven for a further 30 minutes, basting every 10 minutes or so. Check the lamb to see if it's cooked sufficiently; you're aiming for medium, or still pink. Insert a small knife into the thickest part of the lamb and leave it there for 5 seconds. Remove the knife and place it on the fleshy part of your thumb. The knife should be hot to touch, but not burning. If you'd like to cook the lamb longer, return it to the oven and continue cooking.

When the meat is cooked to your liking, remove it from the sauce, cover with foil and tea towels to keep warm and set it aside in a warm place to rest for at least 15 minutes. Spoon excess fat from the top of the sauce and keep the sauce warm until ready to serve.

Slice the lamb and arrange the meat on a serving platter with the sauce poured around it. Garnish with coriander leaves and serve with Steamed Rice and Lentil and Chickpea Salad (page 520).

Red curry of duck

Serves 4

This is another variation on the basic Thai curry theme, but the different herbs produce a slightly more complex result. The dish is smart enough for a dinner party, assuming you are serving several side dishes with it. Add vegetables such as Asian greens or bamboo shoots to balance the dish. You can purchase a Chinese roast duck from an Asian roast house. Barbecued quail also makes a good substitute.

1 Chinese roast duck
500 ml (2 cups) coconut milk
4 tsp Thai red curry paste
2 tbsp grated palm sugar
2 tbsp fish sauce
125 ml (½ cup) chicken stock
4 kaffir lime leaves (optional)
½ cup Thai basil leaves
Steamed Rice (page 198) to serve

Using a sharp knife, remove all the flesh from the duck's carcass, taking care to leave the meat in reasonably large pieces, with the skin intact. Discard the bones and chop the duck meat into 2 cm chunks, if necessary.

Place the coconut milk, curry paste, palm sugar and fish sauce in a large heavy-based saucepan over a medium–high heat. Bring to the boil, reduce heat and simmer for 5–10 minutes. Add the stock, duck meat and kaffir lime leaves (if using). Continue to simmer for 5–10 minutes, taking care not to let it boil or overcook as the duck pieces will start to break up.

Add basil leaves and serve immediately with Steamed Rice.

Malaysian fish curry

Serves 4

Curry pastes sound harder to make than they actually are, but after the first couple of attempts, they become obviously simple. A food processor cuts the work in half. Try doubling the paste and freezing half for next time. The fish in this dish can be left whole or diced, depending on how you like it.

- 50 g tamarind
- 125 ml (½ cup) boiling water
- 1 lemongrass stem, chopped
- 2 dried red chillies, soaked in boiling water and drained
- 2 cloves garlic, peeled
- 1 tbsp grated ginger
- 1 onion, chopped
- 2 tsp ground coriander
- 2 tsp ground cumin
- 1 tsp ground fennel (optional)
- 1 tsp turmeric
- 1 tsp salt
- 60 ml (¼ cup) vegetable oil
- 60 ml (¼ cup) vegetable oil, additional
- 250 ml (1 cup) coconut milk
- 4 firm fish steaks or 750 g diced white fish, such as ling, cod, flathead or trevally
- Steamed Rice (page 198) to serve

Soak tamarind in boiling water for 15–20 minutes. Use your fingers to work pulp free from tamarind seeds. Strain tamarind, reserving liquid.

Place lemongrass, chillies, garlic, ginger and onion in food processor and blend until smooth (can be done in a mortar and pestle if you want to give your biceps a work out). Add spices, salt and oil and blend briefly until smooth.

Heat a large heavy-based saucepan over a medium–high heat. Add additional oil and paste and fry until fragrant. Add tamarind liquid and coconut milk, bring to the boil. Reduce to a simmer and cook for 10–15 minutes.

Remove skin from fish if needed and add fish. Simmer for a further 5–6 minutes, or until fish is just cooked. Serve with Steamed Rice.

Quick Thai fish curry

Serves 4

This curry is ridiculously easy. As the fish and the sauce are prepared separately, junior members of the family can have the sauce or not, while we can get our curry hit and add as much chilli as we like.

1 × 140 ml can coconut cream
3 tsp Thai curry paste (red or green as you prefer)
2 tbsp grated palm sugar
2 tbsp fish sauce
1 × 400 ml can coconut milk
4 firm white fish fillets (blue eye or flathead)

seasoned flour
oil
½ cup coriander leaves
Steamed Rice (page 198) to serve
lime wedges to serve

Heat a small saucepan over a medium heat. Add the coconut cream and cook over a medium–high heat for 5 minutes, until it separates and the oil floats on the surface. Add the curry paste and cook for 5 minutes, stirring constantly, until fragrant. Add the palm sugar and cook briefly before adding the fish sauce and coconut milk. Bring the liquid to the boil, reduce heat and simmer for 5 minutes.

Heat a heavy-based frypan over a medium–high heat. Coat each fish fillet with seasoned flour. Add a generous splash of oil to the frypan and cook the fish for 3–4 minutes on each side, until golden brown and cooked through.

Check seasoning and add coriander leaves. Serve the fish on Steamed Rice with the sauce poured over the top and lime wedges on the side.

Fish curry

Serves 4

For different flavours try madras, Thai or masala curry pastes.

750 g firm white fish, diced into 2 cm chunks
1 small red chilli, sliced
1 tbsp lime juice
salt
oil
1 onion, sliced
1 tbsp grated ginger
2 cloves garlic, crushed
1 tbsp mild curry paste
1 × 140 ml can coconut cream
½ cup coriander leaves
1 lime, cut into wedges
Steamed Rice (page 198) to serve

Toss the fish with the chilli, lime juice and salt.

Heat a heavy-based frypan over a medium–high heat. Add a splash of oil and the onion and cook for 4–5 minutes, stirring often. Add ginger, garlic and curry paste and cook for 2–3 minutes, stirring often, until fragrant. Add the coconut cream and bring to the boil. Reduce heat and simmer, uncovered, until the sauce thickens slightly. Add the fish and cook, covered, for 3–4 minutes, or until the fish is just cooked through.

Sprinkle the fish curry with coriander leaves and serve with lime wedges and Steamed Rice.

Thai prawn and asparagus curry

Serves 4

This impressive seafood curry is actually very easy to make. It follows our basic Thai curry method, then the remaining ingredients are added and it's ready to serve. Who said cooking was hard, eh?

1 × 140 ml can coconut cream
3 tsp Thai red curry paste
2 tbsp grated palm sugar
2 tbsp fish sauce
1 × 400 ml can coconut milk
500 g green (raw) prawns, peeled
150 g asparagus
½ red capsicum, thinly sliced
½ cup coriander leaves
Steamed Rice (page 198) to serve

Place the coconut cream in a heavy-based saucepan and cook over a medium–high heat for 5 minutes, until it separates and the oil floats on the surface.

Add the curry paste and cook for 5 minutes, stirring constantly, until fragrant. Add the palm sugar and cook briefly before adding the fish sauce and coconut milk. Bring the liquid to the boil, then reduce heat and simmer for 8–10 minutes. Add the prawns, asparagus and red capsicum. Return the curry to the boil, then reduce heat and simmer for 2–3 minutes, or until the prawns are cooked.

Add coriander leaves to taste, check seasoning and serve with steamed rice.

Thai red roasted pumpkin, spinach and chickpea curry

Serves 4

This curry follows our method of cooking the curry paste in coconut milk, then adding the other ingredients. Here, these happen to be chickpeas, roasted chunks of pumpkin and tender spinach leaves. All in all, it's a real beauty, and vegetarian to boot.

100 g (½ cup) dried chickpeas, soaked in cold water
350 g pumpkin, peeled, de-seeded and chopped into 3 cm chunks
oil
salt and freshly ground black pepper
1 × 140 ml can coconut cream
3 tsp Thai red curry paste
2 tbsp grated palm sugar
2 tbsp fish sauce
1 × 400 ml can coconut milk
100 g baby spinach leaves
½ cup coriander leaves
Steamed Rice (page 198) to serve

Preheat oven to 180°C.

Drain the chickpeas and place them in a medium-sized saucepan. Cover with plenty of water and cook for 30–40 minutes, until tender. Drain and set aside until needed.

Toss the pumpkin with a little oil, salt and pepper. Roast in the preheated oven for 20–30 minutes, until tender.

Place the coconut cream in a heavy-based saucepan and cook over a medium–high heat for 5 minutes, until it separates and the oil floats on the surface.

Add the curry paste and cook for 5 minutes, stirring constantly, until fragrant. Add the palm sugar and cook briefly before adding the fish sauce and coconut milk. Bring the liquid to the boil, then reduce the heat and simmer for 8–10 minutes. Add the roasted pumpkin and heat through. Add the cooked chickpeas and spinach and cook until the spinach leaves are wilted.

Add coriander leaves to taste, check seasoning and serve with Steamed Rice.

Potato, spinach and chickpea curry

Serves 4

This is one of our absolute favourite stand-bys for a mid-week meal. To make it even faster, use a can of chickpeas, drained.

100 g (½ cup) dried chickpeas, soaked in cold water
oil
1 onion, diced
2 cloves garlic, crushed
2 tbsp curry paste
6 potatoes, peeled and diced
250 ml (1 cup) tomato sugo
250 ml (1 cup) chicken stock
salt
100 g baby spinach leaves
handful of coriander leaves
Steamed Rice (page 198) to serve

Place the drained chickpeas in a saucepan. Cover with plenty of water and cook for 30–40 minutes, or until tender. Drain and set aside until needed.

Heat a large saucepan over a medium–high heat. Add a splash of oil and the onion and cook for 5–6 minutes, or until the onion is soft. Add the garlic and curry paste and cook for 1–2 minutes. Add the potatoes, lower the heat and cook for a further 3–4 minutes, stirring often, until the curry is fragrant. Take care not to burn the curry paste.

Add the tomato sugo and stock and bring to the boil. Season with salt. Reduce heat and simmer for 20 minutes, or until the potatoes are tender. Add the chickpeas and spinach and cook for 1–2 minutes.

Check seasoning. Add coriander leaves and serve with Steamed Rice.

Lentil dhal

Serves 4

Dhal is one of the classic dishes of Indian cooking. We have adapted it by adding finely diced onion and carrot, as well as a little curry paste. We generally use whole green lentils, as they keep their shape and texture. Red lentils will cook much faster and turn into a fine puree.

- 300 g (1½ cups) whole green lentils
- oil
- 1 onion, finely diced
- 1 carrot, finely diced
- 2 tbsp curry paste
- 250–500 ml (1–2 cups) vegetable or chicken stock
- 2 tbsp chopped parsley or coriander
- Steamed Rice (page 198) to serve
- natural yoghurt to serve

Sort through the lentils, discarding any brown ones and pieces of grit, then rinse well.

Heat a heavy-based pan over a medium heat. Add a splash of oil, then cook the onion and carrot for 3–4 minutes, stirring occasionally, until softened. Add the curry paste and cook for 3–4 minutes, until aromatic. Add the lentils, stirring to coat them well with the curry mixture. Pour in enough stock to cover the lentils and bring to the boil. Reduce heat and cook at a simmer for 30–40 minutes, or until the lentils are soft.

Pour in more stock as needed, but take care not to add too much near the end. Add herbs and serve with Steamed Rice and a dollop of natural yoghurt.

Indian spiced beans

Serves 4

This is the type of dish we have when we want a quick spice hit. Once the beans are cooked it only takes about 10 minutes to chop the ingredients and get it all simmering. It's even quicker than waiting in line at the local Indian for a takeaway.

- 200 g (1 cup) black-eye (or borlotti) beans, soaked overnight
- 2 tbsp olive oil
- 1 clove garlic, crushed
- 1 tsp grated fresh ginger
- 2 onions
- 2 tsp curry paste
- 250 ml (1 cup) vegetable or chicken stock
- salt
- 125 g (½ cup) natural yoghurt
- ½ cup coriander leaves
- Steamed Rice (page 198) to serve

Place beans in a medium-sized saucepan, cover with water, and bring to the boil over a medium heat. Reduce heat to medium–low and cook until beans are soft, about 30–40 minutes. Drain, and set aside.

Heat oil in a medium-sized saucepan over medium–high heat and cook garlic, ginger and onion for 5 minutes or until soft.

Add curry paste and cook for a further 3–4 minutes until aromatic, stirring occasionally. Add beans, stock and salt.

Allow to come to the boil, then reduce heat to medium–low and cook for 10–12 minutes, until liquid thickens.

Stir in the yoghurt, sprinkle with coriander leaves and serve with Steamed Rice.

Kidney bean and vegetable chilli

Serves 4

This bean dish, Middle Eastern in inspiration, is just the thing to warm the cockles of the heart.

- 125 g (⅔ cup) kidney beans, soaked overnight
- 2 tbsp olive oil
- 2 onions, diced
- 2 carrots, diced
- 1 red capsicum, diced
- 1 eggplant, diced, salted and rinsed
- 2 cloves garlic, crushed
- 2 small red chillies, de-seeded and finely diced
- 2 tsp ground turmeric
- 2 tsp sweet paprika
- 2 tbsp tomato paste
- 250 ml (1 cup) vegetable stock
- salt and freshly ground black pepper
- 1 tsp harissa paste (optional)
- Steamed Rice (page 198) to serve

Place kidney beans in a medium-sized saucepan, cover with water and bring to the boil over a medium heat. Reduce heat to medium–low and cook until beans are soft, about 30–40 minutes. Drain and set aside.

Heat a medium saucepan over medium–high heat, add oil and cook onions, carrot, capsicum and eggplant for 6–8 minutes, or until softened. Add garlic, chilli and spices and cook for a further 3–4 minutes, until aromatic, stirring occasionally.

Add tomato paste and cook for a further minute. Add stock, salt and pepper, plus harissa if using, and bring to the boil. Reduce heat to a simmer and cook for 10–12 minutes, until liquid thickens and vegetables are tender.

Check seasoning. Serve with Steamed Rice.

Fragrant vegetable curry

Serves 4

The choice of vegetables here can be changed to suit personal tastes or to use what's best in season. During winter we use the mix listed below; during the warmer months we use mostly capsicum, eggplant and zucchini.

oil
1 tsp brown mustard seeds
½ tsp ground cumin
½ tsp ground coriander
½ tsp chilli powder
½ tsp ground turmeric
1 tsp curry powder
¼ tsp ground cardamom
¼ tsp ground cinnamon
1 onion, diced
1 potato, diced
1 parsnip, diced
1 carrot, diced
1 small swede, diced
1 small sweet potato, diced
small wedge pumpkin, peeled and diced
250 ml (1 cup) vegetable stock
salt and freshly ground black pepper
¼ cauliflower, cut into florets, optional
Steamed Rice (page 198) to serve

Heat a heavy-based saucepan over a medium–high heat. Add a generous splash of oil and all the spices, cook for 2–3 minutes until distinctly fragrant but not burning. Add diced vegetables and cook in aromatic spice mix for 1–2 minutes. Add enough stock to just cover, season with salt and pepper and bring to the boil. Reduce to a simmer, cook for 15–20 minutes, or until the vegetables are just tender. Add cauliflower for the last 3–4 minutes of cooking.

Check seasoning, add more stock or water if necessary to adjust consistency. Serve with Steamed Rice.

Sweet potato and cashew nut curry

Serves 4

In this simple curry the sweetness of the potato is a perfect match for the spices, while the cashews add a nutty crunch. You may, of course, add other vegetables if so desired.

oil	250 ml (1 cup) coconut milk
1 tsp brown mustard seeds	250 ml (1 cup) vegetable stock or water
1 tsp ground coriander	90 g (⅔ cup) toasted cashew nuts
1 tsp ground turmeric	handful of basil leaves, torn
2 cloves garlic, crushed	1 tbsp fish sauce
2 tsp grated ginger	squeeze of lime juice
2 medium sweet potatoes, peeled and diced 2 cm	Steamed Rice (page 198) to serve
1 tbsp shaved palm sugar	

Heat a heavy-based saucepan over a medium–high heat. Add a splash of oil and mustard seeds. Cook for 2–3 minutes, or until seeds start to pop. Add coriander and turmeric and cook for a further 2–3 minutes. Add garlic and ginger and cook for another 2–3 minutes, stirring often. Add diced sweet potatoes, sugar, coconut milk and stock. Stir well and bring to the boil.

Reduce to a simmer and cook for 20 minutes, stirring often until potato is cooked. Add nuts, basil, fish sauce and a generous squeeze of lime juice.

Serve with Steamed Rice.

tagines

Tagines use spices in a different way to curries, and they produce quite different results. The name comes from the traditional glazed earthenware dish that the meal is cooked in across North Africa. In a modern sense, we understand a tagine to be a slow-cooked stew where meat and vegetables are combined with spices for flavour, fruit for sweetness and nuts for crunch. We're big on tagines, both for everyday dinners and for entertaining, as they can be left to cook on their own and don't take much looking after.

Things you need to know about tagines

1 Tagines are traditionally cooked in a special earthenware dish, but it's not essential.

2 An everyday earthenware casserole dish with a tightly fitting lid is great if the long, slow cooking is to be done in the oven.

3 Tagines usually use tough, cheaper cuts of meat which become tender during the slow cooking process.

4 Tagines use special ingredients such as pomegranate syrup, preserved lemons and harissa, which bring unique flavours and textures to the finished dish.

5 The best accompaniments include tzatziki to cool down fiery dishes plus rice pilaf, couscous and lots of pita bread.

Quick couscous

We didn't create this method – it's straight from the packet! If kept covered, couscous will stay warm for 10 minutes.

250 ml (1 cup) water or stock
1 tbsp olive oil
pinch of salt
250 g (1¼ cups) instant couscous
small knob of butter

Place water or stock, oil and salt in a saucepan and bring to the boil. Remove from heat, stir in the couscous, cover and allow to rest for 2 minutes. Add the butter to the soaked couscous and place over a low heat. Stir with a fork to break up the grains and mix the butter through.

Serves 4

Spiced couscous

You can change the spices in this couscous to incorporate different flavours, or substitute some of the stock with orange juice.

500 ml (2 cups) chicken or vegetable stock
pinch of allspice
pinch of cinnamon
pinch of nutmeg
¼ tsp ground cumin
¼ tsp ground coriander
salt
1 tbsp oil
500 g (2½ cups) instant couscous
1 tbsp butter

Place the stock in a large saucepan. Add the spices, a pinch of salt and the oil, and bring to the boil. Remove from heat, stir in the couscous, cover and allow to rest for 3–4 minutes. Add the butter to the soaked couscous and place over a low heat. Stir with a fork to break up the grains and mix the butter through.

Serves 6–8

Pine nut and coriander couscous

The pine nuts add texture and flavour, while the coriander adds freshness to the dish.

oil
1 small onion, diced
50 g (⅓ cup) pine nuts
2 tbsp currants (optional)
500 ml (2 cups) chicken or vegetable stock
salt
500 g (2½ cups) instant couscous
1 tbsp butter
1 cup roughly chopped coriander leaves

Heat a heavy-based saucepan over a medium heat. Add oil, the onion and pine nuts and cook for 5 minutes, or until the pine nuts are golden brown. Add the currants (if using), stock and a pinch of salt. Bring to the boil.

Remove from heat, stir in the couscous, cover and allow to rest for 3–4 minutes. Add the butter to the soaked couscous and place over a low heat. Stir with a fork to break up the grains and mix the butter through. Stir in the coriander to serve.

Serves 6–8

Saffron couscous
Add a pinch of saffron threads to the boiling liquid.

Herb couscous
Add 2 tbsp chopped fresh herbs (such as parsley or coriander) as you stir in the butter.

Chicken tagine with mushrooms, chorizo and sherry

Serves 6

This warming chicken dish will take the edge off chilly evenings as the weather starts to cool. The chorizo and mushrooms boost the flavour, making it very hearty. Use wild pine mushrooms, if available, and serve with couscous or mashed potatoes.

oil
1 chorizo sausage (250 g), diced
1½ kg skinless chicken casserole pieces or diced thigh fillet
1 onion, sliced
300 g mushrooms, sliced
2 cloves garlic, crushed
1 tsp harissa
2 tsp ground cumin
2 tsp ground coriander
1 tsp sweet paprika
½ tsp allspice
1 tbsp plain flour
60 ml (¼ cup) dry sherry
250–500 ml (1–2 cups) tomato sugo
500 ml (2 cups) chicken stock
salt and freshly ground black pepper
parsley and coriander leaves

Heat a heavy-based frypan over a medium heat. Add a splash of oil and the chorizo and cook until the fat renders out. Remove from the frypan and drain on absorbent paper.

Return the pan to the heat. Add a generous splash of oil and cook the chicken pieces until golden brown all over. Remove the chicken from the pan and set aside.

Return the frypan to the heat and add more oil, if necessary. Add the onion and cook for 3–4 minutes, until it softens. Add the mushrooms, along with more oil if necessary, and cook until they soften. Add garlic and spices and cook for 1–2 minutes, until fragrant. Sprinkle in the flour, lower the heat and cook for 1–2 minutes. Raise the heat, add the sherry and stir well. Bring to the boil and cook until reduced by half. Add the tomato sugo and stock and bring to the boil.

Return the chorizo and chicken to the pan, and add more sugo if necessary to just cover. Cover with a lid and cook over a low heat for 1 ½ hours.

Check seasoning and add fresh parsley and coriander to serve.

Beef and prune tagine

Serves 4–6

The casseroles and stews of the Middle East and North Africa typically include dried fruit, whose sweetness complements meats, vegetables and spices. This is a classic example of this style of cooking.

1½ tsp sweet paprika
1½ tsp chilli powder
2 tsp ground cumin
2 tsp ground coriander
1 tsp ground white pepper
1 tsp salt
2 tbsp lemon juice
60 ml (¼ cup) olive oil
1 kg diced beef, blade or skirt
750 ml (3 cups) beef stock
250 g (1½ cups) pitted prunes
coriander leaves

Combine the spices, salt, lemon juice and oil to form a smooth paste. Coat the beef with the spice mixture and leave to marinate for at least 4 hours or preferably overnight.

Preheat oven to 180°C.

Place the marinated beef in an ovenproof casserole dish with a tight-fitting lid. Add the stock, cover and cook in the preheated oven for 1 hour.

Add the prunes, replace the lid and return to the oven for a further 45 minutes. Check to see if the beef is nearly cooked. If so, cook for a final 30 minutes with the lid removed to reduce the liquid.

Sprinkle with coriander leaves and serve with Pine Nut, Sultana and Onion Pilaf (page 200).

Moroccan chicken with tomato saffron jam

Serves 6

This is a beauty of a recipe, one we'd serve up every week if time allowed. If you're as keen on this style of cooking as we are, this dish may become one of your favourites, too.

oil
1½ kg skinless chicken casserole pieces or diced thigh fillet
1 onion, diced
2 cloves garlic, crushed
1 tsp ground cinnamon
1 tsp ground ginger
1 tsp ground cumin
¼ tsp ground cardamom

pinch of saffron threads
6 tomatoes (500 g), diced
250 ml (1 cup) chicken stock
salt and freshly ground black pepper
2 tbsp honey
1 tbsp orange-blossom water
2 tbsp flaked toasted almonds
¼ cup coriander leaves
Quick Couscous (page 453) to serve

Heat a heavy-based saucepan over a medium–high heat. Add a generous splash of oil and cook the chicken pieces until golden brown all over. This may need to be done in batches. Remove the chicken and set aside.

Return the pan to the heat. Add more oil, if necessary, and cook the onion for 3–4 minutes, stirring often, until soft. Add the garlic, cinnamon, ginger, cumin, cardamom and saffron. Cook for 1–2 minutes, then add the diced tomatoes. Lower the heat and cook for 5 minutes, stirring occasionally. Raise the heat, add the stock and chicken and bring to the boil. Season with salt and pepper. Reduce the heat and simmer for 30–40 minutes, or until the chicken is cooked.

Remove the chicken pieces and set them aside to keep warm. Raise the heat under the saucepan and reduce the cooking liquid until it's the consistency of thick cream. Add the honey and continue to cook for 5–6 minutes, stirring often, until it's reduced and like jam. Check seasoning, add orange-blossom water and return the chicken to the pan to heat through.

Scatter the chicken with almonds and coriander. Serve with couscous.

Lamb and quince tagine

Serves 6

Lamb is without doubt the classic meat when it comes to making tagines. It has enough flavour to cope with the spices and also sits well with the sweetness of whatever fruit you choose to use. Here we've used quinces, one of our absolutely favourite fruits.

1 kg diced lamb	375 ml (1½ cups) chicken stock
1 tsp ground cumin	2 quinces, peeled, quartered and cored
1 tsp ground coriander	2 tbsp honey
1 tsp ground ginger	salt and freshly ground black pepper
1 tsp paprika	1 piece preserved lemon, soaked, pulp removed, then rind thinly sliced
2 cloves garlic, crushed	
1 onion, diced	coriander leaves
1 cinnamon stick	Quick Couscous (page 453) to serve
pinch of saffron threads	

Place the lamb, spices, garlic, onion, cinnamon and saffron in a large heavy-based saucepan. Cover with stock and bring to the boil. Reduce heat to low, cover with a lid and cook for 1–1½ hours, or until the lamb is tender.

Place the quinces in a small saucepan, cover with water, add honey and cook over a medium heat for 45 minutes, until tender. Drain, reserving the cooking liquid.

Check the lamb to ensure that it is tender. Adjust seasoning. If needed, add some of the quince poaching liquid to adjust the consistency. Add the quinces to the lamb tagine, along with the preserved lemon. Heat through completely.

Sprinkle with coriander leaves and serve with couscous.

Lamb tagine

Serves 4

This is one of my favourite lamb dishes. Extremely simple and impressive, this recipe can be doubled or even trebled if you are feeding lots of people. MC

2 tsp sweet paprika	1 tsp salt
1 tsp ground ginger	2 tbsp lemon juice
1 tsp chilli powder	60 ml (¼ cup) olive oil
1 tsp ground cumin	1 kg diced lamb
1 tsp ground coriander	juice of 1 orange
1 tsp ground white pepper	500 ml (2 cups) chicken stock
½ tsp ground cardamom	90 g (⅔ cup) dried apricots, diced
½ tsp ground cinnamon	90 g (½ cup) sultanas
½ tsp allspice	fresh coriander to serve

Mix spices, salt, lemon juice and oil to form a smooth paste. Coat diced lamb with the spice mixture and leave to marinate for 4 hours or overnight.

Preheat oven to 180°C.

Place lamb in a heavy-based saucepan that has a well-fitting lid, add orange juice and stock. Cook for 1 hour in oven, with lid on, stirring occasionally.

Remove lid, add apricots and sultanas and return to the oven for a further 30–60 minutes, or until lamb is tender. Serve with coriander leaves, Pine Nut and Saffron Pilaf (page 200), and Tzatziki (page 563).

Tunisian lamb shanks

Serves 4–6

Another variation of our lamb tagine – just a bit more up-market. I like to serve the shanks standing upright with a spoonful of sauce drizzled over, just like in a restaurant. My butcher tells me that shanks from the forelegs are better quality than rear legs and so far this has proven true. MC

olive oil	4–6 lamb shanks
2 onions, diced	2 tbsp lemon juice
2 carrots, diced	750 ml (3 cups) chicken stock
1½ tsp sweet paprika	60 g (⅓ cup) dried apricots
1½ tsp chilli powder	90 g (½ cup) sultanas
2 tsp ground cumin	½ preserved lemon, soaked, pulp removed, then rind diced (or zest of 1 lemon)
2 tsp ground coriander	
1 tsp ground white pepper	60 g (⅔ cup) flaked almonds
1 tsp salt	coriander leaves

Heat a large ovenproof casserole pot or saucepan over a medium–high heat. Add oil, onions and carrots and cook for 5–6 minutes, stirring often, until softened. Add spices and salt, then cook for a further 3–4 minutes. Add shanks to the pot and cook briefly. Add lemon juice, stock, apricots and sultanas. Bring to the boil. Cover with a lid, reduce heat and cook for 2 hours.

Check to see whether the lamb is tender. If not, cook for a further 15–20 minutes and try again. Add preserved lemon (or zest), almonds and coriander leaves and serve with Couscous (page 453).

Aromatic vegetable tagine

Serves 4–6

You can add just about any vegetable you like to this dish: capsicum, eggplant, pumpkin, okra, cauliflower or even mushrooms, just to name a few.

olive oil	8 small potatoes, peeled and cut in half
1 onion, diced	2 parsnips, cut into quarters
1½ tsp sweet paprika	1 sweet potato, cut into 3 cm chunks
1½ tsp chilli powder	2 tbsp lemon juice
2 tsp ground cumin	750 ml (3 cups) vegetable stock
2 tsp ground coriander	salt
1 tsp ground white pepper	2 zucchini, cut into quarters
2 carrots, cut into 3 cm chunks	coriander leaves

Preheat oven to 180°C.

Heat a large heavy-based saucepan or ovenproof casserole pot over a medium–high heat. Add oil, onions and spices and cook for 5–6 minutes, stirring often, until softened. Add carrots, potatoes, parsnips and sweet potato. Cook for a further 3–4 minutes, stirring often. Add lemon juice, stock, season with salt. Bring to the boil.

Cover with a lid, reduce heat and cook (or, better still, cook in a 180°C preheated oven) for 45 minutes. Check to see whether vegetables are tender. Add zucchini; cook for a further 5 minutes, check seasoning and serve with coriander leaves.

Moroccan chickpea and pumpkin stew

Serves 4

The natural sweetness of the pumpkin combines really well with the spice.

- 100 g (½ cup) chickpeas, soaked overnight
- 2 tbsp olive oil
- 1 onion, diced
- ½ red capsicum, diced
- 500 g pumpkin, diced 1 cm
- 1 tsp grated ginger
- 1 clove garlic, crushed
- 2 tsp ground cumin
- 2 tsp ground coriander
- 1 tsp sweet paprika
- 1 tbsp tomato paste
- 500 ml (2 cups) vegetable stock
- salt and freshly ground black pepper
- coriander leaves
- Steamed Rice (page 198) to serve

Place chickpeas in a medium-sized saucepan, cover with water and bring to the boil over a medium heat. Reduce heat and cook until soft, about 30–40 minutes. Drain and set aside.

Heat oil in a medium-sized saucepan over medium–high heat and cook onion and capsicum for 5 minutes or until soft. Add pumpkin, ginger, garlic and spices and cook for a further 3–4 minutes until aromatic, stirring occasionally. Add tomato paste and cook for 1–2 minutes. Add chickpeas and stock, plus salt and pepper.

Allow to come to the boil, then reduce heat to a simmer and cook for 10–12 minutes, until liquid thickens and pumpkin is cooked.

Sprinkle with coriander leaves and serve with Steamed Rice.

Pan-fried blue eye with harissa lentils

Serves 6

Lentils provide the perfect background for this stunning fish dish. We prefer to use small green lentils as they keep their shape better.

- oil
- 1 onion, diced
- 1 clove garlic, crushed
- 2 tsp harissa
- 1 tsp ground coriander
- 1 tsp ground cumin
- 125 g (⅔ cup) green lentils
- 500 ml (2 cups) chicken or vegetable stock
- 125 ml (½ cup) tomato sugo
- salt and freshly ground black pepper
- 6 × 150 g blue-eye fillets
- ¼ cup chopped coriander leaves

Heat a medium-sized saucepan over a medium–high heat. Add a splash of oil and cook the onion for 3–4 minutes. Add the garlic, harissa, coriander and cumin. Cook for a further 1–2 minutes, stirring often. Add the lentils, stock and tomato sugo, and bring to the boil. Reduce the heat and cook for 45 minutes, stirring occasionally, until the lentils are cooked and the sauce is reduced. Season to taste.

Heat a heavy-based frypan over a medium–high heat. Add a generous splash of oil and cook the blue-eye fillets for 4–5 minutes on each side, or until cooked through and golden brown. Check the seasoning of the lentils and stir through coriander leaves.

Spoon the lentils into 6 serving bowls, or one large platter. Top with the fish and serve immediately.

Eggplant and root vegetable tagine

Serves 4–6

The earthiness of the eggplants and root vegetables are a perfect match for this spicy dish, while the chickpeas add a lovely crunch.

2 eggplants
salt
oil
1 onion, diced
2 tsp grated ginger
2 cloves garlic, crushed
4 green chillies, chopped
2 tsp ground coriander
2 tsp ground cumin
2 tsp sweet paprika
1 tsp ground ginger

1 tsp allspice
250 ml (1 cup) tomato sugo
500 ml (2 cups) vegetable or chicken stock
salt and freshly ground black pepper
500 g pumpkin, peeled, de-seeded and diced into 2 cm chunks
2 parsnips, peeled and cut into 2 cm sticks
2 potatoes, peeled and diced into 2 cm chunks
1 × 400 g can chickpeas, drained
coriander leaves

Cut the eggplants in half, then slice each half to form 1 cm thick semi-circles. Sprinkle with salt and set aside for 20 minutes, until juices bead on the surface. Rinse the eggplant and dry well, then brush with oil and grill until tender and golden brown on each side. Set aside to cool.

Heat a heavy-based frypan over a medium–high heat. Add a generous splash of oil and the onion and cook for 2–3 minutes. Add the ginger, garlic, chillies and spices and cook for 3–4 minutes, until fragrant. Add the tomato sugo and stock and bring to the boil. Season with salt and pepper, then add the pumpkin, parsnips and potatoes. Cook on a gentle simmer for 25–30 minutes, or until the vegetables are cooked through. Add the eggplant and chickpeas and cook for 5 minutes, allowing them to heat through.

Check seasoning. Serve sprinkled with coriander leaves.

Tunisian vegetable and chickpea tagine

Serves 6

This stunning dish – full of spice, hearty vegetables and earthy chickpeas – is bound to blow away any winter blues.

- 100 g (½ cup) chickpeas, soaked overnight in cold water
- olive oil
- 1 onion, diced
- 1½ tsp sweet paprika
- 1½ tsp chilli powder
- 2 tsp ground cumin
- 2 tsp ground coriander
- 1 tsp ground white pepper
- 2 carrots, cut into 3 cm chunks
- 8 small potatoes, peeled and cut in half
- 2 parsnips, cut into quarters
- 1 sweet potato, cut into 3 cm chunks
- 2 tbsp lemon juice
- 500 ml (2 cups) vegetable stock
- 250 ml (1 cup) tomato sugo
- salt
- 2 zucchini, cut into quarters
- 100 g baby spinach leaves
- ½ cup coriander leaves

Put chickpeas in a medium-sized saucepan, cover with water and bring to the boil over a medium heat. Reduce heat and cook until soft, about 30–40 minutes. Drain and set aside.

Heat a large ovenproof casserole or saucepan over a medium–high heat. Add oil and onion and cook for 5–6 minutes, stirring often, until softened. Add spices, carrots, potatoes, parsnips and sweet potato. Cook for a further 3–4 minutes, stirring often. Add lemon juice, stock, tomato sugo and season with salt. Bring to the boil.

Preheat oven to 180°C.

Cover the tagine with a lid and cook in the preheated oven for 45 minutes. Check to see whether the vegetables are tender. Add zucchini and cooked chickpeas and cook for a further 10 minutes. Add spinach leaves and stir through until they wilt. Check seasoning.

Sprinkle with coriander leaves to serve. Excellent with Spiced Couscous (page 453).

VEGIES

seasonal side dishes

Most people master how to barbecue a steak, pan-fry chicken or grill some bratwurst sausages, but few seem to take the time to learn to prepare vegetables correctly. Or if they do, it's just the basics of peas, carrots and green beans. Well-prepared vegetables should be a part of every meal; in fact, they can even be the highlight. Think of baby carrots drizzled with a little honey, new season's peas with mint and butter, fresh asparagus at the start of spring or something as simple as mashed potatoes.

This chapter gives instructions on how to prepare a wide selection of vegetables correctly, plus ways to jazz them up and add complementary flavours. Always use the season as your guide to ensure what you're buying is ripe and full of flavour. To help you choose, we've included an easy-to-follow seasonal vegetable chart.

Don't forget that Mother Nature can act at will and may bring on plums early with a spell of hot weather, or delay winter greens with a lack of rain. So always use your senses – sight, touch and smell – when choosing the season's best.

vegie recipes

Asparagus with feta	472
Easy green beans	472
Wok-fried snake beans	473
Wok-fried snake beans with cashews	473
Broad beans braised with pancetta	474
Broccoli with toasted pine nuts	474
Stir-fried broccolini with garlic	475
Wok-fried brussels sprouts	475
Brussels sprouts with almonds and parsley	476
Red cabbage with sweet and sour flavours	476
Cabbage with bacon and apples	477
Carrots with butter and sugar glaze	477
Roast carrots	478
Roast cauliflower	478
Cauliflower cheese	479
Stir-fried cauliflower	479
Chinese broccoli and garlic stir-fry	480
Choy sum with ginger	480
Barbecued corn cobs	481
Sichuan eggplant	481
Caponata	482
Braised fennel	482
Fennel fritters	483
Jerusalem artichoke puree	483
Pan-fried mushrooms	484
Garlic mushrooms	484
Mushrooms with fresh herbs	485
Roasted onions	485
Caramelised onions	486
Fresh garden peas	486
Roast parsnips	487
Stir-fried snow peas with cashews and soy	487
Sugar snap peas with lemon butter	488
Mashed potatoes	489
Roast potatoes	489
Baked potatoes	490
Potato wedges	490
Rosemary garlic potatoes	491
Potato gratin	492
Catalan potatoes	492
Roast potatoes with chorizo, chilli and coriander	493
Potato roesti	493
Salt-baked potatoes	494
Pumpkin and parmigiano mash	494
Spiced pumpkin wedges	495
Savoury roast pumpkin	495
Roasted root vegetable chips	496
Sesame sweet potato wedges	496
Mashed swede	497
Spinach with lemon and almonds	497
Roasted Roma tomatoes	498
Toffee tomatoes	498
Zucchini with raisins and pine nuts	499
Wok-fried Asian greens	499

Things you need to know about vegetables

1 Asparagus is one vegetable that really signifies spring. Choose asparagus of an even thickness so that all the spears will cook at the same time. Most commonly you will see green asparagus, though white and purple can be found at the height of the season.

2 Asian greens are more widely available than ever, so they can easily become a part of your weekly menu. When preparing them, ensure they are well washed to remove any dirt.

3 One of our favourite Asian greens is choy sum, which has tender fleshy stems with bright green leaves and yellow flowers. Another is gai laan; it's almost identical in appearance, except the flowers are white.

4 Leafy greens such as brussels sprouts, cabbage and broccoli aren't everyone's cup of tea, but usually it's because they've been overcooked. If leafy greens are cooked for longer than necessary, sulphur compounds are released giving the vegies an unpleasant aroma. The exception is slow-braised red cabbage. However, leafy greens are fabulous when carefully cooked, which in their case means cooked only briefly.

5 When purchasing corn, look for even-coloured cobs with the green husks free from decay. Fine, silky white tassels extending out of the top are another sign of freshness. Corn's natural sweetness means
it is a vegetable that appeals to children and adults alike, so make full use of it throughout the warmer months.

6 The pungent aniseed flavour of fennel can be overpowering for some people. However, cooking transforms fennel from an intense taste to a mild and gentle one. When buying fennel bulbs, choose those with their feather-like tops still attached as a sign of freshness.

7 Green beans are without doubt the most popular of all the bean family. There are lots of other varieties to try at various times of the year, including yellow butter beans, broad beans, borlotti beans and large flat runner beans.

8 The array of mushroom varieties now on offer is fantastic, from the everyday cultivated button and flat mushroom to the more full-flavoured Swiss brown, shiitake, enoki and oyster mushrooms.

9 Wild mushrooms appear in the damp autumn months when the weather conditions are just right. The most widely available are pine mushrooms (saffron milk cap) and slippery jacks. These are usually picked in secret spots dotted around the countryside, usually near pine trees.

10 Fresh garden peas seem to have been replaced in our kitchens by packets of frozen peas. We use them ourselves sometimes, but please make the effort, every now and then, to pod fresh peas, even if it's just to let our kids know that peas don't grow in supermarket freezers.

11 Potatoes can be split into two main groups, both with endless varieties. Potatoes high in starch are called floury, and are ideal for baking, mashing and frying. Waxy potatoes are best suited to boiling, as they will not collapse.

12 It is best to purchase potatoes with the dirt still attached. They will last longer and be protected against some bruising. Unwashed potatoes will keep in a cool, dark place for up to 1 month.

13 Pumpkin has a delightfully sweet flesh and is a great staple in our winter cooking. There are many different varieties to choose from, but there is little discernable difference in flavour between them.

14 Take care when cutting pumpkins due to their uneven shape and tough skin. It is best to chop the top or bottom off, and then stand the pumpkin upright. When balanced like this it is safe to cut into wedges. Peel the tough skin away using a sharp knife. Cut wedges in half and discard the seeds.

15 Root vegetables are one of the largest groups of vegetables and perhaps one of the least utilised. They include parsnips, swedes, turnips, celeriac, Jerusalem artichokes, kohlrabi and, of course, carrots.

16 Good root vegetables should have a deep, earthy aroma and be firm and appealing to the eye. Their harvesting is perfectly timed to coincide with the hearty comfort foods of winter, such as roasts and stews.

17 Spinach is a quick and easy vegetable to prepare, especially now that pre-washed spinach leaves are so readily available. It has a delicate flavour and appeals to those who find cabbage and brussels sprouts too strong.

18 There is nothing quite like a tomato in its prime – sun-kissed, fragrant and oozing with flavour. The arrival of heirloom varieties such as green zebras, black Russians and tigerella means there is now a range of new varieties to include in our cooking.

19 Zucchini is one of the classic summer vegetables. Pan-fry a few slices briefly in butter or olive oil to taste just how good they can be. The flowers that are attached to the ends of baby zucchini are also highly sought after. They are best stuffed and then deep-fried.

Seasonal vegetable chart

We are big fans of seasonal produce – and encourage everyone to use produce at its peak for best quality and fullest flavour. Use the following lists as a general guide, which show when each vegetable is in season.

SPRING
- artichokes
- asparagus
- avocados
- broad beans
- broccoli
- cabbage
- carrots
- cauliflower
- cucumbers
- green beans
- leeks
- lettuce
- peas
- potatoes
- salad onions
- silverbeet
- snow peas
- spinach
- sugar snap peas
- sweetcorn
- tomatoes
- zucchini flowers

SUMMER
- asparagus
- avocados
- borlotti beans
- butter beans
- capsicums
- celery
- cucumbers
- eggplant
- green beans
- leeks
- lettuce
- peas
- radishes
- snow peas
- squash
- sugar snap peas
- sweetcorn
- tomatoes
- zucchini
- zucchini flowers

AUTUMN
- asian greens
- avocados
- beetroot
- borlotti beans
- broccoli
- brussels sprouts
- butter beans
- cabbage
- capsicums
- carrots
- cauliflower
- celery
- cucumbers
- eggplant
- fennel
- green beans
- leeks
- lettuce
- onions
- parsnips
- peas
- potatoes
- pumpkin
- silverbeet
- spinach
- squash
- swedes
- sweet potato
- sweetcorn
- tomatoes
- turnips
- wild mushrooms

WINTER
- asian greens
- avocados
- beetroot
- broccoli
- brussels sprouts
- cabbage
- carrots
- cauliflower
- celeriac
- celery
- fennel
- horseradish
- Jerusalem artichokes
- kale
- kohlrabi
- leeks
- okra
- olives
- onions
- parsnips
- peas
- potatoes
- pumpkin
- silverbeet
- spinach
- swedes
- sweet potato
- turnips

Asparagus with feta

Serves 4

Asparagus goes well with a great variety of sauces and other ingredients. In this recipe, marinated feta melts slightly on the warm asparagus to absolutely delicious effect.

500 g asparagus
oil
salt and freshly ground black pepper
100 g marinated feta
1 tbsp red wine vinegar

Trim the woody ends from the asparagus. You can do this by holding the end of the stalk in one hand and the remainder in the other. The stalk will break at the appropriate point. If preferred, trim off the bottom 5 cm or so with a knife. Toss the asparagus with oil, salt and pepper.

Heat a heavy-based frypan over a medium–high heat. Add the asparagus and a splash of oil and cook for 5–6 minutes, turning regularly.

Arrange the asparagus on a platter, crumble feta on top, drizzle with vinegar and serve.

Asparagus with hollandaise sauce
Cook asparagus in boiling water for 2–3 minutes. Drain and while still warm serve with Hollandaise Sauce (page 555).

Asparagus with prosciutto
Wrap a slice of prosciutto around each asparagus spear and cook as above.

Easy green beans

Serves 4

All beans should be cooked briefly to retain their crispness, and then tossed with a little butter, if preferred. They are without doubt one of the most popular dinner vegetables.

500 g green beans, trimmed
2 tbsp butter

Bring a large saucepan of water to the boil. Cook the beans in boiling water for 3–4 minutes. Drain the beans, toss with butter and serve immediately.

Green beans with almonds
Add toasted almond flakes to the cooked beans, along with chopped parsley or mint.

Green beans with walnuts
Top the cooked green beans with chopped roasted walnuts, a drizzle of walnut oil and a few drops of red wine vinegar.

Wok-fried snake beans

Serves 4

Snake, long or yard beans are a common sight at all markets nowadays, especially those with Asian stallholders. These beans are really great to cook as they always retain a light crunch.

1 tbsp peanut oil
4 spring onions, thinly sliced
1 tsp grated ginger
1 bunch snake beans, cut into 3 cm pieces
1–2 tbsp soy sauce
50 g (⅓ cup) roasted cashews
200 g firm tofu, cut into cubes

Heat a wok over a high heat. Add oil, swirling to cover the sides, then add the spring onions, ginger and snake beans. Toss to coat with oil and cook for 1 minute, until fragrant. Add a generous splash of water and cover with a lid. Allow to steam for 3–4 minutes.

Add soy sauce, cashews and tofu. Toss, cover with the lid and cook for 1–2 minutes. Serve immediately.

Wok-fried snake beans with cashews

Serves 4

A simple side dish with crunch.

oil
4 shallots, sliced
1 bunch snake beans, cut into 5 cm lengths
2–3 tbsp stock
75 g (½ cup) toasted cashew nuts
1–2 tbsp soy sauce

Heat a wok over a high heat, add a splash of oil and shallots and cook for 2–3 minutes, stirring often. Add the snake beans, stir-fry briefly, then add stock, cover with a lid and cook for 3–4 minutes.

Remove lid and check the beans are tender. If not, add more stock if needed and cook for a further 1–2 minutes.

Add cashew nuts, season with soy sauce and serve.

Broad beans braised with pancetta

Serves 4

Broad beans generally have to be double-peeled to be enjoyed at their best. It's a bit of work, but the flavour of these beans makes it worth every minute of effort.

1 kg broad beans
1 tbsp olive oil
1 onion, finely diced
4 slices pancetta, thinly sliced and diced
250 ml (1 cup) chicken stock
50 g butter
salt and freshly ground black pepper

Remove the beans from their large pods. Bring a large saucepan of water to the boil. Add the broad beans and cook for 1 minute. Drain and refresh under cold running water.

Remove the pale green skins from the beans. This is easily done by inserting a small knife or your thumbnail into the skin and creating a slit, then pushing the vivid green bean halves from their skins. Discard the skins.

Heat a saucepan over a medium heat. Add the oil and onion and cook for 3–4 minutes until soft, stirring often. Add pancetta and cook until it begins to colour, stirring often. Add beans and stock and bring to the boil. Reduce to a simmer and cook uncovered until the beans are tender.

Raise the heat and cook until the stock has evaporated. Add butter and season with salt and pepper.

Broad beans with extra-virgin olive oil
Pod the beans and cook them in boiling water for 2–3 minutes. Drizzle with your best extra-virgin olive oil, salt and shavings of parmigiano.

Broccoli with toasted pine nuts

Serves 4

Broccoli needs to be cooked quickly in boiling water, or it can be steamed. Here, it is finished with toasted nuts to give it a little extra flavour.

500 g broccoli
1 tbsp olive oil
50 g (⅓ cup) pine nuts
salt and freshly ground black pepper

Trim the thick stalk off the broccoli and cut the head into small florets.

Bring a large saucepan of water to the boil. Add the broccoli and cook for 3–4 minutes.

Heat a frypan over a medium heat and add the oil and pine nuts. Cook, stirring, until golden brown. Drain the broccoli well and add it to the frypan. Cook for a further 30 seconds.

Season with salt and pepper. Serve immediately.

Stir-fried broccolini with garlic

Serves 4

Bunches of young broccoli, or broccolini, are always a winner in our house. We like to eat them stem and all. Stir-frying adds extra-special flavour.

1 bunch broccolini
oil
2 cloves garlic, crushed
1–2 tbsp chicken stock

Trim the ends from the broccolini and cut into 4 cm lengths.

Heat a wok over a high heat. Add a splash of oil, the broccolini and garlic. Cook for 1 minute, stirring often, making sure the garlic doesn't burn. Add stock, cover with a lid and steam for 2–3 minutes. Serve immediately.

Wok-fried brussels sprouts

Serves 4

This will make you fall in love with brussels sprouts all over again – or for the first time!

500 g brussels sprouts
1 tbsp peanut oil
2 tsp grated ginger
1 tbsp soy sauce
1 tsp sesame oil
1 tsp toasted sesame seeds

Trim the brussels sprouts of their darker green outside leaves and cut the sprouts in half. Bring a large saucepan of water to the boil. Add the brussels sprouts and cook them for 4–5 minutes.

Heat a wok over a high heat. Add the oil, ginger and cook briefly. Add the drained, hot brussels sprouts and toss quickly to coat them with ginger and oil. Add soy sauce and cook for 2–3 minutes, stirring frequently to allow the liquid to evaporate. Add the sesame oil and sesame seeds, and serve.

Brussels sprouts with almonds and parsley

Serves 4

Follow the instructions here to create perfectly cooked brussels sprouts that will reveal just how tasty they can be.

500 g brussels sprouts
10 g butter
100 g (1 cup) flaked toasted almonds
2 tbsp chopped parsley
salt and freshly ground black pepper

Trim the brussels sprouts of their darker green outside leaves and cut the sprouts in half. Bring a large saucepan of water to the boil. Add the brussels sprouts and cook them for 6–8 minutes.

Melt the butter in a pan over a medium heat. Add the drained brussels sprouts and cook for 3–4 minutes, stirring well. Sprinkle with almonds and parsley and season with salt and pepper.

Brussels sprouts with chestnuts
Substitute chunks of cooked chestnut for the almonds.

Red cabbage with sweet and sour flavours

Serves 4

This sweet-and-sour cabbage is perfect with roast pork.

½ red cabbage
75 g butter
80 ml (⅓ cup) red wine vinegar
80 ml (⅓ cup) redcurrant juice or blackcurrant cordial

Cut the cabbage into quarters and trim away the central stalk. Thinly slice the cabbage.

Heat a large heavy-based saucepan over a medium–high heat. Melt the butter, add the cabbage and toss well. Stir in the vinegar and redcurrant juice, cover and cook for 20–30 minutes, stirring often.

Cabbage with bacon and apples

Serves 4

Cabbage, bacon and apple were made to be cooked and served together. This dish is superb with grilled sausages or pork cutlets.

½ cabbage
1 tbsp olive oil
2 slices bacon, chopped
1 onion, sliced
1 green apple, grated
1 tsp caraway seeds
pinch of ground cloves
salt and freshly ground black pepper
2 tbsp white wine

Cut the cabbage into quarters and trim away the central stalk. Thinly slice the cabbage.

Heat a heavy-based pan over a medium–high heat. Add the oil, bacon and onion and cook for 4–5 minutes, stirring often, until the onion just starts to brown.

Add the cabbage, apple, caraway seeds, cloves, salt and pepper and white wine. Stir well. Cover with a lid and cook for 5 minutes. Stir well and cook uncovered for 5 minutes, or until just tender. Serve immediately.

Carrots with butter and sugar glaze

Serves 4

Carrots are an everyday vegetable that everyone enjoys. Other root vegetables such as turnips and swede can also be prepared in this way.

4 carrots
1 tbsp butter
1 tbsp sugar
salt and freshly ground black pepper

Peel the carrots and cut them into even-sized pieces – choose from rings, large dice or thick batons.

Bring a saucepan of water to the boil. Add the carrots and cook for 3–4 minutes. Drain well. They should still be slightly crisp and not completely cooked.

Heat a frypan over a medium–high heat and add the butter and sugar. When completely melted, stir well then add the carrots. Cook the carrots in the sugar glaze for 4–5 minutes, or until they are lightly golden. Season with salt and pepper and serve immediately.

Roast carrots

Serves 6

These carrots can be added to the traditional roast, cooked separately and served as a side dish, or added to salads for their extra-sweet flavour.

- 1 bunch baby carrots or 3 large carrots
- oil
- 1 tbsp balsamic vinegar
- 1–2 sprigs of thyme
- salt and freshly ground black pepper

Preheat oven to 180°C.

If using baby carrots, scrub them lightly. If using normal carrots, peel them and then cut them into even-sized pieces.

Place the carrots in a baking tray. Drizzle with oil, vinegar, thyme, salt and pepper. Cook in the preheated oven for 20–30 minutes, tossing occasionally, until tender.

Honey roasted carrots
Add 1 tbsp honey to the baking dish.

Roast cauliflower

Serves 6

Roasting may not be the first cooking method which springs to mind for cauliflower but it works extremely well. For extra flavour you can also sprinkle the cauliflower with a little spice such as sweet paprika or ground cumin.

- 1 medium cauliflower
- oil
- salt and freshly ground black pepper

Preheat oven to 180°C.

Cut the large stalk out of the cauliflower to leave the separated florets. Try to ensure they are a similar size.

Toss the cauliflower with oil, salt and pepper. Place in a baking tray and cook in the preheated oven for 20 minutes, or until golden brown and tender.

Cauliflower cheese

Serves 4

Cauliflower cheese is a classic Australian dish. It tastes great and encourages children to eat cauliflower – so why not serve it tonight?

- 1 medium cauliflower
- 500 ml (2 cups) milk
- 2 tbsp butter
- 45 g (⅓ cup) flour
- 1 tsp Dijon mustard
- 200 g (1⅔ cups) grated cheddar
- salt and freshly ground black pepper

Preheat oven to 180°C.

Cut the large stalk out of the cauliflower to leave the separated florets.

Bring a large saucepan of water to the boil and cook the cauliflower in boiling water for 6–7 minutes, or until just tender. Drain well and place in a buttered ovenproof baking dish.

Warm the milk to a gentle simmer. Heat a small saucepan over a medium heat and melt the butter. Reduce heat to low and add the flour.

Stir to form a roux and allow to 'cook out' for 1–2 minutes. Raise heat, add warm milk and whisk until a smooth sauce forms. Simmer for 5 minutes, when the sauce will have thickened slightly.

Remove from heat and add the mustard and cheese. Stir until melted. Season to taste. Pour the sauce over the cauliflower and place in the preheated oven. Cook for 20 minutes, or until bubbling and beginning to brown on top.

Stir-fried cauliflower

Serves 4

Make this recipe when you want a quick cauliflower dish with plenty of flavour and oomph.

- ½ cauliflower
- 2 tbsp peanut oil
- ½ tsp sesame oil
- 1 chilli, de-seeded and diced
- 1 onion, diced
- 1 clove garlic, crushed
- salt

Cut the large stalk out of the cauliflower to leave the separated florets. Try to ensure they are a similar size.

Heat a wok and add the oils, chilli, onion, garlic and salt. Cook until the onion is soft.

Add the cauliflower to the wok and toss quickly to coat evenly. Sprinkle with hot water, reduce heat, cover and cook for 10 minutes, or until tender.

Chinese broccoli and garlic stir-fry

Serves 4

These greens are almost obligatory when we serve Asian dishes. Sometimes we use baby bok choy, sometimes Chinese cabbage, but mostly it's gai laan (Chinese broccoli) because it cooks so brilliantly.

1 bunch gai laan
oil
4 cloves garlic, crushed
2 tbsp grated ginger
125 ml (½ cup) chicken stock
1–2 tbsp soy sauce

Wash the gai laan well, taking care to remove all dirt. Discard any big or old leaves. Thinly slice the stems; on the angle is best.

Heat a wok over a high heat. Add a splash of oil, the garlic and ginger and cook for 1 minute, stirring often, making sure the garlic doesn't burn. Add the gai laan and toss for 1–2 minutes. Add the stock and cover with a lid. Cook for 3–4 minutes, tossing occasionally to ensure the greens cook evenly. Remove the lid and season with soy sauce.

Spoon the gai laan and juices onto a platter.

Choy sum with ginger

Serves 4

These steamed greens are ideal with any Asian-influenced meal.

2 tbsp water
2 tbsp fish sauce
1 tsp grated ginger
1 tbsp peanut oil
1 bunch choy sum, chopped

Combine the water, fish sauce and ginger.

Heat a wok and add oil, swirling to cover the sides. Throw in the choy sum and toss quickly to coat with oil. Pour in the ginger and fish sauce mixture. Toss again, then cover the wok with a lid. Allow to cook for 3–4 minutes, stirring occasionally.

Spoon the greens and juices onto a serving platter.

Barbecued corn cobs

Serves 4

This is a must-try recipe as corn is great when it's cooked on the barbecue. If you can get your hands on some Spanish smoky paprika, it'll be an absolute knockout.

4 corn cobs
2 tbsp olive oil
2 tsp sweet paprika
salt and freshly ground black pepper

To prepare the corn, roll back and remove the green husks, then pull off the silky tassels. Wash the cobs briefly to ensure that all tassels have been removed. Cut the cobs in half or into smaller pieces as required.

Brush the cobs all over with oil, then sprinkle with sweet paprika, salt and pepper.

Place the corn cobs on a heated barbecue grill and cook for 10 minutes, turning often.

Sichuan eggplant

Serves 4

Eggplant is a vegetable which seems to go in and out of favour with great regularity. This easy recipe should put it right back up there in the popularity stakes.

2 eggplants
salt
oil
60 ml (¼ cup) kecap manis
2 tsp sesame oil
1 tsp Salt and Pepper and Spice (page 295) (optional)

Preheat oven to 180°C.

Cut eggplants in half, then cut each half into 3 wedges. Sprinkle with salt and set aside for 20 minutes until juices bead. Rinse well and pat dry.

Heat a heavy-based frypan over a medium–high heat. Add a generous splash of oil and cook the eggplant until lightly brown on the flesh side.

Place in a baking tray skin-side down.

Mix the kecap manis and sesame oil together. Brush over the eggplant and sprinkle with Salt and Pepper Spice (if using).

Bake in the preheated oven for 10–15 minutes, until the eggplant is cooked through. Serve immediately.

Caponata

Serves 6

Serve this Sicilian eggplant dish with pan-fried lamb or veal, or with chicken cooked with a hint of spice.

2 eggplants, cut into 1 cm dice
salt
oil
1 onion, diced
2 celery stalks, cut into 1 cm dice
1 red capsicum, cut into 1 cm dice
75 g (½ cup) pitted green olives
2 tsp salted capers, soaked and rinsed
80 ml (⅓ cup) white wine vinegar
2 tbsp caster sugar
chopped basil and parsley
salt and freshly ground black pepper

Place the diced eggplant in a colander and sprinkle with salt. Leave for 20–30 minutes, until juices bead. Rinse well and pat dry.

Place a large heavy-based frypan over a medium heat and add enough oil to cover the base of the pan. Cook the eggplant in batches until golden brown, adding more oil if necessary. Remove from the pan and cook the onion, celery and capsicum until soft.

Return the eggplant to the pan, and add the olives, capers, vinegar and caster sugar. Heat a little until the sugar has dissolved, taking care not to overcook the eggplant. Remove from heat and allow to cool at room temperature.

Before serving, add herbs to taste, and salt and pepper if necessary.

Braised fennel

Serves 4

Braised fennel is a side dish which can accompany dishes such as chicken saltimbocca, risotto or veal schnitzel.

2 fennel bulbs
20 g butter
1 tbsp olive oil
salt and freshly ground black pepper
125 ml (½ cup) chicken stock
1 tbsp chopped parsley
lemon juice

Remove the fennel's tough outer skin and trim off the feathery tops. Cut the bulbs in half and remove the core. Slice the fennel into thick, even-sized wedges.

Heat a large heavy-based frypan over a medium heat and add the butter and oil. Allow the butter to melt, then add the fennel. Cook gently for 5–10 minutes, lowering the heat if necessary, until the fennel starts to soften but not brown.

Season, then add the chicken stock and simmer for 15 minutes, until tender. The stock will slowly be absorbed into the fennel bulbs, softening them along the way.

Sprinkle the fennel with chopped parsley and season again with salt and freshly ground black pepper. Add lemon juice to freshen up the fennel if it tastes too rich.

Fennel fritters

Makes 5–6 fritters

Serve these fritters as a side dish in autumn and winter, when fennel is at its seasonal best.

1 fennel bulb
1 egg
125 ml (½ cup) milk
50 g (½ cup) dry breadcrumbs
40 g (½ cup) grated parmigiano
oil

Remove the fennel's tough outer skin and trim off the feathery tops. Cut the fennel into ½ cm slices across the bulb. Bring a saucepan of water to the boil and cook the fennel briefly in boiling water. Refresh under cold running water and dry well.

Beat the egg and milk together in 1 bowl and combine the breadcrumbs and cheese in another. Dip the fennel first into the egg mixture, and then into the breadcrumbs.

Heat a heavy-based frypan over a medium heat. Add oil and cook the fritters until golden and crispy.

Jerusalem artichoke puree

Serves 4

A fine accompaniment to a classic roast rib of beef.

1 kg Jerusalem artichokes
80 ml (⅓ cup) thickened cream
45 g butter
salt and freshly ground black pepper
chopped parsley

Peel the artichokes and place them in a large saucepan. Cover them with water and bring to the boil. Reduce to a simmer and cook for 10 minutes, until tender.

Drain the artichokes well then return them to the saucepan. Place the saucepan over a low heat and warm the artichokes for 1–2 minutes, shaking the pan occasionally to evaporate excess moisture.

Place the artichokes in a food processor and puree roughly. Add cream and butter and continue pureeing until smooth. Season with salt and pepper.

Gently reheat the artichoke puree in a saucepan over a low heat, stirring well. Stir through chopped parsley and serve immediately.

Pan-fried mushrooms

Serves 4

Mushrooms are one of the simplest things to pan-fry. Try button, Swiss brown or sliced field mushrooms, or a combination of more exotic varieties such as shiitake and enoki. In autumn, try this method with wild orange pine mushrooms.

500 g mushrooms
2 tbsp olive oil
2 tbsp butter
salt and freshly ground black pepper
fresh chopped herbs

Wipe the mushrooms clean, if required. Cut the mushrooms to a similar size, if necessary, to allow even cooking.

Heat a heavy-based frypan over a medium–high heat, then add oil and butter. Add the mushrooms and toss to coat. Continue cooking for 8–10 minutes, moving the mushrooms so that they cook evenly and start to soften. Season with salt and pepper, then add fresh chopped herbs to taste.

Pesto mushrooms
Pan-fry large field mushrooms and serve with a dollop of basil pesto on top.

Garlic mushrooms

Serves 4–6

Mushrooms cope really well with the heat of a barbecue, and taste especially good when they are drizzled with this lovely garlic oil.

12 Swiss brown or field mushrooms
60–80 ml (¼–⅓ cup) olive oil
2 cloves garlic, crushed
salt and freshly ground black pepper

Wipe the mushrooms with a damp cloth. Mix oil with garlic, salt and pepper.

Place the mushrooms on the barbecue plate, brush with oil. Cook for 4 minutes, brushing with oil, rotating once. Turn over and brush with oil. Cook for a further 4 minutes, rotating once.

Mushrooms with fresh herbs

Serves 4–6

A good mix of mushroom varieties as described below will ensure a delicious combination of textures and flavours.

150 g Swiss brown mushrooms
150 g oyster mushrooms
100 g button mushrooms
2 tbsp olive oil
½ cup chopped fresh herbs
salt and freshly ground black pepper

Wipe mushrooms with a damp cloth if required to remove grit. Mix the oil, herbs, salt and pepper together. Toss oil and mushrooms together.

Place the mushrooms on an oiled barbecue plate. Cook mushrooms for 15 minutes, turning often. Add extra oil if required.

Roasted onions

Serves 4–6

Cooking just wouldn't be the same without onions. Their flavour adds something special to every dish.

6 onions
salt and freshly ground black pepper
2 tbsp balsamic vinegar
60 ml (¼ cup) olive oil

Preheat oven to 200°C.

Peel the onions and cut them into rings. Spread the onions out in a baking tray and sprinkle them with salt, pepper, vinegar and oil and toss to mix.

Bake in the preheated oven for 30 minutes, or until the onions soften.

Serve with grilled steak or lamb chops.

Caramelised onions

Serves 4

Serve these caramelised onions with grilled steaks, use them on pizza or toss them through cooked pasta with chopped rocket and parmigiano.

80 ml (⅓ cup) olive oil
4 onions, sliced
2 cloves garlic, peeled
1 small red chilli, halved
2 sprigs of thyme
salt and freshly ground black pepper

Heat the oil in a saucepan and add the onions, garlic, chilli and thyme. Cook for 20–30 minutes on a low heat, stirring often, until the onions soften. Check seasoning.

Fresh garden peas

Serves 4

To pod peas, simply snap the ends off the pod and open it by running your finger along the seam. Remove the peas and discard the pod. A kilo and a half of peas will yield 500 g podded peas.

500 g podded peas
sprig of mint
2 tbsp butter
salt and freshly ground black pepper

Bring a saucepan of water to the boil. Add peas and mint and cook for 5–6 minutes, until tender.

Drain the peas, add butter and season with salt and pepper.

Minty pea mash
Boil the peas as directed. Drain well, remove mint and season the peas with salt and pepper. Add butter and mash roughly. Pea mash is great with pan-fried salmon, lamb cutlets or roast chicken.

Roast parsnips

Serves 4

Parsnips herald the arrival of winter, so what better way to enjoy them than cooked alongside the weekly roast.

1 kg parsnips
60 ml (¼ cup) olive oil
2 tbsp sherry vinegar
salt and freshly ground black pepper

Preheat oven to 180°C.

Peel the parsnips and cut them into even-sized pieces, or just cut them in half lengthways if they are not too big. Place them in a bowl and mix well with the oil and vinegar. Season with salt and pepper.

Spread the parsnips in a shallow baking dish and cook in the preheated oven for 45 minutes, or until golden brown and tender. Turn the parsnips occasionally during cooking to ensure that they brown evenly.

Roast parsnips with Worcestershire sauce and honey
Substitute 2 tbsp honey and 1 tbsp Worcestershire sauce for the olive oil and sherry vinegar.

Stir-fried snow peas with cashews and soy

Serves 4

Snow peas are eaten whole, as their pod is thin and very sweet. They excel in a stir-fry, retaining their crunch and vibrant colour.

600 g snow peas
oil
1 clove garlic, crushed
1 tsp grated ginger
4 spring onions, thinly sliced
2–3 tbsp chicken stock or water
1–2 tbsp soy sauce
75 g (½ cup) roasted cashews

Carefully pull the tip away from each snow pea, then pull the tip along the pod to tear off the string. Repeat from the other end.

Place a wok over a high heat and add a splash of oil and the garlic, ginger and spring onions. Cook for 1 minute, stirring frequently. Add snow peas and stock or water.

Cover the wok with a lid and cook for 3–4 minutes, stirring once or twice. Remove the lid, stir well and add soy sauce and cashews.

Sugar snap peas with lemon butter

Serves 4

Sweet sugar snap peas appeal to young and old alike. If you have younger members in the family, they may prefer their sugar snaps without the lemon.

600 g sugar snap peas
2 tbsp butter
2 tbsp lemon juice
salt and freshly ground black pepper

Carefully pull the tip away from each sugar snap pea, then pull the tip along the pod to tear off the string. Repeat from the other end.

Bring a large saucepan of water to the boil. Add the sugar snaps and cook for 3–4 minutes, until tender. Drain, and add butter and lemon juice.

Check seasoning, and serve immediately.

potato varieties

Variety	Boil	Roast	Mash	Fry	Bake	Chips	Gnocchi
Desiree	**	***		**	**		**
Bintje	***	**	**	**	**		**
Nicola	*	***	**	***	*		
Sebago	**	*	**	**	*		
King Edward	**	***			**	*	
Toolangi delight	**	*	**		**	**	***
Spunta	*	**	**		**	***	
Roseval		***		***	**		
Pink eye	***				*		
Patrone	***			**	**		
Russet burbank				***	**		

* Good   ** Very good   *** Excellent

Mashed potatoes

Serves 6

What could be better to serve for a large family gathering than great mashed potatoes?

1 ½ kg potatoes (bintje, nicola, sebago or spunta)
50 g butter, diced
2–3 tbsp hot milk
chopped parsley
salt and freshly ground black pepper

Peel the potatoes and chop them into even-sized pieces. Place the potatoes in a large saucepan and cover with water. Bring to the boil, reduce heat and cook for 12–15 minutes, until tender.

Drain the potatoes well, then return them to the saucepan and place over a low heat. Warm the potatoes for 1–2 minutes, shaking the pan occasionally to evaporate excess moisture.

Mash the potatoes well, then stir in butter, milk and chopped parsley. Season to taste with salt and pepper.

Champ
When I was growing up as a boy from an Irish background, I would sometimes have hot cooked curly kale stirred into my mashed potatoes to make champ. If curly kale wasn't available, cabbage or spring onion was used. AC

Mashed potatoes with goat's cheese
To give an extra flavour boost to your mashed potatoes, substitute 50 g soft marinated goat's cheese for the hot milk.

Roast potatoes

Serves 6

There's nothing quite like perfectly cooked roast potatoes. They are also delicious when cooked in the same tray as a roast chicken or piece of beef, as the flavour from the meat adds that extra-special something.

1½ kg potatoes (desiree, nicola, king edward or roseval)
olive oil
salt and freshly ground black pepper

Preheat oven to 200°C.

Peel the potatoes and cut them into large, even-sized pieces. Place the potatoes in a baking tray, toss with oil and sprinkle with salt and pepper.

Cook the potatoes in the preheated oven for 1 hour, turning them occasionally. They should be crispy and golden.

Goose-fat roast potatoes
Prepare potatoes as directed then toss with 3 tbsp melted goose fat, salt and freshly ground black pepper. Cook the potatoes in a 200°C oven, turning them occasionally. They should be crispy and golden when ready.

Baked potatoes

Serves 6

Baked potatoes are a wonderful meal in anyone's book – quick, versatile and completely family-friendly.

6 large potatoes (bintje, spunta or nicola)
oil
salt and freshly ground black pepper
butter

Preheat oven to 200°C.

Scrub the potatoes well, if needed. Place the potatoes in a baking tray, toss with oil and sprinkle with salt and pepper.

Bake the potatoes in the preheated oven for 1 hour, or until the potatoes are tender. Turn them over after 30 minutes. The oil will ensure the skins crisp up beautifully.

When ready to serve, cut a cross in each potato and squeeze gently to open them up. Serve with a dollop of butter in each potato.

Baked potato fillings
Try grated cheese, baked beans, bolognaise, coleslaw, ratatouille or avocado and sour cream.

Potato wedges

Serves 4

A simple but fantastic accompaniment to any grilled dish.

1 kg potatoes (desiree, nicola, king edward or roseval)
oil
2 tbsp rosemary leaves
1 tbsp chopped parsley
salt and freshly ground black pepper

Preheat oven to 180°C.

Cut the potatoes into thick wedges. Place the oil, herbs, salt and pepper in a large bowl. Add the potato wedges and toss well.

Place the wedges on a large baking tray, skin-side down. Cook in the preheated oven for 45–55 minutes. The potato wedges will be golden brown when ready.

Spiced potato wedges
Omit herbs and add 1 tsp chilli powder, 1 tsp ground cumin and 1 tsp ground coriander.

Dukkah potato wedges
Omit herbs and add 2–3 tsp dukkah.

Sesame and cumin potato wedges
Omit herbs and add 1 tsp sesame seeds and 1 tsp ground cumin.

Rosemary garlic potatoes

Serves 4

This is a true family favourite at the Campion–Curtis household – try it just once and it may become yours, too. These potatoes go well with roast lamb or any pan-fried meats.

1 kg potatoes (desiree, nicola, king edward or roseval)
oil
2–3 sprigs of rosemary, chopped
20 cloves garlic, unpeeled
salt and freshly ground black pepper

Preheat oven to 180°C.

Peel and dice the potatoes into 2–3 cm chunks. Place them in a deep baking tray with lots of oil, rosemary, garlic, salt and pepper. Mix well.

Bake in the preheated oven for 1 hour, stirring occasionally, until the potatoes are golden and cooked through.

Potato gratin

Serves 6

A gratin is classic dinner party stuff and minimal work once it's in the oven. You might like to serve the potatoes with steamed vegetables or a simple green salad.

1.5 kg potatoes (desiree or bintje)
185 ml (¾ cup) cream
185 ml (¾ cup) milk
2 cloves garlic, sliced
salt and freshly ground black pepper
nutmeg

Preheat oven to 180°C.

Peel the potatoes and place them in a large saucepan. Cover with water and bring to the boil. Cook for 5 minutes; you don't want the potatoes to be completely cooked.

Drain the potatoes well, then return them to the saucepan. Place the saucepan over a low heat and warm the potatoes for 1–2 minutes, shaking the pan occasionally to evaporate excess moisture.

Butter an ovenproof dish, one that you can serve at the table. Slice the potatoes into 5 mm thick slices and arrange in the buttered dish. Mix the cream and milk together and pour over the potatoes. Scatter garlic slices over, season with salt and pepper and grate fresh nutmeg over. Cover with foil.

Cook in the preheated oven for 40 minutes. Remove foil and return the dish to the oven for a further 10 minutes so the potatoes can brown a little.

Catalan potatoes

Serves 6

A mix of braising and roasting occurs in this dish. The stock is absorbed into the potatoes as they cook in the oven, yet they end up crisp and full of flavour from the smoky paprika.

1 ½ kg desiree potatoes
salt and freshly ground black pepper
1 tsp smoky paprika
olive oil
500–750 ml (2–3 cups) chicken stock
salt and freshly ground black pepper

Preheat oven to 200°C.

Peel the potatoes and cut them in half lengthways. Place them in a roasting tray and sprinkle with salt, pepper and paprika. Add a good splash of oil, and toss to coat the potatoes with seasoning.

Carefully pour in enough stock to half-cover the potatoes. Cook for 1 ½ hours, tossing the potatoes occasionally. Cook until they're golden brown and the liquid has been absorbed.

Roast potatoes with chorizo, chilli and coriander

Serves 4

If you haven't fallen in love with chorizo yet, this dish may well be the one that tips you over the edge. When using chorizo always pan-fry first as this removes all excess fat and caramelises the meat, adding a sweet flavour.

500 g baby potatoes
olive oil
salt and freshly ground black pepper
½ spicy or mild chorizo
sliced red chilli
coriander leaves

Preheat oven to 180°C.

Heat a heavy-based frypan over a medium heat, add a generous splash of oil and pan-fry the potatoes until golden brown. Place the potatoes in a roasting tin, season with salt and pepper and cook in the preheated oven. Place the chorizo into the frypan and pan-fry until golden brown. Drain the chorizo on paper towel, and add to the potatoes in the oven. Cook for 30–40 minutes, or until the potatoes are cooked through. Place the roast potatoes and chorizo in a serving dish, and top with sliced red chilli and coriander leaves.

Potato roesti

Serves 4

Use waxy potatoes for this recipe, as they'll hold together best.

4 potatoes (bintje, desiree or spunta)
1 zucchini
chopped fresh herbs
salt and freshly ground black pepper
oil

Preheat oven to 180°C.

Coarsely grate the potatoes and zucchini. Squeeze excess starch away from the potatoes. Place the grated potato and zucchini in a bowl, along with the freshly chopped herbs, salt and pepper. Mix well.

Heat a heavy-based pan over a medium–high heat. Pour in a generous amount of oil and add 6 cm wide mounds of the grated potato mix.

Allow to cook for 3–4 minutes. The mixture will begin to brown and hold itself together.

Flatten the mounds of potato a little using a palette knife, then loosen the base, turn them over and cook for a further 5 minutes.

Remove the potato roesti from the pan, place them on a baking tray and cook in the preheated oven for 15–20 minutes.

Salt-baked potatoes

Serves 6

It takes an awful lot of salt to prepare these potatoes, but miraculously you can't taste it once they're cooked. Luckily for us, salt is not expensive.

- 2–3 kg small baking potatoes (desiree, patrone or spunta)
- 2 tbsp olive oil
- 1 kg fine salt

Preheat oven to 180°C.

Scrub the potatoes well, if needed, and then dry well. Prick the potatoes with a fork and rub them with oil. Pour a 1–2 cm layer of salt into a deep baking tray. Add the potatoes and pour the remaining salt over to cover them.

Cook the potatoes for 2 hours, until they're tender when tested with a fork. The potatoes will keep warm until you are ready to serve.

Break through the salt crust and lift out the potatoes, brushing them gently to remove any salt from the skins.

Pumpkin and parmigiano mash

Serves 4

Mashed pumpkin is not the most inspiring of vegetables. That is, until you give it a lift with parmigiano, chopped basil and a drizzle of your best olive oil.

- 1 kg pumpkin
- 40 g (½ cup) grated parmigiano
- 10 basil leaves, chopped
- 2 tbsp olive oil
- salt and freshly ground black pepper

Peel the pumpkin and remove the seeds. Cut into 2–3 cm dice. Place the pumpkin in a medium-sized saucepan and cover with water. Bring to the boil, then simmer for 10 minutes, until the pumpkin is just tender.

Drain the pumpkin, then return it to the saucepan. Place the saucepan over a low heat and warm the pumpkin for 1–2 minutes, shaking the pan occasionally to evaporate excess moisture.

Remove from heat. Mash the pumpkin and stir in parmigiano, basil and oil. Season with salt and pepper.

Pumpkin and nutmeg mash
Substitute a knob of organic butter and plenty of ground nutmeg for the parmigiano, basil and olive oil.

Sweet potato mash
Substitute sweet potatoes for pumpkin, then mash well and season with salt and freshly ground black pepper. The final touch is to stir in a decent splash of good cream.

Spiced pumpkin wedges

Serves 4

A trio of spices adds flavour to these wedges of pumpkin, then a little pomegranate syrup is drizzled over them to add a sweet–sour finish. If needed, balsamic vinegar can be substituted for the pomegranate syrup.

1 kg pumpkin
oil
1 tsp ground cumin
1 tsp ground coriander
1 tsp ground sweet paprika
salt and freshly ground black pepper
2 tbsp pomegranate syrup

Preheat oven to 180°C.

Cut the pumpkin into thick wedges. Remove the seeds but leave the skin on each wedge.

Heat a heavy-based frypan over a medium–high heat and add a splash of oil. Cook wedges on each side until golden brown. Place on a baking tray.

Combine the cumin, coriander, sweet paprika, salt and pepper. Sprinkle the spices over the wedges and cook them in the preheated oven for 20 minutes, or until tender. Drizzle with pomegranate syrup and serve immediately.

Savoury roast pumpkin

Serves 4–6

Serve this roast pumpkin with roast beef, pan-fried lamb cutlets or a hearty casserole. It can also be stirred into a risotto or added to a rice pilaf.

1 kg pumpkin
oil
1 onion, diced
1 clove garlic, crushed
1 red chilli, de-seeded and diced
1 red capsicum, diced

Preheat oven to 180°C.

Peel the pumpkin and remove the seeds. Cut into 2–3 cm dice.

Heat an ovenproof frypan over a medium heat. Add the oil, onion, garlic and chilli and cook for 3–4 minutes, stirring often, until fragrant. Add the capsicum and pumpkin and cook for 10 minutes, stirring often.

Place in the preheated oven and cook for 30–40 minutes, or until tender.

Roasted root vegetable chips

Serves 6

We're very keen on roasting vegetables in this way, as it gives them such a tasty golden coating. We eat them whether we're having a roast dinner or not.

3 medium swedes
3 large carrots
4 medium parsnips
6 large potatoes
salt and freshly ground black pepper
olive oil

Preheat oven to 180°C.

Peel swedes, carrots and parsnips and cut into long, fat, chip-shape pieces. Place in a bowl. Scrub potatoes and cut into 8 wedges each. Add potatoes to other vegetables, sprinkle salt and pepper over and toss with enough olive oil to coat.

Arrange in a single layer on baking tray(s) and cook on the top shelf of the preheated oven for 40 minutes or until golden brown and crispy.

Sesame sweet potato wedges

Serves 4–6

Sweet potato is excellent for the barbecue as it cooks fairly quickly.

2 medium sweet potatoes
2 tbsp sesame oil or olive oil
salt and freshly ground black pepper

Peel the sweet potatoes then cut in half lengthways. Then cut each half lengthways into 4 wedges. Mix oil with a little salt and pepper.

Place the wedges on an oiled barbecue grill, brush with oil and cook for 10 minutes in total, turning from time to time.

Mashed swede

Serves 4

If you find the flavour of swede a little too strong, try a mash using a mix of swede and potato or carrot.

4 small swedes (1 kg)
3 tbsp butter
salt and freshly ground black pepper

Peel the swedes and cut them into large chunks. Place the swedes in a saucepan of water and bring to the boil. Cook for 15–20 minutes, until tender.

Drain the swedes and return them to the saucepan. Place the saucepan over a low heat and cook for 1–2 minutes, shaking the pan occasionally to evaporate excess moisture.

Remove from heat and mash the swedes until smooth. Stir in butter and season with salt and pepper.

Mashed turnips
Prepare exactly as for mashed swedes and finish with butter, chopped parsley, salt and pepper. This is particularly good with roast duck.

Spinach with lemon and almonds

Serves 4

This dish is easy to make, tasty and nutritious, so ensure that it's on your family menu this week.

2 tbsp olive oil
110 g (⅔ cup) blanched almonds
200 g spinach leaves
2 tbsp lemon juice
salt and freshly ground black pepper

Heat a large heavy-based frypan over a medium–high heat. Add oil and blanched almonds. Cook the almonds by tossing regularly until they're golden brown. Add the spinach leaves and cook, stirring, until they collapse and soften.

Add lemon juice, salt and freshly ground black pepper. Stir well to combine and remove from heat. Serve immediately.

Roasted Roma tomatoes

Serves 4

Egg-shaped Roma tomatoes are at their peak in autumn. They are excellent to cook with as they have lots of flesh, few seeds and little juice, so they hold their shape well when cooked.

250 g Roma tomatoes
60 ml (¼ cup) olive oil
2 cloves garlic, crushed
1 tbsp balsamic vinegar
1 tsp sugar
sprigs of thyme or oregano
salt and freshly ground black pepper

Preheat oven to 180°C.

Cut the tomatoes in half and place them skin side down in a baking tray. Mix the oil, garlic, vinegar and sugar and brush onto the cut side of the tomatoes. Scatter fresh herbs over the tomatoes and sprinkle with salt and pepper.

Place the tray in the preheated oven and cook for 30 minutes, or until the tomatoes are tender.

Roasted roma tomatoes with feta and basil
When the roasted tomatoes come out of the oven, crumble 75 g marinated goat's feta and chopped basil leaves over them.

Toffee tomatoes

Makes 20–25

These make a smart addition to virtually any special Saturday-night dinner party.

1 punnet cherry tomatoes
110 g (½ cup) caster sugar
60 ml (¼ cup) water

Line a flat tray with baking paper. Ensure that the cherry tomatoes are nice and clean, then stick a toothpick into each one and place them on the tray.

To make the toffee, place the caster sugar and water in a saucepan. Cook over a low heat until the sugar dissolves. Increase the heat and boil the liquid. Cook for 12–15 minutes, or until the liquid begins to turn a golden caramel colour. If needed, carefully swirl the saucepan to mix the caramel.

Remove the saucepan from the heat before the mixture becomes dark brown. Working quickly, and holding only the toothpick, dip each tomato into the hot caramel, making sure that the tomato is completely covered. Allow excess caramel to drip back into the saucepan. Place the tomatoes onto the tray and allow to cool.

Zucchini with raisins and pine nuts

Serves 4

This is a classic southern Italian dish which blends pan-fried zucchini with sweet and sour flavours.

250 g small zucchinis
oil
1 clove garlic, thinly sliced
50 g (⅓ cup) pine nuts
55 g (⅓ cup) raisins
6 mint leaves, thinly sliced
2 tbsp lemon juice
salt and freshly ground black pepper

Trim the ends off the zucchini, then cut into ½ cm thick rings. Heat a large frypan over a medium–high heat and add a splash of oil. Add the zucchini and garlic and cook until the zucchini slices are pale gold on each side. Add the pine nuts and stir well for 1–2 minutes.

Add the raisins, mint leaves and lemon juice and remove from heat. Season with salt and pepper.

Zucchini with red wine vinegar and basil
Cook the zucchini as directed in the oil, then remove from heat and drizzle with red wine vinegar and freshly chopped basil. Season with salt and freshly ground black pepper.

Wok-fried Asian greens

Serves 4

In this recipe any greens can be used, such as bok choy, Chinese broccoli, choy sum or water spinach. Adjust cooking times slightly for the larger greens.

2 tbsp peanut oil
2 tsp grated ginger
2 cloves garlic, crushed
1–2 bunches Asian greens, washed
chicken stock or water
½ tsp sesame oil

Heat a wok over a high heat. Add oil, then ginger and garlic and cook for 1 minute until fragrant, stirring often. Add greens and toss well to coat with ginger and garlic until just beginning to wilt. Add a splash of stock (or water), toss and cover wok with lid and allow to cook for 2–3 minutes.

Remove lid, allow any excess water to evaporate. Stir sesame oil through and serve immediately.

SALADS

+ dressings
fresh flavours

Many people think of salads as summer food, when in fact they're an important part of our diets all year round. At the very least we should eat a green salad with a main meal every day. The simplest salads are made up of good, fresh leaves – all you need to do is toss them in a bowl with some vinegar and extra-virgin olive oil, and they're ready to go.

The variety of fresh leaves available these days is phenomenal, from baby cos, frisee, lamb's tongues, oakleaf and mignonette to wild rocket and baby spinach leaves. Of course, salads can be far more than just leaves. They can contain raw or cooked vegetables, olives, feta and other cheeses, seafood and meats. Others are ideal as entrees, offering a perfect blend of flavours but without being too filling.

salad recipes

dressings

Classic salad dressing	504
Lemon dressing	504
Anchovy dressing	504
Pomegranate dressing	504
Nahm jim dressing	504
Caesar dressing	504
Yoghurt dressing	505
Thai dressing	505
Miso dressing	505
Mirin dressing	505
Chinese dressing	505

salads

Green salad	506
Greek salad	506
Rocket, parmigiano and pomegranate salad	506
Baby spinach, bacon and crispy crouton salad	507
Pear, walnut and rocket salad	507
Rocket, fig, blue cheese and crispy prosciutto salad	508
Tomato, bocconcini and basil salad	509
Tomato and white bean salad	509
Tomato and roast capsicum salad	510
Blood orange and fennel salad	510
Caesar salad	511
Salad of fennel, walnuts and parmigiano	513
Potato salad	514
Beetroot salad	514
Beetroot, rocket and yoghurt salad	515
Beetroot fattouche	515
Green bean, almond and feta salad	516
Watercress tabouli	516
Walnut tabouli salad	517
Asian coleslaw	517
Simple bok choy salad	518
Tuna nicoise à la our house	518
Barbecued vegetable salad	519
Chickpea, feta and coriander salad	520
Lentil and chickpea salad	520
Eggplant, pine nut and coriander salad	521
Smoked trout and avocado salad	521
Tuna, cannellini beans and asparagus salad	522
Honey and zaatar carrot salad	522
Middle Eastern carrot salad	523
Roast pumpkin, feta, olive and spinach salad	523
Lively mushroom salad	524
Sweet potato, smoked chicken, bocconcini and rocket salad	524
Moroccan couscous salad	525
Moroccan chicken salad	525
Roast vegetable, brown rice and goat's cheese salad	526
Asian noodle salad	528
Ramen noodle and sesame salad	528
Sichuan chicken salad	529
Thai chicken salad	531
Prawn, roast tomato, green bean and egg salad	532
Vietnamese beef noodle salad	534
Vietnamese prawn and mint salad	535
Hot Thai salmon and lychee salad	536
Thai-style calamari salad	537
Pink grapefruit and coriander salad with prawns	537
Crab, blood orange and panzanella salad	538
Asparagus and green tea noodle salad with Thai prawns	540
Asparagus and broad bean mograbieh salad with barbecued salmon	541
Sumac beef salad with lentils, grapes and parsley	543
Beef salad with hot and sour flavours	544
Spice-crusted quail salad with pomegranate dressing	545

Things you need to know about salads

1 All lettuces must be washed. Some lettuces, such as spinach and frisee, usually need 2 attempts to remove all the grit.

2 Lettuce must be dried well. This keeps it crisp and ensures that the dressing will stick to it.

3 A salad spinner is an essential tool to make sure your lettuce leaves are perfectly dry. You'll also need a large bowl for tossing salads and a couple of good platters and bowls for serving.

4 Most salad dressings are a ratio of 3 parts oil to 1 part vinegar (acid).

5 Add your seasoning to the vinegar or juice to dissolve it. You cannot successfully season dressing once the oil is added.

6 We usually make a small batch of dressing and keep it in a jar in the cupboard. Then all we have to do is shake and drizzle.

7 Different vinegars will add variety to your salads; we generally alternate between red wine, sherry and balsamic vinegar.

8 Likewise, your oil will make a difference; this is where good-quality extra-virgin olive oil shines. We usually have a fruity and a peppery extra-virgin olive oil on hand.

9 Some of our recipes have a separate dressing while in others the dressing is part of the salad itself.

10 We also use mustard, walnut or almond oil, and peanut oil for Asian-influenced salads.

11 To add slivers or shavings of vegetables, use a vegetable peeler. The long, thin strips are much easier to eat in salads than chunky, diced or sliced vegetables.

12 Roasted and barbecued vegetables also work as they introduce flavours and textures that you can't achieve with raw ingredients.

13 We like to soak raw onion slices in hot tap water to remove the worst of the onion's powerful taste. Don't leave them to soak too long or they will lose their crispness.

14 Salads need to be dressed; whether it's a squeeze of lemon juice and a splash of extra-virgin olive oil, or more complex variations.

15 You can swap red vinegar for herb, white wine or balsamic vinegar; use lime juice instead of lemon; exchange the extra-virgin olive oil for lemon-, peanut- or parmesan-infused oil; or go for grain mustard instead of Dijon. Place all the ingredients in a jar, put on the lid and shake well, and the dressing is ready to use.

Classic salad dressing

1 tbsp red wine vinegar
½ tsp Dijon mustard
salt and freshly ground black pepper
60 ml (¼ cup) extra-virgin olive oil

Mix together vinegar, mustard, salt and pepper. Add extra-virgin olive oil and whisk well.

Lemon dressing

1 tbsp lemon juice
½ tsp Dijon mustard
salt and freshly ground black pepper
60 ml (¼ cup) extra-virgin olive oil

Mix together lemon juice, mustard, salt and pepper. Add extra-virgin olive oil and whisk well.

Anchovy dressing

6 anchovy fillets, finely chopped
1 clove garlic, crushed
1 tbsp lemon juice
60 ml (¼ cup) olive oil
freshly ground black pepper

Prepare dressing by whisking all ingredients together.

Pomegranate dressing

1 tbsp lemon juice
1 tbsp pomegranate molasses
1 tsp sumac (optional)
salt and freshly ground black pepper
60 ml (¼ cup) extra-virgin olive oil

Mix together lemon juice, pomegranate molasses, sumac (if using), salt and pepper. Add extra-virgin olive oil and whisk well.

Nahm jim dressing

Make this dressing when you want a burst of flavour in a seafood or chicken salad.

2 small red chillies
1 clove garlic, crushed
2 tbsp grated palm sugar
2 tbsp fish sauce
2 tbsp lime juice
freshly ground black pepper

Split the chillies in half and remove the seeds. Chop finely, and mix with the crushed garlic, palm sugar, fish sauce and lime juice. Check flavour, adding a good burst of black pepper to make the dressing fresh, salty and sweet.

Caesar dressing

This is a great, full-flavoured dressing that can be used in many salads other than the classic caesar.

3 eggs
2 anchovies (optional)
2 tsp Dijon mustard
2 tbsp red wine vinegar
salt and freshly ground black pepper
125 ml (½ cup) extra-virgin olive oil

Place the eggs in a small saucepan. Bring to the boil and cook for 3 minutes. Refresh under cold running water. When cool, peel the shells and place the soft-boiled eggs in a food processor. Add anchovies (if using), mustard, vinegar, salt and pepper. Whiz until creamy. Drizzle in extra-virgin olive oil until it's all incorporated. If the dressing is too thick, add 1–2 tbsp boiling water.

Cheat's caesar dressing
Mix 2 tbsp ready-made mayonnaise with 2 tbsp of Classic Salad Dressing and 2 chopped anchovies.

Yoghurt dressing

Try this dressing in salads which are served with spiced grilled meats.

180 g (¾ cup) natural yoghurt
2 tbsp lemon juice
2 cloves garlic, crushed
salt and freshly ground black pepper
1 tbsp tahini

Mix all the ingredients together. Keep refrigerated.

Thai dressing

As you would expect, this is just the thing for lighter seafood or chicken salads in summer.

1 tbsp grated palm sugar
1 tbsp fish sauce
1 tbsp lime juice
freshly ground black pepper
2 tbsp peanut oil

Dissolve the palm sugar in the fish sauce and lime juice. Add black pepper and oil. Mix together well.

Miso dressing

An excellent dressing for salads with a Japanese flavour base. It's especially good with a beef salad.

2 tbsp miso paste
2 tbsp boiling water
2 tsp caster sugar
1 tsp sesame oil

Dissolve the miso in boiling water. Add the caster sugar and oil.

Mirin dressing

Try this dressing with any Japanese-style salads, especially those using udon or soba noodles.

1 tbsp grated palm sugar
2 tbsp lime juice
1 tbsp fish sauce
2 tbsp mirin
freshly ground black pepper
2 tbsp chopped coriander leaves
60 ml (¼ cup) peanut oil

Dissolve the palm sugar in the lime juice, fish sauce and mirin. Add pepper, coriander and oil. Whisk together well.

Chinese dressing

A sweet dressing for Asian-inspired salads.

2 tsp caster sugar
1 tbsp light soy sauce
1 tbsp Chinese cooking wine
2 tsp sesame oil

Mix the ingredients together, ensuring that the caster sugar dissolves.

Green salad

Serves 6

Green salad doesn't mean all the leaves have to be green. You could just as easily add some bitter radicchio leaves for a striking contrast in both taste and colour.

250 g salad leaves, washed
1 Lebanese cucumber, peeled and thinly sliced
1 tbsp red wine vinegar
½ tsp Dijon mustard
salt and freshly ground black pepper
60 ml (¼ cup) extra virgin olive oil

Toss salad leaves and cucumber together. Mix together vinegar, mustard, salt and pepper. Add oil and whisk well. Toss dressing through salad.

Greek salad

Serves 6

Greek salad is known around the world as a simple yet satisfying combination. It makes regular appearances on our table throughout summer.

1 Lebanese cucumber
½ red capsicum
200 g feta
3 ripe tomatoes
½ red onion, thinly sliced
1 cos lettuce, washed
90 g (½ cup) kalamata olives
2 tbsp chopped parsley
1½ tbsp lemon juice
salt and freshly ground black pepper
60 ml (¼ cup) extra virgin olive oil

Peel cucumber and remove seeds. Slice thinly. Dice capsicum and feta into 1 cm squares. Cut tomatoes into wedges.

Mix cucumber, capsicum, feta and tomatoes, onion, lettuce, olives and parsley in a bowl.

Whisk lemon juice, salt and pepper together. Add oil and whisk well. Toss dressing through salad.

Rocket, parmigiano and pomegranate salad

Serves 6

The textural combination of peppery rocket leaves and crunchy pomegranate seeds is amazing in this salad.

1 pomegranate
100 g rocket
60 g (¾ cup) shaved parmigiano
Pomegranate Dressing (page 504)

Remove the fruit from the pomegranate skin. You need to ensure that all the yellow inside skin has been removed, as it is quite bitter. Toss seeds with the rocket and parmigiano. Dress with pomegranate dressing to serve.

Baby spinach, bacon and crispy crouton salad

Serves 4–6

This salad makes a classic light lunch in the warmer months.

125 g crusty bread
oil
8 slices bacon
100 g baby spinach
2 hard-boiled eggs (optional)
Caesar Dressing (page 504) to serve

Dice the bread into 1 cm chunks. Heat a heavy-based pan over a medium heat, and add a generous splash of oil and the chunks of bread. Stir for 6–8 minutes, until the bread becomes quite toasty. Drain on absorbent paper.

Return the pan to the heat, adding more oil if necessary, and cook the bacon until crispy. Set aside to drain and cool.

Cut the bacon into 1 cm pieces. Place the spinach leaves in a serving bowl, then add the bacon and croutons. Chop the eggs roughly (if using) and scatter on top.

Drizzle Caesar Dressing over and serve.

Pear, walnut and rocket salad

Serves 4

You can add radicchio leaves to this salad to vary it a bit if you wish.

100 g rocket
80 g (⅔ cup) toasted walnuts
1 pear
60 g (¾ cup) shaved parmigiano (optional)
Classic Salad Dressing (page 504)

Place the rocket and walnuts in a bowl. Just before serving, quarter the pear and slice it thinly. Add the pear to the salad, along with parmigiano (if using). Toss with Classic Salad Dressing and serve.

Rocket, fig, blue cheese and crispy prosciutto salad

Serves 4–6

This is a salad with an amazing combination of flavours and textures, combining crispy prosciutto and peppery rocket with succulent figs and pungent blue cheese.

12 slices prosciutto
100 g wild rocket
6 figs, quartered
100 g blue cheese, crumbled
Classic Salad Dressing (page 504)

Heat a large frypan over a medium heat. Add the prosciutto and cook for 1–2 minutes on each side, until crispy. Break into 3 cm pieces.

Place the rocket in a bowl with the figs, blue cheese and crispy prosciutto. Toss gently with dressing when ready to serve.

Tomato, bocconcini and basil salad

Serves 4–6

This classic combination is always at its best in late summer. If the budget allows, upgrade from baby bocconcini to 2 buffalo mozzarella.

4 ripe tomatoes, cut into wedges
½ red onion, thinly sliced
12 baby bocconcini, halved
handful of torn basil leaves
salt and freshly ground black pepper
Classic Salad Dressing (page 504)

Toss all the ingredients together gently.

Tomato and white bean salad

Serves 6

This simple salad is a refreshing mix of ripe tomatoes, crisp cucumbers and tender white beans.

100 g (½ cup) white beans (cannellini), soaked overnight
3 ripe tomatoes, diced
2 Lebanese cucumbers, diced
2 spring onions, thinly sliced
1 tbsp chopped mint leaves
2 tbsp lemon juice
2 tbsp extra virgin olive oil
salt and freshly ground black pepper

Drain soaked beans and rinse under cold running water. Cook in boiling water until tender, about 30 minutes. Drain and cool.

Mix beans with other salad ingredients and season to taste.

Tomato and roast capsicum salad

Serves 4

The flavours of the sun are evident in every bite of this delicious salad.

1 red capsicum
2 tbsp olive oil
4 sun-ripened tomatoes
fresh basil leaves, torn
salt and freshly ground black pepper
1 tbsp sherry vinegar
60 ml (¼ cup) olive oil, additional

Preheat oven to 200°C.

Rub capsicum all over with olive oil and place in a baking tray. Cook for 20–30 minutes, turning occasionally until blistered. Place capsicum in a plastic bag and seal. The steam created will lift the skins away from the flesh. Allow to cool, then remove all skin and seeds and slice into thin strips.

Cut eyes from tomatoes. Cut in half, then into thin wedges. Mix tomato with capsicum, basil leaves, salt, freshly ground black pepper, vinegar and oil. Allow to stand for at least 30 minutes at room temperature, then serve.

Blood orange and fennel salad

Serves 4

The amazing tang of blood oranges and the freshness of fennel are a winning combination in this brilliant salad.

1 red onion, sliced
2 fennel bulbs
4 blood oranges
90 g baby spinach leaves, washed
90 g (½ cup) kalamata olives
generous handful of flat-leaf parsley
1 tbsp sherry vinegar
salt and freshly ground black pepper
60 ml (¼ cup) olive oil

Pour hot tap water onto onion and allow to stand for 2 minutes before draining. Place in a large bowl. Remove tough outer layer from fennel bulbs. Cut in half, remove core and slice fennel thinly. Add this to the onions.

Using a sharp knife remove all the peel and pith from oranges. Then remove the segments from the membrane, so that each segment is free from any pith or seeds. Squeeze any excess juice from orange membrane into a bowl and set aside for the dressing. Add blood orange segments to the fennel, along with the spinach leaves, olives, parsley and vinegar.

Add the salt and pepper to the blood orange juice and whisk together. Add oil. Drizzle dressing over salad and toss together gently.

Caesar salad

Serves 4

There are hundreds of ways to prepare this famous salad. This is how we do it. The dressing will make enough for 2 salads and will keep for 2 weeks in the refrigerator.

3 eggs
2 anchovies (optional)
2 tsp Dijon mustard
2 tbsp red wine vinegar
salt and freshly ground black pepper
125 ml (½ cup) olive oil

4 slices bacon
125 g day-old bread, diced 1 cm
oil
1 cos lettuce
90 g (1 cup) shaved parmigiano
1 tbsp chopped parsley

Place eggs in a small saucepan, bring to the boil and cook for 3 minutes. Refresh under cold water. When cool, peel shells and place soft-boiled eggs in food processor. Add anchovies if using, mustard, vinegar, salt and pepper. Whiz until creamy. Drizzle in oil until all incorporated. If thick add 1–2 tbsp boiling water.

Cut bacon into chunks. Heat a frypan over a medium–high heat and cook the bacon until crispy. Remove from pan and set aside. Return pan to heat, add a generous splash of oil and cook bread until golden brown.

Wash lettuce and tear leaves into bite-sized pieces. Combine lettuce, bacon, croutons and half of the cheese in a bowl. Pour over just enough dressing to coat each piece. Toss to combine and serve with remaining cheese, and parsley on top.

Salad of fennel, walnuts and parmigiano

Serves 4

This is the type of salad that needs no accompaniment; it's simply perfect in its own right. We would serve a salad like this as its own course, after mains but before cheese, on a big dinner party night.

1 red onion, sliced
1 fennel bulb
90 g (1 cup) walnuts, toasted
60 g (¾ cup) shaved parmigiano
handful each of radicchio leaves and baby spinach leaves
1 tbsp sherry vinegar
salt and freshly ground black pepper
60 ml (¼ cup) extra virgin olive oil

Pour hot tap water onto onion and allow to stand for 2 minutes before draining.

Remove tough outer skin layer of fennel. Cut in half, remove core and slice fennel thinly. Roughly chop walnuts and toss with onion, fennel, parmigiano and salad leaves.

Whisk vinegar and salt and pepper together. Whisk in oil. Dress salad when ready to serve.

Potato salad

Serves 6

Potato salad is an essential summer experience, though we often serve it in the cooler months, too, with pan-fried sausages or Danish Beef Burgers (page 259).

1 ½ kg waxy potatoes, washed (peeled if preferred)
6 slices bacon, diced
10 cornichons, chopped
¼ cup chopped flat-leaf parsley leaves
3 hard-boiled eggs, diced
Mayonnaise (page 554)
freshly ground black pepper

Boil the potatoes until just cooked. Drain and allow to cool. Cut into 1 cm slices, or dice if preferred. Place in a bowl.

Heat a small frypan over a medium–high heat. Cook the bacon until crispy, then break it into small pieces.

Mix the potatoes, bacon, cornichons, parsley, eggs and mayonnaise together. Grind fresh black pepper over and serve.

Ruth's potato salad
Cook potatoes with 2 sprigs of Vietnamese mint. Drain, allow to cool and then mix with mayonnaise, a handful of chopped Vietnamese mint leaves and lots of freshly ground black pepper.

Beetroot salad

Serves 4

It's rare that we're without beetroot in our kitchen as it is so easy to prepare. Try this salad to find out for yourself.

1 bunch baby beetroots, or 3 large
1 tbsp red wine vinegar
salt and freshly ground black pepper
2 tbsp mustard seed oil
1 tbsp chopped chives

Remove and discard leaves from beetroots. Place beetroot in a saucepan and cover with water. Bring to the boil, reduce to a simmer and cook until tender, about 30 minutes. Drain and allow to cool. When cool remove skins, cut flesh into evenly sized wedges and place in a bowl.

Whisk together vinegar, salt and pepper and oil. Pour over beetroots and top with chopped chives.

Beetroot salad with tomato and mozzarella
Add 2 tomatoes, cut into wedges, torn basil leaves and slices of fresh mozzarella – buffalo mozzarella if you can get it.

Beetroot, rocket and yoghurt salad

Serves 4–6

We're big fans of beetroot and this is just one of the ways we get to incorporate it in a refreshing salad.

3 beetroots, leaves trimmed
100 g rocket
½ red onion, thinly sliced
Yoghurt Dressing (page 505)

Place the beetroots in a saucepan, cover with water and bring to the boil. Reduce heat, cover with a lid and cook for 30–40 minutes, depending on their size, until tender. Drain, allow to cool, then peel and cut into wedges.

Place the rocket in a bowl and add the beetroot wedges and onion slices. Drizzle Yoghurt Dressing over to serve.

Beetroot fattouche

Serves 4

You may well have noticed our obsession with beetroot, but feel free to make this salad with other vegetables such as tomato, asparagus, green beans or artichokes.

1 bunch baby beetroots, or 3 large
1 red onion, sliced
1 tsp sumac
125 g pide bread, or foccacia
olive oil
1 baby cos, washed
1 Lebanese cucumber, halved and sliced
generous handful of flat-leaf parsley leaves
2 tbsp lemon juice
salt and freshly ground black pepper
60 ml (¼ cup) olive oil

Remove and discard leaves from beetroots. Place in a saucepan and cover with water. Bring to the boil, reduce to a simmer and cook until tender, about 30 minutes. Drain and allow to cool. When cool remove skins, cut flesh into evenly sized wedges and place in a bowl.

Pour hot tap water onto onion and allow to stand for 2 minutes before draining. When cool toss onion slices with sumac.

Dice pide bread into 1 cm chunks. Heat a heavy-based pan over a medium heat, then add a generous splash of olive oil and the bread chunks. Stir until bread becomes quite toasty, about 6–8 minutes. Mix beetroot with onion, bread chunks, lettuce, cucumber and parsley. Whisk lemon juice, salt and pepper together, then whisk in oil. Dress salad when ready to serve.

Green bean, almond and feta salad

Serves 6

This salad has become a modern classic for many people. It was introduced to us by our friend Sue Sloan, to whom we are eternally grateful.

500 g green beans, ends trimmed
100 g (1 cup) flaked almonds, toasted
100 g feta, crumbled
2 tbsp chopped parsley leaves
1 tbsp red wine vinegar
salt and freshly ground black pepper
60 ml (¼ cup) olive oil

Cook beans in boiling water for 2 minutes. Refresh under cold water immediately. Cut beans in half and place on a platter.

Top with toasted almonds, feta and parsley. Whisk vinegar, salt and pepper together. Add oil and whisk well. Drizzle dressing over salad.

Asparagus, almond and feta salad
Use asparagus spears instead of green beans.

Watercress tabouli

Serves 6

Tabouli really gets a lift by using watercress instead of parsley. We often serve this salad with Moroccan turkey at Christmas lunch and on any other salad-friendly days.

150 g (¾ cup) burghul
1 bunch watercress, picked and washed
½ red onion, finely diced
500 g firm ripe tomatoes, diced
2 tbsp lemon juice
60 ml (¼ cup) extra virgin olive oil
salt and freshly ground black pepper

Soak burghul in cold water for 20 minutes, drain well. Chop watercress roughly. Place burghul, watercress, onion and tomatoes in a bowl. Mix well. Add lemon juice and olive oil. Season to taste with salt and pepper.

Rocket tabouli
Swap watercress for 100 g washed and chopped rocket.

Walnut tabouli salad

Serves 4–6

This is a twist on the classic tabouli, with walnuts adding crunch. You may also wish to add a handful of rocket leaves.

- 200 g (1 cup) burghul
- 1 pomegranate (optional)
- 1 red onion, thinly sliced
- 1 cup flat-leaf parsley leaves
- 1 cup coriander leaves
- 120 g (1 cup) toasted walnuts, roughly chopped
- Pomegranate Dressing (page 504)

Soak the burghul in plenty of cold water for 30 minutes. Drain and place in a large bowl.

If using the pomegranate, remove the seeds from the skin, ensuring that all the bitter yellow inside skin is discarded. Set some of the pomegranate seeds aside for a garnish.

Place the majority of the pomegranate in the bowl with the burghul, along with the onion, parsley, coriander and walnuts.

Toss the salad with Pomegranate Dressing just before serving.

Asian coleslaw

Serves 6

This salad is good if you're having a large group over. It is excellent just as it is, or you can top it with roast beef, roast duck or barbecue chicken pieces.

- ½ wonga bok (Chinese cabbage), sliced
- 2 carrots, shredded
- 6 spring onions, thinly sliced
- ½ cup coriander leaves
- 1 tbsp shaved palm sugar
- 2 tbsp fish sauce
- 60 ml (¼ cup) lime juice
- freshly ground black pepper
- 60 ml (¼ cup) peanut oil

Toss wonga bok, carrot, spring onions and coriander together. Dissolve palm sugar in fish sauce and lime juice. Add pepper and whisk in oil. Toss vegetables with dressing and pile onto a platter.

Simple bok choy salad

Serves 6

A salad such as this is excellent with meats from the barbecue or as part of any good feast with food-loving friends.

150 g baby bok choy, washed
½ cup coriander leaves
½ red capsicum, thinly sliced
6 spring onions, thinly sliced
4 red shallots, thinly sliced

2 tbsp lime juice
½ tsp fish sauce
salt and freshly ground black pepper
60 ml (¼ cup) peanut oil

Toss bok choy, coriander, capsicum, spring onions and shallots together. Place in a serving bowl.

Whisk lime juice, fish sauce, salt, pepper and oil together. Pour dressing over salad.

Tuna nicoise à la our house

Serves 4 (or us 2)

When we have had one of those days and it's all too much, we put the children to bed early and make a massive bowl of tuna nicoise, open a bottle of wine and relax. Somehow the worries of the day seem to slip away as we talk, eat and drink together.

1 baby cos, washed and torn into bite-sized pieces
4 potatoes, diced and boiled
500 g green beans, blanched
2 tomatoes, cut into wedges

4 boiled eggs, cut into wedges
100 g (⅔ cup) kalamata olives
300 g canned tuna
Anchovy Dressing (page 504)
chopped parsley to garnish

In a large platter put down first a layer of lettuce, then a second layer comprising potatoes, beans, tomato, egg and olives. Drain tuna and scatter it over the other ingredients. Drizzle the anchovy dressing over, sprinkle parsley and serve with crusty bread and the aforementioned bottle of wine.

Fresh tuna nicoise
Grill 4 x 200 g tuna steaks and serve them on top of the salad in place of the canned tuna.

Salmon nicoise
Grill 4 x 200 g salmon steaks and serve then on top of the salad in place of the canned tuna.

Barbecued vegetable salad

Serves 6–8

This salad is a beauty because it shows once and for all that the barbecue can do much more than just cook steaks and chops.

1 eggplant, cut into 8 wedges, salted and rinsed
2 small zucchini, cut into quarters
1 red capsicum, cut in 6 wedges, seeds removed
100 g small mushrooms
60 ml (¼ cup) olive oil
1 tbsp sherry vinegar
salt and freshly ground black pepper
60 ml (¼ cup) olive oil, additional
1 tbsp sherry vinegar, additional
20 basil leaves, thinly sliced

Toss all vegetables with oil, vinegar, salt and pepper. Place vegetables on oiled barbecue grill. Cook for 20–30 minutes. Turn regularly and brush with more oil if needed.

Place vegetables on a platter. Drizzle with additional oil and vinegar. Sprinkle basil on top.

Chickpea, feta and coriander salad

Serves 4–6

When using feta in salads such as this, go for the softer-style feta in olive oil rather than the usual firm cheese in brine. It adds a rich and salty hit.

- 1 × 400 g can chickpeas, drained
- 1 red onion, thinly sliced
- 150 g feta, crumbled
- 1 cup coriander leaves
- 1 cup flat-leaf parsley leaves
- 2 tbsp lemon juice
- 1 tbsp pomegranate molasses
- 60 ml (¼ cup) olive oil
- salt and freshly ground black pepper

Lightly toss together the chickpeas, onion, feta and herbs. Add the lemon juice, pomegranate molasses, oil, salt and pepper. Serve immediately.

Chickpea, feta and rocket salad
Add 75 g rocket to the salad and omit the coriander.

Lentil and chickpea salad

Serves 6

This salad is an earthy accompaniment to any dish with a hint of spice.

- 1 × 400 g can chickpeas, drained
- 200 g (1 cup) cooked small green lentils
- 1 red onion, finely diced
- 1 cup coarsely chopped parsley leaves
- zest of 1 lemon, chopped
- 2 medium tomatoes, finely diced
- 1 small cucumber, finely diced
- 2 tbsp lemon juice
- 80 ml (⅓ cup) extra-virgin olive oil
- salt and freshly ground black pepper

Place the chickpeas, lentils, onion, parsley, lemon zest, tomatoes and cucumber in a large bowl. The salad can now be refrigerated until 1 hour before serving, or leave it to stand at room temperature, if time permits.

To serve, add lemon juice and extra-virgin olive oil and toss to combine. Season to taste.

Eggplant, pine nut and coriander salad

Serves 4–6

This eggplant salad is seriously good. It's similar to caponata, and has a touch of the Middle East with coriander, currants and pine nuts. It's great with roast beef, barbecued lamb chops and roast chicken.

3 eggplants
salt
oil
¼ cup currants
1 tbsp red wine vinegar
3 tomatoes, diced
1 cup coriander leaves
100 g (⅔ cup) toasted pine nuts
160 g (1 cup) pitted green olives, halved
2 tbsp capers, soaked in cold water
60 ml (¼ cup) extra-virgin olive oil
salt and freshly ground black pepper

Cut the eggplants in half, then slice each half to form 1 cm thick semi-circles. Sprinkle with salt and set aside for 20 minutes until juices bead on the surface. Rinse the eggplant and dry well. Brush the eggplant with oil and grill until tender and golden brown on each side. Set aside to cool.

Soak the currants in vinegar for 20 minutes. Place them in a large bowl, along with the cooled eggplant, diced tomatoes, coriander leaves, pine nuts and olives. Drain the capers, chop coarsely and add to the eggplant salad.

Add extra-virgin olive oil, season with salt and freshly ground black pepper and toss all the ingredients together. Place in a bowl to serve.

Smoked trout and avocado salad

Serves 4

Trout is a great match for creamy avocado, though the other ingredients also play their part in this salad.

500 g asparagus
2 smoked trout fillets
100 g rocket leaves
150 g cherry tomatoes, halved
2 avocados, peeled and sliced
2 tbsp chopped parsley
1 cucumber, sliced
Lemon Dressing (page 504)

Bring a large saucepan of water to the boil. Remove the woody ends from the asparagus and cook the spears in boiling water for 1–2 minutes. Refresh under cold running water, then cut the asparagus into 3 cm pieces on an angle.

Break the trout fillets into chunks, removing all bones. Place in a bowl, along with the asparagus, rocket, tomatoes, avocados, parsley and cucumber.

Toss with dressing to serve.

Tuna, cannellini beans and asparagus salad

Serves 4–6

A quick salad such as this is an appetising way to include oily fish and legumes in your daily diet.

500 g asparagus
350 g canned tuna in olive oil, drained
1 × 400 g can cannellini beans, drained
80 g (½ cup) Ligurian or other small black olives
½ cup flat-leaf parsley leaves
½ red onion, finely diced
1 small cucumber, quartered and sliced
1 punnet cherry tomatoes, quartered
Classic Salad Dressing (page 504)

Bring a saucepan of water to the boil. Remove the woody ends from the asparagus and cut the spears into 3 cm lengths. Cook in boiling water for 2 minutes. Drain and refresh under cold running water.

Place the asparagus in a bowl, along with the tuna, cannellini beans, olives, parsley, onion, cucumber and tomatoes. Toss with dressing to serve.

Honey and zaatar carrot salad

Serves 4

Carrots prepared in this way can be part of a Middle Eastern mezze, as their inherent sweetness makes them a natural match with spices and lemon juice.

oil
4 carrots, peeled and sliced
1 ½ tsp smoky paprika
1 tsp ground cumin
1 tsp ground coriander
1 tsp zaatar
pinch of saffron threads
1 tbsp honey
2–3 tbsp lemon juice
2 tbsp chopped coriander (optional)

Heat a heavy-based frypan over a medium heat. Add enough oil to cover the base of the pan and add the carrots, spices and saffron. Cook until the carrots are golden and beginning to become tender. Add the honey and lemon juice, reduce heat and cook for a further 3–4 minutes.

Remove from heat and place in a serving bowl. Sprinkle coriander over to serve, if desired.

Middle Eastern carrot salad

Serves 4

A stunning salad, best served as a side dish to accompany a tagine or Middle Eastern–inspired dish. Serve at room temperature.

4 carrots
olive oil
2 tsp cumin seeds
1 tsp sweet paprika
juice of ½ lemon, to serve

Preheat the oven to 180°C.

Peel the carrots and cut into slices. Heat a heavy-based frypan over medium heat. Add enough oil to cover the base of the pan, add cumin seeds and carrot slices. Cook until golden and the carrots are beginning to become tender. Sprinkle in the sweet paprika, then cook in the preheated oven until tender, about 10–15 minutes. Squeeze lemon juice over to serve.

Roast pumpkin, feta, olive and spinach salad

Serves 4–6

It's amazing how certain ingredients are transformed by roasting. This is especially true of pumpkin, which changes into a sweet vegetable that's perfect in a salad such as this.

350 g pumpkin, peeled, de-seeded and chopped into 3 cm chunks
oil
salt and freshly ground black pepper
150 g feta, crumbled
100 g baby spinach leaves
90 g (½ cup) kalamata olives
Classic Salad Dressing (page 504)

Preheat oven to 180°C.

Toss the pumpkin with a little oil, salt and pepper. Roast in the preheated oven for 20–30 minutes until tender. Set aside to cool.

Place the pumpkin, feta, spinach and olives in a large bowl. Toss with dressing to serve.

Lively mushroom salad

Serves 6

Make this salad in advance and toss it with the dressing just before serving. You may also like to cook the mushrooms the day before; if so, allow them to reach room temperature before serving.

oil
500 g mushrooms (Swiss brown, oyster and shiitake)
2 cloves garlic, crushed
freshly ground black pepper
60 ml (¼ cup) chicken stock or water

2 tbsp soy sauce
½ cup flat-leaf parsley leaves
¼ cup torn basil leaves
2 tbsp lemon juice
2 tbsp lime juice
60 ml (¼ cup) olive oil

Heat a large frypan over a medium heat. Add a generous splash of oil and the mushrooms and garlic, and season with pepper. Toss to combine and cook for 5–6 minutes, stirring often. Add stock or water and soy sauce, cover with a lid and cook for a further 5 minutes. Remove from frypan and set aside to cool.

When cool, add the herbs, citrus juice (enough to taste) and olive oil. Season to taste, then pile into a serving bowl.

Sweet potato, smoked chicken, bocconcini and rocket salad

Serves 4–6

We're lucky enough to have a local butcher who makes exceptional smoked chicken, so we regularly include it in pasta dishes and salads such as this in warmer weather.

2 sweet potatoes, peeled and diced into 2 cm chunks
oil
salt and freshly ground black pepper
6–8 bocconcini, halved

2 smoked chicken fillets, sliced
100 g wild rocket
75 g semi-dried tomatoes
80 g (½ cup) toasted pine nuts
Classic Salad Dressing (page 504)

Preheat oven to 180°C.

Toss the sweet potatoes with oil, salt and pepper and roast in the preheated oven for 20–30 minutes, until tender. Set aside to cool.

Place the sweet potato, bocconcini, smoked chicken, rocket, tomatoes and pine nuts in a large bowl. Toss with dressing to serve.

Moroccan couscous salad

Serves 6

This recipe involves quite a few different steps but it's well worth the effort.

2 tbsp olive oil
200 g (1 cup) instant couscous
250 ml (1 cup) water
pinch of salt
100 g (½ cup) chickpeas, soaked and cooked
200 g pumpkin, diced 5 mm and roasted
½ red capsicum, diced 5 mm
90 g (⅔ cup) toasted pine nuts
½ cup chopped coriander leaves
salt and freshly ground black pepper
Yoghurt Dressing (page 505)

Heat oil in a saucepan. Add couscous; stir to coat with oil. Add water and salt and bring to the boil. Remove from the heat, cover and leave to soak for 5 minutes.

Use a fork to break up the grains, then tip the couscous into a bowl and allow to cool.

Mix couscous with remaining ingredients. Season to taste. Drizzle Yoghurt Dressing over the top.

Moroccan chicken salad

Serves 6

We love to combine spicy flavours with meat such as chicken, then serve it atop masses of salad ingredients and chickpeas.

90 g (⅔ cup) plain flour
3 tsp ground cumin
3 tsp ground coriander
2 tsp chilli powder
1 tsp turmeric
salt and freshly ground black pepper
olive oil
4 skinless chicken breast fillets
250 g salad leaves, washed
handful of coriander leaves
90 g (½ cup) chickpeas, soaked and cooked
1 Lebanese cucumber, peeled and thinly sliced
1 avocado, peeled and sliced
1 tbsp sherry vinegar
salt and freshly ground black pepper
60 ml (¼ cup) olive oil

Preheat oven to 180°C.

Mix together flour and spices. Lightly coat chicken fillets with spice mixture. Heat a heavy-based frypan over a medium heat. Add a splash of oil and the chicken and cook for 2–3 minutes on each side until well browned. Place on tray and cook in preheated oven for 5–6 minutes, or until cooked. Set aside.

Mix together salad leaves, coriander, chickpeas, cucumber and avocado. Whisk vinegar, salt and pepper together, then slowly whisk in oil. Toss dressing with salad and divide between four plates.

Cut chicken into thick wedges and serve on top of salad.

Roast vegetable, brown rice and goat's cheese salad

Serves 6–8

The nuttiness of brown rice is combined with the sweetness of roasted vegetables to create a really fabulous salad. I have a personal dislike of 'hippy' food, but chef Megan Lilburn has completely turned my mind around with this dish. Thanks for the great recipe. MC

1 eggplant
salt
1 red capsicum, de-seeded and diced into 2 cm chunks
2 carrots, peeled, halved and thickly sliced
2 small zucchini, halved and cut into 2 cm slices
1 red onion, cut into wedges
oil
salt and freshly ground black pepper
100 g (½ cup) brown rice
75 g baby spinach leaves
Lemon Dressing (page 504)
90 g goat's cheese

Preheat oven to 180°C.

Cut the eggplants in half, then slice each half to form 1 cm thick semi-circles. Sprinkle with salt and set aside for 20 minutes until juices bead on the surface. Rinse the eggplant and dry well.

Place all the vegetables in a roasting dish. Toss with oil, salt and pepper and roast for 30–40 minutes, or until the vegetables are tender and golden brown. Set aside to cool.

Place the brown rice in a saucepan. Cover with plenty of water and bring to the boil. Reduce to a simmer, cover and cook for 20–30 minutes, or until the rice is tender. Drain and refresh under cold running water.

Mix the roast vegetables, brown rice and spinach leaves together. Just before serving, toss dressing through. Pile onto a platter and crumble goat's cheese over the top.

Asian noodle salad

Serves 6

A salad such as this is virtually a dish in its own right thanks to the delicious soba noodles that form its base. Cellophane noodles could also be used if you prefer.

125 g soba noodles
100 g snow peas
½ red capsicum, finely diced
1 carrot, shredded
2 Lebanese cucumbers, thinly sliced
4 red shallots, thinly sliced
20 Vietnamese mint leaves, shredded
Mirin Dressing (page 505)

Cook soba noodles in plenty of boiling water for 6–8 minutes. Refresh under cold water. Cook snow peas in boiling water for 2 minutes. Refresh under cold water and slice thinly.

Toss all ingredients together. To serve, mix salad with mirin dressing and pile onto a large platter.

Ramen noodle and sesame salad

Serves 4

This salad is more delicate than the other noodle recipes in this book. It's an ideal accompaniment to Steamed Thai Fish (page 286) or Soy Ginger Salmon (page 286).

180 g ramen noodles
2 spring onions, thinly sliced
¼ cup coriander leaves
1 small cucumber, sliced
1 tsp toasted sesame seeds
6 slices pickled ginger
250 g cooked asparagus (optional)
Chinese Dressing (page 505)

Bring a saucepan of water to the boil. Add the noodles and cook them for 3–4 minutes, or until al dente. Drain and refresh under cold running water.

Mix the noodles with the spring onions, coriander, cucumber, sesame seeds, ginger and asparagus (if using). Toss with dressing and serve.

Sichuan chicken salad

Serves 4–6

This is a quick and easy salad to whip up using leftover roast chicken, or you could use a pre-cooked chicken from a roast shop. The Salt and Pepper Spice really makes it. Make up a batch and keep it on hand in the cupboard. Before you know it, you'll be sprinkling it on everything.

150 g snow peas
½ roast chicken
½ iceberg lettuce, shredded
1 small cucumber, sliced
6 spring onions, thinly sliced
1 tsp chilli flakes
1 tsp Salt and Pepper Spice (page 295)
Chinese Dressing (page 505)

Bring a small saucepan of water to the boil. Remove the tips from the snow peas and cook them briefly in boiling water before refreshing under cold running water. Cut in half.

Remove the skin and bones from the chicken and shred the flesh. Place the chicken in a bowl, along with the snow peas, lettuce, cucumber and spring onions. Mix the chilli and Salt and Pepper Spice together.

Toss the dressing through the salad just before serving and sprinkle chilli and Salt and Pepper Spice over the top.

Thai chicken salad

Serves 4

This is another firm Campion–Curtis favourite, particularly when matched with a glass of lightly chilled riesling on a hot summer's night.

- 2 chicken breast fillets, skin removed
- 250 ml (1 cup) coconut milk
- 1 lemongrass stem, thinly sliced
- 2 small red chillies, halved
- 1 iceberg lettuce, washed and broken into bite-sized pieces
- 1 cucumber, skinned, halved and sliced
- handful of bean sprouts
- 6 shallots, sliced
- 1 cup coriander sprigs
- 150 g (1 cup) roast peanuts
- 1 tbsp shaved palm sugar
- 2 tbsp lime juice
- 1 tbsp fish sauce
- 1 small red chilli, de-seeded and diced
- freshly ground black pepper
- 60 ml (¼ cup) olive oil

Place chicken in a small saucepan and cover with coconut milk. Add lemongrass and chillies. Bring to the boil, lower heat and cook, covered, for 5 minutes. Turn chicken over and cook for a further 5 minutes. Check that chicken is cooked through. Allow to cool completely in coconut milk, then drain and slice thinly. Discard cooking liquid.

Combine lettuce, cucumber, bean sprouts, shallots, coriander, peanuts and cooked sliced chicken.

Prepare salad dressing by dissolving palm sugar in lime juice. Then stir in fish sauce, chilli and black pepper and whisk in olive oil. Toss dressing through salad and arrange on a large platter.

Coconut chicken and noodle salad
Combine cooked chicken with Asian Noodle Salad (page 528) instead of as described.

Thai prawn salad
Substitute 500 g cooked peeled prawns for chicken.

Thai beef salad
Combine 2 tbsp fish sauce and ¼ tsp chilli paste, and spread over 2 x 200 g sirloin steaks. Allow to marinate for at least 20 minutes. Place the steaks on a hot barbecue and cook for 6 minutes, rotating as needed. Turn the steaks over and cook for a further 4–5 minutes, again rotating as needed. Allow the steaks to rest on a cool part of the barbecue for 5 minutes before serving. Thinly slice the steaks and place them on top of the prepared salad in place of chicken.

Prawn, roast tomato, green bean and egg salad

Serves 6

A number of ingredients are layered with cos lettuce in this recipe, then topped with a creamy Caesar Dressing to create a truly impressive salad.

6 Roma tomatoes
oil
salt and freshly ground black pepper
1 tsp zaatar (optional)
250 g green beans
6 eggs
500 g green (raw) prawns
1 baby cos lettuce
Caesar Dressing (page 504)

Preheat oven to 180°C.

Cut the tomatoes in half. Rub with oil, season with salt and pepper, and sprinkle with zaatar (if using). Roast in the preheated oven for 30–40 minutes, or until tender.

Bring a saucepan of water to the boil. Cut the ends off the green beans and cut them in half. Cook in boiling water for 1–2 minutes. Drain and refresh under cold running water.

Place the eggs in a saucepan and cover with water. Bring to the boil, reduce to a simmer and cook for 8 minutes. Drain and refresh under cold running water. Peel the eggs and chop them into 6 segments. Set the eggs aside until needed.

Heat a large frypan over a medium–high heat. Add a splash of oil and cook the prawns, in batches if necessary, for 1–2 minutes on each side, until cooked.

Arrange the cos leaves on a platter. Place the roast tomatoes, eggs and prawns on top of the leaves and scatter with green beans. Drizzle dressing over and serve.

Vietnamese beef noodle salad

Serves 4–6

Lots of zingy flavours and great textures make this dish ideal for a light lunch or entree.

- 500 g beef – girello or scotch fillet
- 2 tbsp fish sauce
- 1 tbsp peanut oil
- 200 g rice vermicelli noodles
- 60 ml (¼ cup) lime juice
- 1 tbsp chilli paste
- 2 tbsp fish sauce, additional
- 1 tbsp shaved palm sugar
- 12 Vietnamese mint leaves, shredded
- freshly ground black pepper
- 60 ml (¼ cup) peanut oil, additional
- 100 g snow peas, blanched and thinly sliced
- ½ red capsicum, thinly sliced
- 100 g shiitake mushroom, finely diced
- 90 g (⅔ cup) cashew nuts, toasted
- 90 g bean sprouts
- 60 g crispy fried shallots

Preheat oven to 190°C.

Rub beef all over with fish sauce and peanut oil and marinate for 30 minutes. Heat a heavy-based pan over a high heat. Add beef and brown all over. Place on a baking tray and cook in oven for 30 minutes or until medium-rare. Remove and leave to cool.

Put the kettle on to boil. Pour boiling water over noodles. Allow to stand for at least 5 minutes, then drain.

Mix together lime juice, chilli paste, additional fish sauce, palm sugar, mint and pepper. Whisk in additional peanut oil. Thinly slice beef, then shred thinly. Place beef into a bowl with any cooking juices and the dressing. Stir until beef is coated and allow to marinate for 30 minutes.

Toss noodles with snow peas, red capsicum, mushrooms, cashew nuts and bean sprouts. Pile high on a platter, spoon the beef and dressing on top and scatter crispy fried shallots over.

Vietnamese prawn and mint salad

Serves 4–6

We often serve this salad as an entree when we have friends over for dinner. It goes well with an aromatic white wine and is packed with flavour and texture. It can also be adapted for chicken or beef, if you prefer.

- 500 g small cooked prawns
- 1 cucumber, peeled and thinly sliced
- 2 carrots, peeled and grated
- 1 small Chinese cabbage, thinly shredded
- 3 shallots, thinly sliced
- 2 kaffir lime leaves, shredded
- 10 mint leaves, shredded
- ½ cup loosely packed coriander leaves
- 45 g (⅓ cup) chopped roasted peanuts
- 2 small red chillies, de-seeded and diced
- 2 cm piece of ginger, grated
- 1 clove garlic, crushed
- 80–100 ml (⅓–½ cup) lime juice
- 2 tbsp vegetable oil
- 2 tbsp fish sauce
- ½ tsp white sugar

Peel the prawns and cut them in half lengthways. Place them in a large bowl with the cucumber, carrots, Chinese cabbage, shallots, kaffir lime leaves, mint leaves, coriander and peanuts. Mix together well.

Place the remaining ingredients in a separate bowl and whisk well.

When ready to serve, toss the dressing through the salad and mix well. Serve on a large platter to share.

Vietnamese chicken and mint salad
Pan-fry 2 chicken fillets. Allow to cool, then slice thinly and use instead of prawns.

Vietnamese beef and mint salad
Pan-fry 500 g beef fillet. Allow to cool, then slice thinly and use instead of prawns.

Hot Thai salmon and lychee salad

Serves 4–6

This salad combines spicy chillies, pungent fish sauce, slippery sweet lychees and chunks of just-cooked salmon.

1 tbsp fish sauce
1 tsp grated palm sugar
2 small red chillies, chopped
2 × 200 g salmon fillets
peanut oil
1 Lebanese cucumber, peeled
3 spring onions, thinly sliced
10 mint leaves, shredded

1 cup coriander sprigs
150 g (1 cup) roasted peanuts
20 lychees, peeled, halved and de-seeded
1 tbsp grated palm sugar
2 tbsp lime juice
1 tbsp fish sauce
2 small red chillies, de-seeded and diced
freshly ground black pepper

Make the marinade by mixing the fish sauce, palm sugar and chopped chillies together. Place the salmon in a shallow dish, pour the marinade over and set aside to marinate for at least 40 minutes, but no longer than 4 hours. Drain the salmon.

To cook the salmon, heat a small frypan or grill pan over a medium–high heat. Add a splash of oil and cook the salmon for 4 minutes on each side, or until the salmon is medium–rare. Set aside to cool.

Use a vegetable peeler to cut long thin strips from the cucumber, discarding the inner seeds. Place the cucumber in a colander and drain for 10 minutes. Place the spring onions, mint leaves, coriander, peanuts and lychees in a large bowl.

Prepare the salad dressing by dissolving the palm sugar in the lime juice, then adding the fish sauce and diced chillies.

Remove the skin and any bones from the salmon. Flake the salmon into pieces and add to the salad, along with the cucumber. Toss the dressing through the salad to taste and season with freshly ground black pepper.

Divide between plates or arrange on a large platter to serve.

Thai-style calamari salad

Serves 4–6

If preferred, the calamari could be swapped with cooked prawns or chunks of hot smoked salmon. The kaffir lime leaves are well worth the trouble of tracking down, though chopped lime zest will add a similar burst of freshness.

3 calamari tubes (750 g)
1 cucumber, peeled
6 shallots, thinly sliced
2 kaffir lime leaves, shredded, or zest of 2 limes
1 cup coriander leaves
1 small red chilli, de-seeded and sliced
1 iceberg lettuce
oil
2 tbsp crispy fried shallots
75 g (½ cup) roasted peanuts
Nahm Jim Dressing (page 504)

Cut the calamari down the side so they open out flat. Score the flesh on the diagonal, 1 cm apart. Cut the calamari into 5 cm × 2 cm pieces. Set aside until ready to cook.

Use a vegetable peeler to cut long strips from the cucumber, discarding the seeds and squeezing away excess moisture. Place the cucumber in a bowl, along with the shallots, kaffir lime leaves (or zest), coriander and chilli. Shred the iceberg lettuce and mix with the other salad ingredients.

When ready to serve, heat a large heavy-based frypan or wok over a high heat. Add a splash of oil and cook the calamari for 2–3 minutes, or until the calamari cooks and curls but is still tender. Remove from heat and drain briefly on kitchen paper.

Add the shallots and peanuts to the salad, along with the dressing and warm calamari. Toss together and divide between plates as an entree.

Pink grapefruit and coriander salad with prawns

Serves 4–6

Pink grapefruit are becoming more readily available, which is great because they are sweeter than the regular variety. That's what makes them perfect for a seafood salad such as this.

2 pink grapefruit
1 cup coriander leaves
½ cup Thai basil leaves
2 shredded kaffir lime leaves (optional)
2 small red chillies, sliced
1 cucumber, shredded
2 shallots, thinly sliced
oil
500 g peeled cooked prawns
Thai Dressing (page 505)

Peel the grapefruit with a sharp knife, removing the peel and outside pith. Cut down along the membrane to remove each segment. Place the grapefruit in a bowl, along with the coriander, basil, kaffir lime leaves (if using), chillies, cucumber and shallots.

Mix the dressing into the salad. To serve, arrange the prawns on a plate and top with salad.

Crab, blood orange and panzanella salad

Serves 4–6

If preparing the crab meat from scratch sounds too hard, substitute cooked prawns or crayfish.

1 kg blue-swimmer crabs or 400 g crab meat
salt
300 g day-old bread (pide or foccacia)
oil
4 blood oranges
½ cucumber, peeled, de-seeded and cut into ½ cm slices
1 radicchio, shredded
1 baby fennel bulb, thinly sliced
¼ cup chopped parsley
2 tbsp chopped basil
2 tbsp lemon juice
60 ml (¼ cup) extra-virgin olive oil
salt and freshly ground black pepper

If the crabs are still alive, put them to sleep by placing them in the freezer for 30 minutes before cooking. Bring a large saucepan of water to the boil. Add a generous handful of salt and the crabs, and cook for 15 minutes. Remove from heat, and allow to cool.

When the crabs are cool, crack their shells open and remove the flesh, taking care that no stray bits of shell make their way into the meat. Refrigerate until needed.

Roughly dice the bread into 1 cm square pieces. Heat a large frypan and add a generous splash of oil and the bread. Cook for 4–5 minutes, tossing often, until golden brown. Drain on absorbent paper and set aside until needed.

Using a sharp knife, remove all the peel and pith from the oranges. Remove the segments from the membrane, so that each segment is free from any pith or seeds. Squeeze any excess juice from the orange membrane into a bowl and set aside for the dressing.

Place the crab meat, bread, orange segments, cucumber, radicchio, fennel and chopped herbs in a large bowl. Add the lemon and orange juice and extra-virgin olive oil to the salad ingredients. Season with salt and pepper and toss lightly to combine. Divide between plates and serve.

Asparagus and green tea noodle salad with Thai prawns

Serves 6

The zingy dressing used in this recipe doubles as a marinade for the prawns.

2 tbsp grated palm sugar
80 ml (⅓ cup) lime juice
60 ml (¼ cup) fish sauce
2 small red chillies, de-seeded and diced
60 ml (¼ cup) peanut or olive oil
200 g green tea noodles

4 bunches asparagus
1 cup coriander leaves
½ cup Vietnamese mint leaves
½ cup Thai basil leaves
1 kg green (raw) prawns

Mix the palm sugar, lime juice and fish sauce together. Stir until sugar dissolves. Add the chillies and oil. Set aside 60 ml (¼ cup) of the liquid for use as a marinade; the remainder will be used as a dressing.

Bring a large saucepan of water to the boil and cook the green tea noodles for 8 minutes, or until al dente. Drain and cool under running water. Place in a bowl.

Bring another saucepan of water to the boil. Snap off and discard the asparagus ends. Cook asparagus in boiling water for 2–3 minutes, depending on thickness. Refresh under cold running water.

Cut asparagus into 5 cm lengths. Place in the bowl with the noodles, and add the herbs. Refrigerate until needed.

Peel the prawns, leaving tails attached, and place in a bowl. Add the 60 ml (¼ cup) of marinade liquid. Marinate prawns for 30 minutes before cooking.

Heat a large frypan or grill. Add prawns and cook for 2–3 minutes on each side. Remove from heat and add to the noodle salad, along with the dressing. Toss to combine. Divide between 6 plates and serve immediately.

Asparagus and broad bean mograbieh salad with barbecued salmon

Serves 6

This mograbieh salad makes an impressive offering on a large white platter.

350 g (1⅔ cup) mograbieh
500 g asparagus
750 g broad beans
100 g rocket, washed
1 red onion, thinly sliced
½ preserved lemon, soaked in cold water, then diced

1 cup flat-leaf parsley leaves
60 ml (¼ cup) lemon juice
1 tsp sumac
salt and freshly ground black pepper
150 ml (⅔ cup) olive oil (preferably fruity)
2 × 200 g salmon steaks

Cook the mograbieh in a saucepan of boiling water for 20–30 minutes, until tender. Drain and refresh under cold running water.

Bring a large saucepan of water to the boil. Remove the woody ends from the asparagus and cook the spears in boiling water for 1–2 minutes. Refresh under cold running water, then cut the asparagus into 3 cm pieces on an angle.

Pod the broad beans and cook for 2–3 minutes in boiling water. Drain and refresh under cold running water, then remove the pale green skins.

Place the asparagus in a large bowl with the broad beans, mograbieh, rocket, onion, preserved lemon and parsley.

Make the dressing by placing the lemon juice, sumac, salt, pepper and oil in a small jar. Shake together to mix.

Cook the salmon on a hot barbecue for 3–4 minutes on each side, or in a frypan over a medium–high heat. Set aside to cool slightly, then break the salmon into chunks, discarding the skin and any bones.

When ready to serve, add the salmon to the salad, plus enough dressing to coat, and arrange on a large platter.

Sumac beef salad with lentils, grapes and parsley

Serves 4–6

We love the contrast of tangy beef and sweet juicy grapes in this salad. If grapes aren't in season, try using olives or fresh pomegranate seeds in their place.

2 tbsp pomegranate syrup
60 ml (¼ cup) extra-virgin olive oil
2 tbsp lemon juice
2 tsp sumac
½ tsp ground coriander
½ tsp ground cumin
pinch of ground allspice
2 cloves garlic, crushed
salt and freshly ground black pepper
2 × 250 g porterhouse steaks
100 g (½ cup) small green lentils
200 g sultana grapes, halved
½ red onion, thinly sliced
½ bunch flat-leaf parsley, coarsely chopped
2 tbsp lemon juice, additional
1 clove garlic, crushed, additional
60 ml (¼ cup) olive oil

Mix the pomegranate syrup, extra-virgin olive oil, lemon juice, spices, 2 cloves garlic, salt and pepper together. Rub over the beef and refrigerate to marinate for 4 hours.

Place the lentils in a saucepan, cover with water and bring to the boil. Reduce to a simmer and cook for 20–30 minutes, until the lentils are tender. Drain and set aside.

Prepare the salad by mixing the grapes, onion, parsley and lentils together. Make the dressing by mixing the additional 2 tbsp lemon juice, garlic and oil together. Season the dressing with salt and pepper.

Drain the excess marinade from the beef. Cook the meat for 3–4 minutes on each side on a hot barbecue grill or in a heavy-based frypan over a medium–high heat. Allow to rest for 5–10 minutes.

Slice the beef and add to the salad. Add enough dressing to coat, toss to combine and serve immediately.

Beef salad with hot and sour flavours

Serves 6

This Thai-influenced salad will wake up anyone's tastebuds. It's worth searching out green mango or papaya as it adds a lovely crunch to the salad.

oil
500 g beef fillet
60 ml (¼ cup) lime juice
60 ml (¼ cup) fish sauce
2 tbsp sweet chilli sauce
freshly ground black pepper
1 green mango or papaya (optional)
2 tomatoes

1 cucumber, peeled
2 spring onions, thinly sliced
½ cup coriander leaves
½ cup Thai basil
4 shallots, thinly sliced
1 small red chilli, de-seeded and diced
1 tbsp toasted sesame seeds

Preheat the oven to 180°C.

Heat a small frypan over a medium heat. Rub oil over the beef and cook for 5 minutes until the beef is brown all over. Place in the preheated oven for 15 minutes. Set aside to cool.

Mix lime juice, fish sauce, sweet chilli sauce and pepper together. Rub 1 tbsp over the beef and marinate until ready to serve.

To peel the mangoes take a small sharp knife, trim top and bottom off so the mango will stand firm and following the curve of the mango cut down over the flesh removing the skin. Then cut down between the flesh and stone removing the cheek of the mango. Slice each cheek thinly. If using papaya, remove skin, cut in half, discard any seeds and slice thinly. Cut the tomatoes into quarters and slice thinly. Slice the cucumber thinly using a peeler. Toss these ingredients with the spring onions, herbs, shallots and chilli.

Slice the beef thinly. Add to the salad, adding enough dressing to just coat. Toss gently and serve on individual plates or as one large platter so guests can help themselves. Scatter sesame seeds over.

Spice-crusted quail salad with pomegranate dressing

Serves 4

We cook with quail quite a lot and our favourite ways of serving it typically include spices and other bold flavours. If fresh pomegranates are in season, add a scattering of the jewel-like seeds over the salad.

- 4 quails, about 160 g each, spatchcocked
- 1 tbsp ground coriander
- 1 tbsp ground cumin
- 1 tbsp sweet paprika
- salt and freshly ground black pepper
- 90 g butter lettuce, washed
- 60 g frisee leaves, washed
- 2 Roma tomatoes, sliced into wedges
- ½ red capsicum, finely diced
- olive oil
- 3 tsp pomegranate syrup
- large pinch of caster sugar
- 60 g (⅓ cup) pine nuts, toasted

Prepare the quail by placing the bird breast side up on a chopping board. Insert knife into cavity and cut down through breast bone with a sharp knife. Press on top of bird to flatten. Turn bird skin side down and trim away bones as desired. Mix together the coriander, cumin, paprika, salt and pepper. Sprinkle spice mix over quails. Leave to marinate for 1 hour.

Divide butter leaves between four plates and top with frisee, tomato wedges and red capsicum.

Heat a heavy-based pan over a medium–high heat. Add a splash of oil. Cook quails for 4–5 minutes on each side. Remove and rest, covered, in a warm place for 5 minutes.

Whisk together pomegranate syrup, sugar and 3 tbsp olive oil. Cut quails in half, arrange on top of salad, scatter with toasted pine nuts and drizzle with pomegranate dressing.

SAUCES

+ preserves
salsa, relish + jams

Many cooks have a fear of making sauces. Somewhere in the past they may have had a bad experience with a cheese sauce and never quite recovered. This is a shame as there is a whole world of sauces out there. From basic bechamel, gravy and hollandaise to the more exotic almond skordalia, green harissa and chilli salsa, there are so many flavours and textures to enjoy.

A steak can be transformed by adding romesco sauce, a pan-fried chicken fillet with green harissa. Add pesto to your pasta, mushroom sauce to your sausages or tzatziki to your lamb chops.

Cold sauces such as pesto, harissa, romesco and salsas will keep for several weeks in the fridge. Simply cover the surface with a layer of olive oil to prevent oxidisation and dip into them whenever you want to add flavour to a sandwich, cold roast meat or a barbecue.

Sweet sauces can spruce up everyday desserts, cakes and tarts. They can be as simple as raspberry sauce to serve with ice-cream or our great recipe for caramel sauce to accompany your favourite steamed pudding.

sauce + preserve recipes

sauces

Quince aioli	550
Almond skordalia	550
Basil pesto	551
Coriander pesto	551
Thai basil pesto	552
Romesco sauce	552
Tapenade	553
Seed mustard	553
Mayonnaise	554
Hollandaise sauce	555
Lemon butter sauce	555
White sauce (bechamel)	556
Cheese sauce	557
Classic mushroom sauce	557
Creamy mushroom sauce	558
Red wine onion gravy	558
Turkey gravy	559
Allan's gravy	559
Bread sauce	560
Apple sauce	560
Tomato sauce	561
Roasted capsicum and tomato sauce	561
Barbecue sauce	562
Pepper sauce	562
Mint sauce	562
Satay sauce	563
Tzatziki	563
Yoghurt and tahini sauce	564
Vietnamese dipping sauce	564
Green olive salsa	564
Chilli salsa	565
Tomato and basil salsa	565
Fresh mango salsa	565
Fennel relish	566
Coriander relish	566
Asian cucumber salsa	567
Sugar syrup	567
Lime and palm sugar syrup	568
Raspberry sauce	568
Brandy orange butter	569
Marmalade cream	569
Caramel sauce	570
Coconut caramel sauce	570
Chocolate sauce	571
Butterscotch sauce	572
Bourbon sauce	572
Thin custard	573
Thick custard (pastry cream)	573

preserves

Preserved lemons	575
Marinated olives	575
Tomato kasoundi	576
Mango chutney	576
Capsicum relish	577
Beetroot relish	577
Chilli jam	578
Sweet chilli sauce	578
Onion marmalade	579
Asian pickles	580
Pickled ginger	580
Berry jam	581
Peach and almond jam	581
Backyard plum jam	582
Fig jam	582
Orange marmalade	583
Cranberry and pear conserve	583
Pumpkin conserve	584
Cumquat jelly	584
Lemon curd (lemon butter)	585
Microwave lemon curd	585

Things you need to know about sauces

1 The simplest sauces can be made in just a few minutes.

2 Savoury sauces can be thickened with flour or cornflour, or simply reduced until they take on a sticky consistency.

3 Sauces such as mayonnaise and hollandaise are an emulsion of egg yolks and melted butter or oil.

4 Learn a sauce such as hollandaise and upgrade to bearnaise, maltaise or saffron in a jiffy.

5 There are also simple no-cook sauces such as fresh tomato salsa and basil pesto.

6 Sweet sauces are great to have on hand to liven up vanilla ice-cream, fresh fruit or pancakes. Butterscotch sauce can be used on just about anything, while chocolate sauce can dress up a cake, muffin or a bowl of fresh berries.

Quince aioli

Makes 250 ml (1 cup)

Classic aioli is a garlic-infused mayonnaise. This quince aioli goes with virtually all pan-fried or barbecued meats, and is an absolute winner with roast pork.

3–4 cloves garlic, peeled
250 g quince paste
165 ml (⅔ cup) olive oil
60–80 ml (¼–⅓ cup) lemon juice
salt and freshly ground black pepper

Peel and crush the garlic. Place in a large bowl with the quince paste and mash well with a fork. Using a whisk, add the oil, whisking it in well. Don't worry if it looks a bit lumpy; it all comes together at the end.

Once all the oil is added, add lemon juice, salt and pepper and whisk until smooth.

The aioli will keep refrigerated for up to 6 weeks. Best served at room temperature.

Almond skordalia

Makes 250 ml (1 cup)

Skordalia is a Greek-style dip which is great served with crumbed calamari rings, barbecued lamb and pan-fried salmon.

100 g day-old bread
110 g (⅔ cup) toasted blanched almonds
100 g cooked potato
2 cloves garlic, crushed
60–80 ml (¼–⅓ cup) lemon juice
60–80 ml (¼–⅓ cup) olive oil
salt and freshly ground black pepper

Place the bread and almonds in a food processor and blend until they form a breadcrumb texture. Add the potato, garlic and enough lemon juice and oil to form a thick paste. Season with salt and pepper, and adjust consistency with hot water if needed.

Basil pesto

Makes 375 ml (1½ cups)

This is our version of the classic Italian condiment. Stir it through spaghetti, add it to a bowl of minestrone or serve a dollop with barbecued meats.

80 g (½ cup) pine nuts
1 clove garlic, peeled
1 bunch basil, leaves only
200 ml (¾ cup) extra-virgin olive oil
100 g (1¼ cups) grated parmigiano

Place the pine nuts and garlic in a food processor and pulse. Add the basil and puree until smooth. Gradually add the extra-virgin olive oil in a thin stream, until everything combines into a creamy consistency. Add the parmigiano and blend. Will keep refrigerated for up to 6 weeks.

Almond pesto
Substitute almonds for pine nuts.

Rocket pesto
Substitute rocket for basil.

Coriander pesto

Makes 375 ml (1½ cups)

This pesto adds zing to barbecues, tagines or marinades.

1 bunch coriander, leaves and stems, well washed
50 g baby spinach leaves
2 large green chillies, de-seeded
2 cloves garlic, peeled
½ tsp grated ginger
2 tbsp lime juice
½ tsp ground coriander
½ tsp ground cumin
½ tsp sweet paprika
¼ tsp salt
¼ tsp freshly ground black pepper
165 ml (⅔ cup) olive oil

Place the coriander, spinach leaves, chillies, garlic, ginger and lime juice in a food processor. Blend until smooth. Add the spices, salt and pepper and blend again. Gradually add the oil in a thin stream until everything combines into a creamy consistency.

Thai basil pesto

Makes 375 ml (1½ cups)

Try a spoonful of this stunning Thai basil pesto stirred through noodles or added to stir-fries.

- 165 ml (⅔ cup) peanut oil
- 75 g (½ cup) raw peanuts
- 1 bunch Thai basil, leaves only
- 25 Vietnamese mint leaves
- 1 large green chilli, de-seeded
- 2 tbsp lime juice
- 1 tbsp fish sauce
- ½ tsp grated ginger
- 1 clove garlic, peeled

Heat the oil over a medium heat. Add the peanuts and cook until just golden, then remove using a slotted spoon.

Allow the peanuts and oil to cool. Place the remaining ingredients in a food processor with the peanuts and oil. Blend until smooth.

Romesco sauce

Makes 500 ml (2 cups)

Romesco is a little like a Spanish-flavoured pesto, and is absolutely amazing served with barbecued chicken, seafood and lamb. Try it just once, and it's sure to become a favourite.

- 1 red capsicum, de-seeded
- 1 small red chilli, de-seeded
- 1 tomato, halved
- 4 cloves garlic, peeled
- olive oil
- 80 g (½ cup) blanched almonds
- 75 g (½ cup) hazelnuts
- 2 tbsp smoky paprika
- large pinch of saffron threads, soaked in 2 tbsp boiling water
- 1 thick slice of bread, toasted and diced
- 1 tbsp chopped parsley
- 2 tbsp red wine vinegar
- ½ tsp salt
- ½ tsp freshly ground black pepper

Preheat oven to 180°C.

Place the capsicum, chilli, tomato and garlic onto a baking tray and drizzle with oil. Place in the preheated oven and cook for 30 minutes, or until all the ingredients are tender.

Place the almonds and hazelnuts on a separate baking tray and cook in the preheated oven for 15 minutes, until golden. Place the hazelnuts in a clean tea towel and rub to remove the skins.

Peel the capsicum and tomato. Add to a food processor, along with all the other ingredients (including the saffron's soaking liquid), and whiz to a coarse paste. Spoon the mix into a bowl, stir well and add more oil, to form a thick paste-like consistency. Season with extra vinegar, salt and pepper as needed. The sauce should have a smoky, full-flavoured taste. Keeps refrigerated for up to 6 weeks.

Tapenade

Makes 750 ml (3 cups)

Try this olive paste on warm toast for a taste sensation. We recommend chopping the ingredients by hand to ensure a coarse texture.

100 g salted capers
700 g (4½ cups) pitted kalamata olives
60 g anchovy fillets, including oil
6 cloves garlic, crushed
2 tbsp chopped parsley
freshly ground black pepper
250–375 ml (1–1½ cups) olive oil

Soak the capers in cold water for 10 minutes and rinse several times to remove excess salt. Drain well and chop finely.

Coarsely chop the pitted olives and the anchovies. Stir the capers, olives, anchovies (and their oil), garlic and parsley together in a large bowl. Season with pepper.

Add enough oil to make a paste-like consistency. Place in an airtight container, cover with a layer of olive oil and refrigerate. It will keep for a few weeks.

Seed mustard

Makes 750 ml (3 cups)

Mustard is a great condiment to make for friends at Christmas – or at any time of the year. It's not difficult to do and the recipe can be easily adapted to incorporate flavours such as walnuts, herbs or brandy, once you get the hang of it.

100 g (⅔ cup) yellow mustard seeds
100 g (⅔ cup) brown mustard seeds
1 tbsp freshly ground black pepper
1 tbsp salt
250 ml (1 cup) vegetable oil
250 ml (1 cup) dry white wine or white vinegar
250 ml (1 cup) vermouth

Place the yellow and brown mustard seeds, pepper, salt, oil, wine (or vinegar) and vermouth in a food processor. Process for 5 minutes.

At this stage the mustard will look like a thin dressing with mustard seeds floating around in it; don't be alarmed, this is normal. Cover and set aside overnight.

Next day, process again for 5 minutes. The mustard will begin to thicken, though it may need a further 5 minutes on the following day to be just right.

When you are happy with the consistency, spoon the mustard into jars. Store in a cool, dark place.

Walnut and sage mustard
Add 100 g (¾ cup) walnuts and 12 sage leaves to the mustard at the final stage in the food processor.

Mayonnaise

Makes 250 ml (1 cup)

If you're going to make your own salads, you might as well make your own mayonnaise as well. This can easily be done in a mixer or food processor, or by hand if you prefer. In fact, making mayonnaise by hand with a simple bowl and whisk doesn't take as long as you might imagine.

- 2 egg yolks
- salt and freshly ground black pepper
- ½ tsp Dijon mustard
- 125 ml (½ cup) extra-virgin olive oil
- 1 tbsp white wine vinegar
- white pepper
- 1–2 tbsp boiling water, if required

Place the egg yolks, a little salt and pepper and the mustard in a food processor or bowl. Blend or whisk for 2–3 minutes, or until white and creamy. Slowly drizzle in the extra-virgin olive oil until a thick, creamy consistency is reached. If the oil is added too fast, the mayonnaise may separate.

Add vinegar and seasoning, if needed. If the mayonnaise is too thick, add a little boiling water to thin it. Keeps refrigerated for 2 weeks.

Rocket mayonnaise
Puree a handful of rocket leaves in the food processor, adding mayonnaise until smooth.

Lemon mayonnaise
Substitute lemon juice for the white wine vinegar. Serve with freshly cooked prawns.

Lime and chilli mayonnaise
Substitute lime juice for the white wine vinegar. Add 1 clove crushed garlic, 1 tsp tomato paste and 2 de-seeded and finely diced small red chillies to the food processor or bowl at the same time as the egg yolks.

Tartare sauce
Add 2 tsp soaked, chopped capers, 30 g chopped cornichons and 1 tbsp chopped parsley to the finished mayonnaise. Great with beer-battered fish.

Aioli
Add 4 (or more if you wish) cloves of crushed garlic to the food processor or bowl at the same time as the egg yolks.

Herb aioli
Add 4 cloves of crushed garlic and ½ cup roughly chopped basil to the food processor or bowl at the same time as the egg yolks.

Hollandaise sauce

Makes 250 ml (1 cup)

It may take a few attempts to master this classic sauce of the French kitchen. Once you do, you can serve it over poached eggs and bacon to create Eggs Benedict (page 19), or with asparagus.

3 egg yolks
2–3 tbsp lemon juice
180 g melted butter
boiling water as required
salt and freshly ground black pepper

Place the egg yolks, lemon juice and a pinch of salt in a food processor or mixer. Blend for 3–5 minutes, until pale and thickened. Slowly add the melted butter in a steady stream. The butter should be just warm rather than hot.

When thick, add boiling water to adjust the consistency and check seasoning. Pour into a bowl and keep warm. Either stand the bowl in another bowl of warm water or wrap it in a tea towel and stand it near something warm. Take care, as too much heat will curdle the sauce.

Bearnaise sauce
Add 2 tbsp chopped tarragon to the egg yolks.

Maltaise sauce
Substitute blood orange juice for lemon juice.

Saffron sauce
Add a pinch of saffron threads to the egg yolks.

Lemon butter sauce

Makes 125 ml (½ cup)

This sauce can be served with all manner of fish dishes, but our favourite way of serving it is with Salmon and Potato Cakes (page 278).

60 ml (¼ cup) white wine
100 g soft butter
2 tbsp lemon juice
salt and freshly ground black pepper

Place the white wine in a small saucepan and allow to reduce by half. Reduce heat and whisk in the butter, piece by piece. Add lemon juice and seasoning. Keep sauce warm on the side of the stove until ready to serve.

Blood orange butter sauce
Substitute blood orange juice for lemon juice and serve with steamed new season's asparagus.

Lime butter sauce
Substitute lime juice for lemon juice and serve with pan-fried fish fillets.

White sauce (bechamel)

Makes 500 ml (2 cups)

This is the base sauce from which Cheese Sauce, Parsley Sauce and a multitude of similar sauces are made.

500 ml (2 cups) hot milk
2 tbsp butter
45 g (⅓ cup) flour
salt and freshly ground black pepper

Warm the milk to a gentle simmer. Place a medium saucepan over a medium heat and melt the butter, without browning. Add the flour and stir well to incorporate. Reduce heat and 'cook' the roux for 2–3 minutes, stirring often.

Raise the heat under the roux and add 1 ladleful of hot milk. Whisk in well, then continue to add milk, 1 ladleful at a time, until it's all incorporated. Reduce heat and cook for 3–4 minutes, stirring often. Season with salt and pepper.

Parsley sauce
Add 2 tbsp chopped parsley.

Mustard sauce
Add 1 tbsp grain mustard.

Onion sauce
Cook 2 sliced onions in 2 tbsp olive oil until soft. Omit butter, add flour and cook as directed above.

Cheese sauce

Makes 500 ml (2 cups)

This is the sauce you need for cauliflower cheese, macaroni cheese, cannelloni and to complete the final layer on a lasagne. If you plan to serve this as a straight cheese sauce, you'll need to simmer it over a low heat for 15 minutes.

500 ml (2 cups) milk
2 tbsp butter
45 g (⅓ cup) plain flour
1 tsp Dijon mustard
200 g (1⅓ cups) grated cheddar
salt and freshly ground black pepper

Warm the milk to a gentle simmer. Heat a small saucepan over a medium heat and melt the butter. Reduce heat to low and add the flour. Stir to form a roux and allow to 'cook out' for 1–2 minutes.

Raise the heat, add the warm milk and whisk until a smooth sauce forms. Simmer for 5 minutes, when it will have thickened slightly.

Remove from heat, add mustard and cheese and stir until melted. Season with salt and pepper.

Goat's cheese sauce
Substitute half of the cheddar with fresh goat's cheese.

Classic mushroom sauce

Makes 500 ml (2 cups)

Use pine or slippery jack mushrooms if they're available; otherwise, a combination of button, oyster and shiitake mushrooms will do just fine. Serve with pan-fried bratwurst sausages and mashed potatoes.

oil
250 g mushrooms of your choice, sliced
125 ml (½ cup) red wine
125 ml (½ cup) beef stock
salt and freshly ground black pepper

Heat a large heavy-based frypan over a medium–high heat. Add a generous splash of oil and the mushrooms. Cook for 4–5 minutes, stirring often.

Add the wine and stock to the pan and season. Cook until the liquid has reduced by half and the mushrooms are tender.

Creamy mushroom sauce

Makes 500 ml (2 cups)

This simple but stylish sauce will add life to steaks, lamb cutlets, beef burgers – in fact, virtually any pan-fried meats.

oil
1 onion, finely diced
250 g Swiss brown mushrooms, cut into wedges
250 ml (1 cup) beef stock
80 ml (⅓ cup) cream
salt and freshly ground black pepper

Heat a heavy-based pan over a medium–high heat. Add a splash of oil, then the onion and mushrooms. Cook for 5–6 minutes, stirring occasionally, until the onion and mushrooms are well softened. Add the stock, bring to the boil and reduce by half. Add the cream to the sauce and simmer for a further 2–3 minutes. Season well, adding lots of pepper.

Red wine onion gravy

Makes 500 ml (2 cups)

A terrific accompaniment to roast meat, beef burgers, sausages or barbecued steak, this recipe uses red wine and beef stock to create a hearty, full-flavoured gravy. We don't like our gravies to be thick; however, if you do, simply add 2 tbsp flour instead of the recommended 1 tbsp.

oil
2 onions, thinly sliced
1 tbsp plain flour
125 ml (½ cup) red wine
250 ml (1 cup) beef stock
salt and freshly ground black pepper

Heat a heavy-based pan over a medium–high heat. Add a splash of oil and the onions. Cook for 3–4 minutes, stirring often, until the onions are well softened and turning a golden colour. Sprinkle in the flour and stir well. Add the wine and stock and bring to the boil, whisking occasionally. Reduce heat and allow to simmer for 10–15 minutes, stirring occasionally.

Check seasoning, add juices from the resting meat and serve the gravy in a warmed jug alongside the roast.

White wine onion gravy
Use white wine and chicken stock instead of red wine and beef stock. This keeps the flavour fairly light, which is excellent when you need a gravy to serve with delicate meats such as pork, veal or chicken.

Turkey gravy

Makes 500 ml (2 cups)

We often roast a turkey on Christmas Eve, then remove the fillets and legs to reheat the following day, leaving us with the bones to make this gravy. The bones are simmered with vegetables, herbs and water for a few hours, then strained and reduced to sticky, gorgeous gravy. It's very easy to do and the gravy is something else.

- bones from a roast turkey, plus any pan juices
- 2 onions, roughly chopped
- 2 carrots, roughly chopped
- 2 celery stalks, roughly chopped
- 1 tomato, chopped
- 2 sprigs of thyme
- 2 bay leaves
- 375 ml (1½ cups) red wine

Chop the bones into pieces that will easily fit into a large saucepan. Place the bones, any pan juices from the roast plus all of the remaining ingredients into the saucepan and add cold water to cover. Place over a high heat and bring to the boil. Skim off any scum that comes to the surface. Reduce to a simmer and cook for 2 hours. Continue skimming as required.

The stock should have reduced by between a third to a half by this stage. Strain the stock into a medium-sized saucepan. You can easily stop the cooking at this point and refrigerate the stock until needed. We usually do this first part of the process on Christmas Eve, strain the stock and then refrigerate it overnight.

Continue to simmer and reduce the stock, skimming as required. It will eventually reduce to a sticky and full-flavoured gravy that's amazing with roasted turkey.

Allan's gravy

Makes 500 ml (2 cups)

This is one of our most popular recipes, and we just had to include it once again for those not already converted to making their own gravy. It takes only 5 minutes to put together, then 15 minutes to simmer gently. There's nothing hard about that.

- 2 tbsp butter
- 2 tbsp plain flour
- 2 tbsp red or white wine
- 1 tbsp tomato paste
- 375 ml (1½ cups) stock
- salt and freshly ground black pepper

If using a roasting dish, pour away excess fat and place the dish over a medium–low heat. If not using a roasting dish, use a small saucepan. Add butter and melt. Stir in the flour and cook for 1–2 minutes, stirring often. Add the wine, tomato paste and stock, and bring to the boil, whisking often. Reduce heat and allow to simmer for 10–15 minutes, stirring often.

Check seasoning, add juices from the resting meat and serve the gravy in a warmed jug alongside the roast.

Bread sauce

Makes 500 ml (2 cups)

This old-fashioned English sauce is usually served with roasted game birds such as pheasant and guinea fowl. It adds a whole new dimension of flavour to a roast.

1 small onion, peeled
6 whole cloves
375 ml (1½ cups) milk
1 bay leaf
salt and freshly ground black pepper
100 g (2 cups) fresh breadcrumbs
knob of butter

Stud the onion with the cloves and place it in a small saucepan. Pour the milk over, add the bay leaf and cook on a low heat for 15 minutes, just simmering, to allow the milk to infuse.

Strain the milk into a clean saucepan and season well with salt and pepper. Add the breadcrumbs and cook over a low heat for 10 minutes. Whisk butter through just before serving. Season to taste and serve.

Apple sauce

Makes 500 ml (2 cups)

The perfect accompaniment to a roast leg of pork or pan-fried pork chops.

3 Granny Smith apples, peeled, cored and thinly sliced
1 tbsp caster sugar
2 tbsp lemon juice
salt and freshly ground black pepper

Place the apple slices in a saucepan over a low heat. Add a few tbsp water, along with the caster sugar and lemon juice. Cover and cook for 15 minutes, keeping the heat low.

Mash the apples with a fork or a potato masher into a nice, smooth puree. Season to taste.

Tomato sauce

Makes 1 litre (4 cups)

The perfect sauce to accompany spaghetti and meatballs, meatloaf or pan-fried fish fillets.

80 ml (⅓ cup) olive oil
2 onions, diced
2 small red chillies, de-seeded and diced
2 cloves garlic, crushed
125 ml (½ cup) dry white wine
500 ml (2 cups) chicken stock
250 ml (1 cup) tomato sugo
salt and freshly ground black pepper

Heat a large saucepan over a medium heat. Add the oil and onions and cook for 7–8 minutes, stirring often, ensuring that the onions don't colour.

Add the chillies and garlic and cook for a further 1–2 minutes, until fragrant. Add white wine, bring to the boil and reduce by half. Add the stock and tomato sugo and bring to the boil. Reduce heat and simmer for 10 minutes. Season with salt and pepper.

Roasted capsicum and tomato sauce

Makes 500 ml (2 cups)

Serve this sauce with potato gnocchi, barbecued chicken fillets, sausages or pan-fried fish.

2 red capsicums, quartered
500 g Roma tomatoes, halved
6 cloves garlic, peeled
2 red chillies
oil
salt and freshly ground black pepper

Preheat oven to 180°C.

Place all the vegetables in a deep baking tray. Drizzle with oil and season with salt and pepper. Roast for 30 minutes.

Remove the capsicums and place them in a plastic bag to allow the steam to lift their skins.

When the capsicums are cool, peel the skin and remove the seeds. Puree all the vegetables together and strain through a sieve.

Add oil to adjust the consistency and check seasoning.

Barbecue sauce

Makes 375 ml (1½ cups)

I thought I had the ultimate recipe for barbecue sauce, until I came across this easy version in one of Keith Floyd's books. AC

2 cloves garlic, peeled
½ tsp salt
½ tsp smoky paprika
80 ml (⅓ cup) honey
60 ml (¼ cup) tomato puree or sauce
80 ml (⅓ cup) orange juice
80 ml (⅓ cup) red wine vinegar
125 ml (½ cup) soy sauce

Put all the ingredients in a food processor and puree until smooth.

Pour into a saucepan and bring to the boil.

Reduce to a simmer and cook for 10 minutes. Season if required.

Pepper sauce

Makes 375 ml (1½ cups)

This sauce is just the thing when you have some big juicy steaks to cook.

2 tbsp butter
45 g (⅓ cup) flour
1 tsp freshly ground black pepper
2 tbsp red wine
1 tbsp tomato paste
375 ml (1½ cups) stock
salt and freshly ground black pepper

Place a small saucepan over a medium–low heat. Add the butter and melt it. Stir in the flour and pepper and cook for 1–2 minutes, stirring often. Add the wine, tomato paste and stock and bring to the boil, whisking often.

Reduce heat and allow to simmer for 10–15 minutes, stirring often. Check seasoning, adding more pepper if required.

Mint sauce

Makes 250 ml (1 cup)

Taste this version of the classic accompaniment to roast lamb and you'll never go back to the supermarket product again.

125 ml (½ cup) boiling water
2 cups chopped mint leaves
1 tbsp caster sugar
125 ml (½ cup) cider or white wine vinegar
salt to taste

Pour boiling water over the mint and caster sugar. Set aside to soak for 30 minutes. Add vinegar and salt to taste. Serve with lamb.

Satay sauce

Makes 250 ml (1 cup)

Serve this fantastic sauce with pan-fried chicken or pork, or if you need a quick dipping sauce.

1 tbsp vegetable oil
1 small onion, diced
1 small red chilli, de-seeded and diced
2 tsp ground coriander
1 tsp ground cumin
1 tsp ground turmeric
¼ tsp ground cinnamon

1 tsp salt
1 tsp sugar
1 tbsp soy sauce
165 ml (⅔ cup) coconut milk
50 g (⅓ cup) roasted peanuts, finely chopped
salt and freshly ground black pepper

Heat a saucepan over a medium heat. Add the oil, onion and chilli. Cook for 3–4 minutes, stirring well. Add the coriander, cumin, turmeric, cinnamon, salt and sugar. Stir well for 1 minute.

Add the soy sauce and coconut milk and bring to the boil. Reduce heat and allow to simmer for 5 minutes. Add the ground peanuts and simmer for a further 2–3 minutes, until a good consistency. Season to taste.

Tzatziki

Makes 250 ml (1 cup)

Tzatziki appears regularly in our kitchen as it goes with everything from barbecued lamb kebabs to spicy tagines, or can simply be served as a dip with Turkish bread.

250 g (1 cup) natural yoghurt
1 clove garlic, crushed
1 Lebanese cucumber, grated

pinch of dried mint
¼ cup coarsely chopped coriander leaves
salt and freshly ground black pepper

Mix all the ingredients together and season to taste.

Yoghurt and tahini sauce

Makes 250 ml (1 cup)

This has a lot more body than regular yoghurt sauces, due to the addition of tahini. Serve with kebabs, barbecued chicken and spicy Middle Eastern stews.

1 tbsp tahini
2 tbsp lemon juice
2 cloves garlic, crushed
180 g (¾ cup) natural yoghurt
salt and freshly ground black pepper

Mix the tahini and lemon juice together to form a smooth paste. Add the garlic and yoghurt and whisk until smooth. Season to taste. Keep refrigerated.

Vietnamese dipping sauce

Makes 60 ml (¼ cup)

This is our version of the classic Vietnamese nuoc cham dipping sauce. It's perfect served with spring rolls, rice-paper rolls and all manner of South East Asian snacks.

2 tsp grated palm sugar
2 tbsp lime juice
60 ml (¼ cup) fish sauce
1 small red chilli, sliced
1 tbsp water

Dissolve the sugar in lime juice. Add the fish sauce, chilli and water. Allow the flavours to infuse for 30 minutes before using.

Green olive salsa

Makes 375 ml (1½ cups)

This salsa is easy to prepare but it tastes as if you've gone to lots of trouble. That's got to be good. Chop the ingredients by hand to ensure a coarse texture.

200 g (1¼ cups) pitted green olives
2 tsp capers, soaked and rinsed
2 anchovies
½ cup chopped flat-leaf parsley leaves
80 ml (⅓ cup) extra-virgin olive oil
freshly ground black pepper

Finely chop the olives, capers and anchovies. Mix together in a bowl and add the parsley and extra-virgin olive oil. Stir well and add lots of freshly ground black pepper to season.

Chilli salsa

Makes 250 ml (1 cup)

A combo of tomato and cucumber with a decent chilli kick. Great when you want to add a burst of flavour to barbecued food or as a pre-dinner dip with sliced baguette.

4 tomatoes
1 Lebanese cucumber
2 tbsp chopped coriander
2 tbsp olive oil
2 tbsp lemon juice
2 small red chillies, de-seeded and diced
salt and freshly ground black pepper

Finely dice the tomatoes and cucumber. Stir through the coriander, oil, lemon juice and chillies. Season with salt and pepper and allow to stand for 30 minutes before using.

Tomato and basil salsa

Makes 250 ml (1 cup)

We use this salsa in a multitude of ways, including on top of crostini and blinis, as a fresh-tasting dip or spooned over barbecued chicken fillets.

4 ripe tomatoes
1 small cucumber
6 basil leaves, thinly sliced
sherry or balsamic vinegar
olive oil
salt and freshly ground black pepper

Dice the tomatoes and cucumber finely. Mix the tomato, cucumber and basil together and season to taste with sherry or balsamic vinegar, oil, salt and pepper.

Tomato and coriander salsa
Substitute coriander leaves for basil.

Fresh mango salsa

Makes 250 ml (1 cup)

A stunning recipe that makes the most of fresh mangoes in season. Best with fish or chicken.

1 ripe mango
1 tsp caster sugar
1 tbsp lime juice
2 tsp fish sauce
2 small red chillies, finely diced
1 tbsp chopped Thai basil or coriander leaves
freshly ground black pepper

Peel the mango. Remove the mango flesh from the stone and dice finely. Dissolve the caster sugar in the lime juice and fish sauce. Add the remaining ingredients and mix to combine. Serve with Asian-flavoured dishes.

Fennel relish

Makes 250 ml (1 cup)

Simple, but a stunner. Try it with pan-fried fish, veal cutlets or sausages.

1 fennel bulb
2 tbsp lemon juice
salt and freshly ground black pepper
2 tbsp olive oil

Remove the core from the fennel and dice the fennel finely. Toss the fennel together with lemon juice, salt, pepper and oil. Serve immediately.

Coriander relish

Makes 250 ml (1 cup)

This fresh-tasting relish is excellent served with pan-fried meat or fish.

½ cucumber
1 cup coriander leaves
1 red onion, diced
salt and freshly ground black pepper
2 tbsp lemon juice
2 tbsp olive oil
2 tbsp pomegranate syrup

Cut the cucumber into quarters lengthways, then slice thinly. Place in a bowl with the coriander and onion. To serve, season with salt and pepper, add lemon juice, oil and pomegranate syrup, then toss to combine.

Asian cucumber salsa

Makes 500 ml (2 cups)

Serve this fresh-tasting salsa with spiced barbecue foods such as Oriental Beef.

1 cucumber
½ small onion, finely diced
2 tbsp sugar
½ tsp salt
½ tsp freshly ground black pepper
2 tbsp white vinegar
2 tsp fish sauce
¼ cup chopped coriander
45 g (⅓ cup) chopped peanuts

Peel the cucumber, cut in half lengthways and scoop out the seeds with a teaspoon. Cut into small dice. Place the cucumber in a bowl with all the remaining ingredients, except the peanuts. Stir well and allow to marinate for at least 30 minutes.

Season to taste and place in a serving bowl. Sprinkle with the chopped peanuts.

Sugar syrup

Makes 200 ml (¾ cup)

Sugar syrup can be used for poaching fruit and as a base for making berry sauces, or it can be reduced to make caramel sauce. If desired, ingredients such as lemon zest or a cinnamon stick can be added to give flavour to the basic sugar syrup.

125 ml (½ cup) water
110 g (½ cup) caster sugar

Place the caster sugar and water in a medium-sized saucepan over a low heat. Stir until the sugar dissolves. Raise heat and bring to the boil.

Simmer for 2–3 minutes. Allow to cool and use as directed.

Lemon syrup
Add 2 tbsp lemon juice and the zest of 1 lemon to the cooled syrup.

Lime syrup
Add 2 tbsp lime juice and the zest of 1 lime to the cooled syrup.

Orange-blossom syrup
Add 2 tbsp orange juice, 1 tbsp orange-blossom water and the zest of 1 orange to the cooled syrup.

Rosewater syrup
Add 1 tbsp rosewater to the cooled syrup.

Lime and palm sugar syrup

Makes 125 ml (½ cup)

Palm sugar and lime juice add a slightly Asian flavour to Sugar Syrup.

65 g (¼ cup) grated palm sugar
125 ml (½ cup) water

60 ml (¼ cup) lime juice

Place the palm sugar and water in a medium-sized saucepan over a low heat. Stir until the sugar dissolves. Raise heat and bring to the boil.

Simmer for 2–3 minutes. Remove from heat and add lime juice.

Raspberry sauce

Makes 250 ml (1 cup)

Try raspberry sauce (also known as raspberry coulis) with almond friands, alongside chocolate cake or over vanilla ice-cream.

125 ml (½ cup) water
110 g (½ cup) caster sugar

250 g raspberries, stalks removed

Heat a medium-sized saucepan over a low heat. Add water and caster sugar and stir until the sugar dissolves. Raise heat and bring to the boil.

Add raspberries and cook for 1 minute, then remove from heat. Puree in a food processor and pass through a sieve to remove seeds.

Rhubarb sauce
Add 100 g chopped rhubarb to the simmering syrup, along with 1 tbsp rosewater. Cook for 2–3 minutes. Remove from heat and allow to cool. Puree if desired.

Strawberry sauce
Replace the raspberries with an equal quantity of strawberries. Or try blackberries, blueberries or loganberries.

Brandy orange butter

Makes 1 × 500 g log

This is the classic accompaniment to a hot plum pudding.

225 g butter, diced
230 g (2 cups) icing sugar
60 ml (¼ cup) brandy
zest of 1 orange, finely grated

Cream the butter and icing sugar together until light and fluffy. Beat in the brandy and orange zest.

Place the butter on a square of greaseproof paper and fold the paper over the top. Using your hands, roll it into a log shape. Twist the ends of the paper to seal well. Refrigerate until completely cold. Unwrap and slice as needed.

Whisky spice butter
Substitute whisky for the brandy and add ½ tsp mixed spice to the butter.

Marmalade cream

Makes 250 ml (1 cup)

Super-simple and super-delicious, this cream goes perfectly with a freshly baked orange and almond cake.

3 tbsp orange marmalade
125 g (½ cup) mascarpone
1 tsp orange-blossom water
⅓ cup Greek yoghurt
icing sugar

Mix the marmalade, mascarpone and orange-blossom water together. Add yoghurt, then icing sugar to taste.

Caramel sauce

Makes 250 ml (1 cup)

This light caramel has a multitude of uses. Try it with a slice of cake or tart, or use it to marinate slices of orange for caramel oranges.

110 g (½ cup) caster sugar
60 ml (¼ cup) water
125 ml (½ cup) water, additional

Place the caster sugar and 60 ml (¼ cup) water in a saucepan. Cook over a low heat until the sugar dissolves. Raise heat and boil the liquid. Stir until the liquid is clear, then stop stirring or the mixture will caramelise.

Cook for 12–15 minutes, until the liquid begins to colour; the desired colour is a mix of gold and caramel, not dark brown. If needed, carefully swirl the saucepan to mix the caramel.

Remove from heat and carefully add the additional 125 ml (½ cup) water; it will probably spit and spurt quite a bit at this stage, so take care. Stir well to make sure all the caramel comes from the bottom of the saucepan.

Coconut caramel sauce

Makes 250 ml (1 cup)

This slightly more decadent caramel sauce is lovely over ice-cream or served with fresh stone fruit such as peaches and nectarines.

110 g (½ cup) caster sugar
60 ml (¼ cup) water
60 ml (¼ cup) water, additional
60 ml (¼ cup) coconut milk

Place the caster sugar and 60 ml (¼ cup) water in a saucepan. Cook over a low heat until the sugar dissolves. Raise heat and boil the liquid. Stir until the liquid is clear, then stop stirring or the mixture will caramelise.

Cook for 12–15 minutes, until the liquid begins to colour; the desired colour is a mix of gold and caramel, not dark brown. If needed, carefully swirl the saucepan to mix the caramel.

Remove from heat and carefully add the additional 60 ml (¼ cup) water; it will probably spit and spurt quite a bit at this stage, so take care. Stir well to make sure all the caramel comes from the bottom of the saucepan. Stir through the coconut milk.

Chocolate sauce

Makes 125 ml (½ cup)

Sometimes I make this sauce with Mars Bars, which adds extra caramel flavour to the sauce. AC

90 g dark chocolate, chopped
1 tbsp butter
2 tbsp brandy
80 ml (⅓ cup) cream

Place all the ingredients in a heatproof bowl. Set the bowl over a saucepan of simmering water and cook for 5–6 minutes. Stir often until everything has melted together smoothly. Serve while hot or warm.

Chocolate brandy sauce
Add 1 tbsp brandy.

White chocolate sauce
Substitute white chocolate for dark.

Butterscotch sauce

Makes 375 ml (1½ cups)

The addition of butter, brown sugar and cream transforms caramel sauce into an amazing butterscotch creation. This is brilliant over ice-cream, served warm with a slice of cake or as the final touch to a steamed pudding.

110 g (½ cup) caster sugar
60 ml (¼ cup) water
60 g butter
100 g (½ cup) brown sugar
125 ml (½ cup) cream

Place the caster sugar and water in a saucepan. Cook over a low heat until the sugar dissolves. Raise heat and boil the liquid. Stir until the liquid is clear, then stop stirring or the mixture will caramelise.

Cook for 12–15 minutes, until the liquid begins to colour; the desired colour is a mix of gold and caramel, not dark brown. If needed, carefully swirl the saucepan to mix the caramel.

Remove from heat and carefully add the butter and brown sugar. Return to the heat and simmer until smooth. Stir in cream and whisk until combined. Set aside to cool. The sauce can be allowed to cool completely, if required; simply melt it over a low heat until it's runny once again.

Bourbon sauce

Makes 250 ml (1 cup)

This sauce works well with vanilla or coffee ice-cream, and can also be served with a steamed pudding.

200 g (1 cup) brown sugar
185 ml (¾ cup) cream
1 vanilla bean
1 tsp honey
2 tbsp bourbon

Place the brown sugar, cream, vanilla bean and honey in a small saucepan. Simmer over a low heat for 20 minutes. Remove from heat, strain and add the bourbon. Serve cold.

Kahlua sauce
Substitute Kahlua for bourbon.

Thin custard

Makes 500 ml (2 cups)

All lovers of dessert need to know how to make custard. Once you master the classic version, you can play around with it and make brandy or muscat custard.

5 egg yolks
110 g (½ cup) caster sugar
500 ml (2 cups) milk
½ tsp vanilla extract

Beat the egg yolks and caster sugar together until pale and thick.

Place the milk and vanilla in a saucepan and bring to simmering point. Whisk the hot milk into the egg-yolk mixture, then pour into a clean saucepan.

Place the custard over a medium–low heat. Using a wooden spoon, stir constantly in a figure of 8 to prevent the custard catching on the bottom of the saucepan. As it approaches (but isn't allowed to reach) the boil, the mixture will begin to thicken.

Remove immediately from the heat and strain into a cold bowl. This will slow the cooking and remove any eggy bits from the custard.

Brandy custard
Add 60 ml (¼ cup) of brandy to the custard just before serving.

Muscat custard
Add 60 ml (¼ cup) of liqueur muscat or tokay to the custard just before serving.

Thick custard (pastry cream)

Makes 500 ml (2 cups)

This is for those who like their custard thick. It's also the custard that will set quite firmly and can be used in many desserts, tarts and slices.

2 egg yolks
55 g (¼ cup) caster sugar
1 tbsp plain flour
500 ml (2 cups) milk
½ tsp vanilla extract

Beat the egg yolks and caster sugar together until pale, then stir in the flour until smooth.

Place the milk and vanilla in a saucepan and bring to the boil. Whisk the hot milk into the egg-yolk mixture, then pour into a clean saucepan.

Place the custard over a low heat and stir constantly as the custard comes to the boil and thickens. Remove from heat.

This custard can be made in advance and reheated gently over a low heat when needed. Cover with cling film if not using immediately to stop a skin forming.

Things you need to know about preserves

1 You need the best-quality produce to make the best preserves. The ingredients have to be just right – neither underripe nor overripe.

2 Some fruit can be roasted before being made into jam to intensify the flavour. Always remove the stones before cooking.

3 Jars must be sterilised before use. The easiest way to do this is in the dishwasher on a hot cycle. Failing this, wash them well and place them in a hot oven for a couple of minutes.

4 Soak the jar lids in boiling water for 10 minutes.

5 When the jars have been filled, check that the lids are airtight; if not, air can get in and ruin all your hard work.

6 Always label the preserves with the name of the product and the date on which it was made.

7 Pass on a few jars to food-loving friends. Hopefully, you'll get a few in return!

Preserved lemons

Makes 8 preserved lemons

Preserved lemons are stored in salty brine for later use. We use them in Middle Eastern salads, rolled up inside a leg of lamb and to add a burst of lemon flavour to tagines and couscous.

8 lemons
4 tbsp salt
2–3 cloves
1 cinnamon stick

Cut the lemons into quarters. Place the salt, cloves and cinnamon in a large saucepan of water and bring to the boil. When boiling, add half the quantity of lemon wedges and allow the water to return to the boil. Cook skin side down for 7–8 minutes. Remove the lemons, drain and cook the next batch. Reserve the cooking liquid.

Squash the lemons into sterilised jars and push down firmly. When each jar is full, cover the lemons with the reserved cooking liquid. Store in a cool, dark place for 3–4 weeks before using.

To use the preserved lemon, soak a wedge in cold water for 10 minutes, cut out and discard the pulpy centre and use the lemon rind in your recipe.

Marinated olives

Makes 1 kg

We've tried numerous recipes over the years in our search for a simple way to prepare fresh olives. This recipe from our friend Daniele gives great results. Daniele prefers to remove the stones completely, while we tend to leave them in – the choice is yours.

1 kg olives
1 lemon, sliced
salt
white vinegar
1 tbsp fennel seeds
2 cloves garlic, sliced
4 bay leaves
4 sprigs of oregano
2 small chillies
olive oil as required

Cut a slit in the base of each olive with a sharp knife. You might like to follow Daniele's example and bash them with a beer bottle so the seed can be completely removed! Place the olives in a large container and cover with water and the sliced lemon. Leave for 24 hours.

Strain and rinse the olives a few times. Dry well. Sprinkle the olives with salt and leave for 24 hours. Rinse well in fresh water. Cover with vinegar and leave for 24 hours. Drain well.

Mix the olives with the fennel seeds, garlic, bay leaves, oregano and chillies. Place in glass jars and cover with olive oil. The olives will take at least 6 weeks to mature. Test regularly until you are happy with the flavour.

Tomato kasoundi

Makes 500 ml (2 cups)

This fantastic tomato chilli pickle is based on a recipe by Christine Manfield, who in turn was inspired by Charmaine Solomon. It is an excellent addition to curries, noodles or barbecued meats.

- 1 tbsp black mustard seeds
- 125 ml (½ cup) cider vinegar
- 2 kg tomatoes
- 2 tbsp cumin seeds
- 125 ml (½ cup) vegetable oil
- pinch of cloves
- 2 tsp ground turmeric
- 2 tbsp grated ginger
- 10 cloves garlic, peeled
- 10 small chillies
- 85 g (⅓ cup) grated palm sugar
- 60 ml (¼ cup) fish sauce
- salt and freshly ground black pepper
- vegetable oil, as needed

Place the mustard seeds and vinegar in a saucepan and cook over a medium heat for 10 minutes. Set aside for 2 hours.

Cut a cross in the base of each tomato and cut out the core. Bring a large saucepan of water to the boil. Add the tomatoes, a few at a time, and cook for 30 seconds, then place them in cold water. The tomatoes can then be peeled and cut into quarters.

Dry-roast the cumin seeds in a dry frypan over a medium heat, stirring well, until fragrant. Cool, then grind to a fine powder.

Heat the oil in a heavy-based saucepan. Fry the cumin, cloves and turmeric gently, until fragrant. Remove from heat.

Place the soaked mustard seeds, ginger, garlic and chillies in a food processor and whiz until smooth. Add the mix to the saucepan with the oil and spices, along with the prepared tomatoes. Bring to a simmer and cook for 1 hour, stirring frequently. Add palm sugar and fish sauce and cook for a further 30 minutes. Season to taste, if needed.

Spoon into sterilised jars and cover with a thin layer of oil.

Mango chutney

Makes 1¼ litres (5 cups)

Mango is one of those quintessential summer ingredients with myriad uses: serve it on top of a pavlova, alongside a panna cotta or in a smoothie. You can also make this simple chutney and enjoy its flavour over the cooler months.

- 165 ml (⅔ cup) white wine vinegar
- 100 g (½ cup) brown sugar
- 1 onion, finely diced
- 4 cloves garlic, peeled
- 1 tsp ground ginger
- 4 mangoes, peeled and sliced

Bring the vinegar, sugar, onion, garlic and ginger to the boil. Reduce by half. Add mango and cook for a further 5 minutes. Remove from heat and pour into sterilised jars.

Capsicum relish

Makes 625 ml (2½ cups)

This relish reminds us of summer. Use it in sandwiches or as an accompaniment to barbecued beef or pork.

- 5 red capsicums
- oil
- 2 onions, diced
- 2 cloves garlic, crushed
- 220 g (1 cup) raw sugar
- 125 ml (½ cup) white wine vinegar
- 1 tsp cinnamon
- 1 tsp freshly ground black pepper
- 125 ml (½ cup) water
- salt and freshly ground black pepper

Preheat oven to 200°C.

Rub the red capsicums with oil and roast in the preheated oven for 20–25 minutes, until their skins blister. Place the capsicums in a plastic bag and seal to allow the steam to lift their skins. When cool, remove the skins and seeds and dice the flesh roughly.

Add a splash of oil to a large saucepan and cook the onions and garlic for 3–4 minutes, until soft. Add the capsicum, sugar, vinegar, cinnamon, ground pepper and water. Allow the sauce to come to the boil, then reduce heat and simmer for 30 minutes, until the sauce thickens slightly.

Season and spoon into sterilised jars.

Beetroot relish

Makes 500 g (2 cups)

Vibrant beetroot relish is stunning with cold meats and is ideal for picnics or in the cold of winter with the weekly roast.

- 3 medium beetroots
- 250 ml (1 cup) water
- 250 ml (1 cup) white wine vinegar
- 60 g (¼ cup) brown sugar
- 2 whole cloves
- 2 tsp grated ginger
- 2 cloves garlic, sliced
- 1 small red chilli, de-seeded and chopped
- 12 peppercorns

Trim the beetroots, wash them well and place them in a saucepan. Cover with water and bring to the boil. Cook for 30–40 minutes, depending on their size, until tender. Drain, and allow to cool before peeling and grating.

Place water, vinegar, sugar, cloves, ginger, garlic, chilli and peppercorns in a small saucepan. Bring to the boil and cook until reduced to 125 ml (½ cup).

Strain the liquid over the grated beetroot, return to a clean saucepan and simmer for 10 minutes.

Store in an airtight container.

Chilli jam

Makes 500 ml (2 cups)

This classic Thai sauce is a cupboard staple in our house. We use it to add flavour to Asian meatballs and noodles and as a great barbecue marinade.

500 ml (2 cups) vegetable oil
500 g red shallots, peeled and thinly sliced
2 cloves garlic, thinly sliced
10 long red chillies, de-seeded and sliced
2 tbsp tamarind pulp
250 ml (1 cup) boiling water
260 g (1 cup) grated palm sugar
25 g dried shrimp paste
60 ml (¼ cup) fish sauce
1 tsp salt

Heat a wok over a high heat. Add oil, then deep-fry the shallots, garlic and chillies in separate batches. Drain on absorbent paper. Allow the oil to cool and then strain.

Place the fried ingredients in a food processor and add a third of the cool cooking oil (100 ml). Process until smooth, adding more oil if needed to obtain a smooth paste.

Soak the tamarind in boiling water for 5–10 minutes. Use your fingers to work the pulp free from the tamarind seeds. Strain the tamarind, reserving the liquid.

Place the paste in a heavy-based pan and add the tamarind liquid and remaining ingredients. Heat over a low heat until the palm sugar dissolves, then bring to the boil. Reduce heat and cook for 5 minutes, stirring frequently, until the jam thickens slightly.

Sweet chilli sauce

Makes 300 ml (1¼ cups)

Why make sweet chilli sauce when you can buy a bottle? Because it tastes about 100 times better, that's why. We find that it's best made with milder long red chillies such as the cayenne, poblano or serrano varieties. You can, of course, use hotter chillies if you prefer.

250 g chillies (cayenne, poblano or serrano)
4 cloves garlic, crushed
375 ml (1½ cups) water
220 g (1 cup) caster sugar
1 tbsp salt
1 tbsp white vinegar

Remove the seeds and membrane from the chillies and slice the flesh thinly. Place in a saucepan with the garlic, water, caster sugar, salt and vinegar. Bring to the boil, then reduce heat and simmer for 30 minutes, until most of the liquid has evaporated.

Whiz the sauce in a blender to produce a thick consistency with speckles of chilli.

Onion marmalade

Makes 750 g (3 cups)

This gorgeous condiment is great with roast meats and in sandwiches of all types, but particularly those with a good cheddar cheese.

80 ml (⅓ cup) olive oil	salt and freshly ground black pepper
4 onions, sliced	1 tsp yellow mustard seeds
2 cloves garlic, peeled	1 tsp mixed spice
1 small red chilli, halved (optional)	125 ml (½ cup) white wine vinegar
2 sprigs of thyme	90 g (½ cup) soft brown sugar

Heat the oil in a saucepan and add the onions, garlic, chilli (if using) and thyme. Season well with salt and pepper. Cook for 20 minutes on a low heat, stirring often, until the onions soften and turn a pale gold colour.

Add the remaining ingredients and bring to the boil. Stir well to ensure the brown sugar dissolves. Reduce to a simmer again and continue cooking until the mix has a shiny, jam-like consistency.

Allow to cool, then spoon into sterilised jars. Keeps in the refrigerator for 3–4 weeks.

Asian pickles

Serves 6–8

Make these pickles in advance and serve them as you need them. They are good as a side dish to Asian food.

500 ml (2 cups) rice vinegar
250 ml (1 cup) water
110 g (½ cup) caster sugar
2 tbsp light soy sauce
2 cloves garlic, sliced
12 black peppercorns
6 slices ginger

2 small red chillies, halved
¼ cauliflower, broken into bite-sized florets
2 carrots, cut into sticks
2 Lebanese cucumbers, cut into sticks
1 daikon, halved and cut into 1 cm slices
¼ Chinese cabbage, cut into 4 cm chunks

Place the rice vinegar, water, caster sugar, soy sauce, garlic, peppercorns, ginger and chillies in a large saucepan. Bring to the boil, stirring initially to dissolve the sugar. Remove from heat.

Bring a large saucepan of water to the boil and blanch the cauliflower and carrots for 1–2 minutes. Refresh under cold running water.

Place all the vegetables in a large jar. Pour pickling liquid over, ensuring that all the vegetables are covered. Set aside to mature for 48 hours before using. Keep refrigerated.

Pickled ginger

Makes 500 ml (2 cups)

Pickled ginger is available at most Asian supermarkets, but when there is plenty of ginger around, you may like to make your own.

500 g ginger
350 ml (1⅓ cups) rice vinegar
150 ml (⅔ cup) water
2 small red chillies, halved

2 cloves garlic, sliced
12 peppercorns
220 g (1 cup) caster sugar

Using a very sharp knife, peel and thinly slice the ginger. Blanch briefly in boiling water.

To prepare the pickling liquid, place the rice vinegar, water, chillies, garlic, peppercorns and caster sugar in a saucepan. Bring to the boil, then simmer for 20 minutes.

Strain, discarding the flavourings. Place the ginger in sterilised jars, cover with the pickling liquid and seal well. The ginger will turn pinkish over time.

Berry jam

Makes 1 litre (4 cups)

You can make this simple jam with a mixture of berries – blackberries, raspberries and strawberries – or just use one kind of berry, such as raspberries.

1 kg berries
2 tbsp lemon juice
1 kg (4½ cups) caster sugar

If using strawberries and a mixture of other berries, cut the strawberries in half. Wash the berries. Place the fruit, lemon juice and caster sugar in a large heavy-based saucepan. Cook over a low heat until the sugar dissolves, stirring often. Raise the heat and cook at a boil for 15–20 minutes.

After 15 minutes, check to see if the jam has reached setting point by placing a teaspoon of the mixture onto a chilled plate. Tip the plate; if the jam runs, cook for a further 5 minutes, then try again. Pour into sterilised jars while still hot.

Peach and almond jam

Makes 500 g (2 cups)

This is the perfect way to capture the flavour of summer peaches and enjoy them in the cooler months.

1 kg peaches
500 g (2¼ cups) caster sugar
2 tbsp amaretto (optional)
70 g (½ cup) slivered toasted almonds

Cut the peaches in half, remove the stones and cut each half into wedges. Place in a large heavy-based saucepan, add the caster sugar and amaretto (or 2 tbsp water if not using amaretto) and bring to the boil. Cook at a gentle boil for 20–30 minutes.

After 20 minutes, check to see if the jam has reached setting point by placing a teaspoon of the mixture onto a chilled plate. Tip the plate; if the jam runs, cook for a further 5 minutes, then try again. Add the toasted almonds and pour into sterilised jars while still hot.

Apricot jam
Substitute apricots for peaches. Omit almonds and use 2 tbsp water instead of amaretto.

Backyard plum jam

Makes 2–3 litres

The plum tree in the backyard is a great Australian tradition, providing plums for summer cooking and the opportunity to make a stunning jam like this one.

2 kg plums, quartered and stoned
250 ml (1 cup) water
2 tbsp lemon juice
1½ kg (6¾ cups) caster sugar

Place the plums, water and lemon juice in a large heavy-based saucepan. Bring to the boil over a medium heat and cook for 20 minutes, or until the fruit is soft.

Meanwhile, warm the caster sugar either by placing it in a heatproof bowl in the oven, or in the microwave. Add the sugar to the stewed fruit and stir well until the sugar dissolves. Raise the heat and cook for 15–20 minutes, stirring often.

After 15–20 minutes, check to see if the jam has reached setting point by placing a teaspoon of mixture onto a chilled plate. Tip the plate; if the jam runs, cook for a further 5 minutes, then try again. Pour into sterilised jars while still hot.

Fig jam

Our friends around the corner have the most magnificent fig tree, and boxes of figs appear as if by magic on our doorstep each summer. This recipe is a bit trickier than most jams, but it works beautifully.

figs
caster sugar

Take your figs, as many as you want, but at least 1 kg is good. Remove the stems. Weigh the figs and then place them in a large bowl. Add half of their weight in caster sugar (if you have a kilo of figs, for example, add 500 g sugar). Leave overnight.

Place the figs and sugar in a large heavy-based saucepan and bring to the boil. Using a slotted spoon, remove the fruit and set aside. Continue to boil the syrup until it reaches 106°C (pearl stage). Carefully return the figs to the syrup and cook gently for 15 minutes, stirring often to prevent the jam from catching.

Fig and ginger jam
For every kilo of fruit, add 50 g (¼ cup) chopped crystallised ginger.

Orange marmalade

Makes 750 ml (3 cups)

You can make this marmalade with any citrus fruit. Try blood oranges, tangelos, mandarins or cumquats, which are our all-time favourite.

1 kg oranges
600 g (2¾ cups) caster sugar
60 ml (¼ cup) Cointreau (optional)

Place the oranges in a large saucepan and cover with water. Bring to the boil and cook for 1 hour, until soft. Remove the oranges and reduce the cooking liquid to 80 ml (⅓ cup). When the oranges have cooled, peel them, discarding the pips, and puree the flesh. Strain the puree and add it to the cooking liquid.

Finely shred the peel – you're aiming to get 100 g – and add it to the cooking liquid, along with the caster sugar. Bring to the boil, add Cointreau (if using) and reduce heat. Cook until it achieves a syrupy consistency, stirring frequently.

Test for setting point by putting a teaspoon of marmalade onto a chilled plate. Tip the plate; if the marmalade runs, cook for a further 5 minutes, then try again. Pour into sterilised jars while still hot and enjoy as soon as it's cool.

Cranberry and pear conserve

Makes 1 litre (4 cups)

The mix of tangy craisin, pear and orange creates an unusual yet sensational conserve.

500 g (3½ cups) craisins or frozen cranberries
4 pears, peeled, cored and chopped
1 orange, peeled and flesh roughly chopped
720 g (4 cups) soft brown sugar
1 tsp ground cinnamon
¼ tsp ground cardamom
170 g (1 cup) raisins

Place all the ingredients in a large bowl and leave it to stand overnight.

Transfer the fruit to a large saucepan and bring to the boil. Reduce heat and simmer for 30–45 minutes, or until thick.

Ladle into sterilised jars while still hot.

Pumpkin conserve

Makes 500 ml (2 cups)

A true autumn treat, this conserve is great on toast in the morning.

500 g (2¼ cups) caster sugar
500 g pumpkin, peeled, de-seeded and flesh grated
zest of 2 limes, grated
60 ml (¼ cup) lime juice
125 ml (½ cup) water
50 g butter

Place all the ingredients in a heavy-based saucepan over a medium heat. Bring to the boil and cook at a gentle boil for 20–30 minutes, or until the jam reaches setting point.

Check to see if the conserve has reached setting point by placing a teaspoon of the mixture onto a chilled plate. Tip the plate; if it runs, cook for a further 5 minutes, then try again. Pour into sterilised jars while still hot.

Cumquat jelly

Makes 750 ml–1 litre (3–4 cups)

Cumquat jelly is incredibly easy to make because you don't have to chop the peels or try to remove hundreds of tiny pips. The end result will be an intensely flavoured citrus jelly that's amazing on hot buttered toast.

1 kg cumquats
caster sugar as required

Cut the cumquats in half and place them in a saucepan. Add enough cold water to cover and bring to a gentle boil. Reduce heat to a simmer and cook the fruit for 2 hours. Regularly skim off the froth as it comes to the surface.

Allow the liquid and fruit to cool slightly, then ladle it into a cloth-lined colander or sieve. A large clean tea towel is fine, or muslin is good if you have it. Allow the liquid to drip through into a large bowl.

When the dripping begins to slow, gather the edges of the cloth together and tie with string. Hang the cloth in an elevated position and allow the remaining liquid to drip through for a few hours, or overnight if time permits.

Measure the cumquat liquid into a saucepan and add equal caster sugar to the liquid. For example, you would add 500 g sugar if you had 500 ml liquid.

Return the liquid and sugar to the heat and bring to the boil. Reduce to a simmer and regularly skim off froth as it comes to the surface. Cook until it achieves a syrupy consistency, stirring frequently.

To see if the jelly has reached setting point, place a teaspoon of the mixture onto a chilled plate. Tip the plate; if the jam runs, cook for a further 5 minutes, then try again. Pour into sterilised jars while still hot.

Lemon curd (lemon butter)

Makes 500 ml (2 cups)

This is arm-breaking work but well worth the effort for this rich and yummy treat.

4 egg yolks
200 g (1 cup) caster sugar
200 g soft butter
grated zest of 2 lemons
80 ml (⅓ cup) lemon juice

Beat egg yolks and sugar in a large heatproof bowl until pale and creamy. Add butter, lemon zest and juice. Place over a simmering pot of water and whisk continuously until thickened, 20–30 minutes. Store in sterilised jars in the refrigerator for up to 3 weeks.

Passionfruit curd
Substitute 60 ml (¼ cup) of passionfruit pulp for lemon juice.

Microwave lemon curd

Makes 500 ml (2 cups)

Instead of the endless whisking over a hot pot, try this microwave version. It's so quick and easy.

125 g butter
grated zest of 3 lemons
125 ml (½ cup) lemon juice
250 g (1 ¼ cups) caster sugar
4 medium eggs

Place butter, grated zest and juice of lemons in a microwave-proof bowl. Cook on high for 3 minutes. Add sugar and cook for 2 minutes. Stir in eggs, one at a time. Cook on low until mixture thickens, about 12–15 minutes. Stir occasionally. Store in sterilised jars in the refrigerator for up to 3 weeks.

PASTRY

sweet + savoury
roll your dough

There's a knack to making pastry, and for many people it takes a few attempts to get it right. Pastry is greatly influenced by the weather: too humid, and the pastry becomes sticky; too cold, and it's too hard to manipulate. A cool, light touch seems to work best, so if your hands are too hot, rinse them under cold water. Working in a cool, well-ventilated spot will also help.

Most importantly, don't give up. Once you've mastered the art of making pastry you will be able to whip up quiches, tarts and pies at the drop of a hat. There are no shortcuts when it comes to making good sweet or shortcrust pastry: it needs to be rested for at least 20 minutes every time it has been worked, or it will shrink during cooking. When it comes to puff pastry, however, we often use frozen all-butter sheets, rather than making our own every time.

Some people swear by a food processor to make pastry, and if that works well for you, congratulations. We've always stuck to the tried-and-tested rubbing-in method, which takes the same amount of time as a food processor but results in less washing up.

pastry recipes

pastry

Shortcrust pastry	590
Sweetcrust pastry	590
Almond sweetcrust pastry	591
Rich sweetcrust pastry	591
Cream cheese pastry	592
Puff pastry	593
Rough puff pastry	594
Choux pastry	594
Hot water pastry	595

savoury

Asparagus and goat's cheese tart	595
Quiche lorraine	596
Haloumi, olive and onion tart	597
Roast pumpkin and blue cheese tart	598
Roast tomato, pancetta and spinach tart	600
Mushroom tart	601
Tomato and anchovy tart	603
Roast chilli tomato and pesto tarts	604
Leek and cheese slice	605
Olive, prosciutto and feta slice	605
Potato, rosemary and goat's cheese tarts	606
Roast pumpkin, feta and pine nut puff slice	606
Olive, fig and goat's cheese slice	607
Moroccan chicken rolls	608
Breakfast tarts	609
Egg and bacon pie	610
Spiced eggplant parcels	612
Chicken and vegetable pasties	613
Cheese and potato pies	614
Sausage rolls	614
Free-form roast summer vegetable tart	615
Vegetable pasties	616
Cheesy choux puffs	617
Spanakopita (Greek cheese pastries)	617
Bistella	618

sweet

Ricotta tart	620
Apricot and frangipane tart	621
Raspberry and mascarpone tart	621
Passionfruit tart	622
Lemon tart	622
Lemon meringue tart	623
Apple tart	623
Bitter chocolate tarts	624
Apple and rhubarb pie	625
Free-form fruit pie	626
Fruit mince pies	628
Blueberry and mascarpone tart	628
Peach and frangipane tart	629
Cherry and marzipan tart	629
Raspberry and limoncello tart	630
Chocolate and pear tart	630
Blood plum and almond tart	631
Roasted apricot, ricotta and almond free-form tart	632
Quince tarte tatin	634
Profiteroles with white chocolate and raspberries	635
Chocolate eclairs	636
Egyptian bread and butter pudding	636
Pistachio, almond and orange blossom baklava	637
Kataifi nests with sweet labne and rosewater-poached rhubarb	639

Things you need to know about pastry

1 Don't be afraid of pastry. We reckon that pastry, like dogs, can sense fear and will play up to it.

2 Making pastry is like riding a bike: make it right once and you'll have the knack forever.

3 Climate will affect pastry. If your kitchen is hot and stuffy, you're not going to have too much luck. Keep ingredients and your work area as cool as possible.

4 Always dust your work surface and rolling pin with a little flour to stop the pastry sticking.

5 To check that you have rolled out your pastry to the right size, place your tin on top of the pastry and allow an extra 2–3 cm for the sides.

6 Try not to roll pastry too thin; 3 mm is perfect.

7 To line a pastry tin, place your rolling pin on top of the pastry at the edge closest to you. Pick up the edge of the pastry and roll the pin, bringing the pastry with it. Transfer the rolling pin to the edge of the tin and unroll the pastry onto the tin. Push the pastry down into the tin and push the edges over it. Roll the rolling pin across the top to trim off excess pastry. Lastly, work your fingers around the side of the tin, making sure the pastry is pushed down into the corners. Trim off any excess pastry using a small knife.

8 Pastry is often cooked in the oven before any filling is added. This is known as blind baking. We typically use rice for this.

Shortcrust pastry

Makes 1 × 25 cm savoury pastry shell

This is the basic pastry used for all savoury tarts. It can also be used for sweet tarts, especially if the filling is very sweet.

300 g (2 cups) plain flour
pinch of salt
150 g butter, diced

60–80 ml (¼–⅓ cup) cold water
plain flour for dusting

PASTRY DOUGH Sift the flour and salt. Rub in the butter to produce a breadcrumb texture. Add enough water to bring the pastry together and knead briefly. Wrap in cling film and chill for 30 minutes.

PASTRY SHELL Preheat oven to 180°C.

Roll the pastry on a lightly floured board to 3 mm thickness. Line a buttered 25 cm flan tin with the pastry, working your fingers around the side of the tin to make sure the pastry is pushed down into the corners. Trim off any excess pastry using a small knife.

Prick the base of the pastry shell with a fork and rest for 30 minutes. Line the pastry with greaseproof paper, then add baking beans, pastry weights or rice. Bake blind for 15 minutes in the preheated oven. Remove the paper and pastry weights and bake for a further 5 minutes to crisp the pastry.

Sweetcrust pastry

Makes 1 × 25 cm sweet pastry shell

Sweetcrust pastry is easier to work with because the sugar breaks down the protein in the flour and makes the pastry more supple. Use it for sweet tarts.

300 g (2 cups) plain flour
150 g soft butter, diced
pinch of salt

1 egg
55 g (¼ cup) caster sugar
plain flour for dusting

PASTRY DOUGH Place the flour, butter and salt in a bowl and rub together until the mixture resembles fine breadcrumbs. Break the egg into a separate bowl, add caster sugar and mix lightly. Add to the flour mixture and mix the until pastry comes together. Wrap in cling film and chill for 30 minutes.

PASTRY SHELL Preheat oven to 180°C.

Roll the pastry on a lightly floured board to 3 mm thickness. Line a buttered 25 cm flan tin with the pastry, working your fingers around the side of the tin to make sure the pastry is pushed down into the corners. Trim off any excess pastry using a small knife.

Prick the base of the pastry shell with a fork and rest for 30 minutes. Line the pastry with greaseproof paper, then add baking beans, pastry weights or rice. Bake blind for 15 minutes in the preheated oven. Remove the paper and pastry weights and bake for a further 5 minutes to crisp the pastry.

Almond sweetcrust pastry

Makes 1 × 25 cm almond sweetcrust pastry shell

Here, almonds replace some of the flour to introduce a nutty flavour to the pastry.

200 g (1⅓ cups) plain flour
100 g (1 cup) ground almonds
pinch of salt
150 g soft butter, diced
2 egg yolks
55 g (¼ cup) caster sugar
plain flour for dusting

PASTRY DOUGH Rub the flour, almonds, salt and butter together until it resembles fine breadcrumbs. Lightly beat the egg yolks and dissolve the caster sugar in them. Make a well in the centre of the flour mix, pour in the egg and sugar and knead lightly to form a ball. Wrap in cling film and chill for 30 minutes.

PASTRY SHELL Preheat oven to 180°C.

Roll the pastry on a lightly floured board to 3 mm thickness. Line a buttered 25 cm flan tin with the pastry, working your fingers around the side of the tin to make sure the pastry is pushed down into the corners. Trim off any excess pastry using a small knife.

Prick the base of the pastry shell with a fork and rest for 30 minutes. Line the pastry with greaseproof paper, then add baking beans, pastry weights or rice. Bake blind for 15 minutes in the preheated oven. Remove the paper and pastry weights and bake for a further 5 minutes to crisp the pastry.

Rich sweetcrust pastry

Makes 1 × 25 cm almond sweetcrust pastry shell

Pastry with a high butter content is often described as short pastry. It produces a stunning eating experience but can be difficult to roll in one piece. If this happens simply push pieces together to line the flan tin.

225 g (1½ cups) plain flour
175 g soft butter, diced
pinch of salt
1 egg yolk
55 g (¼ cup) caster sugar

PASTRY DOUGH Place flour, butter and salt in a bowl and rub together until the mixture resembles fine breadcrumbs. Place egg yolk into a separate bowl, add sugar and mix lightly. Add to flour mixture and mix until pastry comes together. Wrap in cling film and chill for 30 minutes.

PASTRY SHELL Preheat oven to 180°C.

Roll pastry on a lightly floured board to 3 mm thickness and line a greased 25 cm flan tin. If the pastry proves difficult to roll, simply push pieces together to line the flan tin. Work fingers around the side of the tin making sure pastry is pushed down into corners. Trim any excess off the top using a small knife.

Prick base with fork and rest for 30 minutes. Line pastry with greaseproof paper, then baking beans, pastry weights or rice and bake blind for 15 minutes in preheated oven. Remove paper and weights, and bake for a further 5 minutes to crisp pastry.

Cream cheese pastry

Makes 1 × 25 cm cream cheese pastry shell

This fantastic recipe comes from Natalie Paull, a Melbourne-based chef. The cream cheese makes a pastry that's perfect for heartier fillings. You can use a food processor with this recipe, but the pastry will need a longer resting time.

125 g soft cream cheese
125 g soft butter
1 tbsp caster sugar
150 g (1 cup) plain flour
¼ tsp baking powder
pinch of salt
plain flour for dusting

PASTRY DOUGH Place the cream cheese, butter and caster sugar in a food processor and whiz until soft. Sift the flour, baking powder and salt, then add to the food processor. Pulse until the pastry just comes together. Remove the pastry and knead briefly. Wrap in cling film and chill for 2 hours.

PASTRY SHELL Preheat oven to 180°C.

Roll the pastry on a lightly floured board to 3 mm thickness. Line a buttered 25 cm flan tin with the pastry, working your fingers around the side of the tin to make sure the pastry is pushed down into the corners. Trim off any excess pastry using a small knife.

Prick the base of the pastry shell with a fork and rest for 30 minutes. Line the pastry with greaseproof paper, then add baking beans, pastry weights or rice. Bake blind for 15 minutes in the preheated oven. Remove the paper and pastry weights and bake for a further 5 minutes to crisp the pastry.

Puff pastry

Makes 500 g puff pastry

Puff pastry is usually thought best left to the experts, but in fact it's quite easy. It takes a few hours because of all the resting time, but you can do plenty of other things in between.

250 g (1⅔ cups) plain flour
pinch of salt
squeeze of lemon juice
100–120 ml (⅓–½ cup) iced water
250 g butter
plain flour for dusting

Sift the flour and salt together in a large bowl. Add lemon juice and enough iced water to bring the pastry together. Tip onto a floured bench and roll the pastry into a 20 cm square. Wrap in foil and chill for 30 minutes.

Remove the butter from the refrigerator 30 minutes before using and cut into thick slices. It is essential that the butter and pastry share a similar temperature and softness, so the butter will be thoroughly incorporated.

Place the chilled pastry on a floured bench and roll out to a 30 cm square, leaving a thick centre that is about twice as thick as the sides. Place slices of butter in the centre of the pastry and press all over with your fingertips to soften the butter a little more. Fold in all the edges, ensuring that the butter is completely encased in the pastry.

Turn the pastry over, dust with flour and roll it into a long 50–60 cm rectangle. Fold the bottom third of the pastry up over the centre and the top third down to cover it, like a letter. Make a single indentation with your finger on top of the pastry to signify the first fold. Wrap in foil and chill for 30 minutes.

Remove the pastry from the refrigerator. Turn it 90° (a quarter turn) and roll again into a long rectangle. Again fold into 3, like a letter, and mark 2 indentations. Cover and chill for 30 minutes. Repeat until a total of 6 folds have been completed. Remember to mark them as you go. After the last fold, roll the pastry as required and allow to rest 30 minutes before baking.

If not using the pastry immediately, divide into 2 portions and freeze.

Rough puff pastry

Makes 500 g rough puff pastry

This is the 'quick' version of puff pastry. It's perfect when time is tight and you need a top for your pie. What you're doing here is 3 folds in one go, rather than 6 folds with resting time in between, as for true puff pastry.

250 g (1⅔ cups) plain flour
pinch of salt
250 g butter, diced
squeeze of lemon juice
100–120 ml (⅓–½ cup) iced water
plain flour for dusting

Place the flour and salt in a food processor. Add the butter to the flour and pulse 3–4 times. Don't try to make the butter disappear; it should still be nice and lumpy.

Place the pastry in a large bowl, add lemon juice and iced water, then knead lightly to bring the pastry together; don't over-knead. Wrap in cling film and rest in the refrigerator for 30 minutes.

Dust the pastry with flour and roll it into a long 50–60 cm rectangle. Fold the bottom third of the pastry up over the centre and the top third down to cover it, like a letter. Turn it 90° (a quarter turn) and roll again into a long rectangle. Again fold into 3 and turn it 90°. Roll one last time into a long rectangle (3 times in total), fold into 3, wrap in cling film and pop back in the refrigerator for 30 minutes before using as directed by the recipe.

Choux pastry

Makes enough for 40 profiteroles or 10–15 eclairs

Choux pastry makes delectable things such as profiteroles and cheesy puffs.

125 ml (½ cup) water
125 ml (½ cup) milk
pinch of salt
100 g butter
150 g (1 cup) plain flour
5 eggs

Place the water, milk, salt and butter in a saucepan and bring to the boil. Tip in the flour, stir and return to a low heat. Cook for 2–3 minutes, stirring constantly, until the mixture begins to come away from the side of the saucepan.

Tip the contents into a food processor. Start the processor, allowing the mixture to cool slightly.

Break the eggs into a jug and beat lightly. Slowly add the egg mix to the pastry mixture, ensuring that the eggs are well incorporated each time before adding more. Continue adding the eggs until the pastry is of a dropping consistency – not too runny. You may not need to add all the eggs; it tends to vary a bit from batch to batch.

Hot water pastry

Makes enough for 6–8 pasties

This quick pastry is just what you need for making delicious pasties.

- 150 ml (½ cup plus 1 tbsp) cold water
- 100 g butter
- 1 tsp salt
- 300 g (2 cups) self-raising flour

Place the water, butter and salt in a saucepan over a medium heat until butter has completely melted. Remove from heat, rapidly stir in flour and mix until dough forms a ball.

Place dough on a lightly floured board. Allow to cool for a few minutes, dust hands with flour and knead gently for thirty seconds. Divide dough as required and cover with a tea towel to keep warm. Use dough while still warm, as it becomes firm when cold.

Asparagus and goat's cheese tart

Serves 8

Asparagus and goat's cheese appears in a range of dishes, from salads to pasta and, as described here, savoury tarts.

- 150 g asparagus
- 4 eggs
- 125 ml (½ cup) cream
- salt and freshly ground black pepper
- 2 tbsp chopped parsley
- 1 × 25 cm Shortcrust Pastry shell (page 590)
- 100 g goat's cheese

Preheat oven to 180°C.

Bring a saucepan of water to the boil. Trim the woody ends from the asparagus. You can do this by holding the end of the stalk in one hand and the remainder in the other. The stalk will break at the appropriate point. If preferred, trim off the bottom 5 cm or so with a knife. Cook the asparagus in boiling water for 2 minutes. Drain and refresh under cold running water.

Beat the eggs with cream, salt, pepper and parsley. Place the asparagus in the base of the cooked pastry shell, pour in the egg mix and crumble goat's cheese over the top. Bake in the preheated oven for 30 minutes, until golden brown and set.

Quiche lorraine

Serves 8

Quiche lorraine is the type of quiche that most people know, with a filling that includes lots of cooked onion and bacon. No wonder it's so popular.

- 2 tbsp olive oil
- 1 onion, diced
- 4 slices bacon, cut into strips
- 6 eggs
- 250 ml (1 cup) cream
- salt and freshly ground black pepper
- 2 tbsp chopped parsley
- 125 g (1½ cups) parmigiano, grated
- 1 × 25 cm Shortcrust Pastry shell (page 590)

Preheat oven to 180°C.

Heat a heavy-based frypan over a medium heat, add oil and onions and cook for 4–5 minutes, stirring often until onion softens but doesn't colour. Add bacon and cook for a further 3–4 minutes. Remove from heat and allow to cool.

Beat eggs with cream, salt, pepper, parsley and cheese. Spoon onion and bacon mix into cooked pastry shell. Pour egg mix into pastry shell and bake in preheated oven for 30 minutes until golden brown and set.

Leek and goat's cheese quiche
Substitute 2 thinly sliced leeks for onion and goat's cheese for 60 g (¾ cup) parmigiano.

Asparagus quiche
Cook onion until soft, add the bacon if you want to. Place blanched, chopped asparagus spears in pastry shell along with onion before egg mix.

Caramelised onion quiche
Cook 4 sliced onions in 60 ml (¼ cup) olive oil with salt, freshly ground black pepper and a sprig or two of fresh thyme for 30 minutes. Stir often. The onions will turn dark brown and gloriously rich. Drain and allow to cool before placing in cooked pastry shell. Also delicious with goat's cheese rather than parmigiano.

Mushroom quiche
Add 125 g sliced mushrooms to pan while cooking onions. Cook for a further 5–6 minutes, or until mushrooms are softened. Allow to cool, then add to the pastry shell before egg mix.

Olive and spinach quiche
Cook onion until soft, remove and allow to cool. Add 90 g of black olive halves with 100 g (½ cup) blanched, chopped spinach, then complete as described.

Haloumi, olive and onion tart

Serves 8

Cooked onions make a fantastic flavour base in a savoury tart. They're used to great effect in this recipe with kalamata olives and haloumi cheese.

oil	125 ml (½ cup) cream
2 onions, sliced	20 g (¼ cup) grated parmigiano
salt and freshly ground black pepper	2 tbsp chopped parsley
150 g haloumi	1 × 25 cm Shortcrust Pastry shell (page 590)
4 eggs	90 g (½ cup) pitted kalamata olives

Preheat oven to 180°C.

Heat a small saucepan over a medium heat. Add a generous splash of oil and the onions, salt and pepper. Cook for 10–15 minutes, stirring often, until the onions caramelise and turn golden. Set the onions aside in a colander to drain.

Cut the haloumi into ½ cm slices. Heat a small frypan over a medium heat. Add a splash of oil and cook the haloumi slices for 2–3 minutes on each side, until golden brown. Remove from heat and set aside.

Whisk the eggs together with the cream, grated parmigiano, parsley, salt and pepper. Place the onions in the cooked pastry shell and top with haloumi slices. Scatter olives over the top, then pour in the egg custard. Bake in the preheated oven for 30–40 minutes, or until the egg custard is set.

Roast pumpkin and blue cheese tart

Serves 8

The sweetness of the pumpkin is perfectly matched by the saltiness of the blue cheese in this heavenly tart. Try it with a Pear, Walnut and Rocket Salad (page 507).

1 kg pumpkin, peeled, de-seeded and diced into 3 cm chunks	100 g blue cheese
oil	4 eggs
salt and freshly ground black pepper	125 ml (½ cup) cream
1 × 25 cm Shortcrust Pastry shell (page 590)	2 tbsp chopped parsley
	20 g (¼ cup) grated parmigiano

Preheat oven to 180°C.

Toss the pumpkin with oil, salt and pepper and roast in the preheated oven until golden brown.

Place the roasted pumpkin in the cooked pastry shell and crumble over blue cheese. Whisk the eggs together with the cream, parsley, grated parmigiano, salt and pepper and pour over the top. Bake in the preheated oven for 30–40 minutes, or until the egg custard is set.

Roast tomato, pancetta and spinach tart

Serves 8

Tarts offer great opportunities to combine a mix of different flavours and textures. Here, the spicy roasted tomatoes, full-flavoured pancetta, soft onions and spinach encased in a crisp pastry shell are an absolute delight.

4 tomatoes
oil
salt and freshly ground black pepper
1 tsp chilli powder (optional)
1 onion, diced
6 pancetta slices, diced
4 eggs
125 ml (½ cup) cream
20 g (¼ cup) grated parmigiano
2 tbsp chopped parsley
80 g spinach, blanched and chopped
1 × 25 cm Shortcrust Pastry shell (page 590)

Preheat oven to 180°C.

Cut the tomatoes into wedges. Place them on a baking tray, brush with oil and sprinkle with salt, pepper and chilli (if using). Roast in preheated oven for 20–30 minutes, until the tomatoes are soft and golden brown.

Heat a small saucepan over a medium heat. Add a generous splash of oil, the onion and pancetta. Cook for 5–6 minutes, stirring often.

Whisk the eggs together with the cream, grated parmigiano, parsley, spinach and salt and pepper. Arrange the tomato wedges in the base of the cooked pastry shell, add the onion and pancetta mix and pour in the egg custard. Bake in the preheated oven for 30–40 minutes, or until the egg custard is set.

Mushroom tart

Serves 8

If you're using mushrooms in a savoury tart you'll need to pre-cook them to bring out their earthy flavour and remove excess moisture. In this recipe, the mushrooms are lightly pan-fried, then flavoured with a touch of garlic and cream.

oil
1 onion, diced
2 cloves garlic, crushed
250 g Swiss brown mushrooms, sliced
salt and freshly ground black pepper
pinch of grated nutmeg
2 tbsp cream
1 tbsp grated parmigiano
2 tbsp chopped parsley
1 egg, beaten
150 g fromage frais or goat's cheese
1 × 25 cm Shortcrust Pastry shell (page 590)

Preheat oven to 180°C.

Heat a heavy-based frypan over a medium–high heat. Add a splash of oil and the onion and cook for 3–4 minutes, until the onion is soft. Add the garlic and mushrooms and cook for 3–4 minutes, stirring often. Season with salt, pepper and nutmeg. Add the cream and cook until the juices reduce to just 1–2 tbsp. Remove from heat, transfer to a bowl and allow to cool slightly.

Add the parmigiano, parsley and egg to the mushrooms and toss to combine. Lightly mix through fromage frais or goat's cheese, then spoon the mix into the cooked pastry shell. Bake in the preheated oven for 10–12 minutes, or until the filling is set.

Tomato and anchovy tart

Serves 8

This tart is perfect for those of you who love the salty combination of anchovies and olives.

olive oil
1 onion, diced
1 garlic clove, crushed
6 tomatoes, diced
2 tbsp tomato paste
2 eggs
salt and freshly ground black pepper
1 × 25 cm Shortcrust Pastry shell (page 590)
12 anchovy fillets
12 black olives

Preheat oven to 180°C

Heat a heavy-based frypan over medium heat, add a splash of olive oil and cook onion and garlic until soft. Add tomatoes and tomato paste and continue to cook until soft, about 10 minutes. Remove from heat and allow to cool. Add eggs and season to taste.

Pour into cooked pastry shell. Cut anchovy fillets in half lengthways, remove stones from olives and cut in half. Lay the anchovy strips over the tomato in a diamond lattice formation and put one olive half in each diamond.

Bake in preheated oven for 40 minutes, or until tomato filling is set and lightly brown.

Roast chilli tomato and pesto tarts

Serves 10

Whether you make puff pastry from scratch or buy a good quality product, these tarts are a winner for entree on a hot summer's day.

- 10 Roma tomatoes
- 2 tbsp olive oil
- 1 tsp chilli paste
- salt and freshly ground black pepper
- 75 g pesto
- 1 egg yolk
- 1 tbsp milk
- salad leaves to serve (optional)
- basil oil (optional)
- ½ quantity Rough Puff Pastry (page 594) or 2–3 sheets frozen puff pastry

Preheat oven to 180°C.

Cut the tomatoes in half and place skin side down on a lined baking tray. Mix the oil and chilli paste together and brush liberally over tomato halves. Sprinkle with salt and pepper. Roast in the preheated oven for 20–25 minutes, until softened and lightly browned.

Cut the pastry into 10 equal rectangles, approximately 10 × 8 cm. Arrange on lined baking trays. Place 1 tsp pesto in the centre of each piece of pastry, spread it out but leave 1 cm of pastry free around the edge. Arrange 2 tomato halves on top of the pesto. Mix egg yolk and milk together to form egg wash. Fold over 1 cm of the edge to form a lip, brush the edge with egg wash.

Bake the tarts in the preheated oven for 15–20 minutes until the pastry is golden brown.

Place a tart on each plate, with a handful of salad leaves if desired. Drizzle basil oil around tart and serve.

Leek and cheese slice

Serves 6–8

Cut this simple tart into small squares and serve it as a nibble with drinks, or cut larger squares and serve it with salad for lunch.

2 leeks
generous knob of butter
½ quantity Puff Pastry (page 593) or 2–3 sheets frozen puff pastry
100 g taleggio or gruyere cheese
thyme leaves
freshly ground black pepper
1 egg yolk
1 tbsp milk

Preheat oven to 200°C.

Trim, wash and thinly slice the leeks. Heat a heavy-based frypan over a medium heat. Add the butter and cook leeks over a low heat, covered, until they soften but do not brown.

Roll out the pastry on a lightly floured board to a square 3 mm thick. Place the pastry on a lined baking tray. Spoon the leeks evenly onto the pastry, leaving a 1 cm gap around the edge. Crumble taleggio or gruyere over the top, scatter with thyme leaves and season with freshly ground black pepper.

Mix the egg yolk with milk to make an egg wash. Fold the 1 cm edge of pastry to form a lip, and brush with the egg wash. Bake in the preheated oven for 15–20 minutes, or until golden brown.

Olive, prosciutto and feta slice

Serves 8

This slice has a beautiful tangy taste, and is ideal as an appetiser or for lunch for four people. If they are in season, add figs for a lovely sweetness. If you'd like to make your own Puff Pastry, see page 593.

2 sheets Puff Pastry, each approximately 20 × 20 cm
1 egg yolk
1 tbsp milk
⅓ cup olive paste or tapenade
200 g feta
1 tbsp baby capers, soaked and chopped if necessary
1 tbsp chopped thyme and rosemary
4 figs, cut into quarters (optional)
8 slices prosciutto

Place puff pastry sheets on a lined baking tray. Mix egg yolk with milk to make egg wash. Brush an egg wash border around the edges of the pastry. Spread tapenade or olive paste over pastry leaving a 1 cm edge free. Crumble feta over olive paste, scatter capers and herbs over the top. Arrange figs on top of other ingredients. Fold over 1 cm of the edge to form a lip, brush edge with egg wash.

Preheat oven to 200°C.

Add slices to preheated oven and cook for 15–18 minutes, until pastry is cooked and golden brown.

To serve, lay prosciutto over the top of the slice. Cut into portions as preferred for an appetiser or entree.

Potato, rosemary and goat's cheese tarts

Makes 4

The secret to the success of this tart is to use good-quality potatoes and goat's cheese. Opt for kipflers for maximum flavour and try a quality cheese such as Holy Goat.

4 peeled potatoes
½ quantity Puff Pastry (page 593) or 2–3 sheets frozen puff pastry
2 tbsp chopped rosemary
200 g goat's cheese
olive oil
salt and freshly ground black pepper

Cook the peeled potatoes in boiling water until just tender. Drain the potatoes, allow to cool and cut into ½ cm slices.

Preheat oven to 180°C.

Roll puff pastry to a rectangle 3 mm thick and cut into 4 smaller rectangles measuring about 12 cm × 16 cm. Place on baking trays lined with baking paper. Divide the potato slices between each rectangle, leaving a 1 cm border. Scatter with chopped rosemary and add 2–3 slices of goat's cheese on top. Drizzle with olive oil and season with salt and pepper. Bake in the preheated oven for 20–25 minutes, until puffed and golden brown. Serve with a simple green salad.

Roast pumpkin, feta and pine nut puff slice

Serves 4

An absolute winner on the menu at Ludo Foodstore whenever it's made. A glorious combination of sweet roast pumpkin, salty feta and crunchy pine nuts.

1 kg pumpkin, diced 2 cm chunks
olive oil
salt and freshly ground black pepper
¼ quantity Puff Pastry (page 593) or 2–3 sheets frozen puff pastry
100 g rocket leaves
200 g feta
80 g (½ cup) pine nuts

Preheat oven to 180°C.

Toss the pumpkin with olive oil, salt and pepper and roast in the preheated oven for 30 minutes or until the pumpkin is tender and golden brown.

Place the pastry in a lined baking tray measuring about 20 × 20 cm. Scatter rocket leaves over the base and top with cooked pumpkin. Crumble feta over the pumpkin and scatter pine nuts on top.

Bake in the preheated oven for 15–20 minutes or until the pastry is crisp and golden brown. Cut into 4 pieces. Serve with salad.

Olive, fig and goat's cheese slice

Serves 8

We often make slices such as this as a pre-dinner nibble when friends come around. The slices use puff pastry as a base, and are incredibly easy to make.

- 1 quantity Puff Pastry (page 593) or 4–6 sheets frozen puff pastry
- 1 egg yolk
- 1 tbsp milk
- ⅓ cup olive paste or tapenade
- 4 figs
- 200 g goat's cheese
- 1 tbsp baby capers, soaked and chopped if necessary
- 1 tbsp chopped thyme and rosemary
- 8 slices prosciutto (optional)
- rocket leaves to serve

Preheat oven to 200°C.

Divide the pastry in half and, on a lightly floured board, roll each piece into a square 3 mm thick. Place the pastry sheets on lined baking trays.

Mix the egg yolk with milk to make an egg wash. Brush a border of egg wash around the edges of the pastry. Spread tapenade or olive paste over the pastry, leaving a 1 cm gap around the edge. Slice the figs into 0.5 cm slices and arrange on top of the olive paste. Crumble on goat's cheese and scatter capers and herbs over the top. Fold the 1 cm edge of pastry to form a lip, and brush with egg wash.

Bake in the preheated oven for 15–18 minutes, until the pastry is cooked and golden brown.

Arrange the prosciutto slices over the top of the slice (if using). Cut into portions as preferred for an appetiser or entree, and serve with a rocket salad.

Olive, prosciutto and feta slice
Use olive paste as directed, then top with figs and feta. When cooked, arrange prosciutto slices over the top and slice.

Moroccan chicken rolls

Makes 20

If you like your food spicy, double the quantities of spice recommended in this recipe.

- 1 onion, finely diced
- oil
- 500 g chicken mince
- 2 tsp ground cumin
- 2 tsp ground coriander
- 1 tsp smoky paprika
- 2–3 tbsp chopped coriander
- 1 egg yolk
- salt and freshly ground black pepper
- 1 quantity Puff Pastry (page 593) or 4–6 sheets frozen puff pastry
- plain flour for dusting
- 1 egg yolk, additional
- 1 tbsp milk
- sesame seeds

Heat a small frypan over a medium–high heat. Add a splash of oil and the onion. Cook for 4–5 minutes, stirring often, until soft.

Mix the onion, chicken mince, spices, coriander, egg yolk, salt and pepper together.

Roll out the pastry on a lightly floured board to 3 mm thickness – either a square or a rectangle will do. Roll the chicken mince to form a long snake, 2 cm wide. Place the mince on the puff pastry; you may need 2–3 'snakes', depending on the length of your pastry.

Mix the additional egg yolk with milk to make an egg wash. Brush 1 edge of the puff pastry with egg wash and fold the pastry over to totally enclose the meat. Crimp the pastry to ensure that it sticks together, then cut into 20 small rolls. Place the chicken rolls on a lined baking tray.

Brush the rolls with egg wash and slash each top with a knife in a few places to expose the filling. Sprinkle with sesame seeds. Rest for 30 minutes.

Preheat oven to 200°C.

Bake the chicken rolls for 15–20 minutes, or until the pastry is cooked and golden brown, ensuring the chicken is cooked through.

Breakfast tarts

Makes 12

Perfect for social brunches, or even picnics, what better way to eat bacon and eggs than to wrap them up in flaky pastry?

12 cherry tomatoes
12 button mushrooms
salt and freshly ground black pepper
olive oil
6 bacon rashers, rind removed
½ quantity Puff Pastry (page 593) or 2–3 sheets frozen puff pastry
40 g (½ cup) grated parmigiano
12 eggs
¼ cup chopped parsley

Preheat oven to 180°C.

Place tomatoes and mushrooms on a baking tray. Sprinkle with salt and pepper and drizzle with oil. Bake in the preheated oven for 15–20 minutes or until soft and golden brown. Place the bacon on another baking tray and cook in the preheated oven for 5–8 minutes or until crispy.

Grease a 12 cup muffin tray. Roll out the pastry on a lightly floured board to 3 mm thickness. Cut circles of pastry using a 10 cm cutter and place each pastry circle into the muffin tray. Sprinkle 1 tbsp grated parmigiano in each tart shell. Arrange half a bacon slice in each shell, along with one mushroom. Crack an egg into each shell. Cut the cherry tomatoes in half and add 2 halves to each tart. Sprinkle with chopped parsley, salt and pepper.

Bake in the preheated oven for 15–18 minutes or until the eggs have set. Serve while still warm.

Egg and bacon pie

Serves 6–8

A good egg and bacon pie is a beautiful thing. If you like, you could also use smoked chicken, pancetta or prosciutto, or make individual pies.

- 1 quantity Rough Puff Pastry (page 594) or 4–6 sheets frozen puff pastry
- plain flour for dusting
- 2 tbsp olive oil
- 2 onions, finely diced
- 400 g slices bacon, cut into strips
- freshly ground black pepper
- 2 tbsp chopped parsley
- 4 eggs
- 1 egg yolk
- 1 tbsp milk

Preheat oven to 190°C.

Divide the pastry in half and roll out each piece on a lightly floured board to 3 mm thickness. Line a 25 cm buttered pie dish with 1 piece of pastry.

Heat a heavy-based frypan over a medium heat. Add the oil and onions and cook for 3–4 minutes, stirring often, until the onions soften. Add the bacon and cook for a further 3–4 minutes, stirring often to stop the bacon catching. Season well with pepper. Add the parsley and eggs and stir well to combine. Spoon the filling into the prepared pie dish.

Mix the egg yolk with milk to make an egg wash. Brush the edge of the bottom piece of pastry with egg wash and cover with the remaining piece of pastry. Crimp the edges to join the pastry pieces together. Brush the pastry top with egg wash and bake in the preheated oven for 30 minutes, or until the pastry is risen and golden brown.

Spiced eggplant parcels

Makes 36

Eggplant is a vegetable which seems to polarise people – you either love it or loathe it. We fall into the love category, and if you do too, then these small spiced eggplant parcels will be just up your alley.

oil
1 onion, diced
1 eggplant, diced into 1 cm chunks
1 clove garlic, crushed
1 tsp grated ginger
2 tsp harissa
pinch of saffron threads
1 tsp ground coriander
1 tsp ground cumin
¼ tsp ground cardamom
¼ tsp allspice
1 tbsp tomato paste
250 ml (1 cup) chicken or vegetable stock
salt and freshly ground black pepper
¼ cup chopped coriander
2 quantities Puff Pastry (page 593) or 8–12 sheets frozen puff pastry
plain flour for dusting
1 egg yolk
1 tbsp milk
cumin or sesame seeds

Heat a large frypan over a medium–high heat. Add a generous splash of oil, the onion and eggplant and cook for 3–4 minutes, stirring often. Add the garlic, ginger, harissa, saffron and spices. Cook for 1–2 minutes, stirring often, until fragrant. Add the tomato paste and cook briefly, then add the stock and bring to the boil. Season, reduce the heat and simmer for 10–15 minutes, or until the eggplant is cooked and the liquid has reduced to form a thick sauce. Remove from heat and allow to cool. Check seasoning and add chopped coriander.

Divide pastry into 4 pieces and roll each one out on a lightly floured board to form a square (30 cm × 30 cm). Cut each square into 9 squares. Place 1 heaped tsp of the eggplant mixture in each square.

Mix the egg yolk with milk to make an egg wash. Brush 2 edges of the pastry with egg wash and fold over diagonally to form small triangles. Crimp the pastry edges to ensure that the pastry sticks together.

Place the parcels on a lined baking tray, brush with egg wash and sprinkle with cumin or sesame seeds. Rest for 30 minutes.

Preheat oven to 200°C.

Bake the parcels for 10–12 minutes, or until the pastry is cooked and golden brown. Serve while still warm.

Chicken and vegetable pasties

Makes 6

On a long car trip, a picnic or bushwalk, a good chicken pastie can be just the thing. They can also be made into small cocktail-sized nibbles and served with tomato relish.

- 2 × 200 g chicken fillets
- 2 tbsp olive oil
- 1 onion, finely diced
- 2 medium potatoes, finely diced
- 1 small carrot, finely diced
- 1 clove garlic, finely crushed
- 1 tbsp tomato paste
- 250 ml (1 cup) chicken or vegetable stock
- 2 tbsp chopped parsley
- salt and freshly ground black pepper
- 1 quantity Puff Pastry (page 593) or 4–6 sheets frozen puff pastry
- plain flour for dusting
- 1 egg, lightly beaten

Cut the chicken fillets into 2 cm dice. Heat the oil in a saucepan over a medium–low heat and add the chicken and onion. Stir together and cook for 5 minutes. Add the potatoes, carrot, garlic and tomato paste and cook for a further 5 minutes, stirring well. Add the stock and bring to a simmer. Cover and cook for 10 minutes. Uncover the saucepan, raise the heat to high, and cook for 6–7 minutes, stirring, until the liquid has evaporated. Stir in chopped parsley, season to taste and allow to cool.

Preheat oven to 180°C.

Divide the puff pastry into 6 equal pieces and keep warm. Roll out each piece of pastry on a lightly floured board to a rough circle, 18 cm wide. Brush generously with beaten egg. Place ⅙ of the chicken mix in the centre of each pastry circle in a heaped oval. Raise the 2 sides together and press to seal on top of the chicken mix. Crimp the edges to give them a decorative look. Continue until all 6 pasties are made. Place on a buttered baking tray and brush with beaten egg.

Cook for 30 minutes or until golden brown.

Cheese and potato pies

Makes 8

Scrumptious for lunch or afternoon tea, and perfect for packing into the picnic basket for a day at the beach.

1 quantity Shortcrust Pastry dough (page 590)
500 g potatoes, diced 1 cm and cooked until tender
150 g (1½ cups) tasty cheese, grated
2 tbsp sour cream
1 tbsp chopped parsley
salt and freshly ground black pepper
1 egg yolk
1 tbsp milk

Preheat oven to 180°C.

Roll pastry out to 3 mm thickness. Cut 8 × 15 cm circles. Combine potatoes, cheese, sour cream, parsley, salt and pepper. Spoon the mixture onto the bottom half of each pastry circle. Mix egg yolk with milk to make egg wash. Brush top half of pastry with egg wash. Fold pastry over to enclose filling. Crimp edges together and place on lined baking tray. Set aside to rest for 30 minutes.

Brush pies with egg wash and bake in preheated oven for 15–20 minutes, or until golden brown.

Sausage rolls

Makes 20

The sausage meat typically offered for sausage rolls is not something we're all that keen to eat. We buy really good sausages and use them instead; then we know exactly what's in there.

1 quantity Puff Pastry (page 593) or 4–6 sheets frozen puff pastry
20 small skinless frankfurter sausages or baby bratwurst
Dijon or grain mustard (optional)
1 egg yolk
1 tbsp milk

Roll pastry out to 3 mm thickness – either a square or a rectangle will do. Use one sausage as a guide to cut out 20 evenly sized rectangles. They should be wide enough to wrap completely around the sausage 1½ times.

Spread a small amount of mustard onto the lower half of each rectangle. Mix egg yolk with milk to make egg wash. Place a sausage on top of the mustard and brush the top half of the pastry with egg wash. Roll the sausage up in the pastry.

Preheat oven to 200°C.

Place sausage rolls on lined baking tray with the pastry join underneath. Brush with egg wash, slash each top with a knife in a few places to expose sausage. Rest for 30 minutes.

Bake sausage rolls for 15–20 minutes, or until pastry is cooked and golden brown.

Free-form roast summer vegetable tart

Serves 6

A delicious summer tart, perfect for lunch or as an entree before dinner.

1 eggplant
3 tomatoes
2 zucchini
1 red onion
5–6 cloves garlic, left whole
olive oil
salt and freshly ground black pepper
2 thyme sprigs
handful of basil leaves
2–3 oregano sprigs
1 quantity Shortcrust Pastry dough (page 593)
1 egg yolk
1 tbsp milk

Preheat oven to 180°C.

Cut the eggplant in half, then cut each half into 6 wedges. Cut the tomatoes into quarters. Cut the zucchini in half lengthways and then into 4 cm chunks. Cut the red onion into thick wedges. Place the vegetables and garlic in a deep baking tray and toss them with the olive oil, salt and pepper. Roughly chop the herbs and scatter on top. Roast for 30–40 minutes or until the vegetables are cooked and golden brown. Set aside to cool.

Roll the pastry on a lightly floured surface to make a circle about 40 cm wide and 3 mm thick. Place the pastry on a tray lined with baking paper and leave to rest for 30 minutes.

Arrange the roasted vegetables on the pastry, leaving a 5 cm border. Fold the pastry over the edge of the vegetables to form the sides of the tart. Mix the egg yolk with milk to make an egg wash and brush the egg wash over the sides of the tart. Bake the tart in the oven for 30–35 minutes, or until the pastry is cooked and golden brown.

Vegetable pasties

Makes 6

These are great for lunches and picnics, or they can be made into small cocktail-sized party food and served with tomato relish.

- 2 tbsp olive oil
- 1 onion, finely diced
- ½ red capsicum, finely diced
- 2 medium potatoes, finely diced
- 2 tomatoes, roughly chopped
- 200 g pumpkin, peeled and cut into 2 mm dice
- 1 small carrot, finely diced
- 1 clove garlic, finely crushed
- 1 tbsp tomato paste
- 1 tsp curry paste
- 250 ml (1 cup) cold water
- 2 tbsp chopped parsley
- 1 quantity Hot Water Pastry (page 595)
- 1 egg, lightly beaten

Heat olive oil in a saucepan over a medium–low heat. Add prepared vegetables, tomato paste and curry paste. Stir together and cook for 5 minutes. Add water, bring to a simmer, cover and cook for 10 minutes. Uncover saucepan, raise heat to high and stir until liquid has evaporated, about 6–7 minutes. Stir in chopped parsley, season to taste and allow to cool.

Preheat oven to 180°C.

Divide Hot Water Pastry into 6 equal pieces and keep warm. Roll out each pastry to a rough circle about 18 cm across. Brush generously with beaten egg. Place one-sixth of vegetable mix in the centre of each pastry circle in a heaped oval. Raise the two sides together and press to seal on top of vegetable mix. Crimp edges to give a decorative look. Continue until all six pasties are made. Place on a greased baking tray and brush with beaten egg.

Cook for 30 minutes or until golden brown.

Cheesy choux puffs

Makes 30

These are ideal as a nibble before dinner. We find their light cheese flavour is perfect with a glass or two of sparkling wine.

1 quantity Choux Pastry (page 594)

90 g (1 cup) gruyere or parmigiano, grated

Preheat oven to 200°C.

Add cheese to choux pastry mixture. Spoon teaspoonfuls of choux pastry onto lined baking trays. Place trays in the oven at the same time. With choux pastry it is important not to open the door in the first 10 minutes of cooking, as cold drafts will make the pastry sink.

Cook for 10 minutes, then turn oven temperature down to 180°C. Cook for another 10 minutes, then try one. They should be quite brown (more than golden-brown) and relatively dry inside. Resist the urge to pull them out too soon, as they will be doughy inside. When ready, set aside to cool.

Spanakopita (Greek cheese pastries)

Serves 4–6

The classic Greek spanakopita (cheese pie) is a winning light meal in our book. It can also be made into small cocktail-sized party food.

150 g spinach leaves
125 g (½ cup) ricotta
1 egg
150 g mashed feta
pinch of nutmeg

freshly ground black pepper
2 tbsp chopped parsley
6 sheets filo pastry
100 g melted butter

Preheat oven to 180°C.

Blanch spinach leaves in boiling water. Refresh immediately under cold running water, squeeze excess water out and chop finely. Mix spinach with ricotta, egg, feta, nutmeg, pepper and chopped parsley until smooth.

Brush 1 sheet of filo pastry with melted butter, lay another sheet of filo pastry on top, brush again with butter and repeat until you have 6 sheets of filo pastry buttered together. Lay filo pastry layers in a 23 cm flan tin. Spoon in spinach/ricotta mix. Fold pastry ends over to enclose filling completely. Brush top with melted butter.

Bake in preheated oven for 30 minutes, or until golden brown and slightly puffy.

Bistella

Serves 6–8

We've come to love these Moroccan chicken pastries through the cooking and writing of Melbourne-based chef Greg Malouf. Traditionally, they're made with pigeon but we find that chicken pies are easier to re-create in the home kitchen. While it may seem unusual to sprinkle the pastry with icing sugar to serve, it is an essential part of the finished dish.

oil	1 tbsp tomato paste
1 onion, diced	salt and freshly ground black pepper
1 clove garlic, crushed	2 tbsp chopped coriander
500 g skinless chicken thigh fillets, diced	8 sheets filo pastry
½ tsp ground ginger	150 g melted butter
½ tsp ground cinnamon	150 g (1½ cups) flaked toasted almonds
½ tsp ground allspice	45 g (⅓ cup) icing sugar
125 ml (½ cup) chicken stock	1 tsp ground cinnamon

Heat a heavy-based frypan over a medium heat. Add a splash of oil and the onion and cook for 3–4 minutes, stirring often. Add the garlic and chicken and cook for 5–6 minutes, or until the chicken is golden brown. Add the spices and cook for 1–2 minutes, until fragrant. Add the stock and tomato paste and season with salt and pepper. Bring to the boil. Reduce to a simmer and cook for 6–8 minutes, stirring often, until the chicken is cooked and most of the stock has been absorbed. Check seasoning and add chopped coriander.

Preheat oven to 180°C.

Brush each sheet of filo pastry with melted butter. Lay 3–4 sheets in the base of a buttered 25 cm flan tin, allowing plenty of pastry to hang over the edges. Add the chicken filling and sprinkle on the toasted almonds. Top with another 3–4 pieces of buttered filo. Fold the edges over to totally encase the filling.

Bake in the preheated oven for 15–20 minutes, or until golden brown and the chicken is heated through.

Sieve the icing sugar and cinnamon together. Dust the bistella with icing sugar and serve hot.

Ricotta tart

Serves 8

A simple and easy tart to make, and one that can be adapted in many ways. The list of variations below should keep most tart lovers happy for a long time.

1 × 25 cm Sweetcrust Pastry shell (page 590)
250 g (1 cup) ricotta
110 g (½ cup) caster sugar
3 eggs
1 tsp vanilla extract
125 ml (½ cup) cream
2 tbsp plain flour
grated zest of 1 lemon
2 tbsp lemon juice
ground cinnamon

Preheat oven to 180°C.

In a bowl, whisk together ricotta, caster sugar, eggs, vanilla, cream and flour with the grated zest and lemon juice. Spoon ricotta mix into cooked pastry shell. Sprinkle with cinnamon and bake in preheated oven for 40 minutes, or until firm.

Quince and ricotta tart
Slice 2 cooked quinces. Add to cooked pastry shell, then pour ricotta mix over.

Date and orange ricotta tart
Substitute orange for lemon juice and zest. Add 300 g fresh dates to cooked pastry shell, then pour ricotta mix over.

Port-soaked prune and ricotta tart
Soak 300 g pitted prunes in 2 tbsp port for 20 minutes. Add to cooked pastry shell, then pour ricotta mix over.

Other ideas
Add any fruit you like, such as raspberries, pear slices, or roasted nectarine wedges. You can also swap the ricotta for fresh goat's curd, mascarpone or fromage frais.

Apricot and frangipane tart

Serves 8

Frangipane is a gorgeous almond tart filling that is delicious on its own and even better when you pour it over roasted apricots. Tempting isn't it?

8 ripe apricots
3 tbsp caster sugar
100 g soft butter
110 g (½ cup) caster sugar, additional
2 eggs
100 g (1 cup) ground almonds
1 tbsp plain flour
1 × 25 cm Sweetcrust Pastry shell (page 590)

Preheat oven to 180°C.

Cut apricots in half and discard stones. Place on a baking tray skin side down. Sprinkle with sugar and roast in preheated oven for 20–30 minutes, until apricots soften and brown slightly.

Prepare frangipane by creaming butter and additional sugar until white. Add eggs and combine. Add ground almonds and flour and stir until well combined.

Place roasted apricot halves skin side down in tart shell. Spoon frangipane over them and bake for 30 minutes, until frangipane is set and golden brown.

Other fruits
The variations of this tart could go on forever. Add any fruit you like, such as raspberries or roasted nectarine or peach wedges.

Raspberry and mascarpone tart

Serves 8

Raspberries are among our favourite fruits and we especially love them in tarts, where their acidic taste adds a lovely contrast. Use either basic Sweetcrust Pastry (page 590) or Almond Sweetcrust Pastry (page 591).

250 g (1 cup) mascarpone
2 eggs
1 tsp vanilla extract
60 ml (¼ cup) tokay or port
55 g (¼ cup) caster sugar
250 g (2 cups) raspberries
1 x Almond Sweetcrust Pastry shell (page 591)
icing sugar to serve

Preheat oven to 180°C.

Lightly beat together mascarpone, eggs, vanilla, tokay or port and sugar until combined. Scatter raspberries over the cooked pastry base and pour mascarpone mix over. Bake in preheated oven for 20 minutes, or until set and golden brown. Dust with icing sugar to serve.

Passionfruit tart

Serves 8

If we offer to bring a dessert to a friend's house, more often than not it's our passionfruit tart they'll ask for. It combines the exquisite tropical flavour of passionfruit and the creamy richness of mascarpone. In this recipe it's best to pour the filling directly into the still-warm, just-baked pastry shell.

6 eggs
125 g (½ cup) mascarpone
200 g (¾ cup + 1 tbsp) caster sugar
250 ml (1 cup) passionfruit pulp, from about 12–15 passionfruits
grated zest of 2 lemons
80 ml (⅓ cup) lemon juice
1 × 25 cm Rich Sweetcrust Pastry shell (page 591)

Preheat oven to 180°C.

Beat eggs, mascarpone, sugar, passionfruit pulp and lemon zest and juice together. Allow to stand for 30 minutes before straining to remove passionfruit seeds. Pour strained filling into still-warm blind-baked pastry shell.

Reduce oven to 140°C. Place tart in oven and cook for 30 minutes if using a fan-forced oven (a non fan-forced oven will take 5–10 minutes longer). By this stage the filling will be just set on top. This is the time to remove it from the oven for a perfect consistency. Allow to cool, during which time it will finish setting.

Lemon tart

Serves 8

Few people can say no to a classic lemon tart, especially when it's as delectable as this.

4 eggs
220 g (1 cup) caster sugar
grated zest of 2 lemons
80 ml (⅓ cup) lemon juice
250 g melted butter
125 g (1¼ cups) ground almonds
1 × 25 cm Sweetcrust Pastry shell (page 590)
cream to serve

Preheat oven to 180°C.

Beat eggs and sugar until light and doubled in bulk, about 10 minutes. Add lemon zest and juice, butter and almonds, then mix to incorporate.

Pour into blind-baked tart shell. Bake in preheated oven for about 40 minutes, or until golden brown and set.

Serve at room temperature with cream.

Lemon meringue tart

Serves 8

I dreamed of a lemon meringue tart this good. Instead of using a traditional filling based on lemon curd or cornflour, I decided to take my favourite lemon tart recipe and give it a make-over. What a dish! MC

4 eggs
185 ml (¾ cup) thickened cream
150 g (⅔ cup) caster sugar
100 ml (⅓ cup) lemon juice
zest of 2 lemons
1 × 25 cm Sweetcrust Pastry shell (page 590)
4 egg whites
300 g (1⅓ cups) caster sugar, additional

Preheat oven to 180°C.

Beat the eggs, cream, caster sugar, lemon juice and zest in a bowl. Strain and pour into the still-warm blind-baked pastry shell. Place in the oven and bake for 30 minutes, or until the filling is just set. Set aside to cool.

While the tart is cooking, make the meringue topping. Beat egg whites until stiff. Add additional caster sugar, a third at a time, and continue beating until meringue is glossy and firm.

Once the lemon tart has cooled, spoon the meringue over the top of the tart, forming peaks (you may like to use a piping bag to get a more uniform look).

Place the tart under a very hot preheated grill or in a 220°C preheated oven for 3–4 minutes, until just golden brown on top. Allow to cool, then serve.

Apple tart

Serves 8

We make this tart only when good-quality apples are in season, which is mostly throughout autumn and winter.

30 g butter
6 Granny Smith apples, peeled, cored and thinly sliced
60 ml (¼ cup) brown sugar
1 tsp ground cinnamon
2–3 tbsp apricot jam
1 tbsp water
1 × 25 cm Sweetcrust Pastry shell (page 590)

Preheat oven to 180°C.

Heat a heavy-based saucepan over a medium heat. Melt butter, then add apples, sugar and cinnamon. Cook briefly until apples just begin to soften, stirring carefully.

Place jam in small saucepan over a low heat with water. Bring to the boil and stir well. Brush pastry shell with apricot glaze. Arrange apple slices in the base of the baked pastry shell. Brush top apple slices with apricot glaze, then bake in preheated oven for 20 minutes or until golden brown and crisp. Serve with pure cream.

Bitter chocolate tarts

Makes 18 tarts

These tiny chocolate tarts are incredibly decadent, especially if you can source some gold leaf to decorate the tops. Make them in mini tart shell trays or mini muffin tins and serve with coffee at the end of a meal.

- 1 quantity Sweetcrust Pastry dough (page 590)
- 150 ml (⅔ cup) cream
- 150 g dark chocolate, chopped
- 1 tsp tokay or brandy
- 2 egg yolk
- gold leaf (optional)

Preheat oven to 180°C.

Roll pastry out on a lightly floured board. Cut out 7½ cm circles. Lightly butter mini tart shells or mini muffin tins and place a pastry circle in each. Press circles down gently with fingers. Prick pastry with a fork.

Cook in preheated oven for 6–8 minutes, or until pastry is dry and just beginning to colour. Allow pastry shells to cool.

Place cream in a saucepan and bring to the boil. Remove from the heat and add chocolate. Whisk until chocolate is completely melted. Set aside to cool, whisking occasionally. Whisk in tokay or brandy and egg yolks. Spoon chocolate mixture into tart shells. Allow to cool completely. If desired, decorate with a tiny sprinkle of gold leaf to serve.

Apple and rhubarb pie

Serves 8

This is a proper winter dessert that begs to be served with hot custard. The pastry shell for the pie is baked as normal, then the apple filling is added. A raw pastry top is laid over the apple and the whole thing is baked again.

2 quantities Sweetcrust Pastry dough (page 590)
30 g butter
60 g (¼ cup) brown sugar
½ tsp ground cinnamon
6 Granny Smith apples, peeled, cored and sliced
1 bunch rhubarb, trimmed of green leaves and sliced
1 egg yolk
1 tbsp milk
caster sugar, additional

Preheat oven to 180°C.

Roll out half of the pastry and line a 23 cm flan tin. Rest for 30 minutes and bake blind. Roll out remaining pastry to 25 cm across.

Heat a heavy-based saucepan over a medium–high heat. Add the butter, sugar and cinnamon and stir until melted. Add sliced apples and rhubarb, stir and cook for 5 minutes. Pile fruit immediately into blind baked pastry shell and cover with remaining pastry, pushing down and crimping the edges. Trim excess pastry. Make a small cross in centre of the pastry to allow steam to escape. Mix egg yolk with milk to make egg wash. Brush pastry with egg wash and sprinkle liberally with caster sugar.

Bake in preheated oven for 20 minutes or until golden brown. Allow to cool for 20 minutes before slicing.

Apple and raspberry pie
Omit rhubarb. Cook apple on its own. Place cooked apple slices on cooked pastry base. Arrange 250 g (2 cups) fresh raspberries on top. Cover with pastry and continue.

Apple and rhubarb crumble tart
Forget the pastry top, cover with the crumble mix from Rhubarb Crumble (page 650) and bake for 15–20 minutes, or until golden brown and crunchy.

Free-form fruit pie

Serves 4–6

Make this with your choice of berries or whatever is in season. I love it with raspberries and blackberries, or gooseberries. But most of all I love it with lashings of runny cream. MC

200 g (1⅓ cups) plain flour
pinch of salt
125 g soft butter, diced
cold water as required
plain flour for dusting

800 g fresh or frozen berries
75 g (⅓ cup) caster sugar
1 egg yolk
1 tbsp milk

Sift the flour with the salt, then rub in the butter to produce a breadcrumb texture. Add enough water to bring the pastry together, then knead briefly. Wrap in cling film and chill for 30 minutes.

Preheat oven to 200°C.

Roll out the pastry on a lightly floured board to form a rough circle, 5 mm thick. Place the pastry on a flat buttered baking tray. Arrange the berries in the middle, sprinkle them with caster sugar and pinch the pastry up to overlap and form sides (don't expect them to meet in the middle).

Mix the egg yolk with milk to make an egg wash. Brush the edges of the pastry with the egg wash. Bake in the preheated oven for 30–35 minutes, or until the pastry is cooked and golden brown.

Fruit mince pies

Makes 18

What would Christmas celebrations be without a few mince pies to munch on?

- 75 g (½ cup) currants
- 90 g (½ cup) sultanas
- ½ apple, grated
- 40 g (¼ cup) blanched almonds
- 40 g (¼ cup) brown sugar
- ½ tsp ground cinnamon
- zest of 1 lemon, chopped
- zest of 1 orange, chopped
- 1 tbsp lemon juice
- 1 tbsp orange juice
- 1 tbsp brandy or rum (optional)
- 1 quantity Shortcrust Pastry dough (page 590)
- 1 egg yolk
- 1 tbsp milk
- 2–3 tbsp caster sugar, additional

Preheat oven to 180°C

Combine fruits, nuts, sugar, spice, citrus zest and juice and alcohol if using. Stir well and set aside to macerate for 2 hours.

Roll two-thirds of the pastry out on a lightly floured board. Cut out 7 ½ cm circles. Lightly butter mini tart shells or mini muffin tins and place a pastry circle in each. Press circles down gently with fingers. Prick pastry with a fork. Cook in the preheated oven for 6–8 minutes, or until pastry is dry and just beginning to colour. Allow pastry shells to cool.

Fill shells with fruit mince. Roll remaining pastry out and cut into 5 cm circles or stars and place on top of fruit mince. Mix egg yolk with milk to make egg wash. Brush the pastry pie tops with egg wash and sprinkle with additional sugar. Bake in preheated oven for 6–8 minutes, or until pastry tops are cooked.

Blueberry and mascarpone tart

Serves 8

Mascarpone can be used to create a marvellous creamy filling by combining it with eggs, vanilla, a little alcohol and sugar. Try this with raspberries or blackberries too.

- 250 g (1 cup) mascarpone
- 2 eggs
- 1 tsp vanilla extract
- 60 ml (¼ cup) tokay or port
- 55 g (¼ cup) caster sugar
- 200 g (2½ cups) blueberries
- 1 × 25 cm Sweetcrust Pastry shell (page 590) or Almond Sweetcrust Pastry shell (page 591)
- icing sugar to serve

Preheat oven to 180°C.

Lightly beat together the mascarpone, eggs, vanilla, tokay or port and caster sugar, until combined. Scatter blueberries over the cooked pastry base and pour in the mascarpone mix. Bake in the preheated oven for 20 minutes, or until set and golden brown.

Dust with icing sugar to serve.

Peach and frangipane tart

Serves 8

We often prepare this tart for a simple dessert using apricots, quinces, raspberries, nectarines, blueberries or peaches. When using stone fruit, we usually roast them first to add a caramelised flavour.

2 peaches
55 g (¼ cup) caster sugar
100 g soft butter
110 g (½ cup) caster sugar, additional
2 eggs
75 g (¾ cup) ground almonds
1 tbsp plain flour
1 × 25 cm Sweetcrust Pastry shell (page 590)

Preheat oven to 180°C.

Cut the peaches into wedges and discard the stones. Place them on a baking tray, skin side down. Sprinkle with caster sugar and roast in the preheated oven for 20–30 minutes, until the peaches soften and brown slightly.

Prepare the frangipane by creaming the butter and additional 110 g caster sugar until white. Add the eggs and combine. Add ground almonds and flour and stir well.

Place the roasted peach wedges, skin side down, in the cooked tart shell. Spoon frangipane over them and bake for 30 minutes, until the frangipane is set and golden brown.

Pear and frangipane tart
Substitute poached pear slices for peaches.

Cherry and marzipan tart

Serves 8

We look forward with great anticipation to the first cherries of the season. They're luscious in their natural state, and gorgeous when included in this marzipan tart filling.

200 g soft butter
220 g (1 cup) caster sugar
4 eggs
150 g (1½ cups) ground almonds
2 tsp almond essence
1 tbsp plain flour
300 g cherries, halved and pitted
1 × 25 cm Sweetcrust Pastry shell (page 590)

Preheat oven to 180°C.

Prepare the marzipan by creaming the butter and caster sugar until white. Add the eggs and combine. Add the ground almonds, almond essence and flour, and stir until well combined.

Place the cherry halves in the cooked tart shell. Spoon marzipan over them and bake for 30 minutes, until the marzipan is set and golden brown. Serve with pure cream.

Raspberry and limoncello tart

Serves 8

Limoncello is an Italian liqueur with a gutsy lemon flavour and a more than reasonable alcohol kick. We use it in a number of custards and tarts, and as a drink straight from the freezer on hot summer nights.

150 g (1¼ cup) raspberries
1 × 25 cm Sweetcrust Pastry shell (page 590)
4 eggs
150 g (⅔ cup) caster sugar
zest of 2 lemons
100 ml (⅓ cup) lemon juice
2 tbsp limoncello
185 ml (¾ cup) cream
icing sugar to serve (optional)

Preheat oven to 160°C.

Scatter the raspberries in the base of the cooked pastry shell. Beat together the eggs, caster sugar, lemon zest, lemon juice, limoncello and cream. Pour over the raspberries and bake in the preheated oven for 30 minutes, or until the egg mix is just set. Allow to cool.

Serve at room temperature. Dust with icing sugar, if you wish.

Chocolate and pear tart

Serves 8

This tart is extremely rich, so it's best to serve it in small portions.

220 g (1 cup) caster sugar
500 ml (2 cups) water
4 pears, peeled, quartered and cored
200 ml (¾ cup) thickened cream
125 g chocolate, chopped
2 egg yolks
110 g (½ cup) caster sugar, additional
1 × 25 cm Sweetcrust Pastry shell (page 590)

Preheat oven to 180°C.

Place 220 g caster sugar and water in a medium-sized saucepan over a low heat. Stir until the sugar dissolves. Raise the heat and bring to the boil, then simmer for 2–3 minutes. Add the pears to the simmering syrup and poach for 4–5 minutes. Remove from heat and set aside until needed.

Place the cream in a saucepan and bring to the boil. Remove from heat and add the chocolate. Whisk until the chocolate is completely melted. Set aside to cool, whisking occasionally. Whisk in egg yolks and 110 g caster sugar.

Arrange the pear quarters in the cooked pastry shell. Pour chocolate mix over and refrigerate until set.

Blood plum and almond tart

Serves 4–6

This tart is best made in late summer or early autumn, when plums are at their best.

50 g soft butter	1 tbsp brandy
55 g (¼ cup) caster sugar	½ quantity Puff Pastry (page 593) or 2–3 sheets frozen puff pastry
1 egg	
35 g (⅓ cup) ground almonds	plain flour for dusting
1 tbsp plain flour	4 blood plums, halved and stoned
¼ tsp ground nutmeg	1 egg yolk
¼ tsp ground cinnamon	1 tbsp milk

Preheat oven to 180°C.

Cream the butter and caster sugar until pale and creamy. Add the egg, almonds, flour, nutmeg, cinnamon and brandy. Whisk until well combined.

Roll out the puff pastry on a lightly floured board to form a rectangle (30 cm × 15 cm), 3 mm thick. Place the pastry on a lined baking tray. Spread the almond mix over the puff pastry, leaving a 2 cm border all round.

Arrange the plums along the centre of the pastry rectangle, flesh side up. Pinch the pastry up to overlap and form the sides of the tart (this can look quite rustic).

Mix the egg yolk with milk to make an egg wash. Brush the edges of the pastry with the egg wash. Bake in the preheated oven for 15–20 minutes, or until the edges are golden and the fruit is tender.

Pear and almond tart
Substitute poached pear slices for the plums.

Roasted apricot, ricotta and almond free-form tart

Serves 4–6

This is a very rustic fruit tart. There's no need for a pastry tin as, quite simply, the pastry is rolled into a circle, the filling is piled into the centre and the edges are pinched up to create rough sides. It's as easy as that.

- 200 g (1⅓ cups) plain flour
- pinch of salt
- 125 g soft butter, diced
- cold water as required
- 6 apricots, quartered
- 2 tbsp caster sugar
- 2 tbsp ground almonds
- 2 tbsp caster sugar, additional
- zest of 1 lemon, diced
- plain flour for dusting
- 150 g (⅔ cup) ricotta
- 1 egg yolk
- 1 tbsp milk

Sift the flour with the salt, then rub in the butter to produce a breadcrumb texture. Add enough water to bring the pastry together, then knead briefly. Wrap in cling film and chill for 30 minutes.

Preheat oven to 200°C.

Sprinkle the apricots with caster sugar and roast in the preheated oven for 10–12 minutes, until soft and slightly golden brown.

Mix the ground almonds, additional 2 tbsp caster sugar and lemon zest together.

Roll out the pastry on a lightly floured board to form a rough circle, 5 mm thick. Place the pastry on a flat buttered baking tray and spread with ricotta, leaving a 3–4 cm border free. Sprinkle the almond mix over the ricotta and add the roasted apricots. Pinch the pastry up to overlap and form sides (don't expect them to meet in the middle).

Mix the egg yolk with milk to make an egg wash. Brush the edges of the pastry with the egg wash and scatter the top with caster sugar. Bake in the preheated oven for 30–35 minutes, or until the pastry is cooked and golden brown.

Roasted peach, ricotta and almond free-form tart
Use peaches instead of the apricots.

Quince tarte tatin

Serves 4–6

Tarte tatin is an incredible pie experience and one we enjoy as often as our waistlines permit. It's traditionally prepared by topping cooked apples with puff pastry, then flipping the cooked pie over onto a platter to serve, so the pastry ends up on the bottom and the fruit on the top. While we enjoy the traditional version, we also love it when prepared with quinces.

1 litre (4 cups) water
220 g (1 cup) caster sugar
1 vanilla pod
1 lemon, halved
4 quinces
½ quantity Puff Pastry (page 593) or 2–3 sheets frozen puff pastry

plain flour for dusting
75 g butter
150 g (⅔ cup) caster sugar, additional
1 egg yolk
1 tbsp milk

Place the water, caster sugar, vanilla and lemon in a saucepan. Bring the liquid to a rolling boil. Peel, quarter and core the quinces, and add them immediately to the poaching liquid to prevent discolouration. Reduce to a simmer and cook for 1 ½ hours, or until the quinces are tender and ruby red. Drain the quinces well and set them aside.

Roll out the pastry on a lightly floured board to 5 mm thickness and set aside to rest for 30 minutes.

Heat a frypan over a medium–high heat. Add the butter and additional 150 g (⅔ cup) caster sugar and cook for 8–10 minutes, stirring constantly. Cook until the sugar and butter have cooked to a golden caramel colour. Carefully add the quince pieces, watching out for splashes, and cook for 2–3 minutes, stirring or tossing to coat the quinces with caramel. Set the frypan aside to cool a little.

Preheat oven to 190°C.

Either leave the quinces in the frypan you cooked them in, and arrange them neatly, or transfer them to a 22 cm pie dish. Place the pastry over the quinces and tuck down the sides to completely cover the fruit, then trim away excess pastry.

Mix the egg yolk with milk to make an egg wash. Brush the pastry with the egg wash and place in the preheated oven. Cook for 20–25 minutes, or until the pastry is risen, golden brown and cooked. Remove from oven.

Place a large plate or platter over the frypan or pie dish. Using oven gloves or tea towels, tip the frypan or dish over and remove it, leaving the quinces on top and the pastry on the bottom. Take care, as the frypan or dish will be very hot.

Serve immediately with thick cream.

Profiteroles with white chocolate and raspberries

Makes 30

In this great variation on the theme of choux pastry profiteroles, the profiteroles are filled with white chocolate custard, drizzled with white chocolate sauce then scattered with raspberries. This would be a sensational dessert to complete a summer dinner party.

1 quantity Choux Pastry (page 594)
2 egg yolks
55 g (¼ cup) caster sugar
1 tbsp plain flour
500 ml (2 cups) milk
½ tsp vanilla extract
100 g white chocolate, chopped
1 quantity White Chocolate Sauce (page 571)
300 g (2⅓ cup) raspberries

Preheat oven to 200°C.

Spoon teaspoonfuls of choux pastry onto lined baking trays. Place the trays in the oven at the same time. It is important not to open the door during the first 10 minutes of cooking, as cold draughts will make the pastry sink.

Cook for 10 minutes, then reduce oven temperature to 180°C. Cook for another 10 minutes, then try one. They should be quite brown (more than golden brown) and relatively dry inside. Resist the urge to take them out too soon, because you will not fit enough cream into them if they are doughy inside. When ready, set aside to cool.

Beat the egg yolks and caster sugar together until pale, then stir in flour until smooth. Bring the milk and vanilla to the boil. Whisk the hot milk into the egg yolk mixture and return to a clean saucepan over a low heat. Stir constantly as the custard comes to the boil and thickens. Remove from heat. Add chopped chocolate and stir until it dissolves.

When cold, spoon the custard into a piping bag, if you have one, then poke the piping nozzle into the choux pastry base and squeeze to fill each one. If not using a piping bag, slit the profiteroles with a knife and fill with custard. Refrigerate until ready to serve.

To serve, either arrange 3–4 profiteroles on each plate (piled if you wish) or the entire batch on a large platter. Warm the chocolate sauce until it melts, then drizzle it over the profiteroles. Scatter raspberries over and serve.

Passionfruit profiteroles
Fill pastry balls with Passionfruit Curd (page 585) and drizzle with Lemon Icing (page 702).

Chocolate eclairs

Makes 12–15

We're big fans of a well-made chocolate eclair and have been known to travel quite a distance to our favourite cake shop to get a fix. Alternatively, we whip up a batch at home and indulge to our hearts' content.

1 quantity Choux Pastry (page 594)
1 quantity Thick Custard (page 573)
1 quantity Chocolate Ganache (page 702)

Preheat oven to 200°C.

Pipe 8 cm lengths of choux pastry onto lined baking trays. Place the trays in the oven at the same time. It is important not to open the door during the first 10 minutes of cooking, as cold draughts will make the pastry sink.

Cook for 10 minutes, then reduce oven temperature to 180°C. Cook for another 10 minutes, then try one. They should be quite brown (more than golden brown) and relatively dry inside. Resist the urge to take them out too soon, as they will end up doughy inside. When ready, set aside to cool.

Spoon the thick custard into a piping bag, if you have one, then poke the piping nozzle into the choux pastry base and squeeze to fill with pastry cream. If not using a piping bag, slit the eclairs with a knife and fill with custard.

Spread ganache over the top of each eclair.

Egyptian bread and butter pudding

Serves 6–8

Nothing is original, it seems. We've been playing around with this recipe since spotting it in an old cookbook. Recently we've seen two or three other variations on the same theme. Such is life.

100 g filo pastry, 8–10 sheets
50 g melted butter
60 g (⅓ cup) dried apricots, diced
60 g (⅓ cup) sultanas
30 g (⅓ cup) flaked almonds, toasted
30 g (¼ cup) shelled pistachios, toasted
30 g (¼ cup) pine nuts, toasted
500 ml (2 cups) milk
150 ml (⅔ cup) thick cream
55 g (¼ cup) caster sugar
2 tbsp pomegranate syrup
whole nutmeg

Preheat oven to 160°C.

Brush each sheet of filo with butter, crumple loosely and arrange on two baking trays. Bake in preheated oven for 20 minutes, or until crisp and golden.

Turn oven up to 220°C.

Butter a 20 cm pie dish. Crumple filo sheets, retaining some largish pieces. Mix together dried fruit and nuts and layer alternatively with filo pastry in the pie dish. Place milk, cream and sugar in a saucepan and bring to the boil. Pour boiling milk over the pastry and fruit, drizzle with pomegranate syrup and grate fresh nutmeg over. Bake in preheated oven for 15–20 minutes.

Pistachio, almond and orange-blossom baklava

Serves 12

This recipe is inspired by Claudia Roden's *A New Book of Middle Eastern Food*. This book is well worth checking out if you're at all interested in food of the Middle East.

220 g (1 cup) caster sugar
125 ml (½ cup) water
60 ml (¼ cup) lemon juice
1 tbsp orange-blossom water
325 g (3¼ cup) ground almonds
100 g (⅔ cup) ground pistachios
½ tsp ground coriander
125 g melted butter
8 filo pastry sheets, cut in half

Preheat oven to 170°C.

Place sugar, water and lemon juice in a saucepan. Simmer until sugar has dissolved. Allow to cool completely, then stir in the orange blossom water. Mix together the almonds, pistachios and ground cardamom.

Brush a 24 × 22 cm baking dish with melted butter. Lay two sheets of filo in the bottom. Sprinkle a thin layer of nuts on top, fold hanging edges over. Place two sheets filo on top and brush with melted butter. Continue adding layers of nuts and filo until all ingredients are used. Brush top with plenty of butter.

With a sharp knife cut baklava into small diamond shapes and bake in preheated oven for 45 minutes.

When the baklava comes from the oven pour the orange-blossom syrup over and allow to cool completely. To serve, run a knife along the lines previously cut.

Kataifi nests with sweet labne and rosewater-poached rhubarb

Serves 6

Despite all the small steps, this is an easy dessert to make, and very impressive. You can easily increase the recipe to serve more by making more nests and cooking extra rhubarb.

375 g (1½ cups) natural yoghurt	200 g kataifi pastry
½ tsp ground cardamom	150 g melted butter
1 tbsp icing sugar	750 ml (3 cups) water
½ tsp ground cardamom, additional	110 g (½ cup) caster sugar, additional
½ tsp ground allspice	2 tbsp rosewater
1–2 tbsp caster sugar	8 stems of rhubarb, cut into 3 cm lengths
75 g (¾ cup) ground almonds	

Make the sweet labne by mixing yoghurt, cardamom and icing sugar together. Set a sieve over a bowl, line with muslin or a clean tea towel. Spoon the yoghurt into the sieve, cover and refrigerate for at least 4 hours.

Preheat oven to 180°C.

Mix extra ground cardamom, allspice, caster sugar and ground almonds together. Take the kataifi pastry and divide it into 6 × 20 cm lengths, approximately 2 cm wide. Drizzle melted butter over the pastry and sprinkle almond mixture over. Twirl the pastry up to form circular 'nests'. Transfer to a lined baking tray. Drizzle with a little extra butter. Bake in the preheated oven until crisp, about 10–12 minutes. Remove and set aside.

To poach the rhubarb, put water, additional caster sugar and rosewater into a large saucepan. Cook over a low heat until the sugar dissolves. Bring to the boil. Add rhubarb pieces. Cook gently; you want the rhubarb to retain its shape. Remove the rhubarb when tender and set aside. Return syrup to the heat and cook until reduced by half. Return rhubarb to the syrup when the syrup is cool.

Remove the labne from fridge, discard the whey. Arrange a nest on each plate and add a spoonful of labne in its centre. Arrange 5–6 pieces of rhubarb around nest, drizzle with a spoonful of the poaching syrup and serve.

DESSERTS

+ puddings sweet treats

Dessert can be as simple as a platter of seasonal fruit or as decadent as a chocolate tart with lashings of cream. In winter we enjoy self-saucing puddings, crumbles and souffles, while in summer it's mousses, panna cotta and trifles. Both our children have a sweet tooth, and they almost always insist on having dessert. Luckily, they are now old enough to make their own, usually pancakes, rice pudding or chocolate-dipped strawberries.

The kind of dessert we serve takes into consideration the meal we are having, the weather and which fruit is in season. It's difficult, for example, to really enjoy a hot pudding after a summer's lunch, especially if that lunch has been a barbecue, or to appreciate a cold summer pudding on a chilly winter's night.

These recipes can be mixed and matched to make amazing flavour combinations. Poached Quinces (page 645) can be served with Vanilla Panna Cotta (page 662) or Meringues (page 685) with Chocolate Mousse (page 656). Check out the Pastry, Cakes and Biscuits chapters for more ideas.

dessert + pudding recipes

desserts

Vanilla poached fruit	644
Poached quinces	645
Spiced poached pears	645
Sugar-roasted stone fruit with fresh cheese and honey	646
Baked peaches with limoncello cream	646
Poached pears with chocolate sauce and caramel cream	647
Baked plums with amaretti biscuits	648
Rhubarb crumble	650
Autumn crumble	651
Cherry clafoutis	652
Caramel oranges	652
Crème caramel	653
Summer pudding	654
Lemon mousse	655
Coffee and cardamom mousse	656
Chocolate mousse	656
Zabaglione	657
White chocolate and butterscotch mousse cake	657
Luke's lemon and sugar pancakes	658
Chocolate souffle	659
Tiramisu	661
Tiramisu cake	661
Vanilla panna cotta	662
Coconut panna cotta with spiced quinces	663
Wobbly berry jelly	664
Caroline's (vodka and blood orange) jelly	665
Chestnut creams with rich chocolate sauce	667

puddings

Molten chocolate puddings	668
Lemon delicious pudding	670
Self-saucing lemon and coconut pudding	670
Steamed lemon pudding	671
Chocolate self-saucing pudding	672
Self-saucing sticky date and pecan pudding	673
Christmas pudding	674
Bread and butter pudding	675
Panettone and raspberry pudding	675
Ginger parkin with spiced cream	676
Christmas trifle	677
Raspberry and gin trifle	678
Mango and orange-blossom trifle	680
Rice pudding	681
Risotto of chocolate and nougat	683
Pavlova	684
Meringues	685
Baby pavlovas with banana and honeycomb	686
Rosewater meringue stack with red summer berries	687
Nectarine and limoncello meringue slice	688
Vanilla ice-cream	689
Frozen nougat	690
Raspberry and Campari sorbet	691
Watermelon granita with summer fruit	692
Tiramisu ice-cream	694
Strawberry, rosewater and pistachio semifreddo	696
Espresso semifreddo with butterscotch sauce	696
Moroccan rocky road ice-cream	697
Praline	697

Things you need to know about desserts and puddings

1 Don't be afraid to try something new, but it's best to tackle the more complicated desserts only when time permits.

2 Sheet gelatine is miles better than powdered, which often doesn't dissolve easily and has an unusual taste. (Check the sheet size; all of our recipes use sheets that weigh 5 g.)

3 A tub of ice-cream in the freezer can be your stand-by dessert if you have a complete failure.

4 Melt some chocolate and cream together to serve over the top of your ice-cream for an instant dessert.

5 Try a shot of limoncello over ice-cream for a great adult dessert.

Quick dessert ideas

Here are some ideas for simple desserts for those times when you have unexpected guests or just have a craving for something sweet.

1 Vanilla ice-cream with fresh berries and Raspberry Sauce (page 568).

2 Grilled peaches with honey-flavoured mascarpone.

3 Sliced bananas, chocolate ice-cream and Butterscotch Sauce (page 572).

4 Strawberries tossed with 1–2 tbsp balsamic vinegar.

5 Affogato – vanilla ice-cream with a shot of espresso and liqueur.

6 Make banana splits with ice-cream, Chocolate Sauce (page 571) and flaked toasted almonds.

7 Cut figs in half, top with a splash of sweet wine and serve with vanilla ice-cream.

8 Peel and slice oranges, pour over 1–2 tbsp orange-blossom water and serve with Marmalade Cream (page 569).

9 Grill or bake nectarine halves and serve with a drizzle of honey and fresh goat's cheese.

10 Sprinkle plums with ground cinnamon, ginger and sugar, and roast until tender; serve with cream.

11 Make a rhubarb fool by folding whipped cream through rhubarb puree.

Vanilla poached fruit

Serves 4

Poaching fruit is extremely easy – it's nothing more than heating water and sugar in a saucepan, adding a few aromatic spices if you feel like it, and simmering the fruit of your choice until it's tender. This will take anything from 5 minutes for berries to up to 1½ hours for quinces. Poached fruit retains its shape during cooking; that's why we prefer it to stewed fruit, which disintegrates during cooking. Try berries, cherries, apricots, rhubarb, pineapple, peaches, pears or plums.

500 ml (2 cups) water
220 g (1 cup) caster sugar
juice of 1 lemon
1 vanilla pod
500 g fruit

Place water, sugar, lemon juice and vanilla pod in a large heavy-based saucepan over medium heat. Stir until sugar is dissolved. Bring to a gentle boil. Cut fruit if needed, place in poaching syrup and cook until just softened. Remove and either serve warm with some poaching liquid or allow to cool and serve in poaching liquid.

Spiced poached fruit
Add cardamom pods, cinnamon sticks, star anise, sliced fresh ginger or even chillies to add a touch of spice.

Dessert wine poached fruit
Substitute half of the water with dessert wine and reduce sugar by half.

Try using poached fruit

- with ice-cream, custard or alongside a simple cake
- on pancakes with a little of the syrup over the top
- in clafoutis, tarts, steamed puddings and cakes
- with rice pudding
- under a rich layer of crème brûlée
- in crumbles, tarts and mousses

Poached quinces

Serves 4–6

The bright yellow quince is one of our favourite autumn fruits - not only because their perfume will scent a room for weeks but also because of the incredible transformation they undergo during cooking. Virtually rock hard and inedible when ripe, they develop a deep ruby-red colour and an intense, glorious flavour as a result of poaching.

1 litre (4 cups) water
220 g (1 cup) caster sugar
1 vanilla pod
1 lemon, cut in half
2 cloves
4–6 quinces
cream or vanilla ice-cream to serve

Prepare poaching liquid by placing water, sugar, vanilla, lemon and cloves in a large heavy-based saucepan. Bring liquid to a rolling boil.

Peel, quarter and core the fruit, adding quinces immediately to poaching liquid to prevent discolouration. Reduce to a simmer, cover and cook for about 1½ hours, or until the quinces are tender and ruby red.

Serve quinces with a little of the warm syrup along with cream or vanilla ice-cream.

Spiced poached pears

Serves 6

Pears are one of the most popular fruits for poaching, and they match really well with aromatic spices such as cinnamon, vanilla and cloves.

440 g (2 cups) caster sugar
1 litre (4 cups) water
1 star anise
1 cinnamon stick
2 cardamom pods
2 whole cloves
1 vanilla pod, spilt
pinch of saffron threads
5 cm fresh ginger, sliced
6 pears, peeled

Place sugar and water in a large saucepan, one that will fit the pears snugly, and dissolve sugar over a low heat. Add the star anise, cinnamon, cardamom, cloves, vanilla, saffron and ginger. Bring to the boil, reduce heat and simmer gently for 10 minutes.

Add peeled pears to simmering liquid. Cover saucepan and cook until fruit is soft. (Expect anything from 20 to 40 minutes, depending on pear variety.)

Test softness of pears by inserting a skewer into them; if not ready, continue cooking for a few minutes more.

Serve pears with a little of the warm syrup and cream or vanilla ice-cream.

Sugar-roasted stone fruit with fresh cheese and honey

Serves 4–6

This is one of our favourite easy-to-prepare desserts. Roasting the stone fruit with a little sugar on top intensifies all the natural flavours. It is best done in summer when stone fruit is at its best; ripe nectarines, plums, peaches or apricots will all work a treat.

8 nectarines or peaches or 16 apricots or small plums
55 g (¼ cup) caster sugar
100 g (½ cup) ricotta or goat's curd
full flavoured honey

Preheat oven to 200°C.

Cut fruit in half and remove the stones. Place the fruit halves, flesh side up, on a baking tray. Sprinkle sugar on top. Place into preheated oven and cook for 20–30 minutes, or until they are beginning to brown on top.

Place sugar-roasted fruit on a platter, spoon a dollop of ricotta or curd into the centre of each, then drizzle with honey.

Spiced roasted stone fruit
Sprinkle ground cinnamon, nutmeg, allspice, cardamom or ginger onto fruit before cooking.

Sugar-grilled stone fruit
Cook stone fruit under a hot grill for 3–4 minutes.

Baked peaches with limoncello cream

Serves 6

This simple dessert is ideal on a hot summer's day. Limoncello can be bought from good Italian food shops or wine stores.

3 egg yolks
55 g (¼ cup) caster sugar
2 tbsp plain flour
zest of 1 lemon
250 ml (1 cup) milk
250 ml (1 cup) cream
60 ml (¼ cup) limoncello
6 peaches
caster sugar, additional

Beat egg yolks, sugar and flour together until pale and creamy. Put lemon zest, milk and cream in a small saucepan. Bring to the boil over a medium heat. Pour the boiling milk onto the egg/sugar mix and whisk to combine. Return to the saucepan and gently bring to the boil, stirring constantly.

Remove from heat, stir through limoncello, transfer to a bowl, cover and refrigerate.

Preheat oven to 180°C. Cut the peaches in half and remove stones. Place on a baking tray skin side down, sprinkle with additional caster sugar and bake in the preheated oven for 10–15 minutes, or until the peaches soften slightly and turn golden brown.

Remove peaches from the oven, place 2 peach halves on each plate, add a spoonful of limoncello cream to each half and serve.

Poached pears with chocolate sauce and caramel cream

Serves 6

Chocolate sauce is a favourite in our house. We pour it over ice-cream, dip strawberries in it and drizzle it over chocolate desserts. We like trying different types of chocolate for different experiences and once made this dessert with Green & Black's caramel chocolate: heavenly!

- 220 g (1 cup) caster sugar
- 1 litre (4 cups) water
- 1 cinnamon stick
- 1 vanilla pod, spilt
- 6 pears, williams or red sensations
- 110 g (½ cup) caster sugar, additional
- 250 ml (1 cup) water, additional
- 250 ml (1 cup) thickened cream
- Chocolate Sauce (page 571)
- 30 g (¼ cup) toasted almond flakes

Combine the caster sugar and water in a large saucepan that will fit the pears snugly, and dissolve sugar over a low heat. Add the cinnamon and vanilla. Bring to the boil, reduce heat to low and simmer gently for 10 minutes. Peel the pears, cut them in half lengthwise and scoop out the cores. Add pears to the simmering liquid, cover the pan and cook until the pears are soft. (This may take 20–40 minutes, depending on the pear variety.) Test whether the pears are soft by inserting a skewer into one; if not ready, continue cooking for a few minutes more. Once cooked, remove pears from the poaching liquid and set aside to cool.

To make the caramel cream, place the additional caster sugar and 80 ml (⅓ cup) water in a small saucepan and cook over a low heat until the sugar dissolves. Increase heat and bring to the boil. Continue boiling until sugar turns a dark caramel. Remove from heat and very carefully add the remaining 160 ml (⅔ cup) water; it will splutter as it hits the hot caramel. Bring back to the boil, stir well, remove from the heat and allow to cool. When cool, stir through the cream and refrigerate until needed.

To serve, place 2 pear halves in each serving bowl, add a dollop of caramel cream and allow each guest to pour over the warm Chocolate Sauce and sprinkle with almond flakes.

Baked plums with amaretti biscuits

Serves 4

Plums are best for this simple but stunning dessert, but you can use nectarines or peaches if you prefer. We had the most success with this recipe when we used the giant plums which appear towards the end of the stone fruit season in early autumn.

8 plums, halved and stoned
75 g amaretti biscuits
2 tbsp brown or raw sugar
2 tbsp butter, diced
pinch of ground cinnamon
pinch of grated nutmeg
2 tbsp sweet sherry
185 ml (¾ cup) cream
150 g mascarpone
1 tbsp icing sugar
1 tbsp sweet sherry, additional

Preheat oven to 200°C.

Place the plum halves, flesh side up, in a deep baking tray so they fit snugly. Crush the biscuits using your hands and place them in a bowl along with the sugar, butter and spices. Toss to combine. Spoon the amaretti crumble into the plums. Don't worry if some of the filling spills into the base of the baking dish.

Drizzle sweet sherry over the top and bake in the preheated oven for 15–20 minutes, or until the crumble mixture is golden brown and the plums have cooked through.

Whip the cream until it forms soft peaks. Fold through the mascarpone, icing sugar and additional sweet sherry.

Serve 2 plum halves per person with a dollop of the sherry cream.

Baked peaches with amaretti biscuits
Substitute peaches for plums in the recipe.

Rhubarb crumble

Serves 4–6

Rhubarb crumble, along with apple, is probably the most popular of all crumbles. Crumbles are a great thing for teenagers to try if they show an interest in cooking, as they are virtually foolproof.

2 bunches of rhubarb
55 g (¼ cup) caster sugar
2 tbsp water
150 g soft butter, diced
250 g (1⅔ cups) plain flour
150 g (¾ cup) soft brown sugar

Trim off the leaves and root ends from the rhubarb and cut into 2 cm chunks. Heat a heavy-based pot over medium heat. Add rhubarb, sugar and water. Reduce the heat to low, cover with a lid and cook for 5–10 minutes, stirring often. Remove from the heat and allow to cool.

Preheat oven to 180°C.

Rub together soft butter, flour and brown sugar until they resemble fine breadcrumbs. Place stewed rhubarb in a baking dish, top with crumble mixture and bake in preheated oven for 20 minutes, or until golden brown. Serve with cream or custard.

Nutty rhubarb crumble
Add 60 g (⅔ cup) flaked almonds or chopped hazelnuts to the crumble mix.

Rhubarb oat crumble
Substitute 60 g (⅓ cup) flour with rolled oats.

Cinnamon rhubarb crumble
Add 1 tsp ground cinnamon to the crumble mixture.

Autumn crumble

Serves 4–6

Crumbles make terrific family desserts, as they seem to hit the spot with all age groups. We always follow the seasons when trying to decide which flavour to make – will it be apple, rhubarb, nectarine or quince? This is a good crumble to make in autumn.

1 bunch rhubarb	250 g (1⅔ cups) plain flour
4 plums, halved and stoned	150 g (¾ cup) soft brown sugar
2 apples, peeled, cored and sliced	¼ tsp ground nutmeg
55 g (¼ cup) caster sugar	¼ tsp ground cinnamon
2 tbsp water	80 g (½ cup) sultanas
150 g soft butter, diced	50 g (½ cup) flaked almonds

Trim the leaves and roots from the rhubarb and cut into 2 cm chunks. Cut the halved plums into wedges.

Heat a heavy-based saucepan over a medium heat and add the rhubarb, plums, apples, caster sugar and water. Reduce the heat to low, cover with a lid and cook for 5–10 minutes, stirring often. The fruit should be reduced to a chunky paste. Remove from heat and allow to cool.

Preheat oven to 180°C.

Rub together the soft butter, flour, brown sugar, nutmeg and cinnamon until they resemble fine breadcrumbs.

Stir the sultanas and almonds into the stewed fruit, then spoon the fruit into a baking dish. Top with the crumble mixture and bake in the preheated oven for 20 minutes, or until golden brown.

Serve with cream or custard.

Cherry clafoutis

Serves 4

Clafoutis is a really simple dessert – a sweet batter poured over fruit and baked in the oven. This French dessert is traditionally made with cherries, but try it with peaches, figs, berries, nectarines or even plums.

3 eggs
80 g (⅓ cup) caster sugar
250 g (1 cup) natural yoghurt
250 ml (1 cup) milk
2 tbsp self-raising flour
1 tsp vanilla extract
500 g pitted cherries

Preheat oven to 180°C.

To make clafoutis batter beat eggs in a bowl together with sugar, yoghurt, milk, flour and vanilla extract.

Lightly butter an ovenproof dish, then scatter the cherries (or other fruit) into it. Pour mixture over fruit and bake in preheated oven for 45 minutes. When ready, the clafoutis will be puffed and golden.

Caramel oranges

Serves 6

Caramel oranges are a classic 1970s dinner party dessert. Now, call us old-fashioned if you will, but this is a classic match of flavours that should still be enjoyed today, regardless of trends.

6 oranges, or other citrus fruit
Caramel Sauce (page 570)
60 g (1 cup) shaved coconut, lightly toasted (optional)
cream to serve

Use a sharp knife to remove skin from oranges and slice the fruit thickly, discarding any pips. Place orange slices into a serving bowl and pour Caramel Sauce over. Allow to marinate for 2–3 hours before serving.

Serve fruit and syrup with toasted coconut and cream.

Crème caramel

Serves 6

Crème caramel is a light, refreshing dessert. Do you need more temptation? No? Good, then make it tonight.

90 g (⅓ cup) caster sugar
60 ml (¼ cup) water
600 ml (2⅓ cups) milk
½ tsp vanilla extract
zest of 1 orange
3 eggs
3 egg yolks
55 g (¼ cup) caster sugar, additional

Place sugar and water in a saucepan. Cook, stirring over a low heat until sugar dissolves. Raise heat and boil liquid. Stop stirring once liquid is clear; otherwise mixture will caramelise. Cook for 12–15 minutes, or until liquid begins to colour; the desired colour is a lovely mix of gold and caramel, not dark brown. If needed, carefully swirl the saucepan to mix the caramel. Allow to cool for 1 minute, then pour the caramel into 6 × 175 ml individual ovenproof moulds. Tilt and turn the dish so that the caramel covers the base and goes up the sides a little.

Preheat the oven to 160°C.

Warm milk, vanilla and orange zest in a saucepan over a medium heat. Remove just as it comes to the boil and infuse for 10 minutes. Beat eggs, egg yolks and additional sugar together until pale and thick. Whisk warm milk into egg mixture. Strain the mixture, then pour it in on top of the caramel.

Place dishes into a deep baking tray. Pour hot water around to come halfway up the sides. Cook in preheated oven for 35–45 minutes. Custard should be firm to touch, with a slight wobble when ready. Refrigerate overnight.

To serve run a knife around the edge of the custard, then place a plate upside-down over the top of the dish and quickly turn over.

Summer pudding

Serves 6–8

Summer pudding is an old-fashioned English dessert; it's the sort of thing to serve when you're having a large group over on a hot summer's day.

- 10–15 slices day-old white bread, crusts removed
- 500 g (3¾ cups) strawberries
- 200 g (1½ cups) raspberries
- 200 g (1⅔ cups) blackberries
- 200 g redcurrants
- 200 g loganberries
- 500 ml (2 cups) water
- 220 g (1 cup) caster sugar
- clotted cream for serving

Line a 1-litre pudding bowl with day-old sliced white bread.

Sort berries and remove any stalks. Bring water and sugar to the boil. Place berries and currants in the hot syrup and allow to heat through for 1 minute. Drain immediately, reserving the liquid.

Return cooking liquid to the saucepan and boil until reduced by half. Allow berries and syrup to cool completely before gently mixing the two together again.

Spoon fruit into bread-lined bowl. Add enough cooking liquid to cover, then top with more bread. Place a small plate onto the top of the pudding (one which fits inside the rim of the bowl) and put a heavy weight on it. Refrigerate overnight.

To serve, remove pudding from bowl by placing a plate over the top of the bowl, turning it upside down and shaking gently. Serve with clotted cream.

Cherry berry pudding
Replace the strawberries with 500 g pitted cherries and cook them for 1 minute before adding the remaining fruit. The cherries add a great richness to the pudding.

Lemon mousse

Serves 4–6

Fruit mousses are seen by most people as fairly old-fashioned – the sort of thing Granny used to serve up. This is a pity, as mousses are easy to make and last for a couple of days refrigerated. They can be made with almost any fruit and are as light as air, which is perfect in warmer weather or after a big meal.

zest of 2 lemons, chopped
125 ml (½ cup) lemon juice
2 × 5 g gelatine sheets
3 eggs, separated
110 g (½ cup) caster sugar
250 ml (1 cup) whipping cream

Place lemon zest and juice in a small saucepan and bring to the boil over a medium heat. Remove from heat, add gelatine and stir until dissolved.

Whisk egg yolks and sugar until pale and creamy. Fold lemon mixture into egg yolks. Beat egg whites until stiff. Whip cream until soft peaks form.

Add a spoonful of cream and egg whites to lemon base. Stir in until well combined; this will allow you to fold remaining egg whites and cream in without losing their 'air'. Gently fold in remaining egg whites and cream.

Spoon into serving bowl(s). Refrigerate until set, about 3–4 hours, or overnight.

Passionfruit mousse
Reduce lemon zest to 1 and substitute strained passionfruit pulp for lemon juice.

Birgit's easy mousse
This is my mum's easy mousse, made with just two ingredients: a pack of lemon jelly crystals and a tin of evaporated milk. It's easy to make and it's as light a feather to eat. Chill evaporated milk for 2 hours, then whip until thick. Dissolve jelly crystals in 125 ml (½ cup) boiling water, then drizzle into whipped milk. Beat to incorporate. Spoon into serving bowl(s) and allow to set. This is traditionally made with lemon-flavoured jelly, but any jelly is okay. MC

Coffee and cardamom mousse

Serves 4–6

We are keen on blending the flavours of coffee and cardamom, so you'll find it in lots of our dessert recipes, including here, in this mousse.

2 × 5 g gelatine sheets
125 ml (½ cup) hot strong black coffee
3 eggs, separated
80 g (⅓ cup) caster sugar
¼ tsp ground cardamom
250 g (1 cup) mascarpone

Dissolve gelatine in hot coffee, stir well and strain. Set aside until cool and just beginning to set, about 10–15 minutes.

Beat egg yolks, sugar and cardamom until white and creamy. Add mascarpone and the cooled coffee/gelatine. Mix well. Beat egg whites until stiff peaks form. Stir 1 tbsp egg white into coffee mixture, then fold rest through gently.

Spoon into serving bowl(s) and allow to set. Serve with Orange and Walnut Florentines (page 773).

Chocolate mousse

Serves 4–6

A good chocolate mousse is a joy to behold – and to eat, of course. This is our favourite chocolate mousse because it tastes brilliant, it's incredibly simple to make and it can easily have lots of other flavours added to it.

200 g dark chocolate, chopped
3 eggs, separated
250 ml (1 cup) whipping cream

Melt the chocolate by placing it in a bowl over a saucepan of simmering water or in a microwave on low for 1–2 minutes.

Whip the egg whites until soft peaks form. In a separate bowl, whip the cream until soft peaks form. Gently whisk the egg yolks into the melted chocolate. Add a spoonful of cream and a spoonful of egg whites and stir in; this will allow you to fold in the remaining egg whites and cream without losing their 'air'.

Gently fold in the remaining egg whites and cream, spoon into a serving dish and allow to set for 2–3 hours or overnight.

Serve with fresh raspberries and cream.

Chocolate coffee mousse
Add 2 tbsp strong black coffee to the melted chocolate with the egg yolks.

Jaffa mousse
Add the chopped zest of 2 oranges to the melted chocolate.

Chocolate brandy mousse
Add 2 tbsp brandy to the egg yolks.

Frozen chocolate mousse
Line a log tin with plenty of cling film, leaving lots of overhang. Spoon the chocolate mousse into the tin and smooth the top. Completely cover the top of the mousse with cling film and freeze overnight. Cut thin slices to serve.

Zabaglione

Serves 4

Zabaglione is a rich, marsala-flavoured Italian dessert. It's usually made, poured into tall glasses and served while still warm. It can also be chilled and used in many other ways. It is a particularly impressive and decadent dish to offer friends.

6 egg yolks
110 g (½ cup) caster sugar
60 ml (¼ cup) marsala

Place egg yolks, sugar and marsala in a large stainless-steel bowl and whisk lightly. Sit bowl over a pot of simmering water and whisk mixture continually until it thickens and doubles in bulk, about 5 minutes.

Pour zabaglione into tall glasses and serve immediately.

Zabaglione mousse
Remove from heat and continue to whisk until zabaglione cools. Whisk in 200 g mascarpone and spoon into glasses to set.

Zabaglione ice-cream
Stir zabaglione into homemade Vanilla Ice-Cream (page 689).

White chocolate and butterscotch mousse cake

Serves 8

We've taken the base ingredients of tiramisu and come up with this white chocolate mousse cake, and it's guaranteed to go down a treat. MC

200 g white chocolate, chopped into chunks
3 eggs, separated
250 g (1 cup) mascarpone
150 g Italian sponge fingers
Butterscotch Sauce (page 572)
2 bananas, sliced (optional)

Line a cake tin with baking paper.

Melt the chocolate by placing it in a bowl over a saucepan of simmering water or in a microwave on low for 1–2 minutes.

Beat the egg yolks and mascarpone together until pale and creamy. Add the melted chocolate to the mascarpone mix and stir until well mixed. Whip the egg whites until stiff, then fold them into the mascarpone mix.

Lay half the sponge fingers in the bottom of the prepared cake tin and drizzle with Butterscotch Sauce. Pour on the mascarpone mix, top with sliced banana (if using) and the remaining sponge fingers, then drizzle with more Butterscotch Sauce. Cover with cling film and refrigerate for 3–4 hours or overnight, until set.

Carefully remove the cake from the tin and serve.

Luke's lemon and sugar pancakes

Serves 4

Luke is the sweet tooth in our family and he's recently mastered the art of making pancakes. He's happy to make everyone else pancakes, too, as long as they're with lemon and sugar.

1 egg
250 ml (1 cup) milk
pinch of salt
150 g (1 cup) plain flour
2 tbsp melted butter
caster sugar to serve
2 lemons, cut into wedges, to serve

Place the egg, milk and salt in a bowl and whisk lightly. Whisk in the flour, a little at a time, until the pancake batter has the consistency of thin custard. Allow to rest for 30 minutes. Strain the batter if there are any lumps.

Heat a heavy-based pan over a medium heat. When hot, brush the base of the pan with melted butter, then pour in just enough batter to coat the bottom of the pan thinly. Allow to cook until golden, then turn over and cook the other side. Repeat until the mixture is used up, adding more melted butter as needed.

Luke usually serves each pancake with a sprinkle of caster sugar and a wedge of lemon as they are ready, but you could keep the cooked pancakes warm in a 180°C oven if you want to serve them together.

Berry pancakes
Top pancakes with fresh berries (or stewed apricots or sliced banana) and roll up. Place the filled pancakes in a buttered ovenproof dish and cook in a preheated 180°C oven for 10 minutes. Serve with cream or ice-cream.

Chocolate souffle

Serves 6

We expect that the name 'chocolate souffle' might get your attention, but it will go in the too-hard basket before you move on to the next page. Well, don't! This way of making a souffle is how I was taught at catering college and if seventeen-year-old apprentices can make it, so can you. Go on, give it a go, just this once… MC

2 eggs, separated
55 g (¼ cup) caster sugar
2 tbsp plain flour
500 ml (2 cups) milk
125 g dark chocolate, chopped
2 egg whites, additional
6 × 175 ml souffle dishes, buttered and sprinkled with caster sugar

In a bowl, beat egg yolks and sugar until pale, stir in flour until smooth. Heat milk and chocolate in a saucepan until chocolate melts. Whisk milk on to egg yolk mixture and return to a clean saucepan over low heat. Stir constantly as custard comes to the boil and thickens. Remove from heat.

Preheat oven to 200°C.

Whip egg whites until stiff, then carefully fold them into warm chocolate mix.

Place buttered souffle dishes on a flat ovenproof tray. Divide souffle mixture between dishes, allowing room for rising. Cook in preheated oven until the souffles are well risen and firm to the touch, about 12–15 minutes. Remove carefully from the oven and serve immediately.

Coffee souffle
Omit chocolate. Instead add 2–3 tbsp strong black coffee to the milk as it comes to the boil.

Raspberry souffle
Omit chocolate. Puree 60 g (½ cup) raspberries and strain to remove the seeds. Stir puree into cooked custard. Scatter a few extra raspberries onto the top of each souffle as they go into the oven.

Tiramisu

Serves 4–6

No book about contemporary Australian cooking would be complete without a recipe for tiramisu. This creamy, chocolate- and coffee-flavoured Italian trifle is always popular when it is served, and there is almost no cooking involved, other than making the coffee essence.

6 eggs, separated
55 g (¼ cup) caster sugar
500 g (2 cups) mascarpone
60 ml (¼ cup) sweet marsala

24 Italian sponge finger biscuits
125 ml (½ cup) strong black coffee
cocoa powder, or grated chocolate

Beat egg yolks with sugar until pale and creamy. Gently whisk in mascarpone and marsala. Whip egg whites until stiff, then fold them into the mascarpone mix.

Lay half the sponge fingers in the bottom of a serving dish and drizzle with half of the coffee.

Pour half of the mascarpone mix over. Top with remaining biscuits, drizzle with remaining coffee. Top with remaining mascarpone mix. Refrigerate for 3–4 hours to allow the flavours to develop fully. Sift cocoa, or grate chocolate, over the top just before serving.

Tiramisu cake

Serves 8

This cake came about by combining classic tiramisu with our friend Daniele's diplomatica cake. Daniele gave our recipe the thumbs up, but she'd double the amount of alcohol if she had her way.

200 g chocolate, chopped into chunks
3 eggs, separated
60 ml (¼ cup) marsala
250 g (1 cup) mascarpone

150 g Italian sponge fingers
125 ml (½ cup) strong black coffee
cocoa powder to serve

Line a cake tin with baking paper.

Melt the chocolate by placing it in a bowl over a saucepan of simmering water or in a microwave on low for 1–2 minutes.

Beat the egg yolks with marsala until pale and creamy. Add the mascarpone and beat until smooth. Add the melted chocolate to the mascarpone mix and stir until well mixed. Whip the egg whites until stiff, then fold them into the mascarpone mix.

Lay half the sponge fingers in the bottom of the prepared cake tin and drizzle with half the coffee. Pour the mascarpone mix on top, add the remaining sponge fingers and drizzle over the remaining coffee. Cover with cling film and refrigerate for 3–4 hours or overnight, until set.

Carefully remove the tiramisu cake from the tin, dust with cocoa powder and serve.

Vanilla panna cotta

Serves 6

This is a simple yet stylish dessert. You can add just about any flavouring to the base mix, such as citrus zest, spices or flavour extracts. Panna cotta is delicious served with fresh berries, figs or roasted stone fruit.

375 ml (1½ cups) milk
375 ml (1½ cups) cream
80 g (⅓ cup) caster sugar
1 tsp vanilla extract
3 × 5 g gelatine sheets
fruit to serve

Bring milk, cream, sugar and vanilla to the boil. Remove from heat. Add gelatine and stir until dissolved. Strain liquid, then pour into 6 × 125 ml moulds. Refrigerate overnight.

To serve use a small spatula or knife to work the pudding away from the edges, then stand moulds in boiling water for 4–5 seconds. Place a plate on top of each mould, then turn over carefully so the plate is on the bottom. Shake to dislodge the pudding. Remove the ramekin and serve with fruit of your choice.

Rosewater panna cotta
Add 2 tbsp rosewater to strained liquid.

Liquorice panna cotta
Add 1–2 tsp liquorice extract to strained liquid.

Lime panna cotta
Add the chopped zest of 2 limes to the milk/cream, then bring to the boil.

Cardamom panna cotta
Crush 2 cardamom pods and add to milk/cream and heat. Add 2 tbsp orange-blossom water to strained liquid. Serve with 130 g (1 cup) raspberries tossed with 2 tbsp orange-blossom water.

Coffee panna cotta
Substitute 125 ml (½ cup) milk for strong black coffee. Add 2 crushed cardamom pods to milk/cream mixture for additional pleasures.

Jelly-topped panna cotta
Heat 125 ml (½ cup) fruit juice, such as raspberry, add 1 gelatine sheet and dissolve. Divide between 7 × 125 ml (½ cup) moulds and set. Pour cool panna cotta onto firm jelly and refrigerate until set.

Coconut panna cotta with spiced quinces

Serves 8

The smooth richness of the coconut panna cotta and the contrasting spice of the quinces is a combination we love. Make it once and it is sure to become a family favourite.

500 ml (2 cups) milk
500 ml (2 cups) coconut cream
80 g (⅓ cup) caster sugar
3 × 5 g gelatine sheets

500 ml (2 cups) water
220 g (1 cup) sugar
2 star anise
4–6 quinces

Bring the milk, coconut cream and caster sugar to the boil. Remove from heat, add gelatine and stir until dissolved. Strain the liquid, then pour into 8 × 125 ml plastic moulds. Cover and refrigerate overnight.

Prepare the poaching liquid for the quinces by placing the water, sugar and star anise in a large heavy-based saucepan. Bring the liquid to a rolling boil.

Peel, quarter and core the quinces, adding them to the poaching liquid immediately in order to prevent discolouration. Reduce to a simmer, cover and cook for 1½ hours, or until the quinces are tender and ruby red. Set aside until needed.

Use a small spatula or knife to work the puddings away from the edge of the moulds, then stand the moulds in boiling water for 4–5 seconds. Place a plate on top of each mould, then turn each one over carefully so the plate is on the bottom. Shake to dislodge the panna cotta.

Remove the mould and serve each panna cotta with 2–3 quarters of quince and a spoonful of poaching liquid.

Wobbly berry jelly

Serves 8

We love jellies as they look very impressive and are easy to make. They are best made the day before to ensure they set well. You could set the jelly in a kugelhopf tin or other decoratively shaped mould.

5 × 5 g gelatine sheets
110 g (½ cup) caster sugar
500 ml (2 cups) water
375 ml (1½ cups) dessert wine

600 g mixed berries – raspberries, blueberries and strawberries
8 × 125 ml dariole moulds

Soak gelatine sheets in cold water for 2–3 minutes or until soft, then squeeze and set aside. Put sugar and water in a saucepan and cook over a low heat to dissolve the sugar. Bring to the boil, add dessert wine and bring back to the boil. If you want to evaporate most of the alcohol in the wine, continue boiling for 5 minutes. If not remove from the heat, add gelatine and stir until dissolved. Strain into a jug. Allow to cool slightly: you don't want to pour hot liquid over the berries as this will cook and soften them.

Wash berries and drain well; if necessary cut strawberries in half. Divide berries equally between the 8 moulds. Pour the just-warm liquid over and cover the moulds. Refrigerate to set, at least 4–6 hours, or overnight.

Use a small spatula or knife to work the jellies away from the moulds' edges, and then stand dariole moulds in boiling water for 4–5 seconds. Place a plate on top of each mould, then turn over carefully so the plate is on the bottom. Shake to dislodge the jelly.

Caroline's (vodka and blood orange) jelly

Serves 6

Caroline is a new friend. As we're all ex-chefs, we've had many food discussions, mostly centred around dessert, and jelly kept popping up in conversation. It became a bit of an in-joke and I promised her a jelly recipe with her name, so here it is. MC

250 ml (1 cup) blood orange juice
110 g (½ cup) caster sugar
400 ml (1⅔ cups) water
60 ml (¼ cup) vodka (optional)
4 × 5 g gelatine sheets
6 × 125 ml dariole moulds

4 tangelos
3 pink grapefruits
4 blood oranges
60 ml (¼ cup) Cointreau
2 tbsp lemon juice

Place blood orange juice, sugar, water and vodka (if using) in a saucepan and bring to the boil. Remove from heat. Add gelatine and stir until dissolved. Strain and pour into 6 × 125 ml moulds. Refrigerate until set, 3–4 hours or overnight.

Use a sharp knife to remove the skins and pith of the citrus fruits. Remove the segments from the membranes so that each segment is free from any pith or seeds. Combine all fruits in a bowl with Cointreau and lemon juice and set aside to marinate for up to 4 hours.

To serve, stand moulds in boiling water for a few seconds. Place serving plate on top of each mould and shake to unmould jelly. Warm citrus salad by heating gently in a pan until steaming, or microwave on medium heat for 2–3 minutes. Serve jellies with fruit segments.

Chestnut creams with rich chocolate sauce

Serves 6

An unusual dessert, but beautifully decadent and perfect in the cooler months. Chestnut puree is available from most good food shops.

1 × 5 g gelatine sheet
250 ml (1 cup) cream
125 ml (½ cup) milk
55 g (¼ cup) caster sugar
1 × 435 g can unsweetened chestnut puree
75 g cooked chopped chestnuts (optional)
½ tsp vanilla extract
90 g dark chocolate, chopped into chunks
1 tbsp butter
2 tbsp brandy
80 ml (⅓ cup) cream
6 × 125 ml dariole moulds

Soak gelatine sheet in cold water for 2–3 minutes, until soft. Squeeze excess water off and set aside. Put cream, milk and sugar in a small saucepan and bring to the boil. Remove from heat, add gelatine and stir until dissolved. Add chestnut puree. Strain through a sieve. Add chopped chestnuts if using them – they add a bit of texture if you like that. Pour mix into greased dariole moulds. Refrigerate to set, 3–4 hours or overnight.

Make chocolate sauce by putting all remaining ingredients into a heatproof bowl. Set bowl over a saucepan of simmering water and cook for 5–6 minutes. Stir often until everything has melted together smoothly. Keep warm.

Use a small spatula or knife to work the puddings away from the moulds' edges, and then stand dariole moulds in boiling water for 4–5 seconds. Place a plate on top of each mould, then turn over carefully so the plate is on the bottom. Shake to dislodge the pudding. Remove the mould and serve pudding with warm chocolate sauce.

Molten chocolate puddings

Serves 6

No dinner party is complete without a decadent chocolate dessert. You can make the pudding mix in advance and put it to one side until ready to cook after the main course. It's lovely with a glass of tokay, our favourite dessert wine.

- 350 g dark chocolate, chopped into chunks
- 50 g soft butter
- 150 g (⅔ cup) caster sugar
- 4 eggs, lightly beaten
- 2 tbsp plain flour
- cream to serve

Grease 6 × 125 ml ramekins and place them on a baking tray.

Melt the chocolate by placing it in a bowl over a saucepan of simmering water or in a microwave on low for 1–2 minutes.

Beat the butter and caster sugar together until light and fluffy. With the mixer still going, gradually add the beaten eggs. Add the flour and ensure that all ingredients are well combined. Add the melted chocolate and beat to a smooth paste.

Divide the chocolate mixture evenly between the ramekins. If you wanted to, you could now set the puddings aside until you are ready to cook them.

Preheat oven to 180°C.

Place the ramekins in the preheated oven and cook for 18–20 minutes. Check the puddings by inserting a skewer: you want them to be gooey in the middle, but cooked at least 1 cm inside from the edge.

When ready, turn the puddings out onto serving plates and serve immediately with cream.

Lemon delicious pudding

Serves 4–6

With its light-as-a-feather crust floating over a tangy lemon sauce, it's no wonder that few people can resist Lemon Delicious Pudding. It's the type of pudding that is perfectly at home as a weeknight family dessert and at a weekend dinner party. We often make it with other citrus fruit such as lime, orange or tangelo.

75 g soft butter
zest of 2 lemons, grated
330 g (1½ cups) caster sugar
3 eggs, separated
125 ml (½ cup) lemon juice
250 ml (1 cup) milk
100 g (⅔ cup) self-raising flour

Preheat oven to 180°C.

Butter a 1-litre pudding bowl and sprinkle with caster sugar.

Cream the butter with the lemon zest and caster sugar. Add the egg yolks and mix well. Add lemon juice, milk and flour, and mix to incorporate. Beat the egg whites until stiff and fold through the batter.

Spoon the mixture into the pudding bowl and place the bowl in a deep baking dish. Pour hot water into the dish until it comes halfway up the bowl.

Cook in the preheated oven for 45 minutes, or until golden brown and puffed.

Self-saucing lemon and coconut pudding

Serves 4–6

We seem to have developed a thing for self-saucing puddings.

200 g (1⅓ cups) self-raising flour
110 g (½ cup) caster sugar
45 g (⅔ cup) desiccated coconut
zest and juice of 1 lemon
125 ml (½ cup) milk
1 egg
60 g melted butter
150 g (⅔ cup) caster sugar, additional
1 tbsp cornflour
150 ml (⅔ cup) boiling water
80 ml (⅓ cup) lemon juice
1-litre ovenproof dish, buttered and sprinkled with caster sugar
cream to serve

Preheat oven to 180°C.

Mix flour, caster sugar and coconut together in a bowl. Whisk together lemon zest and juice, milk, egg and melted butter until smooth, then pour onto the flour mixture. Mix until smooth. Spoon into the greased ovenproof dish.

Mix the additional caster sugar and cornflour together and sprinkle over the pudding mix. Stir boiling water and lemon juice together and pour over the pudding. Place in the preheated oven and cook for 45 minutes, or until a skewer comes out clean when inserted. Serve with cream.

Steamed lemon pudding

Serves 4–6

A good steamed pudding is one of the most popular desserts. Despite the minimal ingredients and the easy cooking method, a huge variety of different puddings can be made by swapping the lemon with other flavours.

125 g soft butter
125 g (½ cup) caster sugar
2 medium eggs
200 g (1⅓ cups) self-raising flour
chopped zest and juice of 2 lemons

Cream butter and sugar until light and fluffy. Add eggs one by one, allowing each to be incorporated before adding the next. Stir in flour, then stir in lemon zest and juice.

Butter a 1-litre pudding bowl and spoon in the pudding mixture. Cover with buttered greaseproof paper and foil. Tie down tightly with string under the rim of the pudding bowl or, easier still, use a large elastic band.

Place pudding bowl into a large pot and pour in enough water to come three-quarters of the way up the bowl. Bring water to the boil; reduce to a simmer, place the lid on the saucepan and cook for 1½ hours. Check the water level from time to time and add more if needed.

Remove pudding bowl from the water and allow to stand for 10 minutes. Remove the foil and greaseproof paper. Run a small spatula around the edge of the pudding and unmould onto a platter. Serve with thin custard.

Steamed orange pudding
Substitute orange, tangelo or blood orange zest and juice for lemon.

Steamed chocolate pudding
Replace 60 g (⅓ cup) of the flour with cocoa. Sift the two together. Omit lemon zest and juice. Add 90 g (½ cup) small chocolate chips as an optional extra.

Steamed jam or marmalade pudding
Spoon 100 g of your favourite jam or marmalade into bottom of bowl, then spoon pudding mix over the top. Omit lemon juice and zest and add ½ tsp vanilla extract.

Steamed ginger pudding
Add 2 tsp ground ginger to the pudding mix and omit lemon juice and zest. Stir in 60 g (⅓ cup) chopped glace ginger.

Steamed treacle or maple syrup pudding
Spoon 100 g golden syrup or maple syrup into bottom of bowl, then spoon pudding mix over the top. Omit lemon juice and zest and add ½ tsp vanilla extract.

Steamed rhubarb pudding
Chop 1 bunch rhubarb into 1 cm pieces. Toss with 2 tbsp raw sugar, ½ tsp nutmeg and ½ tsp cinnamon. Omit lemon juice and zest and stir in rhubarb, sugar and spices instead.

Chocolate self-saucing pudding

Serves 4

This is an incredibly popular style of dessert – partly because it is so easy and partly because of the apparently magical way the sauce starts on the top of the pudding and ends up on the bottom.

- 60 g melted butter
- 125 ml (½ cup) milk
- 75 g (¼ cup) caster sugar
- 1 egg
- 150 g (1 cup) self-raising flour
- 20 g (¼ cup) cocoa
- 20 g (¼ cup) cocoa, additional
- 55 g (¼ cup) caster sugar, additional
- 250 ml (1 cup) boiling water
- 1-litre ovenproof dish, buttered and sprinkled with caster sugar

Preheat oven to 180°C.

Whisk melted butter, milk, sugar and egg together lightly. Sift flour and cocoa together, then whisk into the milk. Pour this into an ovenproof dish.

Place additional cocoa and sugar together into a bowl, whisk in boiling water until smooth, then pour this over the chocolate pudding.

Place in preheated oven and cook for 30–40 minutes, or until skewer comes out clean when tested.

Chocolate and peppermint pudding
Add 1 tsp peppermint essence with melted butter.

Chocolate and walnut pudding
Add 60 g (½ cup) chopped walnuts with flour and cocoa.

Self-saucing sticky date and pecan pudding

Serves 4–6

Thoughts of open fires and chilly nights spring to mind when we think about this dish. You could swap the pecans for walnuts or hazelnuts if you prefer.

- 175 g (1 cup) dried dates, pitted and chopped
- 1 tsp bicarbonate of soda
- 250 ml (1 cup) boiling water
- 60 g butter
- 150 g (¾ cup) brown sugar
- 2 eggs
- 175 g (1 cup plus 2 tbsp) self-raising flour
- 60 g (½ cup) chopped pecans
- 100 g (½ cup) brown sugar, additional
- 1 tbsp cornflour
- 300 ml (1¼ cups) boiling water
- 2 tbsp golden syrup
- cream to serve

Preheat oven to 180°C.

Butter a 1-litre ovenproof dish and sprinkle with caster sugar.

Mix the dates and bicarbonate of soda in a bowl. Pour boiling water over and leave to stand.

Cream the butter and brown sugar until pale and thick. Add the eggs, one by one, incorporating the first one well before adding the next. Fold in the flour until well mixed, then fold through the date mixture and the pecans.

Spoon the pudding mixture into the buttered dish. Mix the additional 100 g (½ cup) brown sugar and cornflour together and sprinkle over the pudding mix. Pour boiling water onto the golden syrup, then gently pour over the pudding.

Place the pudding in the preheated oven and cook for 35–45 minutes, or until a skewer comes out clean when tested. Serve with cream.

Christmas pudding

Makes 3 large puddings

This is the pudding recipe we have been making for years and will no doubt continue to make for years to come, as Christmas just wouldn't be the same without it. It uses stout to give it a delicious richness, which is the giveaway that it originated in Ireland, the country my family and I emigrated from in 1973. This mix makes three large puddings – one for the day itself, one as a gift and one to put away for mid-year Christmas. AC

175 g (1¼ cups) self-raising flour
½ tsp ground nutmeg
1 tsp ground cinnamon
1 tsp mixed spice
225 g (4½ cups) fresh breadcrumbs
500 g (2½ cups) brown sugar
450 g (3 cups) currants
225 g (1⅓ cups) raisins
225 g (1⅓ cups) sultanas

50 g (⅓ cup) slivered almonds
100 g (⅔ cup) mixed peel or candied orange peel
zest of 1 orange
zest of 1 lemon
225 g margarine
3 eggs
65 ml (¼ cup) brandy
275 ml (1 cup) Guinness

3 × 1-litre pudding bowls, buttered

Sift together flour and spices. Stir in breadcrumbs, brown sugar, currants, raisins, sultanas, mixed peel, almonds and citrus zest. Melt margarine and mix with eggs, brandy, stout and margarine. Stir wet mix into dry mix, combining both fully. It may look quite runny at this stage but will thicken in the refrigerator. Cover mixture and refrigerate overnight.

Divide pudding mixture between three bowls. Cover with buttered greaseproof paper and foil. Tie down tightly with string under the rim of each pudding bowl, or easier still, use a large elastic band.

Place each pudding bowl into a large pot. Pour in enough water to come three-quarters of the way up the bowl. Bring to the boil, reduce to a simmer, cover and cook for 4 hours.

Check water level from time to time and add more if needed. Test the puddings with a skewer as you would a cake, to make sure they are cooked. Either serve while still hot or wrap carefully and store in a cool dark place for up to 6 months.

Australian Christmas pudding

This is the variation we developed as we grew to love great Australian ingredients. It is quite different from the original, but delicious also. Add to the pudding mix 1 tsp ground ginger, ¾ tsp ground wattle seed, 175 g (1 cup) chopped glace ginger in place of mixed peel and 150 g (1 cup) macadamias in place of almonds. Swap Australian dark rum for brandy and South Australian stout for Guinness.

Bread and butter pudding

Serves 4

Bread and butter pudding is best made with day-old bread to absorb the egg mixture better. A simple dish that any member of the family could make.

10 slices white bread, crusts removed
butter as required
30 g (¼ cup) sultanas
3 eggs
55 g (¼ cup) caster sugar
500 ml (2 cups) milk
1 tsp vanilla extract

Preheat oven to 180°C.

Lightly butter each slice of bread, then cut each into quarters to form triangles. Butter a pie dish and lay the bread triangles into it so that they overlap each other. Scatter the sultanas over the top. Beat eggs, sugar, milk and vanilla extract together in a bowl. Pour egg mixture over the bread slices. Allow to stand for 10–15 minutes, then push bread down to soak up egg mixture, adding the remaining egg mix if there is any.

Bake in preheated oven for 45 minutes. When ready, the pudding will be puffed and golden.

Bread and jam pudding
Spread strawberry or raspberry jam onto the buttered bread triangles.

Pain au chocolat pudding
Substitute 2-3 pains au chocolat (chocolate-filled 'croissants') for bread and butter.

Panettone and raspberry pudding

Serves 4–6

This is a marvellous way to use up any leftover panettone from Christmas Day. It's a simple variation on a bread and butter pudding but with a heady aroma from the panettone and little bursts of flavour courtesy of the berries.

10 slices panettone
150 g (1 ¼ cup) raspberries
3 eggs
55 g (¼ cup) caster sugar
500 ml (2 cups) milk
1 tsp vanilla extract
1–2 tbsp caster sugar, additional

Preheat oven to 180°C.

Butter a pie dish and arrange the panettone slices so that they overlap each other. Scatter raspberries over the top.

Beat the eggs, caster sugar, milk and vanilla together in a bowl, then pour over the panettone slices. Allow to stand for 10–15 minutes, then push the panettone down to soak up the egg mixture. Sprinkle additional caster sugar over the top.

Bake in the preheated oven for 40–45 minutes. When ready, the pudding will be puffed and golden.

Ginger parkin with spiced cream

Serves 8

If you thought British food was a write-off, you have never tried this dessert, which is heavenly on a cold winter's night. The parkin improves with age, becoming even gooier and stickier, so make it in advance if you can. To complete the dessert, serve the parkin with poached pears.

100 g (⅔ cup) self-raising flour
pinch of salt
2 tsp ground ginger
½ tsp mixed spice
½ tsp ground nutmeg
100 g (1 cup) rolled oats
175 g (½ cup) golden syrup
50 g black treacle

100 g soft butter
90 g (½ cup) soft brown sugar
1 egg
1–2 tbsp milk
300 ml (1¼ cups) thick cream
1 tsp mixed spice
½ tsp ground ginger

Preheat oven to 140°C.

Sift the flour, salt and spices together in a large bowl. Add the oats and stir through. Place the golden syrup, treacle, butter and brown sugar in a small saucepan and melt over a gentle heat. Do not boil. Add to the flour, along with the egg and milk, to create a soft cake consistency. If needed, add a little more milk. Spoon the mixture into a buttered cake tin and bake in the preheated oven for 1 hour.

Check if the cake is cooked by inserting a skewer into the centre. If the skewer comes out clean, the cake is cooked. If not, cook for a further 5 minutes and try again. Allow the cake to cool in the tin for 10 minutes before turning it out on a cooling rack. Once cold, wrap in cling film and store in an air-tight container for up to 2 weeks.

Mix the cream, spice and ginger together. Warm the parkin by either heating it in the microwave for 2 minutes or by wrapping it in foil and heating it in a preheated 180°C oven for 10 minutes.

Cut the parkin into 8 wedges and serve with spiced cream.

Christmas trifle

Serves 6–8

We love trifle, particularly in summer when fresh fruit is so magnificent. We usually have panettone left over after Christmas and so we use it in this dish instead of sponge. Combined with the sparkling wine jelly and real custard, this is a spectacular dish.

3 × 5 g gelatine leaves
250 ml (1 cup) apple juice
110 g (½ cup) caster sugar
500 ml (2 cups) sparkling wine
4 peaches, sliced
150 g (1¼ cups) raspberries
6–8 slices panettone

2 egg yolks
55 g (¼ cup) caster sugar, additional
1 tbsp plain flour
500 ml (2 cups) milk
½ tsp vanilla extract
300 ml (1¼ cups) whipping cream
2 tbsp pistachios, sliced, or 2 tbsp flaked almonds

Soak the gelatine sheets in cold water for 2–3 minutes, or until soft. Remove from soaking dish and squeeze away excess water. Set aside.

Place the apple juice and caster sugar in a saucepan and bring to the boil. Remove from the heat, add the gelatine leaves and sparkling wine and stir until dissolved. Strain into a large serving bowl and refrigerate for 4–6 hours, until almost set. Add the peach slices and raspberries at this point; if you add the fruit too early it will sink to the bottom. Arrange the panettone slices on top of the jelly.

Make the custard by beating the egg yolks and additional 55 g (¼ cup) caster sugar together until pale, then stir in the flour until smooth. Bring the milk and vanilla to the boil. Whisk the hot milk into the egg yolk mixture and return to a clean saucepan over a low heat. Stir constantly as the custard comes to the boil and thickens. Remove from heat and allow to cool. Spread the custard over the panettone and chill until ready to serve.

To serve, whip the cream, spread it over the custard and sprinkle with nuts.

Raspberry and gin trifle

Serves 8–10

A huge bowl of trifle will have your friends coming back for seconds. If you don't have any gin in the house, use any other white spirit or dessert wine.

3 × 5 g gelatine leaves
750 ml (3 cups) apple juice
40 g (2 tbsp) caster sugar
60 ml (¼ cup) gin
4 peaches, sliced
150 g (1¼ cups) raspberries
6–8 slices panettone

2 egg yolks
55 g (¼ cup) caster sugar, extra
1 tbsp plain flour
500 ml (2 cups) milk
½ tsp vanilla extract
300 ml (1¼ cups) whipping cream
2 tbsp pistachios, sliced, or 2 tbsp flaked almonds

Soak gelatine sheets in cold water for 2–3 minutes or until soft, then squeeze and set aside. Remove and squeeze excess water away. Set aside.

Put apple juice and sugar in a saucepan and bring to the boil. Remove from heat, add the gelatine leaves and gin and stir until dissolved. Strain into a large serving bowl. Refrigerate until almost set, at least 3–4 hours. Only then add the peach slices and raspberries – if you add them too early they will sink to the bottom. Arrange panettone slices on top of the jelly. Refrigerate.

Make the custard by beating the egg yolks and extra sugar until pale, then stir in flour until smooth. Bring milk and vanilla to the boil. Whisk milk into the egg yolk mixture and return to a clean saucepan over low heat. Stir constantly as the custard comes to the boil and thickens. Remove from the heat. Allow to cool. Spread custard over the panettone and chill until ready to serve.

Whip cream, spread over the custard and sprinkle with nuts.

Mango and orange-blossom trifle

Serves 8

The combination of mangoes, citrus jelly and almond-flavoured biscuits is hard to beat. Once the jelly is made, the rest of the preparation is plain sailing. The pistachio praline is an additional extra, but it's like air-conditioning in the heat of summer – you've just got to have it.

- 110 g (½ cup) caster sugar
- 250 ml (1 cup) water
- zest of 2 oranges
- zest of 2 lemons
- 250 ml (1 cup) orange juice
- 80 ml (⅓ cup) lemon juice
- 250 ml (1 cup) apple juice
- 3 × 5 g gelatine sheets
- 2 tbsp orange-blossom water
- 2 mangoes, peeled and diced into 1 cm pieces
- 110 g (½ cup) caster sugar, additional
- 80 ml (⅓ cup) water, additional
- 75 g (½ cup) shelled pistachios
- 200 g amaretti biscuits, crushed
- 2 tbsp orange-blossom water, additional
- 250 g (1 cup) mascarpone
- icing sugar to taste (optional)

Place caster sugar and water in a saucepan and heat gently until the sugar dissolves. Add the citrus zest and fruit juices and bring to the boil. Remove from heat, add the gelatine sheets and stir until dissolved. Strain, discarding the zest, and cool slightly. Add the orange-blossom water and stir to combine. Pour into a large glass bowl, or 8 individual glasses. Place in the refrigerator until almost set, then add the diced mango. If you add the mango before this stage it will sink to the bottom. Refrigerate the jelly until set.

To make the caramel for the pistachio praline, place the additional 110 g caster sugar and 80 ml water in a saucepan. Cook over a low heat until the sugar dissolves. Raise the heat and boil the liquid. Cook for 12–15 minutes, or until the liquid begins to colour. The desired colour is a mix of gold and caramel, not dark brown. If needed, carefully swirl the saucepan to mix the caramel. Remove from heat, add the pistachios and tip onto a tray lined with baking paper. Allow the praline to cool, then chop roughly.

Lightly crush the amaretti biscuits and spoon onto the jelly. Sprinkle with the additional 2 tbsp orange-blossom water. Beat the mascarpone until smooth and add icing sugar to taste, if desired. Spoon the mascarpone on top of the biscuits and refrigerate until ready to serve.

Serve the trifle topped with the chopped praline.

Rice pudding

Serves 4

This is the easiest rice pudding recipe we know. We often serve it with a dollop of raspberry jam. It's also a recipe children enjoy learning how to make, including our daughter Mia, who has mastered it.

1 litre (4 cups) milk
110 g (½ cup) caster sugar
1 tsp vanilla extract
220 g (1 cup) short-grain rice

Place the milk, caster sugar, vanilla and rice in a large heavy-based saucepan. Bring to the boil, then reduce to a very low heat and cook for 20 minutes, stirring often. When the rice is tender, remove from heat, cover and allow to rest for 15 minutes before serving. This will allow time for any remaining liquid to be absorbed.

Spoon the warm rice pudding into serving bowls.

Middle Eastern rice pudding
Prepare the pudding as directed, then add 50 g (⅓ cup) toasted pine nuts and 50 g (⅓ cup) currants. Drizzle with pomegranate syrup to serve.

Chocolate rice pudding
Add 60 g chopped dark chocolate to the pudding once cooked. Stir until melted.

Adult's rice pudding
Soak 110 g (⅔ cup) sultanas in 125 ml (½ cup) liqueur muscat or tokay as the rice is simmering, then add them to the pudding.

Risotto of chocolate and nougat

Serves 4

It may seem odd to have a risotto recipe in a chapter on desserts, but a dessert it is. Think of a gorgeous rice pudding dotted with glace fruit and chunks of chocolate and nougat.

1 litre (4 cups) milk
110 g (½ cup) caster sugar
1 tsp vanilla extract
220 g (1 cup) short-grain rice
2 tbsp cream
80 g glace fruit (citron, quinces or figs), diced (optional)
100 g dark chocolate, roughly chopped
100 g almond nougat, chopped

Place the milk, caster sugar, vanilla and rice in a large heavy-based saucepan. Bring to the boil, then reduce to a very low heat and cook for 20 minutes, stirring often. When the rice is tender, remove from heat, cover and allow to rest for 15 minutes before serving. This will allow time for any remaining liquid to be absorbed. Stir through the cream and glace fruit (if using).

Spoon the warm rice into serving bowls. Scatter chocolate and nougat over the risotto and serve immediately.

Pavlova

Serves 8–10

The pavlova is a marvellous version of meringue, almost always topped with cream, then finished with berries and passionfruit. There's no real secret to making one; if you can whip egg whites you can whip up a pavlova. It's traditionally served at barbecues all through summer, so who are we to break a great custom?

6 egg whites
440 g (2 cups) caster sugar
1 tsp vanilla extract
1 tbsp cornflour

1½ tsp white vinegar
250 ml (1 cup) whipping cream
pulp from 6 passionfruit
200 g (1½ cups) raspberries

Preheat oven to 180°C.

Beat egg whites until stiff peaks form. Add sugar, a third at a time, allowing each third to be well incorporated so that you end up with a thick glossy meringue. Fold through vanilla, cornflour and vinegar.

Either spoon into a greased and lined 23 cm springform cake tin or spread in a high circle on a sheet of baking paper on a tray. Place in oven, lower temperature to 120°C and bake for 45 minutes. Turn the oven off, leaving the pavlova to cool inside the oven, preferably overnight.

Place cool pavlova on a serving platter and cover with whipped cream. Scoop passionfruit pulp on top and scatter raspberries over.

Baby pavs
Spoon pavlova mix into 12 individual rounds and bake for 30 minutes. Allow to cool in oven. Serve one per guest.

Meringues

Makes about 20

A delicate white meringue is one of the wonders of baking. How is it that two basic ingredients, namely egg whites and sugar, can be transformed into such a delicious food by mere beating and cooking? The technique becomes irrelevant with the first mouthful of these crispy delights with their marshmallow centres.

6 egg whites   300 g (1⅓ cups) caster sugar

Preheat oven to 160°C.

Beat egg whites until stiff. Add the caster sugar a third at a time and continue beating until the meringue is glossy and firm. Spoon large dollops of meringue onto lined baking trays (you should get around 20 meringues). Bake in preheated oven for 30 minutes. Turn oven off, and leave to cool for 30 minutes more. Enjoy them as they are!

Meringues with chocolate sauce
Place one meringue on each plate. Add a dollop of whipped cream and another meringue. Pour over hot Chocolate Sauce (page 571) and serve.

Meringues with berries
Layer meringues with whipped cream and berries.

Chocolate meringues
Sprinkle 40 g (⅓ cup) cocoa over meringue mixture, then add 1 tsp vinegar and fold in carefully, before baking.

Chocolate meringue discs
Make meringue as described. Line 3 flat trays with paper and divide meringue between them. Smooth into large circles, about 20 cm. They don't have to be perfect. Cook for 1 hour and leave in oven overnight. Use these 3 circles to make meringue mousse stacks, right.

Mousse and meringue stacks
Make chocolate meringues as described. Top each meringue with Coffee and Cardamom Mousse (page 656) before it sets and layer meringues on top of each other. Refrigerate for 2–3 hours until mousse sets before serving.

Baby pavlovas with banana and honeycomb

Serves 6–8

Pavlova is a must-have food at many celebrations and serving individual baby versions makes them much more dinner-party fare. Topped with banana and honeycomb they are quite amazing. As an alternative, drizzle pavlovas with Butterscotch Sauce (page 572).

6 egg whites
440 g (2 cups) caster sugar
1 tsp vanilla extract
1 tbsp cornflour
1½ tsp white vinegar
300 ml (1¼ cups) whipping cream
4 bananas
Honeycomb (page 795)

Preheat oven to 180°C.

Beat the egg whites until stiff peaks form. Add sugar, one-third at a time, allowing each third to be well incorporated so that you end up with a thick glossy meringue. Fold through the vanilla, cornflour and vinegar.

Spoon tablespoons of meringue on to baking trays lined with baking paper: the mix should make 12–16, depending on the size. Place in the oven, lower the temperature to 120°C and bake for 30 minutes. Turn the oven off, leaving the pavlovas to cool inside the oven.

Whip cream to soft peaks. Peel bananas and cut into slices. Arrange one pavlova on each plate, spoon cream on top of each. Place 2–3 pieces of banana on each, add chunks of honeycomb and serve.

Rosewater meringue stack with red summer berries

Serves 8–10

This dessert is basically an overgrown layered pavlova with lots of extras. You'll definitely need one of these if you're entertaining a large group of people over summer. Serve it in all its glory and allow everyone to help themselves.

6 egg whites
440 g (2 cups) caster sugar
2 tbsp rosewater
1 tbsp cornflour
1½ tsp white vinegar

600 ml (2⅓ cups) thickened cream
500 g cherries, pitted
250 g redcurrants, destalked
300 g (2 cups) raspberries

Preheat oven to 180°C. Line 3 baking trays with baking paper.

Beat the egg whites until stiff peaks form. Add the caster sugar, a third at a time, allowing each third to be well incorporated so that you end up with a thick, glossy meringue. Fold through the rosewater, cornflour and vinegar.

Shape 1 disc of meringue onto the 3 prepared baking trays, the first 20 cm wide, the second 15 cm and the last 10 cm in width. Place the trays in the oven, lower the temperature to 120°C and bake for 45 minutes. Turn the oven off, leaving the meringue to cool inside the oven.

Whip the cream until thick. Combine the fruit in a bowl. Place the largest meringue disc on a serving platter, spread it with cream and top with almost half the fruit. Add the medium-sized meringue disc and top with cream and fruit. Repeat with the final meringue, using up the remaining cream and fruit.

Nectarine and limoncello meringue slice

Serves 8–10

The perfect dessert for a hot summer's night. This slice is best made the day before, or at least early in the day you want to serve it. The meringue doesn't freeze completely, so you get a crisp texture and the contrast of a creamy filling.

4 egg whites
300 g (1⅓ cups) caster sugar
6 nectarines
60 ml (¼ cup) limoncello
4 eggs, separated
55 g (¼ cup) caster sugar, additional
250 g (1 cup) mascarpone

Preheat oven to 160°C.

Line 3 baking trays with baking paper. Roughly draw a rectangle (10 cm × 20 cm) on each piece of paper.

Beat the egg whites until stiff. Add the caster sugar, a third at a time, and continue beating until the meringue is glossy and firm. Divide the mixture between the 3 baking trays, spreading the mixture to reach the 4 corners of each rectangle. Bake in the preheated oven for 30 minutes. Turn the oven off, and leave to cool for 30 minutes.

Dice 2 nectarines into 1 cm chunks and marinate in limoncello for at least 40 minutes. Beat the 4 egg yolks with the additional 55 g caster sugar. Beat in the mascarpone until smooth. Add the diced nectarines and limoncello. Beat the egg whites until stiff peaks form. Whisk a spoonful of egg white through the limoncello mixture, then carefully fold the remaining egg whites through.

Place 1 meringue rectangle on a tray that will fit in the freezer. Spoon half of the limoncello mixture on top, spreading out to the corners. Add another meringue layer, the remaining limoncello mix and then the final layer of meringue. Cover loosely and freeze for at least 6 hours before serving, or preferably overnight.

Slice the remaining nectarines. Remove the meringue from the freezer, cut slices to suit and arrange each slice on a plate. Garnish with nectarine slices and serve.

Vanilla ice-cream

Serves 8–10

This recipe, which has a high proportion of cream, enabled us to get by for years without an ice-cream machine. The cream is folded through at the last minute before the mix goes into the freezer. You just have to give it a stir each hour until it freezes – around 4 or 5 times.

4 eggs
125 g (½ cup) caster sugar
2 tsp vanilla extract
500 ml (2 cups) whipping cream

Beat eggs, caster sugar and vanilla until thick and doubled in size, about 5 minutes. Whip cream until it forms stiff peaks. Fold whipped cream gently into egg mixture.

If you have an ice-cream machine, churn ice-cream according to machine's instructions; if not, pour the mixture into a bowl. Place in freezer. Remove after 1 hour and stir well to break up ice particles. Return to the freezer and repeat every hour for 4–5 hours or until just about frozen. On the last stir transfer ice-cream into a sealable container.

Allow to set in the freezer for at least 24 hours before serving.

Christmas cake ice-cream
Add ¼ tsp ground cinnamon, ¼ tsp ground nutmeg and 60 ml (¼ cup) brandy to the mixture with eggs and sugar. Follow the basic recipe. When the ice-cream is almost frozen, stir in 100 g (⅔ cup) mixed fruit 50 g (⅓ cup) roasted almonds and 50 g (⅓ cup) candied cherries.

Chocolate ice-cream
Add 250 g melted dark chocolate to the mix just before adding the whipped cream. You can also add 100 g chocolate chunks.

Hazelnut ice-cream
Add 200 g (1⅓ cup) roasted hazelnuts and 60 g (½ cup) ground roasted hazelnuts to the mix just before adding the whipped cream.

Frozen nougat

Serves 6

Melbourne chef Arnie Sleeman created this method for what he calls frozen nougat. We've persuaded him to allow us to use it here. His recipe uses glucose, which means the ice-cream never really freezes, so in many ways it's more like a semifreddo than an ice-cream. It doesn't require an ice-cream machine and can have virtually any flavour added. How good is that?

100 g (¼ cup) honey
65 g glucose (obtainable from chemist shops)
8 egg whites
4 egg yolks
130 g (⅔ cup) caster sugar
330 ml (1⅓ cups) cream
165 g flavouring of your choice

Place honey and glucose in a saucepan, cook over a medium heat until it boils, remove and allow to cool slightly. Beat egg whites until soft peaks appear, then slowly pour honey mixture onto whites and continue beating until incorporated.

In a separate bowl beat egg yolks and sugar until white and silky in appearance. Whip cream until soft peaks form.

Gently whip a large spoonful of beaten egg white and whipped cream into egg yolks. When this is fully incorporated gently fold in remaining egg white and cream. Fold in flavouring of your choice.

Place the mixture in a freezer-proof bowl, cover with foil and freeze overnight.

Liquorice frozen nougat
Melt 165 g liquorice with the honey and glucose; it will take an extra 2–3 minutes to melt.

Chocolate and chestnut frozen nougat
Add 90 g melted chocolate and 90 g peeled chestnuts (or hazelnuts).

Frozen nougat ice-cream cake
Because of the no-churn policy this can be poured into a 22 cm springform cake tin and frozen. Perfect for birthday parties. Add Strawberry Sauce (page 568) or 165 g melted chocolate.

Raspberry and Campari sorbet

Serves 6–8

This is where an ice-cream machine becomes indispensable, but if you don't have one you can still give it a go. Best eaten within 2 days of making it.

200 g (1 cup) caster sugar
375 ml (1½ cups) water
300 g (2 cups) raspberries
1½ tbsp lemon juice
2 tbsp Campari
additional Campari for serving

Prepare syrup by placing sugar and water in a saucepan. Stir over a medium heat until sugar dissolves. Allow to cool for 5 minutes.

Place berries, lemon juice and cooled syrup in a food processor and whiz until smooth. Strain liquid to remove the raspberry seeds. Add Campari to the strained liquid.

Pour into ice-cream machine and churn according to the manufacturer's instructions. Alternatively pour the liquid into a shallow freezer-proof tray and freeze for 1 hour. Remove tray and stir the sorbet well. Freeze for 1 hour more and repeat the stirring. Pour into a freezer-proof bowl, cover and freeze overnight. Place sorbet in refrigerator for 10 minutes before serving.

Serve scoops of sorbet with additional Campari drizzled over.

Watermelon granita with summer fruit

Serves 6

This semi-frozen dessert is refreshing in the summer months. Spoon the dessert into chilled glass bowls to prevent the granita from melting too quickly when it's served.

1 kg watermelon
75 g (⅓ cup) caster sugar
60 ml (¼ cup) white spirit (vodka, tequila or rum)
3 pink grapefruit or 4 oranges
½ cantaloupe
200 g strawberries

Chop the watermelon, discarding the skin and pips. Place the melon in a food processor, along with the caster sugar and white spirit, and blend until smooth. Strain through a sieve and discard any remaining pulp. Tip the watermelon juice into a shallow baking tray and freeze overnight.

Remove the skins and pith of the citrus fruit. Remove the segments from the membrane so that each segment is free from any pith or seeds. Either dice the cantaloupe or scoop into balls using a melon baller. Remove the leaves from the strawberries, cut in half if necessary and wash. Combine all the fruit in a bowl and set aside.

Remove the granita from the freezer and flake with a fork. Divide the fruit salad between 6 chilled glass bowls, add a large spoonful of granita and serve.

Tiramisu ice-cream

Serves 6

If you're a fan of tiramisu – and that's probably about 90 per cent of the population – then you're going to love this frozen version. A big thank you to Rosemary Di Benedetto for the recipe.

125 ml (½ cup) strong black coffee
2 tbsp coffee liqueur
1 × 395 g can sweetened condensed milk
600 ml (2⅓ cups) cream
60 ml (¼ cup) cup milk
12 sponge fingers

Line a medium (21 cm × 9 cm × 6 cm) loaf tin with cling film. Mix the coffee and liqueur together and allow to cool.

Place the condensed milk, cream and milk in a large bowl and beat until thick. Add half of the coffee mixture and beat well.

Lay 6 sponge fingers in the prepared tin, spoon in the milk and cream mixture and drizzle over half of the remaining coffee mixture. Top with 6 sponge fingers, then drizzle with the remaining coffee mixture. Freeze overnight.

Remove from tin and cut into 1 cm slices to serve. Cut each slice in half diagonally. Delicious with Bourbon Sauce (page 572) or Butterscotch Sauce (page 572).

Strawberry, rosewater and pistachio semifreddo

Serves 6–8

A beautiful dessert heralding the arrival of the new season's berries. Light and delicate, it is the essential taste of summer.

500 g strawberries, washed and hulled
1 tbsp rosewater
6 egg yolks
110 g (½ cup) caster sugar
350 ml (1⅓ cups) thickened cream
75 g (½ cup) shelled unsalted pistachios
1 tbsp finely chopped mint leaves

Place half of the strawberries in a bowl with the rosewater and mash roughly (a potato masher is ideal).

Beat the egg yolks and caster sugar until pale and creamy. Whip the cream until it forms stiff peaks. Add a spoonful of cream to the egg yolk mixture and stir until well combined. Fold through the remaining cream, mashed strawberries and pistachios. Pour into a sealable plastic container and place in the freezer. For the next 3–4 hours, about every hour, remove the semifreddo from the freezer and stir well to break up ice crystals. Line a 1½ litre (6 cup) capacity loaf-shaped tin with plastic wrap and spoon in the mixture. Cover the top with plastic wrap and place in the freezer overnight.

Chop the remaining strawberries into quarters and toss with the mint. Allow to stand at room temperature for 2–3 hours before serving.

Remove the semifreddo from the freezer 10 minutes before serving to allow it to soften. Slice the semifreddo into 1 ½ cm thick slices. Arrange on serving plates, add minted strawberries and serve immediately.

Espresso semifreddo with butterscotch sauce

Serves 8

Butterscotch Sauce can be used in many ways – drizzle it over vanilla ice-cream, baby pavlovas or this espresso semifreddo.

200 g chocolate, chopped into chunks
6 egg yolks
110 g (½ cup) caster sugar
165 ml (⅔ cup) strong black coffee
350 ml (1⅓ cups) cream
Butterscotch Sauce (page 572)

Line a medium (21 cm × 9 cm × 6 cm) loaf tin with cling film.

Melt the chocolate by placing it in a bowl over a saucepan of simmering water or in a microwave on low for 1–2 minutes.

Beat the egg yolks and caster sugar until pale and thick. Add the coffee and chocolate and beat to incorporate. Whip the cream to form soft peaks. Add a spoonful of whipped cream to the chocolate base and stir through, then gently fold through the remaining cream. Spoon into the prepared loaf tin, cover and freeze overnight.

To serve, allow the semifreddo to stand in its tin at room temperature for 10 minutes. Turn out onto a board and cut into slices.

Arrange slices on plates and drizzle with Butterscotch Sauce.

Moroccan rocky road ice-cream

Serves 8–10

This recipe works well without an ice-cream machine, and you could also make it with a good-quality store-made vanilla ice-cream if you wished. The rocky road influence comes from chef Natalie Paull.

4 eggs
110 g (½ cup) caster sugar
2 tsp vanilla extract
500 ml (2 cups) whipping cream
1 quantity Moroccan Rocky Road (page 796)

Beat the eggs, caster sugar and vanilla together for 5 minutes, until thick and doubled in size. Whip the cream until it forms stiff peaks, then gently fold the cream into the egg mixture.

If you have an ice-cream machine, churn the ice-cream according to your machine's instructions. If you don't have an ice-cream machine, pour the mixture into a bowl and place it in the freezer. Remove it after 1 hour and stir well to break up the ice particles. Return it to the freezer and repeat every hour for 4–5 hours, or until just about frozen.

Chop the rocky road into bite-size pieces. On the last stir of the ice-cream, add the chopped rocky road then spoon the ice-cream into a sealable container. Cover and allow to set in the freezer for at least 24 hours before serving.

To serve, allow the ice-cream to stand in its container at room temperature for 10 minutes before scooping.

Praline

Use praline to garnish desserts such as panna cotta or pavlova, or fold through mousse and ice-cream. Almost any nut can be swapped for the almonds.

80 g (⅓ cup) caster sugar
2 tbsp water
80 g (½ cup) blanched almonds, toasted

Place sugar and water in a small saucepan, heat gently to dissolve sugar, then bring to the boil. Swirl the liquid over the heat (do not stir) to prevent sugar crystals forming, and cook to a light brown colour.

Remove from heat and stir in toasted almonds. Pour onto a lightly oiled baking tray and leave until set hard. When completely cold, remove from tray and chop into bite-size pieces.

CAKES

stickybuns, cheesecakes + muffins

There is nothing more welcoming than the aroma of a cake baking in the oven, nothing that rekindles childhood memories more than the scent of a tray of cupcakes cooling on a rack or a still-warm sponge being spread with raspberry jam.

For kids today, however, these delights are an increasingly rare occurrence. Many people are too busy to cook dinner, let alone go to the bother of dipping cubes of sponge into chocolate and coconut to make lamingtons or whipping up a batch of cupcakes. Sadly, the result will be adults who have no experience of home baking whatsoever. To ensure that this is not the future for your household, we've gathered a selection of recipes that may well become your family favourites.

Cakes make great desserts, and all the work is done before your guests arrive. A fairly easy cake such as our Sherry-Soaked Raisin and Almond Cake (page 721) can easily be dressed up by serving it with Marmalade Cream (page 569). We're big cheesecake fans so we've included recipes for a few beauties, including our Raspberry Ripple Cheesecake (page 738) and Amaretto-Cherry Cheesecake (page 737).

cake recipes

toppings

Basic icing	702
Butter icing	702
Chocolate ganache	702
Cream cheese frosting	702
Chocolate fudge icing	703
White chocolate frosting	703
Maple syrup frosting	703
Coconut frosting	703
Royal icing	703

cakes

Allan's easy sponge cake	704
One-pot chocolate cake	705
Chocolate fudge cake	706
Rich chocolate and almond cake	708
Choc chip pound cake	709
Chocolate and coconut cake	709
Chocolate and cardamom fudge cake	710
Chocolate ripple log	710
Sicilian orange cake with marmalade cream	711
Passionfruit roulade	712
Passionfruit ring cake	713
Lemon and walnut cake	713
Boil-and-bake fruit cake	714
Chocolate and hazelnut panforte	715
Spiced Italian fruit cake	716
Chadwick family Christmas cake	717
Elizabeth's hiking cake	718
Apricot streusel crumble cake	719
Sherry-soaked raisin and almond cake	721
Rhubarb lemon cake	722
Upside-down pear and ginger cake	723
Orange marmalade cake	724
Almond cake	724
Orange and yoghurt syrup cake	725
Lemon sour cream cake	726
Green cake	727
Lemon tea cake	728
Coconut cake	729
Gingerbread cake	729
Banana and walnut cake	730
Apple, fig and pecan cake	730
Carrot cake	731
Pumpkin cake	732
Date and coconut loaf	732
Pecan coffee cake	733
Plum cake	733
Linzertorte made easy	734

cheesecakes

Lemon cheesecake	734
Cherry cheesecake	735
My kind of cheesecake	736
Amaretto-cherry cheesecake	737
Raspberry ripple cheesecake	738
Pedro Ximenez cheesecake with boozy prunes	739
White chocolate cheesecake	740
Cheesecake brownies	740
Chocolate brownies	741
Lamingtons	742
Killer cupcakes	743
Cupcakes	744
Friands	746

muffins

Basic muffins	747
Triple chocolate muffins	748
Raspberry and white chocolate muffins	748
Rhubarb, cinnamon and yoghurt muffins	749
Blueberry and coconut muffins	749
Spiced apple and sour cream muffins	750
Banana and maple syrup muffins	750
Chocolate cheesecake muffins	751
Peanut butter muffins	751
Banana muffins	752
Morning glory muffins	752
Coffee and walnut muffins	753
'Doughnut' muffins	753
Flourless chocolate muffins	754
Spicy cheddar muffins	755
Polenta herb muffins	755

stickybuns

Scones	756
Strawberry shortcakes	757
Simple brioche	757
Sticky currant buns	758
Chelsea buns	759
Sticky cinnamon buns	760
Doughnuts	761

Things you need to know about cakes

Basic baking equipment:
20 cm cake tin
22 cm cake tin
23 cm cake tin
loaf tin (21 x 9 x 6 cm)
muffin tins, either 2 x 6 large or 3 x 6 small
cooling rack

1 Grease tins with the fat you are cooking with. This means butter with most cakes, oil when used, and so on. Grease the tin, line it with paper, then grease again.

2 Needless to say, a mixing machine will make light work of any beating, whisking or blending to be done.

3 Always line tins with baking paper to make sure cakes come out easily and to keep washing up to a minimum. The easiest way to line a round cake tin is to tear off a square piece of paper that's big enough to sit the tin on without much excess. Fold the paper in half, then in half again (sideways), then in half again diagonally to end up with a wedge-shaped piece of paper. Mark a curve on the paper with your scissors, using the cake tin as a gauge, then cut along the curve. Unfold the paper and it should fit perfectly.

4 It's much easier to make a cake with soft butter than with hard. Zap hard butter in the microwave for 20 seconds, or grate to soften it quickly. We usually use unsalted butter for baking.

5 The better the quality of your chocolate, the better your cakes, so when a recipe calls for chocolate use cooking couverture. Dark couverture is best, and buttons (or chips) melt more easily.

6 Vanilla extract has a far superior flavour to vanilla essence. Yep, it's more expensive too, but you only have to use half as much.

7 Use Dutch cocoa for better flavour; again, the better the quality, the better the cake.

8 All eggs are medium (59 g).

9 For preference, use espresso coffee where coffee is called for, adding extra coffee grounds for a stronger brew. A stovetop espresso machine makes great cooking coffee. Otherwise, the simplest thing to do is to dissolve 1-2 tsp instant coffee in the required amount of boiling water.

10 To test whether a cake is ready, insert a skewer or cake tester into the centre of the cake. The skewer should come out free of cake mix or crumbs. If it doesn't, cook for a further 5 minutes, then try again.

11 When the cake is cooked, place it on a cooling rack and allow to stand for 10-15 minutes before removing the cake tin.

12 A simple way to jazz up a cake is to dust it with icing sugar or cocoa.

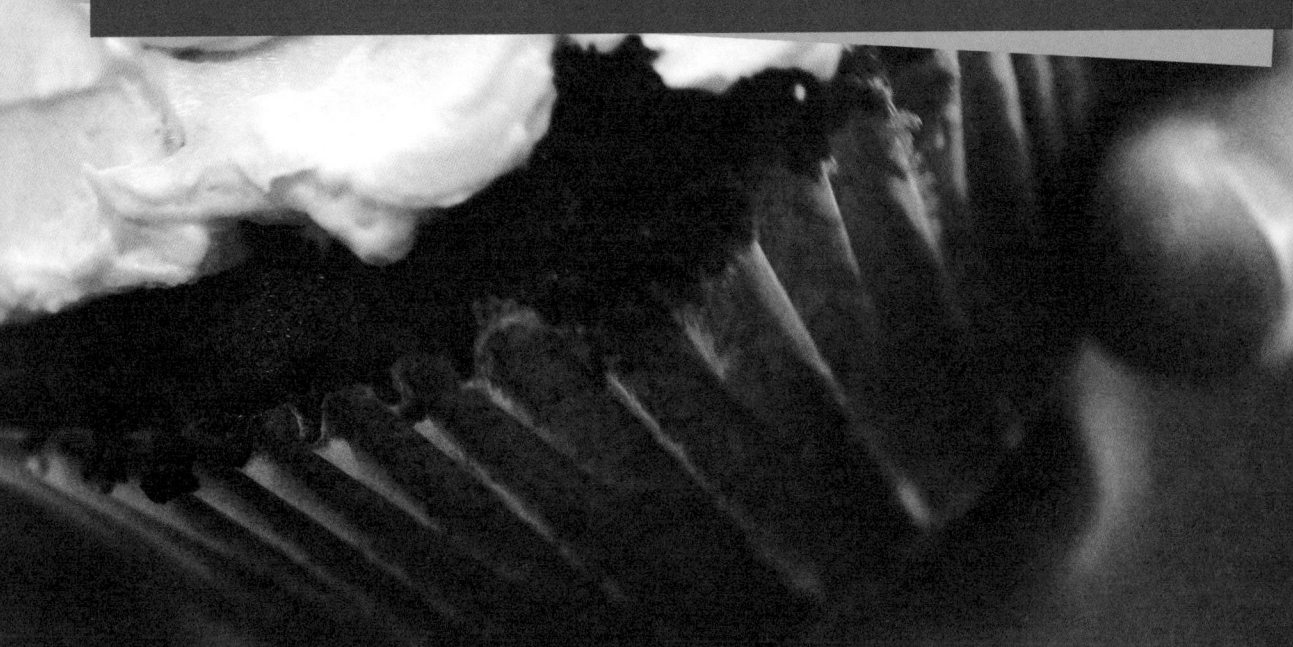

Basic icing

This basic icing is what you'll need for everyday cakes.

1½ tbsp water
2 tbsp melted butter
130 g (1 cup) icing sugar

Whisk the water and butter together. Add it to the icing sugar, bit by bit, until you reach the desired consistency.

Coffee icing
Substitute strong coffee for water.

Chocolate icing
Substitute cocoa powder for 30 g of the icing sugar.

Passionfruit icing
Strain 2 passionfruit and use in place of water.

Lemon icing
Substitute lemon juice for water and add the finely chopped zest of 1 lemon.

Orange icing
Substitute orange juice for water and add the finely chopped zest of 1 orange.

Butter icing

Another basic icing, but with a butter base.

250 g soft butter
130 g (1 cup) icing sugar
1 tsp vanilla extract

Place all the ingredients in a mixer and beat for 5–6 minutes, until white and fluffy.

Chocolate ganache

This is the shiny icing used on the delicacies sold in European cake shops. Be sure to place your cake on a cooling rack over a plate before pouring the warm ganache over.

2 tbsp cream
90 g dark chocolate, chopped

Warm the cream to just below boiling, then remove from heat. Add chocolate and whisk to incorporate. Pour over the cake, taking care to cover the sides as well as the top.

White chocolate ganache
Substitute white chocolate for dark.

Cream cheese frosting

This is the classic icing for carrot cake, but we love its fresh, creamy flavour and use it on lots of other cakes, too.

200 g soft cream cheese
110 g (½ cup) caster sugar
2 tbsp lemon juice

Place all the ingredients in a food processor and blend until smooth.

Chocolate fudge icing

A rich chocolate icing that's great for Killer Cupcakes (page 743).

220 g (1 cup) caster sugar
50 g (½ cup) cocoa
125 g butter
60 ml (¼ cup) milk
390 g (3 cups) icing sugar

Place the caster sugar and cocoa in a saucepan and whisk in the butter and milk. Bring to the boil and cook for 3 minutes, stirring well. Remove from heat and allow to cool until the saucepan is cool enough to touch. Whisk in the icing sugar and stir until thick. Allow to cool completely before using.

White chocolate frosting

A slightly simpler chocolate frosting to use on cakes, muffins or brownies.

250 g white chocolate buttons
300 ml (1¼ cups) sour cream

Melt the chocolate by placing it in a bowl over a saucepan of simmering water or in a microwave on low for 1–2 minutes. Beat into the sour cream.

Maple syrup frosting

This frosting is delicious on muffins with a sprinkle of toasted shredded coconut.

100 g soft cream cheese
2 tbsp maple syrup

Place ingredients in a bowl and beat until smooth.

Coconut frosting

A richer frosting that's good on fruit- and nut-based cakes.

60 ml (¼ cup) coconut milk
130 g (1 cup) icing sugar
35 g (½ cup) desiccated coconut

Place ingredients in a bowl and beat until smooth.

Royal icing

Royal icing can be used for more formal cakes such as Christmas and wedding cakes. We've included it here to adorn the top of the Chadwick Family Christmas Cake (page 717).

2 egg whites
195 g (1½ cups) icing sugar
2 tsp lemon juice

Place the egg whites in a bowl and beat slightly with a wooden spoon. Add the icing sugar very gradually, beating with a spoon. When thick and smooth, add lemon juice and beat again. Using a palette knife spread the icing onto your cake.

Allan's easy sponge cake

Serves 6–8

There's something special about a good sponge cake filled with a little whipped cream and a layer of raspberry jam. This is a really easy recipe, and it cooks in no time.

4 eggs
110 g (½ cup) caster sugar
100 g (⅔ cup) plain flour
raspberry jam as required
250 ml (1 cup) thickened cream, whipped
icing sugar to serve

Preheat oven to 180°C.

Butter a 20 cm springform cake tin and line the sides and bottom with greaseproof paper. Butter the paper and sprinkle it with a little plain flour to ensure that the batter won't stick.

Beat the eggs and caster sugar together until very thick and light. Carefully fold in the flour, then spoon the mix into the prepared cake tin and cook in the preheated oven for 15–20 minutes. Test the cake by inserting a skewer. If it comes out clean, the cake is ready; if it doesn't, cook for a further 2–3 minutes and test again.

Allow the cake to cool on a wire rack. When cool, remove the cake from the cake tin and peel away the greaseproof paper. Cut the sponge in half, and spread a layer of jam and whipped cream on the bottom half of the cake. Replace the top, then sprinkle with icing sugar.

Passionfruit sponge cake
Fill the sponge with a layer of Passionfruit Curd (page 585) instead of jam.

One-pot chocolate cake

Serves 6–8

This has to be the best, most simple chocolate cake in the whole world! There's no need for a mixer or any equipment at all, other than a pot and a wooden spoon. The further in advance you make it, the moister and deeper the flavours become.

250 g soft butter
150 g dark chocolate, chopped
220 g (1 cup) caster sugar
250 ml (1 cup) strong coffee

150 g (1 cup) plain flour
100 g (⅔ cup) self-raising flour
50 g (½ cup) cocoa
2 eggs

Preheat oven to 180°C.

Butter a 22 cm springform cake tin, line the sides and bottom with greaseproof paper and butter lightly.

Place the butter, chocolate, caster sugar and coffee in a large saucepan. Cook over a medium heat, stirring occasionally, until everything melts. Remove from heat and allow to cool slightly.

Sift the flours and cocoa together and add to the cooled chocolate mixture, along with the eggs. Beat well until all ingredients are combined.

Spoon into the prepared cake tin and bake in the preheated oven for 45 minutes. Test the cake by inserting a skewer. If it comes out clean, the cake is ready; if it doesn't, cook for a further 5 minutes and test again.

Chocolate fudge cake

Serves 6–8

Similar to the One-Pot Chocolate Cake, but just a tad more sophisticated and fudgy.

250 g soft butter, diced
150 g dark chocolate, chopped
220 g (1 cup) caster sugar
250 ml (1 cup) strong coffee
150 g (1 cup) self-raising flour
50 g (½ cup) cocoa
2 eggs
100 g (¾ cup) ground almonds
Chocolate Ganache (page 702) or extra cocoa powder, for topping

Preheat oven to 180°C.

Place butter, chocolate, sugar and coffee in a large saucepan. Cook over a medium heat, stirring occasionally, until everything melts. Remove from the heat and allow to cool slightly. Sift flour and cocoa together and add to cooled chocolate mixture, along with eggs and ground almonds. Beat well until all ingredients are combined. Spoon into a greased and lined 22 cm springform cake tin. Bake for 45 minutes.

Test the cake by inserting a skewer. If it comes out clean the cake is ready; if it doesn't, cook for a further 5 minutes and test again. Top with Chocolate Ganache or dust with cocoa powder.

Rich chocolate and almond cake

Serves 6–8

Our variation on this classic Elizabeth David cake, which we find every bit as good as everyone says it is.

250 g dark chocolate, chopped
1 tbsp brandy
130 g (1⅓ cup) ground almonds
250 g soft butter
220 g (1 cup) caster sugar
6 eggs, separated
2 tbsp caster sugar, additional
Chocolate Ganache (page 702), for topping

Preheat oven to 180°C.

Melt chocolate gently, then mix in brandy and ground almonds. Cream the butter and sugar until light and fluffy. Add egg yolks, then beat to incorporate. Add chocolate and almond mixture, stir lightly to blend. Beat egg whites with additional caster sugar until they form stiff peaks. Add 1 tbsp egg white to chocolate mixture and stir in well. Gently fold through remaining egg white.

Spoon into a greased and lined 23 cm springform tin and bake in preheated oven for 50 minutes.

Test with a skewer. If it comes out clean, the cake is ready; if it doesn't, cook cake for a further 5 minutes before trying again. Allow cake to cool in tin for 15 minutes before removing on to a cooling rack.

When cool, cover with Chocolate Ganache.

Rich chocolate and hazelnut cake
Replace the ground almonds with roasted ground hazelnuts.

Choc chip pound cake

Serves 6–8

This is afternoon tea fare at its best – a simple plain cake studded with chocolate chips.

200 g soft butter
200 g soft cream cheese
330 g (1 ½ cups) caster sugar
3 eggs
grated zest of 1 lemon
75 g (¼ cup) sour cream, or natural yoghurt
350 g (2 ⅓ cups) self-raising flour
250 g small chocolate chips

Preheat oven to 180°C.

Cream together butter, cream cheese and sugar until white. Add eggs, one by one, until incorporated. Add lemon zest and sour cream and mix well. Finally add flour, then stir through chocolate chips. Spoon into a greased and lined 22 cm springform cake tin. Bake in preheated oven for 40 minutes. Check the cake with a skewer. If it comes out clean the cake is cooked; if it doesn't, cook for a further 5–10 minutes and try again.

Blueberry pound cake
Substitute blueberries for chocolate chips.

Mascarpone and raspberry pound cake
Substitute mascarpone for cream cheese and fresh raspberries for chocolate chips.

Chocolate and coconut cake

Serves 6–8

The coconut in this chocolate cake adds a great background flavour and texture that appeals to adults and children alike.

185 g soft butter
220 g (1 cup) caster sugar
3 eggs
225 g (1½ cups) self-raising flour
50 g (½ cup) cocoa
125 ml (½ cup) sour cream
35 g (½ cup) desiccated coconut
icing sugar to serve

Preheat oven to 180°C.

Butter a 22 cm springform cake tin, line the sides and bottom with greaseproof paper and butter lightly.

Cream the butter and caster sugar until light and fluffy. Add the eggs, one by one, fully incorporating each one before adding the next. Sift the flour and coconut together, add to the wet mix and beat well. Add the sour cream and coconut and beat until combined.

Spoon the mixture into the prepared cake tin and bake in the preheated oven for 40 minutes. Test the cake by inserting a skewer. If it comes out clean, the cake is ready; if it doesn't, cook for a further 5 minutes and test again. Allow to cool, dust with icing sugar and serve.

Chocolate and cardamom fudge cake

Serves 6–8

This recipe comes from our foodie friend Siu Ling Hui, although it originally included sour cherries. It needs no accompaniment, except perhaps some cream and a glass of tokay.

350 g dark chocolate, chopped into chunks
100 g unsalted butter
6 eggs, separated
110 g (½ cup) caster sugar
50 g (½ cup) cocoa
2 tsp ground cardamom
75 g (⅓ cup) caster sugar, additional

Preheat oven to 175°C.

Butter a 22 cm springform cake tin, line the sides and bottom with greaseproof paper and butter lightly.

Place the chocolate and butter in a heatproof bowl and set over a saucepan of simmering water, stirring occasionally, until they have melted. In a large bowl, beat the egg yolks with caster sugar until light and fluffy. Beat in the chocolate mixture, then carefully fold in the cocoa and cardamom.

Whisk the egg whites to soft peaks, then gradually beat in the additional 75 g caster sugar until the mixture forms stiff peaks. Stir a quarter of this meringue through the chocolate mixture to lighten it, then fold in the remaining meringue gently but thoroughly.

Transfer the mix to the prepared cake tin and bake in the preheated oven for 40 minutes, or until the centre is just set and a skewer comes out clean. Cool on a rack for 20 minutes before turning out to cool completely.

Chocolate ripple log

Serves 6

I fell in love with chocolate ripple cake during my first summer in Melbourne. It's the simplicity of this cake that makes it so good. Even better, our children are now old enough to make it and they love it too. MC

300 ml (1 ¼ cups) cream
1 tsp caster sugar
1 tsp vanilla extract
1 × 250 g packet Chocolate Ripple biscuits
crushed nuts or grated chocolate
fresh berries to serve

Pour the cream into a large bowl, add caster sugar and vanilla, then whip until very stiff.

Spread a biscuit with a generous amount of cream, stand it on its side and add another biscuit to form a sandwich. Continue until all the biscuits are joined together in a log shape.

Spread the remaining cream over the biscuits to cover them completely.

Refrigerate for at least 4 hours before serving. Sprinkle with crushed nuts or grated chocolate and serve with fresh berries.

Sicilian orange cake with marmalade cream

Serves 8

Cakes are great for dessert as they can be baked in advance and thus save you the drama of any last-minute assembling. This one is wonderful after any Mediterranean-influenced main course as it's rich, moist and full of flavour.

2 oranges
5 eggs
220 g (1 cup) caster sugar
250 g (2 cups) ground almonds
1 tsp baking powder
icing sugar
Marmalade Cream (page 569) to serve

Put oranges in a small saucepan, cover with water and bring to the boil.

Reduce heat to a simmer and cook for 30–40 minutes, or until the fruit is soft. Allow to cool. Cut into quarters, removing pips. Puree in a food processor until smooth.

Preheat oven to 180°C.

Beat eggs and sugar together until pale and doubled in bulk, about 5 minutes. Mix almonds and baking powder together. Add orange puree and almond mixture to the beaten eggs and beat to incorporate completely. Pour mixture into a greased and lined 22 cm springform cake tin.

Bake in the preheated oven until light brown and firm in the centre, about 1 hour. Allow to cool. Dust the cake with icing sugar, cut into slices and serve with Marmalade Cream.

Baby orange and almond cakes
Line 18 x 125 ml (½ cup) muffin pans with paper cases then spoon the mixture into the prepared muffin pans and bake in the preheated oven for 20 minutes, or until light brown and firm in the centre. Test the cakes by inserting a skewer into one of them. If it comes out clean, they are ready; if it doesn't, cook for a further 5 minutes and test again. Allow to cool on a wire rack.

Passionfruit roulade

Serves 6–8

A simple dish that is perfect to serve on a hot summer's day as dessert after a long lazy lunch.

4 eggs
110 g (½ cup) caster sugar
100 g (⅔ cup) plain flour
1 cup Lemon Curd (page 585)
250 ml (1 cup) thickened cream, whipped
pulp of 6 passionfruit
sifted icing sugar

Preheat oven to 180°C.

Butter a 25 × 30 cm Swiss roll tin and line the sides and bottom with baking paper. Butter the paper and sprinkle over a little plain flour to ensure that the batter won't stick.

Beat the eggs and sugar until very thick and light. Carefully fold in the flour, then spoon the mixture into the prepared tin. Transfer to the oven and bake for 12–15 minutes. Test the cake by inserting a skewer in the centre. If it comes out clean, the cake is ready; if it doesn't, cook for a further 2–3 minutes and test again.

Allow the cake to cool on a wire rack for 5–10 minutes, then peel away the baking paper. Place a clean tea towel on the work surface, cover with another sheet of baking paper and sprinkle over a little caster sugar. While still warm, turn the cake onto the paper-lined tea towel and, using the tea towel as a guide, carefully roll the cake up widthwise, rolling the paper inside the cake. Set aside to cool completely.

Carefully unwrap the cake, spread Lemon Curd over the base and spread whipped cream over the top of that. Spoon over passionfruit pulp and carefully re-roll, without the paper. Place the roulade, seam-side down, on a platter and dust with icing sugar.

Passionfruit ring cake

Serves 6–8

We love using passionfruit in cakes, tarts and desserts. This recipe follows the classic French method called 'quatre-quart', which combines equal quantities of ingredients. A kugelhopf tin is ideal if you have one; if not, a 22 cm springform cake tin will work.

250 g soft butter
250 g (1 cup plus 2 tbsp) caster sugar
4 eggs
250 g (1 ⅔ cups) self-raising flour, sifted
Passionfruit Icing (page 702)

Preheat oven to 180°C.

Butter a 22 cm springform cake tin, line the sides and bottom with greaseproof paper and butter lightly.

Cream the butter and caster sugar until light and fluffy. Add the eggs, one by one, fully incorporating each one before adding the next. Carefully fold in the flour.

Spoon the mixture into the prepared cake tin and bake in the preheated oven for 40 minutes. Test the cake by inserting a skewer. If it comes out clean, the cake is ready; if it doesn't, cook for a further 5 minutes and test again. Set aside to cool.

Turn the cake out of the tin and pour the icing over, allowing it to run down the sides.

Lemon and walnut cake

Serves 6–8

The zesty lemon and chunks of walnut make this cake a real beauty. Perfect to serve for afternoon tea.

250 g butter
1 tsp vanilla extract
zest of 2 lemons, chopped
220 g (1 cup) caster sugar
3 eggs
150 g (1 cup) self-raising flour
1 tsp cinnamon
120 g (1 cup) chopped walnuts
80 ml (⅓ cup) lemon juice
60 ml (¼ cup) milk
Lemon Icing (page 702)
90 g (¾ cup) chopped walnuts, additional

Preheat oven to 180°C.

Butter a 22 cm springform cake tin, line the sides and bottom with greaseproof paper and butter lightly.

Cream the butter, vanilla, lemon zest and caster sugar until light and fluffy. Add the eggs, one by one, fully incorporating each one before adding the next. Sift the flour and cinnamon together and add to the eggs, stirring in well. Add the walnuts, lemon juice and milk, and stir until combined.

Spoon the mixture into the prepared cake tin and bake in the preheated oven for 40 minutes. Test the cake by inserting a skewer. If it comes out clean, the cake is ready; if it doesn't, cook for a further 5 minutes and test again. Allow to cool.

Drizzle Lemon Icing over the cake and decorate with the additional walnuts.

Boil-and-bake fruit cake

Serves 8–10

This is easy to make and great for taking away on a weekend camping trip or just for having on hand in the cupboard.

150 g butter
300 g (2 cups) sultanas
300 g (2 cups) currants
200 g (1 cup) brown sugar
1 tsp ground allspice
1 tsp ground cinnamon
1 tsp ground ginger
1 tsp bicarbonate of soda
250 ml (1 cup) water
2 eggs, beaten
150 g (1 cup) plain flour
150 g (1 cup) self-raising flour

Preheat oven to 180°C.

Combine butter, sultanas, currants, sugar, spices, soda and water in a saucepan. Cook over a medium heat until mixture comes to the boil, stirring often. Remove from heat and allow to cool.

Add eggs and beat well. Sift flours together, add to the mixture and beat well. Spoon into a greased and lined 22 cm springform tin and bake for 1 hour. Check the cake with a skewer. If it comes out clean the cake is cooked; if it doesn't, cook for a further 5–10 minutes and try again.

Apple fruit cake
Swap half of the dried fruit for grated fresh apple.

Fig or date fruit cake
Replace half of the currants with figs or dates.

Chocolate and hazelnut panforte

Serves 18–20

This is our own version of panforte, a firm toffee-like cake of Italian origin. Use new season's hazelnuts and the best chocolate you can afford. You must line the cake tin with greaseproof paper for this recipe.

150 g dark chocolate, chopped
150 g (⅔ cup) caster sugar
350 g (1 cup) honey
500 g (3⅓ cups) hazelnuts, skins removed
200 g citron, diced
50 g (⅓ cup) plain flour

50 g (½ cup) Dutch cocoa
2 tsp ground cinnamon
1 tsp ground nutmeg
¼ tsp ground black pepper
¼ tsp ground cloves
¼ tsp mixed spice

Preheat oven to 150°C. Prepare a 23 cm springform cake tin by lining base and sides with greaseproof paper. Lightly grease with hazelnut or olive oil.

Place chocolate, sugar and honey in a large saucepan and dissolve over low heat, stirring regularly.

Place hazelnuts and citron in a large bowl. Sift flour, cocoa and spices, add to nut mix and combine well. Pour hot chocolate mixture over dry ingredients and stir together quickly. Press firmly into prepared tin. Bake in preheated oven for 60 minutes.

During cooking the mixture will start to bubble at the edges of the tin. When bubbles have almost reached the middle, the cake is ready. Remove and, if necessary, smooth top using a butter knife. Cool for 15 minutes, then remove from tin. Allow to cool completely before cutting.

To serve, cut into quarters then into thin slices with a sharp knife and serve with coffee.

Panforte can be wrapped in silicon paper and stored in a cool dark place for up to 6 months.

Spiced Italian fruit cake

Serves 8–10

This is a glorious blending of candied fruits, chocolate, a multitude of spices and the heady aroma of marsala. Resistance is useless. When the cake mix is in the tin you can add additional sliced glace fruit in a decorative pattern on top if you wish.

125 g (¾ cup) sultanas
80 ml (⅓ cup) marsala
250 g (1⅔ cup) blanched almonds, chopped
90 g (⅔ cup) pine nuts
250 g candied fruit, such as orange, apricots, figs, pears or lemon, chopped
125 g dark chocolate, chopped
125 g (½ cup) caster sugar
125 g (¾ cup) plain flour

1 tsp ground cinnamon
¼ tsp ground cloves
½ tsp nutmeg
½ tsp ground cardamom
½ tsp baking powder
2 tbsp honey
60 g butter
3 eggs

Soak sultanas in marsala for at least 1 hour, but ideally overnight. Cooking the sultanas in the Marsala for 1–2 minutes in the microwave will hurry the soaking along.

Preheat oven to 180°C.

Mix sultanas with nuts, candied fruit and chocolate. Add sugar and mix together. Sift flour with spices and baking powder. Mix through nut mixture. Melt honey and butter together. Beat eggs until light and fluffy and doubled in size. Add warm butter and honey mixture to eggs and fold through fruit/nut mixture until well combined.

Spoon into a greased and lined 22 cm springform cake tin. Bake in preheated oven for 45–50 minutes, or until a skewer comes out clean.

Chadwick family Christmas cake

Serves 20

Our friends John and Ann Marie Chadwick have agreed to share their Christmas cake recipe. John first made the cake to remind himself of his English roots and it's now become their family tradition. They recommend making it at the beginning of December to allow the fullest flavour to develop in time for the big day. It takes 5 hours to cook but is well worth the time and effort.

BATTER
- 250 g butter
- 300 g (1½ cups) brown sugar
- 4 eggs
- 250 g (1⅔ cups) plain flour, sifted
- ½ tsp baking powder
- ½ tsp salt

FRUIT
- 320 g (2 cups) sultanas
- 300 g (2 cups) dried apricots, sliced
- 170 g (1 cup) pitted dried dates, sliced
- 190 g (1 cup) dried figs, sliced
- 125 g (¾ cup) mixed peel
- 100 g (½ cup) glace cherries
- 55 g (⅓ cup) blanched almonds
- 50 g (½ cup) walnuts
- 250 ml (1 cup) sweet sherry
- 2–3 tbsp brandy

ICING
- apricot jam
- 250 g marzipan icing (store-bought)
- Royal Icing (page 703)

Preheat oven to 200°C.

Butter a 25 cm square cake tin, line the sides and bottom with greaseproof paper and butter lightly. If you have a smaller tin use it instead and allow a little longer cooking time.

Cream the butter and brown sugar until light and fluffy. Add the eggs, one by one, fully incorporating each one before adding the next. Sift the flour, baking powder and salt together. Stir this into the butter and sugar mix.

Place all of the dried fruit and nuts together in a large bowl. Add the sherry and stir to combine. Add the fruit and nuts to the batter and stir to mix well. The secret here is for every member of the family to have a stir and make a wish!

Spoon the mixture into the prepared cake tin and smooth the top. Cover with foil and bake in the preheated oven for 20 minutes. Reduce oven temperature to 175°C and bake for another 20 minutes, then remove the foil and reduce the temperature to 125°C to bake the cake for a further 3 hours and 20 minutes. Test the cake by inserting a skewer. If it comes out clean, the cake is ready. If not, cook for a further 20 minutes and test again.

Allow the cake to cool for 10 minutes. Remove the cake from the tin and place it upside down on a wire rack. The bottom of the cake is quite flat and will now become the top. This will make icing the cake much easier. Brush the top and sides of the cake with the brandy while still warm, then allow to cool completely on a cooling rack. Wrap the cool cake in foil and store in a cool place. Wait a few days before icing.

To ice the cake, thickly spread the jam over the top and sides. Roll out the marzipan and cover the top and sides with a thin layer. Use a palette knife to spread a layer of royal icing all over the cake. Decorate further if desired.

Elizabeth's hiking cake

Serves 6–8

Every year we hike to the lighthouse at the southern tip of Wilsons Promontory National Park with a great group of friends. Fellow hiker Elizabeth always brings this cake for morning tea and, along with the great views and conversations on the way, it's become an essential part of our trip.

- 240 g (1½ cups) mixed dried fruit (for example, apricots, figs and apple)
- 160 g (1 cup) sultanas
- 1 × 440 g can crushed pineapple in natural juices
- 150 g butter
- 1 tbsp mixed spice
- ½ tsp ginger
- ½ tsp cinnamon
- 2 eggs
- 200 g (1⅓ cups) self-raising flour

Preheat oven to 170°C.

Butter a 22 cm springform cake tin, line the sides and bottom with greaseproof paper and butter lightly.

Place the dried fruit, pineapple, butter and spices in a saucepan and heat until the butter melts. Allow to cool. Add the eggs to the fruit mixture and stir well. Add flour and stir through well.

Spoon the mixture into the prepared cake tin and bake in the preheated oven for 40 minutes. Test the cake by inserting a skewer. If it comes out clean, the cake is ready; if it doesn't, cook for a further 5 minutes and test again. Allow to cool.

Apricot streusel crumble cake

Serves 6–8

We love to prepare this cake when fresh apricots are at their best in midsummer. The almond topping makes this a cake and a crumble, all at the same time.

180 g soft butter
150 g (⅔ cup) caster sugar
2 eggs
150 g (1 cup) self-raising flour
120 g (⅔ cup plus 2 tbsp) plain flour
80 ml (⅓ cup) milk
8–10 apricots, halved and stoned

50 g (⅓ cup) plain flour, additional
60 g soft butter, additional
75 g (⅓ cup) raw sugar
1 tsp ground cinnamon
50 g (½ cup) flaked almonds
icing sugar to serve

Preheat oven to 180°C.

Butter a 22 cm springform cake tin, line the sides and bottom with greaseproof paper and butter lightly.

Cream the butter and caster sugar until light and fluffy. Add the eggs, one by one, allowing the first to be incorporated before adding the second. Sift the flours together and add to the cake mixture, along with the milk. Beat until combined. Spoon the mix into the prepared cake tin and arrange the apricots on top of the cake mix.

Combine the additional 50 g (⅓ cup) flour, 60 g butter, raw sugar and cinnamon until the mix forms a breadcrumb texture. Stir the flaked almonds through, then sprinkle the crumble mixture over the apricots.

Bake in the preheated oven for 40–45 minutes. Test the cake after 40 minutes by inserting a skewer. If it comes out clean, the cake is ready; if it doesn't, cook for a further 5 minutes and test again. When cool, dust the cake with icing sugar and serve.

Apple streusel crumble cake
Use slices of poached apple instead of apricots.

Sherry-soaked raisin and almond cake

Serves 6–8

We've been making almond cakes for many years now and they always go down a treat. In this variation, raisins soaked in sherry add richness to the cake, which also makes a great dessert when served with Marmalade Cream (page 569).

170 g (1 cup) raisins	125 g (1¼ cups) ground almonds
60 ml (¼ cup) sweet sherry	225 g (1½ cups) self-raising flour
125 g soft butter	250 g (1 cup) natural yoghurt
220 g (1 cup) caster sugar	1 tsp almond essence
2 eggs	icing sugar to serve

Soak the raisins in sherry overnight. If time is tight, microwave on high for 1 minute or place in a small saucepan and warm through for a few minutes. Cool before using.

Preheat oven to 180°C.

Butter a 22 cm springform cake tin, line the sides and bottom with greaseproof paper and butter lightly.

Cream the butter and caster sugar until light and fluffy. Add the eggs, one by one, allowing the first to be incorporated before adding the second. Fold in the almonds, flour, yoghurt and almond essence.

Spoon the mix into the prepared cake tin and bake in the preheated oven. Test the cake after 35 minutes by inserting a skewer. If it comes out clean, the cake is ready; if it doesn't, cook for a further 5 minutes and test again. When cool, dust the cake with icing sugar and serve.

Rhubarb lemon cake

Serves 6–8

The best kind of fruit to include in cakes is those with a good amount of acid. That's why plums, apricots, quinces and rhubarb feature so heavily in our baking. We find they balance the sweetness and richness of cakes. Try this rhubarb lemon cake, and you'll see exactly what we mean.

4–5 rhubarb stalks, cut into 2 cm pieces
65 g (⅓ cup) brown sugar
125 g soft butter
220 g (1 cup) caster sugar
zest of 1 lemon
3 eggs
2 tbsp lemon juice
150 g (1 cup) plain flour
50 g (⅓ cup) self-raising flour
100 ml (⅓ cup) sour cream
icing sugar to serve

Preheat oven to 180°C.

Butter a 20 cm springform cake tin, line the sides and bottom with greaseproof paper and butter lightly.

Toss the rhubarb with brown sugar and set aside.

Cream the butter and caster sugar until light and fluffy. Add the lemon zest and then the eggs, one by one, fully incorporating each one before adding the next. Stir through lemon juice. Sift the flours together and fold in carefully, alternating with sour cream. Finally, fold the rhubarb through.

Spoon the mix into the prepared cake tin and bake in the preheated oven for 40 minutes. Test the cake by inserting a skewer. If it comes out clean, the cake is ready; if it doesn't, cook for a further 5 minutes and test again.

Allow to cool for 15 minutes, then remove from the tin. Dust with icing sugar to serve.

Upside-down pear and ginger cake

Serves 6–8

There's something magical about preparing a cake from the base up. We love the fact that the top starts on the bottom, and when it's flipped over it looks amazing. This pear and ginger version tastes particularly fine.

2 tbsp butter
2 tbsp brown sugar
4 firm pears, peeled, cored and sliced
2 tbsp lemon juice
125 g butter
65 g (⅓ cup) brown sugar
2 eggs
225 g (1½ cups) self-raising flour
2 tsp ground ginger
2 tbsp lemon juice
icing sugar to serve

Preheat oven to 180°C.

Butter a 22 cm springform cake tin, line the sides and bottom with greaseproof paper and butter lightly.

Place the butter and brown sugar in a medium saucepan and cook over a low heat for 1–2 minutes, until the sugar dissolves. Add the pears and lemon juice and cook for 3–4 minutes, stirring all the time. Remove from the heat and allow to cool.

Arrange pear slices in the base of the prepared cake tin. Reserve any cooking liquid.

Cream the butter and brown sugar until light and fluffy. Add the eggs, one by one, fully incorporating the first before adding the second. Sift the flour and ginger together and fold in carefully. Add lemon juice and enough cooking liquid to form a soft cake mix.

Spoon into the cake tin over the pear slices and bake in the preheated oven for 40 minutes. Test the cake by inserting a skewer. If it comes out clean, the cake is ready; if it doesn't, cook for a further 5 minutes and test again.

Allow the cake to cool for 15 minutes, then remove from tin and turn over to reveal the top. Dust with icing sugar to serve.

Orange marmalade cake

Serves 6–8

This rich, buttery orange cake with a hint of marmalade is just the thing for autumnal afternoons. Brew a pot of your favourite tea as the perfect accompaniment.

- 220 g soft butter
- 180 g (¾ cup plus 1 tbsp) caster sugar
- zest of 1 orange, chopped
- 3 eggs
- 300 g (2 cups) self-raising flour, sifted
- 60 ml (¼ cup) orange juice
- ½ cup orange marmalade

Preheat oven to 180°C.

Butter a 22 cm springform cake tin, line the sides and bottom with greaseproof paper and butter lightly.

Cream the butter, caster sugar and orange zest until light and fluffy. Add the eggs, one by one, fully incorporating each one before adding the next. Carefully fold in the flour, along with the orange juice. Finally, fold in the marmalade.

Spoon the mixture into the prepared cake tin and bake in the preheated oven for 40 minutes. Test the cake by inserting a skewer. If it comes out clean, the cake is ready; if it doesn't, cook for a further 5 minutes and test again.

Almond cake

Serves 6–8

This almond cake is perfect for afternoon tea, it's so beautifully moist and rich.

- 125 g soft butter
- 220 g (1 cup) caster sugar
- 2 eggs
- 125 g (1¼ cups) ground almonds
- 225 g (1½ cups) self-raising flour
- 250 g (1 cup) natural yoghurt
- a few drops of almond essence
- icing sugar for dusting

Preheat oven to 180°C.

Cream butter and sugar until light and fluffy. Add eggs one by one, fully incorporating each one before adding the next. Fold in almonds and flour, yoghurt and almond essence. Spoon into a greased and lined 22 cm springform cake tin and bake in preheated oven.

Test the cake after 35 minutes by inserting a skewer. If it comes out clean the cake is ready; if it doesn't, cook for a further 5 minutes and test again. When cool, dust cake with icing sugar and serve.

Orange and yoghurt syrup cake

Serves 6–8

This style of cake is always wonderfully moist because you pour flavoured syrup over it not long after it emerges from the oven.

125 g soft butter
220 g (1 cup) caster sugar
3 eggs, separated
zest of 2 oranges
60 ml (¼ cup) orange juice
250 g (1 cup) natural yoghurt
300 g (2 cups) self-raising flour
zest of 2 oranges, additional
100 ml (⅓ cup) orange juice, additional
2 tbsp lemon juice
80 g (⅓ cup) caster sugar

Preheat oven to 180°C.

Cream butter and sugar until light and fluffy. Add egg yolks along with the zest. Add orange juice and yoghurt. Mix briefly, then add flour and beat until smooth. Beat egg whites until stiff, then fold through cake mix. Spoon into a greased and lined 22 cm springform cake tin and bake in preheated oven for 40 minutes. Test the cake by inserting a skewer. If it comes out clean the cake is ready; if it doesn't, cook for a further 5 minutes and test again.

Prepare syrup by placing additional zest and juice in a small saucepan with sugar. Stir to dissolve, then bring to the boil. Allow to simmer for 2–3 minutes. Pour warm syrup topping over cake and allow to cool.

Orange poppyseed cake
Add 150 g poppyseeds. Forget the syrup topping.

Lemon sour cream cake

Serves 6–8

This has a great gutsy lemon flavour and stays moist because of the sour cream in it.

125 g soft butter
220 g (1 cup) caster sugar
zest of 1 lemon
3 eggs
2 tbsp lemon juice

150 g (1 cup) plain flour
60 g (⅓ cup) self-raising flour
100 g sour cream
icing sugar for dusting

Preheat oven to 180°C.

Cream butter and sugar until light and fluffy. Add lemon zest, then add eggs one by one, fully incorporating each one before adding the next. Stir through lemon juice. Sift flours together and fold in carefully, alternating with sour cream. Spoon into a greased and lined 20 cm springform cake tin.

Bake for 40 minutes. Test the cake by inserting a skewer. If it comes out clean the cake is ready; if it doesn't, cook for a further 5 minutes and test again.

Allow to cool for 15 minutes, then remove from tin. Dust with icing sugar to serve.

Green cake

Serves 6–8

Don't be put off by the name; this is a great-tasting cake with a hint of almond flavour. My mum made this cake for my brother and me for every birthday we had as children, and it always came with chocolate icing. Even now, I find it irresistible. Our children want to change it to a blue, or even a red, cake; but for me it always was, and always will be, green cake. MC

200 g soft butter
250 g (1¼ cups) caster sugar
3 eggs
225 g (1½ cups) self-raising flour
1½ tsp almond essence
1 tsp green food colouring

Preheat oven to 180°C.

Cream butter and sugar until light and fluffy. Add eggs one by one, fully incorporating each one before adding the next. Add flour with almond essence and colouring. Beat until smooth.

Spoon into a greased and lined 23 cm springform cake tin and bake in preheated oven for 40 minutes. Test the cake by inserting a skewer. If it comes out clean the cake is ready; if it doesn't, cook for a further 5 minutes and test again.

Allow to cool for 15 minutes, then remove from tin. When cool, top with Chocolate Icing (page 702).

Lemon tea cake

Serves 6–8

Also known as Madeira cake, this is one of our favourite types of cake: quiet and unassuming, but somehow extremely more-ish. If you can leave it alone for a few days, it gets better with age.

220 g soft butter
180 g (¾ cup) caster sugar, plus additional for sprinkling
grated zest of 2 lemons
3 eggs
200 g (1⅓ cup) self-raising flour
90 g (⅔ cup) plain flour
60 ml (¼ cup) lemon juice

Preheat oven to 170°C.

Cream butter and sugar until light and fluffy. Add lemon zest. Add eggs one at a time, allowing each to be incorporated before adding the next. Stir in flour and lemon juice and keep stirring until incorporated.

Spoon into a greased and lined loaf tin 23½ × 13½ × 7 cm, sprinkle with additional caster sugar and bake for 1 hour. Test the cake by inserting a skewer; if it comes out clean the cake is ready. If it doesn't, cook for a further 5 minutes and test again. Allow to cool in tin before removing.

Lemon and poppyseed tea cake
Add 1 tbsp poppyseeds to flour.

Orange tea cake
Substitute orange zest and juice for lemon.

Cinnamon and lemon tea cake
Add 1 tsp ground cinnamon to flour.

Coconut cake

Serves 6–8

This is a beautiful cake with a dense texture that can easily be sliced and passed around. Try it as your next birthday cake.

250 ml (1 cup) coconut milk
100 g (1¾ cup) desiccated coconut
200 g soft butter
330 g (1½ cups) caster sugar
4 eggs
250 g (1⅔ cups) self-raising flour

Preheat oven to 180°C.

Place coconut milk and coconut in a small saucepan over a medium heat. Allow to simmer for 2–3 minutes, then allow to cool.

Cream butter and sugar until light and fluffy. Add eggs one by one, fully incorporating each one before adding the next. Alternatively fold in sifted flour and coconut mixture until well combined. Spoon mixture into greased and lined 22 cm springform cake tin. Bake in preheated oven for 40 minutes.

Test the cake by inserting a skewer. If it comes out clean the cake is ready; if it doesn't, cook for a further 5 minutes and test again. Allow to cool, dust with icing sugar and serve.

Gingerbread cake

Serves 6–8

This cake comes from the oven smelling sweetly of ginger, mixed spice, treacle and golden syrup. Tempting, eh?

100 g soft butter
100 g (¼ cup) treacle
100 g (½ cup) brown sugar
100 g (¼ cup) golden syrup
300 g (2 cups) self-raising flour
3 tsp ground ginger
1 tsp mixed spice
2 eggs
125 ml (½ cup) milk

Preheat oven to 170°C.

Melt butter, treacle, sugar and golden syrup together in a saucepan. Allow to cool. Sift flour with spices and fold into the butter and sugar mixture. Add eggs and milk and combine well. Spoon into a greased and lined loaf tin 23½ × 13½ × 7 cm and bake in preheated oven for 30 minutes.

Test the cake by inserting a skewer. If it comes out clean the cake is ready; if not, cook for a further 5 minutes and test again. Allow to cool before slicing.

Banana and walnut cake

Serves 6–8

At last, we've found a use for those bananas lurking at the bottom of the fruit bowl. The riper the bananas and the blacker the skins, the better this cake will be.

125 g soft butter
220 g (1 cup) caster sugar
2 eggs
225 g (1½ cups) self-raising flour
1 tsp vanilla extract
2 ripe bananas, mashed
90 g (¾ cup) walnuts, chopped, optional

Preheat oven to 180°C.

Cream butter and sugar until light and fluffy. Add eggs, one by one, incorporating well after each addition. Stir through flour, vanilla, mashed banana and walnuts.

Spoon into a greased and lined log tin 23½ × 13½ × 7 cm and bake in preheated oven for 20–25 minutes. Check the cake with a skewer. If it comes out clean the cake is cooked; if not, cook for a further 5–10 minutes and try again.

Apple, fig and pecan cake

Serves 6–8

This is a rich, moist cake that will keep well for several days.

zest of 1 orange
125 ml (½ cup) orange juice
150 g (⅔ cup) raw sugar
150 g (½ cup) honey
100 g (½ cup) dried figs, chopped
60 g (⅓ cup) raisins
1 apple, grated
150 g (1 cup) plain flour
150 g (1 cup) self-raising flour
1 tsp baking powder
½ tsp ground cinnamon
1 tsp mixed spice
2 eggs, lightly beaten
60 ml (¼ cup) vegetable oil
90 g (¾ cup) pecan nuts, roughly chopped
Cream Cheese Frosting (page 702)

Preheat oven to 180°C.

Combine orange zest, juice, sugar, honey, figs and raisins in a saucepan. Bring to the boil over a medium heat, then remove and allow to cool. Add the grated apple. Sift flours, baking powder and spice together and add to mixture. Add eggs, oil and pecans and mix well until combined.

Spoon into a greased and lined 22 cm springform cake tin. Bake for 45 minutes. Check the cake with a skewer. If it comes out clean the cake is cooked; if it doesn't, cook for a further 5–10 minutes and try again. Allow to cool in tin for 15 minutes, then remove and cool on a cooling rack.

Top with Cream Cheese Frosting.

Carrot cake

Serves 8–10

When we first heard about carrot cakes in the 1980s, we were very sceptical of the whole idea. This delicious cake proves just how wrong we were.

300 g (2 cups) self-raising flour
1 tsp cinnamon
1 tsp mixed spice
4 eggs
330 g (1½ cups) caster sugar
1 tsp vanilla extract
300 ml (1¼ cups) olive or vegetable oil
pinch of salt
60 g (⅓ cup) hazelnuts
60 g (½ cup) walnut pieces
150 g (1 cup) sultanas
3 large grated carrots
Cream Cheese Frosting (page 702)

Preheat oven to 180°C.

Sift flour, cinnamon and mixed spice together into a large bowl. Add eggs, sugar, vanilla, oil and a pinch of salt. Mix lightly, then incorporate hazelnuts, walnuts, sultanas and grated carrots.

Pour into a greased and lined 23 cm greased cake tin. Bake in preheated oven for 1 hour. Check the cake with a skewer. If it comes out clean, the cake is cooked; if it doesn't, cook for a further 5–10 minutes and try again. Allow to cool in tin for 15 minutes, then remove and cool on cooling rack.

Top with Cream Cheese Frosting.

Carrot, cardamom and cashew cake
Substitute ground cardamom for cinnamon, and omit mixed spices. Substitute cashews for hazelnuts and walnuts.

Pumpkin cake

Serves 6–8

Pumpkin is a particularly sweet vegetable and it produces a cake that has a lovely crust on the outside and is moist on the inside.

100 g (⅔ cup) sultanas
250 ml (1 cup) hot tea
225 g soft butter
220 g (1 cup) caster sugar
3 eggs
375 g (2½ cups) self-raising flour
500 g pumpkin, steamed or boiled and pureed
1 tsp mixed spice
icing sugar for dusting or Cream Cheese Frosting (page 702)

Preheat oven to 180°C.

Soak sultanas in hot tea for 15 minutes, drain well and discard tea. Set sultanas aside. Cream butter and sugar until light and fluffy. Add eggs one by one, beating well after each addition. Add flour and pumpkin puree, beat well. Stir in sultanas and mixed spice. Pour into a greased and lined 22 cm springform cake tin and bake in preheated oven for 50–60 minutes.

Check the cake with a skewer. If it comes out clean the cake is ready; if it doesn't, cook for a further 5 minutes and try again.

To serve, dust with icing sugar or Cream Cheese Frosting.

Date and coconut loaf

Serves 6–8

This very healthy-looking, and -tasting, cake will keep for up to a week in an airtight container.

175 g (1 cup) dates, chopped
125 ml (½ cup) boiling water
125 g soft butter
110 g (½ cup) caster sugar
1 egg
100 g (⅔ cup) self-raising flour
70 g (1 cup) desiccated coconut

Preheat oven to 180°C.

Soak chopped dates in boiling water until well softened and water has been absorbed.

Cream butter and sugar until light and fluffy. Beat in egg.

Add flour and beat until smooth. Add dates and coconut and stir well until combined.

Spoon into a greased and lined loaf tin (23½ × 13½ × 7 cm) and bake in the preheated oven for 40 minutes. Test by inserting a skewer. If it comes out clean, it's ready; if it doesn't, cook for a further 5 minutes and try again.

Pecan coffee cake

Serves 6–8

This is a very simple tea cake, or should that be coffee cake?

150 g soft butter
90 g (⅓ cup) caster sugar
2 eggs
150 g (1 cup) self-raising flour
1 tsp baking powder
60 ml (¼ cup) strong coffee
90 g (¾ cup) chopped pecans
pecan halves and Coffee Icing (page 702) to serve

Preheat oven to 180°C.

Cream butter and sugar until light and fluffy. Add eggs, one by one, incorporating well after each addition. Sift together flour and baking powder. Add flour and coffee and mix until well combined. Fold through chopped nuts.

Spoon into a greased and lined 20 cm springform cake tin and bake in preheated oven for 30–35 minutes. Check the cake with a skewer. If it comes out clean the cake is cooked; if it doesn't, cook for a further 5 minutes and try again.

Allow to cool, then top with Coffee Icing and pecan halves.

Plum cake

Serves 6–8

This cake is one of our favourite ways to enjoy summer plums.

200 g soft butter
165 g (¾ cup) caster sugar
4 eggs
1 tsp vanilla extract
125 g (⅔ cup plus 1 tbsp) plain flour
100 g (⅔ cup) self-raising flour
pinch of salt
12 blood plums
icing sugar for dusting

Preheat oven to 180°C.

Cream butter and sugar until light and fluffy. Add eggs, one at time, allowing each one to be incorporated well. Add vanilla, sifted flours and salt together and stir in well.

Spoon into a greased and lined 23 cm springform cake tin. Cut fruit in half, remove stones and arrange on top of cake mixture. Bake in preheated oven for 30–35 minutes. Check that cake is cooked by inserting skewer. If it comes out clean, the cake is cooked; if it doesn't, cook for a further 5 minutes and try again. Allow to cool, and dust with icing sugar to serve.

Linzertorte made easy

Serves 6–8

Here we replace the traditional linzertorte pastry lattice top with flaked almonds. But if you have one of the lattice gadgets, feel free to reserve a small amount of the dough to form the lattice strips and lay them across the top.

175 g (1 cup plus 2 tbsp) plain flour
75 g (⅔ cup) ground hazelnuts
60 g (½ cup) icing sugar
zest of 1 lemon
1 tsp ground cinnamon

100 g soft butter, diced
2 egg yolks
350 g (1 cup) plum jam
1 tbsp lemon juice
60 g (⅔ cup) flaked almonds

Preheat oven to 180°C.

Combine flour, hazelnuts, icing sugar, lemon zest and cinnamon in a large bowl. Rub in butter until mixture develops a breadcrumb texture. Add egg yolks and form mixture into a smooth dough. Press dough into a greased and lined 22 cm springform cake tin, pushing some of the dough up the sides to form a pastry edge, like a tart.

Mix plum jam and lemon juice together and spoon onto dough, taking care not to let it go over the edge. Sprinkle flaked almonds on top and bake in preheated oven for 30–40 minutes, or until filling is beginning to set.

Allow the torte to cool completely before cutting and serving.

Lemon cheesecake

Serves 6–8

This is the simplest cheesecake of all, with lots of chopped lemon zest and lemon juice to balance the creamy filling. One to be enjoyed regularly.

150 g digestive biscuits
60 g melted butter
500 g soft cream cheese
150 g (⅔ cup) caster sugar

125 ml (½ cup) lemon juice
2 × 5 g gelatine sheets
125 ml (½ cup) cream
zest of 2 lemons, chopped

Place the biscuits in a food processor and whiz to form small crumbs. Add the melted butter and process briefly. Press the biscuit mix into the bottom of a 20 cm springform cake tin and place in the refrigerator to set for at least 20 minutes.

Beat the cream cheese and caster sugar until well softened and creamy. Bring the lemon juice to the boil, add gelatine sheets and stir until dissolved. Add the cream and lemon zest and stir until well combined. Stir the lemon mixture into the cream cheese until combined. Pour on top of the biscuit base and chill until set.

Cherry cheesecake

Serves 6–8

This cheesecake has a similar texture to My Kind of Cheesecake (page 736) as it is also cooked in a deep baking tray surrounded by hot water. The cherry topping makes it even more enjoyable.

150 g digestive biscuits
60 g melted butter
200 g soft cream cheese
110 g (½ cup) caster sugar
zest of 1 lemon
2 eggs
150 g (⅔ cup) curd cheese or ricotta
200 g cottage cheese
500 g pitted cherries, halved
80 ml (⅓ cup) water
2 tbsp caster sugar, additional
1 tbsp arrowroot
1 tbsp cold water, additional

Place biscuits in a food processor and whiz to form small crumbs; add melted butter and process briefly. Press biscuits into the bottom of a 22 cm springform cake tin. Place in the refrigerator to set, for at least 20 minutes.

Beat cream cheese, sugar and lemon zest until smooth. Add eggs one at a time, beating after each addition. Fold through curd and cottage cheese.

Take the cake tin and wrap the outside base with foil, using two pieces to cover the base. This prevents water seeping into the cake during cooking.

Place the cake tin in a deep baking tray. Pour in cheesecake filling over biscuit base. Pour boiling water into the baking dish to come halfway up the cake tin. Place carefully in the oven. Cook for 1 hour, or until the cake is just set, with some hint of wobble still. Allow to cool on a cooling rack before refrigerating, preferably overnight.

Place water and sugar in a saucepan and bring to the boil. Add cherries. Dissolve arrowroot in cold water and add to cherry mixture; stir until thick. Pour cherry mixture over cold cheesecake and return to the refrigerator for about 30 minutes, or until set.

Raspberry cheesecake
Substitute raspberries for cherries.

My kind of cheesecake

Serves 6–8

This cheesecake is made in the traditional way but is cooked in a deep baking tray surrounded by hot water. This gentle cooking means the cheesecake cooks slowly. The result is my kind of cheesecake: one with an extraordinarily soft, silky texture. MC

150 g digestive biscuits
60 g melted butter
500 g cream cheese
110 g (½ cup) caster sugar
zest of 2 lemons
2 eggs
3 egg yolks
150 ml (⅔ cup) thick cream
100 ml (⅓ cup) lemon juice

Place biscuits in a food processor and whiz to form small crumbs; add melted butter and process briefly. Press biscuits into the bottom of a 22 cm springform cake tin. Place in the refrigerator to set, for at least 20 minutes.

Preheat oven to 170°C.

Beat cream cheese until smooth, add sugar and lemon zest, then whisk in eggs and yolks one at a time. Stir in cream and lemon juice. Take the cake tin and wrap the outside base with foil, using two pieces to cover the base. This prevents water seeping into the cake during cooking.

Place the cake tin in a deep baking tray. Pour in cheesecake filling over biscuit base. Pour boiling water into the baking dish to come halfway up the cake tin. Place carefully in the oven. Cook for 1 hour, or until the cake is just set, still with some hint of wobble. Allow to cool on a cooling rack before refrigerating, preferably overnight.

Passionfruit cheesecake
Substitute strained passionfruit pulp for lemon juice and serve chilled cake with additional pulp on top.

Baked orange cheesecake
Substitute orange juice and zest for lemon juice and zest.

Amaretto-cherry cheesecake

Serves 8

We have a fondness for cheesecake, as you will have already guessed by the number of recipes we've included in this book! This version has the contrasting flavours of bitter almonds and hot cherry sauce.

200 g digestive biscuits
80 g (½ cup) chopped blanched almonds
75 g melted butter
375 g soft cream cheese
150 g (⅔ cup) caster sugar
zest of 1 lemon
2 eggs
300 g cottage cheese
1 tbsp amaretto

CHERRY SAUCE
80 ml (⅓ cup) water
1 tbsp amaretto
2 tbsp caster sugar
500 g cherries, halved and pitted
1 tbsp arrowroot
1 tbsp cold water, additional

Preheat oven to 170°C.

Wrap the outside of a 22 cm springform cake tin with a double layer of foil; this will prevent water seeping into the cake during cooking.

Place the biscuits in a food processor and whiz to form small crumbs. Add the chopped almonds and melted butter and process briefly. Press the biscuits into the bottom of the cake tin and place in the refrigerator to set for at least 20 minutes.

Beat the cream cheese until smooth, then add caster sugar and lemon zest. Whisk in the eggs, one at a time. Fold through the cottage cheese and amaretto.

Place the cake tin in a deep baking tray and spread the cheesecake filling over the biscuit base. Pour enough boiling water into the baking dish to come halfway up the cake tin.

Place the tray carefully in the oven and cook for 1 hour, or until the cake is just set but still has a hint of wobble.

Remove the cake tin from the water and allow to cool on a cooling rack before refrigerating, preferably overnight.

Place the water, amaretto and caster sugar in a saucepan and bring to the boil. Add the cherries and bring back to the boil. Dissolve the arrowroot in 1 tbsp cold water, then add it to the hot cherries, stirring well to thicken the sauce. Remove from heat.

Remove the cheesecake from the cake tin and place on a large plate. Serve hot cherry sauce with each slice of cheesecake.

Raspberry ripple cheesecake

Serves 8–10

This brilliant cheesecake is a Campion–Curtis favourite. It's baked standing in water to achieve a light texture, and the ripple effect is created by using fresh berries.

- 150 g digestive biscuits
- 60 g melted butter
- 80 ml (⅓ cup) water
- 2 tbsp caster sugar
- 2 punnets raspberries
- 500 g soft cream cheese
- 110 g (½ cup) caster sugar, additional
- zest of 2 lemons, chopped
- 2 eggs
- 3 egg yolks
- ½ tsp vanilla extract
- 125 ml (½ cup) thick cream
- 2 tbsp lemon juice

Wrap the outside of a 22 cm springform cake tin with a double layer of foil; this will prevent water seeping into the cake during cooking.

Place the biscuits in a food processor and whiz to form small crumbs. Add the melted butter and process briefly. Press the biscuits into the bottom of the cake tin and place in the refrigerator to set for at least 20 minutes.

Preheat oven to 170°C.

Place the water and 2 tbsp caster sugar in a small saucepan and bring to the boil. Add the raspberries and return to the boil, then strain immediately. Return the syrup to the saucepan and simmer until reduced to a thick, sticky sauce. Add the syrup to the berries and refrigerate.

Beat the cream cheese until smooth, then add caster sugar and lemon zest. Whisk in the eggs and yolks, one at a time. Stir in the vanilla, cream and lemon juice. Using a wooden spoon, gently stir the raspberries into the cheesecake mix. Try not to mix them in completely as you're aiming for a swirling effect.

Place the cake tin in a deep baking tray and spread the cheesecake filling over the biscuit base. Pour enough boiling water into the baking tray to come halfway up the cake tin. Place the tray carefully in the oven and cook for 1 hour, or until the cake is just set but still has a hint of wobble.

Remove the cake tin from the water and allow to cool on a cooling rack before refrigerating, preferably overnight.

Pedro Ximenez cheesecake with boozy prunes

Serves 8

We love really good Pedro Ximenez, an intensely sweet Spanish sherry. Combined with cheesecake and prunes, it's a taste sensation.

- 150 g digestive biscuits
- 60 g melted butter
- 80 ml (⅓ cup) Pedro Ximenez
- 500 g cream cheese
- 110 g (½ cup) caster sugar
- zest of 2 lemons
- 2 eggs
- 3 egg yolks
- 125 ml (½ cup) thick cream
- 2 tbsp lemon juice
- 125 ml (½ cup) Pedro Ximenez, additional
- 250 ml (1 cup) water
- 60 g (¼ cup) caster sugar, additional
- 200 g (1¼ cup) pitted prunes
- 2 tbsp lemon juice, additional

Take a 22 cm springform cake tin and wrap the outside base with foil, using two pieces to cover the rim; this prevents water seeping into the cake during cooking. Put biscuits in a food processor and whiz to form small crumbs, add the melted butter and process briefly. Press biscuits into the bottom of the cake tin. Place in the refrigerator to set, for at least 20 minutes.

Preheat oven to 170°C. Put Pedro Ximenez in a small saucepan and reduce by half. Beat cream cheese until smooth, add the sugar and lemon zest, and then whisk in eggs and yolks one at a time. Stir in the cream, lemon juice and reduced Pedro Ximenez. Place the cake tin in a deep baking tray. Pour cheesecake filling over the biscuit base. Pour boiling water into the baking dish to come halfway up the cake tin. Place carefully in the oven. Cook for 1 hour, or until the cake is just set, still with some hint of wobble. Allow to cool on a rack before refrigerating, preferably overnight.

To make the boozy prunes, put additional Pedro Ximenez, water and caster sugar in a small saucepan. Cook over a low heat until the sugar dissolves, then bring to the boil. Add prunes. Cover and cook for 2–3 minutes. Remove the prunes from the liquid and return the saucepan to the heat. Continue cooking until the syrup reduces by half. Remove from the heat. Add lemon juice and return the prunes to the syrup.

Serve the cheesecake in slices with warm boozy prunes and a glass of Pedro Ximenez.

White chocolate cheesecake

Serves 6–8

If white chocolate isn't your thing, simply use dark chocolate instead.

150 g Chocolate Ripple biscuits
60 g melted butter
150 g white chocolate
500 g soft cream cheese
150 g (⅔ cup) caster sugar
250 ml (1 cup) sour cream

Place the biscuits in a food processor and whiz to form small crumbs. Add the melted butter and process briefly. Press the biscuit mix into the bottom of a 20 cm springform cake tin and place in the refrigerator to set for at least 20 minutes.

Melt the chocolate by placing it in a bowl over a saucepan of simmering water or in a microwave on low for 1–2 minutes. Beat the cream cheese and caster sugar until well softened and creamy. Add the sour cream and melted chocolate and stir into the cream cheese mixture until combined. Pour on top of the biscuit base and chill until set.

Cheesecake brownies

Makes 12

Here it is: the combination that lovers of cheesecake and lovers of brownies have been looking for. A recipe that combines both!

100 g chocolate
100 g butter
3 eggs
50 g (⅓ cup) plain flour
150 g (⅔ cup) caster sugar
250 g soft cream cheese
zest of 1 lemon, chopped
1 egg, additional
75 g (⅓ cup) caster sugar, additional

Preheat oven to 180°C.

Butter and line a lamington tin.

Melt the chocolate and butter by placing them in a bowl over a saucepan of simmering water or in a microwave on low for 1–2 minutes. Beat the eggs, flour and caster sugar together until white and doubled in bulk. Add the melted chocolate and pour into the prepared lamington tin.

Beat the cream cheese, lemon zest, additional egg and 75 g (⅓ cup) caster sugar until combined. Pour onto the chocolate mix. Swirl to incorporate, aiming for a marbled effect.

Bake in the preheated oven for 40 minutes, or until cooked through and bouncy to the touch. Allow to cool before cutting.

Chocolate brownies

Makes 12

A good chocolate brownie is a wondrous thing, and that's exactly what you'll get with this recipe. We've been making and enjoying these brownies for years, and we hope to do so for many more to come.

180 g butter
180 g dark chocolate, chopped
3 eggs
1 tsp vanilla extract
250 g (1 cup plus 2 tbsp) caster sugar
110 g (⅔ cup plus 1 tbsp) plain flour
½ tsp salt
180 g (1½ cups) chopped walnuts

Preheat oven to 180°C.

Butter and line a lamington tin.

Melt the butter and chocolate together by placing them in a bowl over a saucepan of simmering water or in a microwave on low for 1–2 minutes. Beat the eggs, vanilla and caster sugar together until light and doubled in bulk. Sift the flour and salt together. Add the flour, melted chocolate and walnuts to the beaten eggs and mix to combine.

Pour into the prepared lamington tin and bake in the preheated oven for 25 minutes. Take care not to overcook the brownies or they will lose their deliciously gooey texture. Allow to cool before cutting.

Lamingtons

Makes 18

Lamingtons are one of the classics of Australian baking. The simple squares of sponge dipped in light chocolate icing and rolled in coconut are worth making for the tradition alone. Luckily, they taste great, too.

4 eggs
110 g (½ cup) caster sugar
100 g (⅔ cup) plain flour
390 g (3 cups) icing sugar
50 g (½ cup) cocoa
185 ml (¾ cup) water
280 g (4 cups) desiccated coconut

Preheat oven to 180°C.

Line a lamington tin with greaseproof paper, ensuring there is plenty of overhang. This will allow the sponge to rise but without going over the edge. Butter the paper and sprinkle with a little plain flour to ensure that the batter won't stick.

Beat the eggs and caster sugar together until very thick and light. Carefully fold in the flour.

Spoon the sponge mixture into the lamington tin, ensuring it is relatively flat on top. Bake in the preheated oven for around 10 minutes, or until risen and golden.

Allow to cool for 5 minutes on a wire rack, then carefully lift the sponge onto a chopping board and peel away the greaseproof paper. Allow to cool completely.

Place the icing sugar, cocoa and water in a saucepan and bring to the boil, whisking well. Reduce heat and simmer for 1–2 minutes. Remove from heat and allow to cool slightly.

Place the coconut in a shallow dish. Using a serrated knife, carefully cut the sponge into 18 even-sized cubes. Dip pieces of sponge into the chocolate icing until well covered and place on a cake rack to drain. When most of the excess icing has dripped off, dunk the sponge into the coconut, ensuring that each side is coated. Leave to dry on a cooling rack.

Jam-filled lamingtons
Cut sponge pieces in half lengthways. Spread with jam and sandwich back together. Dip in chocolate icing and roll in coconut.

Killer cupcakes

Makes 10

Children and adults alike will be won over by these chocolate-enriched cupcakes.

100 g soft butter
130 g (⅔ cup) brown sugar
1 egg
1 tsp vanilla extract
95 g dark chocolate, melted and cooled
200 g (1 ⅓ cups) self-raising flour
60 ml (¼ cup) milk
Chocolate Fudge Icing (page 703)

Preheat oven to 180°C.

Line 10 × 125 ml (½ cup) muffin pans with paper cases.

Cream the butter and brown sugar until light and fluffy. Add the egg and vanilla and beat until well incorporated. Stir in the melted chocolate. Fold through flour and milk, and mix until just combined.

Spoon the mixture into the prepared muffin tins and bake in the preheated oven for 15 minutes, or until a skewer inserted into the centre comes out clean. Cool completely, then top with Chocolate Fudge Icing to serve.

Cupcakes

Makes 10

All cupcakes should be beautifully light and sponge-like, just like these ones. The real fun of cupcakes is in the decorating. You can go simple, perhaps chocolate ganache and silver cachous, or try white icing with those pretty iced flowers from cake decorating shops. I love dolly mixture on mine, but you can use jelly beans, smarties, M&Ms, crushed honeycomb and just about any form of chocolate. MC

175 g butter
150 g (⅔ cup) caster sugar
1 tsp vanilla extract
3 eggs
225 g (1½ cups) self-raising flour
Basic Icing, to decorate (page 702)

Preheat oven to 180°C.

Line 10 × 125 ml (½ cup) muffin pans with paper cases.

Cream butter and sugar until light and fluffy. Add vanilla, then eggs one by one, fully incorporating each one before adding the next. Sift flour and fold in carefully. Spoon mixture into the cases. Bake for 15 minutes or until a skewer inserted into the centre comes out clean. Cool completely.

Spread frosting onto the cakes and decorate as you wish.

Friands

Makes 9

Australian food writer Jill Dupleix popularised these little oval-shaped cakes, for which we are all eternally thankful. These friands are based on her classic recipe, using a base of ground almonds, icing sugar and egg whites.

180 g butter
160 g (1¼ cups) icing sugar
75 g (½ cup) plain flour
125 g (1¼ cups) ground almonds
5 egg whites
zest of 1 lemon, chopped
icing sugar to serve

Preheat oven to 200°C.

Butter 9 friand moulds or line 9 × 125 ml (½ cup) muffin pans with paper cases.

Melt the butter and allow to cool. Sift the icing sugar and flour into a bowl, and mix in the ground almonds. Lightly beat the egg whites with a fork for 30 seconds, then stir into the dry ingredients. Add the melted butter and lemon zest and stir well.

Divide the mix between the buttered friand moulds and bake in the preheated oven for 15 minutes. Test the friands by inserting a skewer into one of them. If it comes out clean, they are ready; if it doesn't, cook for a further 5 minutes and test again.

When ready, cool for 10 minutes then un-mould onto a cooling rack. Dust the friands with icing sugar to serve.

Hazelnut friands
Replace the ground almonds with ground roasted hazelnuts.

Orange and poppyseed friands
Replace the lemon zest with the grated zest of 1 orange. Add 2 tbsp ground poppyseeds.

Blueberry friands
Dot 3-4 blueberries on the top of each friand just before they go into the oven.

Raspberry friands
Dot 3-4 raspberries on the top of each friand just before they go into the oven.

Basic muffins

Makes 6 large muffins

Our basic muffin mixture is exceptionally easy to make and you can vary it by adding berries, chocolate chips or anything else that takes your fancy.

150 g (1 cup) self-raising flour
pinch of salt
110 g (½ cup) caster sugar
1 tsp vanilla extract
1 egg
125 ml (½ cup) milk
50 g melted butter

Preheat oven to 180°C.

Line 6 × 125 ml (½ cup) muffin pans with paper cases.

Mix the flour, salt and caster sugar together. Add vanilla, egg, milk and butter and beat until smooth.

Spoon the mixture into the prepared muffin tins and bake in the preheated oven for 15–20 minutes, or until risen and golden brown. Allow to cool.

Chocolate muffins
Substitute 30 g cocoa for 30 g of the flour.

Triple chocolate muffins

Makes 8

Triple chocolate muffins are created by studding dark and white chocolate chips through a chocolate muffin base, then topping the finished product with chocolate icing. Not the sort of thing you'd want to eat every day, but fantastic every now and then.

150 g (1 cup) self-raising flour
50 g (½ cup) cocoa
90 g (½ cup) soft brown sugar
165 ml (⅔ cup) milk
60 g butter, melted and cooled
1 egg
45 g (¼ cup) dark chocolate chips
45 g (¼ cup) white chocolate chips
Chocolate Fudge Icing (page 702)

Preheat oven to 180°C.

Line 8 × 125 ml (½ cup) muffin pans with paper cases.

Sift the flour and cocoa together, then add brown sugar and stir through. Whisk the milk, melted butter and egg together. Add the wet mix to the dry mix and whisk together until it forms a smooth batter. Fold through chocolate chips.

Spoon the mix into the prepared muffin tins and bake in the preheated oven for 20 minutes, or until risen and golden brown. Allow to cool, then top with frosting.

Raspberry and white chocolate muffins

Makes 10

Tart raspberry and creamy white chocolate is a great combo in treats such as these muffins.

200 g (1 ⅓ cups) self-raising flour
150 g (⅔ cup) caster sugar
zest of 1 lemon, chopped
60 g melted butter
125 ml (½ cup) milk
1 egg
100 g (¾ cup) raspberries
95 g (½ cup) white chocolate chips
icing sugar to serve

Preheat oven to 180°C.

Line 10 × 125 ml (½ cup) muffin pans with paper cases.

Mix the flour, caster sugar and lemon zest together. Beat the butter, milk and egg together in a separate bowl. Mix the dry and wet mixes together to form a smooth batter, then fold through the raspberries and chocolate.

Divide the mix between the prepared muffin tins and bake in the preheated oven for 20 minutes, or until risen and golden brown. Allow to cool, then dust with icing sugar to serve.

Rhubarb, cinnamon and yoghurt muffins

Makes 10

Creamy yoghurt is the perfect contrast for tart pieces of rhubarb in these muffins.

200 g (1⅓ cups) self-raising flour
1 tsp ground cinnamon
150 g (⅔ cup) caster sugar
60 g butter, melted and cooled
1 egg
125 g (½ cup) natural yoghurt
125 ml (½ cup) milk
3 rhubarb stalks, cut into thin slices
icing sugar to serve

Preheat oven to 180°C.

Line 10 × 125 ml (½ cup) muffin pans with paper cases.

Mix the flour, cinnamon and caster sugar together in a bowl. In a separate bowl, whisk together the melted butter, egg, yoghurt and milk. Add the dry mix to the wet mix and whisk to a smooth batter. Fold in the slices of rhubarb.

Spoon the mix into the prepared muffin tins and bake in the preheated oven for 20–25 minutes, or until golden brown and risen. Allow to cool, then dust with icing sugar to serve.

Blueberry and coconut muffins

Makes 10

Coconut cream adds flavour and aroma to these blueberry muffins.

100 g butter
150 g (⅔ cup) caster sugar
1 egg
125 ml (½ cup) coconut cream
200 g (1⅓ cups) self-raising flour
35 g (½ cup) desiccated coconut
150 g (1 cup) blueberries
icing sugar to serve

Preheat oven to 180°C.

Line 10 × 125 ml (½ cup) muffin pans with paper cases.

Beat the butter and caster sugar together until light and fluffy. Add the egg and beat until combined. Stir through the coconut milk, followed by the flour and desiccated coconut, then most of the blueberries.

Spoon the mix into the prepared muffin tins and top each muffin with the remaining blueberries. Bake in the preheated oven for 20 minutes, or until risen and golden brown. Allow to cool, then dust with icing sugar to serve.

Spiced apple and sour cream muffins

Makes 10

Apples and spices are a great match, so we just had to include this recipe for a muffin where they have a starring role.

100 g soft butter
150 g (⅔ cup) caster sugar
1 egg
1 tsp vanilla extract
125 ml (½ cup) sour cream
200 g (1⅓ cups) self-raising flour
½ tsp ground cinnamon
¼ tsp grated nutmeg
2 apples, peeled, cored and finely diced
icing sugar to serve

Preheat oven to 180°C.

Line 10 × 125 ml (½ cup) muffin pans with paper cases.

Cream the butter and caster sugar until light and fluffy. Add the egg and vanilla and beat well, then stir in the sour cream to combine completely. Sift flour and spices together and stir through until combined. Stir in the diced apple.

Spoon the mix into the prepared muffin tins and bake in the preheated oven for 15–20 minutes, or until risen and golden brown. Allow to cool, then dust with icing sugar to serve.

Banana and maple syrup muffins

Makes 10

Ripe bananas add great texture and flavour to these muffins, but it's the maple syrup frosting that turns them into something really special.

3 ripe bananas
165 g (¾ cup) caster sugar
1 egg
1 tbsp maple syrup
75 g melted butter
225 g (1½ cups) self-raising flour
Maple Syrup Frosting (page 703)

Preheat oven to 180°C.

Line 10 × 125 ml (½ cup) muffin pans with paper cases.

Mash the bananas with caster sugar. Beat in the egg, maple syrup and butter, then add the flour. Stir until well combined.

Spoon the mix into the prepared muffin tins and bake in the preheated oven for 20 minutes, or until risen and golden brown. Allow to cool, then top with frosting.

Banana, walnut and maple syrup muffins
Add 60 g (½ cup) chopped walnuts to the muffin mix along with the flour.

Chocolate cheesecake muffins

Makes 8 large or 16 small muffins

These are a bit trickier to make than some of our other muffin recipes, but they are well worth the extra hassle.

90 g cream cheese
30 g (2 tbsp) caster sugar
150 g (1 cup) self-raising flour
30 g (⅓ cup) cocoa
pinch of salt
110 g (½ cup) caster sugar, additional
1 egg, beaten
175 ml (⅔ cup) milk
80 ml (⅓ cup) vegetable oil

Preheat oven to 180°C.

Beat cream cheese and sugar until soft and smooth. Set aside.

Sift flour, cocoa and salt together into a large bowl. Add additional sugar and mix together. Beat egg, milk and oil together, then add to the flour mix and beat until well combined.

Half-fill greased muffin tins with chocolate batter. Add about 1 tsp cream cheese mix, then cover with remaining chocolate batter. Bake in preheated oven for 15–20 minutes, or until risen and golden brown.

Peanut butter muffins

Makes 12 large muffins

These are incredibly easy to make and will appeal to peanut butter lovers everywhere.

125 g soft crunchy peanut butter
75 g soft butter
110 g (½ cup) caster sugar
2 eggs
250 ml (1 cup) milk
225 g (1½ cups) self-raising flour

Preheat oven to 180°C.

Cream butters, sugar and eggs together until smooth. Add milk, mix well, then add flour and stir to combine. Spoon into greased muffin tins. Bake in preheated oven for 15–20 minutes until risen and golden brown.

Banana muffins

Makes 6 large or 12 small muffins

The banana in these muffins gives them a great fruity flavour and texture.

3 ripe bananas, mashed
180 g (¾ cup) caster sugar
1 egg
75 g melted butter
225 g (1½ cups) self-raising flour

Preheat oven to 180°C.

Mix mashed bananas and sugar together well. Beat egg in, add melted butter, stir to combine, then add flour, stirring well until combined.

Spoon into greased muffin tins and bake in preheated oven for 20 minutes, or until risen and golden brown.

Banana and walnut muffins
Add 60 g (½ cup) chopped walnuts.

Banana, pecan and maple syrup muffins
Substitute 2 tbsp maple syrup for 30 g of the sugar. Add 60 g (½ cup) chopped pecans.

Morning glory muffins

Makes 12 large muffins

Apparently these are the ultimate morning muffin, but we never seem to get around to making them until at least lunchtime.

150 g (1 cup) self-raising flour
1 tsp ground cinnamon
pinch of salt
110 g (½ cup) caster sugar
1 carrot, grated
60 g (⅓ cup) raisins
60 g (½ cup) chopped nuts
60 g (¾ cup) desiccated coconut
1 apple, grated
2 eggs
60 ml (¼ cup) vegetable oil
1 tsp vanilla extract

Preheat oven to 180°C.

Sift flour, cinnamon and salt into a large bowl. Add sugar, carrot, raisins, nuts, coconut and apple and mix until combined. Add eggs, oil and vanilla and mix until combined.

Spoon into greased muffin tins and bake in preheated oven for 20 minutes, or until risen and golden brown.

Coffee and walnut muffins

Makes 8 large or 16 small muffins

These muffins are great as they are, but if you want to jazz them up even further you can spoon a little Coffee Icing (page 702) on top and add a walnut half.

125 ml (½ cup) strong coffee
125 ml (½ cup) cream
1 egg, lightly beaten
125 ml (½ cup) vegetable oil

225 g (1½ cups) self-raising flour
pinch of salt
80 g (⅓ cup) caster sugar
100 g (¾ cup) chopped walnuts

Preheat oven to 180°C.

Whisk coffee, cream, egg and oil together. Sift flour and salt together into a separate bowl. Add sugar and nuts and stir through. Pour coffee mixture onto flour mixture and whisk until well combined. Spoon into greased muffin tins and bake in preheated oven for 20 minutes, or until risen and golden brown.

'Doughnut' muffins

Makes 10–12 large muffins

No tricky names here, just muffins that taste like a doughnut, with only a fraction of the work.

250 g (1⅔ cup) self-raising flour
pinch of salt
1 tsp ground cinnamon
80 ml (⅓ cup) vegetable oil
150 g (⅔ cup) caster sugar

1 egg
175 ml (⅔ cup) milk
75 g melted butter
110 g (½ cup) caster sugar, additional
1 tsp ground cinnamon, additional

Preheat oven to 180°C.

Sift flour, salt and cinnamon into a large bowl. In a separate bowl mix oil, sugar, egg and milk together. Add to flour and stir well until combined. Spoon into greased muffin tins and bake in preheated oven for 20 minutes, or until risen and golden brown. While cooking, melt butter. Mix additional sugar and cinnamon together.

When muffins are cooked, remove from tins and dip tops into melted butter, then into cinnamon/sugar mixture. Place on a cooling rack to cool.

Jam doughnut muffins
Half-fill muffin tins, then add ½ tsp strawberry jam to each muffin. Cover with more batter and cook in the same way.

Flourless chocolate muffins

Makes 20 small or 10 large muffins

As with flourless cakes, these muffins use ground almonds to keep them moist.

150 g dark chocolate, chopped
125 g soft butter
3 eggs, separated
90 g (⅓ cup) caster sugar
90 g (1 cup) ground almonds
2 tbsp caster sugar, additional

Preheat oven to 170°C.

Place chocolate and butter in a bowl over a pot of simmering water to melt. Remove from heat and add egg yolks, sugar and ground almonds. Whisk egg whites until stiff peaks form, then fold in additional sugar. Fold egg mixture into chocolate mixture.

Spoon into greased muffin trays and bake in preheated oven for 30–35 minutes, or until a skewer comes out clean when tested.

Flourless white chocolate and raspberry muffins

Add 50 g white chocolate chips and 125 g (1 cup) raspberries to chocolate mixture before folding in egg whites.

Spicy cheddar muffins

Makes 6 large or 12 small muffins

It's worth searching out the best farmhouse cheddar you can for these muffins as they are worth the extra expense. The recipe was supplied by food writer and friend Siu Ling Hui.

250 ml (1 cup) milk
2 tbsp melted butter
1 egg, lightly beaten
generous pinch of cayenne pepper
200 g (1⅓ cups) plain flour
1 tbsp baking powder
1 tbsp caster sugar
pinch of salt
150 g (1½ cups) grated farmhouse cheddar
100 g (¾ cup) walnuts, lightly roasted and chopped; or 1 grated apple

Preheat oven to 180°C.

Combine milk, butter, egg and cayenne pepper in a large bowl. Sift together the flour, baking powder, sugar and salt. Toss grated cheddar with flour to mix well. Add the cheese and flour mixture to the wet mixture and stir well. Add the walnuts or grated apple.

Spoon into greased muffin trays, cook in preheated oven for 15–20 minutes, or until risen and golden brown.

Polenta herb muffins

Makes 6 large or 12 small muffins

These are a great savoury option for when you want to give the sweet things a miss.

90 g (½ cup) polenta
150 g (1 cup) self-raising flour
1 tsp baking powder
60 g soft butter, diced
2 eggs
100 ml (⅓ cup) milk
2 tbsp chopped fresh herbs

Preheat oven to 180°C.

Stir polenta, flour and baking powder together. Add butter and rub in until mixture resembles fine breadcrumbs. Add eggs, milk and herbs, then mix well.

Spoon into greased muffin tins and bake in preheated oven for 20 minutes, or until muffins are risen and golden brown in colour.

Scones

Makes 6–8

Many people claim that they, and only they, know how to make the perfect scone. Try the recipe below and you'll realise that now you have that knack too!

300 g (2 cups) self-raising flour
pinch of salt
2 tsp caster sugar
125 ml (½ cup) cream
125 ml (½ cup) milk
additional cream
jam and whipped cream for serving

Preheat oven to 200°C.

Sift together flour, salt and sugar into a bowl. Mix cream and milk together, then stir the wet mix onto the dry mix. Stir gently until the mixture is just combined. Tip mixture onto a lightly floured bench top.

Pat scone dough out with lightly floured hands until it is 2 cm thick. Cut out scones with a 5½ cm cutter. Mix together leftover bits and roll and cut them out also.

Place scones on a lined baking tray touching together, brush tops with additional cream. Cook in preheated oven for 12–15 minutes.

Remove tray and cover scones with a clean tea towel until cool. Split scones and spread with jam and whipped cream.

Cinnamon scones
Sift 1 tsp cinnamon with the flour.

Date scones
Add 6-8 finely chopped dates to the scone dough.

Strawberry shortcakes

Makes 8

These shortcakes make a great Sunday afternoon treat.

325 g (2 cups plus 1 tbsp) plain flour
pinch of salt
1 tbsp baking powder
55 g (¼ cup) caster sugar
125 g soft butter, chopped
1 egg, beaten
125 ml (½ cup) cream
2 tbsp caster sugar, additional
1 egg white, lightly beaten
300 g strawberries
250 ml (1 cup) whipped cream

Preheat oven to 220°C.

Sift flour, salt and baking powder into a bowl. Add sugar and butter and rub in to produce a fine breadcrumb texture. Whisk egg into cream and pour into flour mixture, bit by bit, stirring it with a fork until mixture holds together.

Turn dough out onto a lightly floured surface and roll to a thickness of 2 cm. Cut out circles using a 6 cm cutter. Continue re-rolling dough and cutting out circles – you should get 8 in total.

Place shortcakes on a greased baking tray, brush with egg white and sprinkle with remaining caster sugar. Bake for 10–15 minutes, until golden brown.

Split while still warm and fill with sliced strawberries and whipped cream and serve immediately.

Simple brioche

Makes 1 large brioche

Brioche is a yeast loaf usually served at breakfast in France. This recipe is for one large brioche, although they are often made small, as individual serves. Brioche is scrumptious toasted and served with butter and jam, and it makes the most amazing bread-and-butter pudding.

2 sachets (14 g) dried yeast
1 tsp sugar
2 tbsp warm water
200 g (1⅓ cups) plain flour
1 tsp salt
2 eggs, beaten
60 g melted butter

Mix yeast with sugar and warm water and set aside until yeast bubbles. Sift flour and salt together. Add yeast, eggs and butter to the flour. Mix briefly, then tip dough onto a lightly floured surface. Knead until smooth and no longer sticky, around 6–8 minutes. Place dough in a large bowl and cover with cling film. Allow to prove in a warm place until dough doubles in size, 1–2 hours.

Preheat oven to 190°C.

Take proven dough and knead for 1–2 minutes. Shape dough into a loaf and place in a greased loaf tin 23½ × 13½ × 7 cm. Cover with a cloth and leave to prove in a warm place for 20 minutes.

Bake in preheated oven for 15–20 minutes, or until golden brown and bottom sounds hollow when tapped.

Sticky currant buns

Makes 12 buns

I adore currant buns and it has to be said that my only disappointment with Australia – and it's only this small one – is that there aren't enough currant buns in the baker's shops. MC

400 g (2⅔ cup) plain flour
1 tsp mixed spice
2 sachets (14 g) dried yeast
55 g (¼ cup) caster sugar
pinch of salt
100 g butter
2 eggs, lightly beaten
125 ml (½ cup) milk
90 g (⅔ cup) currants
Sugar Syrup (page 567)

Sift flour and spice together into a large bowl. Add yeast, sugar and salt, and mix briefly. Melt butter and mix with beaten eggs and milk. Pour onto flour, mix briefly with a wooden spoon, then tip out onto a floured bench. Knead for 4–5 minutes or until dough is smooth and silky. Place dough in a bowl, cover with cling film and set aside in a warm place to prove until doubled in bulk, about 1 hour.

When proven, tip dough onto floured surface, add currants and knead well to mix in fruit. Divide dough into 12 equal-sized pieces. Roll each one into a small bun shape and place all on a greased and lined baking tray. Cover tray with a tea towel and prove in a warm place for 20 minutes.

Preheat oven to 200°C.

Place buns in oven and bake for 15–20 minutes, or until risen and golden brown. When buns are cooked brush liberally with Sugar Syrup and allow to cool slightly before eating them warm.

Sticky orange and currant buns
Add 60 g (⅓ cup) diced candied orange peel along with currants.

Chelsea buns

Makes 12 buns

Chelsea buns are a touch more complicated to make than currant buns, but the end result is well worth the effort.

400 g (2⅔ cups) plain flour
2 sachets (14 g) dried yeast
55 g (¼ cup) caster sugar
pinch of salt
100 g melted butter
2 eggs, lightly beaten
125 ml (½ cup) milk
60 g melted butter, additional
55 g (¼ cup) caster sugar, additional
30 g (¼ cup) currants
60 g (⅓ cup) sultanas
Sugar Syrup (page 567)

Sift flour into a large bowl. Add yeast, sugar and salt and mix briefly. Mix melted butter with beaten eggs and milk. Pour onto flour, mix briefly with a wooden spoon, then tip out onto a floured bench. Knead for 4–5 minutes or until dough is smooth and silky. Place dough in a bowl, cover with cling film and set aside in a warm place to prove until doubled in bulk, about 1–2 hours.

Tip dough onto floured surface and knead well. Roll out to a large square, about 30 cm. Brush with additional melted butter, then sprinkle liberally with additional caster sugar. Sprinkle with dried fruits. Roll up from one end to form a large Swiss roll shape. Cut into 2 cm slices. Place slices, cut side up, onto a lined baking tray. Cover tray with a tea towel and prove in a warm place for 20 minutes.

Preheat oven to 200°C.

Place proved buns in oven and bake for 15–20 minutes, or until risen and golden brown. When buns are cooked brush liberally with Sugar Syrup and allow to cool slightly before eating them warm.

Swiss buns
Drizzle cooked buns with Basic Icing (page 702).

Jam swirls
Omit butter, sugar and fruit and spread dough with jam instead.

Cheat's hot cross buns
Add 60 g (⅓ cup) chopped candied orange peel or mixed peel to bun dough. Slash tops with a knife to form cross shapes.

Sticky cinnamon buns

Makes 12 buns

These cinnamon buns are rich, sticky and very more-ish. They're guaranteed to make your morning tea better than ever.

400 g (2⅔ cup) plain unbleached flour	200 ml (¾ cup) milk
55 g (¼ cup) caster sugar	75 g soft butter
½ tsp salt	75 g (⅓ cup) caster sugar
2 sachets (14 g) dried yeast	1 tsp ground cinnamon
50 g butter	1 egg yolk
1 egg	1 tbsp milk, additional

Sift flour, sugar, salt and yeast together into a large bowl. Melt butter and mix with egg and milk. Pour onto flour, mix briefly with a wooden spoon, then tip out onto a floured bench. Knead for 4–5 minutes or until dough is smooth and silky. Place dough in a bowl, cover with cling film and set aside in a warm place to prove until doubled in bulk, about 1–2 hours.

Tip dough onto floured surface and knead well. Roll dough out to a large square about 30 cm. Mix soft butter, sugar and cinnamon together and spread liberally over dough. Roll up from one end to form a large Swiss roll shape. Cut into 2 cm slices. Place slices, cut side up into a lined deep baking tray. Cover tray with a tea towel and prove in a warm place for 20 minutes.

Preheat oven to 200°C.

Mix the egg yolk and additional milk to make an egg wash. Brush buns with egg wash. Place proved buns in oven and bake for 15–20 minutes, or until risen and golden brown. Best eaten warm.

Doughnuts

Makes 10 doughnuts

We don't make these every day, but we're always glad when we do. You can pipe a dollop of jam or custard into the centre when the doughnuts have cooled – if they last that long.

pinch of salt
55 g (¼ cup) caster sugar
1 sachet (7 g) dry yeast
2 tbsp tepid water
300 g (2 cups) unbleached plain flour
150 g soft butter, diced
3 eggs
oil for frying
caster sugar, additional
a little ground cinnamon

Mix salt, sugar, yeast and water. Leave in a warm place until mixture bubbles. Place flour in a large bowl, add butter and rub in until a breadcrumb texture is achieved. Make a small well in the centre, add proven yeast and mix lightly. Add eggs one by one, mixing well in between. Then turn dough onto a floured surface. Knead until smooth and no longer sticky, around 6–8 minutes. Place dough in a bowl, cover with cling film and set aside in a warm place to prove until doubled in bulk, about 1 hour.

Tip dough onto floured surface and knead well for 1–2 minutes. Divide dough into 10 evenly sized pieces. Shape into balls and place on greased baking tray. Cover with a cloth and leave to prove in a warm place for 20 minutes.

Heat oil to 175°C or until a cube of bread turns golden.

Cook doughnuts in batches until golden brown, turning once. Drain briefly; then roll in caster sugar and cinnamon mix while still warm.

BISCUITS
+ slices
bite-sized delights

You'll find many of our favourite sweet things in this chapter. There's a recipe here for every occasion, from afternoon tea to children's birthday parties, or for a rainy Saturday afternoon when you're in need of a little something sweet.

Biscuits are great because one batch seems to go quite a long way – unlike a cake, which can disappear almost as soon as it's made. It's also possible to jazz up simple biscuits such as macaroons by sandwiching them together with chocolate ganache. The simplest slice mixture takes only a few minutes to stir together and requires simply spooning into a baking tray and popping in the oven. There is very little chance that it will fail.

We've also provided a collection of sweets. We make such things as rocky road and nougat at Christmas time to give as gifts to friends. Many of these are simple enough to make with children, though some do require a sugar thermometer to ensure accuracy. Always take care when boiling sugar as it can lead to nasty burns.

biscuit + slice recipes

biscuits

Anzac biscuits	767
Biscotti	767
Raspberry jam drops	768
Almond macaroons	769
Viennese biscuits	769
Shortbread	770
Snickerdoodles	770
Coconut wafers	771
Passionfruit yoyo biscuits	771
Hazelnut and vanilla creams	772
Gingerbread hearts	772
Orange and walnut Florentines	773
Cardamom spiced wafers	773
Mini rum and raisin garibaldi	774
Almond bread	774
Brandy snaps	775
Coconut biscuits	775
Gingernuts	776
Double chocolate chip cookies	776
Chocolate peanut cookies	777
Spiced pecan cookies	777
Muesli munchies	778
Oatcakes	778
Goat's cheese biscuits	779
Cheese bickies	779

slices

Millionaire's shortbread (caramel slice)	780
Hedgehog	782
Mars Bar slice	782
Toffee almond squares	783
Flapjacks	783
Vanilla and caramelised apricot slice	784
Raspberry, vanilla and almond slice	785
Viennese plum slice	785
Raspberry coconut slice	786
Munchie muesli slice	788
Fruity polenta slice	788
Robyn's caramel, macadamia and hazelnut slice	789
Nutmeg slice	790
Nanaimo bars	791
Marzipan bars	792
Lemon slice	793
White Christmas	793
Almond nougat	794
Coconut ice	794
Chocolate truffles	795
Honeycomb	795
Rocky road	796
Moroccan rocky road	796
Honey joys	798
Chocolate crackles	798
Caramel popcorn	798
Toffee apples	799

Things you need to know about biscuits and slices

BASIC BAKING EQUIPMENT

1 lamington or slice tin (275 x 175 mm)
2–3 flat baking trays
a cooling rack

1 Grease trays with butter and line them with greaseproof paper to give yourself a better chance of removing slices in 1 piece and keep washing up to a minimum.

2 We often cut slices into smallish squares and offer a selection.

3 On average, each slice recipe can be cut into 10 or 12 regular portions, or a number of thin fingers. It's difficult to accurately estimate how many people each recipe will feed, because it depends how much they can eat!

4 It's much easier to make a slice or biscuits with soft butter than with hard. Zap hard butter in the microwave for 20 seconds, or grate to soften it quickly. We usually use unsalted butter for baking.

5 Vanilla extract has a far superior flavour to vanilla essence. It's more expensive, but you only have to use half as much.

6 The better the quality of your chocolate, the better your baking, so when a recipe calls for chocolate use cooking couverture. Dark couverture is best, and buttons (or chips) melt more easily.

7 Use Dutch cocoa for better flavour; again, the better the quality, the better the result.

8 All eggs are medium (59 g).

9 Test to see whether a slice is cooked in the same way as for cakes: insert a skewer or cake tester into the centre of the slice. The skewer should come out free of mix or crumbs. If it doesn't, cook for a further 5 minutes, then try again.

10 Needless to say, a mixing machine will make light work of any beating, whisking or blending to be done.

Cooking with sugar

Sugar is used for many different purposes when baking sweet treats, and is cooked to different stages. A sugar thermometer will make life much easier when testing these different stages, but you can get by without one if you use the following practical method.

TO COOK SUGAR

1 Place the sugar in the pan with water and cook over a low heat until the sugar melts. Raise the heat and allow the liquid to boil.

2 Don't stir, but do keep the sides of the pan clear of any splatters as they will crystallise and may cause the sugar to also crystallise. A pastry brush dipped in cold water is best for this purpose.

3 To test the different cooking stages without a sugar thermometer, drop small quantities of the sugar into iced water.

SOFT BALL (116°C): If the sugar is ready, you will be able to roll it into a soft ball with your fingers.

HARD BALL (121°C): As above but the sugar will roll into a firmer ball.

SMALL CRACK (140°C): The sugar should peel off your fingers in a pliable film which sticks to your teeth when chewed.

HARD CRACK (153°C): The sugar will break like glass.

CARAMEL (176°C): Continue cooking until golden brown.

Anzac biscuits

Makes 24

Traditional Anzacs are one of the easiest and most popular biscuits to make.

100 g (1 cup) rolled oats
70 g (1 cup) desiccated coconut
185 g (1¼ cups) plain flour
130 g (⅔ cup) brown sugar
125 g butter
80 ml (⅓ cup) water
2 tbsp golden syrup
1 tsp bicarbonate of soda

Preheat oven to 180°C.

Line baking trays with baking paper.

Mix the oats, coconut, flour and brown sugar together in a large bowl. Place the butter, water and golden syrup in a small saucepan and bring to the boil. Remove from heat, add bicarbonate of soda and stir until the mixture becomes frothy. Pour the frothy mixture onto the dry ingredients and mix quickly.

Roll the mixture into small balls and place on the prepared trays, allowing some room for spreading. Press down gently.

Bake in the preheated oven for 15–20 minutes, or until golden brown but still slightly soft. Allow to cool for 5 minutes. Remove from trays and leave to cool on a cooling rack, then store in an airtight container.

Macadamia Anzacs
Substitute 150 g (1 cup) macadamias for dessicated coconut.

Biscotti

Makes 24–30

Biscotti are an Italian-style dry biscuit, usually served after a meal with coffee and grappa. We prefer them at 11 a.m. with a cup of tea.

250 g (1⅔ cup) plain flour
1 tsp baking powder
250 g (1 cup plus 2 tbsp) caster sugar
1 tsp vanilla extract
2 eggs
1 egg yolk
100 g (⅔ cup) blanched toasted almonds

Preheat oven to 180°C.

Sift flour, baking powder and sugar into a large bowl. Add vanilla, eggs and egg yolk to the mixture and mix until ingredients form a ball. Add almonds and knead until they are combined.

Divide dough into two and form into two log-shaped pieces, about 25 cm in length. Place both pieces on a lined baking tray, allowing room for spreading. Bake in preheated oven for 30 minutes, or until firm to touch and golden brown. Remove and allow to cool.

Reduce oven temperature to 140°C. Slice logs on the diagonal, 1 cm thickness. Place slices on lined baking trays and return to the oven for 20 minutes, or until quite dry.

Pistachio biscotti
Substitute pistachios for almonds.

Chocolate and hazelnut biscotti
Substitute hazelnuts for almonds and cocoa for 30 g of the flour.

Raspberry jam drops

Makes 30

These have become a real favourite at our place in recent years – no doubt due to the two mini food lovers named Mia and Luke. The quality of the jam you use will make a big difference, and you can use jams other than raspberry if preferred. It's best to dust your hands with flour when making these biscuits, in order to roll the mixture successfully into balls for baking.

150 g soft butter
150 g (⅔ cup) caster sugar
65 g (½ cup) icing sugar
2 eggs
a few drops of vanilla extract

185 g (1¼ cups) self-raising flour
75 g (½ cup) plain flour
pinch of salt
plain flour for dusting
150 g (½ cup) raspberry jam

Preheat oven to 180°C.

Line baking trays with baking paper.

Cream the butter and sugars until pale and fluffy. Beat in the eggs and vanilla. Sift the flours and salt together, then stir in gently. Place the mix in the refrigerator for 15 minutes to make it easier to handle.

Dust your hands with flour and roll heaped spoonfuls of the biscuit mixture into balls. Place the biscuits on the prepared baking trays. Flatten each biscuit slightly, then use a teaspoon to make an indent in the middle. Spoon jam into indent. Bake in the preheated oven for 12–15 minutes, or until golden. Remove from trays and leave to cool on a cooling rack, then store in an airtight container.

Silver darlings
Luke's own creation: sprinkle silver cachou balls onto the biscuits before baking.

Lemon gems
Substitute lemon curd for jam.

Chocolate drops
Replace jam with one large chocolate chip on each biscuit (or use Smarties if the biscuits are for a child's party).

Chocolate vanilla drops
Melt 100 g dark chocolate by placing it in a bowl over a saucepan of simmering water or in a microwave on low. Using a spoon, drizzle melted chocolate over the biscuits. Allow the chocolate to set before storing the biscuits in an airtight container.

Almond macaroons

Makes 48

The variations on these biscuits are enormous and are limited only by the different types of nuts available.

3 egg whites
300 g (1⅓ cup) caster sugar
300 g (3 cups) ground almonds
2 tbsp plain flour
additional plain flour as required

Preheat oven to 180°C.

Beat egg whites to stiff peaks. Slowly beat in sugar until thick and glossy. Mix together almonds and flour. Fold dry mix into beaten egg whites.

Dust hands with a little flour and roll heaped teaspoonfuls of the biscuit mixture into balls. Place biscuits on a lined baking tray. Bake in preheated oven for 10–15 minutes, or until golden brown and firm to touch.

Cinnamon almond macaroons
Add 1½ tsp ground cinnamon to the almond/flour mix.

Chocolate macaroons
Substitute cocoa powder for 30 g of the ground almonds. Be really decadent and sandwich cooked macaroons with Chocolate Ganache (page 702).

Coconut macaroons
Substitute desiccated coconut for ground almonds.

Viennese biscuits

Makes 40

This is a classic biscuit mixture that has its origins in Austria. It is perfect when you want to make a biscuit mixture that can be used in a piping bag. You can pipe rounds or fingers as you need. They can then be sandwiched together with butter icing or dipped into melted chocolate.

250 g soft butter
130 g (1 cup) icing sugar
2 eggs
250 g (1⅔ cup) plain flour

Preheat oven to 200°C.

Cream butter and sugar until white and fluffy. Add eggs, beat well, then beat in flour. Place mixture into a piping bag and pipe onto buttered baking trays or trays lined with baking paper.

Bake in preheated oven for 8–10 minutes, or until beginning to brown at the edges.

Shortbread

Makes 30

There's something essentially wholesome about shortbread; it's always so crisp and satisfying. It can also be adapted to produce new versions with flavours such as orange, chocolate and spice.

- 260 g (1¾ cups) plain flour
- 115 g (¾ cup) rice flour
- 250 g soft butter, diced
- 125 g (½ cup) caster sugar
- pinch of salt
- water, if required

Preheat oven to 170°C.

Rub together flours, butter, sugar and salt. Knead well until combined. Add a little water if it is very dry. Roll to ½ cm thickness and cut into large fingers or 5 cm circles. Bake in preheated oven until crisp, about 10–12 minutes.

Orange shortbread
Add the zest of 2 oranges to the basic mixture.

Chocolate shortbread
Substitute cocoa for 30 g of the plain flour.

Spiced shortbread
Add 1 tsp mixed spice to the basic mixture.

Snickerdoodles

Makes 20–24

Love the name, but we have no idea what it means. Which is pretty irrelevant when they taste so good.

- 125 g soft butter
- 165 g (¾ cup) caster sugar
- 1 egg
- 1 egg yolk
- 225 g (1½ cup) self-raising flour
- ½ tsp nutmeg
- 165 g (1⅓ cups) walnuts, chopped
- 65 g (½ cup) currants
- 2 tsp caster sugar, additional
- 2 tsp ground nutmeg, additional

Preheat oven to 180°C.

Cream together butter and sugar until light and fluffy. Beat in egg and egg yolk. Add flour, nutmeg, walnuts and currants and mix until smooth. Drop teaspoonfuls onto a greased baking tray. Mix together additional sugar and nutmeg and sprinkle onto biscuits. Bake in preheated oven for 10–15 minutes.

Coconut wafers

Makes 12–15

Coconut wafers are excellent to serve with desserts such as mousses, chilled puddings and panna cotta.

100 g soft butter
100 ml (⅓ cup) coconut cream
110 g (½ cup) caster sugar
75 g (½ cup) self-raising flour
25 g (⅓ cup) flaked coconut

Preheat oven to 180°C.

Cream butter, coconut cream and sugar together until smooth. Stir in flour and flaked coconut.

Gently shape heaped teaspoonfuls of the mixture into rounds, place on a floured baking tray and flatten slightly. Cook in preheated oven for 10–12 minutes, or until golden brown.

Passionfruit yoyo biscuits

Makes 18

Yoyo biscuits are a classic combination in which two simple biscuits are joined with a vanilla filling. We like to think we have improved on this classic by using a passionfruit filling – we'll leave it to you to decide.

300 g (2 cups) plain flour
300 g soft butter
100 g (⅔ cup) icing sugar
100 g (¾ cup) custard powder
pinch of salt
½ tsp vanilla extract
2 passionfruit
60 g melted butter
250 g (1½ cups) icing sugar

Preheat oven to 180°C.

Beat together flour, butter, icing sugar, custard powder, salt and vanilla. Roll into small balls and place on a greased baking tray. Press down with the prongs of a fork to form a round biscuit. Bake in preheated oven for 10–15 minutes, until cooked but not coloured. Allow to cool completely.

Strain the pulp from passionfruit to remove seeds. Mix with butter and icing sugar until smooth. Spoon a small amount of passionfruit butter onto one biscuit half and top with another biscuit. Continue until all biscuits are ready.

Hazelnut and vanilla creams

Makes 18

These are quite rich, full-flavoured biscuits that are great with a strong, long black coffee.

125 g soft butter
150 g (¾ cup) brown sugar
1 egg
½ tsp ground nutmeg
300 g (2 cups) self-raising flour

75 g (½ cup) roasted hazelnuts, skins removed
125 g soft butter, additional
250 g (2 cups) icing sugar
½ tsp vanilla extract

Preheat oven to 180°C.

Cream butter and sugar until light and fluffy. Beat in egg until well combined, then stir in nutmeg and flour. Roughly chop hazelnuts and add to mixture.

Roll teaspoonfuls of the biscuit mixture into balls and place on a lined tray. Press down with the prongs of a fork to form a round biscuit. Bake in preheated oven for 10–15 minutes, or until golden brown. Remove and allow to cool.

Make vanilla cream by beating additional butter, slicing sugar and vanilla until light and fluffy.

Match up same-size biscuits in pairs. Spoon a small amount of vanilla cream on to one biscuit and top with its match. Continue until all biscuits are ready.

Gingerbread hearts

Makes 30 biscuits

Ginger is a flavour that people either love or can't stand at all; this one is for all the ginger lovers we know.

125 g soft butter
70 g (⅓ cup) brown sugar
zest of 1 orange, finely chopped
1 egg
125 ml (½ cup) warm honey
450 g (3 cups) self-raising flour

4 tsp ground ginger
½ tsp ground cinnamon
30 blanched almonds
1 egg, lightly beaten
raw sugar

Preheat oven to 170°C.

Cream butter and sugar until light and fluffy. Add zest and egg and beat until smooth. Stir in honey. Sift together flour, ginger and cinnamon and stir into wet mixture. Wrap biscuit mixture in cling film and chill for 30 minutes.

Roll biscuit mixture out onto a floured surface and cut out heart shapes. Lay biscuits on a lined baking tray. Push an almond into the centre of each. Brush each biscuit with beaten egg and sprinkle raw sugar over. Bake in preheated oven for 8–10 minutes.

Allow biscuits to cool.

Orange and walnut Florentines

Makes 24

This twist on the classic Florentine recipe brings a great orange taste to the existing toffee and chocolate flavours.

45 g butter
125 ml (½ cup) pure cream
125 g (½ cup plus 1 tbsp) caster sugar
100 g (¾ cup) walnuts, roughly chopped
zest of 1 orange, finely chopped
50 g (⅓ cup) plain flour
100 g dark chocolate, chopped

Preheat oven to 160°C.

Place butter, cream and sugar in a small saucepan and bring to the boil over a medium heat, then remove immediately. Stir in the nuts, orange zest and flour. Leave to cool for 5 minutes.

Drop heaped teaspoons of the mix onto lined baking trays, leaving 4 cm between each one.

Bake in preheated oven for 15–20 minutes. Biscuits should be golden at the edges and firm to the touch. Allow to cool on the trays.

Melt chocolate and spread onto the back of each biscuit. Allow chocolate to set completely before storing.

Cardamom spiced wafers

Makes 18–20 biscuits

This recipe is based on tuile biscuits, which made obligatory appearances on all restaurant dessert menus in the 1980s.

60 g soft butter
60 g (¼ cup) caster sugar
2 egg whites
60 g (⅓ cup) plain flour
¼ tsp ground cardamom

Preheat oven to 180°C.

Beat butter and sugar until pale and light. Lightly whisk in egg whites. Sift together the flour and ground cardamom, then fold into the mixture.

Drop teaspoons of the mix onto lined baking trays. Use a spatula to spread it paper thin into 10 cm long wafers. Bake in preheated oven for 5 minutes. They should be just golden at the edges and pale in the centre. Allow to cool, then transfer to an airtight container.

Tuiles
Omit the ground cardamom to make plain tuiles. These biscuits can be made in any shape but traditionally they are shaped into 10 cm circles, baked, then draped over moulds or rolled around rolling pins while still warm to make basket shapes.

Mini rum and raisin garibaldi

Makes 15 biscuits

These are a decadent sandwich-style biscuit, with crisp pastry circles enveloping a rich, moist, rum-flavoured fruit filling. They deserve to be eaten regularly.

60 g (¼ cup) raw sugar
75 ml (⅓ cup) water
1½ tbsp muscat
1 tbsp dark rum
pinch of mixed spice
pinch of cinnamon
320 g (2 cups) sultanas
1 quantity Sweetcrust Pastry (page 590)
1 egg yolk
1 tbsp milk
caster sugar

Preheat oven to 180°C.

Place sugar, water, muscat, rum and spices in a saucepan. Heat to simmering and stir until sugar dissolves. Add the sultanas and simmer for 10 minutes, stirring regularly. If most of the liquid has not been absorbed into the fruit, continue cooking for a few minutes more. Allow mix to cool but do not refrigerate.

Roll pastry to 3 mm thickness. Cut out 7½ cm circles. Lay half of the pastry circles onto lined baking trays.

Mix the egg yolk with milk to make an egg wash. Brush edges of pastry circles with egg wash. Spoon a tablespoon of sultanas onto each pastry circle, then press another pastry circle on top. Press down gently. Brush pastry tops with egg wash and sprinkle with a little sugar.

Bake in a preheated oven for 10–12 minutes, or until golden brown.

Almond bread

Makes 18

A perfectly crisp slice of almond bread is a beautiful thing, particularly when served alongside a dessert or simply piled on a plate for afternoon tea.

6 egg whites
180 g (¾ cup) caster sugar
180 g (1¼ cups) plain flour
180 g (1¼ cups) blanched almonds

Preheat oven to 180°C.

Beat egg whites to stiff peaks. Slowly beat in sugar until mixture is thick and glossy. Fold through flour and almonds. Spoon into a greased log tin 23.5 × 13.5 × 7 cm and bake in preheated oven for 45 minutes. Allow to cool, then slice very thinly.

Lower oven temperature to 140°C. Place slices on baking tray and dry in preheated oven until crisp, about 10 minutes.

Pistachio bread
Substitute pistachios (or any other nut that takes your fancy) for almonds.

Brandy snaps

Makes 20–24

Brandy snaps are considered the epitome of dinner party chic by many. Although we don't hold them quite that high, these traditional biscuits, often filled with brandy cream and berries, are well worth knowing how to make.

90 g butter
90 g (¼ cup) golden syrup
200 g (1¼ cups) icing sugar
90 g (⅔ cup) plain flour
pinch of salt
1 tsp ground ginger

Place butter, golden syrup and icing sugar in a saucepan over a medium heat. Stir until melted, then remove from heat. Sift flour, salt and ginger together and add to melted mixture. Beat until well combined.

Drop teaspoons of the mix onto lined baking trays. Use a spatula to spread mixture into 8 cm circles. Bake in preheated oven for 5 minutes. They should be just golden at the edges and pale in the centre. Allow to cool then transfer to an airtight container.

Brandy snap baskets
Brandy snaps, while still warm, can be draped over moulds to form basket shapes or rolled around the handle of a large wooden spoon to form tubes.

Coconut biscuits

Makes 24

These are great when you need to make a little something for afternoon tea but time is short.

100 g butter
220 g (1 cup) caster sugar
1 egg
200 g (1⅓ cups) self-raising flour
50 g (½ cup) ground almonds
25 g (⅓ cup) desiccated coconut
plain flour for dusting

Preheat oven to 180°C.

Line baking trays with baking paper.

Cream the butter and caster sugar until light and fluffy. Beat in the egg completely, then stir in the flour, followed by the ground almonds. Place the coconut in a flat tray.

Dust your hands with a little flour and roll heaped teaspoonfuls of the biscuit mixture into balls. Roll them in the coconut, then place the biscuits on the prepared baking trays.

Bake in the preheated oven for 10–12 minutes, or until just beginning to colour. Remove from trays and leave to cool on a cooling rack, then store in an airtight container.

Gingernuts

Makes 16

An oldie but a goodie, these classic biscuits will brighten up any afternoon tea. If you are feeling truly dedicated, you can make a batch to use as the base in the Amaretto-Cherry Cheesecake recipe (page 737).

100 g (⅔ cup) self-raising flour
½ tsp bicarbonate of soda
1 tsp ground ginger
¼ tsp ground nutmeg
¼ tsp ground allspice
65 g (⅓ cup) brown sugar
50 g butter, diced
2–3 tbsp golden syrup

Preheat oven to 180°C.

Line baking trays with baking paper.

Sift the flour, bicarbonate of soda, ginger, nutmeg and allspice together. Add the brown sugar and butter, and rub until the mix has a fine breadcrumb texture. Add 2 tbsp golden syrup and mix together to form a firm dough. Add more golden syrup as required.

Divide the mixture into 16 and shape into even-sized balls. Place the balls on the prepared baking trays, allowing room for spreading. Press each biscuit gently with the prongs of a fork.

Bake in the preheated oven for 10–12 minutes. Remove from trays and leave to cool on a cooling rack, then store in an airtight container.

Double chocolate chip cookies

Makes 35

These rich double chocolate cookies have cocoa in the mix and chocolate chips studded through them.

150 g soft butter
150 g (⅔ cup) caster sugar
100 g (½ cup) brown sugar
1 tsp vanilla extract
1 egg
150 g (1 cup) self-raising flour
100 g (⅔ cup) plain flour
50 g (½ cup) cocoa
190 g (⅔ cup) small chocolate chips (a mix of dark and white)

Preheat oven to 180°C.

Line baking trays with baking paper.

Cream the butter, sugars and vanilla until light and fluffy. Add the egg, then beat well until combined. Sieve the flours and cocoa together, then stir into the mix. Finally, stir through the chocolate chips.

Roll level teaspoons of the mixture into balls and place them 3 cm apart on the prepared baking trays. Flatten slightly using a fork.

Bake in the preheated oven for 12–15 minutes. They should be dry on top and still slightly soft in the centre. Remove from trays and leave to cool on a cooling rack, then store in an airtight container.

Double chocolate chip and walnut cookies
Add 60 g (½ cup) chopped walnuts along with the chocolate chips.

Chocolate peanut cookies

Makes 30

Peanut butter and chocolate chips sounds like an unusual combination, but it really works. Trust me! MC

125 g soft butter
125 g (½ cup) crunchy peanut butter
100 g (½ cup) brown sugar, firmly packed
110 g (½ cup) caster sugar
1 tsp vanilla extract
1 egg
225 g (1½ cups) self-raising flour
95 g (½ cup) chocolate chips

Preheat oven to 180°C.

Line baking trays with baking paper.

Cream the butter, peanut butter, sugars and vanilla until pale and fluffy. Add the egg and beat until combined. Add the flour and mix together, then stir in the chocolate chips.

Roll level teaspoons of the mixture into balls and place them 3 cm apart on the prepared baking trays. Flatten slightly using a fork.

Bake in the preheated oven for 10–12 minutes, or until golden brown. Remove from trays and leave to cool on a cooling rack, then store in an airtight container.

Spiced pecan cookies

Makes 24

These spiced pecan biscuits are great to have on hand for an afternoon snack.

150 g butter
110 g (½ cup) caster sugar
100 g (½ cup) brown sugar
1 tsp vanilla extract
1 egg
250 g (1⅔ cups) self-raising flour
60 g (½ cup) chopped pecans
½ tsp ground nutmeg
½ tsp ground cinnamon
pinch of allspice

Preheat oven to 180°C.

Line baking trays with baking paper.

Cream the butter, sugars and vanilla until light and fluffy. Add the egg and beat until well combined. Fold the flour into the mix, followed by the pecans, nutmeg, cinnamon and allspice. Stir well.

Roll level teaspoons of the mixture into balls and place 3 cm apart on the prepared baking trays. Flatten slightly using a fork.

Bake in the preheated oven for 10–15 minutes. Remove from trays and leave to cool on a cooling rack, then store in an airtight container.

Muesli munchies

Makes 30

Natural muesli adds flavour and texture to these biscuits, but be warned: it's hard to stop at just one!

150 g butter
110 g (½ cup) caster sugar
100 g (½ cup) brown sugar
1 tsp vanilla extract

1 egg
250 g (1⅔ cups) self-raising flour, sifted
110 g (1 cup) natural muesli
½ tsp cinnamon

Preheat oven to 180°C.

Line baking trays with baking paper.

Cream the butter, sugars and vanilla until light and fluffy. Add the egg and beat well until combined. Fold the flour into the mix, followed by the muesli and cinnamon.

Roll level teaspoons of the mixture into balls and place them 3 cm apart on the prepared baking trays. Flatten slightly using a fork.

Bake in the preheated oven for 10–15 minutes. Remove from trays and leave to cool on a cooling rack, then store in an airtight container.

Oatcakes

Makes 20

These are wonderful with cheese – cheddar in particular – and make a change from packets of water crackers, which are pretty unexciting.

110 g (¾ cup) wholemeal flour
75 g (½ cup) plain flour
110 g (1 cup) oatmeal

110 g soft butter, diced
60 g (¼ cup) brown sugar
1 egg

Preheat oven to 190°C.

Mix flours and oatmeal together and rub in butter to produce a breadcrumb texture. Add sugar and egg and mix together until a smooth dough forms. Roll with a rolling pin until 3 mm thick and cut into 5 cm circles. Place circles on a tray lined with baking paper and cook for 20–25 minutes, or until biscuits are crisp. Store in an airtight container.

Goat's cheese biscuits

Makes 40

These biscuits are great spread with a little tapenade, or topped with fresh goat's curd and a slice of roasted tomato. A formal thank you to Grace.

350 g soft butter
250 g fresh goat's cheese
60 g (¾ cup) parmigiano, grated
pinch of salt
½ tsp cayenne
425 g (2¾ cups) plain flour

Preheat oven to 160°C.

Beat butter, goat's cheese, parmigiano, salt and cayenne to a smooth paste in a food processor. Place in a bowl and mix in flour. Roll into 5 cm logs and wrap in cling film. Freeze for 30 minutes to allow easy slicing. Slice logs into discs 1 cm thick. Place on a tray lined with baking paper and bake in preheated oven for 20–25 minutes, until pale gold in colour. Allow to cool, then store in an airtight container.

Cheese bickies

Makes 20–25

Easy to make, easy to cook and easy to eat. What more could you want in life?

150 g soft butter
225 g (1½ cups) plain flour
125 g (1¼ cups) grated cheddar
pinch of salt
½ tsp cayenne pepper

Place all ingredients in mixing bowl. Beat until mixture forms a ball. Roll into 2 long sausage shapes, about 3 cm thick. Wrap in cling film and refrigerate for 30 minutes.

Preheat oven to 180°C.

Slice logs into discs 1 cm thick. Place on a tray lined with baking paper and bake in preheated oven for 10–12 minutes or until slightly browned.

Millionaire's shortbread (caramel slice)

Makes 12

We always knew this recipe as caramel slice, but have recently found out that it's also called millionaire's shortbread – a much more fitting name.

90 g soft butter
90 g (⅓ cup) raw sugar
1 egg
60 g (⅓ cup) self-raising flour
60 g (¾ cup) desiccated coconut

395 ml can condensed milk
125 g butter, additional
125 g (½ cup) caster sugar, additional
150 g dark chocolate, chopped

Preheat oven to 180°C.

Cream butter and sugar until light and fluffy. Add egg, beat well. Add flour and coconut and stir to combine. Spread mixture in lined lamington tin. Bake in heated oven for 15–20 minutes, or until just cooked. (It's going to go back into the oven for another 15 minutes, so it doesn't have to be brown.)

Place condensed milk, butter and additional sugar in a small saucepan. Place over a medium heat and bring to the boil, stirring often to prevent condensed milk catching and burning. When sugar is dissolved and mixture has just started to boil, pour it over the cooked pastry base. Return to oven and cook for a further 10–15 minutes, or until caramel has turned golden brown. Set aside to cool.

When caramel is set, melt chocolate and coat caramel. Top evenly, leave to set, then cut into squares.

Hedgehog

Makes 24

This is one of those 'stir together and pour into a tin' recipes that is incredibly quick and easy to make. Hedgehog is best kept chilled as it softens at room temperature.

250 g Marie biscuits
75 g (⅔ cup) walnuts, chopped
250 g butter
150 g (⅔ cup) caster sugar
50 g (½ cup) cocoa
2 eggs
100 g dark chocolate, chopped

Preheat oven to 180°C.

Break biscuits into approximately 1 cm pieces. Mix with walnuts and set aside. Melt butter over a medium heat. Add sugar and cocoa to the saucepan; return to the heat and stir until sugar dissolves. Remove from heat and allow to cool.

Beat in eggs, then add broken biscuits and nuts. Spoon into a lined lamington tin, press down well until biscuits are covered with chocolate mix and refrigerate until set. Melt chocolate and coat top evenly. Allow to set, then cut into small squares.

Mars Bar slice

Makes 12 large or 24 small slices

I'd like to claim that I only make this for kids' parties, but then I would be a liar. MC

3 Mars Bars
90 g butter
90 g (3 cups) Rice Bubbles

Chop Mars Bars roughly and place in a small saucepan with butter. Cook over a medium heat until Mars Bars and butter have melted. Whisk together well to combine the two.

Place Rice Bubbles in a good-sized bowl and pour hot melted ingredients over. Stir well to combine the two together. Pour mixture into a lamington tin or spoon into 24 patty pans and refrigerate until set. If using a lamington tin, cut into 12 bars when set.

Toffee almond squares

Makes 12

These squares are delicious and quite rich, certainly decadent enough to stand up to a strong espresso after dinner.

60 g soft butter
125 g (1 cup) ground almonds
100 g (½ cup) caster sugar
2 eggs
2 tbsp plain flour
90 g butter, additional
125 g (½ cup) caster sugar, additional
60 g (⅔ cup) flaked almonds

Preheat oven to 180°C.

Cream butter, ground almonds and sugar until light and fluffy. Add eggs and flour and beat well to combine. Spoon into greased and lined lamington tin. Bake in preheated oven for 15–20 minutes, or until set and golden brown.

Place additional butter and sugar in a small saucepan. Bring to the boil over medium–high heat and cook for 5–10 minutes, or until sugar starts to caramelise, stirring often. Remove from heat, add flaked almonds and pour and spread evenly over baked base. Set aside to cool before slicing into squares.

Flapjacks

Makes 12

These may sound as if they are a small pancake or pikelet, but they are in fact a simple yet delicious slice that is great for children's lunch boxes.

150 g butter
200 g (½ cup) golden syrup
90 g (½ cup) soft brown sugar
250 g (2½ cups) rolled oats
100 g (⅔ cup) plain flour
80 g (½ cup) sultanas (optional)

Preheat oven to 180°C.

Butter a lamington tin, line the sides and bottom with greaseproof paper and butter lightly.

Place the butter, golden syrup and brown sugar in a small saucepan. Cook over a medium heat until melted and foaming. Remove from heat and allow to cool.

Mix the oats and flour together. Add the warm butter mixture and combine well. Add sultanas (if using), and mix through.

Press the mixture into the prepared lamington tin and bake in the preheated oven for 20–25 minutes. Allow to cool before cutting into small rectangles.

Vanilla and caramelised apricot slice

Makes 12

Ripe apricots are lightly roasted, then topped with cake batter to make a simple dessert or treat for afternoon tea.

6 apricots, halved and stoned
1–2 tbsp caster sugar
165 g (¾ cup) caster sugar
200 g (1⅓ cups) self-raising flour
100 g soft butter
125 ml (½ cup) milk
1 tsp vanilla extract
1 egg
2–3 tbsp flaked almonds

Preheat oven to 180°C.

Butter a lamington tin, line the sides and bottom with greaseproof paper and butter lightly.

Place the apricot halves skin side down in the base of the prepared lamington tin and sprinkle with caster sugar. Bake in the preheated oven for 20 minutes, or until the apricots are golden brown.

Rub 165 g (¾ cup) caster sugar, flour and butter together. Add the milk, vanilla and egg to the mix and beat until smooth. Pour over the caramelised apricots and sprinkle flaked almonds on top. Return to the oven and cook for 20 minutes, or until risen and firm to the touch. Slice into wedges to serve.

Raspberry, vanilla and almond slice

Serves 8

This is an easy slice to make. All you have to do is make a simple base and place half of it in a tin and bake it. The remaining mixture is combined with berries and almonds to create the topping.

350 g (1⅔ cups) caster sugar
300 g (2 cups) self-raising flour
125 g soft butter
250 ml (1 cup) milk
1 tsp vanilla extract
1 egg
250 g (2 cups) raspberries
60 g (⅔ cup) flaked almonds

Preheat oven to 180°C.

Rub together sugar, flour and butter. Divide mixture in half. Press half into lined 23 cm cake tin and press down firmly. Bake in preheated oven for 20 minutes.

Add milk, vanilla and egg to remaining mix. Scatter baked half with raspberries and pour remaining mixture over. Sprinkle almonds on top.

Return to the oven and cook for a further 30 minutes, or until risen and firm to touch. Slice into wedges to serve.

Viennese plum slice

Makes 12

Unlike a tart, a slice is quite stable and easy to handle without cracking. This makes it a great thing to take along on a picnic, where it should happily arrive in one piece.

200 g (1⅓ cups) plain flour
¼ tsp ground cinnamon
100 g soft butter
165 g (¾ cup) caster sugar
pinch of salt
1 egg yolk
1 tsp vanilla extract
1–2 tbsp milk
4–6 blood plums, halved and stoned
2 tbsp raw sugar
200 g (⅔ cup) redcurrant jelly

Butter a lamington tin, line the sides and bottom with greaseproof paper and butter lightly.

Sift the flour and cinnamon into a bowl. Add butter and rub together until the mixture has a breadcrumb texture. Mix in the caster sugar and salt, then add the egg, vanilla and enough milk to bring it to a soft dough. Press the dough into the prepared lamington tin. Refrigerate for 30 minutes.

Preheat oven to 180°C.

Cut the halved plums into threes and place them skin side down over the pastry. Sprinkle with raw sugar. Bake in the preheated oven for 30–40 minutes, or until the pastry is cooked and the plums have softened.

Leave to cool completely. Melt the redcurrant jelly and spoon it over the plums. Leave to set, then cut into small rectangles.

Raspberry coconut slice

Makes 12

We've tasted a few versions of this slice, and then taken the best aspects of each one and blended them to make our own variation. The combination of a simple pastry base with berries and coconut is hard to beat.

125 g soft butter
55 g (¼ cup) caster sugar
½ tsp vanilla extract
1 egg
225 g (1½ cups) self-raising flour
60 ml (¼ cup) milk
160 g (½ cup) raspberry jam

150 g (1¼ cups) raspberries
100 g soft butter, additional
110 g (½ cup) caster sugar, additional
2 eggs, additional
225 g (2½ cups) shredded coconut
50 g (⅓ cup) plain flour, additional
icing sugar to serve

Preheat oven to 180°C.

Butter a lamington tin, line the sides and bottom with greaseproof paper and butter lightly.

Cream the butter, caster sugar and vanilla in a mixer until white and fluffy. Add the egg, then fold in flour and milk. Mix until it forms a sticky dough. Press the dough into the prepared lamington tin. Spread jam over the uncooked base, then sprinkle evenly with raspberries.

Cream the additional butter and caster sugar together until pale and fluffy. Add the eggs, one at a time and beating well after each addition. Stir in the coconut and flour, then gently spoon the mix over the raspberry base.

Bake in the preheated oven for 35–40 minutes. Check that the topping is cooked in the centre. If not, cook for another 5–10 minutes. Allow to cool before cutting into slices. Dust with icing sugar to serve.

Munchie muesli slice

Makes 12

This is packed with good things, including dried fruit, rolled oats, sunflower seeds and honey. We've been making it for years and it never fails to satisfy.

110 g (½ cup) caster sugar
150 g (1 cup) self-raising flour
90 g (1 cup) shredded coconut
90 g (1 cup) rolled oats
80 g (½ cup) sultanas
75 g (½ cup) raisins
75 g (½ cup) chopped dates
60 g (⅓ cup) sunflower seeds (optional)
125 g butter
2 tbsp water
60 g honey
1 egg

Preheat oven to 180°C.

Mix together sugar, flour, coconut, oats, dried fruit and seeds. Melt butter, water and honey together and pour over combined ingredients while still hot. Stir well until mixture comes together, then stir in the egg. Spoon mixture into a lined lamington tin and bake in preheated oven for 40 minutes, or until set and golden brown. Allow to cool before cutting into slices.

Fruity polenta slice

Makes 12

Polenta gives this slice a slight crunch and a lovely contrast to the honey-soaked fruit.

1 tbsp honey
250 ml (1 cup) hot tea
320 g (2 cups) dried fruit (for example, sultanas, currants and raisins)
180 g (1 cup) polenta
250 g (1⅔ cups) self-raising flour
100 g (½ cup) brown sugar
110 g (½ cup) caster sugar
200 g butter
½ tsp cinnamon
zest of 1 lemon, chopped
2 tbsp lemon juice
3 eggs

Preheat oven to 180°C.

Dissolve the honey in hot tea, add the dried fruit and set aside to soak. Allow to cool while you prepare the remaining ingredients.

Butter a lamington tin, line the sides and bottom with greaseproof paper and butter lightly.

Combine the polenta, flour, sugars, butter and cinnamon. Rub together until the mixture has a fine breadcrumb texture. Add the lemon zest, juice and eggs, and mix well. Drain the dried fruit thoroughly and add it to the mix. Stir well.

Spoon the mixture into the prepared lamington tray and smooth the top. Bake in the preheated oven for 30–40 minutes, or until set and golden brown. Slice into wedges to serve.

Robyn's caramel, macadamia and hazelnut slice

Makes 12

Like most foodies, we're always scanning the food pages of newspapers and magazines for good ideas. This recipe appeared in the *Age* newspaper, and it's a beauty.

BASE
- 90 g dark chocolate
- 80 g butter
- 150 g (1 cup) plain flour
- ½ tsp cinnamon
- 60 g (½ cup) hazelnut meal
- 100 g (½ cup) brown sugar
- 1 egg, lightly beaten

TOPPING
- 100 g (⅔ cup) hazelnuts
- 1 × 395 g can condensed milk
- 2 tbsp golden syrup
- 50 g butter
- 100 g (⅔ cup) macadamias
- 100 g dark chocolate, melted

Preheat oven to 180°C.

Butter a lamington tin, line the sides and bottom with greaseproof paper and butter lightly.

Place the chocolate and butter in a small saucepan and cook over a low heat until just melted. Sift the flour and cinnamon into a bowl, then stir in the hazelnut meal and brown sugar. Add the melted chocolate, along with the egg, and mix well. Press the mixture into the prepared lamington tin and bake in the preheated oven for 15 minutes.

Roast the hazelnuts in the oven until golden brown. Place them in a tea towel and rub well to remove the skins.

To make the topping, place the condensed milk, golden syrup and butter in a saucepan and place over a medium heat, stirring until it almost boils. Pour this mixture over the cooked base and top with hazelnuts and macadamias. Bake in the preheated oven for 15 minutes and leave to cool.

When cool, drizzle melted chocolate over the top until covered.

Nutmeg slice

Makes 12

This is a super-simple slice with a double-layered base.

400 g (2 cups) brown sugar
300 g (2 cups) self-raising flour
125 g butter, diced
250 ml (1 cup) milk
1 egg
1 tsp ground nutmeg
50 g (½ cup) flaked almonds

Preheat oven to 180°C.

Butter a lamington tin, line the sides and bottom with greaseproof paper and butter lightly.

Place the brown sugar, flour and butter in a bowl and rub together until it forms a breadcrumb texture. Spoon half of this mixture into the prepared lamington tin.

Add the milk, egg and nutmeg to the remaining dry mix and stir well. Spoon over the base, then scatter flaked almonds over the top.

Bake in the preheated oven for 30 minutes, then test with a skewer to ensure it is ready. If the skewer comes out clean, the slice is ready; if not, cook for a further 5 minutes and test again. Allow to cool before slicing into squares.

Ginger slice
Replace the ground nutmeg with ground ginger and add 100 g (½ cup) chopped glace ginger.

Nanaimo bars

Makes 12

Another delicious recipe, and one that requires no baking.

BASE	TOPPING
375 g digestive biscuits	125 g butter
250 g butter	585 g (4½ cups) icing sugar
90 g (⅓ cup) caster sugar	2 tbsp custard powder
50 g (½ cup) cocoa	60 ml (¼ cup) hot water
1 egg	125 g dark chocolate
1 tsp vanilla extract	60 g butter, additional
140 g (2 cups) desiccated coconut	65 g (½ cup) icing sugar, additional
125 g chopped nuts	

Butter a lamington tin, line the sides and bottom with greaseproof paper and butter lightly.

Crush the biscuits into crumbs. Place the butter, caster sugar and cocoa in the top of a double boiler and stir until blended. Add the egg and vanilla and cook for 1 minute. Remove from heat and add the biscuit crumbs, coconut and nuts. You should have quite a stiff mixture. Pat into the prepared tin and place in the refrigerator for 30 minutes.

To make the topping, place the butter, icing sugar, custard powder and hot water in a small saucepan. Bring to the boil and cook for 1–2 minutes, stirring often. Remove from heat and allow to cool. Spread over base and return to the refrigerator for 30 minutes.

Finally, melt the chocolate and additional 60 g butter by placing them in a bowl over a saucepan of simmering water or in a microwave on low for 1–2 minutes. Add the additional 65 g icing sugar and beat until smooth. Spread over the custard layer and return to the fridge until the chocolate sets. Cut into small rectangles.

Marzipan bars

Makes 12

I get to enjoy these bars all by myself as no one else in the family likes the flavour of marzipan. For that reason alone, this has to be one of my favourite recipes. MC

100 g soft butter
220 g (1 cup) caster sugar
2 eggs
1 tsp vanilla extract
½ tsp almond essence
225 g (1½ cups) plain flour

100 g marzipan, grated
75 g (¾ cup) ground almonds
140 g (1 cup) craisins (dried cranberries)
50 g (½ cup) flaked almonds
icing sugar to serve

Preheat oven to 180°C.

Butter a lamington tin, line the sides and bottom with greaseproof paper and butter lightly.

Cream the butter and caster sugar until light and fluffy. Beat in the eggs, one by one, fully incorporating the first before adding the second. Add the vanilla and almond extracts. Add the flour and mix until just combined. Finally, add the marzipan, ground almonds, craisins and flaked almonds. Stir until just combined.

Spoon the mixture into the prepared lamington tin and bake in the preheated oven for 40 minutes, or until golden brown. Test the slice by inserting a skewer. If it comes out clean, the slice is ready; if it doesn't, cook for a further 5 minutes and test again. Allow to cool. Dust with icing sugar and cut into small rectangles.

Lemon slice

Makes 18

A slice that is refreshing and zesty, ideal for a hot summer's afternoon.

BASE
125 g soft butter
220 g (1 cup) caster sugar
200 g (1⅓ cups) self-raising flour

TOPPING
220 g (1 cup) caster sugar
2 eggs
zest of 2 lemons, chopped
125 ml (½ cup) lemon juice
50 g (⅓ cup) self-raising flour
icing sugar to serve

Preheat oven to 180°C.

Butter a lamington tin, line sides and bottom with greaseproof paper and butter lightly.

Cream the butter and caster sugar until light and fluffy. Add the flour and mix through. Press the mixture into the prepared lamington tin and bake in the preheated oven for 10 minutes, or until firm and golden.

Make the topping by placing the caster sugar, eggs and lemon zest in a mixer. Beat for 5 minutes. Add lemon juice and flour, and beat until combined.

Pour the mixture over the baked base and return to the oven for 20–25 minutes, or until the topping is just set. Allow to cool. Slice into wedges and dust with icing sugar to serve.

White Christmas

Makes 12–16

What better treat to serve at Christmas? If preferred, spoon the mix into patty pan cases rather than serving it as a slice.

180 g white chocolate
70 g (1 cup) desiccated coconut
70 g (2 cups) Rice Bubbles
130 g (1 cup) icing sugar

160 g (1 cup) sultanas
150 g (1 cup) dried apricots, diced
140 g (1 cup) craisins (dried cranberries)
250 ml (1 cup) coconut cream

Line a lamington tray with greaseproof paper.

Set the chocolate to melt, either in a bowl over a saucepan of simmering water or in a microwave.

Mix coconut, Rice Bubbles, icing sugar, sultanas, apricots and craisins in a large bowl and toss until well combined. Add the coconut cream and melted chocolate and stir together.

Pour into the prepared lamington tin and press down firmly to form a flattish surface, taking care not to squash the Rice Bubbles too much. Leave to set. Cut into wedges to serve.

Almond nougat

Makes 18

This nougat has endless variations: you can swap almonds with hazelnuts, pistachios or macadamias, or add chocolate or glace fruit such as oranges and figs.

rice paper (optional)
550 g (2½ cups) caster sugar
250 ml (1 cup) liquid glucose
60 ml (¼ cup) honey

2 egg whites
200 g (1¼ cups) blanched almonds
100 g glace fruit (optional)

Line a lamington tin with rice paper, with enough set aside to put on top at a later stage. Rice paper is traditionally used to set nougat in, but you could line the tin with baking paper instead.

Combine the caster sugar, glucose and honey in a saucepan and stir over a medium heat until the sugar has dissolved. Increase the heat to high and boil until the mixture reaches the small crack stage, 140°C on the sugar thermometer.

When the sugar is just about at 140°C, beat the egg whites until stiff. Carefully pour the boiling sugar onto the egg whites while still beating; a mixer is ideal for this. Beat until well combined. Fold through almonds and glace fruit (if using).

Pour into the prepared dish, cover with rice paper (if using) and put aside until set. Cut into long bars and wrap in cellophane.

Chocolate hazelnut nougat
Add 100 g melted chocolate and substitute 200 g (1⅓ cups) hazelnuts for the almonds.

Christmas nougat
Use pistachios instead of almonds and add 95 g (⅔ cup) craisins.

Coconut ice

Makes 18

This is another copha-based recipe that I've had to adjust. It calls for a hideous amount of icing sugar, but luckily we only eat a little of this confection at a time. MC

1 egg white
650 g (5 cups) icing sugar
350 g (5 cups) desiccated coconut

1 × 270 ml can coconut cream
pink food colouring

Line a lamington tin with greaseproof paper.

Beat the egg white slightly. Sift the icing sugar into a large bowl, then add the coconut, coconut cream and egg white. Mix until well combined. Place half the mixture in the prepared lamington tin. Press down firmly to ensure that it's even (I use an empty jar as a rolling pin).

Add a few drops of pink food colouring to the remaining coconut mix and mix well so the colour is evenly distributed. Spread on top of the white coconut ice and press down firmly until evenly spread. Refrigerate until set.

Cut into long rectangles or small squares as desired. Keep refrigerated

Chocolate truffles

Makes 25–30

This recipe is extremely versatile. You can use milk chocolate instead of dark, and add different types of alcohol or flavoured essences to create myriad flavours.

90 g butter
125 ml (½ cup) double cream
300 g dark chocolate
2 tbsp brandy
cocoa

Place the butter and cream in a medium-sized saucepan and heat over a gentle heat until the butter melts. Add the chocolate and heat until it melts. (You can melt this in the microwave if you prefer.)

Remove from heat and let it stand for 2–3 minutes. Add brandy and set aside to cool, stirring occasionally to keep the butter incorporated. When cool, place in the refrigerator to firm up.

Take teaspoon-sized balls of the mix and roll them into round shapes. You'll have to work quickly as the mixture will quickly melt when it comes into contact with your warm hands. Roll the truffles in cocoa until well covered. Refrigerate.

Kahlua truffles
Swap brandy with Kahlua.

Grand Marnier truffles
Swap brandy with Grand Marnier.

White chocolate and rosewater truffles
Swap dark chocolate with white chocolate and brandy with rosewater.

Honeycomb

Makes 18

Honeycomb is simply amazing to make. Once you add the bicarbonate of soda, it explodes upwards and outwards, so take care as it is essentially boiling sugar. Use good-quality baking paper for this rather than greaseproof paper, as greaseproof often tears when the honeycomb hardens.

220 g (1 cup) caster sugar
100 ml (⅓ cup) honey
2 tbsp water
1 tbsp bicarbonate of soda, sifted

Line a baking tray with good-quality baking paper.

Place the caster sugar, honey and water in a heavy-based saucepan. Cook over a low heat until the sugar dissolves, stirring once or twice. Once the sugar has dissolved, raise the heat and bring to the boil. Cook for 3–4 minutes, until the liquid starts to change colour. Remove from heat.

Fold through the bicarbonate of soda; be careful, as it grows quickly. Spoon into the prepared baking tray and allow to cool.

Chocolate-coated honeycomb
Simply cover the honeycomb with melted chocolate. I once saw chef Raymond Capaldi set honeycomb in a cake tin, then coat it with melted chocolate – giant Violet Crumble at your disposal!

Rocky road

Makes 12

Rocky road is all about personal taste. Some people like it with coconut, others prefer Turkish delight or chocolate-coated marshmallows. Personally, I make it a different way each time, but my all-time favourite addition has to be Clinkers, inspired by chef and friend Megan Lilburn. MC

- 125 g dark chocolate
- 125 g milk chocolate
- 75 g mini marshmallows
- 100 g Clinkers (optional)
- 75 g nuts (almonds, brazil nuts, macadamias ... whatever)
- 300 g rosewater Turkish delight
- 35 g (½ cup) desiccated coconut

Line a deep log tin with baking paper.

Set the chocolates to melt, either in a bowl over a saucepan of simmering water or in a microwave.

Prepare the marshmallows, Clinkers, nuts and Turkish delight so they are all a similar size. Place them in a large bowl and toss well to evenly mix.

Pour the melted chocolate over the ingredients and mix well to combine – use your hands, it's more fun. Tip into the prepared baking tray and refrigerate until set.

Cut into slices.

Moroccan rocky road

Makes 18

We love the addition of spices to create Nat Paull's fabulous Moroccan rocky road.

- 100 g white marshmallows, cut into ½ cm pieces
- 100 g rosewater Turkish delight, cut into ½ cm pieces
- 50 g (⅓ cup) chopped roasted hazelnuts
- ¼ tsp ground nutmeg
- 1 tsp ground cardamom
- 1 tsp vanilla powder (optional)
- ½ tsp ground black pepper
- 1 tsp ground cinnamon
- 150 g chocolate, chopped into chunks

Line a flat baking tray with baking paper.

Place the marshmallows, Turkish delight and hazelnuts in a bowl. Mix all the spices together and toss together with the marshmallow mixture. Place the chocolate in a heatproof bowl and set over a saucepan of simmering water until it has melted.

Spread half the melted chocolate in the prepared baking tray, then scatter half the marshmallow mixture over the top. Cover with the remaining chocolate and repeat with the remaining marshmallow mix. Put aside until the chocolate sets. Chop into chunks.

Honey joys

Makes 24

It wouldn't be a proper party without honey joys.

100 g butter
100 g (¼ cup) honey
125 g (4¼ cups) Corn Flakes
24 paper patty pans

Preheat oven to 180°C.

Place butter and honey in a small saucepan and cook over a low heat, stirring until sugar has dissolved. Then bring to the boil and remove from heat.

Place Corn Flakes in a bowl and stir in hot butter mixture. Divide mixture between patty pans. Bake for 10 minutes.

Chocolate crackles

Makes 12

I love chocolate crackles, but being a food snob I can't stand copha. So I remade the classic. I know, don't mess with it if it ain't broke, but I had to. Besides, proper chocolate is so much better for you than a manufactured solidified fat. MC

140 g (4 cups) Rice Bubbles
195 g (1½ cups) icing sugar
70 g (1 cup) desiccated coconut
250 g chocolate, melted

Place the Rice Bubbles, icing sugar and coconut in a large bowl. Mix well to combine. Pour melted chocolate over and mix together. You'll need to work quickly as the chocolate will start to set as it cools. Spoon into patty pan cases and refrigerate until set.

Caramel popcorn

Makes 30

A kids' party favourite, quick and easy to make and very more-ish.

2–3 tbsp olive oil
110 g (½ cup) popping corn
150 g butter
200 g Jersey caramels
30 paper patty pans

Heat a saucepan over a medium heat. Add oil, heat, then add popping corn. Cover and allow to cook until all the corn is popped. Shake the saucepan regularly to encourage this. Tip the popcorn into a bowl.

Place butter and Jersey caramels in a small saucepan and cook over a low heat. Stir until melted, then pour over the popcorn. Stir until popcorn is completely coated with the caramel, then spoon into patty pans.

Toffee apples

Makes 4

Eating a toffee apple reminds me of going to a carnival as a child in Ireland. We find they work best with small apples as we like lots of toffee and not too much apple. AC

4 small apples
4 lollipop sticks
220 g (1 cup) caster sugar
60 ml (¼ cup) water
1 tsp white vinegar

Line a tray with baking paper.

Wash and dry the apples thoroughly, then insert lolly sticks into the stem ends of the fruit.

Combine the caster sugar, water and vinegar in a small, heavy-based saucepan. Stir constantly over a low heat, without boiling, until the sugar has completely dissolved. Increase the heat and bring to the boil. Simmer, without stirring, until the liquid turns to a golden toffee colour. Remove from heat.

Dip an apple in the toffee and turn it to evenly coat. Stand it upright on the prepared tray to set. Repeat with the remaining apples.

When cool, wrap the toffee apples in clear cellophane and tie with string. Store them in a cool, dry place, away from direct sunlight, but not in the fridge. They are best made and eaten within 2–3 days.

LUNCHBOX
healthy + quick

The word 'lunchbox' will no doubt send a shiver down the spine of any parent with primary school-aged children. If there's one culinary challenge we could all do without, it's the dilemma of how to pack a healthy and appealing lunch that can be eaten quickly.

Some children are born with the ability to eat anything put in front of them, while others are fussy eaters who cause major headaches for all concerned. Our children fall somewhere in the middle. We've seen enough lunchboxes returning full at the end of the day to cause us misery, but on other days it's, 'Why didn't you pack me more lunch? I was starving!'

Hopefully this chapter will give you some ideas for how to send your little darlings off to school with a healthy lunch that they are going to enjoy.

lunchbox ideas

Most children's lunchboxes focus on the sandwich, be it Vegemite, cheese, ham, peanut butter or Nutella. An important part of our job as parents is to encourage our children to eat a wide variety of foods, and to make sure that they know about healthy eating options. We need to show by example that a good diet is one that incorporates balance, diversity and the five food groups. Above all, it must taste good.

Research has shown that humans, whatever their age, often need to try a new food up to 15 times before they will accept it as part of their diet. By continuing to offer your children a wide range of food, you will expand their culinary horizons and give them the start in life they need to grow into healthy adults.

Most children eat far too many lollies, chips, snack foods and chocolate. Unfortunately, such 'bad' food is on offer more often than 'good' food. Just think of the television ads, supermarket displays and fast-food chains. We are slowly beginning to realise the impact this is having on our next generation. Don't wait for the government to introduce new rulings reducing the amount of junk-food advertising. Turn the television off and drag your children down to the park to kick the footy around or hit a tennis ball. Not only will it be good for your kids, it will be good for you, too.

Changing your child's attitude to diet isn't going to happen overnight, but small changes can make a big difference.

Let's start with bread. We don't care how much fibre or other supposedly 'healthy' ingredients have been added to processed bread – we wouldn't feed it to our dog, never mind our children. One of the greatest pleasures in life is a slice of crusty bread, a crisp baguette, a nutty wholegrain roll or some chewy pita bread. Two slices of white processed bread don't have the same appeal. Children love texture and they love good bread; it's the adults who love the convenience of processed foods. Keep your food as unrefined as possible – the less your bread is processed, the fewer chemicals or added flavours it has, the better it is for you.

If you are reading this and thinking there's no way my little angel is going to eat wholegrain bread instead of sliced white bread, you need to change your attitude. If you eat good-quality bread, your little angel will, too. As parents, we have the biggest influence on our children's diets.

Lunchbox checklist

1 Include a variety of food: fruit, vegetables, dairy and bread.

2 Include a bottle of water each day.

3 Avoid 'super-sized' lunchboxes; keep them small, especially for younger children.

4 Avoid pre-packaged food as much as possible – it's over-processed and all that packaging is bad, bad, bad for the environment.

5 Ensure there are no high-risk foods such as meat and dairy in the warmer months.

6 Variety is the spice of life, so move away from Vegemite sandwiches and try other options.

7 Try to get your child's school to adopt a healthy lunch day.

Start slowly by moving up from sliced white bread to sliced wholemeal or wholegrain, then try a soft roll from the local hot bread shop. Finally, offer your child a roll from a decent bakery, one that doesn't use premixes or improvers, just good, old-fashioned bread-making techniques. A good sourdough loaf will do the trick.

Pita bread is marvellous stuff, and kids love it. A spread of peanut butter, some grated carrot and lettuce, and lunch is looking good. You can try tuna, leftover roast chicken, hummus, grated cheese – anything, in fact, that your child likes to eat. For difficult eaters, try making the Pita Crisps on page 43. Get your kids to help you make them, and before you know it they will be eating the pita bread on its own. Then it's just a matter of time before you can slip a cheese and salad pita wrap into their lunchbox. Pita wraps are also excellent because they can be cut into small pieces, making them ideal for small hands.

So, now that we have healthy bread on the menu, what are we going to put in it? Vegemite, Nutella, peanut butter and all those other supermarket spreads are okay, in moderation, particularly on those days when you all wake up late and it's suddenly one of 'those' mornings. For the rest of the time, make an effort and try some healthy, unprocessed options such as:

- chicken, lettuce and mayonnaise
- hummus and cheddar
- tuna and salad
- ham, lettuce and tomato
- bacon, lettuce and tomato (BLT)
- grated carrot, tzatziki and lettuce.

Make sure your child's lunchbox isn't left sitting in full sun until lunchtime, and avoid risky foods such as chicken, sliced meats and dairy on extremely hot days. Small ice packs can be used to help keep lunches cool.

Lunch doesn't have to mean sandwiches every day, however. Think about a small salad with leftover roast chicken, a small can of tuna, chunks of cheddar or a boiled egg. Leftover meatballs with tomato sauce, baby quiches, sausage rolls,

last night's pasta or pizza, or a small flask of soup. Favourite dips such as hummus, tzatziki or beetroot with crackers or pita chips all go down a treat with our children for lunch.

Most kids like fruit, but they don't like bruised apples, squishy bananas or pulped pears. They like mandarins, small apples, just-ripe bananas, strawberries, a handful of cherries, apricots, a bunch of grapes, slices of watermelon, wedges of orange and fruit salad. Try making a big bowl of fruit salad for brekkie and put a small container in the lunchbox. If all else fails, or it's that bleak time of the year when there's not a lot of fruit in season, try a small bag of dried apple or apricots.

Dairy food is an important part of a child's diet, but lukewarm yoghurts and sweaty slices of cheese are just not going to cut it. Cheese sticks and triangles aren't even cheese; according to the Food Standards Australia New Zealand's website, processed cheese is 'a product manufactured from cheese and products obtained from milk that is heated and melted, with or without added emulsifying salts, to form a homogenous mass'. Sounds delicious, doesn't it! Offer real cheddar and brie with crackers when the weather is cooler.

Now, let's move on to something vaguely healthy that children can snack on for morning tea. Forget potato chips; once again, try the Pita Crisps (page 43) or go for corn or rice cakes, sultanas, nuts, home-made muffins, carrot sticks, plain popcorn or rice crackers.

Lastly, what to drink? Water is best, and that's it. There's no need for juice, flavoured milk, cordial or, heaven forbid, fizzy drinks. Get your kids used to drinking water – remember, we are supposed to drink six glasses a day, and you're never too young to start.

For more information on healthy eating plans for children, or adopting healthy lunch days at your child's school, visit these websites:
www.healthinsite.gov.au/topics/Healthy_Lunch_Boxes
www.goforyourlife.vic.gov.au
www.nutritionaustralia.org
www.kitchengardenfoundation.org.au
www.edibleschoolyard.org

NOTES
glossary, references + inspirations, index

Glossary

Acidulated water Water that has had lemon juice added to it to prevent ingredients such as artichokes and quinces discolouring during preparation. 1 litre (4 cups) water requires 60 ml (¼ cup) lemon juice.

Arborio rice A short-grain rice from northern Italy used for making risotto.

Barbecue pork A boneless piece of pork marinated in soy sauce, hoisin sauce, salt, sugar and colouring, then roasted by hanging in a special oval-shaped oven. Also known as char siew.

Black beans Fermented salted black beans that require soaking for at least 10 minutes before being rinsed, drained and chopped.

Blanch Briefly cook ingredients in boiling water.

Bok choy A Chinese variety of cabbage with crunchy white stalks and dark green leaves.

Bouquet garni A bundle of fresh herbs that includes bay leaves, thyme, parsley and celery leaves, tied with string or wrapped in muslin. It is added to stocks and soups for flavour and removed during straining.

Chilli paste A widely available fiery chilli mixture. Adjust amounts to suit your taste. Also called sambal oelek.

Chinese rice wine Chinese rice wine with a delicate fragrance and amber colour. Dry sherry can be substituted at a pinch. Also known as shao-hsing rice wine.

Chocolate When we cook with chocolate we usually use couverture. This chocolate, specially made for cooking, has a high cocoa fat content and less sugar than other chocolate. Dark chocolate is a pretty good substitute.

Chorizo Spanish air-cured sausage made with paprika.

Clarified butter Butter that has been melted and had milk solids removed. It has very good keeping qualities and will not burn during cooking. Also known as ghee.

Coconut milk and cream Made from grated coconut soaked in hot water. Coconut milk is lighter and thinner than coconut cream.

Cornichons Baby pickled cucumbers.

Couscous This staple of North African cooking comes in different grades. 'Instant' couscous only needs to be soaked in boiling water and then it's ready.

Dashi A Japanese ingredient made from bonito (fish) that's used as a base flavouring for soups.

Dukkah An Egyptian mixture consisting of roasted and crushed spices, nuts and sesame seeds.

Fish sauce A tangy, thin sauce made from salted fish. It's essential in many Asian cuisines and wonderful for adding a salty burst of flavour.

Gelatine A substance used to set desserts and puddings. Sheet gelatine is considerably better than powdered, and comes in various sheet sizes.

Ghee See clarified butter.

Grated ginger A 5 cm piece of fresh root ginger will produce 1 tsp grated ginger. Ginger graters (small, textured white ceramic 'plates') are available from Asian grocers.

Haloumi Cheese made from ewe's milk, usually salty and squeaky in texture.

Harissa A Tunisian chilli paste with a smoky flavour.

Kaffir lime leaves These leaves, with a pungent citrus flavour, are used whole in broths or finely shredded for salads and marinades. Each leaf has 2 oval sections. Search out fresh leaves from Asian grocers.

Kecap manis A thick, sweet Indonesian soy sauce that's widely available at all Asian grocery stores and larger supermarkets. You could substitute a combination of soy sauce and sugar.

Lebanese cucumber Short, thin cucumbers.

Liquid glucose Used when cooking sugar, available from chemists or cake decorating shops.

Mascarpone Fresh Italian cheese with a rich sour-cream flavour.

Mirin Sweetened Japanese sake used for cooking.

Miso paste A Japanese paste made from soybeans. Yellow, red or brown miso pastes are most commonly used to form the base of soups and entrees.

Mograbieh Large couscous available from good food shops and Middle Eastern shops. Requires up to 30 minutes' cooking time.

Nori sheets Sheets of dried seaweed that is essential in Japanese cooking, particularly in making California rolls.

Palm sugar Sugar made from the sap of palm trees and set into thick, dense cakes. It's best grated using the fine side of a grater, or one of those wonderful microplane graters, and is usually dissolved in an acidic liquid such as lemon juice or fish sauce.

Pancetta An Italian ham that's shaped like a fat sausage.

Paprika A powdered seasoning made from sweet red pepper. Smoky paprika is dried naturally over a wood fire, and comes in both sweet and spicy varieties.

Polenta Ground cornmeal much used in Italy to produce either a soft mixture to accompany stews or firm blocks to be grilled or pan-fried.

Pomegranate syrup A thick, bittersweet fruit syrup available from Middle Eastern grocery stores.

Prosciutto A salted, air-dried ham which adds a salty bacon flavour to dishes. Also known as Parma ham.

Rice flour Finely ground rice used to make shortbread and other biscuits.

Rice vinegar A Japanese vinegar. Make sure you purchase pure rice vinegar, not flavoured 'sushi vinegar'.

Rosewater Rose-scented liquid from the Middle East. Available at good delicatessens and Middle Eastern grocery stores.

Saffron Saffron is one of the world's most expensive spices, with each thread coming from the centre of the crocus flower. Luckily, only a few threads are needed to enjoy saffron's aroma and flavour.

Seasoned flour A little salt and pepper is added to flour to coat meats before cooking or crumbing.

Sesame oil A rich aromatic oil made from roasted sesame seeds. Only a small amount is needed to add flavour to dishes.

Shallots Small brown or red onion-shaped vegetables. Red shallots are used extensively in Asian cuisines, and have a flavour between garlic and onion.

Sichuan pepper The small red berries aren't actually a member of the pepper family, but they have a peppery taste. Best toasted before use. Also known as Szechwan pepper.

Sumac Ground red berries with a sweet flavour. Available from Middle Eastern grocery stores.

Tahini A paste made from sesame seeds. Available from Middle Eastern grocery stores or the health-food section of the supermarket.

Tamarind The pulp of the tamarind fruit, sold in clear plastic packets. Soak 60 g of the sour tamarind pulp in 250 ml (1 cup) boiling water. Strain and cool, then use the soaking liquid.

Tofu Soy milk set into firm blocks. Also called bean curd.

Tom yum A Thai paste that's usually used to make spicy soup and broths.

Truffle oil Oil infused with truffles, available from specialist Italian importers or delicatessens.

Vine leaves Usually purchased in brine. Soak in cold water for at least 30 minutes before using.

Wasabi A fiery lime-green paste extracted from the wasabi root, used extensively in Japanese cuisine.

Zaatar Traditionally made with wild thyme, sesame seeds and sumac, zaatar is used as a seasoning in many Middle Eastern dishes.

References + inspirations

We are inspired by the many books below, as well as countless meals in restaurants and at the dining tables of home cooks who have welcomed us. Our sincere thanks to all.

Alexander, Stephanie. *The Cook's Companion*. Viking, Ringwood, 1996.
Beck, Simone, Bertholle, Louisette and Child, Julia. *Mastering the Art of French Cooking* (Vols 1 and 2). Penguin, Harmondsworth, 1973.
Boetz, Martin. *Longrain*. Hardie Grant Books, South Yarra, 2003.
Brissenden, Rosemary. *South East Asian Food*. Penguin, Ringwood, 1996.
Ceserani, Victor and Kinton, Ronald. *Practical Cookery*. The Chaucer Press, London, 1983.
Dupleix, Jill. *Old Food*. Allen & Unwin, St Leonards, 1998.
Freeman, Meera and Le, Van Nhan. *The Vietnamese Cookbook*. Viking, Ringwood, 1995.
Hazan, Marcella. *Marcella's Kitchen*. Macmillan, London, 1988.
Henry, Diana. *Crazy Water, Pickled Lemons*. Mitchell Beazley, London, 2002.
—*The Gastro Pub Cookbook*. Mitchell Beazley, London, 2003.
Johnson, Phillip. *Classic Ecco*. Murdoch Books, Sydney, 2000.
The Kitchen Handbook. Reader's Digest, Sydney, 1982.
Lawson, Nigella. *How to Be a Domestic Goddess*. Chatto & Windus, London, 2000.
Luard, Elisabeth. *European Peasant Cookery*. Corgi, London, 1988.
Manfield, Christine. *Spice*. Viking, Ringwood, 1999.
Passmore, Jacki. *Encyclopedia of Asian Food & Cooking*. Doubleday Books, Sydney, 1991.
Perry, Neil. *Simply Asian*. Viking, London, 2000.
Roden, Claudia. *A New Book of Middle Eastern Food*. Penguin, Harmondsworth, 1986.
Solomon, Charmaine. *Charmaine Solomon's Encyclopedia of Asian Food*. William Heinemann Australia, Port Melbourne, 1996.
—*Thai Cookbook*. Viking, Ringwood, 1989.
Thompson, David. *Classic Thai Cuisine*. Simon & Schuster, East Roseville, 1993.
What's Cooking in Japan. Kikkoman Corporation, Tokyo, 1993.

Some of the recipes in this book have appeared in our other books, too:
Campion and Curtis in the Kitchen. Hardie Grant Books, South Yarra, 2002.
Chilli Jam. Allen & Unwin, St Leonards, 1997.
Every Day Cooking. Hardie Grant Books, Prahran, 2006.
Every Day in the Kitchen. Hardie Grant Books, South Yarra, 2003.
Food with Friends. Hardie Grant Books, South Yarra, 2004.
Fresh. Purple Egg, Melbourne, 2001.
The Seasonal Produce Diary. Purple Egg, Melbourne, 1995–2000 and Hardie Grant Books, Prahran, 2005–2009.
Sizzle! Purple Egg, Melbourne, 2000.
Tucker for Tots. Lothian, Melbourne, 1996.

Acknowledgements

In the Kitchen has been many years in the making. You'd expect that of a recipe collection drawn from the best of our work since we began writing about food in 1993. The recipes within these pages were prepared for special occasions and family celebrations long past; they are everyday meals and family favourites. This book is a celebration of modern Australian cooking as we see it.

Acknowledgements have to go to the many food stylists, editors, book designers, photographers, typesetters and publishers who have been involved in the 30 books over the years. While there may be just two names on the cover of this book, there's a huge team of people required to make it come to fruition. Our biggest thanks go to Mary Small and the entire team at Hardie Grant Books, who have worked tirelessly to make *In the Kitchen* the best it can be.

Thanks also to family and friends, many of whom sampled our recipes in the development stage and gave us honest feedback. All of our recipes are better for it. Thanks also to those who donated their favourite recipes and allowed us to include them. We hope this book becomes an essential part of your kitchen, one you refer to often.

Index

A

Adult's rice pudding 681
Aioli 554
    Herb aioli 554
    Quince aioli 550
Allan's easy sponge cake 704
Allan's gravy 559
almonds
    Almond bread 774
    Almond cake 724
    Almond macaroons 769
    Almond nougat 794
    Almond pesto 551
    Almond skordalia 550
    Almond sweetcrust pastry 591
    Baby orange and almond cakes 711
    Blood plum and almond tart 631
    Cinnamon almond macaroons 769
    Peach and almond jam 581
    Pear and almond tart 631
    Pistachio, almond and orange-blossom baklava 637
    Raspberry, vanilla and almond slice 785
    Rich chocolate and almond cake 708
    Roasted apricot, ricotta and almond free-form tart 632
    Roasted peach, ricotta and almond free-form tart 632
    Sherry-soaked raisin and almond cake 721
    Toffee almond squares 783
    Vanilla and caramelised apricot slice 784
    Viennese plum slice 785
amaretti
    Baked peaches with amaretti biscuits 648
    Baked plums with amaretti biscuits 648
Amaretto-cherry cheesecake 737
American pork ribs 311
anchovies
    Anchovy dressing 504
    Tomato and anchovy tart 603
Anzac biscuits 767
apples
    Apple fruit cake 714
    Apple sauce 560
    Apple streusel crumble cake 719
    Apple tart 623
    Apple, fig and pecan cake 730
    Spiced apple and sour cream muffins 750
    Toffee apples 799

apricots
    Apricot and almond muesli 6
    Apricot and frangipane tart 621
    Apricot jam 581
    Apricot streusel crumble cake 719
    Raspberry, vanilla and almond slice 785
    Roasted apricot, ricotta and almond free-form tart 632
    Vanilla and caramelised apricot slice 784
Arancini 217
Artichoke, prosciutto and buffalo mozzarella parcels 51
Asian chilli pork steaks 311
Asian coleslaw 517
Asian cucumber salsa 567
Asian lamb steaks 306
Asian marinade 292
Asian noodle salad 528
Asian pickles 580
Asian vegetables
    Chinese broccoli and garlic stir-fry 480
    Choy sum with ginger 480
    Simple bok choy salad 518
    Wok-fried Asian greens 499
asparagus
    Asparagus and broad bean mograbieh salad with barbecued salmon 541
    Asparagus and goat's cheese tart 595
    Asparagus quiche 596
    Asparagus soup 120
    Asparagus with feta 472
    Asparagus and green tea noodle salad with Thai prawns 540
    Asparagus with hollandaise sauce 472
    Asparagus with prosciutto 472
    Asparagus, almond and feta salad 516
    Chicken and asparagus risotto 205
    Smoked trout and asparagus cream sauce 168
    Spaghetti with smoked chicken and asparagus 168
    Thai prawn and asparagus curry 445
    Tuna, cannellini bean and asparagus salad 522
Autumn crumble 651
avocado
    Smoked trout and avocado salad 521
    Smoked trout and avocado toasts 106

B

Baba ghanoush 43
Baby orange and almond cakes 711
Baby pavlovas with banana and honeycomb 686
Baby spinach, bacon and crispy crouton salad 507
Baccala 57
Backyard plum jam 582
bacon
    Baby spinach, bacon and crispy crouton salad 507
    Bacon and eggs 20
    Broad bean and bacon pasta sauce 167
    Cabbage with bacon and apples 477
    Carbonara 160
    Corn fritters with crisp bacon and spiced tomatoes 34
    Egg and bacon pie 610
    Grilled tomatoes with basil butter and bacon 16
    Tomato sauce with bacon 163
Bahjis 68
Baked beans with smoky ham hock 36
Baked eggs with spinach and cheddar 26
Baked fish parcels with coconut milk and kaffir lime 287
Baked orange cheesecake 736
Baked peaches with amaretti biscuits 648
Baked plums with amaretti biscuits 648
Baked potatoes 490
baklava
    Pistachio, almond and orange-blossom baklava 637
bananas
    Banana and maple syrup muffins 750
    Banana and walnut cake 730
    Banana muffins 752
    Banana pikelets 12
    Banana, walnut and maple syrup muffins 750
    Gingerbread waffle cakes with honeycomb butter and banana 14
barbecues 290–1
    Barbecue baste 292
    Barbecue sauce 562
    Barbecued chermoula prawns 320
    Barbecued lime and chilli chicken wings 299
    Barbecued oysters 329
    Barbecued vegetable salad 519
Basic icing 702

Basic muffins 747
basil
    Basil and pine nut stuffed lamb 362
    Basil frittata with smoked salmon 29
    Basil pesto 551
    Eggplant, tomato and basil sauce 164
    Grilled tomatoes with basil butter and bacon 16
    Linguini with chilli, anchovies, breadcrumbs and basil 172
    Roasted roma tomatoes with feta and basil 498
    Spiced beef balls in basil leaves 304
    Thai basil pesto 552
    Tomato and basil salsa 565
    Tomato, bocconcini and basil salad 509
    Zucchini-flower, stuffed with feta and basil 64
beans, dried
    Baked beans with smoky ham hock 36
    Braised lamb with cannellini beans 403
    Cheesy bean and tomato pasta bake 184
    French roast lamb with haricot beans and green olive salsa 366
    Indian spiced beans 448
    Kidney bean and vegetable chilli 449
    Mediterranean bean stew with feta 420
    Mexican bean cakes with chilli salsa 332
    Tuna, cannellini bean and asparagus salad 522
    Tuscan bean risotto 211
    Tuscan bean stew 421
    see also chickpeas; lentils
beans, green
    Easy green beans 472
    Green bean, almond and feta salad 516
    Green beans with almonds 472
    Green beans with walnuts 472
    Prawn, roast tomato, green bean and egg salad 532
    see also broad beans
beans, snake
    Wok-fried snake beans 473
    Wok-fried snake beans with cashews 473
Bearnaise sauce 555
Bechamel sauce 556
beef
    Basic beef stew 394
    Beef and Guinness casserole with dumplings 396
    Beef and Guinness pie 401
    Beef and prune tagine 455
    Beef chow mein 235
    Beef goulash 399
    Beef pot-roast 360
    Beef rendang 435
    Beef salad with hot and sour flavours 544
    Beef stew with dumplings 394
    Beef stew with mushrooms 394
    Beef stock 116
    Beef stroganoff 264
    Beef, black bean and cashew nut stir-fry 227
    Bloody good beef curry 434
    Braised steak with onions 395
    Chilli beef and mushroom stir-fry 228
    Chilli beef stir-fry 228
    Chilli rump steak 302
    Chimichuri barbecued beef 305
    Classic beef and mushroom kebabs 303
    Corned beef 263
    Garlic confit with braised beef 400
    Hot and sour beef curry 436
    Indian beef curry 437
    Indian beef, spinach and potato curry 438
    Oriental beef 304
    Pan-fried steak with mushroom sauce 263
    Pinchito beef kebabs 303
    Pomegranate-glazed beef 358
    Roast beef with Yorkshire puddings 356
    Roast eye fillet with chilli and garlic marinade 358
    Roast rib of beef with potato gratin 357
    Roast sirloin with mustard and balsamic crust 359
    Savoury mince 265
    Sour and spicy beef braise 434
    Sour beef with lemongrass 230
    Spezzatino 398
    Spiced beef balls in basil leaves 304
    Steak with oven chips 262
    Sumac beef salad with lentils, grapes and parsley 543
    Swedish meatballs 266
    Teriyaki beef 226
    Thai beef salad 531
    Thai red beef and bok choy curry 433
    The perfect porterhouse 302
    Vietnamese beef and mint salad 535
    Vietnamese beef noodle salad 534
beer
    Deep-fried fish fillets in beer batter 281
beetroot
    Baked mushrooms with beetroot salad 88
    Beetroot dip 44
    Beetroot fattouche 515
    Beetroot relish 577
    Beetroot salad 514
    Beetroot salad with tomato and mozzarella 514
    Beetroot soup 129
    Beetroot, rocket and yoghurt salad 515
Beijing dumpling soup 147
berries
    Berry jam 581
    Berry pancakes 658
    Cherry berry pudding 654
    Meringues with berries 685
    Rosewater meringue stack with red summer berries 687
    Summer pudding 654
    Wobbly berry jelly 664
    see also blueberries; cranberries; raspberries; strawberries
Best soft polenta 192
Big brekkie 20
Bircher muesli 6
Birgit's easy mousse 655
Birgit's frikadella 265
Biscotti 767
biscuits 767–79
    Almond bread 774
    Anzac biscuits 767
    Biscotti 767
    Brandy snap baskets 775
    Brandy snaps 775
    Cheese bickies 779
    Chocolate drops 768
    Chocolate peanut cookies 777
    Chocolate vanilla drops 768
    Coconut biscuits 775
    Double chocolate chip and walnut cookies 776
    Double chocolate chip cookies 776
    Flapjacks 783
    Gingerbread hearts 772
    Gingernuts 772
    Goat's cheese biscuits 779
    Hazelnut and vanilla creams 772
    Hedgehog 782
    Lemon gems 768
    Mars bar slice 782
    Marzipan bars 792
    Millionaire's shortbread 780
    Mini rum and raisin garibaldi 774
    Muesli munchies 778
    Oatcakes 778
    Orange and walnut florentines 773
    Passionfruit yoyo biscuits 771
    Pistachio biscotti 767
    Raspberry jam drops 768
    Shortbread 770
    Silver darlings 768
    Snickerdoodles 770
    Spiced pecan cookies 777
    Toffee almond squares 783
    Viennese biscuits 769

see also macaroons
Bistella 618
Blinis 46
blood oranges *see* oranges
blue cheese
    Dates with blue cheese 54
    Gnocchi with blue cheese sauce 189
    Risotto with rocket and gorgonzola 210
    Roast pumpkin and blue cheese tart 598
    Rocket, fig, blue cheese and crispy prosciutto salad 508
blueberries
    Blueberry and coconut muffins 749
    Blueberry and mascarpone tart 628
    Blueberry friands 746
    Blueberry pikelets 12
Boil-and-bake fruit cake 714
bok choy
    Barbecue pork and bok choy stir-fry 230
    Chicken, bok choy and udon miso 146
    Simple bok choy salad 518
    Thai red beef and bok choy curry 433
bolognaise
    Beef and mushroom bolognaise 160
    Bolognaise pasta bake 184
    Quick-and-easy bolognaise 160
    Spicy bolognaise 160
Boreks 68
Bourbon sauce 572
braises
    Braised fennel 482
    Braised lamb chop 402
    Braised lamb with cannellini beans 403
    Braised pork belly with chorizo sausage 410
    Braised pork with star anise 408
    Braised rabbit with cider and rosemary 417
    Braised steak with onions 395
    Garlic confit with braised beef 400
    Sour and spicy beef braise 434
    Soy-braised chicken 393
    see also casseroles; stews
brandy
    Brandy custard 573
    Brandy orange butter 569
    Brandy snaps 775
    Brandy snap baskets 775
bread 150–5
    A great crusty loaf 152
    Bread rolls 151
    Bread sauce 560
    Focaccia 154
    Fruity soda bread 150
    Garlic focaccia 154

    Garlic naan 155
    Knot rolls 151
    Naan bread 155
    Olive focaccia 154
    Polenta bread 153
    Poppyseed rolls 151
    Rosemary focaccia 154
    Rosemary polenta bread 153
    Sesame seed rolls 151
    Soda bread 150
    Spice naan 155
    Square white loaf 151
    see also pizza
Bread and butter pudding 675
    Egyptian bread and butter pudding 636
    Panettone and raspberry pudding 675
breakfast
    Breakfast tarts 609
    Hangover breakfast 21
    The big breakfast 20
Brioche 757
broad beans
    Asparagus and broad bean mograbieh salad with barbecued salmon 541
    Broad bean and bacon pasta sauce 167
    Broad bean and crispy prosciutto soup 128
    Broad beans braised with pancetta 474
    Broad beans with extra-virgin olive oil 474
broccoli
    Broccoli frittata 24
    Broccoli with toasted pine nuts 474
    Chicken, broccoli and noodle stir-fry 225
    Chinese broccoli and garlic stir-fry 480
    Stir-fried broccolini with garlic 475
broths
    Italian spring vegetable and pasta broth 135
    Lamb shank, vegetable and barley broth 138
    Pan-fried salmon with chilli coriander udon broth 284
brownies
    Cheesecake brownies 740
    Chocolate brownies 741
Bruschetta 47
brussels sprouts
    Brussels sprouts with almonds and parsley 476
    Brussels sprouts with chestnuts 476
    Wok-fried brussels sprouts 475
buffalo mozzarella
    Buffalo mozzarella and cherry tomato sticks 50

    Prosciutto, buffalo mozzarella and artichoke parcels 51
buns
    Cheat's hot cross buns 759
    Chelsea buns 759
    Jam swirls 759
    Sticky cinnamon buns 760
    Sticky currant buns 758
    Sticky orange and currant buns 758
    Swiss buns 759
burgers
    Caramelised onion and chickpea burgers 333
    Danish beef burgers 259
    Haloumi and couscous burgers 331
    Lemony chicken and veal burgers 296
    Lentil and ricotta burgers 334
    Spiced green lentil burgers 330
Burghul-coated calamari 72
butter
    Brandy orange butter 569
    Crayfish with roasted red capsicum butter 321
    Honeycomb butter 14
    Lemon curd 585
    Microwave lemon curd 585
    Passionfruit curd 585
Butter icing 702
butterscotch
    Butterscotch sauce 572
    Espresso semifreddo with butterscotch sauce 696
    White chocolate and butterscotch mousse cake 657

C

cabbage
    Cabbage with bacon and apples 477
    Red cabbage with sweet and sour flavours 476
caesar salads
Caesar dressing 504
    Caesar salad 511
    Cheat's caesar dressing 504
cakes
    Allan's easy sponge cake 704
    Almond cake 724
    Apple fruit cake 714
    Apple streusel crumble cake 719
    Apple, fig and pecan cake 730
    Apricot streusel crumble cake 719
    Baby orange and almond cakes 711
    Banana and walnut cake 730
    Boil-and-bake fruit cake 714
    Carrot cake 731
    Carrot, cardamom and cashew cake 731
    Chadwick family Christmas cake 717
    Choc chip pound cake 709
    Chocolate and cardamom fudge cake 710

Chocolate and coconut cake 709
Chocolate fudge cake 706
Chocolate ripple log 710
Cinnamon and lemon tea cake 728
Coconut cake 729
Date and coconut loaf 732
Elizabeth's hiking cake 718
Fig or date fruit cake 714
Frozen nougat ice-cream cake 690
Gingerbread cake 729
Green cake 727
Lemon and poppyseed tea cake 728
Lemon and walnut cake 713
Lemon sour cream cake 726
Lemon tea cake 728
Linzertorte made easy 734
One-pot chocolate cake 705
Orange and yoghurt syrup cake 725
Orange marmalade cake 724
Orange poppyseed cake 725
Orange tea cake 728
Passionfruit ring cake 713
Passionfruit roulade 712
Passionfruit sponge cake 704
Pecan coffee cake 733
Plum cake 733
Pumpkin cake 732
Rhubarb lemon cake 722
Rich chocolate and almond cake 708
Rich chocolate and hazelnut cake 708
Sherry-soaked raisin and almond cake 721
Sicilian orange cake with marmalade cream 711
Spiced Italian fruit cake 716
Tiramisu cake 661
Upside-down pear and ginger cake 723
see also brownies; cheesecakes; friands; lamingtons; slices

calamari
    Burghul-coated calamari 72
    Calamari with soy and chilli glaze 238
    Deep-fried Thai calamari 71
    Pan-fried calamari 71
    Seared calamari with chilli and balsamic dressing 105
California rolls 55
calzone, Roasted vegetable 249
Caponata 482
capsicums
    Capsicum relish 577
    Chicken casserole with red capsicum 384
    Crayfish with roasted red capsicum butter 321
    Moroccan eggplant and capsicum kebabs 330
    Roast capsicum soup 122
    Roasted capsicum and tomato sauce 561
    Tomato and roast capsicum salad 510
    Tomato sauce with roasted capsicum 162
caramel
    Caramel oranges 652
    Caramel popcorn 798
    Caramel sauce 570
    Caramel slice 780
    Crème caramel 653
    Poached pears with chocolate sauce and caramel cream 647
    Robyn's caramel, macadamia and hazelnut slice 789
Caramelised onion and chickpea burgers 333
Carbonara 160
cardamom
    Cardamom panna cotta 662
    Cardamom spiced wafers 773
    Carrot, cardamom and cashew cake 731
    Chocolate and cardamom fudge cake 710
    Coffee and cardamom mousse 656
    Roast duck with orange and cardamom caramel sauce 375
Caribbean fish marinade 294
Caroline's (vodka and blood orange) jelly 665
carrots
    Carrot and coriander soup 125
    Carrot cake 731
    Carrot, cardamom and cashew cake 731
    Carrots with butter and sugar glaze 477
    Honey and zaatar carrot salad 522
    Middle Eastern carrot salad 523
    Roast carrots 478
casseroles
    Beef and Guinness casserole with dumplings 396
    Chicken casserole with mushrooms 384
    Chicken casserole with red capsicum 384
    Chicken casserole with wine 384
    Chickpea and vegetable casserole 421
    French chicken casserole 386
    Hungarian chicken casserole 389
    Mediterranean chicken casserole 385
    Mediterranean fish stew 418
    Rabbit casserole 416
    Seafood casserole with saffron and cream 418
    Simple chicken casserole 384
    see also braises; stews
Cassoulet 412
Catalan chicken 387
Catalan potatoes 492

cauliflower
    Cauliflower cheese 479
    Cauliflower polpetti 60
    Cauliflower, chilli and coconut soup 124
    Roast cauliflower 478
    Stir-fried cauliflower 479
Cevapcici 317
Chadwick family Christmas cake 717
Champ 489
Cheat's caesar dressing 504
Cheat's hot cross buns 759
cheese
    Cauliflower cheese 479
    Cheese and potato pies 614
    Cheese and zaatar kataifi parcels 67
    Cheese bickies 779
    Cheese sauce 557
    Cheesy bean and tomato pasta bake 184
    Cheesy choux puffs 617
    Cheesy wedgies 193
    Macaroni cheese 181
    Risotto of chicken, mushroom and taleggio cheese 206
    Roast vegetable and goat's cheese lasagne 186
    Spanakopita 617
    Spicy cheddar muffins 755
    see also blue cheese; goat's cheese
cheesecakes
    Amaretto-cherry cheesecake 737
    Baked orange cheesecake 736
    Cheesecake brownies 740
    Cherry cheesecake 735
    Chocolate cheesecake muffins 751
    Lemon cheesecake 734
    My kind of cheesecake 736
    Passionfruit cheesecake 736
    Pedro Ximenez cheesecake with boozy prunes 739
    Raspberry cheesecake 735
    Raspberry ripple cheesecake 738
    White chocolate cheesecake 740
Chelsea buns 759
chermoula
    Barbecued chermoula prawns 320
    Chermoula chicken 344
    Chermoula prawns 70
cherries
    Amaretto-cherry cheesecake 737
    Cherry berry pudding 654
    Cherry cheesecake 735
    Cherry clafoutis 652
    Duck confit with cherry and verjuice sauce 378
Cherry tomato and buffalo mozzarella sticks 50
chestnuts
    Brussels sprouts with chestnuts 476

Chestnut creams with rich chocolate sauce 667
Chestnut stuffing 342
Chestnuts roasted with jamon 49
Troffiette with chestnuts and smoked ham hock 176

chicken
- Barbecued lime and chilli chicken wings 299
- Catalan chicken 387
- Cheesy schnitzel 252
- Chermoula chicken 344
- Chicken and asparagus risotto 205
- Chicken and corn soup 132
- Chicken and mushroom pie 390
- Chicken and mushroom risotto 205
- Chicken and pea risotto 205
- Chicken and pistachio dolmades 66
- Chicken and veal polpettini 259
- Chicken and vegetable pasties 613
- Chicken bistella 618
- Chicken casserole with mushrooms 384
- Chicken casserole with red capsicum 384
- Chicken casserole with wine 384
- Chicken chow mein 235
- Chicken drumsticks with Italian flavours 255
- Chicken fajitas 254
- Chicken fillets poached in soy and star anise 256
- Chicken laksa 143
- Chicken liver pate 56
- Chicken noodle soup 132
- Chicken nuggets 252
- Chicken pandan parcels 75
- Chicken parmigiano 252
- Chicken pilaf 201
- Chicken saltimbocca 251
- Chicken saltimbocca skewers 299
- Chicken satay kebabs 300
- Chicken schnitzel 252
- Chicken stock 117
- Chicken tagine with mushrooms, chorizo and sherry 454
- Chicken tandoori in naan bread 300
- Chicken, almond and harissa pilaf 201
- Chicken, black bean and noodle stir-fry 225
- Chicken, broccoli and noodle stir-fry 225
- Chicken, cashew and noodle stir-fry 225
- Chicken, ginger and noodle stir-fry 225
- Chicken, mushroom and olive sauce 169
- Chicken, oyster sauce and noodle stir-fry 225
- Chicken, sultana and sweet spice pilaf 204

Chinese chicken noodle soup 132
Coconut chicken and noodle salad 531
Coconut chilli chicken curry 430
French chicken casserole 386
Hungarian chicken casserole 389
Indian chicken curry 429
Indian chicken, potato and spinach curry 429
Indian spiced schnitzel 252
Indonesian marinated baby chickens 312
Lemon and herb schnitzel 252
Lemon chicken polpettini 260
Lemon spice chicken 296
Lemony chicken and veal burgers 296
Luke's favourite chicken dinner 253
Malaysian chicken curry 431
Mediterranean chicken casserole 385
Moorish chicken skewers 298
Moroccan chicken pie 392
Moroccan chicken rolls 608
Moroccan chicken salad 525
Moroccan chicken with tomato saffron jam 456
Moroccan chicken with tomatoes and olives 391
Oriental roast chicken 345
Pan-fried herb chicken fillets 250
Pan-fried chicken with mushroom sauce 250
Paper-wrapped chicken 74
Piri-piri chicken 301
Risotto of chicken, mushroom and taleggio cheese 206
Roast chicken 344
Sichuan chicken and fungi salad 92
Sichuan chicken salad 529
Simple chicken casserole 384
Southern fried chicken 255
Soy-braised chicken 393
Spaghetti with braised chicken meatballs in tomato sugo 182
Spaghetti with smoked chicken and asparagus 168
Spiced coriander and yoghurt chicken 256
Spicy lip-smacking drumsticks 298
Spring Spanish rice with chicken, peas and lemon 220
Steamed ginger chicken 258
Teriyaki chicken udon stir-fry for Mia 226
Thai chicken balls 260
Thai chicken salad 531
Thai green chicken and cashew curry 428
Thai green chicken and spinach curry 428
Thai red chicken curry 428
Veal schnitzel 252
Vietnamese chicken and mint salad 535

Vietnamese chicken noodle soup 132
Whole barbecued chicken with lemon and herbs 301
Yakitori chicken kebabs 326

chickpeas
- Caramelised onion and chickpea burgers 333
- Chickpea and vegetable casserole 421
- Chickpea, feta and coriander salad 520
- Chickpea, feta and rocket salad 520
- Indian chickpea and spinach curry 429
- Lamb, chickpea and saffron pilaf 204
- Lentil and chickpea salad 520
- Moroccan chickpea and pumpkin stew 462
- Nine-spiced roasted vegetables with chickpeas 379
- Potato, spinach and chickpea curry 447
- Pumpkin, chickpea and saffron pilaf 204
- Thai red roasted pumpkin, spinach and chickpea curry 446
- Tunisian vegetable and chickpea tagine 465

chilli
- Chilli and balsamic dressing 105
- Chilli and garlic marinade 293
- Chilli beef and mushroom stir-fry 228
- Chilli beef stir-fry 228
- Chilli crabs 324
- Chilli fish balls 69
- Chilli jam 578
- Chilli kangaroo stir-fry 228
- Chilli prawn balls 69
- Chilli rump steak 302
- Chilli salsa 565
- Chilli stir-fried vegetables with noodles 239
- Lime and chilli mayonnaise 554
- Sweet chilli sauce 578

Chimichuri barbecued beef 305
Chinese broccoli and garlic stir-fry 480
Chinese crispy-skin chicken 347
Chinese dressing 505
Chinese roast duck 374
Chinese twice-cooked pork spare ribs 274

chocolate
- Bitter chocolate tarts 624
- Chestnut creams with rich chocolate sauce 667
- Choc chip pound cake 709
- Chocolate and cardamom fudge cake 710
- Chocolate and coconut cake 709
- Chocolate and hazelnut panforte 715
- Chocolate and pear tart 630
- Chocolate and peppermint self-saucing pudding 672
- Chocolate and walnut pudding 672
- Chocolate brandy mousse 656
- Chocolate brandy sauce 571

Chocolate brownies 741
Chocolate cheesecake muffins 751
Chocolate coffee mousse 656
Chocolate crackles 798
Chocolate drops 768
Chocolate eclairs 636
Chocolate fudge cake 706
Chocolate fudge icing 703
Chocolate ganache 702
Chocolate hazelnut nougat 794
Chocolate ice-cream 689
Chocolate icing 702
Chocolate macaroons 769
Chocolate meringue discs 685
Chocolate meringues 685
Chocolate mousse 656
Chocolate mousse and meringue stack 685
Chocolate muffins 747
Chocolate peanut cookies 777
Chocolate rice pudding 681
Chocolate ripple log 710
Chocolate sauce 571
Chocolate self-saucing pudding 672
Chocolate soufflé 659
Chocolate truffles 795
Chocolate vanilla drops 768
Chocolate-coated honeycomb 795
Double chocolate chip and walnut cookies 776
Double chocolate chip cookies 776
Flourless chocolate muffins 754
Frozen chocolate mousse 656
Jaffa mousse 656
Mars Bar slice 782
Moroccan rocky road 796
One-pot chocolate cake 705
Poached pears with chocolate sauce and caramel cream 647
Profiteroles with white chocolate and raspberries 635
Rich chocolate and almond cake 708
Rich chocolate and hazelnut cake 708
Rich chocolate puddings 668
Risotto of chocolate and nougat 683
Rocky road 796
Steamed chocolate pudding 671
Triple chocolate muffins 748
see also white chocolate
chorizo
   Braised pork belly with chorizo sausage 410
   Chicken tagine with mushrooms, chorizo and sherry 454
   Mediterranean eggs with tomato and chorizo 32
   Mussels with tomato, chorizo and couscous 101
   Roast potatoes with chorizo, chilli and coriander 493
Choux pastry 594

Choy sum with ginger 480
chowder
   Fish and fennel chowder 141
   Sweetcorn chowder 141
Christmas
   Australian Christmas pudding 674
   Chadwick family Christmas cake 717
   Christmas cake ice-cream 689
   Christmas nougat 794
   Christmas pudding 674
   Christmas roast turkey with all the trimmings 354
   Christmas trifle 677
   White Christmas 793
chutney
   Mango chutney 576
   see also relish
cinnamon
   Cinnamon almond macaroons 769
   Cinnamon and lemon tea cake 728
   Cinnamon rhubarb crumble 650
   Cinnamon scones 756
   Rhubarb, cinnamon and yoghurt muffins 749
   Sticky cinnamon buns 760
Classic beef and mushroom kebabs 303
Classic mushroom sauce 557
Classic salad dressing 504
Classic tomato soup 122
coconut
   Blueberry and coconut muffins 749
   Chocolate and coconut cake 709
   Coconut biscuits 775
   Coconut cake 729
   Coconut caramel sauce 570
   Coconut chicken and noodle salad 531
   Coconut chilli chicken curry 430
   Coconut frosting 703
   Coconut ice 794
   Coconut macaroons 769
   Coconut panna cotta with spiced quinces 663
   Coconut rice 198
   Coconut spiced prawn kebabs 322
   Coconut wafers 771
   Date and coconut loaf 732
   Pan-fried fish with coconut curry sauce 280
   Raspberry coconut slice 786
   Self-saucing lemon and coconut pudding 670
coffee
   Coffee and cardamom mousse 656
   Coffee and walnut muffins 753
   Coffee icing 702
   Coffee panna cotta 662
   Espresso semifreddo with butterscotch sauce 696
   Pecan coffee cake 733

confit
   Duck confit 378
   Duck confit with cherry and verjuice sauce 378
conserves
   Cranberry and pear conserve 583
   Pumpkin conserve 584
   see also jams; marmalades
coriander
   Chickpea, feta and coriander salad 520
   Coriander pesto 551
   Coriander relish 566
   Coriander-cured salmon 108
   Deep-fried eggs with sweet chilli, coriander and lime sauce 27
   Eggplant, pine nut and coriander salad 521
   Green chilli and coriander steamed mussels 95
   Lime coriander lamb cutlets 308
   Pine nut and coriander couscous 453
   Pumpkin and coriander soup 124
   Roast duck with chilli and coriander rolls 79
   Roast potatoes with chorizo, chilli and coriander 493
   Roast tomato and coriander soup with coriander pesto 121
   Spiced coriander and yoghurt chicken 256
corn
   Barbecued corn cobs 481
   Corn fritters with crisp bacon and spiced tomatoes 34
   Creamy corn soup 128
   Sweetcorn and ricotta hotcakes with smoked salmon 31
   Thai corn fritters 62
Corned beef 263
Country pork, veal and pistachio terrine 58
couscous
   Asparagus and broad bean mograbieh salad with barbecued salmon 541
   Haloumi and couscous burgers 331
   Herb couscous 453
   Moroccan couscous salad 525
   Moroccan spiced breakfast couscous 7
   Mussels with chorizo, tomato and couscous 101
   Pine nut and coriander couscous 453
   Quick couscous 453
   Saffron couscous 453
   Spiced couscous 453
crab
   Chilli crabs 324
   Crab cakes with Thai cucumber salad 103

Crab, blood orange and panzanella salad 538
Egg nets with crab noodle salad 91
Spaghetti with blue-swimmer crab, fennel and tomato 180
Stir-fried with black beans and ginger 104

cranberries
  Cranberry and pear conserve 583
  Roast turkey breast with cranberry, walnut and orange stuffing 355

Crayfish with roasted red capsicum butter 321
Cream cheese frosting 702
Cream cheese pastry 592
Creamy corn soup 128
Creamy mushroom sauce 558
Crème caramel 653
Crispy duck with spiced plum sauce 377
Crispy skin fish with spring onions 281
Crispy-skin quail with Sichuan pepper and salt 111
Crispy stuffed mushrooms 59
Croque monsieur 16
Crostini 46
Croutons 148

crumbles 650
  Apple and rhubarb crumble tart 625
  Apple streusel crumble cake 719
  Apricot streusel crumble cake 719
  Autumn crumble 651
  Cinnamon rhubarb crumble 650
  Nutty rhubarb crumble 650
  Rhubarb crumble 650
  Rhubarb oat crumble 650

Cumquat jelly 584
Cupcakes 744
  Killer cupcakes 743

curd
  Lemon curd 585
  Passionfruit curd 585
  Microwave lemon curd 585

Curried parsnip soup 129

curries
  Beef rendang 435
  Bloody good beef curry 434
  Coconut chilli chicken curry 430
  Fish curry 445
  Fragrant vegetable curry 450
  Hot and sour beef curry 436
  Indian beef curry 437
  Indian beef, spinach and potato curry 438
  Indian chicken curry 429
  Indian chicken, potato and spinach curry 429
  Indian chickpea and spinach curry 429
  Indian lamb, spinach and potato curry 438
  Indian spiced beans 448
  Indian vegetable curry 429
  Kidney bean and vegetable chilli 449
  Lentil dhal 448
  Malaysian chicken curry 431
  Malaysian fish curry 443
  Potato, spinach and chickpea curry 447
  Quick Thai fish curry 444
  Red curry of duck 442
  Sweet potato and cashew nut curry 451
  Thai green chicken and cashew curry 428
  Thai green chicken and spinach curry 428
  Thai prawn and asparagus curry 445
  Thai red beef and bok choy curry 433
  Thai red chicken curry 428
  Thai red fish curry 433
  Thai red roasted pumpkin, spinach and chickpea curry 446

curry pastes
  Green Thai curry paste 426
  Red Thai curry paste 426
  Rendang curry paste 427

custards
  Brandy custard 573
  Muscat custard 573
  Thick custard 573
  Thin custard 573

D

Danish beef burgers 259

dates
  Date and coconut loaf 732
  Date scones 756
  Dates with blue cheese 54
  Fig or date fruit cake 714
  Self-saucing sticky date and pecan pudding 673

Deep-fried eggs with sweet chilli, coriander and lime sauce 27

dips
  Baba ghanoush 43
  Beetroot 44
  Guacamole 45
  Hummus 44
  White bean 45

dolmades
  Chicken and pistachio dolmades 66
  Lamb and mint dolmades 66

Double chocolate chip cookies 776
Doughnuts 761
  'Doughnut' muffins 753
  Jam doughnut muffins 753

dressings
  Anchovy dressing 504
  Caesar dressing 504
  Cheat's caesar dressing 504
  Chilli and balsamic with seared calamari 105
  Chinese dressing 505
  Classic salad dressing 504
  Lemon dressing 504
  Lime dressing 110
  Mirin dressing 505
  Miso dressing 505
  Nahm jim dressing 504
  Pan-fried fish with yellow miso dressing 282
  Pomegranate dressing 504
  Steamed fish with yellow miso dressing 282
  Thai dressing 505
  Yoghurt dressing 505

duck
  Barbecue duck and hokkien noodles 231
  Cassoulet 412
  Chinese roast duck 374
  Crispy duck with spiced plum sauce 377
  Duck and macadamia wonton soup 147
  Duck and pine mushroom bread soup 133
  Duck confit 378
  Duck confit with cherry and verjuice sauce 378
  Duck liver pate 56
  Duck stock 117
  Japanese glazed duck 313
  Peking duck and hoisin rice-paper rolls 80
  Pomegranate and sumac glazed duck 313
  Red curry of duck 442
  Rich duck sauce 165
  Roast duck 374
  Roast duck with chilli and coriander rolls 79
  Roast duck with orange and cardamom caramel sauce 375
  Sumac and pomegranate roast duck 374

Dukkah 48
  Dukkah potato wedges 490

dumplings
  Beef and Guinness casserole with dumplings 396
  Beef stew with dumplings 394
  Horseradish dumplings 395

E

Easy green beans 472

eggplant
  Caponata 482
  Eggplant and feta rolls 52
  Eggplant and root vegetable tagine 436
  Eggplant, pine nut and coriander salad 521
  Eggplant, tomato and basil sauce 164

Moroccan eggplant and capsicum kebabs 330
Roasted eggplant risotto cakes 217
Sichuan eggplant 481
Spiced eggplant parcels 612
eggs
  Baked eggs with spinach and cheddar 26
  Deep-fried eggs with sweet chilli, coriander and lime sauce 27
  Egg nets with crab noodle salad 91
  Egg nets with noodle and herb salad 91
  Egg nets with prawn noodle salad 91
  Eggs and bacon 20
  Eggs Benedict 19
  Eggs Florentine 19
  Egyptian spiced eggs 30
  Mediterranean eggs with tomato and chorizo 32
  Poached eggs 18
  Prawn, roast tomato, green bean and egg salad 532
  Scrambled eggs 19
Egyptian bread and butter pudding 636
Egyptian spiced eggs 30
Elizabeth's hiking cake 718
Espresso semifreddo with butterscotch sauce 696

F

Fajitas 254
fattouche
  Tunisian prawn fattouche 94
fennel
  Blood orange and fennel salad 510
  Braised fennel 482
  Fennel fritters 483
  Fennel relish 566
  Tomato and fennel soup 120
feta
  Asparagus with feta 472
  Asparagus, almond and feta salad 516
  Chickpea, feta and coriander salad 520
  Eggplant and feta rolls 52
  Green bean, almond and feta salad 516
  Mediterranean bean stew with feta 420
  Olive, prosciutto and feta slice 605
  Roast pumpkin, feta and pine nut puff slice 606
  Roast pumpkin and feta frittata 24
  Roast pumpkin, feta and pine nut risotto 215
  Roast pumpkin, feta, olive and spinach salad 523
  Roasted roma tomatoes with feta and basil 498
  Zucchini and feta fritters 35
  Zucchini-flower fritters stuffed with feta 64
figs
  Apple, fig and pecan cake 730
  Fig and ginger jam 582
  Fig jam 582
  Fig or date fruit cake 714
  Olive, fig and goat's cheese slice 607
  Rocket, fig, blue cheese and crispy prosciutto salad 508
fish
  Baked fish parcels with coconut milk and kaffir lime 287
  Barbecued whole fish 328
  Barbecued whole snapper in banana leaves 319
  Caribbean fish marinade 294
  Crispy skinned fish with spring onions 281
  Deep-fried fish fillets in beer batter 281
  Fish curry 445
  Fish fingers 279
  Fish stock 119
  Malaysian fish curry 443
  Mediterranean fish stew 418
  Moroccan fish stew 420
  Pan-fried blue eye with harissa lentils 462
  Pan-fried fish fillets 279
  Pan-fried fish with coconut curry sauce 280
  Pan-fried fish with yellow miso dressing 282
  Quick Thai fish curry 444
  Salt and pepper sardines 328
  Seafood casserole with saffron and cream 418
  Seven-spice fish fillets 280
  Simple barbecued fish 317
  Steamed fish with yellow miso dressing 282
  Steamed Thai fish 286
  Thai fish cakes 318
  Thai red fish curry 433
  see also salmon; swordfish
Flapjacks 783
Florentines
  Orange and walnut Florentines 773
Flourless chocolate muffins 754
Flourless white chocolate and raspberry muffins 754
Focaccia 154
Free-form fruit pie 626
French chicken casserole 386
French onion soup 134
French roast lamb with haricot beans and green olive salsa 366
French toast sandwiches filled with chocolate 13
Friands 746
  Blueberry friands 746
  Hazelnut friands 746
  Orange and poppyseed friands 746
  Raspberry friands 746
Fried tofu with cellophane noodles, shiitake and cashews 241
Frikadella 265
frittata
  Basil frittata with smoked salmon 29
  Broccoli frittata 24
  Cherry tomato and parmigiano frittata 24
  Prosciutto and olive frittata 24
  Roast pumpkin and feta frittata 24
  Roast vegetable frittata 24
fritters
  Corn fritters with bacon and spiced tomatoes 34
  Spinach and haloumi fritters 61
  Thai corn fritters 62
  Zucchini and feta fritters 35
  Zucchini-flower fritters stuffed with feta and basil 64
frosting
  Coconut frosting 703
  Cream cheese frosting 702
  Maple syrup frosting 703
  White chocolate frosting 703
Frozen chocolate mousse 656
nougat
  Chocolate and chestnut frozen nougat 690
  Frozen nougat 690
  Frozen nougat ice-cream cake 690
  Liquorice frozen nougat 690
fruit
  Free-form fruit pie 626
  Fruit compote 8
  Fruit mince pies 628
  Spiced roasted stone fruit 646
  Sugar-grilled stone fruit 646
  Sugar-roasted stone fruit with fresh cheese and honey 646
  Winter fruit compote 9
Fruity polenta slice 788
Fruity soda bread 150

G

Game stock 116
ganache
  Chocolate ganache 702
  White chocolate ganache 702
garlic
  Garlic and fennel olives 49
  Garlic and rosemary roast lamb 361
  Garlic confit with braised beef 400
  Pot-roasted chicken with 40 cloves of garlic 352
Gazpacho soup 140
ginger
  Chicken, ginger and noodle stir-fry 225

Choy sum with ginger 480
Ginger mirin salmon 324
Ginger parkin with spiced cream 676
Ginger slice 790
Gingerbread waffle cakes with honeycomb butter and banana 14
Gingernuts 776
Parsnip, lemon and ginger soup 129
Pickled ginger 580
Soy and ginger salmon kebabs 325
Steamed ginger chicken 258
Stir-fried crabs with black beans and ginger 104
Sweet potato and ginger soup 124
Tofu and ginger stir-fry 242
Upside-down pear and ginger cake 723
Gingerbread cake 729
Gingerbread hearts 772
gnocchi
Gnocchi with blue cheese 189
Goat's cheese gnocchi 187
Potato gnocchi 187
Roast tomato, pancetta and sweet onions with gnocchi 189
Semolina gnocchi 188
goat's cheese
Asparagus and goat's cheese tart 595
Goat's cheese biscuits 779
Goat's cheese gnocchi 187
Goat's cheese sauce 557
Goat's cheese souffle 86
Linguini with roasted pumpkin, spinach and goat's cheese 175
Mashed potatoes with goat's cheese 489
Olive, fig and goat's cheese slice 607
Potato, rosemary and goat's cheese tarts 606
Roast vegetable and goat's cheese lasagne 186
Roast vegetable, brown rice and goat's cheese salad 526
Twice-cooked goat's cheese souffle 87
see also blue cheese; cheese
Goose-fat roast potatoes 489
goulash
Beef goulash 399
Grand Marnier truffles 795
granita
Watermelon granita with summer fruit 692
gravy
Allan's gravy 559
Red wine onion gravy 558
Turkey gravy 559
White wine onion gravy 558
Greek leg of lamb 309
Greek salad 506
Green cake 727

Green chilli and coriander steamed mussels 95
Green salad 506
Guacamole 45
Guinness
Beef and Guinness casserole with dumplings 396
Beef and Guinness pie 401
Gyoza 75

H

haloumi
Grilled haloumi in vine leaves 51
Haloumi and couscous burgers 331
Haloumi and potato cakes with smoked salmon 35
Haloumi, olive and onion tart 597
Spinach and haloumi fritters 61
Ham and tomato omelette 22
ham hock
Lentil and ham hock soup 137
Smoky ham hock with baked beans 36
Troffiette with chestnuts and smoked ham hock 176
Hangover breakfast 21
harissa
Braised lamb shanks with mint and harissa 406
Chicken, almond and harissa pilaf 201
Harissa pork 310
Oysters with jamon and harissa 73
Pan-fried blue eye with harissa lentils 462
hazelnut
Chocolate and hazelnut panforte 715
Chocolate hazelnut nougat 794
Hazelnut and vanilla creams 772
Hazelnut friands 746
Hazelnut ice-cream 689
Rich chocolate and hazelnut cake 708
Robyn's caramel, macadamia and hazelnut slice 789
Hedgehog 782
herbs
Eggs nets with noodle and herb salad 91
Herb aioli 554
Herb couscous 453
Herb scrambled eggs 19
Herby baby chicken with rocket and red onion salad 348
Italian herb and salt rub 343
Lemon and herb schnitzel 252
Lemon, herb and almond stuffing 341
Mushrooms with fresh herbs 485
Polenta herb muffins 755
Stuffed leg of lamb with zaatar, preserved lemon and herbs 365
Whole barbecued chicken with lemon and herbs 301

Hoisin chicken 346
hollandaise
Asparagus with hollandaise sauce 472
Hollandaise sauce 555
honey
Grilled peaches with goat's curd and honey 8
Honey and zaatar carrot salad 522
Honey joys 798
Honey roast pork with stir-fried noodles 233
Roast parsnips with Worcestershire sauce and honey 487
Sichuan pepper and honey pork fillet 312
Honeycomb 795
Baby pavlovas with banana and honeycomb 686
Chocolate-coated honeycomb 795
horseradish
Horseradish dumplings 395
Hot and sour beef curry 436
Hot and sour crispy salad with lime dressing 110
Hot and sour crispy salmon salad with lime dressing 110
Hot water pastry 595
hotcakes
Ricotta hotcakes with poached raspberries 10
Sweetcorn and ricotta hotcakes with smoked salmon 31
Hummus 44
Hungarian chicken casserole 389

I

ice-cream
Chocolate and chestnut frozen nougat 690
Chocolate ice-cream 689
Christmas cake ice-cream 689
Frozen nougat 690
Frozen nougat ice-cream cake 690
Hazelnut ice-cream 689
Liquorice frozen nougat 690
Moroccan rocky road ice-cream 697
Tiramisu ice-cream 694
Vanilla ice-cream 689
Zabaglione ice-cream 657
see also sorbet; granita
icing
Basic icing 702
Butter icing 702
Chocolate fudge icing 703
Chocolate icing 702
Coffee icing 702
Lemon icing 702
Orange icing 702
Passionfruit icing 702
Royal icing 703
see also ganache; frosting

Indian cooking
    Indian beef curry 437
    Indian beef, spinach and potato curry 438
    Indian chicken curry 429
    Indian chicken, potato and spinach curry 429
    Indian chickpea and spinach curry 429
    Indian lamb, spinach and potato curry 438
    Indian spice mix 293
    Indian spiced beans 448
    Indian vegetable curry 429
Indonesian marinated baby chickens 312
Italian cooking
    Chicken drumsticks with Italian flavours 255
    Italian herb and salt rub 343
    Italian spring vegetable and pasta broth 135
    Spiced Italian fruit cake 716

J

Jaffa mousse 656
jam
    Apricot jam 581
    Backyard plum jam 582
    Berry jam 581
    Fig and ginger jam 582
    Fig jam 582
    Jam doughnut muffins 753
    Jam swirls 759
    Jam-filled lamingtons 742
    Peach and almond jam 581
    Steamed jam or marmalade pudding 671
    see also marmalade; conserves
jamon
    Jamon with roasted chestnuts 49
    Oysters with jamon and harissa 73
Japanese glazed duck 313
jelly
    Caroline's (vodka and blood orange) jelly 665
    Cumquat jelly 584
    Jelly-topped panna cotta 662
    Wobbly berry jelly 664
Jerusalem artichoke puree 483

K

Kahlua
    Kahlua sauce 572
    Kahlua truffles 795
Kashmiri lamb 440
Kasoundi 576
Kataifi
    Kataifi cheese and zaatar parcels 67
    Kataifi nests with sweet labne and rosewater-poached rhubarb 639

Katsudon 276
kebabs
    Chicken satay kebabs 300
    Classic beef and mushroom kebabs 303
    Coconut spiced prawn kebabs 322
    Lebanese lamb kebabs 307
    Moroccan eggplant and capsicum kebabs 330
    Pinchito beef kebabs 303
    Pork shish kebabs 310
    Rosemary lamb kebabs 305
    Soy and ginger salmon kebabs 325
    Swordfish kebabs 319
    Yakitori chicken kebabs 326
Kidney bean and vegetable chilli 449
Killer cupcakes 743

L

laksa 143
    Chicken laksa 143
lamb
    Asian lamb steak 306
    Basil and pine nut stuffed lamb 362
    Braised lamb chops 402
    Braised lamb with cannellini beans 403
    Crumbed lamb chops 252
    French roast lamb with haricot beans and green olive salsa 366
    Garlic and rosemary roast lamb 361
    Greek leg of lamb 309
    Indian lamb, spinach and potato curry 438
    Kashmiri lamb 440
    Lamb and mint dolmades 66
    Lamb and quince tagine 458
    Lamb cutlets with red onions 267
    Lamb hot-pot 404
    Lamb kofta skewers 268
    Lamb navarin with root vegetables and rosemary 405
    Lamb shank, vegetable and barley broth 138
    Lamb souvlaki 307
    Lamb tagine 459
    Lamb topsides with roasted ratatouille 484
    Lamb, chickpea and saffron pilaf 204
    Lebanese lamb kebabs 307
    Lime coriander lamb cutlets 308
    Moorish lamb with quince glaze 272
    Moroccan lamb cutlets 306
    Moussaka 269
    Mustard roast lamb 361
    North African lamb 308
    Pesto roast lamb 361
    Rosemary lamb kebabs 305
    Sicilian lamb stew with pecorino 406
    Slow-cooked leg of lamb with lemon and oregano 402
    Slow-roasted lamb shoulder 363
    Spanish lamb stew 407
    Spiced lamb steaks 267
    Stuffed leg of lamb with zaatar, preserved lemon and herbs 365
    Tikka-yoghurt lamb chops 268
    Whole leg of lamb in spicy yoghurt sauce 441
Lamb shanks
    Braised lamb shanks with mint and harissa 406
    Tunisian lamb shanks 460
Lamingtons 742
    Jam-filled lamingtons 742
lasagne
    Beef lasagne 161
    Roast vegetable and goat's cheese lasagne 186
    Traditional lasagne 161
Lebanese lamb kebabs 307
leek
    Leek and cheese slice 605
    Leek and goat's cheese quiche 596
    Potato and leek soup 119
lemon
    Cinnamon and lemon tea cake 728
    Lemon and poppyseed tea cake 728
    Lemon and walnut cake 713
    Lemon butter sauce 555
    Lemon cheesecake 734
    Lemon chicken polpettini 260
    Lemon curd 585
    Lemon delicious pudding 670
    Lemon gems 768
    Lemon icing 702
    Lemon mayonnaise 554
    Lemon meringue tart 623
    Lemon mousse 655
    Lemon slice 793
    Lemon sour cream cake 726
    Lemon spice chicken 296
    Lemon syrup 567
    Lemon tart 622
    Lemon tea cake 728
    Lemon, herb and almond stuffing 341
    Lemony chicken and veal burgers 296
    Microwave lemon curd 585
    Passionfruit tart 622
    Preserved lemons 575
    Rhubarb lemon cake 722
    Self-saucing lemon and coconut pudding 670
    Steamed lemon pudding 671
    Whole barbecued chicken with lemon and herbs 301
lentils
    Barbecued pork sausage with spiced lentils 271
    Lentil and chickpea salad 520
    Lentil and ham hock soup 137
    Lentil and ricotta burgers 334
    Lentil balls with chilli and paprika 65

Lentil dhal 448
Moroccan eggplant and capsicum kebabs 330
Pan-fried blue eye with harissa lentils 462
Roast pumpkin and Moroccan lentil soup 130
Spiced green lentil burgers 330
Sumac beef salad with lentils, grapes and parsley 543

lime
Baked fish parcels with coconut milk and kaffir lime 287
Barbecued lime and chilli chicken wings 299
Deep-fried eggs with sweet chilli, coriander and lime sauce 27
Hot and sour crispy salad with lime dressing 110
Lime and chilli mayonnaise 554
Lime butter sauce 555
Lime coriander lamb cutlets 308
Lime panna cotta 662
Lime syrup 567

Limoncello
Baked peaches with limoncello cream 646
Nectarine and limoncello meringue slice 688
Raspberry and limoncello tart 630

Linguini with chilli, anchovies, breadcrumbs and basil 172
Linguini with roasted pumpkin, spinach and goat's cheese 175
Linzertorte made easy 734
Lion's head meatballs 275
Liquorice panna cotta 662
Luke's favourite chicken dinner 253
Luke's lemon and sugar pancakes 658
Lunchboxes 800–5

M

macaroons
Almond macaroons 769
Chocolate macaroons 769
Cinnamon almond macaroons 769
Coconut macaroons 769

macadamias
Robyn's caramel, macadamia and hazelnut slice 789

Malaysian cooking
Malaysian chicken curry 431
Malaysian curry prawns 70
Malaysian fish curry 443

Maltaise sauce 555

mangoes
Fresh mango salsa 565
Mango and orange-blossom trifle 680
Mango chutney 576

maple syrup
Banana and maple syrup muffins 750

Banana, walnut and maple syrup muffins 750
Maple syrup frosting 703
Steamed treacle or maple syrup pudding 671

marinades
Asian marinade 292
Barbecue baste 292
Caribbean fish marinade 294
Chilli and garlic marinade 293
Simple Moroccan blend 293
Soy and garlic marinade 293
Spicy Mexican marinade 293
Sweet sticky marinade 295
Ultimate barbecue marinade 292
Wine marinade 292

Marinated olives 575

marzipan
Cherry and marzipan tart 629
Marzipan bars 792

marmalade
Marmalade cream 569
Orange and yoghurt syrup cake 725
Orange marmalade 583
Orange marmalade cake 724
Orange poppyseed cake 725
Sicilian orange cake with marmalade cream 711
see also jams; conserves

Mars Bar slice 782
Master stock 118

mayonnaise
Lemon mayonnaise 554
Lime and chilli mayonnaise 554
Rocket mayonnaise 554
Tartare sauce 554
see also aioli

meatballs
Lion's head meatballs 275
Spaghetti with braised chicken meatballs in tomato sugo 182
Swedish meatballs 266
see also polpetti

Mediterranean bean stew with feta 420
Mediterranean chicken casserole 385
Mediterranean eggs with tomato and chorizo 32
Mediterranean fish stew 418

meringues
Baby pavlovas with banana and honeycomb 686
Baby pavs 684
Chocolate meringue discs 685
Chocolate meringues 685
Chocolate mousse and meringue stack 685
Lemon meringue tart 623
Meringues with berries 685
Nectarine and limoncello meringue slice 688

Pavlova 684
Rosewater meringue stack with red summer berries 687

Mexican bean cakes with chilli salsa 332
Middle Eastern carrot salad 523
Middle Eastern fruit and nut stuffing 343
Middle Eastern rice pudding 681
Millionaire's shortbread 780
Minestrone 133

mint
Braised lamb shanks with mint and harissa 406
Lamb and mint dolmades 66
Mint sauce 562
Minty pea mash 486
Moorish prawn and mint salad 93
Penne with prosciutto, peas and mint 167
Vietnamese beef and mint salad 535
Vietnamese chicken and mint salad 535
Vietnamese prawn and mint salad 535

Mirin dressing 505

miso
Chicken, bok choy and udon miso 146
Miso dressing 505
Miso with tofu 146
Pan-fried fish with yellow miso dressing 282
Steamed fish with yellow miso dressing 282
Udon soup with shiitake and roast duck 146

Moorish chicken skewers 298
Moorish lamb with quince glaze 272
Moorish prawn and mint salad 93
Morning glory muffins 752

Moroccan cooking
Moroccan chicken pie 392
Moroccan chicken rolls 608
Moroccan chicken salad 525
Moroccan chicken with tomato saffron jam 456
Moroccan chicken with tomatoes and olives 391
Moroccan chickpea and pumpkin stew 462
Moroccan couscous salad 525
Moroccan eggplant and capsicum kebabs 330
Moroccan fish stew 420
Moroccan lamb cutlets 306
Moroccan mussel and fennel salad 97
Moroccan roast turkey 351
Moroccan rocky road ice-cream 697
Moroccan spiced breakfast couscous 7

Moussaka 269

mousse
Birgit's easy mousse 655
Chocolate brandy mousse 656
Chocolate coffee mousse 656
Chocolate mousse 656

    Coffee and cardamom mousse 656
    Frozen chocolate mousse 656
    Jaffa mousse 656
    Lemon mousse 655
    Passionfruit mousse 655
    White chocolate and butterscotch mousse cake 657
    Zabaglione mousse 657
muesli
    Apple and hazelnut muesli 6
    Bircher muesli 6
    Date and walnut muesli 6
    Muesli munchies 778
    Munchie muesli slice 788
    Quick bircher muesli 6
muffins
    Banana and maple syrup muffins 750
    Banana muffins 752
    Banana, walnut and maple syrup muffins 750
    Basic muffins 747
    Blueberry and coconut muffins 749
    Chocolate cheesecake muffins 751
    Chocolate muffins 747
    Coffee and walnut muffins 753
    'Doughnut' muffins 753
    Flourless chocolate muffins 754
    Flourless white chocolate and raspberry muffins 754
    Jam doughnut muffins 753
    Morning glory muffins 752
    Peanut butter muffins 751
    Polenta herb muffins 755
    Raspberry and white chocolate muffins 748
    Rhubarb, cinnamon and yoghurt muffins 749
    Spiced apple and sour cream muffins 750
    Spicy cheddar muffins 755
    Triple chocolate muffins 748
Muscat custard 573
mushrooms
    Baked mushrooms with beetroot salad 88
    Beef stroganoff 264
    Chicken and mushroom pie 390
    Chicken and mushroom risotto 205
    Chicken tagine with mushrooms, chorizo and sherry 454
    Chilli beef and mushroom stir-fry 228
    Classic beef and mushroom kebabs 303
    Classic mushroom sauce 557
    Creamy mushroom sauce 558
    Crispy stuffed mushrooms 59
    Duck and pine mushroom bread soup 133
    Garlic mushrooms 484
    Lively mushroom salad 524
    Mushroom quiche 596
    Mushroom risotto cakes 217
    Mushroom risotto with truffle oil 213
    Mushroom soup 120
    Mushroom tart 601
    Mushrooms on toast 17
    Mushrooms with fresh herbs 485
    Orecchietti with rich mushroom sauce 170
    Pan-fried chicken with mushroom sauce 250
    Pan-fried mushrooms 484
    Pan-fried steak with mushroom sauce 263
    Porcini and truffle oil risotto 213
    Risotto of chicken, mushroom and taleggio cheese 206
    Roasted pork loin with porcini mushrooms and sherry 372
    Sichuan chicken and noodle salad 92
    Wild mushroom risotto 216
mussels
    … how to clean 96
    Moroccan mussels and fennel salad 97
    Mussels with chorizo, tomato and couscous 101
    Mussels with garlic 96
    Mussels with Thai broth 98
    Steamed mussels with green chilli and coriander 95
mustard
    Mustard roast lamb 361
    Mustard sauce 556
    Roast sirloin with mustard and balsamic crust 359
    Seed mustard 553
    Walnut and sage mustard 553
My kind of cheesecake 736

N

naan bread
    Garlic naan 155
    Spice naan 155
Nahm jim dressing 504
Nanaimo bars 791
Nectarine and limoncello meringue slice 688
nicoise salad
    Fresh tuna nicoise 518
    Salmon nicoise 518
    Tuna nicoise à la our house 518
noodles 222–4
    Asian noodle salad 528
    Asparagus and green tea noodle salad with Thai prawns 540
    Barbecue duck and Hokkien noodles 231
    Barbecue pork and noodle stir-fry 231
    Barbecue pork and sweet chilli noodles 231
    Beef chow mein 235
    Beef, black bean and cashew nut stir-fry 227
    Chicken chow mein 235
    Chicken, black bean and noodle stir-fry 225
    Chicken, broccoli and noodle stir-fry 225
    Chicken, cashew and noodle stir-fry 225
    Chicken, ginger and noodle stir-fry 225
    Chicken, oyster sauce and noodle stir-fry 225
    Chilli prawns with asparagus, shiitake mushrooms and cellophane noodles 237
    Chilli stir-fried vegetables with noodles 239
    Chinese stir-fried vegetables and egg with noodles 239
    Chinese stir-fried vegetables with noodles 239
    Chinese stir-fried vegetables with tofu and noodles 239
    Chow mein 235
    Eggs nets with noodle and herb salad 91
    Fried tofu with cellophane noodles, shiitake and cashews 241
    Honey roast pork with stir-fried noodles 233
    Pad Thai 234
    Ramen noodle and sesame salad 528
    Singapore noodles 236
    Spicy Sichuan noodles 237
    Stir-fried noodles with prawns and snow peas 238
    Teriyaki beef 226
    Teriyaki chicken udon stir-fry for Mia 226
    Vegetable chow mein 235
    Vegetable stir-fry with Hokkien noodles and chilli jam 240
North African lamb 308
nougat
    Almond nougat 794
    Chocolate and chestnut frozen nougat 690
    Chocolate hazelnut nougat 794
    Christmas nougat 794
    Frozen nougat 690
    Frozen nougat ice-cream cake 690
    Liquorice frozen nougat 690
    Risotto of chocolate and nougat 683
Nutmeg slice 790
nuts
    Beef, black bean and cashew nut stir-fry 227
    Carrot, cardamom and cashew cake 731
    Chicken, cashew and noodle stir-fry 225

Fried tofu with cellophane noodles, shiitake and cashews 241
Nutty rhubarb crumble 650
Spiced nut rice 198
Spiced nuts 48
Stir-fried snow peas with cashews and soy 487
Sweet potato and cashew nut curry 451
Thai green chicken and cashew curry 428
Wok-fried snake beans with cashews 473
see also almonds; hazelnuts; pecans; pistachios; pine nuts; walnuts

O

Oatcakes 778
olives
    Chicken, mushroom and olive sauce 169
    Green olive salsa 564
    Haloumi, olive and onion tart 597
    Marinated olives 575
    Moroccan chicken with tomatoes and olives 391
    Olive and thyme crumbed pork schnitzels 270
    Olive focaccia 154
    Olive prosciutto and feta slice 607
    Olive, fig and goat's cheese slice 607
    Olive, prosciutto and feta slice 605
    Pan-fried swordfish with olive ratatouille 283
    Penne tossed with caramelised onion, rocket and olive 170
    Prosciutto and olive frittata 24
    Roast pumpkin, feta, olive and spinach salad 523
    Tapenade 553
    Tomato sauce with olives 162
    Tomato, olive, anchovy pasta sauce 164
    Warm olives with garlic and fennel 49
omelettes
    Ham and tomato omelette 22
    Mushroom omelette 22
    Omelette wraps with smoked salmon 23
    Spinach and feta omelette 22
One-pot chocolate cake 705
onions
    Caramelised onion quiche 596
    Caramelised onions 486
    Creamy onion soup 134
    French onion soup 134
    Lamb cutlets with red onions 267
    Onion bahjis 68
    Onion marmalade 579
    Onion sauce 556
    Roasted onions 485

orange-blossom water
    Mango and orange-blossom trifle 680
    Orange-blossom syrup 567
    Pistachio, almond and orange-blossom baklava 637
oranges
    Baby orange and almond cakes 711
    Baked orange cheesecake 736
    Blood orange and fennel salad 510
    Blood orange butter sauce 555
    Brandy orange butter 569
    Caramel oranges 652
    Caroline's (vodka and blood orange) jelly 665
    Crab, blood orange and panzanella salad 538
    Date and orange tart 620
    Orange and poppyseed friands 746
    Orange and walnut Florentines 773
    Orange icing 702
    Orange marmalade 583
    Orange tea cake 728
    Sicilian orange cake with marmalade cream 711
    Steamed orange pudding 671
Orecchietti with rich mushroom sauce 170
Oriental beef 304
Osso buco 413
Oxtail soup 139
oysters
    Barbecued oysters 329
    Oyster shooters 72
    Oysters with jamon and harissa 73
    Oysters with Vietnamese flavours 73
    Steamed oysters with Asian flavours 74

P

Paella 219
pancakes
    Berry pancakes 658
    Luke's lemon and sugar pancakes 658
pancetta
    Broad beans braised with pancetta 474
    Pot-roasted veal with pancetta and mustard 415
    Roast pumpkin, pancetta and sweet onions with gnocchi 189
    Roast tomato, pancetta and spinach tart 600
    Roast tomato, pancetta and sweet onions with gnocchi 189
    Sweet potato, pancetta and pea risotto 207
Pandan chicken parcels 75
Panettone and raspberry pudding 675
panforte
    Chocolate and hazelnut panforte 715

panna cotta
    Cardamom panna cotta 662
    Coconut panna cotta with spiced quinces 663
    Coffee panna cotta 662
    Jelly-topped panna cotta 662
    Lime panna cotta 662
    Liquorice panna cotta 662
    Rosewater panna cotta 662
    Vanilla panna cotta 662
Paper-wrapped chicken 74
Parsley sauce 556
parsnips
    Curried soup 129
    Parsnip, lemon and ginger soup 129
    Roast parsnips 487
    Roast parsnips with Worcestershire sauce and honey 487
passionfruit
    Passionfruit curd 585
    Passionfruit icing 702
    Passionfruit mousse 655
    Passionfruit profiteroles 635
    Passionfruit ring cake 713
    Passionfruit roulade 712
    Passionfruit sponge cake 704
    Passionfruit tart 622
    Passionfruit yoyo biscuits 771
pasta 160–89
    Beef lasagne 161
    Bolognaise pasta bake 184
    Broad bean and bacon pasta sauce 167
    Cheesy bean and tomato pasta bake 184
    Chicken, mushroom and olive sauce 169
    Chicken, mushroom and spinach sauce 169
    Gnocchi with blue cheese sauce 189
    Goat's cheese gnocchi 187
    Linguini with chilli, anchovies, breadcrumbs and basil 172
    Linguini with roasted pumpkin, spinach and goat's cheese 175
    Macaroni cheese 181
    Michele's macaroni cheese 181
    Orecchietti with rich mushroom sauce 170
    Pasta with tuna and artichokes 177
    Penne tossed with caramelised onion, rocket and olive 170
    Penne with Italian sausage, tomato and red wine sauce 166
    Penne with prosciutto, peas and mint 167
    Potato gnocchi 187
    Roast pumpkin, pancetta and sweet onions with gnocchi 189
    Roast tomato, pancetta and sweet onions with gnocchi 189

Roast vegetable and goat's cheese lasagne 186
Semolina gnocchi 188
Smoked trout and asparagus cream sauce 168
Spaghetti with blue-swimmer crab, fennel and tomato 180
Spaghetti with braised chicken meatballs in tomato sugo 182
Spaghetti with breadcrumbs, tuna, parsley and lemon 179
Spaghetti with silverbeet, raisins and pine nuts 173
Spaghetti with smoked chicken and asparagus 168
Spaghetti with tuna, rocket and lemon 177
Spaghettini carbonara 160
Traditional lasagne 161
Troffiette with chestnuts and smoked ham hock 176

pasties
    Chicken and vegetable pasties 613
    Vegetable pasties 616

pastry 588–9
    Almond sweetcrust pastry 591
    Choux pastry 594
    Cream cheese pastry 592
    Hot water pastry 595
    Puff pastry 592
    Rich sweetcrust pastry 591
    Rough puff pastry 594
    Shortcrust pastry 590
    Sweetcrust pastry 590

Pastry cream 573

pâté
    Chicken liver pâté 56
    Duck liver pâté 56
    Smoked mackerel pâté 57
    Smoked trout pâté 57

Pavlova 684
    Baby pavlovas with banana and honeycomb 686
    Baby pavs 684

peaches
    Baked peaches with amaretti biscuits 648
    Baked peaches with limoncello cream 646
    Grilled peaches with goat's curd and honey 8
    Peach and almond jam 581
    Peach and frangipane tart 629
    Roasted peach, ricotta and almond free-form tart 632

peanut
    Chocolate peanut cookies 777
    Peanut butter muffins 751

pears
    Chocolate and pear tart 630
    Cranberry and pear conserve 583
    Pear and frangipane tart 629
    Pear, walnut and rocket salad 507
    Poached pears with chocolate sauce and caramel cream 647
    Spiced poached pears 645
    Upside-down pear and ginger cake 723

peas
    Chicken and pea risotto 205
    Fresh garden peas 486
    Minty pea mash 486
    Penne with prosciutto, peas and mint 167
    Spring pea soup 126
    Spring Spanish rice with chicken, peas and lemon 220
    Stir-fried snow peas with cashews and soy 487
    Sugar snap peas with lemon butter 488
    Sweet potato, pancetta and pea risotto 207

pecans
    Apple, fig and pecan cake 730
    Pecan coffee cake 733
    Self-saucing sticky date and pecan pudding 673
    Spiced pecan cookies 777

Peking duck and hoisin rice-paper rolls 80
Penne tossed with caramelised onion, rocket and olive 170
Penne with Italian sausage, tomato and red wine sauce 166
Penne with prosciutto, peas and mint 167
Pepper sauce 562

pesto 551–2
    Almond pesto 551
    Basil pesto 551
    Coriander pesto 551
    Pesto roast lamb 361
    Roast chilli tomato and pesto tarts 604
    Roast tomato and coriander soup with coriander pesto 121
    Rocket pesto 551
    Thai basil pesto 552
    Tomato sauce with pesto 163

pickles
    Asian pickles 580
    Pickled ginger 580

pies
    Beef and Guinness pie 401
    Cheese and potato pies 614
    Chicken and mushroom pie 390
    Egg and bacon pie 610
    Free-form fruit pie 626
    Fruit mince pies 628
    Moroccan chicken pie 392

Pikelets 12
    Banana pikelets 12
    Blueberry pikelets 12
    Summer berry pikelets 12

pilaf
    Chicken pilaf 201
    Chicken, almond and harissa pilaf 201
    Chicken, sultana and sweet spice pilaf 204
    Lamb, chickpea and saffron pilaf 204
    Pine nut, sultana and onion pilaf 200
    Preserved lemon, almond and parsley pilaf 199
    Pumpkin, chickpea and saffron pilaf 204

Pinchito beef kebabs 303

pipis
    Spiced pipis with risoni 102

Piri-piri chicken 301
Pissaladiere 59

pistachios
    Chicken and pistachio dolmades 66
    Country pork, veal and pistachio terrine 58
    Pistachio biscotti 767
    Pistachio bread 774
    Pistachio, almond and orange-blossom baklava 637
    Strawberry, rosewater and pistachio semifreddo 696

Pita crisps 42
    Cheese and sesame seed pita crisps 42
    Lemon and pepper pita crisps 42

Pizza 248

platters
    Antipasto platter 41
    Middle Eastern platter 41
    Vegetable crudité platter 41

plums
    Backyard plum jam 582
    Baked plums with amaretti biscuits 648
    Blood plum and almond tart 631
    Crispy duck with spiced plum sauce 377
    Plum and pork steaks 275
    Plum cake 733

Poached eggs 18
Poached fruit 644
    Dessert wine poached fruit 644
    Kataifi nests with sweet labne and rosewater-poached rhubarb 639
    Poached pears with chocolate sauce and caramel cream 647
    Poached quinces 645
    Ricotta hotcakes with poached raspberries 10
    Spiced poached fruit 644
    Spiced poached pears 645
    Vanilla poached fruit 644

Polenta 190–3
    Cheesy wedgies 193
    Fruity polenta slice 788
    Grilled polenta with garlic vegetables 335
    Polenta bread 153
    Polenta herb muffins 755
    Polenta wedgies 193
    Rosemary polenta bread 153
    The best soft polenta 192
polpetti
    Cauliflower polpetti 60
    Zucchini polpetti 60
polpettini
    Chicken and veal polpettini 259
    Lemon chicken polpettini 260
pomegranate
    Pomegranate and sumac glazed duck 313
    Pomegranate and sumac glazed quail 313
    Pomegranate dressing 504
    Pomegranate-glazed beef 358
    Rocket, parmigiano and pomegranate salad 506
    Spice-crusted quail with pomegranate dressing 545
    Sumac and pomegranate roast duck 374
poppyseed
    Lemon and poppyseed tea cake 728
    Orange and poppyseed friands 746
    Orange poppyseed cake 725
pork
    American pork ribs 311
    Asian chilli pork steaks 311
    Barbecue pork and noodle stir-fry 231
    Barbecue pork and sweet chilli noodles 231
    Barbecued pork sausage with spiced lentils 271
    Braised pork belly with chorizo sausage 410
    Braised pork with star anise 408
    Chinese twice-cooked pork spare ribs 274
    Harissa pork 310
    Honey roast pork with stir-fried noodles 233
    Katsudon 276
    Lion's head meatballs 275
    Olive and thyme crumbed pork schnitzels 270
    Plum and pork steaks 275
    Pork gyoza 75
    Pork shish kebabs 310
    Pork terrine with veal and pistachio 58
    Prosciutto-wrapped pork fillet with roasted quinces 370
    Roast rack of pork 369
    Roasted pork loin with porcini mushrooms and sherry 372
    Rodriguez pork 409
    San choy bau 274
    Satay pork sugar-cane sticks 309
    Sichuan pepper and honey pork fillet 312
    Slow-cooked belly pork with Catalan potatoes and quince aioli 411
    Slow-roasted pork belly with fennel and garlic 371
    Sweet sticky pork 371
    The pork dish 408
Porridge 7
potatoes
    Baked potato fillings 490
    Baked potatoes 490
    Catalan potatoes 492
    Champ 489
    Cheese and potato pies 614
    Dukkah potato wedges 490
    Goose-fat roast potatoes 489
    Mashed potatoes 489
    Mashed potatoes with goat's cheese 489
    Potato and haloumi cakes with smoked salmon 35
    Potato and leek soup 119
    Potato and watercress soup 119
    Potato gnocchi 187
    Potato gratin 492
    Potato roesti 493
    Potato salad 514
    Potato tortilla 26
    Potato wedges 490
    Potato, rosemary and goat's cheese tarts 606
    Potato, spinach and chickpea curry 447
    Roast potatoes 489
    Roast potatoes with chorizo, chilli and coriander 493
    Roast rib of beef with potato gratin 357
    Rosemary garlic potatoes 491
    Salt-baked potatoes 494
    Sesame and cumin potato wedges 490
    Spiced potato wedges 490
pot-roast
    Beef pot-roast 360
    Pot-roasted chicken with 40 cloves of garlic 352
    Pot-roasted chicken with apples and cider 350
    Pot-roasted chicken with red wine and mushrooms 350
    Pot-roasted veal shanks 414
    Pot-roasted veal with pancetta and mustard 415
Praline 697
prawns
    Asparagus and prawn risotto 209
    Asparagus and green tea noodle salad with Thai prawns 540
    Barbecued chermoula prawns 320
    Chermoula prawns 70
    Chilli prawns with asparagus, shiitake mushrooms and cellophane noodles 237
    Coconut spiced prawn kebabs 322
    Egg nets with prawn noodle and herb salad 91
    Malaysian curry prawns 70
    Moorish prawn salad 93
    Prawn and coconut tom yum 144
    Prawn and smoked salmon kedgeree 37
    Prawn chilli balls 69
    Prawn cocktail 86
    Prawn rice paper rolls 80
    Prawn, roast tomato, green bean and egg salad 532
    Risotto of prawns with pea and radicchio 208
    Sizzlin' garlic prawns 320
    Stir-fried noodles with prawns and snow peas 238
    Thai barbecued prawns 321
    Thai prawn and asparagus curry 445
    Thai prawn salad 531
    Tunisian prawns with fattouche 94
    Vietnamese prawn and mint salad 535
Preserved lemons 575
preserves *see* chutney; conserves; curds; jam; marmalade; pickles; relish
profiteroles
    Passionfruit profiteroles 635
    Profiteroles with white chocolate and raspberries 635
prosciutto
    Artichoke, prosciutto and buffalo mozzarella parcels 51
    Asparagus with prosciutto 472
    Chicken saltimbocca skewers 299
    Olive, prosciutto and feta slice 605
    Penne with prosciutto, peas and mint 167
    Prosciutto and truffle oil grissini sticks 50
    Prosciutto-wrapped pork fillet with roasted quinces 370
    Rocket, fig, blue cheese and crispy prosciutto salad 508
puddings
    Australian Christmas pudding 674
    Bread and butter pudding 675
    Cherry berry pudding 654
    Chocolate and peppermint self-saucing 672
    Chocolate and walnut pudding 672
    Chocolate rice pudding 681
    Chocolate self-saucing pudding 672
    Christmas pudding 674
    Egyptian bread and butter pudding 636

Lemon delicious pudding 670
Middle Eastern rice pudding 681
Panettone and raspberry pudding 675
Rice pudding 681
Rich chocolate puddings 668
Self-saucing lemon and coconut pudding 670
Self-saucing sticky date and pecan pudding 673
Steamed chocolate pudding 671
Steamed ginger pudding 671
Steamed jam or marmalade pudding 671
Steamed lemon pudding 671
Steamed orange pudding 671
Steamed rhubarb pudding 671
Steamed treacle or maple syrup pudding 671
Summer pudding 654
Puff pastry 593
   Rough puff pastry 594
pumpkin
   Asian-inspired soup 123
   Linguini with roasted pumpkin, spinach and goat's cheese 175
   Pumpkin and coriander soup 124
   Pumpkin and nutmeg mash 494
   Pumpkin and parmigiano mash 494
   Pumpkin cake 732
   Pumpkin conserve 584
   Pumpkin, chickpea and saffron pilaf 204
   Roast pumpkin and blue cheese tart 598
   Roast pumpkin and Moroccan lentil soup 130
   Roast pumpkin, feta and pine nut puff slice 606
   Roast pumpkin, feta and pine nut risotto 215
   Roast pumpkin, feta, olive and spinach salad 523
   Roast pumpkin, pancetta and sweet onions with gnocchi 189
   Savoury roast pumpkin 495
   Spiced pumpkin wedges 495
   Thai red roasted pumpkin, spinach and chickpea curry 446

Q

quail
   Crispy-skin quail with Sichuan pepper and salt 111
   Pomegranate and sumac glazed quail 313
   Shiraz-glazed quails 314
   Spanish barbecued quail 316
   Spice-crusted quail with pomegranate dressing 545

quiche
   Quiche lorraine 596
   Asparagus quiche 596
   Caramelised onion quiche 596
   Leek and goat's cheese quiche 596
   Mushroom quiche 596
   Olive and spinach quiche 596
Quick bircher muesli 6
Quick couscous 453
Quick Thai fish curry 444
Quick-and-easy bolognaise 160
quince
   Lamb and quince tagine 458
   Moorish lamb with quince glaze 272
   Poached quinces 645
   Prosciutto-wrapped pork fillet with roasted quinces 370
   Quince aioli 550
   Quince and ricotta tart 620
   Quince tarte tatin 634
   Slow-cooked belly pork with Catalan potatoes and quince aioli 411

R

rabbit
   Braised rabbit with cider and rosemary 417
   Rabbit casserole 416
Ramen noodle and sesame salad 528
raspberries
   Apple and raspberry pie 625
   Flourless white chocolate and raspberry muffins 754
   Panettone and raspberry pudding 675
   Poached raspberries 10
   Profiteroles with white chocolate and raspberries 635
   Raspberry and campari sorbet 691
   Raspberry and gin trifle 678
   Raspberry and limoncello tart 630
   Raspberry and mascarpone tart 621
   Raspberry and white chocolate muffins 748
   Raspberry coconut slice 786
   Raspberry friands 746
   Raspberry jam drops 768
   Raspberry sauce 568
   Raspberry, vanilla and almond slice 785
ratatouille
   Lamb topsides with roasted ratatouille 364
   Pan-fried swordfish with olive ratatouille 283
Red cabbage with sweet and sour flavours 476
Red curry of duck 442
Red Thai curry paste 426
Red wine onion gravy 558

relish
   Beetroot relish 577
   Capsicum relish 577
   Coriander relish 566
   Fennel relish 566
   see also chutney
Rendang curry paste 427
   Beef rendang 435
rhubarb
   Apple and rhubarb crumble tart 625
   Apple and rhubarb pie 625
   Cinnamon rhubarb crumble 650
   Kataifi nests with sweet labne and rosewater-poached rhubarb 639
   Rhubarb crumble 650
   Rhubarb lemon cake 722
   Rhubarb oat crumble 650
   Rhubarb sauce 568
   Rhubarb, cinnamon and yoghurt muffins 749
   Steamed rhubarb pudding 671
rice 197–221
   Chocolate rice pudding 681
   Coconut rice 198
   Middle Eastern rice pudding 681
   Nasi goreng 221
   Paella 219
   Perisan rice 202
   Rice pudding 681
   Risotto of chocolate and nougat 683
   Roast vegetable, brown rice and goat's cheese salad 526
   Saffron rice 198
   Spiced nut rice 198
   Spring Spanish rice with chicken, peas and lemon 220
   Steamed rice 198
   Sushi rice 55
   see also pilaf; risotto
Rice paper rolls 80
ricotta
   Port-soaked prune and ricotta tart 620
   Ricotta hotcakes with honeycomb butter and banana 10
   Ricotta hotcakes with poached raspberries 10
   Ricotta tart 620
   Roasted apricot, ricotta and almond free-form tart 632
   Roasted peach, ricotta and almond free-form tart 632
rillettes
   Smoked salmon rillettes 107
risoni
   Spiced risoni with pipis 102
risotto
   Arancini 217
   Asparagus and prawn risotto 209
   Chicken and asparagus risotto 205
   Chicken and mushrooms risotto 205

Chicken and pea risotto 205
Mushroom risotto cakes 217
Mushroom risotto with truffle oil 213
Porcini and truffle oil risotto 213
Risotto of chicken, mushrooms and taleggio cheese 206
Risotto of chocolate and nougat 683
Risotto of prawns with peas and radicchio 208
Risotto with rocket and gorgonzola 210
Roast pumpkin, feta and pine nut risotto 215
Roasted eggplant risotto cakes 217
Spezzatino risotto 211
Spring risotto 212
Sweet potato, pancetta and pea risotto 207
Tuscan bean risotto 211
Vegetable risotto cakes 218
Wild mushroom risotto 216
roasts 336–340
   Basil and pine nut stuffed lamb 362
   Chermoula chicken 344
   Chinese crispy-skin chicken 347
   Chinese roast duck 374
   Christmas roast turkey with all the trimmings 354
   French roast lamb with haricot beans and green olive salsa 366
   Garlic and rosemary roast lamb 361
   Herby baby chicken with rocket and red onion salad 348
   Hoisin chicken 346
   Honey roast pork with stir-fried noodles 233
   Lamb topsides with roasted ratatouille 364
   Moroccan roast turkey 351
   Mustard roast lamb 361
   Nine-spiced roasted vegetables with chickpeas 379
   Oriental roast chicken 345
   Pesto roast lamb 361
   Pomegranate-glazed beef 358
   Pot-roasted chicken with 40 cloves of garlic 352
   Prosciutto-wrapped pork fillet with roasted quinces 370
   Roast beef with Yorkshire puddings 356
   Roast capsicum soup 122
   Roast carrots 478
   Roast cauliflower 78
   Roast chicken 344
   Roast duck 374
   Roast duck with orange and cardamom caramel sauce 375
   Roast duck, chilli and coriander rolls 79
   Roast eye fillet with chilli and garlic marinade 358
   Roast pumpkin and Moroccan lentil soup 130
   Roast rack of pork 369
   Roast rib of beef with potato gratin 357
   Roast sirloin with mustard and balsamic crust 359
   Roast tomato and coriander soup with coriander pesto 121
   Roast tomato soup 121
   Roast turkey breast with cranberry, walnut and orange stuffing 355
   Roast vegetable and goat's cheese lasagne 186
   Roasted onions 485
   Roasted pork loin with porcini mushrooms and sherry 372
   Roasted root vegetable chips 496
   Roasted vegetable calzone 249
   Roasted vegetable gazpacho 140
   Savoury roast pumpkin 495
   Slow-roasted lamb shoulder 363
   Slow-roasted pork belly with fennel and garlic 371
   Stuffed leg of lamb with zaatar, preserved lemon and herbs 365
   Stuffed turkey breast 351
   Sumac and pomegranate roast duck 374
   Sweet sticky pork 371
   see also pot-roast
rocket
   Beetroot, rocket and yoghurt salad 515
   Chickpea, feta and rocket salad 520
   Herby baby chicken with rocket and red onion salad 348
   Pear, walnut and rocket salad 507
   Penne tossed with caramelised onion, rocket and olive 170
   Risotto with rocket and gorgonzola 210
   Rocket mayonnaise 554
   Rocket pesto 551
   Rocket tabouli 516
   Rocket, fig, blue cheese and crispy prosciutto salad 508
   Rocket, parmigiano and pomegranate salad 506
   Sweet potato, smoked chicken, bocconcini and rocket salad 524
Rocky road 796
   Moroccan rocky road 796
   Moroccan rocky road ice-cream 697
Rodriguez pork 409
Romensco sauce 552
rosemary
   Braised rabbit with cider and rosemary 417
   Garlic and rosemary roast lamb 361
   Lamb navarin with root vegetables and rosemary 405
   Potato, rosemary and goat's cheese tarts 606
   Rosemary garlic potatoes 491
   Rosemary lamb kebabs 305
   Rosemary polenta bread 153
rosewater
   Kataifi nests with sweet labne and rosewater-poached rhubarb 639
   Rosewater meringue stack with red summer berries 687
   Rosewater panna cotta 662
   Rosewater syrup 567
   Strawberry, rosewater and pistachio semifreddo 696
   White chocolate and rosewater truffles 795
Rough puff pastry 594
Royal icing 703
Ruth's potato salad 514

S

saffron
   Lamb, chickpea and saffron pilaf 204
   Lentil and chickpea salad 520
   Moroccan chicken with tomato saffron jam 456
   Moroccan chickpea and pumpkin stew 462
   Nine-spiced roasted vegetables with chickpeas 379
   Potato, spinach and chickpea curry 447
   Pumpkin, chickpea and saffron pilaf 204
   Saffron and almond couscous stuffing 342
   Saffron couscous 453
   Saffron rice 198
   Saffron sauce 555
   Saffron scrambled eggs 19
   Seafood casserole with saffron and cream 418
Sage and onion stuffing 341
salads 506–545
   Asian coleslaw 517
   Asian noodle salad 528
   Asparagus and broad bean mograbieh salad with barbecued salmon 541
   Asparagus and green tea noodle salad with Thai prawns 540
   Asparagus, almond and feta salad 516
   Baby spinach, bacon and crispy crouton salad 507
   Barbecued vegetable salad 519
   Beef salad with hot and sour flavours 544
   Beetroot fattouche 515
   Beetroot salad 514
   Beetroot salad with tomato and mozzarella 514

Beetroot, rocket and yoghurt salad 515
Blood orange and fennel salad 510
Caesar salad 511
Chickpea, feta and coriander salad 520
Chickpea, feta and rocket salad 520
Coconut chicken and noodle salad 531
Crab, blood orange and panzanella salad 538
Eggplant, pine nut and coriander salad 521
Fresh tuna nicoise 518
Greek salad 506
Green bean, almond and feta salad 516
Green salad 506
Honey and zaatar carrot salad 522
Lentil and chickpea salad 520
Lively mushroom salad 524
Middle Eastern carrot salad 523
Moroccan chicken salad 525
Moroccan couscous salad 525
Pear, walnut and rocket salad 507
Potato salad 514
Prawn, roast tomato, green bean and egg salad 532
Ramen noodle and sesame salad 528
Roast pumpkin, feta, olive and spinach salad 523
Roast vegetable, brown rice and goat's cheese salad 526
Rocket tabouli 516
Rocket, fig, blue cheese and crispy prosciutto salad 508
Rocket, parmigiano and pomegranate salad 506
Ruth's potato salad 514
Salmon nicoise 518
Sichuan chicken and fungi 92
Sichuan chicken salad 529
Simple bok choy salad 518
Smoked trout and avocado salad 521
Spice-crusted quail with pomegranate dressing 545
Sumac beef salad with lentils, grapes and parsley 543
Sweet potato, smoked chicken, bocconcini and rocket salad 524
Thai beef salad 531
Thai chicken salad 531
Thai prawn salad 531
Tomato and roast capsicum salad 510
Tomato and white bean salad 509
Tomato, bocconcini and basil salad 509
Tuna nicoise à la our house 518
Tuna, cannellini bean and asparagus salad 522
Vietnamese beef and mint salad 535
Vietnamese beef noodle salad 534
Vietnamese chicken and mint salad 535
Vietnamese prawn and mint salad 535
Walnut tabouli salad 517
Watercress tabouli 516
salmon
   Asparagus and broad bean mograbieh salad with barbecued salmon 541
   Coriander-cured salmon 108
   Ginger mirin salmon 324
   Hot and sour crispy salad with lime dressing 110
   Pan-fried salmon with chilli coriander udon broth 284
   Salmon and potato cakes 278
   Salmon nicoise 518
   Soy and ginger salmon kebabs 325
   Soy ginger salmon 286
   Whole smoky salmon 329
salsa
   Asian cucumber salsa 567
   Chilli salsa 565
   Fresh mango salsa 565
   Green olive salsa 564
   Tomato and basil salsa 565
salt
   Italian herb and salt rub 343
   Salt and pepper sardines 328
   Salt cod fritters 57
   Salt-baked potatoes 494
San choy bau 274
satay
   Chicken satay kebabs 300
   Satay pork sugar-cane sticks 309
   Satay sauce 563
sauces, savoury
   Allan's gravy 559
   Almond skordalia 550
   Apple sauce 560
   Barbecue sauce 562
   Bearnaise sauce 555
   Blood orange butter sauce 555
   Bread sauce 560
   Cheese sauce 557
   Chilli jam 578
   Classic mushroom sauce 557
   Creamy mushroom sauce 558
   Goat's cheese sauce 557
   Hollandaise sauce 555
   Lemon butter sauce 555
   Lime butter sauce 555
   Maltaise sauce 555
   Mint sauce 562
   Mustard sauce 556
   Onion marmalade 579
   Onion sauce 556
   Parsley sauce 556
   Pepper sauce 562
   Quince aioli 550
   Red wine onion gravy 558
   Roasted capsicum and tomato sauce 561
   Romensco sauce 552
   Saffron sauce 555
   Satay sauce 563
   Sweet chilli sauce 578
   Tapenade 553
   Tomato sauce 561
   Turkey gravy 559
   Tzatziki 563
   Vietnamese dipping sauce 564
   White sauce (bechamel) 556
   White wine onion gravy 558
   Yoghurt and tahini sauce 564
   see also mayonnaise; mustard; pesto; salsa; tomato sauce; relish
sauces, sweet
   Bourbon sauce 572
   Butterscotch sauce 572
   Caramel sauce 570
   Chocolate brandy sauce 571
   Chocolate sauce 571
   Coconut caramel sauce 570
   Kahlua sauce 572
   Raspberry sauce 568
   Rhubarb sauce 568
   Strawberry sauce 568
   White chocolate sauce 571
   see also syrups; custard
sausages
   Barbecued pork sausage with spiced lentils 271
   Cevapcici 317
   Penne with Italian sausage, tomato and red wine sauce 166
   Sausage rolls 614
   see also chorizo
Savoury roast pumpkin 495
Savoury mince 265
schnitzel
   Cheesy schnitzel 252
   Chicken nuggets 252
   Chicken parmigiano 252
   Chicken schnitzel 252
   Crumbed lamb chops 252
   Fish fingers 279
   Indian spiced schnitzel 252
   Katsudon 276
   Lemon and herb schnitzel 252
   Olive and thyme crumbed pork schnitzels 270
   Parmigiano crumbed veal cutlets 277
   Veal schnitzel 252
Scones 756
   Cinnamon scones 756
   Date scones 756
Scrambled eggs 19
   Herb scrambled eggs 19
   Saffron scrambled eggs 19

Seafood casserole with saffron and cream 418
Seed mustard 553
self-saucing puddings
    Chocolate and peppermint self-saucing pudding 672
    Chocolate and walnut pudding 672
    Chocolate self-saucing pudding 672
    Self-saucing lemon and coconut pudding 670
    Self-saucing sticky date and pecan pudding 673
semifreddo
    Strawberry, rosewater and pistachio semifreddo 696
    Espresso semifreddo with butterscotch sauce 696
Semolina gnocchi 188
sesame
    Cheese and sesame seed pita crisps 42
    Ramen noodle and sesame salad 528
    Sesame and cumin potato wedges 490
    Sesame seed rolls 151
    Sesame sweet potato wedges 496
Sherry-soaked raisin and almond cake 721
Shiraz-glazed quails 314
Shortbread 770
Shortcrust pastry 590
Sichuan cooking
    Sichuan chicken and fungi salad 92
    Sichuan chicken salad 529
    Sichuan eggplant 481
    Sichuan pepper and honey pork fillet 312
    Sichuan pepper and salt with crispy-skin quail 111
Sicilian lamb stew with pecorino 406
Sicilian orange cake with marmalade cream 711
Silver darlings 768
Simple brioche 757
slices
    Fruity polenta slice 788
    Ginger slice 790
    Leek and cheese slice 605
    Lemon slice 793
    Marzipan bars 792
    Munchie muesli slice 788
    Nanaimo bars 791
    Nutmeg slice 790
    Olive, fig and goat's cheese slice 607
    Olive, prosciutto and feta slice 605
    Raspberry coconut slice 786
    Raspberry, vanilla and almond slice 785
    Roast pumpkin, feta and pine nut puff slice 606
    Robyn's caramel, macadamia and hazelnut slice 789
    Vanilla and caramelised apricot slice 784
    Viennese plum slice 785
slow cooking 381–3
    Slow-cooked belly pork with Catalan potatoes and quince aioli 411
    Slow-cooked leg of lamb with lemon and oregano 402
    Slow-roasted lamb shoulder 363
    Slow-roasted pork belly with fennel and garlic 371
    see also braises; casseroles; pot-roasts; stews
smoked chicken
    Spaghetti with smoked chicken and asparagus 168
    Sweet potato, smoked chicken, bocconcini and rocket salad 524
smoked salmon
    Haloumi and potato cakes with smoked salmon 35
    Smoked salmon and prawn kedgeree 37
    Smoked salmon omelette wraps 23
    Smoked salmon rillettes 107
    Smoked salmon with basil frittata 29
    Sweetcorn and ricotta hotcakes with smoked salmon 31
smoked trout
    Smoked trout and asparagus cream sauce 168
    Smoked trout and avocado salad 521
    Smoked trout and avocado toasts 106
    Smoked trout pâté 57
snake beans
    Wok-fried snake beans 473
    Wok-fried snake beans with cashews 473
Snickerdoodles 770
sorbet
    Raspberry and campari sorbet 691
souffle
    Chocolate souffle 659
    Coffee souffle 659
    Goat's cheese souffle 86
    Raspberry souffle 659
    Twice-cooked goat's cheese souffle 87
soups 119–147
    Asian-inspired pumpkin soup 123
    Asparagus soup 120
    Beetroot soup 129
    Beijing dumpling soup 147
    Broad bean and crispy prosciutto soup 128
    Carrot and coriander soup 125
    Cauliflower, chilli and coconut soup 124
    Chicken and corn soup 132
    Chicken laksa 143
    Chicken noodle soup 132
    Chicken, bok choy and udon miso 146
    Chinese chicken noodle soup 132
    Classic tomato soup 122
    Creamy corn soup 125
    Creamy onion soup 134
    Curried parsnip soup 129
    Duck and macadamia wonton soup 147
    Duck, pine mushroom and bread soup 133
    Fish and fennel chowder 141
    French onion soup 134
    Italian spring vegetable and pasta broth 135
    Laksa 143
    Lamb shank, vegetable and barley broth 138
    Lentil and ham hock soup 137
    Minestrone 133
    Miso 146
    Miso with tofu 146
    Mushroom soup 120
    Oxtail soup 139
    Parsnip, ginger and lemon soup 129
    Pasta e fagioli 136
    Potato and leek soup 119
    Potato and watercress soup 119
    Prawn and coconut tom yum 144
    Pumpkin and coriander soup 124
    Roast capsicum soup 122
    Roast pumpkin and Moroccan lentil soup 130
    Roast tomato and coriander soup with coriander pesto 121
    Roast tomato soup 121
    Roasted vegetable gazpacho 140
    Spring pea soup 126
    Sweet potato and ginger soup 124
    Sweetcorn chowder 141
    Tom yum 142
    Tomato and fennel soup 120
    Udon soup with shiitake and roast duck 146
    Vegetable soup 120
    Vietnamese chicken noodle soup 132
Southern fried chicken 255
soy
    Calamari with soy and chilli glaze 238
    Chicken fillets poached in soy and star anise 256
    Soy and garlic marinade 293
    Soy and ginger salmon kebabs 325
    Soy ginger salmon 286
    Soy-braised chicken 393
spaghetti
    Spaghetti with blue-swimmer crab, fennel and tomato 180
    Spaghetti with braised chicken meatballs in tomato sugo 182

Spaghetti with breadcrumbs, tuna, parsley and lemon 179
Spaghetti with silverbeet, raisins and pine nuts 173
Spaghetti with smoked chicken and asparagus 168
Spaghetti with tuna, rocket and lemon 177
Spaghettini carbonara 160
Spanakopita 617
Spanish cooking
    Spanish barbecued quail 316
    Spanish lamb stew 407
    Spring Spanish rice with chicken, peas and lemon 220
Spezzatino 398
    Spezzatino risotto 211
spices
    Creole spice blend 295
    Indian spice mix 293
    Nine-spiced roasted vegetables with chickpeas 379
    Salt and pepper spice mix 295
    Simple Moroccan blend 294
    Spiced beef balls in basil leaves 304
    Spiced coriander and yoghurt chicken 256
    Spiced couscous 453
    Spiced eggplant parcels 612
    Spiced Italian fruit cake 716
    Spiced lamb steaks 267
    Spiced nuts 48
    Spiced pecan cookies 777
    Spiced pipis with risoni 102
    Spiced poached fruit 644
    Spiced poached pears 645
    Spiced roasted stone fruit 646
    Spicy cheddar muffins 755
    Spicy lip-smacking drumsticks 298
spinach
    Baked eggs with spinach and cheddar 26
    Indian beef, spinach and potato curry 438
    Indian chicken, potato and spinach curry 429
    Indian chickpea and spinach curry 429
    Indian lamb, spinach and potato curry 438
    Linguini with roasted pumpkin, spinach and goat's cheese 175
    Olive and spinach quiche 596
    Potato, spinach and chickpea curry 447
    Roast tomato, pancetta and spinach tart 600
    Spinach and haloumi fritters 61
    Spinach with lemon and almonds 497
    Thai green chicken and spinach curry 428
    Thai red roasted pumpkin, spinach and chickpea curry 446
    Tomato sauce with spinach 163
Spring rolls 78
steak
    Asian chilli pork steaks 311
    Braised steak with onions 395
    Chilli rump steak 302
    Pan-fried steak with mushroom sauce 263
    Plum and pork steaks 275
    Spiced lamb steaks 267
    Steak with oven chips 262
    The perfect porterhouse 302
stews
    Basic beef stew 394
    Beef stew with dumplings 394
    Beef stew with mushrooms 394
    Mediterranean bean stew with feta 420
    Mediterranean fish stew 418
    Moroccan chickpea and pumpkin stew 462
    Moroccan fish stew 420
    Sicilian lamb stew with pecorino 406
    Spanish lamb stew 407
    Tuscan bean stew 421
    see also casseroles; braises
Sticky cinnamon buns 760
Sticky currant buns 758
Sticky orange and currant buns 758
stir-fries
    Barbecue duck and hokkien noodles 231
    Barbecue pork and bok choy stir-fry 230
    Barbecue pork and noodle stir-fry 231
    Barbecue pork and sweet chilli noodles 231
    Beef chow mein 235
    Beef, black bean and cashew nut stir-fry 227
    Calamari with soy and chilli glaze 238
    Chicken chow mein 235
    Chicken, black bean and noodle stir-fry 225
    Chicken, broccoli and noodle stir-fry 225
    Chicken, cashew and noodle stir-fry 225
    Chicken, ginger and noodle stir-fry 225
    Chicken, oyster sauce and noodle stir-fry 225
    Chilli beef and mushroom stir-fry 228
    Chilli beef stir-fry 228
    Chilli kangaroo stir-fry 228
    Chilli prawns with asparagus, shiitake mushrooms and cellophane noodles 237
    Chilli stir-fried vegetables with noodles 239
    Chinese stir-fried vegetables and egg with noodles 239
    Chinese stir-fried vegetables with noodles 239
    Chinese stir-fried vegetables with tofu and noodles 239
    Fried tofu with cellophane noodles, shiitake and cashews 241
    Honey roast pork with stir-fried noodles 233
    Pad Thai 234
    Singapore noodles 236
    Sour beef with lemongrass 230
    Spicy Sichuan noodles 237
    Stir-fried crabs with black beans and ginger 104
    Stir-fried noodles with prawns and snow peas 238
    Stir-fried rice 221
    Teriyaki beef 226
    Teriyaki chicken udon stir-fry for Mia 226
    Tofu and ginger stir-fry 242
    Vegetable chow mein 235
    Vegetable stir-fry with Hokkien noodles and chilli jam 240
stocks
    Asian chicken stock 117
    Beef stock 116
    Chicken stock 117
    Duck stock 117
    Fish stock 119
    Game stock 116
    Master stock 118
    Rich chicken stock 117
    Turkey stock 117
    Veal stock 116
    Vegetable stock 118
strawberries
    Strawberry sauce 568
    Strawberry shortcakes 757
    Strawberry, rosewater and pistachio semifreddo 696
Stuffed turkey breast 351
stuffings
    Chestnut stuffing 342
    Lemon, herb and almond stuffing 341
    Middle Eastern fruit and nut stuffing 343
    Roast turkey breast with cranberry, walnut and orange stuffing 355
    Saffron and almond couscous stuffing 342
    Sage and onion stuffing 341
sugar, cooking with 766
Sugar syrup 567
    Lime and palm sugar syrup 568
Sugar-grilled stone fruit 646
Sugar-roasted stone fruit with fresh cheese and honey 646

sumac
- Pomegranate and sumac glazed duck 313
- Pomegranate and sumac glazed quail 313
- Sumac and pomegranate roast duck 374
- Sumac beef salad with lentils, grapes and parsley 543

Summer vegetable terrine 85
Sushi rice 55
Swede, mashed 497
Swedish meatballs 266
Sweet chilli and mirin steamed tofu 287
Sweet chilli sauce 578
sweet potato
- Sesame sweet potato wedges 496
- Sweet potato and cashew nut curry 451
- Sweet potato and ginger soup 124
- Sweet potato mash 494
- Sweet potato, pancetta and pea risotto 207
- Sweet potato, smoked chicken, bocconcini and rocket salad 524

sweet sauces *see* sauces
Sweet sticky marinade 295
Sweet sticky pork 371
sweetcorn see corn
Sweetcrust pastry 590
- Rich sweetcrust pastry 591

Swiss buns 759
swordfish
- Pan-fried swordfish with olive ratatouille 283
- Swordfish kebabs 319

Summer pudding 654
syrups
- Lemon syrup 567
- Lime and palm sugar syrup 568
- Lime syrup 567
- Orange and yoghurt syrup cake 725
- Orange-blossom syrup 567
- Rosewater syrup 567

T

tabouli
- Rocket tabouli 516
- Walnut tabouli salad 517
- Watercress tabouli 516

tagines 452–3
- Aromatic vegetable tagine 461
- Beef and prune tagine 455
- Chicken tagine with mushrooms, chorizo and sherry 454
- Eggplant and root vegetable tagine 436
- Lamb and quince tagine 458
- Lamb tagine 459
- Tunisian lamb shanks 460
- Tunisian vegetable and chickpea tagine 465

tahini
- Yoghurt and tahini sauce 564

tandoori
- Chicken tandoori in naan bread 300

Tapenade 553
Tartare sauce 554
tarts
- Apple and raspberry pie 625
- Apple and rhubarb crumble tart 625
- Apple and rhubarb pie 625
- Apple tart 623
- Apricot and frangipane tart 621
- Asparagus and goat's cheese tart 595
- Bitter chocolate tarts 624
- Blood plum and almond tart 631
- Blueberry and mascarpone tart 628
- Breakfast tarts 609
- Cherry and marzipan 629
- Chocolate and pear tart 630
- Date and orange tart 620
- Free-form roast summer vegetable tart 615
- Haloumi, olive and onion tart 597
- Lemon meringue tart 623
- Lemon tart 622
- Mushroom tart 601
- Passionfruit tart 622
- Peach and frangipane tart 629
- Pear and almond tart 631
- Pear and frangipane tart 629
- Port-soaked prune and ricotta tart 620
- Potato, rosemary and goat's cheese tarts 606
- Quince and ricotta tart 620
- Quince tarte tatin 634
- Raspberry and limoncello tart 630
- Raspberry and mascarpone tart 621
- Ricotta tart 620
- Roast chilli tomato and pesto tarts 604
- Roast pumpkin and blue cheese tart 598
- Roast tomato, pancetta and spinach tart 600
- Roasted apricot, ricotta and almond free-form tart 632
- Roasted peach, ricotta and almond free-form tart 632
- Tomato and anchovy tart 603
- *see also* quiche; slices; pies

teriyaki
- Teriyaki beef 226
- Teriyaki chicken udon stir-fry for Mia 26
- Tuna teriyaki skewers 326

terrines
- Country pork, veal and pistachio terrine 58
- Summer vegetable terrine 85

Thai cooking
- Asparagus and green tea noodle salad with Thai prawns 540
- Crab cakes with Thai cucumber salad 103
- Deep-fried Thai calamari 71
- Green Thai curry paste 426
- Quick Thai fish curry 444
- Red Thai curry paste 426
- Steamed Thai fish 286
- Thai barbecued prawns 321
- Thai basil pesto 552
- Thai beef salad 531
- Thai chicken balls 260
- Thai chicken salad 531
- Thai chilli broth with mussels 98
- Thai corn fritters 62
- Thai dressing 505
- Thai fish cakes 318
- Thai green chicken and cashew curry 428
- Thai green chicken and spinach curry 428
- Thai prawn and asparagus curry 445
- Thai prawn salad 531
- Thai red beef and bok choy curry 433
- Thai red chicken curry 428
- Thai red fish curry 433
- Wontons with Thai curry sauce 76

Thick custard 573
Thin custard 573
Tikka-yoghurt lamb chops 268
Tiramisu cake 661
Tiramisu ice-cream 694
toffee
- Toffee almond squares 783
- Toffee apples 799
- Toffee tomatoes 498

tofu
- Chinese stir-fried vegetables with tofu and noodles 239
- Fried tofu with cellophane noodles, shiitake and cashews 241
- Miso soup with tofu 146
- Sweet chilli and mirin steamed tofu 287
- Tofu and ginger stir-fry 242

tomato sauces
- Eggplant, tomato and basil sauce 164
- Roasted capsicum and tomato sauce 561
- Tomato sauce 561
- Tomato sauce # 1 162
- Tomato sauce # 2 163
- Tomato sauce with bacon 163
- Tomato sauce with basil 162
- Tomato sauce with chilli 163
- Tomato sauce with mushrooms 163
- Tomato sauce with olives 162
- Tomato sauce with pesto 163
- Tomato sauce with roasted capsicum 162
- Tomato sauce with roasted eggplant 162

Tomato sauce with spinach 163
Tomato sauce with tuna 162
Tomato, olive and anchovy pasta sauce 164
tomatoes
    Classic tomato soup 122
    Grilled tomatoes with basil butter and bacon 16
    Moroccan chicken with tomato saffron jam 456
    Prawn, roast tomato, green bean and egg salad 532
    Roast chilli tomato and pesto tarts 604
    Roast tomato and coriander pesto soup 121
    Roast tomato soup 121
    Roast tomato, pancetta and spinach tart 600
    Roasted roma tomatoes 498
    Roasted roma tomatoes with feta and basil 498
    Spiced tomatoes with corn fritters and crisp bacon 34
    Toffee tomatoes 498
    Tomato and anchovy tart 603
    Tomato and basil salsa 565
    Tomato and fennel soup 120
    Tomato and roast capsicum salad 510
    Tomato and white bean salad 509
    Tomato kasoundi 576
    Tomato, bocconcini and basil salad 509
trifles
    Christmas trifle 677
    Mango and orange-blossom trifle 680
    Raspberry and gin trifle 678
Troffiette with chestnuts and smoked ham hock 176
truffle oil
    Porcini and truffle oil risotto 213
    Truffle oil and prosciutto sticks 50
truffles (sweet)
    Chocolate truffles 795
    Grand Marnier truffles 795
    Kahlua truffles 795
    White chocolate and rosewater truffles 795
Tuiles 773
tuna
    Fresh tuna nicoise 518
    Pasta with tuna and artichokes 177
    Spaghetti with breadcrumbs, tuna, parsley and lemon 179
    Spaghetti with tuna, rocket and lemon 177
    Spice-coated tuna 325
    Tuna nicoise à la our house 518
    Tuna teriyaki skewers 326
    Tuna, cannellini bean and asparagus salad 522
Tunisian cooking
    Tunisian lamb shanks 460
    Tunisian prawn with fattouche 94
    Tunisian vegetable and chickpea tagine 465
turkey
    Christmas roast turkey with all the trimmings 354
    Moroccan roast turkey 351
    Roast turkey breast with cranberry, walnut and orange stuffing 355
    Stuffed turkey breast 351
    Turkey gravy 559
    Turkey stock 117
Twice-cooked goat's cheese souffle 87
Tzatziki 563

U
Ultimate barbecue marinade 292
Upside-down pear and ginger cake 723

V
vanilla
    Chocolate vanilla drops 768
    Hazelnut and vanilla creams 772
    Raspberry, vanilla and almond slice 785
    Vanilla and caramelised apricot slice 784
    Vanilla ice-cream 689
    Vanilla panna cotta 662
    Vanilla poached fruit 644
veal
    Chicken and veal polpettini 259
    Lemony chicken and veal burgers 296
    Osso buco 413
    Parmiagiano crumbed veal cutlets 277
    Pot-roasted veal shanks 414
    Pot-roasted veal with pancetta and mustard 415
    Veal ragu 161
    Veal schnitzel 252
    Veal stock 116
    Veal, sage and onion meatloaf 277
vegetarian meals
    Aromatic vegetable tagine 461
    Barbecued vegetable salad 519
    Chickpea and vegetable casserole 421
    Chilli stir-fried vegetables with noodles 239
    Chinese stir-fried vegetables with noodles 239
    Eggplant and root vegetable tagine 436
    Fragrant vegetable curry 450
    Free-form roast summer vegetable tart 615
    Grilled polenta with garlic vegetables 335
    Haloumi and couscous burgers 331
    Indian vegetable curry 429
    Moroccan eggplant and capsicum kebabs 330
    Nine-spiced roasted vegetables with chickpea 379
    Potato, spinach and chickpea curry 447
    Roast vegetable, brown rice and goat's cheese salad 526
    Roasted vegetable calzone 249
    Spiced green lentils burgers 330
    Thai red roasted pumpkin, spinach and chickpea curry 446
    Vegetable and egg rice-paper rolls 80
    Vegetable chow mein 235
    Vegetable pasties 616
    Vegetable risotto cakes 218
    Vegetable soup 120
    Vegetable stir-fry with Hokkien noodles and chilli jam 240
    Vegetable terrine 85
vegies, side dishes 469–99
    Asparagus with feta 472
    Asparagus with hollandaise sauce 472
    Asparagus with prosciutto 472
    Baked potatoes 490
    Barbecued corn cobs 481
    Braised fennel 482
    Broad beans braised with pancetta 474
    Broad beans with extra-virgin olive oil 474
    Broccoli with toasted pine nuts 474
    Brussels sprouts with almonds and parsley 476
    Brussels sprouts with chestnuts 476
    Cabbage with bacon and onions 477
    Caponata 482
    Carrots with butter and sugar glaze 477
    Catalan potatoes 492
    Cauliflower cheese 479
    Champ 489
    Chinese broccoli and garlic stir-fry 480
    Choy sum with ginger 480
    Dukkah potato wedges 490
    Easy green beans 472
    Fennel fritters 483
    Fresh garden peas 486
    Garlic mushrooms 484
    Goose-fat roast potatoes 489
    Green beans with almonds 472
    Green beans with walnuts 472
    Jerusalem artichoke puree 483
    Mashed potatoes 489
    Mashed potatoes with goat's cheese 489
    Mashed swede 497
    Minty pea mash 486
    Mushrooms with fresh herbs 485
    Pan-fried mushrooms 484
    Potato gratin 492

Potato roesti 493
Potato wedges 490
Pumpkin and nutmeg mash 494
Red cabbage with sweet and sour
 flavours 476
Roast carrots 478
Roast cauliflower 478
Roast parsnips 487
Roast parsnips with Worcestershire
 sauce and honey 487
Roast potatoes 489
Roast potatoes with chorizo, chilli and
 coriander 493
Roasted onions 485
Roasted roma tomatoes 498
Roasted roma tomatoes with feta and
 basil 498
Roasted root vegetable chips 496
Rosemary garlic potatoes 491
Salt-baked potatoes 494
Savoury roast pumpkin 495
Sesame and cumin potato wedges 490
Sesame sweet potato wedges 496
Sichuan eggplant 481
Spiced potato wedges 490
Spiced pumpkin wedges 495
Spinach with lemon and
 almonds 497
Stir-fried broccolini with garlic 475
Stir-fried cauliflower 479
Stir-fried snow peas with cashews
 and soy 487
Sugar snap peas with lemon
 butter 488
Sweet potato mash 494
Toffee tomatoes 498
Wok-fried Asian greens 499
Wok-fried brussels sprouts 475
Wok-fried snake beans 473
Wok-fried snake beans with
 cashews 473
Zucchini with raisins and pine nuts
 499
Zucchini with red wine vinegar and
 basil 499
Viennese biscuits 769
Viennese plum slice 785
Vietnamese cooking
 Oysters with Vietnamese flavours 73
 Vietnamese beef and mint salad 535
 Vietnamese beef noodle salad 534
 Vietnamese chicken and mint
  salad 535
 Vietnamese chicken noodle soup 132
 Vietnamese dipping sauce 564
 Vietnamese prawn and mint salad 535
vine leaves
 Chicken and pistachio dolmades 66
 Dolmades 66
 Grilled vine leaves with haloumi 51
 Lamb and mint dolmades 66

W

wafers
 Cardamom spiced wafers 773
 Coconut wafers 771
 Tuiles 773
waffles
 Gingerbread waffle cakes with
  honeycomb butter and banana 14
walnuts
 Banana and maple syrup muffins 750
 Banana and walnut cake 730
 Banana, walnut and maple syrup
  muffins 750
 Chocolate and walnut pudding 672
 Coffee and walnut muffins 753
 Double chocolate chip and walnut
  cookies 776
 Lemon and walnut cake 713
 Orange and walnut florentines 773
 Walnut and sage mustard 553
watercress
 Watercress and potato soup 119
Watermelon granita with summer
 fruit 692
White bean dip 45
white chocolate
 Flourless white chocolate and
  raspberry muffins 754
 Raspberry and white chocolate
  muffins 748
 White chocolate and butterscotch
  mousse cake 657
 White chocolate and rosewater
  truffles 795
 White chocolate frosting 703
 White chocolate ganache 702
 White chocolate sauce 571
 see also chocolate
White Christmas 793
White sauce (bechamel) 556
White wine onion gravy 558
Wine marinade 292
Wobbly berry jelly 664
Wok-fried brussels sprouts 475
Wontons with Thai curry sauce 76

Y

Yakitori chicken kebabs 326
yoghurt
 Beetroot, rocket and yoghurt salad
  515
 Orange and yoghurt syrup cake 725
 Rhubarb, cinnamon and yoghurt
  muffins 749
 Spiced coriander and yoghurt
  chicken 256
 Tikka-yoghurt lamb chops 268
 Whole leg of lamb in spicy yoghurt
  sauce 441
 Yoghurt and tahini sauce 564

Yoghurt dressing 505
Yorkshire puddings 356

Z

zaatar
 Honey and zaatar carrot salad 522
 Stuffed leg of lamb with zaatar,
  preserved lemon and herbs 365
zabaglione
 Zabaglione ice-cream 657
 Zabaglione mousse 657
zucchini
 Zucchini and feta fritters 35
 Zucchini flower fritters with feta and
  basil 64
 Zucchini with raisins and pine
  nuts 499
 Zucchini with red wine vinegar and
  basil 499

In the Kitchen is dedicated to our two wonderful children, Mia and Luke. May they always eat well!

This edition published in 2009
First published in 2008 by
Hardie Grant Books
85 High Street
Prahran, Victoria 3181, Australia
www.hardiegrant.com.au
www.hardiegrant.co.uk

All rights reserved. No part of this publication may be reproduced, stored in a retrieval system or transmitted in any form by any means, electronic, mechanical, photocopying, recording or otherwise, without the prior written permission of the publishers and copyright holders.

The moral rights of the authors have been asserted.

Copyright text © Michele Curtis and Allan Campion 2008
Copyright photography © Steve Brown, Lisa Cohen, Greg Elms and Matt Harvey 2008

Cataloguing-in-Publication data is available from the National Library of Australia.

ISBN 978 1 74066 836 1

Cover and internal design concept by Greendot Design
Photography by Steve Brown, Lisa Cohen, Greg Elms and Matt Harvey
Recipe styling by Sara Backhouse
Colour reproduction by Splitting Image Colour Studio
Printed and bound in China by C&C Offset Printing

10 9 8 7 6 5 4 3 2 1